Intelligent action is directed, fore-sightful, and innovative. How does it get produced by the brain? Dalbir Bindra here outlines a theoretical scheme that represents a renewed start toward answering this question. The approach is broad, neglecting neither instincts nor consciousness, and it is rigorous.

Bindra's theory rests on findings of the last twenty-five years in ethological, psychological, clinical, and neural disciplines. He defines certain fundamental neuropsychological processes and shows how these processes combine and operate in concert to produce the diverse phenomena of perception, meaning, learning, motivation, attention, choice, memory, and problem-solving. The theory thus provides a unified basis for the analysis and understanding of the varied aspects of the behavior of man and related animals.

Several earlier theories have tried to explain intelligent behavior exclusively in terms of either sensory-motor, or motivational, or cognitive processes. Bindra shows how the neural processes underlying cognitive knowledge, motivational arousal, and sensory-motor coordination are integrated to produce finely adaptive actions. This is the first major theory in several years to offer a coherent and workable framework for investigating problems in many different fields of behavioral study. As such, the theory will prove of interest to research workers, teachers, and students in the biological, neural, psychological, and medical disciplines concerned with the theoretical and practical aspects of adaptive behavior.

A Theory of
Intelligent Behavior

A Theory of
Intelligent Behavior

Dalbir Bindra
Professor of Psychology
McGill University

A Wiley-Interscience Publication

JOHN WILEY & SONS

New York / London / Sydney / Toronto

Library of Congress Cataloging in Publication Data:

Bindra, Dalbir.

A theory of intelligent behavior.

"A Wiley-Interscience publication."
Bibliography: p.
Includes indexes.
1. Psychology.   2. Adaptability (Psychology).

I. Title.

BF38.B53   150   75–46519
ISBN 0–471–07320–2

Printed in the United States of America

10 9 8 7 6 5 4 3 2 1

Preface

This volume is concerned with the explanation of intelligent behavior—the type of purposive, foresightful, and innovative actions that characterize the biological adaptation of man and related animals. I have sought to define the major theoretical questions, and by trying to answer them, however tentatively and incompletely, to indicate what might be the general form of a coherent explanatory account of behavior.

Explanation is not an all-or-none thing; understanding is gained gradually. Like explorers in uncharted jungles, science operates from uncertain positions, vulnerable and temporary, which serve as transient bases for investigatory probes into the surrounding unknown. Serendipity aside, progress depends on organizing the information gained from previous probes into a conceptual model, using the model to define the task of new probes, and then revising the model as something new is discovered or some improved synthesis imagined. Theory in science is a model-in-being. What I offer here is just such a transient theoretical scheme, organized quite speculatively from the discoveries of the past quarter of a century, with the aim of summarizing what is known and guiding the search ahead for improved understanding of intelligent behavior.

Because science assumes monism—unity underlying apparent diversity—the most satisfying explanations are those that successfully attribute the phenomena of one domain of science to the phenomena of a more molecular science. Thus a theory of behavior should aim at showing how the elemental behavioral concepts are translatable into the language of the neural sciences. In fact, progress in understanding adaptive behavior goes hand-in-hand with progress in the neural sciences; knowledge of behavioral functions elucidates neural mechanisms, and the study of neural mechanisms helps in the analysis of behavioral functions. There is nothing to be gained by ignoring behavioral evidence in the search for neurological principles or from ignoring neurological findings in the search for elemental behavioral processes. Thus, even if one's concern were only in elucidating behavioral principles, it would repay

v

to take into account relevant neurological and neurophysiological evidence.

I have, therefore, tried to build a theoretical scheme that may be described as neurobehavioral or neuropsychological. It emphasizes phylogenetic or comparative, ontogenetic or developmental, and brain-function or neurological considerations. The evidence I have used comes from studies lying on opposite sides of several popular dichotomies: behavioral vs. neurophysiological, ethological vs. laboratory, animal vs. human, adult vs. developmental, experimental vs. clinical, etc. In fact, it is the rapid progress in these branches of biological and psychological inquiry that prompted me to explore how far one could now go toward formulating some sort of a coherent theoretical scheme to deal with the phenomena of intelligent behavior. The exploration has resulted in this volume.

It has been long in the making, spanning two sabbatical leaves: The first, in 1967, was spent at the Berkeley campus of the University of California, and the second, in 1974, was spent at Oxford. During this long period many students and colleagues, at several universities, read and criticized various drafts of chapters and made useful suggestions for improving the sense and substance of the manuscript. To all these generous and thoughtful readers I am thankful. I am especially indebted to those who, steadfastly over the years, served as willing and patient interlocutors and helped me clarify the ideas presented here; they are M. C. Corballis, D. O. Hebb, R. Melzack, P. M. Milner, M. J. Morgan, and my wife, Jane Stewart. I also acknowledge with great pleasure the concern and superb competence that my secretary, Barbara Vien, brought to the task of producing the manuscript.

DALBIR BINDRA

Montreal
January, 1976

Contents

A Theory of
Intelligent Behavior

CHAPTER 1

The Problem

Actions of man and other creatures are said to be intelligent when they are more purposive than haphazard, more intentional than accidental, and more foresightful and innovative than impulsive and stereotyped. Though they have a mentalistic, unscientific ring, terms like purpose, intention, and foresight are useful as initial rough pointers to what intelligence might mean in the context of adaptive behavior. It is not necessary to renounce such common-sense terms for fear that they would hinder the search for naturalistic, bio-logical explanations of animal intelligence; as descriptive labels purpose and foresight need not imply teleology, nor need intention imply an autonomous soul or an homuncular inner agent. In studying intelligence as an adaptive capacity, it is imperative that we begin by trying to define the particular characteristics of behavior to which these terms refer. This realization has emerged only gradually.

Early investigators of evolutionary continuities in behavior (e.g., C. L. Morgan, 1903; Romanes, 1883; Yerkes, 1905) sought to define animal intelligence with reference to phylogenesis. Their work rested on the classical doctrine that all animals have a place on a hierarchy, the *scala naturae* or Great Chain of Being (see A. O. Lovejoy, 1936), on which man, the most superior creature, is at the top and the other species are removed from him to varying degrees. This idea of a linear phylogenetic *scale* was the basis of the customary division of animals into the relatively more intelligent or "higher" species and the relatively less intelligent or "lower" species. This division was consistent with the intuitive impression that the ape is more intelligent than the monkey, the monkey than the dog, and the dog than the rat; and that these mammals are more intelligent than birds and reptiles, and they than the fish. But these estimates of differences in intelligence level them-selves seemed to depend not so much on demonstrated differences in the behavioral capabilities of various species as on the relative closeness of their ancestors to those of man along the assumed phylogenetic *scale*.

The theory of natural selection (Darwin, 1859) had contained the idea

1

that the interrelations among species are more accurately described in terms of a phylogenetic *tree* that depicts numerous branches representing parallel but more or less independent lines of evolutionary descent. The implications of this idea have come to be elaborated only gradually (Dobzhansky, 1962; Simpson, 1961, 1967). One implication now well understood is that each surviving species has been shaped by a unique set of pressures of natural selection and, while some species have evolved more recently than others, there are no evolutionary grounds for regarding the younger species as necessarily the more intelligent, complex, specialized, or "higher." The phylogenetic tree depicts species geneology or ancestral communality, not species "status" in respect to intelligence or any other specific characteristic. Phylogenesis then is not a sound criterion for grading species intelligence, especially when species from unrelated taxa (independent branches) are involved (see Hodos & Campbell, 1969).

The level of development of the brain (see Jerison, 1969, 1973) may appear to be a more meaningful basis for deciding how intelligent a species is, but this criterion too presents difficulties. The question is, which index of brain development is best correlated with our intuitive estimates of species differences in intelligence? The index of brain development that is now widely used for species comparisons is the relative size of the neocortex (Stephan & Andy, 1969). As a proportion of the total size of the brain, the neocortex size is about 50 per cent in prosimians (e.g., lemur, bush baby), about 67 per cent in monkeys, about 75 per cent in apes, and about 80 per cent in man. However, what is probably more important than the relative size of the neocortex is the relative size of the different functional areas of the neocortex. For example, in the opossum and the rat most of the neocortex is taken up by the motor and sensory areas, while in apes and man a great part of the neocortex is "association" neocortex (Diamond & Hall. 1969). Further, within the "association areas" the prefrontal neocortex has a greater proportional size in primates than in other mammals, but there may be no difference in this regard between other primates and man (von Bonin, 1948; Passingham, 1973). Man's neocortex differs from that of other primates in having an enlarged angular gyrus, which is implicated in language (Geschwind, 1971). Man's neocortex is the most asymmetric; there is typically a larger planum temporale in the left hemisphere than in the right hemisphere, and this anatomical fact parallels the typical localization of the language function in the left hemisphere (Geschwind & Levitsky, 1968).

Clearly, it is not the relative size of the neocortex that parallels our intuitive estimates of species differences in intelligence, but the behavioral functions served by the particular parts of the neocortex. Knowledge about the neuro-anatomical features of the brain of a species can tell us something about its intelligence only to the extent that we already know the relation of those brain features to intelligence estimated from the animal's behavior. But this relation cannot be determined without specifying the characteristics of actions that we accept as signs of intelligence. Thus knowledge of the neuroanatomical or neurophysiological organization of the brain cannot, in itself, provide a meaningful criterion of animal intelligence, and the search for the criteria of animal intelligence must fundamentally be tied to the analysis of behavioral capabilities. Of course, we should be guided and aided by any correlations we may find between our tentative behavioral estimates of intelligence on the one hand and phylogenetic, neuroanatomical, or neurophysiological variables on the other, but the criteria of intelligence must be formulated in behavioral terms alone. This returns us to the problem of defining the essential behavioral capabilities represented in the commonsense characterization of intelligent actions.

BEHAVIORAL CRITERIA OF INTELLIGENCE

Behavioral capabilities in terms of which discussions of animal intelligence have been carried on may be grouped into five interrelated concepts. These are goal-direction, learning capacity, foresight, volition, and consciousness. Here I shall examine how each of these concepts applies to the actions of phylogenetically diverse species and try to define some of the behavioral characteristics or dimensions that may be regarded as legitimate criteria of animal intelligence.

Goal Direction

Actions, such as eating, drinking, nursing the young, exploring, copulating, attacking, escaping, playing, and problem-solving, tend to be prolonged; an animal may persist in one such activity for several minutes before it is completed or abandoned. Further, such actions are not unitary, indivisible wholes, but are made up of smaller segments. For the present purpose, it is convenient to recognize three levels of action segments or behavioral units: The highest-level or the most molar unit is the *response*; and the two lower-level or more molecular units I shall call, respectively, the *act* and the *movement*. For example, a rat's response of "lever-pressing for food" may be described as consisting of acts of pressing a lever, walking to the food receptacle, eating the food, and returning to the lever. The act of lever pressing, in turn, may be said to consist of the movements of standing on the rear legs, extending a paw, and leaning on the lever. How broadly or narrowly responses, acts, and movements are defined, depends on the nature of the investigation. For most investigations it may make no difference whether a rat presses a food-delivering lever with its right paw, or its left paw, or by sitting on it, or whether a hallucinating schizophrenic looks to his right or left while listening to what he believes to be cosmic messages. However, if the interest lies in the "handedness" of the rat or in the relation of auditory hallucinations to deafness, then it would be important to identify the smaller units which comprise lever-pressing or listening. Note, however, that the definition of neither response, nor act, nor movement need refer to any specific muscles; with rare exceptions, behavioral units are defined in terms of some specific effects or the end produced by effector activity rather than in terms of effector activity itself.

A significant aspect of animal actions is that the acts comprising a response may vary considerably from one occasion to another even though the response as defined with reference to a specific end remains the same. For example, "drinking" may involve going to a water fountain, bending, and opening one's mouth, or it may involve opening a thermos, pouring some water into a glass, and bringing the glass to the mouth. Because the same effect (ingestion of water) is achieved, we identify the two responses as "drinking," even though the acts involved in the two are quite different. The constituent acts are themselves made up of movements that may vary from time to time; thus, "going to the water fountain" may involve walking, crawling, or moving one's wheelchair. This means that several different movements may be functionally equivalent so far as the production of an act is concerned, and several different acts may be functionally equivalent components of a response. In general, then, each time it occurs, a response may be made up of different sets of functionally equivalent, substitutable, lower-level units. And the same lower-level units (movements and acts) may form parts of several different higher-level units (responses). This flexible, hierarchical arrangement—one in which the smaller segments are not necessarily fixed but can be varied without altering the end—is shown in Figure 1.1.

Animal actions are said to be goal-directed when the production of lower-level units can, to some extent, be adjusted to variations in the circumstances under which a defined response is being studied. The rat-catching response of a cat is goal-directed when variations in the momentary location of the rat are matched by acts that move the cat in the direction of its prey. In general, goal-directedness of a response is demonstrated when any variations in the location or other stimulus features of a specified goal-object are accompanied by appropriate alterations of acts (Bindra, 1959, Chap. 3; Sommerhoff, 1950). The processes by which goal-direction in the above sense is achieved in particular animal actions may vary greatly from one instance to another and can be determined only after careful study (see Hinde & Stevenson, 1970). But the descriptive feature of goal-direction is clear enough; it resides in the selection of particular acts that are, at the time, appropriate for

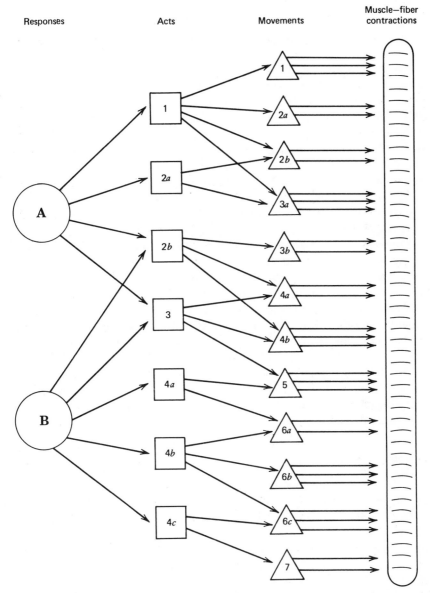

Responses	Acts	Movements	Muscle–fiber contractions

Figure 1.1. Hierarchical arrangement of behavioral segments. Higher-level units are made up of progressively lower-level or smaller segments. Some of the lower-level units are functionally equivalent and can be substituted for each other; the functionally equivalent units have the same designation but different subscripts. The figure shows that response **A** requires the performance of acts 1, either 2*a* or 2*b*, and 3, while response **B** requires acts 2*b*, 3, and either 4*a* or 4*b* or 4*c*. Similarly, act 1 requires movements 1, either 2*a* or 2*b*, and 3*a*; act 2*a* requires movements 2*b* and 3*a*; and so on. A similar hierarchical arrangement, with considerable functional equivalence, exists between each individual movement and its constituent muscle-fiber contractions.

5

the production of a specified response—that is, the attainment of a certain end.

Species differences in goal-direction relate to the range of stimulus conditions and alternative acts which can lead to the production of a specified, goal-directed response. In non-mammalian species, such as the frog and the lizard, any given response, such as catching a prey, is critically dependent on a highly specific stimulus configuration and highly specific acts. This rigid mode of goal-direction may be contrasted with the more flexible goal-direction seen in mammals. The flexibility is one of linkage between acts and the end in terms of which the response is defined; the response on different occasions is made up of acts that are not at all particular but highly variable, depending on the momentary stimulus configurations. Thus a squirrel transports edible objects to its nest by carrying or dragging them along a variety of alternative routes; a small chimpanzee gets a banana from a bigger one by trickery, begging, or stealing; and a man gets his message across by sentences of varying construction, now in one language, now in another. In these examples the behavior may be said to be flexibly goal-directed because, while the end (i.e., the response-as-defined) remains constant, the acts are varied to suit the situation; this contrasts with the rigid goal-direction seen in the nonmammalian species. Thus the critical behavioral characteristic which varies with species is not the presence or absence of goal-direction, but the flexibility of goal-direction; it is this flexibility that may be taken as a criterion of animal intelligence. The basis of the flexibility lies in the nature of the selection mechanisms and the repertoire of available acts; these will be discussed in later chapters.

Learning Capacity

Search for species differences in learning capacity was for many years focused on comparisons of the performance of different vertebrate species on standard laboratory learning tasks, such as those requiring the acquisition of conditioned responses, maze habits, and stimulus discriminations. These comparisons have failed to reveal any consistent differences in the rates of learning that could with confidence be attributed to species differences in learning capacity. Similarly, careful species comparisons on "cognitive tasks," such as those requiring the learning of double-alternation, delayed-response, oddity problems, and conditional stimulus discriminations, have not produced any convincing evidence for the existence of species differences in learning capacity (see Warren, 1965).

These negative findings do not mean that there are no species differences in learning capacity, but rather reflect the difficulty of making meaningful species comparisons (Lashley, 1949). One question usually asked is whether a given species (e.g., a fish, a bird, a rodent, or a primate) is at all capable of learning a certain type of task. If one species is found not to learn the task, it can be argued that the task is "unsuitable" for the species; indeed when tasks are modified to take into account species differences in sensory and motor equipment, as well as behavioral dispositions in relation to various types of experimental situations and incentives, the same species may be found to be quite capable of learning the previously failed task (Hodos & Campbell, 1969; Warren, 1965). But, now, if the experimental situations are quite different (but suitable for each species), it becomes meaningless to compare their rates of learning the task. And even if two species learn a black vs. white discrimination task at the same rate as judged by the measures of discrimination, one species may learn much more about other features of the learning situation than the other species. Such "incidental learning" (see Postman, 1964) may well differentiate between species that perform equally well on the assigned task.

A related difficulty in demonstrating species differences in learning capacity lies in the fact that the same task may be learned by the exercise of qualitatively different behavioral capacities. Consider an oddity problem. The task of the learner is to select the odd one of three simultaneously presented stimuli (e.g., select the circle from an array of two triangles and a circle, △ △ ○). The intent of studies of the oddity problem is to determine whether an animal is capable of acquiring the "principle of oddity." But it is obvious that an animal may perform successfully on the above task simply by learning that the circle is the correct (or rewarded) stimulus. To avoid this, the experimenter makes a stimulus array on each trial by selecting three out of a population of four stimuli, two triangles and two circles; now the circle may be correct on some trials (△ △ ○) but the triangle may be correct on other trials (○ △ ○). But now an animal may learn to perform correctly by learning which ones of the six trials (three of two triangles and one circle, △ △ ○, △ ○ △, ○ △ △, and three of two circles and one triangle, ○ ○ △, ○ △ ○, △ ○ ○) are the correct ones. Clearly in order to be sure that an animal has learned the concept of oddity, the investigator must determine the *basis* of the animal's correct performance; correct performance is not a proof of the capacity to learn the principle of oddity. This means that the investigator must arrange oddity trials of different stimuli to determine whether the animal has learned something about the particular stimuli or about the oddity principle. Now, intuitively it appears plausible that a bird or a rat would learn to perform correctly on the basis of particular stimulus arrays, but that a monkey or a child may well perform correctly on the basis of learning the principle. The contrast is similar to that between a rote learner and someone who applies a mathematical principle of calculation. The former can answer instantly that 19×18 is 342, but the latter takes some time to calculate; however, the former is limited by the multiplication tables he has memorized, while the latter can extend his principle to new sets of figures. The latter possibility may be determined by testing the subject for the same principle but with different stimuli.

The above analysis suggests that a meaningful approach to grading species on what we intuitively call learning capacity would be to compare how different species increase their efficiency of learning by prior experiences in learning similar or different tasks. The tasks may well be different and suitable for each species. The critical point is to determine how much a given species improves its rate of learning a new task on the basis of what it has learned before; in other words, how much does the previously acquired knowledge influence the learning of a new task. Thus, even though we cannot meaningfully compare the rate of initial learning, we should be able to compare the capacity to benefit from previous learning. This is what has traditionally been called the *transfer* of prior learning to new learning. The studies of "learning to learn" or the acquisition of "learning set" (Harlow, 1959) fit the transfer paradigm. In the typical learning-set experiment, the animal is required to master in succession a series of discrimination tasks, usually involving two discriminanda. The testing situation remains constant but the discriminanda change from one problem to the next. Interproblem improvement in learning is then measured; the usual measure is the proportion of correct responses on the second trial (the one following the first or informational trial for the given problem) of each successive block of problems. The rate of improvement in the learning of successive blocks of problems is an index of the capacity to develop learning set or transfer capacity; this appears to be the only meaningful measure for species comparisons of learning capacity.

Hodos (1970) has brought together the results of learning set experiments on certain commonly studied species and has drawn curves comparing their learning capacity in this sense. As seen in Figure 1.2, these curves show marked species differences: the tree shrew, the rat, and the squirrel appear incapable of acquiring the ability to transfer, while the human child and chimpanzee seem to become capable of transfer quickly, frequently performing correctly after only one informational trial. Such one-trial learning is not observed in other species. Note that the order of different species does not completely agree with the classical ordering of species intelligence; the pigeon is higher in ability to transfer than the rat, and the mink is higher than some of the monkeys. Though the grading of different species on the ability-to-transfer dimension is open to revision (in view of uncertainties of species comparisons mentioned earlier), it seems plausible to regard this dimension to be a meaningful criterion of animal intelligence. Actually the relative placing of the species in Figure 1.2 parallels closely their level of neocortical development. It is also noteworthy that some of the newer tests for measuring human intelligence (e.g., Sullivan & Skanes, 1971) are explicitly based on a transfer interpretation of human abilities (Ferguson, 1954).

Another dimension of learning capacity along which species may be differentiated is the retention ability. Some species seem to forget less in a given time and thus master a task more quickly than other species. In a successive alternation experiment (go to A on trial n and to B on trial $n + 1$),

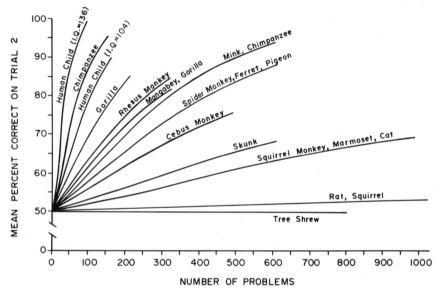

Figure 1.2. A family of ideal curves representing the development of learning set in various animals. [From W. Hodos, Evolutionary interpretation of neural and behavioral studies of living vertebrates, In F. O. Schmitt, Ed., *The neurosciences, second study program* (New York: The Rockefeller University Press, 1970), p. 35. With permission.]

Masterton and Skeen (1972) compared the performance of the hedgehog, the tree shrew, and the bush baby, three species that lie at different points on the anthropoid line of descent, and differ in the neural development of the prefrontal system. They found that the bush baby showed no performance deterioration in the alternation task even when the intertrial interval was raised to 256 sec, while the shrew began to perform at a chance level at the 128-sec interval, and the hedgehog at the 64-sec interval. This order of their capacity to retain information over the delay periods corresponds to the degree of development of their prefrontal systems. Neonatal dogs retain more—tend to learn faster—than neonatal mice or kittens (Stanley, Barret, & Bacon, 1974). However, some of the observed species differences in this regard may be attributable to differences in neurological maturity at the time of original learning (Campbell, Misanin, White, & Lytle, 1974). Differences in retention ability between age-groups within a species have been frequently observed. Campbell & Spear (1972) have reviewed the evidence showing that in the learning of both appetitive and aversive tasks immature animals forget more than adults. It has also been demonstrated that, compared to immature rats, adult rats show greater savings of habituation to novel stimuli (Feigley, Parsons, Hamilton, & Spear, 1972; Parsons, Fagan, & Spear, 1973).

It seems reasonable then to regard the ability to transfer prior learning to new tasks and the ability to retain acquired information as two meaningful dimensions of learning capacity, and these may be taken as criteria of animal intelligence.

Foresight

The concept of foresight refers to the observation that the response of an animal at a given moment may be determined in part by probable future events, to the extent they are predictable from the current stimulus information. Any anticipatory response elicited by a training signal, such as the fish's anticipatory avoidance response at the presentation of a signal that has been consistently followed by an electric shock, illustrates foresight in its simplest form. However, the degree of foresight—the extent to which probable future events determine present behavior—varies greatly among species. A hungry rat that adjusts to a fixed-interval schedule of food availability, by distributing the bulk of its responding at a period just before the time that the food is to be delivered, may be said to be capable of greater foresight than the fish, which, though influenced by it, are probably unable to adjust their responding to the specific time of food delivery. The rat is also capable of adjusting its behavior simultaneously to two reward variables; for example, for a given amount of work requirement per response, a one-pellet reward delayed by one second results in the same level of performance as a ten-pellet reward delayed by ten seconds (Logan, 1965). The rat can also perform effectively in a choice situation (e.g., a T-maze) in which each of two or more different alternatives lead to different consequences or utilities (i.e., benefit vs. cost). However, the rat appears capable of doing so only when it is in the choice situation, in the presence of the choice stimuli in relation to which it has to respond. In the absence of the choice stimuli the rat shows no evidence of planning actions in advance of encountering the choice stimuli. A chimpanzee, on the other hand, seems able to assess the utility of different choice stimuli and make preparatory responses in the absence of some of the critical stimuli in relation to which the final action is to be performed. For example, a chimpanzee may fill its mouth with water, sit nonchalantly at the front of its cage, and then, when a passing attendant comes near enough, spit the water at him (Hebb, 1946a). This ability to plan a certain course of action "in the head"—in advance of encountering the situation—is probably found only in primates. In man such planning may involve several different operations, such as estimating probabilities, comparing, extrapolating, ordering, making analogies, and calculating; thus a man may calculate the profits and losses anticipated from a business deal before committing his participation. It is the making of such "in absentia" estimates of the probable consequences of each alternative and the comparison of the utility estimates in planning a future action that describe what is called "intention." Foresight thus appears to be mainly a matter of anticipatory responding in the case of nonmammalian species, a matter of choice in the case of nonprimate mammals and most primates, and a matter of planning or intentionality in the case of certain primates, such as man. The degree of foresight, the extent to which an animal is capable of adjusting to predictable events of varying remoteness, is then a dimension of foresight that may be taken as a criterion of animal intelligence.

Volition

We are inclined to use the term "voluntary" to describe an action when a casual knowledge of the animal and its immediate circumstances leaves us uncertain as to whether that action or some other will be performed by the animal. In this sense, there is a continuum of involuntary-voluntary actions, which runs from the simple reflex (e.g., the eye-blink) to the more complex elicited acts (e.g., visual-tracking of a target), from these to motivationally determined action patterns (e.g., eating or fighting) and choice responses (e.g., in a preference test), and from these to verbally directed and intentional actions (e.g., in judgmental decisions). The typical behavior of different species differs in this regard.

There is relatively little uncertainty in predicting the behavior of invertebrates. The number of different types of actions of which such organisms are capable is small, and each action occurs reliably on the presentation of fairly specific stimuli. Thus, given that the organism is alive, its actions at any particular time are readily predictable from a knowledge of the eliciting stimuli; the actions are described as "involuntary" or "automatic." Some uncertainty exists concerning predictions of the behavior of fishes. They not only have a wider repertoire of actions, but the actions are determined by complex stimulus configurations as well as by many maturational and organismic-state factors. Casual observation of the animal thus provides insufficient basis for predicting what it will do, except under conditions of overriding intense environmental stimulation. In reptiles, the prior learning experiences of individual animals, as distinct from species-typical experiences, further increases uncertainty of prediction. In birds, owing to the relatively greater role of learning through distinctive individual experience, response-instigating properties of environmental stimuli may vary greatly from one individual to another, so that even highly detailed knowledge about the environment and the internal conditions would not be sufficient for making reliable predictions about what a given bird is likely to do.

The highest degree of uncertainty accompanies attempts to predict what mammals will do under a given set of conditions. Here, since several individual acts can be combined flexibly into certain patterns, the number of different types of actions that an animal can perform is much greater than in birds.

Parker (1974) examined the behavior of 10 different species of nonhuman primates while they performed a manipulative task. A certain act performed by a certain part of the body in relation to a particular aspect of the manipulandum was called a response. He found that the great apes (chimpanzee, orangutan, and gorilla) made about 400 different responses, while primates such as the macaque, gibbon, and lemur made about 150 different responses, and species like the langur and spider monkey made no more than 50 different responses. An index of diversity (or uncertainty) showed these primate species to be highly different from each other. Further, the proportion of total behavior that could be accounted for by the 30 most frequent response categories was less than 50 per cent for the great apes but was over 80 per cent for the other species. In man, even nonlanguage response categories in a comparable situation would undoubtedly surpass the number of response categories of the great apes. These considerations make it nearly impossible to predict reliably—even in probabilistic terms—what certain primates will do even when a great deal of information about the animal and its current circumstances is known. It is this great uncertainty that usually prompts the adjective "voluntary" and characterizes behavior called "intelligent." The type of factors that make behavior highly variable and idiosyncratic will be discussed later; here we need to note simply that as a descriptive adjective "volitional" is often used, not to specify any special class of behavior, but to refer to a dimension of uncertainty of prediction.

The term volition also has two other, more substantive, meanings. In some contexts, volition refers to the subjective experience of choice or intention that appears to supervene in determining certain actions. In other contexts the concept is used as a descriptive characteristic of behavior to refer to the extent to which some aspect of behavior (e.g., eating, urination, heart rate) appears to have come under the subject's "own" control and relatively independent of the conditions that might have initially controlled it. In both these cases a volitional response is thought of as one that depends on certain special processes that can modify what an animal might otherwise have done. The nature of these processes, as well as the question of their special status, will be discussed in the later chapters of this volume. The point that should be noted here is that neither of these meanings of volition necessarily denies determinism. Whether determinism is challenged or not depends on the type of processes that are invoked to explain the phenomena of choice, intention, and self-control.

Consciousness

The term "consciousness" is used in two different senses. Sometimes it is used to refer to the fact of conscious awareness or immediate knowledge of entities that we privately experience "within ourselves," and presume that other mammals, primates, or, at least, human beings do too; in this sense, consciousness is a phenomenon of experience (real or illusory) to be studied, explained, etc., as all other phenomena of nature. At other times, consciousness is used to refer to a special, higher-level capacity or function, developed in evolution, that underlies the phenomena of both conscious awareness and the more intelligent forms of actions discussed above; in this sense "consciousness function" is a hypothetical explanatory concept and must compete with other explanations of the same phenomena. There are thus two problems of consciousness. One is the problem of explaining the phenomena of conscious awareness, and the other is that of examining the merits of the consciousness-function hypothesis relative to the other hypotheses of intelligent actions and conscious awareness.

Though independent, the two problems often get confused because the phenomena of conscious awareness tend to be used to support the hypothesis of consciousness function. The usual argument (e.g., Shallice, 1972; Sperry, 1969) is that the phenomena of conscious awareness *require* some such explanatory concept as a consciousness function. But the case for requirement of a particular explanatory concept can be made convincingly only if it is given a detailed formulation within the broad framework of present-day science and then is shown to be better than competing hypotheses. Serious attempts have recently been made by Sperry (1969) and Shallice (1972) to give a clear formulation to the consciousness hypothesis in neurophysiological terms. However, on closer examination both these formulations are seen, in effect, to regard consciousness as an extraneural agent, whose operations are not completely determined by neural events (see Bindra, 1970). The nature and mechanisms of this agent must then become the objects of a new hypothesis! Further, both Sperry and Shallice propose their formulations within the assumption of "dual-aspect" or the identity view of brain and mind, and this creates another difficulty. As Gray (1971a) has pointed out, if consciousness is a part of brain function, then the explanatory value of consciousness is included in the explanatory value of brain processes, and it becomes meaningless to try to hypothesize a consciousness function as an extraneural process that somehow influences brain processes.

There is another question that must be asked before the hypothesis of a consciousness function can be usefully entertained: Can the explanation of the facts of intelligent actions and conscious awareness be approached in terms of neural events, without postulating a special consciousness function? The postulation of an extraneural agent would be more plausible if the answer to the above question is found to be negative. At present it seems some progress is being made toward understanding the phenomena of intelligent action in terms of neural function, and some potentially testable hypotheses about the nature of consciousness are beginning to be formulated or at least talked about in several different contexts (e.g., Festinger, Ono, Burnham, & Bamber, 1967; Hebb, 1968, 1974; Shallice, 1972; Sperry, 1952). So long as some progress continues to be made in this, it would appear to be unnecessary to postulate an ad hoc extraneural consciousness function to explain the phenomena of consciousness awareness and intelligent actions.

It should be clear that neither as a private phenomenon nor as an explanatory idea can the concept of consciousness be regarded as a meaningful criterion of animal intelligence. However, it must be noted that conscious awareness is often, but not always, an accompaniment of intelligent actions.

In summary, then, actions called intelligent are characterized by flexible goal direction, a high capacity for retaining acquired information and for the transfer of prior knowledge to new situations, foresight characterized by anticipatory choice and planning, and their intuitive invitation of global adjectives like "volitional" and "conscious." These rough criteria of animal intelligence are not mutually exclusive; in fact, their connotations are overlapping. And our search for the explanation of the above characteristics of behavior will show that they arise largely from common processes.

EXPLAINING INTELLIGENT BEHAVIOR

In the nineteenth century it was customary to assume that intelligent actions are produced by certain mental processes, such as perception, learning, thinking, memory, emotion, and will, which can be subjectively experienced, that is, form a part of conscious awareness. On the assumption that intelligent actions were consequences of, and hence secondary to, mental processes, the chief concern of scholars lay in introspectively analyzing and describing the mental processes—the content and operations of conscious awareness—and this is what the first formal body of psychologists undertook to do experimentally toward the close of that century (see Boring, 1946). But developments in the study of brain function during the eighteenth and nineteenth centuries increasingly suggested the priority of brain processes over both mental processes and actions. The belief that the brain was merely the organ through which mental processes expressed themselves into action was gradually replaced by the idea that mental processes themselves are the products of brain processes. This challenged the legitimacy of experienced mental processes as explanatory entities, and required that, like actions, mental processes too be considered as phenomena to be explained in terms of brain processes (Pavlov, 1927; Sechenov, 1965, first published 1886).

With mental processes discarded as plausible explanatory concepts, and not enough known about brain function to encourage linking observed behavior directly to brain processes, the new theoretical schemes that began to develop in the first quarter of this century were neither mentalistic nor truly neural. Rather they made use of a variety of hypothetical intervening or "mediational" entities to account for particular classes of behavioral phenomena. A mediational entity could be a hypothetical organismic state (e.g., hunger, anxiety), a learned variable (e.g., habit strength, expectancy), a developmental concept (e.g., sensorimotor stage, or egocentric thought), a disposition (frustration tolerance, impulsivity), a function (e.g., ego, inhibition), or some other factor (e.g., set, memory, attention). Whatever the name and exact theoretical role assigned to a postulated mediational entity, it may be described as a transformational process (hypothetical or real) with the capability (within certain limits) of receiving certain behaviorally relevant input ("information," stimulus change, motivational arousal, etc.), transforming it in some way, and producing an output which can influence behavior in a particular way. The current theoretical schemes for explaining intelligent behavior may be discussed in terms of the type of transformational processes they postulate.

The Current Scene

Speaking broadly and simplifying considerably, the present-day theoretical schemes may be grouped into two classes, *associational models* and *cognitive models*. The main difference between them lies in the type of *central* transformational processes and the underlying structures they postulate; the sensory, motor, and metabolic processes assumed by the two types of models are essentially the same. In the case of associational models, the transformational process is associational instigation, which requires a central transformational structure made up of some sort of connection or linkage of two or more elements (stimuli, responses, images, feelings, etc.). The linkages are assumed to be specific both in relation to inputs and outputs, so that a certain input into the transformational structure must produce, through its internal linkage mechanisms, a certain specific output, as shown in Figure 1.3a.

In the case of cognitive models, on the other hand, various transformational processes, such as attention, expectancy, perceptual reorganization, are postulated. They are thought to be produced by central transformational structures described merely as "cognitive," and their internal mechanisms or fine structures are not specified. Thus the cognitive models fail to provide a theoretical basis for predicting what output would occur with a certain input, as shown in Figure 1.3b. This lack of specificity, of course, makes cognitive models incapable of being proved wrong, for any behavioral outcome can be used, post hoc, as indicating what the transformation must have been; prediction is impossible but postdiction is perfect. In effect, then, cognitive transformational structures tend to be autonomous homunculi that always make the transformations that are appropriate at the time, but whose exact workings remain unspecified.

It should be evident that both associational and cognitive models are inadequate for explaining intelligent behavior. While the associational model

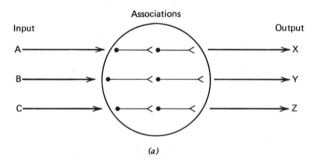

(a)

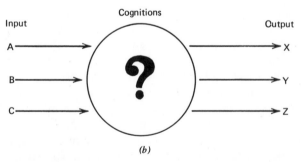

(b)

Figure 1.3. A comparison of the (*a*) associative and (*b*) cognitive models of transformational structures. In the associative structure, since connections or linkages are rigidly specified, the output is fully predictable by the input. In the cognitive structure the internal workings of the structure are not specified, so the output is not predictable.

can explain how particular responses may be produced under specified stimulus conditions, it cannot explain the flexibility of action so characteristic of intelligent behavior. For example, the stimulus-response associational model (Hull, 1943; Skinner, 1938, 1953) may be considered as reasonably successful in dealing with the interpretation of repetitive and stereotyped habits produced in unchanging, fixed training situations (e.g., mazes, lever-boxes, word-list learning tasks, etc.), but it has been found to be completely inadequate for explaining the production of flexible and innovative responses in situations that allow such responses to be made (e.g., insight experiments, problem-solving tasks, recall of stories, etc.). On the other hand, the cognitive model is not sufficiently specific; it can always be found consistent with whatever flexibility and innovativeness is observed in behavior by the simple expedient of postulating, post hoc, certain processes that are asserted as somehow effecting the required transformations. A great variety of transformational processes or structures has been postulated, such as "schema" (Bartlett, 1932; Head, 1920), "expectancy," "cognitive map" (Tolman, 1932), rigidity (Wertheimer, 1945), "categorizing system" (Bruner, 1957), "plan" (Miller, Galanter, & Pribram, 1960), "deep structure" (Chomsky, 1968), and feedback control systems (McFarland, 1971; Powers, 1973), to account for different instances of intelligent behavior. However, since the mode of operation or the internal mechanisms are not specified, nor is it indicated, even in general terms, what specific types of transformations may be performed by them, the cognitive accounts of intelligent behavior tend not to be satisfying as explanatory concepts. While the postulated cognitive structures may serve as initial, rough specifications of the transformations required for producing certain types of behavior, they remain essentially descriptive concepts.

The cognitive model that has managed to rise above the vagueness of the earlier cognitive accounts and dominates the current scene is the "information-processing model." Several fairly coherent versions of this model have been formulated (e.g., Broadbent, 1958, 1971; Neisser, 1967; Newell & Simon, 1971; Norman, 1970). The model is built on an analogy between the brain and communication networks. This is fundamentally a good analogy, for there are several parallel concepts, such as sensory channels and communication channels, neural networks and communication networks, sensory transmission and message transmission, neural coding and message coding, neural trace and message storage, and so on. Applied to human performance in perceptual and memory tasks, this model portrays response output as the end result of progressive "processing" or "coding" of input information through several transformational stages until it is transformed into a response. By ingenious and careful experiments investigators have been able to define the type of transformations (e.g., acoustic confusion, meaning code, organization, interference, icon degradation) that the information must go through in order to produce the observed response characteristics. Together with this, they have isolated the variables that are important in determining what type of processing is likely to take place in a given set of circumstances. This knowledge has been of great value in many practical situations (Broadbent, 1973).

However, it must be noted that the information-processing model does not provide satisfactory explanations of the phenomena it studies in terms of an independent theoretical account; it describes and predicts in a closed hypothetico-deductive system (see Hull, 1943). The investigators seem not to be interested in specifying how the required transformations are produced and how it is decided that one rather than another transformation will occur at a certain time. Transformations are not attributed to postulated structures with specified transformational mechanisms, but to certain implied operators, agents, or transformational homunculi, such as the "attentional filter," which excludes or attenuates certain messages, the "memory retriever," which searches the memory store, the "decision comparator," which compares output to certain criteria, and so on. Even those who recognize the problem—what Neisser (1967) calls "the problem of the executive"—have not undertaken even to try to specify the structures necessary for the proposed transformational processes. For example, Neisser suggests that the operator parallels the *executive routine* of the modern stored-program computer; an executive routine transfers control to particular subroutines (e.g., search through register A rather than B) on the basis of the demands of the task. This, however, is not an adequate answer, for the neural structures that serve as executive routines or operators in animals are certainly different than the tape or card structures that the programmer builds into the software of the computer. Neisser realizes that without a specification of the types of structure that correspond to executive routines or other transformational processes, the model does not really come to grips with the problem of explanation. He asks, rhetorically, "do not predictions become impossible and explanations ad hoc?" (Neisser, 1967, p. 304). Newell (1973) too has expressed doubts about the future fruitfulness of the information-processing approach.

It appears, then, that the information-processing approach has come to the end of the line; this is as far as a closed hypothetico-deductive method can go. Starting with certain working postulates which appear plausible in view of certain analogies, this method enables one to elaborate an internally consistent model of a certain class of phenomena with good specification of relevant variables and transformational processes. Such a model can produce remarkably accurate predictions and may be of great practical use. It can be used to analyze, integrate, and interpret new findings within a consistent framework. In all these ways experimental work within the information-processing framework contributes to the formulation of an explanation.

However, this approach cannot by itself produce an explanation of the phenomena it so successfully analyzes, integrates, and orders, unless it looks beyond the aim of internal consistency and seeks to interpret behavioral phenomena in terms of a more fundamental science built on the independent study of phenomena of a different order.

The Present Approach

To explain intelligent behavior, then, is to show in terms of a more or less plausible theoretical scheme that the fundamental concepts used in the description of behavior are translatable into (or reducible to) the principles of neural sciences. This does *not* mean that the objective of explaining behavior is to replace all descriptions of behavioral phenomena and laws by neural descriptions; explanation of chemical reactions in terms of the principles of physics (physical chemistry) has not led to the discarding of chemical descriptions, nor has the discovery of genetic code meant an end to the descriptive laws of inheritance. What translatability means is simply a statement of equivalence (hypothetical or demonstrable) of the main concepts of the higher-level science to certain functional principles of lower-level (more fundamental) science. The purpose of formulating such explanations is not to replace one science by another, but to close the gap between two sciences—to proclaim their unity, in principle.

Nor should the present view of explanation be taken to mean that the explanation of behavior should be left to the neural sciences—that once neural sciences have developed to a high level, no behavioral studies would be required, for the laws of behavior would follow from the neural principles. It may be true in the eyes of an ultimate knower, or when the whole task of science is done, that all behavioral principles may be implicit in the neural sciences, and that chemistry may be only unexplicated physics, but this has no relevance for those who are still trying to discover the various principles of nature. In practice, laws of higher-level sciences (say, chemistry or psychology) have not been deduced or extrapolated from the laws of lower-level sciences (say, physics or neurology). In fact, it is the empirically determined principles of higher-level sciences that often aid in the elucidation of lower-level mechanisms. This is probably so because knowing how a higher-level system functions indicates how the lower-level systems might be put together to achieve that function. Empirical study of inheritance helped in the discovery of the double-helix model of genetic code; investigation of the discriminative sensory capacities of animals is contributing to the elucidation of the neuroanatomy and neurophysiology of the sensory systems; and the behavioral principles of learning are contributing to the understanding of the mechanisms of neural plasticity.

The explanation of behavior in neural terms must be a cooperative venture, involving both the neural and the behavioral sciences. In practice what this means is that the mediating processes postulated to explain how actions are produced should be neurobehavioral or neuropsychological; they should be neither purely neural nor purely behavioral but should, as far as possible, be consistent with both domains of knowledge. Further, any attempt to specify the exact mechanism underlying a neuropsychological process should be made in explicit neurophysiological terms. However, in this volume I shall not be concerned with the specification of the neural mechanisms that might underlie neuropsychological processes; it is premature to try that. My purpose here is to develop a broad neuropsychological scheme that would serve as a basis for an integrated account of the phenomena of intelligent behavior; my effort is directed at defining certain fundamental neuropsychological structures and processes that would explain intelligent behavior and yet be plausible extensions of the known principles of neural sciences.

In developing a neuropsychological theory, it is of course important that special attention be paid to the biological aspects of intelligent behavior. There are three such biological aspects. One is phylogenetic, concerned with the evolutionary relation of a species to its typical environment and to other species; this makes ethology and the comparative study of behavior important. The second is ontogenetic, concerned with the maturation of behavioral capacities and the learning of specific adaptive patterns during the life of an individual; this makes developmental psychology important. The third is neurophysiological, concerned with the relation of behavior to particular aspects of brain function; this makes physiological psychology and clinical neurology important. Findings in all these fields of research have helped to shape the theoretical scheme developed in the following chapters.

CHAPTER 2

Integrative Processes of the Brain

A neuropsychological theory is a theory about the way in which the brain generates intelligent behavior. How are neural events organized to yield the appropriate selectivity and spatiotemporal ordering of acts that make up adaptive actions? I start with a brief account of the development of general ideas about how the brain works to produce adaptive actions. Following this, I outline a rough sketch, necessarily overgeneralized and faulty in detail, intended to remind the reader of aspects of present knowledge about brain function that are particularly relevant to the task of explaining behavior. This sketch will then serve as a tentative framework for developing more detailed neuropsychological concepts in later chapters.

FROM THE HIERARCHICAL-CONTROL TO THE INTERACTIONAL MODEL OF BRAIN FUNCTION

The view of brain function in terms of which the problem of adaptive behavior was approached in the first half of this century stemmed from the concept of the reflex, which provides a simple model of movement selectivity in relation to environmental demands. According to it, each of a certain set of environmental stimuli (say, S_1, S_2, or S_3) activates one of a corresponding set of sensory processes (s_1, s_2, s_3), and this leads, by activating particular motor processes (m_1, m_2, m_3), to the production of a particular movement (M_1, M_2, M_3). Attempts to extend this reflex concept to explain the more intelligent forms of behavior resulted in the hierarchical control model of brain function, which was elaborated in the writings of early physiologists and neurologists such as Jackson (1887), Sechenov (1965, first published, 1886), Sherrington (1961, first published, 1906), and Pavlov (1927).

Hierarchical-Control Model

Elaborating the idea of reflex arc, this model assumes a series of hierarchically arranged centers or levels, each higher level being capable of more complex sensory-motor integrations and of exercising some control over the integrations at the level or levels below it (see Figure 2.1). Three essential ideas

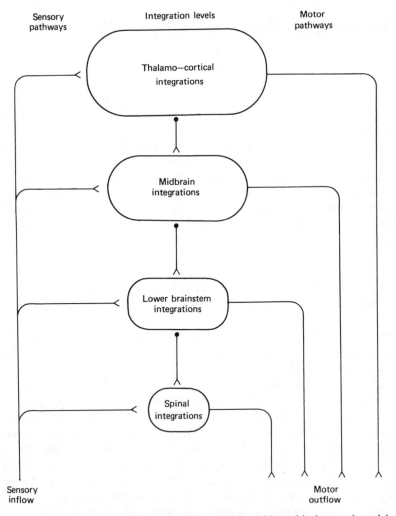

Figure 2.1. A schematic representation of the traditional hierarchical-control model of brain function. There are several levels of sensory-motor integration made up of specific sensory-motor routes, with the higher levels exercising unidirectional control over the lower levels.

characterize this model. One is that the production of different movements requires the activation of a distinctive or "labeled" sensory-motor route, and that the occurrence of any given movement requires the activation of a particular labeled route; this is the assumption that the brain works like a telephone switchboard. The second idea is that the activation of a neural route is determined quite decisively by the momentary sensory inflow, which may arise from a particular stimulus configuration or from sensory-feedback loops within the nervous system; this is the assumption of sensory determination of animal action. The third is the idea that the mental functions of the brain represent the activity of the higher integration levels, and that neural output from higher levels can influence the lower levels, but not vice versa; this is the assumption of unidirectional hierarchical control.

All three assumptions of the hierarchical model have been challenged and considerably revised. The idea that a distinctive sensory-motor route is involved in the occurrence of each different movement is opposed by Lashley's (1924, 1931) demonstration that damage to the cerebral cortex typically does not produce inability to perform specific responses but rather results in a general impairment of behavioral capacity. Consistent with this are Chow's (1967) findings that, for example, destruction of a large proportion (up to 90 per cent) of the visual pathways may not impair performance on fairly complex visual discrimination tasks. Workers in clinical neurology (for a review, see Luria, 1966, Chap. 1) too have continually stressed the variable and ephemeral nature of the symptoms associated with various types of brain damage; for example, aphasia-producing cortical lesions do not make the patient completely incapable of uttering particular words, but result in a general deficiency in the language function (Schuell, Jenkins, & Jimenéz-Pabón, 1964). These facts suggest that the occurrence of a certain movement need not be exclusively dependent on the activation of any particular labeled neural route, and as such are irreconcilable with the switchboard notion of brain function.

The idea that the occurrence of a certain response is determined decisively by the current sensory inflow, together with its inherent or acquired connections, is contradicted by the fact that animals can learn a double-alternation task (AA, BB, AA . . .), which requires two different responses to be made on the successive presentations of the same stimulus (Hunter, 1929). It is also contradicted by the demonstrations that the response to a given stimulus may vary depending on the way in which the subject has been prepared ("set" or "instructed") to respond. The preparation does not consist of any continuing external or internal stimulus input, but can be centrally maintained (e.g., Mowrer, 1940). The observations led Hebb (1949) to conclude that in the production of a response a certain momentary sensory inflow must function jointly with some "semiautonomous" ongoing central neural processes that are independent of *that* sensory inflow. The fact that the brain is spontaneously active, and that sensory inflow does not so much initiate neuronal activity as result in a redistribution of the pattern of neuronal activity, also argues against any sense-dominated view of brain function (Burns, 1968).

The idea of unidirectional hierarchical control—that the central neural influences flow only from the higher to the lower levels of sensory-motor integration—implies first a rostrally ascending information flow through the sensory pathways and then a caudally descending executive flow through the motor pathways. This assumption of unidirectional flow of neural discharge is called into question by electrophysiological recordings obtained simultaneously from various brain structures while an animal is performing a specified response. In general, these recordings show little evidence of unidirectional neural transmission from one structure to another. For example, John (1972) has examined evoked potentials from several brain structures produced by stimuli conditioned to particular approach or avoidance responses. His finding is that changes in neural activity go on simultaneously in almost all the major structures of the brain, and that the characteristic neural activity that is correlated with responding may be recorded from all of them. Consistent with this, neuroanatomical studies indicate that neural pathways and structures form a complex system which is characterized by multiple projecting pathways and reciprocally connected structures. These findings make wholly untenable any model in which the higher structures are conceived of as the pontifical controllers of activity in the lower structures. However, the idea of multiple representation of the same stimuli and movements at several levels of the brain, emphasized by Hughlings Jackson, has been supported by the subsequent work.

Interactional Model

The interactional model is not a formally proposed model; it simply represents the implicit climate of opinion that has gradually developed over the past three decades. The main tenet of the interactional view is that adaptive behavior is the outcome of simultaneously ongoing activity in several interacting neural systems. "System" is a rough but convenient term to refer to a collection of pathways and structures which appear to serve a unitary function. The afferent input into a system is transformed in important ways before it exits as efferent output of the system. Of course, the neuronal structure of a system need not be homogeneous; typically, a system consists of certain afferent neurons that discharge to a structure made up of a specific arrangement of interneurons of several different types, which transform the afferent input in a certain way. The exact properties of the interneurons by which any system produces a certain transformation are still far from being understood, and I shall not be concerned with that level of mechanism in this volume. The point to note is that the brain is more a collection of transformational systems than of switchboard connections of sensory and motor transmission lines.

Another point that is emphasized in the interactional view is that the production of adaptive behavior is dependent in important ways on neural systems that can be called neither sensory, nor motor, nor sensory-motor, because they are several synapses removed from both receptors and effectors and are not parts of the sensory and motor projection areas. These "other" transformational systems are as indispensable to the production of adaptive behavior as are the sensory and motor systems. The activation of particular sensory-motor coordinations is thus dependent not only on the momentary sensory inflow but also on neural discharges from more remote transformational systems.

The type of interactional model that appears to be consistent with recent findings about brain function is shown in Figure 2.2. One important feature of this model is that sensory inflow from receptors is projected to various brain structures simultaneously through three distinguishable transmission systems. The classical or "primary system" projects, mainly through certain nonreticular nuclei of the thalamus, to the sensory areas of the cortex. The more recently discovered "reticular system" projects, through the reticular parts of the lower brainstem and thalamus, to the same sensory areas of the cortex as the classical channel. The even more recently discovered "third" system projects, through a variety of brainstem nuclei to the hypothalamus and forebrain limbic structures. The simultaneous sensory projections in the three systems thus cover virtually the whole of the brain. Though the three systems overlap, and a lot remains to be learned about them, it may be surmised that they correspond roughly to three types of functions. The first system transforms the sensory inflow into neural discharges that represent detailed stimulus features of the environment; it generates "cool" or highly differentiated information and has been called the discriminative or *analyzer* system. The second system transforms the sensory inflow into neural discharges that promote or depress the activity of certain sensory cortical locations; it generates momentary changes in excitatory discharges to the site of projections of the primary system, and has been called the modulating or *activation* system. The third system projects the sensory inflow that generates the emotional arousal connected with different sense modalities (e.g., visual, tactual, gustatory, olfactory, and visceral inflow) to the hypothalamic and limbic structures, and may be called the *affective* system.

The projection of motor outflow to motoneurons and muscles also involves several different neural systems. These motor discharges appear to be coordinated through reciprocal connections between motor structures at different levels of the brain as well as through the cerebellum, which forms a part of the neural loops between the cortical and subcortical motor structures. A small portion of the cortical motor discharge is transmitted through direct

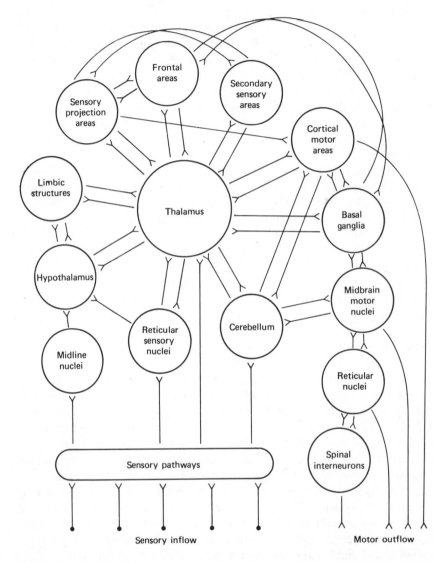

Figure 2.2. A schematic drawing of the interactional model of brain function, as it appears to be emerging. Adaptive behavior is the outcome of simultaneously ongoing activity in several interacting neural systems. The presumed pathways of fairly direct interaction are shown here; not all the pathways shown have been anatomically verified.

corticospinal (mainly pyramidal) fibers, while the remainder is transmitted through extrapyramidal fibers that synapse in the basal ganglia as well as at the lower levels.

According to the interactional model, the coordination of sensory inflow with motor outflow in the production of a response occurs through sensory-motor coordination structures at several levels, from the spinal to the cortical. Each sensory-motor coordination structure receives highly specific sensory projections from the primary sensory system, as well as projections from the lower and higher sensory-motor coordination structures. In the intact animal the normal production of a response involves integrated outflow from all levels of sensory-motor coordinations to motoneurons. The activation of the sensory-motor coordinations involved in a response is, of course, also influenced by neural discharges from other structures of the brain.

This type of model of brain function requires the neural connections that form the basis of the interactions to be highly specific; otherwise it would be impossible to integrate all the particular neural events needed for the production of a response. Recent neuroanatomical and neurophysiological work has confirmed the existence of a great deal of such specificity of neuronal connections. For example, the cortical representation of cutaneous receptors is in multicellular architectonic columns, several of which form a functional unit or "barrel" that receives sensory input of a certain modality from a highly defined peripheral receptive field; in the mouse a barrel in the somatosensory cortex receives input from only one vibrissa (Woolsey & Van der Loos, 1970; Zucker & Welker, 1969). Further, the arrangement of these cortical barrels parallels topographically the arrangement of their peripheral receptive fields. Similar specificities have been found in the projections of the reticular system (earlier regarded as a "nonspecific projection system") to sites in the cortical sensory areas (Jasper, 1958). Even greater specificity exists in the axodendritic synapses on the dendrites of the pyramidal cells of the hippocampus: axons from three different sources synapse in separate, particular sections of the dendritic tree of single pyramidal cell (Cowan, 1972). Without such specificity of neuronal connections, neural interactions would be diffuse and unlikely to produce accurately directed adaptive behavior.

The interactional model makes untenable the concept of distinctive neural centers for particular types of behavioral categories (e.g., eating, attacking, maze learning, or problem solving). The fact that, for example, eating can be induced by electrical stimulation of a particular hypothalamic site does not make that site an "eating center," for the actual response of eating involves simultaneous activity in several different systems of the brain, including perceptual and associational systems. A response as such is *not* localizable in the brain. What one can say is that certain types of neural transformations that are important or necessary for a particular type of action are carried out by particular neural organizations that may occupy a circumscribed site. In this sense, one may talk of a center or substrate of a particular type of *process*, but such a center is not an exclusive or distinctive site for the organization or production of any particular type of *response*. Neural processes may have neural centers, but adaptive actions do not. Though the inapplicability of the concept of center to behavioral phenomenon has been pointed out by several authors (Goldstein, 1927; Luria, 1966, 1973), the concept continues to find its way back into discussions under new guises, such as "the critical neural site for attacking," "neural locus of perceiving," "substrate underlying attending," etc. It is obvious that the same neural processes must contribute to a variety of, if not all, types of behavior, and no instance of behavior can be regarded as the outcome of the operation of a single neural system or process.

Turn now to a brief review of the basic concepts of neural function in terms of which the integrative activity of the brain may be described. There are three main types of concepts: concepts describing the sensory representation of the environment, concepts describing the organization of motor outflow, and concepts describing neural plasticity.

SENSORY REPRESENTATION OF THE ENVIRONMENT

An animal's environment gets represented in its brain by two main processes. One is the transduction of various types of environmental stimulus energies by modality-specific receptors into afferent neural inflow. This inflow represents the main physical dimensions (e.g., waveform, intensity, complexity, duration) of the stimuli. The second is the progressive transformation of the sensory inflow of each modality by a number of sensory nuclei (including the sensory cortex) into the activation of specialized neurons that represent particular features of the stimuli. Each specialized neuron is activated by a specific combination of stimulus features; different specialized neurons are sensitive to different but overlapping combinations of stimulus features. For example, certain neurons in the visual cortex are activated only when their receptive fields contain stimuli of particular figure-background relations, contours, orientations, colors, or directions of motion, or some combinations of these. Similarly, specialized neurons in the auditory cortex are activated by sounds that lie in a certain frequency range and occupy a certain location in relation to the animal's head. Such specialized neurons in the various sensory systems serve as *feature detectors* whose activation represents certain biologically important stimulus features in the animal's environment. The exact mechanisms of transduction and neural transformations involved in the activation of particular feature detectors need not concern us; for our purposes the activation of a feature detector may be regarded as the unit of sensory representation of the environment (*see* Uttal, 1973).

Stimulus Prominence

An animal's environment consists of an extensive field, with some of the stimuli appearing as relatively prominent figures on a somewhat amorphous background, for example, a round fruit in a clump of foliage, a prey on an expanse of sand, a moving object against a stationary background or vice versa, a pink kite in the blue sky, etc. Such figure-ground or signal-noise contrast defines stimulus *prominence*; it is the degree to which the features of a given stimulus (e.g., its location, size, shape, color, motion, texture) are different from the stimulus features present in the rest of the field. Stimulus prominence, described in physical terms, may be assumed to be represented in sensory systems by the *distinctiveness* of the set of feature detectors activated by the given stimulus (figure or signal) relative to the set of feature detectors activated by the stimulus field as a whole ("background" or "noise").

The distinctiveness of the activated feature detectors is not wholly dependent on stimulus prominence (in physical terms); it is also dependent upon the properties of the animal's sensory systems. For one thing, the proportions of feature detectors of particular classes present in an animal's brain are species-specific; evolutionary selection has presumably resulted in higher proportions of feature detectors for those stimulus features that distinguish the important objects and events in the typical environment of the species. For another, the proportions of feature detectors of particular classes also depend on the maturational experience of the individual animal (Blakemore & Cooper, 1970; Hubel & Wiesel, 1965; Wiesel & Hubel, 1965). Correspondingly, it has been shown, for example, that cats reared in an environment containing contours of only one orientation are subnormal in their ability to discriminate contours of other orientations (Hirsch & Spinelli, 1970; Muir & Mitchell, 1973). Similar deficits may result from uncorrected ocular astigmatism in human subjects (Freeman & Thibos, 1973). An early injury to a vibrissa on the muzzle of the mouse results in the failure of the corresponding cortical barrel to develop normally (Van der Loos & Woolsey, 1973). For all normal members of a species, however, the relative (neural) distinctiveness of the sensory representation of a stimulus may be expected to be roughly the same.

Stimulus Difference

In any stimulus field the difference between particular features of different objects may be great (e.g., between a large red ball and a strip of grey paper) or small (e.g., between two strips of grey paper differing in the shade of grey). Stimulus differences are represented in the sensory systems by the activation of different sets of feature detectors. Some feature detectors can be activated by a fairly wide range of stimulus features, while others can be activated only by highly specific stimulus features. Thus feature detectors may be said to be relatively broadly or relatively sharply "tuned"; that is, they vary in their *selectivity* or the degree of specificity of stimulus features that can activate them. For example, certain feature detectors in the cat's visual cortex are activated by a slit, but not by a bar or an edge of the same length. By contrast, in the cat's superior colliculus, visual feature detectors are not selective in respect to size, shape, and orientation, but are selective in respect to the location of a stimulus and its direction of movement. Stimulus differentiation capacity (or acuity) of a system seems to depend both on the number of detectors and on the sharpness of their tuning (quite apart from the sensitivity of individual detectors). In general, then, greater neural mass is likely to be required to detect detailed stimulus features than to detect gross ones; roughly speaking, the greater the differentiating capabilities of a sensory system, the greater its neural mass may be expected to be. The development of four different classes of visual detectors during the maturational period of the frog tadpole has been shown to match the growth of four types of ganglion-cell dendritic trees (Pomeranz & Chung, 1970).

Spatial Location of Stimuli

The behavioral reference point for describing the location of a stimulus is the animal's head. Stimuli at various points of its body and extracorporeal space are represented more or less topographically, at least in the visual, auditory, and somatosensory modalities. There are spatial feature detectors in each of these "spatial senses" that are activated differentially by stimuli at various locations in the stimulus field. In the case of the activation of visual and auditory spatial detectors, variations in the position of eyes and ears are somehow corrected for, so that the animal can tell the direction of an object in relation to its body regardless of the position of its eyes and ears in relation to the rest of the body. The widely held view has been that such corrections in the representation of spatial location—what Helmholtz (1866, quoted by Herrnstein & Boring, 1965) called "unconscious inference"—involve making an adjustment for variations in the positions of head receptors. A parallel neurophysiological finding is that the orientation selectivity of the cat's cortical neurons changes as its body is tilted in relation to the head (Denney & Adoijani, 1972; Horn & Hill, 1969). Further, Bridgeman's (1972) experiments suggest that certain neurons in the visual cortex may be selectively responsive to the relative location of a stimulus in reference to background stimuli while others may be responsive to absolute location in terms of retinal points stimulated. The location of a stimulus *in relation to the observer's body* may then be derived from the joint influence of these two types of cells on spatial-detection cells. This is a possible mechanism of correction for receptor position, but its existence remains to be established.

The representations at the lower brain levels seem to be less finely differentiated in respect to spatial locations than are the representations at the cortical levels. For example, in the posterior group of thalamic nuclei, a cutaneous feature detector may be activated by a stimulus applied anywhere on the left body surface, or anywhere on the right body surface, or on the right top quadrant of the body, etc.; finer differentiations of the location of cutaneous stimuli appear not to be made at this level (Mountcastle, 1961). However, at the level of the somatosensory cortex, spatial differentiation is very fine indeed, and each feature detector may be activated differentially by the stimulation of locations that are only a couple of millimeters apart.

The above remarks apply to the representation of directional information (horizontal and vertical planes) about stimuli. In the case of the visual system, the representation of the distance of particular stimuli from the animal is also an important aspect of spatial representation. There is little doubt that we learn to estimate distance of familiar objects on the basis of certain cues, such as superposition, parallax, linear and aerial perspective, and ocular convergence. However, until recently the question of the existence of any direct sensory representation of distance was not resolved. Considerable evidence has now been accumulated to indicate that binocular disparity serves as the basis of direct sensory representation of the relative distance of objects in the visual field. Julesz (1964) has shown that binocular disparity can create an illusion of relative distance when the visual field consists of random patterns of dots so that no familiar objects are recognizable. Further, a-few-weeks-old human infants fixate objects at different distances for different durations of time even when the retinal size of the object and other relevant variables are kept constant (McKenzie & Day, 1972). Neurophysiological evidence for sensory representation of relative distance has been found in experiments with the cat. It has been shown that there are feature detectors in the cat's visual cortex that are activated differentially by the degree of binocular disparity produced by presenting a stimulus at different distances from the animal (Barlow, Blakemore, & Pettigrew, 1967; Bishop, 1970; Blakemore, 1970).

Time and Number Representation

Certain temporal features of a stimulus, such as its duration, its repetition rate, and temporal pattern, are of course inherently tied to the onset and termination of the environmental stimulation and are thus directly represented in sensory inflow. However, the representation of the location of a stimulus in the flow of time, that is, its temporal relation to other stimuli, is a different matter. There is little doubt that mammals can respond differentially to differences in temporal order of stimuli and to differences in intervals between stimuli. Thus it must be assumed that some time-marking or "clock" mechanism exists that forms the basis of temporal discriminations. Sokolov (1966) has suggested that the output of a certain type of neuronal net to a summating neuron could produce steady discharges firing at fairly regular intervals; such a summating neuron could be described as a "pacemaker" or *timing neuron* of a fixed period. The exact periods of such neurons may be expected to vary between neurons but to be fixed for any particular neuron (within certain metabolic limits). Regularly firing neurons, with highly stable interspike intervals, have been found in mammillary bodies and related structures (Gray, 1971; Komisaruk, 1970; Sokolov, 1966; Stumpf, 1965; Vinogradova, 1970), but their relation to temporal discrimination remains to be elucidated.

Another aspect of the neural representation of environment is the representation of the property of *number*. It has been found that there are certain neurons in the cat's cortex that are activated by a particular numbered item in a series (Thompson, Mayers, Robertson, & Patterson, 1970). Thompson and his collaborators exposed cats to a series of stimuli consisting of clicks, flashes, and shock impulses. They found neurons that were activated when, say, the second, or fourth, or seventh stimulus in the series was presented. The activation of number detectors or "counting neurons" appeared to be independent of stimulus modality and intensity. This finding remains to be replicated. If substantiated, a neural basis would exist for the direct representation of the number of serial stimuli, which would make it possible for an animal to differentiate between, say, four and seven occurrences of a certain event.

Organization of Sensory Cortex

The 2- or 3-mm thickness of the cortex contains several discrete layers made up of different types of cells. The exact distribution of the cells of different shapes and sizes, and the layers they comprise, vary a great deal, not only between cortical regions but also within a region. However, the general functional arrangement of cells in the sensory areas of the cortex remains columnar, vertical to the cortical surface. The top of each column is made up of pyramidal cells whose upward pointing dendrites form an outer surface of apical dendrites and whose axons descend into the white matter below. The middle of a cortical column contains the outer stellate cells, with short, profusely branching dendrites and axons. It is the dendritic fields of the stellate cells that receive afferents from the nuclei of the thalamus; the branching axonal endings of a single thalamic afferent may fall within the dendritic field of 5000 stellate cells. Essentially, the stellate cells distribute the thalamic sensory inflow to the pyramidal cells, which in turn send the efferent cortical discharge to the subcortical structures. The bottom of the column consists of other layers of pyramidal and stellate cells and also contains most of the activating afferents from the reticular nuclei of the thalamus. The dendrites of the pyramidal cells, especially those at the top, also receive input from other parts of the cortex, but the efferent flow from the cortex is mainly downward; any long distance lateral transmission along these surface fibers appears unlikely (Milner, 1970, Chap. 7).

A very rough and generalized account of the functioning of sensory cortex in primates may be given with reference to Figure 2.3, which reproduces Brodmann's anatomical map of the human cortex. The sensory cortex contains the primary, secondary, and tertiary projection areas for each major sensory system; the latter two projection areas are commonly called sensory "association" areas. The visual projections are in the occipital lobe, the primary in area 17, the secondary in areas 18 and 19, and the tertiary in the inferotemporal cortex (area 20) and parts of the transitional zones between the occipital and temporal lobes (areas 37 and 39). The auditory projections are in the temporal lobe, the primary in area 41 (largely hidden in the figure), the secondary in areas 22 and a part of 21, and the tertiary in parts of areas 21, 39, and 40. The somatosensory (cutaneous and proprioceptive) projections are in the parietal cortex of the post-central lobe, the primary in area 3, the secondary in areas 1, 2, 5, and a part of 40, and the tertiary in areas 7 and parts of areas 39 and 40.

The functional relations of the primary, secondary, and tertiary projection areas are beginning to be understood in the case of vision. It appears that the primary visual cortex (striate area 17) receives highly topographic projections from the retina via the lateral geniculate body of the thalamus. Lesions of the striate cortex produce circumscribed field defects (Teuber, Battersby, & Bender, 1960). The secondary visual projection areas or the prestriate areas (18 and 19) receive direct projections of the primary visual cortex as well as indirect projections from the superior colliculus via the inferior pulvinar of the thalamus. Totally destriated animals can detect visual stimuli but are incapable of fine discriminations, suggesting that the collicular projections alone are capable of providing at least amblyopic vision. Though the striate cortex is essential for fineness of discrimination, the secondary projection areas appear to be necessary for the identification of objects as such despite stimulus transformations, orientation, and size (Weiskrantz, 1972); according to Luria (1973), the secondary projection areas serve the

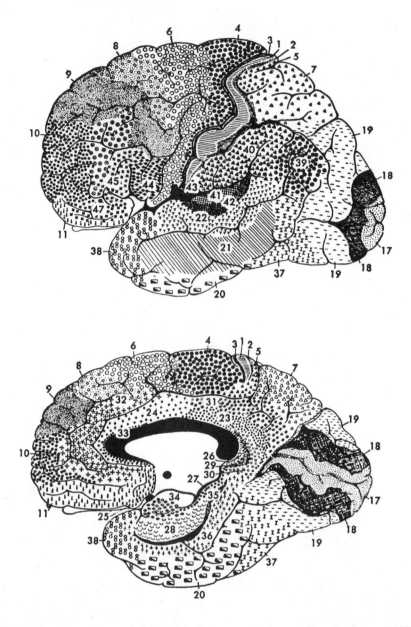

Figure 2.3. Cytoarchitectonic fields of the human cerebral cortex from Brodmann (1909). The upper view is of the outside surface of the left hemisphere; the lower view depicts a midline sagittal section revealing the enfolded cortex of the right hemisphere. (Reprinted with permission of Macmillan Publishing Co., Inc., from W. Penfield & T. Rasmussen, *The cerebral cortex of man.* Copyright 1950 by Macmillan Publishing Co., Inc.)

synthetic function of combining incoming information into usable patterns that are not tied to specific points of retinal excitation. The tertiary projection areas (the inferotemporal cortex) receive projections from the lateral pulvinar and from the prestriate cortex; these seem to subserve the function of recognition of objects, that is, the perception of objects as meaningful entities. Thus there appears to be a hierarchical arrangement of projections from the primary to tertiary areas (Hubel & Wiesel, 1965, 1968). This arrangement, together with independent subcortical inputs, is the basis of the different functions of the three visual cortical areas; jointly they transform the representations of isolated stimulus features into representations of identifiable objects. How far this general arrangement also holds for the primary, secondary, and tertiary areas of the auditory and somatosensory modalities remains to be established.

ORGANIZATION OF MOTOR OUTFLOW

Movements produced by muscular contractions may be divided into three rough categories: large, medium-sized, and small. Large movements involve large muscles and the displacement of large bodily parts, such as the leg, arm, or head, which are attached to trunk or axial joints, such as the hip, shoulders, or neck. Medium-sized movements involve medium-sized muscles and the displacement of somewhat smaller bodily parts, such as the foot, hand, or lower jaw, which are attached to intermediate joints, such as the ankle, wrist, or jaw-hinge. Small movements involve very small muscles and the displacement of small bodily parts, such as the finger, eye, lip, tongue, or vocal cord, which are attached to distal joints, such as the finger joints, and the "joints" that anchor the muscles of eyes, tongue, lips, or vocal cords. There are several points to be noted about the organization of the motor outflow that results in the production of these varieties of movements.

Motor Innervation

In mammals, repetitive activation of a few, say, five to ten, motor neurons of a certain class appears to be sufficient to produce a movement (Asanuma & Rosen, 1972). And the activation of a motor neuron occurs when a certain minimum amount of excitatory neural discharge has summated at its dendrites, and the rate at which this happens depends on the density of neural impulses reaching the neuron (Doty & Bosma, 1956). The obvious next question concerns the origin of the afferent fibers that discharge nerve impulses to the dendrites of motor neurons.

Recent neuroanatomical and neurophysiological studies of the motor cortex (see Chow & Leiman, 1970; Masterton & Berkley, 1974) indicate roughly how the afferent input to individual motor neurons might be organized. As shown in Figure 2.4, each neuron has well developed dendritic processes and the dendrites of one neuron are intermingled with those of others, as well as with the dendrites of some interneurons, forming a dendritic field. Axons of several afferent fibers, presumably arising from the motor commands of different levels of the brain, end on the dendritic fields of motor neurons, maintaining overlapping but differentiated access to the dendrites of individual neurons. This arrangement means that any one afferent axon discharges divergently on the dendrites of several neurons, and several different afferent axons discharge convergently on the dendrites of a single neuron. Neurons with common dendritic fields are arranged in a column; such columns, with inhibitory horizontal connections to surrounding columns, may well serve as functional motor elements (Colonnier, 1966).

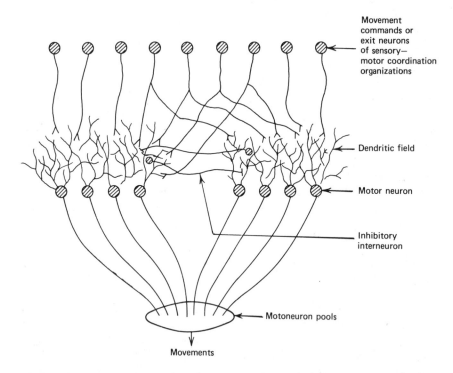

Figure 2.4. A schematic drawing of the proposed hypothetical arrangement of motor neurons, their common dendritic fields, and the overlapping input to the dendritic fields from exit neurons or the movement commands of sensory-motor coordination organizations. Motor neurons with common dendritic fields form a column, and the columns may be connected by inhibitory horizontal interneurons.

Until more specific information is available, it may be assumed that the motor neurons at the subcortical levels are organized in roughly the same way.

Studies of hand movements in the monkey have shown that a burst of discharge of cortical motor neurons is followed about 50 msec later by the onset of electromyographic activity in the corresponding muscles, and about 70 msec later by the onset of movement. Kinesthetic feedback from the muscles activated by such a motor discharge can be observed in the postcentral (somatosensory) cortex about 80 msec after the cortical motor discharge (Evarts, 1971).

Though there are marked species and individual differences, the general picture of muscular innervation in primates, suggested by recent findings (see Brinkman & Kuypers, 1972; Porter, 1973; Towe, 1973), is sketched in Figure 2.5. It shows that motor neurons originating in the lower brainstem, which innervate the proximal muscles and to a lesser degree the intermediate medium-sized muscles, project bilaterally, so that at this level either hemisphere can control large and medium-sized muscles on both sides of the body. The motor neurons originating in the midbrain, which innervate intermediate medium-sized muscles, project mainly contralaterally to the medium-sized muscles, so that at this level one hemisphere can control mainly contralateral medium-sized muscles. The motor neurons originating in the cortex, which innervate all sizes of muscles, project contralaterally to the small and medium-sized muscles and bilaterally to the medium-sized and large muscles, so that at this level one hemisphere can control small muscles only on the contralateral side of the body and medium-sized and large muscles on both sides of the body. Cortical influences on motor neurons are not exclusively transmitted through direct corticospinal pathways, but also through fibers from various parts of the cortex that descend on the midbrain and lower-brainstem motor neurons. Muscles involved in human speech are controlled bilaterally by only one hemisphere, typically the left.

Movement Production

The production of a movement by an animal typically requires coordinated activity of several muscles, hence ordered discharge to the motoneuron pools of those muscles. It is now generally agreed that a movement is not a collection of independently evoked muscular contractions, but an integrated muscular activity which occurs as a whole through the activation of a central motor organization or "movement command." The activation of each movement command results in a spatiotemporally ordered motor outflow required for producing the coordinated muscular activity comprising a movement. Such commands have been identified as individual "motor command

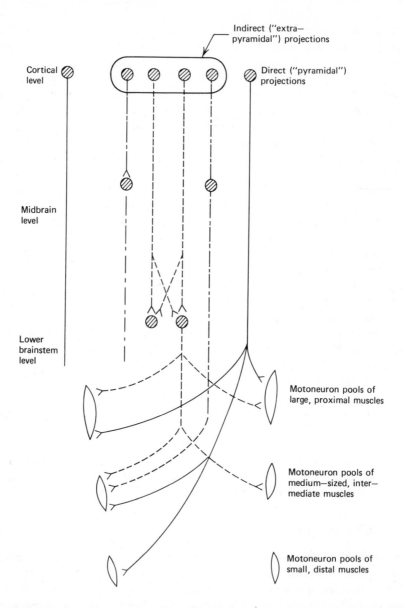

Figure 2.5. A schematic, generalized diagram of the organization of motor innervation of different types of muscles in primates. The efferent projections from different levels show considerable overlap in the muscles they innervate and in the origins (ipsilateral, contralateral, or bilateral) of the motor outflow.

neurons" in certain invertebrates, and the neural events that lead to and follow from their activation are being investigated (e.g., Burke, 1971; Kennedy, 1968). In vertebrates the movement commands may well be more complicated, each involving more than one neuron. Whatever their fine structure, for the purpose of this volume I shall assume that movement commands are the units of neural organization underlying the production of a movement. Collectively, movement commands may be said to comprise a keyboard on which the spatiotemporal arrangements corresponding to various movements that make up any adaptive action can be "played."

Movement commands are located in several structures at different levels of the brain; their stimulation by appropriate means immediately produces the corresponding movements. At the cortical level they are located in the precentral motor areas (motor and premotor zones); at the midbrain level they are located in the red nucleus, the tegmentum, and the superior and inferior colliculi, and at the lower-brainstem level they are located in the vestibular and pontine nuclei, as well as in certain nuclei of the medial bulbar reticular formation. The neural discharge carried by movement commands is distributed, through their terminations at different points of descent, to the motoneuron pools of various muscles.

In order for an effective, directed, movement to occur, the motor outflow must be influenced by sensory information about (a) the position and state of the muscles which are to be activated by a command, and (b) the environmental stimuli in relation to which the movement is to be made. The information about the position and state of muscles is provided by the vestibular and proprioceptive afferent inflow originating in the receptors of the vestibular organs, the joints, and the muscles. The information about the environmental target of a movement is provided mainly by visual, auditory, and cutaneous exteroceptive systems. These two types of information are not projected directly to the dendritic fields of motor neurons, but are first integrated in some way that coordinates the position and muscular state of the muscles to be moved with the spatial features of the stimulus in relation to which the movement is to be made. This integration is carried out by a highly complex and poorly understood system of which the cerebellum, the basal ganglia, the ventrolateral and the intralaminar nuclei of the thalamus, and substantia nigra are important components. Topographic representation of both proprioceptive and exteroceptive stimuli is preserved in these structures. It appears that the cerebellum is rather more involved in the integration of proprioceptive with cutaneous information, while the basal ganglia are rather more involved in the integration of proprioceptive with visual and auditory information. Whatever the exact roles of the various structures, it should be clear that, except in the case of spinal reflexes, a sensory-motor coordination is achieved not by direct sensory discharge into the dendritic

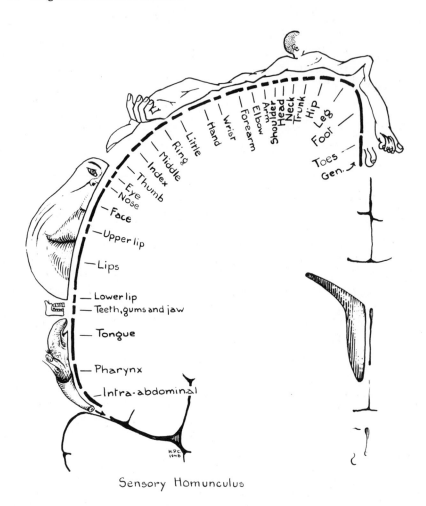

Sensory Homunculus

Figure 2.6. Sensory and motor homunculi. Parts of the body are drawn somewhat in proportion to the extent of cortex devoted to them. The length of the underlying block lines indicates more accurately the comparative extent of each representation. (*a*) Sensory homunculus, (*b*) motor homunculus. (Reprinted with permission of Macmillan Publishing Co., Inc., from W. Penfield & T. Rasmussen, *The cerebral cortex of man.* Copyright 1950 by Macmillan Publishing Co., Inc.)

fields of motor neurons, but by neural discharge that represents prior integration of vestibular, proprioceptive, and exteroceptive information in some *sensory-motor coordination organizations* that lie between the structures receiving direct sensory projections and the structures containing motor neurons. The exit neurons of sensory-motor coordination organizations may be taken

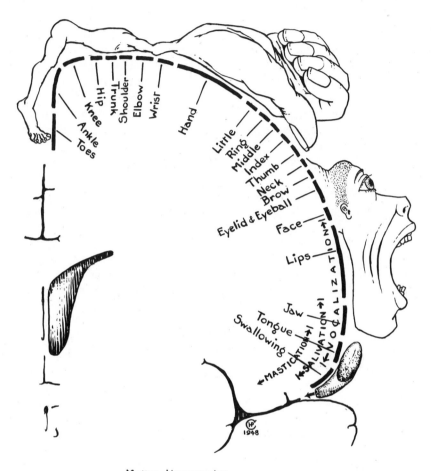

Motor Homunculus

to be movement commands. The movement-command axons carrying the neural output from specific sensory-motor coordination organizations reach the dendritic fields of a particular set of motor neurons.

The lower-brainstem, midbrain, and thalamocortical levels of sensory systems have feature detectors of progressively greater differentiating capability, and this parallels the increasingly refined muscular innervation by the three levels of motor commands arising from the corresponding levels of sensory-motor coordination organizations. Thus the sensory-motor coordination organizations at the three levels would appear to integrate sensory inflow of a certain degree of differentiation with motor outflow of a corresponding degree of refinement. In general, the feature detectors of the lower-brainstem level would be capable of only gross stimulus differentiations, and the corresponding sensory-motor coordination organizations and motor command neurons would be able to produce only gross movements. Sensory-motor coordination organizations at the midbrain level would be able to produce both gross and semirefined movements, and those at the cortical level would be able to produce gross, semirefined, and highly refined movements. This overlapping arrangement of sensory-motor coordination may make it possible for each of the three levels to function in the absence of the others within its own capabilities. In the intact animal the activity of the three levels of sensory-motor coordination organizations would be integrated by their reciprocal connections.

It follows from the above that the most refined movements would be made by the parts of the body having the most detailed sensory and motor representation in the cortex. A look at the cortical homunculi of somatosensory and motor representations of the human body (see Figure 2.6) leaves little doubt that the parts of the body such as the hands, feet, and mouth that are involved in skilled movements have the greatest proportional representation in the cortex. It is noteworthy that the somatosensory (proprioceptive and cutaneous) homunculus matches the motor homunculus in size (Penfield & Rasmussen, 1950). The close relation between cutaneous and proprioceptive inflow and motor outflow, especially in the production of highly skilled movements, appears to be reflected in the juxtaposition of the cortical somatosensory and motor homunculi, indicating their parallel evolutionary origin.

The highly specific, progressively refined, and somewhat duplicated organization of the sensory, motor, and sensory-motor coordination structures of the brain means that the effects of a certain damage on the capacity to produce particular movements may be hard to predict. This is illustrated in an experiment by Brinkman and Kuypers (1972) in which they used monkeys with sectioned corpus collosum ("split-brain" preparation). Their finding is this: If a split-brain monkey is given spatial information about the location of a food pellet to the left eye, it can use its right arm to reach accurately for the food pellet and to retrieve the pellet from a recessed trough by refined, independent movements of the index finger. But if the spatial information is given to the right eye, the monkey uses the right arm normally so far as the reaching movement is concerned, but is unable to make the refined hand and finger movements required to retrieve the pellet; instead of refined finger movements, the monkey uses its hands and fingers to explore tactually (i.e., without visual guidance) the point reached by the arm movement. Thus, with visual information provided only ipsilaterally, the monkey appears to be "blind" so far as the finer movements of the hand and fingers are concerned. The inability to make a fine movement is not a motor deficit, but one of inaccessibility of the appropriate visual information to the contra-lateral sensory-motor coordination organizations required for activating the motor command neurons of the small distal muscles (see Figure 2.3). These findings support the general idea that there are several independently oper-ating sensory-motor coordination regions, that they lie in different parts of the brain, and that, roughly speaking, the more refined a movement, the higher the brain level at which it is organized. The findings also indicate the importance of using pertinent and refined behavioral tasks in analyzing the sensory-motor coordinations underlying any type of movement.

NEURAL PLASTICITY

Persisting changes in the functional properties of the nervous system as a consequence of its own prior activity are usually labeled "plastic changes," and this capability of the nervous system is called *neural plasticity*. A plastic change is inferred when an observed modification of a certain type of neural activity or of a defined segment of behavior is shown, by appropriate control experiments, to have resulted from a particular type of prior physiological activity or environmental encounter. For example, a plastic neural change is inferred from the observation of apparently irreversible reduction in the threshold of electrical stimulation required for producing a neural seizure at a hippocampal site as a consequence of repeated exercise of that neural system. Similarly, a plastic neural change is inferred from the observation that a hungry rat's behavior in a maze is modified when it is trained in that maze. Though all learned modifications of adaptive behavior depend on neural plasticity, not all plastic changes in neural activity may be relevant to any given instance of learned modification of behavior. This section is concerned with the nature of the neural plasticity that underlies learned modifications of adaptive behavior.

Transient Changes in Synaptic Efficacy

Learning may be short-lived, the behavioral modification persisting only minutes or hours, or long-lived, lasting days or years. Whether transient or stable, it must be a matter, essentially, of changes in the pattern of neural transmission from certain neurons to others. For this discussion, then, a plastic neural change is assumed to be an alteration (increase or decrease) in *synaptic efficacy*, that is, the probability of transmission of impulses from the presynaptic to the postsynaptic neuron across a certain synapse.

Evidence that plastic neural changes are fundamentally alterations in synaptic efficacy comes from detailed studies of transient changes in the elicitability of certain reflexes. For example, the gill-withdrawal reflex of a marine molusk, *Aplysia*, has been studied by Kandel and his associates (e.g., Kandel & Tauc, 1965; Castellucci, Pinsker, Kupfermann, & Kandel, 1970). They have shown that the repeated elicitation of this reflex results in a decrement of the reflex movement, and that this habituation decrement is usually quite short-lived. By simultaneously measuring the magnitude of excitatory postsynaptic potentials and the magnitude of reflex movement, they have demonstrated that the basis of the habituation decrement is a transient decrease in the probability of transmission from the axon of the sensory neuron to the postsynaptic interneuron (Castellucci et al., 1970). Studies of the habituation of the spinal flexion reflex in the cat (see Groves & Thompson, 1970) also show that the habituation decrement represents a lower probability of transmission across the synapse between the sensory neuron and the postsynaptic interneuron. Further, sensitization or dishabituation (i.e., increment in reflex movement) has also been found to be closely related to an increase in transmission probability over the same postsensory synapse (Castellucci et al., 1970; Groves & Thompson, 1970). It is safe to conclude that, in general, reflex habituation and reflex sensitization reflect variation in the probability of firing of the interneuron that is efferent to the sensory neuron.

Not all synapses are plastic, and it has been suggested (e.g., Milner, 1957, 1960) that there may be specialized "learning synapses." In their habituation experiments Groves and Thompson (1970) have identified three types of excitatory synapses in the spinal cord of the cat. One of these types is relatively stable in its transmission efficacy with repeated stimulation; this they call the *nonplastic synapse*. A second type decreases in transmission efficacy with repeated stimulation; this is the *habituating synapse*. The third type increases in transmission efficacy as a consequence of the initial few repetitions of the stimulation but decreases in efficacy with further stimulation; this is the *sensitizing synapse*. Groves and Thompson suggest that the combined functioning of a number of such synapses in any reflex would result in the sensitization and habituation effects usually observed with repeated stimulation. They attribute sensitization (dishabituation) effects to extrinsic excitatory discharge arriving at the sensitizing synapse from neurons other than those comprising the reflex arc. Thus, while decrement in the transmission efficacy of a synapse is regarded as an intrinsic consequence of prior transmission through the synapse, the incremental effect is attributed to an extrinsic excitatory influence (see Figure 2.7). Castellucci et al. (1970) have come to a similar conclusion on the basis of their work on the gill-withdrawal reflex of *Aplysia*.

The relatively short-lived changes in efficacy of the synapses involved in habituation and sensitization are probably attributable to such factors as the

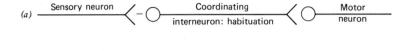

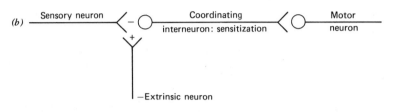

Figure 2.7.   Habituation and sensitization synapses in the spinal arc of the leg-flexion reflex. (*a*) The habituation synapse is an intrinsic part of the reflex arc. (*b*) Sensitization results from excitatory input from an extrinsic neuron.

depletion of excitatory transmitter substance, aftereffects of high-intensity stimulation, monosynaptic low-frequency depression (Thompson & Spencer, 1966), changes in membrane sensitivity (Sharpless, 1964), etc. These are all reversible factors whose effect on synaptic efficacy should be quite transient, dissipating within days if not within a few hours (see Bruner & Kehoe, 1970).

Long-Term Changes in Synaptic Efficacy

Since the mammal is capable of behavioral modifications more lasting than the transient habituation and sensitization effects seen in invertebrates and spinal preparations, the mammalian brain must contain learning synapses that can undergo relatively long-lasting changes. It may be assumed that in the higher structures of the brain a long-term plasticity mechanism is superimposed on the transient mechanisms demonstrated in spinal habituation and sensitization. Presumably synapses capable of long-term plasticity changes include both inhibitory and excitatory neurons. It may also be supposed that the locus of such learning synapses may be quite far removed from the sensory or motor neurons involved in the movements by which learning is tested (see Figure 2.8).

Long-term plasticity would require more or less irreversible strengthening of synaptic junctions, and this in turn would require a stable structural change at the synapse. The fact that learning may not be obliterated by such drastic insults as general anesthesia, electroconvulsive shock, or prolonged cooling of the brain, makes the hypothesis of a structural change as the basis of long-term plasticity unchallengeable.

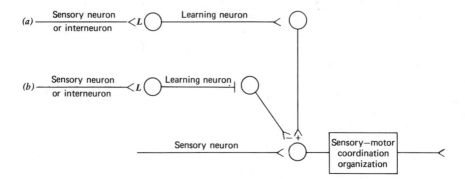

Figure 2.8.   Long-term learning involving structural changes at certain synapses (L). The Learning neuron is an excitatory one in (*a*) and an inhibitory one in (*b*). The learning neurons modulate the transmission efficacy of the synapse between the sensory neuron and the sensory-motor coordination organization or within the sensory-motor coordination organization.

Evidence is now forthcoming that an animal's experience of particular types of rearing situations can result in specific structural changes in its brain. Rosenzweig and his collaborators (see Rosenzweig, Bennett, & Diamond, 1970) have shown that, compared to the brains of rats reared in the normal laboratory environment, the brains of rats reared in impoverished environments are smaller in weight, amount of cortical depth, glial number, and cross-sectional area of certain nuclei. More recently this group (Globus, Rosenzweig, Bennett, & Diamond, 1973) has shown that significant differences between the two groups exist also in the size and number of dendritic spines in the occipital cortex; rats reared under "enriched" conditions, as compared to their impoverished-condition littermates, had a greater density of dendritic spines. Consistent with this is the finding of Valverde (1971) that apical dendrites of the visual cortex of the mouse show deficient growth when the mice are reared in darkness, but only a few days of exposure to normal conditions restores normal growth. Further, Volkmar and Greenough (1972) have shown that higher-order dendritic branching in the occipital cortex is greater in rats reared in a complex environment than those reared in less complex environments. And there is some indication that the growth of dendritic spines of cortical neurons is deficient in retarded human infants and children (Purpura, 1974).

How do experiences of a particular type lead to synaptic growth in particular neurons? Use or "exercise" of the synapse would appear to be a necessary condition of selective growth: the strengthening of a synaptic junction occurs when the synapse is exercised either by the firing of a presynaptic neuron or by some extrinsic influences on some presynaptic or sub-synaptic process. It should be clear that the changes in synaptic efficacy under-lying learning do not involve the making of synaptic junctions *de novo*, but consist in the selective strengthening (further growth) of existing synaptic junctions. For example, the finding of Volkmar and Greenough (1972) that experience increases higher-order dendritic branching but not the growth of primary dendritic branches indicates that the growth of synaptic junctions in learning is an extension of the growth that has already taken place in the course of maturation up to the time of the specific learning experience.

Woody and Engel (1972) have shown that the threshold for eliciting an electromyographic response from a muscle by electrical microstimulation of the appropriate motor cortex site is decreased as a consequence of condition-ing of a response (e.g., nose twitching or eye blinking) involving that muscle. On the basis of this and other findings, Woody (1974) has suggested that the lowered thresholds may represent conditioned, persistent increases in post-synaptic excitability of motor cortex neurons. The origins of such conditioned increases in postsynaptic excitability may well lie in other parts of the brain.

Ultimately, of course, the basis of the growth in synaptic processes must lie in the biochemical mechanisms responsible for neuronal growth and elaboration. The biochemical mechanisms usually invoked are linked to ribonucleic acid (RNA) activity and protein synthesis (see Gaito, 1971; Horn, Rose, & Bateson, 1973; Milner, 1970, Chap. 21; Ungar, 1972). For the present purpose it is not necessary to try to examine the claims of the various hypotheses of the biochemical basis of learning or memory. Any mechanisms that would yield selective synaptic growth as a consequence of the exercise of the neurons concerned could be appended to the present account of the neural basis of learning.

The Problem of Consolidation

A related question concerns the time it takes for the synaptic growth insti-gated by a learning experience to be completed. In the past, some indirect evidence has been taken to mean that a certain period following the learning experience is required for "consolidation" of whatever neuronal changes are involved in the learning. This evidence comes from studies of experimental retrograde amnesia in which the subject is given a traumatic brain insult (e.g., electroconvulsive shock, cortical spreading depression, deep anesthetic stupor, hypothermia) at varying intervals after a single learning trial, and the maximum interval between the learning trial and the trauma that always produces retrograde amnesia for that learning experience (i.e., no saving in learning the task or failure of recall in a memory task) is then determined. This maximum interval could be considered as the time required for the learning to be completed, the memory to be "consolidated," the labile perseveration trace to be turned into a permanent engram, etc.

Though the usual finding in such studies has been that of considerable retrograde amnesia, which diminishes as the interval between the learning trial and the trauma is increased, several recent experiments have shown that under certain conditions no retrograde amnesia may occur even at very short intervals (Chorover & Schiller, 1966; Hine & Paolino, 1970; Lewis, Miller, & Misanin, 1968; Mendoza & Adams, 1969). Indeed the fact that little or no retrograde amnesia may be obtained even when the interval is one second or less (Lewis, Miller, & Misanin, 1968), suggests that the interval at which complete retrograde amnesia is always produced may be no longer than the interval (a few hundred milliseconds) within which perceptual masking occurs—in effect, an interval within which no learning could have taken place (Weiskrantz, 1970). It may be concluded, then, that whatever the explanation of retrograde amnesia when it is obtained, there is no necessary reason to postulate that synaptic growth in learning must always require a post-transmission time of stabilizing or consolidation. Synaptic growth, if it parallels learning, could be instantaneous.

But how is the commoner finding of a temporal gradient of retrograde amnesia (decreasing amnesia with increasing interval between the learning trial and the trauma) to be explained? This has been a controversial question. Some attribute the amnesia gradient to a consolidation process that fixes the hitherto unstable "memory trace" (e.g., Burnham, 1903; Glickman, 1961; McGaugh, 1966), while others attribute it to performance variables that influence "memory expression" or retrieval in learning and memory tasks (e.g., Lashley, 1918; Lewis, 1969; Weiskrantz, 1966). The performance variables that have been shown to affect the retrograde amnesia gradient include post-learning-trial experiences during the learning-trauma interval (Chorover & Schiller, 1966; Miller, Misanin, & Lewis, 1969), "reminder" stimuli (Koppenaal, Jagoda, & Cruce, 1967; Misanin, Miller, & Lewis, 1968; Quatermain, Paolino, & Miller, 1965), competing responses (Lewis & Maher, 1965), and "state-dependence" of learning (Chute & Wright, 1973; Thompson & Grossman, 1972). Since no direct evidence for a consolidation process is available, and since the time-dependent aspects of retrograde amnesia are also consistent with the retrieval hypothesis, there is at present no evidence that uniquely supports the hypothesis of a consolidation process.

The consolidation-versus-retrieval controversy appears to be wrongly drawn. The consolidation hypothesis is of little value unless it specifies what is the nature of the "memory trace" that is consolidated and in what sense it is "consolidated." Similarly, the retrieval hypothesis is of little value unless it specifies what is the nature of the "memory" that is "stored" and in what sense it is stored or retrieved. In the absence of these specifications the most meaningful approach would appear to be that of trying to interpret the phenomena of retrograde amnesia in terms of the general conditions that promote learning of particular associations, say, A:B, and those that promote the recall of B by A. These conditions will be discussed in some of the following chapters. What may be noted here is that the conditions that influence learning and recall go far beyond what is usually called a "learning trial" in the consolidation-versus-retrieval controversy. A study of these conditions suggests that what an animal learns in a learning experience depends not only on what happens in the learning trial as defined, but on several other circumstances that precede and follow the learning trial. The basis of the controversy may lie at least partly in ambiguity about the definition of a learning trial.

Maturation and Learning

The idea that neuronal growth is the basis of relatively long-term learning makes possible a unified conceptualization of maturation and learning. For the question, "How are synaptic junctions strengthened in learning?" is an inherent part of the broader question, "How are neuronal connections formed or obliterated generally?" The factors that determine the direction of growth of a neuron, its rate of growth or degeneration, its branching, and its ultimate synaptic junctions, are relevant to both maturation and learning. For a review of the recent advances in knowledge about the factors controlling neuronal growth and synaptogenesis the reader is referred to the works of Gaze (1970), Horridge (1968), and Jacobson (1969), as well as to a summary by Edds, Barkley, and Fambrough (1972).

A feature of neuronal growth particularly relevant to a discussion of learning is that, in many cases, maturational growth and functional specification of synaptic junctions of a neuron depend on the exercise of that neuron. There is considerable evidence showing that the stimulation of certain neurons is essential if those neurons are to form or maintain their normal, species-typical junctions. For example, Wiesel and Hubel (1965) have shown that, by preventing visual input into one eye of a kitten for about three months, it is possible to reduce greatly the proportion of cortical cells which can be activated by stimulation of the deprived eye. The proportion of responsive cortical cells also declines progressively if the visual input is restricted to diffuse light. If the requisite conditions for the formation of species-typical junctions are not present during a certain critical period, the neurons degenerate or form abnormal (species-atypical) junctions, and this abnormality then appears to be irreversible (Wiesel & Hubel, 1963, 1965). Findings of this type suggest that the synaptic junctions formed or maintained by one neuron may be determined, apart from other maturational factors, by the activity of that neuron during the maturational period.

Clearly, no sharp distinction can be drawn between the formation of synaptic junctions during species-specific "maturation" and their further (postmaturational) strengthening during individual "learning." If neural plasticity is defined as enhancement of synaptic efficacy, then both maturational and postmaturational modifications of behavior involve the same process of synaptic growth. The actual physicochemical processes underlying neuronal growth, whether attributed to maturation or to learning, are presumably the same. Thus, in terms of changes in synaptic junctions, the only workable distinction between maturation and learning could be in terms of changes that take place *partly* as a consequence of exercise of neurons during the "maturational period" of neuronal growth and those that take place *primarily* as a consequence of exercise of neurons after the maturational period. It is futile to try to separate the maturational from the learned modifications of behavior in terms of synaptic growth.

The period of synaptic growth varies greatly for different neurons; in general, the connections of large, long neurons become permanently specified very early in life, but the small, short neurons retain the capacity to grow and form new connections until late in development (Jacobson, 1969). On this basis, it appears likely that the type of behavioral changes that are usually described as learned (postmaturational), as opposed to those described as maturational, are more likely to arise from the growth of small interneurons lying within the (transformational) structures of the brain than from the growth of large transmission neurons that interconnect those structures.

CHAPTER 3

Elicitation of Directed Movements

The adaptiveness of any action is ultimately dependent on the effectiveness of the particular movements that comprise it, and the effectiveness of an individual movement is largely a matter of its directedness. Every movement has an address—it is projected at some point in space, it has a certain direction in relation to environmental objects, including parts of the animal's own body. The present account of the production of movements therefore starts with an examination of the basis of their directedness.

DIRECTEDNESS OF MOVEMENTS

A man can look at an object in space and reach for it with an arm in one quick motion. The muscular activity involved in such a directed movement would vary depending on the direction of the object in relation to the body (whether the object is to the right or left, up or down, etc.), as well as on the exact initial position of the responding arm (whether it is relaxed, flexed at the elbow, extended above his head, etc.) relative to the current orientation of the body as a whole (whether standing, sitting, lying, etc.). Clearly, the production of an accurate movement in this case requires the coordination of the visual information about the location of the object with the proprioceptive information about the initial arm position, as well as with information about body orientation and posture. Similarly, in order to point an arm at an unseen sound-source, the proprioceptive arm-position information must be coordinated with the auditorily represented sound location. The required information about limb position need not always be proprioceptive; position of the parts of the body may be known visually or cutaneously, and the orientation of the body as a whole may be known visually or through the vestibular sensory apparatus. Whatever the sensory modality or modalities that may provide the necessary spatial information, the main point to note is that normally every movement requires the coordination of spatial information about the target stimulus with spatial information about the orientation of the body and the position of the responding limb.

Spatial Information About the Target

Information about the location of a target in the environment is provided by both exteroceptive distance receptors and exteroceptive contact receptors. It is mainly the visual and auditory systems that represent the direction and distance of target stimuli relative to the animal's position in space. From any given fixed position an animal can extend the spatial information available to it by moving the body parts containing particular exteroceptors. Thus adjustments of neck (e.g., head turning), eyes (e.g., visual scanning), ears (e.g., a rabbit's ear cocking), and nose (e.g., an elephant's trunk extension) may add to distal spatial information. Similarly, extension of limbs and tongue, together with manipulation and palpation, may add to proximal spatial information.

A subcortical structure that is important in the representation of the location of environmental stimuli is the superior colliculus. Its importance lies in the fact that it is a polysensory structure and is directly involved in production of head and eye movements. The superior colliculus receives topographic projections from visual, auditory, and somatosensory systems. The feature detectors in the superior colliculus are activated differentially by stimulus changes that occur at different locations in relation to the animal; the nonspatial stimulus features within a modality appear not to be represented in the superior colliculus. This structure may thus be regarded as a "pure" spatial representation structure; it tells where a stimulus event is occurring, not what it is. However, the spatial differentiation in the superior colliculus is quite gross; the receptive fields of spatial feature detectors are large, sometimes covering large proportions of the left or right stimulus fields (Gordon, 1972). The output from the superior colliculus appears to provide the basis for directed eye and head movements (orienting, fixating, and tracking) in relation to the location and motion of environmental stimuli; undercutting the superior colliculus abolishes the ability to orient accurately (Schneider, 1969). Through its connections with the cerebral cortex, which has a much finer representation of spatial information, the superior colliculus provides the basis for finely controlled eye and head movements in relation to environmental stimuli.

Spatial Information About the Body

Spatial information about the body is provided by the vestibular, proprioceptive, kinesthetic, and somatosensory systems.

The vestibular system represents information about the orientation of the body as a whole. Vestibular receptors discharge mainly when some change in head orientation (e.g., tilting the body from a vertical to horizontal position) is in the process of occurring. Similarly, information about the motion of the body as a whole is available only when some change in speed or direction of motion (e.g., linear or rotational acceleration) is taking place. The vestibular receptors of the inner ear, which are sensitive to changes in orientation and speed, are largely incapable of generating tonic, steady-state neural signals representing continuously maintained bodily orientations and speed; they produce mainly phasic signals representing change.

The proprioceptive system provides spatial information about movable bodily parts. The position of limbs and of other jointed parts is represented by the position of the joints to which they are attached (hip, shoulder, wrist, jaw, etc.). Information about the maintained position of a joint depends on the static joint receptors, which discharge steadily and are resistant to adaptation. Joints also contain dynamic receptors, which are sensitive to the speed of joint displacement (and the attached limb); these receptors respond during the kinematic phase of displacement and adapt quickly. Together, these two types of joint receptors provide information about the initial position of a limb (e.g., whether an arm is level with the shoulder or is in line with the length of the trunk, whether an elbow is flexed or extended, whether it is the index or the middle finger that is flexed), and about the speed and acceleration of the displacement of the limb from one position to another, as well as about the terminal position of the limb.

The kinesthetic system provides information about the states of tendons and muscles. Information about phasic changes in the states of tendons, whether produced actively (by central efferent discharge) or passively (by mechanical deformation), is apparently transduced by the Golgi receptors, which are found in the tendons joining the muscles to joints. These receptors have a high threshold of excitation and thus appear to be well suited for transmitting information about large phasic displacement of tendons superimposed on a certain steadily maintained state of the tendons, but their exact function remains to be elucidated. The organs of true "muscle sense" are the muscle spindles. Information about the maintained tonic level of muscle tension, as well as about abrupt phasic changes in tension, is generated at the sensory endings of the muscle spindle. These nerve endings are highly sensitive to stretch, which reflects the degree of contraction of muscle fibers. Changes in the extent of stretch of the muscle spindle, produced actively or passively, cause corresponding changes in the volume of nerve impulses along the sensory fibers.

Though the central projections of the kinesthetic systems are somatotopically organized in the cortex, it is not established whether the kinesthetic system per se contributes to conscious awareness of muscular contraction. Earlier evidence suggested that kinesthetic discharge from a certain muscle does *not* provide a direct basis for telling that the muscle has contracted. For example, Merton (1964) found that, if a subject's eye is temporarily blinded by blackening of the cornea, and the eye and skin around it are treated with a local anesthetic (to eliminate cutaneous information), the subject reports no awareness of movement when the eye is moved passively with forceps. This means that kinesthetic discharge from the eye muscles cannot by itself tell us about the position of eye muscles—in which direction the eyes are pointing. Similarly, it was reported that, if the terminal joint of the thumb is anesthetized by a local injection, the subject is unable to tell of any movement of the thumb when it is moved passively (Marsden, Merton, & Morton, 1971, 1972). However, recent evidence obtained by Goodwin, McCloskey, and Matthews (1972a, 1972b) and Skavenski (1972) indicates that subjects may be aware of their movements in their experiments on the basis of kinesthetic input alone. But the degree of movement required to produce a reliable estimate of eye movements was probably too great to be useful in the normal control of eye movements, and the possibility of other sources of information cannot be ruled out. Whether or not there is awareness of kinesthetic stimulation as such, there is good reason to believe that kinesthetic inflow may play an important part in the determination of movement production. There are topographically precise connections between the primary somatosensory ("sensorimotor") cortex and motor ("motorsensory") cortex (Jones & Powell, 1968). Further, the evoked response in the somatosensory cortex produced by peripheral or thalamic stimulation precedes the response in the motor cortex, and highly localized evoked responses in motor cortex can be reliably produced by electrical microstimulation of the somatosensory cortex (Asanuma, Stoney, & Abzug, 1968; Thompson, Stoney, & Asanuma, 1970).

The somatosensory system transmits information about the location on the skin of pressure (touch), warmth, cold, and tissue-damaging (pain) stimuli. While the cutaneous representation in the cortex is highly refined topographically, the visceral representation is crude.

As described in Chapter 2, the proprioceptive, kinesthetic, and somatosensory systems, transmitting several modalities of information from different parts of the body, are projected somatotopically to the primary and secondary somatosensory areas of the cortex. The modality-unspecific spatial aspects of this information are projected to the tertiary, polysensory areas of the (posterior) parietal and adjoining region of the cortex.

Coordination of Spatial Information

Spatial information from two sources may be said to be coordinated when the neural inputs from the two sources reach and influence some common neurons. The production of a movement requires two types of coordination. First, it requires the coordination of all the neural inputs that provide bodily information (vestibular, proprioceptive, kinesthetic, and somatosensory). This coordination of bodily information is probably achieved through the activity of the somatosensory cortex, which has important connections with the cerebellum through the nucleus ventralis lateralis of the thalamus (Sasaki, Matsuda, & Mizuno, 1973). The second type of coordination is the true spatial coordination involving the integration of spatial information about the environmental (exteroceptive and interoceptive inputs) with the bodily information. The locus of this coordination appears to be the tertiary or non-specific areas of the (posterior) parietal cortex. Neurons in this region are activated by exteroceptive stimuli of various modalities (Thompson, Johnson, & Hoopes, 1963). Neuroanatomical studies of the opossum have shown that three separate nuclei in the thalamus project convergently to the parietal cortex (Killackey & Ebner, 1973). It is also known that single neurons projecting from the somatosensory cortex to the motor cortex receive multiple inputs from the basal ganglia and the cerebellum (Frigyesi & Machek, 1971; Purpura, Frigyese, McMurtry, & Scarff, 1966).

The axons of the converging subcortical fibers, together with inputs from the secondary somatosensory cortex, are presumably distributed in a multiple, overlapping arrangement to the spatial stellate cells of the posterior parietal cortex. It may be supposed, then, that these stellate cells serve as the coordinators of the environmental and bodily spatial information. Different combinations of spatial information would activate different stellate cells, so that a unique pattern of excitation of stellate cells would exist at any moment, representing the current environmental and bodily information. When a sufficient number of the stellate cells of a certain column were activated, a neural discharge would be distributed to the sensory-motor coordination organizations in the thalamus, basal ganglia, and the cortex. This hypothetical, structural arrangement is shown in Figure 3.1.

As may be expected, then, lesions of the posterior parietal lobe result in marked disturbances of spatial integration (Semmes, Weinstein, Ghent, & Teuber, 1963). Human patients with such lesions frequently lose their spatial orientation and confuse spatial relations within their immediate surroundings. For example, they may miss finding their bed in a hospital ward, be unable to follow a map, misalign stimuli that are meant to be parallel, and be incapable of constructing a figure from its component parts or to copy letters such as k, b, and w. In milder cases such disturbances appear only when the patient is asked to perform the task from memory and not when he is dealing with stimuli directly in front of him (Luria, 1973, p. 150). These disorders appear to arise from a failure of coordination of exteroceptive,

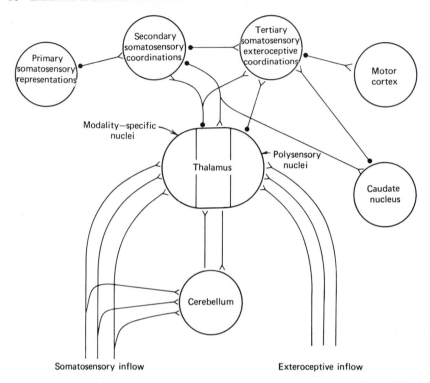

Figure 3.1. A schematic diagram of possible projections involved in the integration of spatial information.

mainly visual, information about certain target stimuli and bodily information about the limbs that are to be moved in relation to those stimuli. The exact neural mechanisms of such spatial coordinations are now being experimentally analyzed by several investigators (e.g., Mountcastle, 1961; Pohl, 1973).

FORM AND PROBABILITY OF MOVEMENT

Turn now to the problem of the production of any specific movement. Assuming that a movement is produced when a number of motor neurons of a certain movement command are activated, we may ask: What factors determine the activation of a particular type of movement command? It should be clear from the preceding discussions that, in general, the occurrence of any movement is determined critically by sensory information about: (*a*) the location of the target stimulus in relation to which the movement is made, (*b*) other features (color, shape, distance, texture, etc.) of the target stimulus and of its background, and (c) the position and state of the muscular apparatus of the various movable parts of the body. In other words, a movement is determined by the momentary sensory pattern arising from a current stimulus configuration made up from all these sources of stimulus input. The essential idea I want to elaborate in this section is that both the form and the probability of occurrence of a movement are determined by the effective strength or potency of the momentary sensory pattern, which in turn is determined partly by the current stimulus configuration and partly by influences from other parts of the brain that modulate the strength of the sensory projections to particular sensory-motor coordination organizations.

A Model of Movement Selection

A hypothetical model of movement selection based on the above consideration is presented in Figure 3.2. In this model each of several alternative movements is designated M_1, M_2, M_3, etc. Each movement command, m_1, m_2, m_3, etc., receives the output of a certain sensory-motor coordinating organization, c_1, c_2, c_3, etc., and projects in an overlapping arrangement to motor neurons, as described in Chap. 2 (Figure 2.4). The probability of activation of a certain motor command, say m_2, depends on the volume of net excitatory discharge (total excitatory minus total inhibitory) projected to the sensory-motor coordination organization from which m_2 exits. In turn, the probability of activation of each sensory-motor coordination organization depends on the sensory complexes, s_1, s_2, s_3, etc., formed by the projections of the feature detectors activated by particular environmental stimulus configurations, S_1, S_2, S_3, etc., as well as by sensory inflow representing bodily information. Each sensory-motor coordination organization has connections with all modalities of sensory projection, so that a common set of coordination organizations subserves all types of sensory inflow. Thus, all the sensory information required for making a directed movement in relation to certain features of the current stimulus configuration is integrated in the sensory-motor coordination organization. Since decorticate animals can make directed movements, it is clear the required sensory-motor coordination organizations also exist at other levels of the brain (e.g., the collicular and midbrain levels).

Note, in Figure 3.2, that each sensory-motor coordinating organization may receive projections from several environmental stimulus feature detectors as well as several bodily stimulus feature detectors. Assuming, for the sake of simplicity, that all other brain systems (e.g., motivational, cognitive) are in a steady state, this model makes the production of a movement dependent on the momentary sensory complex, representing a certain stimulus configuration. That is, other factors remaining constant, it is the momentarily

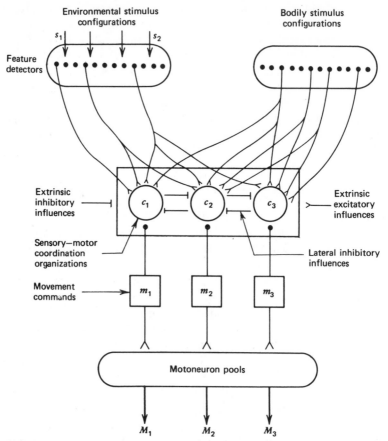

Figure 3.2. Production of movement. A schematic plan showing the converging inflow to and diverging outflow from sensory-motor coordination organizations. In the absence of any major extrinsic influences or intensity differences, S_1 would lead to M_1 and S_2 to M_3. An intermediate stimulus configuration may lead to M_2. See text for explanation.

active feature detectors representing the current environmental and bodily stimulus configurations that determine which sensory-motor coordination organization would be activated—which movement would occur. And the probability that any given movement would occur at a certain moment depends on the relative momentary potency of the various sensory complexes required for particular movements. The *potency* of a sensory complex or its corresponding stimulus configuration refers to the density (volume per unit time) of the net excitatory neural discharge that the sensory complex transmits across the afferent synapses of any given sensory-motor coordination organization. The net excitatory neural discharge depends in turn on the intensity of the stimulus configuration, as well as on the intrinsic excitatory and inhibitory discharges on the synaptic junctions between the sensory projections and the sensory-motor coordination organizations. The extrinsic discharges represent the activity of any neural systems that may be connected to particular classes of sensory-motor coordination organizations. According to this model, then, both the form and the probability of occurrence of a movement is determined by the relative momentary density of the net excitatory afferent discharge delivered to the sensory-motor coordination organization that generates that movement. If extrinsic contributions to the momentary afferent density are ignored, the most critical determiners of movement production are the nature and intensity of the momentary stimulus configuration and the strength of the neural sensory complex it generates.

Since usually there is little apparent evidence of competition among movements, and, in general, movements occur smoothly, it is likely that the more highly excited coordination organizations are capable of inhibiting the less excited coordinations, so that the sensory-motor coordination organizations corresponding to one movement, once slightly excited, could quickly dominate the others. Such a mechanism would imply that each sensory-motor coordination organization has reciprocal inhibitory connections with other sensory-motor coordinations.

As noted above, the efficacy of a stimulus configuration in producing a movement is also determined by the extrinsic excitatory and inhibitory discharges at the afferent synapses of the relevant sensory-motor coordination organizations. In general, habituation to a stimulus configuration would increase the extrinsic inhibitory discharge, decrease synaptic efficacy, and thus tend to decrease the effectiveness of the relevant sensory pattern in activating the sensory-motor coordination organization. Habituation decrement in the production of a response is then attributable to decreased efficacy of a stimulus configuration owing to the operation of some inhibitory mechanism dependent on the repetition of that stimulus configuration in the absence of any associated incentive (aversive or appetitive motivation) stimulation. I shall suggest later that the association of a stimulus configuration with a punishing or rewarding incentive stimulus increases synaptic efficacy through the operation of other extrinsic mechanisms, and hence increases the efficacy of the stimulus configuration.

Role of Stimulus Configuration

The statement that stimulus *configurations* are the critical environmental determinants of movements is meant to emphasize that simple stimuli, such as those that elicit specific reflexes, do not provide sufficient stimulus conditions for the production of a directed movement. Movements are instigated not by target stimulus features alone but by target stimulus features embedded in proper background stimulus contexts. The importance of the background in the determination of movement is shown by several observations. For example, the herring gull will approach an egg (an object of certain size, color, and shape) only when it is presented on an appropriate background (Tinbergen, 1951); the human infant will gaze for long periods at line drawings only when they form patterns of certain optimum figure-ground complexity (Fantz, 1963); and the rat may not approach a familiar target stimulus when the overall test situation (the background) is unfamiliar, but may approach an unfamiliar target stimulus when the test situation is familiar (Sheldon, 1969). Even minor differences in figure-ground complexity have been shown to produce different degrees of electroencephalographic desynchronization in human subjects (Berlyne, McDonnell, Nicki, & Parham, 1967).

The concept of the critical stimulus configuration for the production of particular movements is similar to the concept of "releasing stimulus" found in the writings of ethologists (e.g., Hinde, 1970; Lorenz, 1950, 1966; Tinbergen, 1951), and that of the "unconditioned stimulus" in the conditioning literature (Pavlov, 1927). The difference is that while these concepts regard a particular stimulus by itself as *the* elicitor of a certain specific type of "fixed action patterns" or "unconditioned responses," the concept of critical stimulus configuration refers to a total stimulus configuration. rather than any specific isolatable stimulus. Critical stimulus configuration is a more general concept; what are called "releasing" or "unconditioned" stimuli are a part of the environmental components of the total (environmental and bodily) stimulus configuration that is essential for the production of a certain movement.

Note that the above statement does *not* mean that there is an exclusive one-to-one linkage between particular stimulus configurations and particular movements, as in the case of reflexes. It means rather that, while any particular type of movement may be produced by many different types of stimulus configurations, any given stimulus configuration can contribute to the production of only a limited variety of movements. In other words, each sensory-motor coordination organization receives convergent afferent inputs from many feature detectors, but each feature detector sends divergent efferents to only a limited number of sensory-motor coordination organizations. This arrangement makes it possible for one motor system to cope with all the environmental circumstances which impinge on the animal through several sensory systems.

At first it may be hard to accept the idea that the form of movement is critically determined largely by the influence of momentary sensory complexes on maturationally fixed sensory-motor coordination organizations. But such an assumption is inescapable. Adaptive behavior is environmentally addressed, and the only way in which behavior can be directed at particular target stimuli in the environment is that certain sensory representations of those stimuli and of the movable parts of the body be critical factors in the production of any movement. Ordinarily it is difficult to observe directly a clear relation between a movement and certain types of stimulus configurations. This is so because the situations to which animals are typically exposed are highly complex and are continually changing in their exact stimulus characteristics. The observed relation between stimulus configurations and movement, therefore, is highly statistical or probabilistic, even though, as suggested here, the underlying connections of the sensory-motor coordinating organizations are highly specific and fixed. The observation that the behavior of animals is variable and richly diverse does not contradict the broad assumption of specific and fixed neuronal connections at this level of organization. The variability and diversity of behavior arises partly from the variability and diversity of momentary stimulus configurations. But there are other factors that will be discussed in later chapters.

The above discussion implies that the movements that an animal produces under experimental conditions can be controlled, though only in a probabilistic way, by controlling environmental stimulus configurations. Some of the relations between particular stimulus configurations and movements they promote are well known, and this knowledge is routinely used in the design of experimental situations. Thus the pattern of the rat's activity in an observation box may be controlled by manipulating detailed stimulus features of the box. For example, it is known that box walls with vertical black-and-white stripes are likely to produce more rearing acts and head movements in the vertical plane than walls with horizontal black-and-white stripes. Further, if the top of the box is left uncovered or is transparent, the animal is more likely to jump toward the top than it would in a covered box. The presentation of a noise of a certain intensity is likely to produce orienting acts, but a noise of somewhat greater intensity is likely to produce freezing. In general, if the animal's acts are recorded by a time-sampling method, the relative frequency and sequences of various acts that comprise its "general activity" seem to depend on the details of the momentary sensory complex (Bindra, 1961; Bindra & Spinner, 1958; Zucker & Bindra, 1961). It is this type of information about the control of movement by manipulating stimulus configurations that constitutes the "background knowledge" necessary for arranging experiments that require animals of a certain species to perform specified types of acts, such as lever-pressing, freezing, nose-poking, grooming, burrowing, nursing, and attacking (see Bindra, 1961; Breland & Breland, 1961; Seligman, 1970).

Perhaps the most convincing evidence for the important role of environmental stimulus configurations comes from studies of the approach and withdrawal, preference and aversion, and the behavior of neonates. For example, Kovach (1971) examined the approach responses of neonatal chicks to flickering lights of different colors and found that there was a significantly lower tendency to approach green than to approach blue, yellow, and red. The important role of contact and sound in eliciting filial responses has been demonstrated in neonatal guinea pigs (Harper, 1970). And human infants have been shown to respond differentially to normal and distorted faces (Kagan, Henker, Hen-Tov, Levine, & Lewis, 1966).

An interesting finding that supports the suggested relation between stimulus configurations and movements is that of Condon and Sander (1974). They studied the relation between the movements made by neonate human infants to certain adult speech sounds. They found that certain sustained segments of movements of head, shoulders, elbows, hips, and feet corresponded with the utterances of particular adult speech sounds. For example, on hearing the sound kk of "come," an infant's head is turned to the right, the elbow extended slightly, the left shoulder rotated outwards, the big toe of the left foot adducted, etc., and these movements were sustained for 0.07 sec, the duration for which the sound lasts. Further, the transitions in speech sounds were accompanied by changes in movements. These findings indicate that the relation between stimulus configurations and movements may be highly refined and specific, and deserves detailed experimental analysis.

Stimulus-Movement "Belongingness"

Since it is unlikely that the sensory projections of various modalities are distributed equally and uniformly to all sensory-motor coordination organizations, it is to be expected that certain movements would be linked more closely to stimuli of certain modalities than to others. Thus movements involving parts of the snout (nose, mouth, and lips) appear to be more strongly connected to the olfactory and gustatory sensory projections than to those of other sensory modalities. Vestibular, auditory, and visual modalities appear to be more strongly linked to head, eye, and ear movements, while the cutaneous and proprioceptive sensory projections appear to be more strongly linked to movements of the limbs. Such preferential linkage or "belongingness" of sensory projections and motor outflow has obvious adaptive significance.

In general, information about any one side of an animal's environment ("left field" or "right field") stimulates receptors on that side of the body, while the ensuing neural information is usually transmitted to both hemispheres. However, the information in the two hemispheres is *not* equally utilizable for the production of movements from the two sides of the body. At least at the cortical level, each hemisphere is more directly linked to the muscles of the contralateral side of the body. Since frequently the stimuli in any part of the stimulus field are more directly represented in the contralateral hemisphere (at least in the visual and cutaneous modalities), there should be greater readiness of animals to perform movements with parts of the body that are on the same side of the body as the stimulus—that is, with muscles that are controlled by the same hemisphere as the one that receives direct projections from the stimulus.

This differential readiness for responding with muscles that are on the same side of the body as the target stimulus may be seen quite early in life. In reaching an attractive object presented to it, a human infant uses its right arm if the object is presented in the right visual field, the left arm if the object is presented in the left visual field, and, often, both arms if the object is presented in the middle (White, 1971). Such ipsilateral preference in responding is also evident in certain studies of reaction time. In a simple reaction time experiment, if a tactual stimulus is presented on the right hand and the subject is required to respond with a finger of the left hand, the reaction time is longer (slower reaction speed) than if stimulation and responding parts are on the same side of the body; the difference in time (about 10 msec) is of the same order as the estimates of time required for transcallosal transfer of information from one hemisphere to the other (Muram & Carmon, 1972). Similarly, in reaction time experiments on stimulus-response "compatibility" it has been found that reactions to auditory or visual stimuli presented in the left or right fields are faster when the responding hand is ipsilateral to the side of stimulation than when it is contralateral (Broadbent & Gregory, 1962; Simon, Hinrichs, & Craft, 1970; Wallace, 1971). The difference remains even if the subject is unable to see his responding hand (Wallace, 1972); this means that the left-right spatial information about the target stimuli need not be integrated with visual information about the hand but can be integrated directly with proprioceptive information about the hand.

DEVELOPMENT OF MOVEMENTS

Studies of neonatal development have shown that discrete movements emerge through a process of differentiation of gross bodily motions into specific movements. For example, Bridges (1932) observed in human infants that identifiable emotional reactions such as "anger," "disgust," and "fear," are differentiated between the third and the sixth month of life from an earlier, primitive state of general distress. Bolles and Woods (1964) found that the neonatal rat pup is capable of side-to-side movements of the head but that these are part of a gross pattern of locomotion; the head movements do not become independent of walking until about 8 days of age. Reviewing similar observations from a variety of sources, Schneirla has offered a general account that serves well as a broad working assumption.

According to Schneirla (1959, 1965), specific movements emerge from two types of undifferentiated primitive excitement, "delight" and "distress." The motor output of undifferentiated delight excitement is made up of a preponderance of abduction and extension of limbs and head, which are accompanied by a steady visceral condition, characterized by the predominance of parasympathetic autonomic reactions. The motor output of undifferentiated distress excitement is made up of a preponderance of adduction and flexion of limbs and head, which are accompanied by an interruptive visceral condition, produced by a temporary predominance of sympathetic autonomic reactions. The distress excitement is more generalized and vigorous than the delight excitement. The overall impression given by delight reactions is one of expansive, environment-accepting attitude (e.g., extending neck and arms, visual fixation, ingestion into mouth, smiling), and that given by distress reactions is one of circumspect, environment-rejecting attitude (e.g., flexing arms, averting eyes, ejection from mouth, crying).

Neural Basis of Differentiation

The differentiation process that makes an animal capable of making specific and discrete individual movements is apparently a part of the process of neuronal growth and branching during the maturational period. Though much remains to be learned about the nature and control of neuronal growth, three points relevant to the present discussion appear to be reasonably well established (Horridge, 1968; Jacobson, 1969). One is that during maturational growth axons and dendrites of neurons are elaborated in particular directions and that they form highly specific synaptic links at their terminal locations. A second is that while during the maturational period a neuron may be pluripotent, in that it is capable of forming several alternative synaptic links, once the maturational growth is completed, its links become uniquely specified and fixed. The third point is that in vertebrates the specification of terminal synaptic locations seems to proceed from the periphery (receptors and muscles) to different levels of the central nervous system (Horridge, 1968). For example, the central representation of the receptive fields of sensory neurons is specified during maturation partly by their distal connections with the receptors; the connections made by the axonal endings of a first-order sensory neuron with the dendrites of a second-order neuron are determined by the events at the receptor surface, and the connections made by the axonal endings of the second-order neurons with more central neurons are determined by events at the first-order and second-order neurons. Thus the functional properties of neurons are, at least in part, specified from neuron to neuron in a peripheral-to-central direction. This pattern of neuronal growth and branching means that peripheral sensory stimulation and muscular innervation influence the development of the receptive and innervation fields of central neurons. Thus the sensory-motor coordinations established centrally depend to some extent on the types of sensory input the animal has undergone in its own life in its own environment.

The above observations suggest that the basis of differentiation of specific movements lies in the formation of progressively more refined linkages between sensory inflow and motor outflow during the maturational period. That is, the process of movement differentiation involves the development of refined sensory-motor coordination organizations. Further, on the assumption that sensory and motor neurons are the ones with long axons, it seems likely that the connections that make up sensory-motor coordination organizations would become uniquely specified and fixed relatively early in life. On this basis I assume that the central connections of the input and exit neurons of a sensory-motor coordination organization are determined during the maturational period and thereafter remain fixed and unalterable (except through tissue damage). This implies that the basis of any learned modifications of behavior would lie in structures other than those containing sensory-motor coordination organizations.

Reaching Targets in Space

If an infant reaches for a toy, the first movement of the arm puts the hand, say, in a location nearer the toy but off target to the left (see Figure 3.3). Then the infant makes another movement based on the new current information about the location of the hand and the toy, and now its hand ends up still nearer to the toy but slightly off target to the right. The third movement is made on the basis of the then current information and this may lead to contact with the toy. Such progressive correction of directional error requires continual information about the relative locations of the target and the hand at the end of the responding arm. The accuracy of such a visually guided act of reaching depends on the extent to which the error, or the discrepancy in the alignment of the eyes, hand, and target, can alter the next movement. It is the stimulus configuration of the spatial discrepancy in alignment that serves as the eliciting stimulus for the next movement. Each successive "error stimulus configuration" elicits a movement with less error until the hand reaches the target and touches it.

The spatial-motor coordinations required for reaching targets in space may be modified through experience. Mammals, at least, can compensate for experimentally introduced alterations of the required sensory information. For example, distortion of visual information by lenses produces errors of reaching targets that mammals manage to correct with continued experience under the distorting conditions, but frogs and birds appear incapable of making the necessary adjustments (see Taub, 1968). Such adjustments are probably made continually during development, for example, as an infant's bodily parts get larger, or as astigmatism, unilateral deafness, and other sensory defects require some spatial corrections in reaching environmental targets.

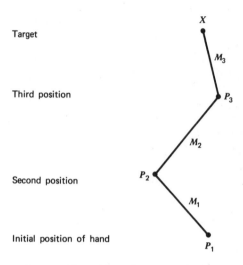

Figure 3.3. Guidance of an act of reaching. The progressive improvement of aim is the consequence of the redirection of successive movements by the coordination of visual spatial information about the target object and the hand with proprioceptive spatial information about the current location of the joints of the arm.

The basis on which appropriate adjustments in reaching targets in space are made is not wholly understood and is being studied through experiments in which accurate performance is disrupted by experimental intervention and then the course of adjustment to the intervention is examined. Consider the experiments of Harris (1965). If a normal adult wears lenses that displace his field of vision, say, to the right by 20°, and is asked to reach a visual target with, say, his right arm (without viewing the arm), he will initially miss the target by tending to point or reach too far to the right; his visual space has been displaced to the right in relation to his right arm as well as the body. However, with a little practice of reaching while observing his arm through the lenses (adaptation trials), he will adapt and begin to perform accurately again. Now, if the lenses are removed and the subject is asked to reach the same visual target (with his arm not visible), he will go too far to the left;

this error indicates the degree of compensation or *adaptive shift*. The observed initial decrement of accuracy is evidence of disruption of an existing inter-modal coordination between visual space and the proprioceptive location of the right arm; and the restoration of accurate performance or adaptation is evidence of the rapid recalibration of the proprioceptive information about the position of the right arm in relation to the representation of the environ-mental auditory-visual space. This is shown by the fact that, following the visual adaptation, test trials with a new auditory target (a sound source) also yield an adaptive shift, so long as the subject continues to use the right arm—the one he observed through his lenses during the adaptation trials. However, when the subject is asked to point to a visual or auditory target with his left ("unadapted") arm, he may point accurately.

These findings show that the adaptation trials, with distorted visual infor-mation about the arm location, as well as about the location of the target, make the proprioceptive information about the right arm discordant not only with the representation of audio visual space, but also with the proprio-ceptive information about the rest of the body; proprioceptive information about the body excluding the right arm may remain concordant with the representation of audio-visual space. The discoordination of the right-arm position sense from the body-as-a-whole position sense may be shown by the fact that the subject is unable to point accurately with his right arm to the other locations or parts of his body. It may be assumed that prolonged experience with the lenses, involving seeing the movements of various parts of the body through the lenses, would result in recoordination of the right-arm position sense with the rest-of-the-body position sense. Now an adaptive shift obtained with the right arm would "transfer" to the left arm, and the same adaptive shift would be shown by both arms even without any specific adap-tation trials with the left arm.

The main question of interest concerns the exact basis of the recoordination of any two sources of information in relation to each other: Is A calibrated to be congruent with B, or vice versa? For example, in Harris' experiments described above, is the visual information about the arm recalibrated to con-form to the proprioceptive information about the arm, or is the proprio-ceptive information about the arm recalibrated to conform to visual information about the arm? In this case, and several others, we know that it is the proprioceptive information that is recalibrated to conform to the visual information; visual information serves as the criterion to which the proprioceptive information is coordinated. But does visual information have a general priority or "dominance" over other types of information in the face of discordance (indicated by inaccuracy of performance)? Rock and Harris (1967) are inclined to think so. But Taub (1968, p. 87 f.) has argued that the information that is more veridical, and thus leads to more accurate performance, will be the dominant one, and that visual information has no general priority in this regard.

The question of the dominance or priority of one type of spatial information over another may not be a proper one, because it assumes that congruence is achieved by adjusting (recalibrating) one source of information in relation to another. It is more likely that congruence is achieved by separate calibrations of the different sources of spatial information in respect to the actions required to reach specific environmental targets. In the displacing lens experiments, for example, the lack of congruence between the visual and proprioceptive information about the position of the responding arm is overcome on the basis of their individual relations to the target to which the pointing act is directed. If the information about the accuracy of performance in relation to the target is provided visually, as is typically the case, then both the visual and proprioceptive information about the arm position will be recalibrated in terms of the common visual information about the target and accuracy of performance. If, on the other hand, the information about the accuracy of performance is provided by, say, auditory or cutaneous cues (e.g., a person finding his way by echo-location or tactual cues), then the auditory or cutaneous information will serve as the calibration criterion for the visual and proprioceptive bodily information. The point is that what recalibration makes congruent are the two sources of spatial information (say, visual and proprioceptive) about bodily parts, and this congruence is achieved by the recalibration of each source in respect to information about the accuracy of performance. In attaining recoordination, then, any modality that provides information about the accuracy of performance will serve as the criterion for recalibration; the modality in which this information is usually presented is visual, but it need not be visual.

It follows from this interpretation of recoordination that if, after adaptation to displacing lenses by practice with the right arm, the subject were asked to perform a reaching act that can be performed without any visual-auditory reference (e.g., scratching his knee or relocating his right arm in some previously designated posture), little or no adaptive shift may be seen. Some experiments show that this is the case (Efstathiou, Bauer, Green, & Held, 1967). In general, the greater the extent to which a certain act is performed independently of the sense modality that indicates accuracy of performance during adaptation trials, the less will be the adaptive shift observed in the performance of that act.

About the mechanism underlying recalibration little is known. Hardt, Held, and Steinbach (1971) have proposed that adaptation to prisms involves a change "in the system that controls and assesses coincidence of the directions indicated by the exposed arm with those of objects. . . ." (p. 230). More specifically, it may be suggested that the process of recalibration involves the generation of a correction factor based on information about misalignment and the movements required to correct that misalignment; this correction factor is then applied to both exteroceptive and proprioceptive information involved in the production of movement. Presumably this takes place in some perceptual system, whose output is then transmitted to appropriate sensory-motor coordination organizations.

It is likely that the infant's ability to reach targets in space is initially acquired by the same kind of calibration process as the one that leads to the correction of experimentally induced error by adults.

CHAPTER 4

Development of Voluntary Acts

This chapter is concerned with the way in which discrete movements develop into the larger behavioral units—acts. An act is a sequence of movements that typically occurs as a unit. There are three main questions to consider: (1) How are unified acts "shaped" from individually elicited, discrete movements? (2) What is the role of reafference, or movement-related information, in the development and performance of acts? (3) How do acts become "voluntary"?

THE SHAPING OF ACTS

When it is about 10 weeks old, a human infant will visually fixate any attractive object a few inches away, and may take a wide swipe at it with one— the nearer—arm. This swipe is simply a movement; its direction and form are determined critically by the spatial location and particular features of the object. Further, there is no indication that the aim of the swipe is to grasp or reach the object; the hand is fisted at the time of the swipe, and the arm is withdrawn to its initial position whether or not the object has been touched in the course of the swipe. The 20-week old infant behaves quite differently. It raises its nearer arm until the hand is in view and then, in small movements, visually guides the hand to the object by alternatively fixating at the object and the hand; directional adjustments are made in successive movements. Further, the successive movements are clearly aimed at reaching or grasping the object; the infant opens its hand, moves its fingers in anticipation of contact with the object, and, once in contact, may manipulate the object for a while. Later still, reaching and grasping become highly precise, smooth, and speedy, without showing much of the midcourse adjustments; well practiced acts are ballistic and accurate. Observations of this type (Piaget, 1952; White, 1971) show that a unified, smooth, efficient, and voluntarily emitted act of reaching or grasping a nearby object is gradually "shaped" from the discrete, disjointed, awkward, and automatically elicited movements of earlier infancy.

Earlier Theories of Act Shaping

The problem posed by the shaping of unified acts from discrete, individually elicited movements may be approached in terms of an example. Consider how an act of reaching and grasping may be developed from three discrete movements, M_1: lifting the arm at the shoulder; M_2: extending the arm; and M_3: opening the hand from a clenched to a grasp formation. Initially each of these three movements is elicited by separate stimulus configurations, S_1, S_2, and S_3, which, through their sensory representations, s_1, s_2, and s_3, activate certain already matured sensory-motor coordination organizations, $(s\text{-}m)_1$, $(s\text{-}m)_2$, $(s\text{-}m)_3$, leading to the observed movements, M_1, M_2, and M_3. Initially, as seen in Figure 4.1a, each of the three movements is elicited separately by its corresponding stimulus configuration. The temporal order in which the three movements occur reflects the temporal order in which the eliciting conditions (environmental and bodily stimulus complex) for each movement are created, say, $S_1\text{-}S_2\text{-}S_3$. If the conditions that lead to the occurrence of the movements in close succession are frequently repeated (practice), a unified act of reaching and grasping would be shaped. Now, the occurrence of S_1 (and s_1) would be able to produce the movement sequence M_1, M_2, and M_3 in the absence of at least some of the stimulus conditions (S_2 and S_3) initially required for the elicitation of M_2 and M_3. The movements would be integrated into an act $M_1\text{-}M_2\text{-}M_3$ in the sense that they would be produced in the correct sequence by S_1 alone; M_2 and M_3 would not require to be individually elicited by S_2 and S_3. The problem, then, is this: What kind of neural change has occurred during practice that enables one stimulus configuration, S_1, to produce the whole sequence comprising the act?

Several hypotheses about the basis of act shaping have been proposed (see Figure 4.1b, c, d). One is that practice results in the linking of the movement commands of the successive movements ($m_1\text{-}m_2\text{-}m_3$), so that the activation of the first movement command would trigger the whole sequence. In other words, movement commands may in some way become linked by direct connections without the intervention of sensory-motor coordination organizations; this is shown in Figure 4.1b. Such a motor-chaining hypothesis is untenable. There is no evidence that the repeated activation of a sequence of movement commands results in a facilitation of the whole sequence. For example, Pinneo (1966) implanted up to six electrodes in the various brain-stem and cerebellar nuclei. The electrical stimulation at each electrode site produced a specific movement, such as right-arm flexion from elbow, spreading of the fingers of the right hand, bringing an arm to the mouth, tightly

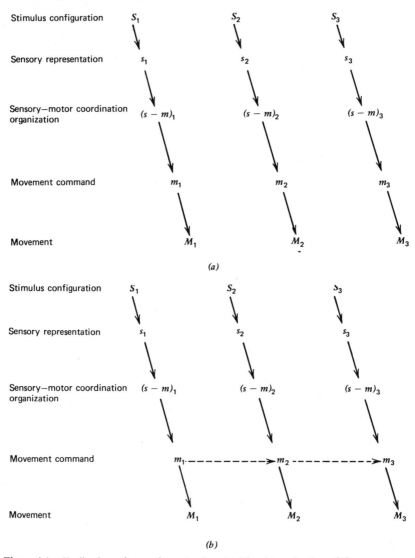

Figure 4.1.   Earlier hypotheses of act shaping. (*a*) The determination of three movements before their integration into a unitary act, (*b*) motor-chaining hypothesis, (*c*) feedback-chaining hypothesis, (*d*) central-chaining hypothesis.

closing both fists, etc. Pinneo then activated each site in succession in predetermined programs. He could produce many lifelike combinations of movement sequences by using different orders and durations of stimulation. However, apparently he found no practice effect; a particular movement

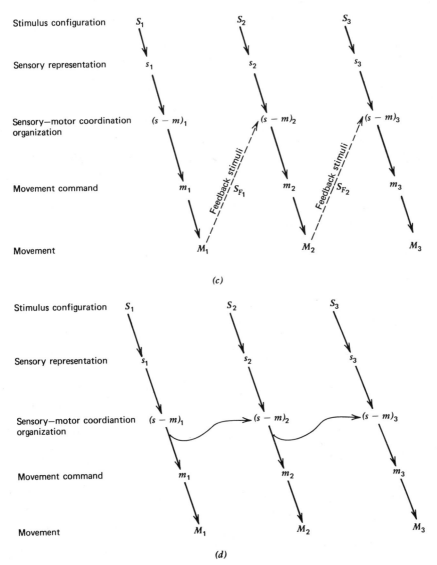

Stimulus configuration S_1 S_2 S_3

Sensory representation s_1 s_2 s_3

Sensory–motor coordination organization $(s - m)_1$ $(s - m)_2$ $(s - m)_3$

Movement command m_1 S_{F_1} m_2 S_{F_2} m_3

Movement M_1 M_2 M_3

(c)

Stimulus configuration S_1 S_2 S_3

Sensory representation s_1 s_2 s_3

Sensory–motor coordiantion organization $(s - m)_1$ $(s - m)_2$ $(s - m)_3$

Movement command m_1 m_2 m_3

Movement M_1 M_2 M_3

(d)

sequence as a whole could not be triggered by the activation of the first movement, but could be produced only by electrically instigating each of the successive movements individually. In his work on the elicitation of complex movement patterns by stimulation of sites in the red nucleus, Delgado (1964, 1965) also has not reported any evidence for the conditioning of the movement sequences to environmental stimuli. This apparent nonexistence of practice effects makes it highly unlikely that the neural organizations underlying the production of movement sequences comprising acts involve any motor-motor connections; by implication it may be said that there is no such thing as "motor program." In general, since the same movement commands must be involved in different acts, the integration of any motor program would be inconsistent with the observed flexibility of linkage between momentary environmental demands and movements.

The feedback-chaining hypothesis of act shaping, proposed by Watson (1929), is shown in Figure 4.1c. According to it, the first movement M_1, elicited by S_1, results in a specific kinesthetic feedback F_1, which, during practice, becomes linked to the sensory-motor coordinating organization that produces the next movement M_2. Similarly, the specific feedback F_2, produced by M_2, becomes linked to the sensory-motor coordinating organization of M_3. According to this view, each movement comprising an act is individually elicited, but instead of each movement being elicited by particular environmental configurations, the later movements come to be elicited by the specific sensory feedbacks of the earlier movements. As noted in Chapter 1, this hypothesis fails to account for the fact that a repeated movement may be linked to two different subsequent movements (e.g., in the sequence M_1-M_1-M_2 at first M_1 produces M_1, and then it produces M_2). Further, if the feedback from one movement is linked to a specific subsequent movement, it is hard to see how acts can be completed by alternative movements. As explained earlier, an important feature of acts is that the movements that make up an act are substitutable, so that an act as defined (e.g., a lever-press) may remain the same but the movements that comprise it may vary from occasion to occasion. Finally, as will become evident in the following section, it is possible for animals to perform and learn acts in the absence of kinesthetic or other sensory feedback from the responding limb. This last objection may be avoided by postulating that the linking of successive movements does not involve peripheral sensory feedback but depends on purely central feedback between the sensory-motor coordination organizations of successive movements, as shown in Figure 4.1d. However, such a central-chaining or mediational hypothesis (Deutsch, 1960; MacCorquodale & Meehl, 1953; Osgood, 1953) would still be open to the other criticisms of the feedback-chaining concept. The general idea of chaining in any form does not seem to work.

The Act-Assembly

The above considerations suggest that the shaping of acts may involve the development of new functional organizations rather than the mere linking or chaining of the mechanisms that produce individual movements. We may suppose, then, that the occurrence of an act reflects the activation of a central neural organization of a higher order than the sensory-motor coordination organization. Such a higher-order neural organization underlying an integrated act will be called an *act-assembly*; it is assumed that there exists a class of act-assemblies corresponding to each class of acts of which an animal is capable.

A convenient way to explain the concept of act-assembly is to imagine a concrete act A that requires the execution of three movements in succession, the first movement belonging to a class of movements M_1, the second to a class M_2, and the third to a class M_3; say, a rat rears in front of a lever (M_1), extends its forepaw to the lever (M_2), and presses the lever (M_3). Each movement may occur in several different ways. The rat may rear with its weight mainly on the right leg (M_{1a}), with its weight mainly on the left leg (M_{1b}), or with its weight equally distributed on the two legs (M_{1c}); it may reach for the lever with its left forepaw (M_{2a}), with its right forepaw (M_{2b}), or with both forepaws (M_{2c}); it may press the lever by hitting it (M_{3a}), by bending its rear legs and pulling the lever down (M_{3b}), or by pressing the top of the lever with its snout (M_{3c}). The shaping of the three movements into the lever-pressing act means that a neural organization—an act-assembly—has been developed that can send sequentially ordered discharges to those sensory-motor coordination organizations whose activation produces the required movements. This discharge has the net effect of providing extraneous excitatory discharges to particular sensory-motor coordinations at particular moments in time, and thus activates particular movements in a particular sequence.

As shown in Figure 4.2, the actual production of each movement in the course of execution of the act remains partly dependent on whatever sensory complexes may directly reach the particular sensory-motor coordination organizations; the sequentially ordered discharge from an act-assembly provides enough input to determine the exact time of activation of each sensory-motor coordination organization. Presumably an act-assembly generates impulses that both initiate and terminate each of the movements comprising an act.

It may be supposed that act-assemblies develop at both the subcortical and cortical levels. It may be expected that act-assemblies for species-typical gross acts, such as those of walking, climbing, or copulation, are located at subcortical levels, while act-assemblies for refined acts, such as those of manipulating, talking, and perceptual-motor skills, are located at the cortical level. At the cortical level act-assemblies appear to be located in the premotor zones, which take up Broadmann's areas 6 and 8 in the human cortex (see Figure 2.3). Compared with other mammals, the premotor areas of man occupy a much larger proportion of the precentral cortex. Luria has suggested (1973, p. 179) that the premotor zones are responsible for arranging the discharge of motor impulses temporally into "consecutive kinetic melodies."

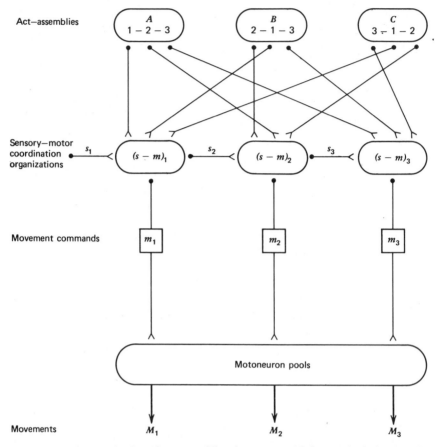

Figure 4.2. The organization of act-assemblies. An act-assembly is organized when certain movements, M_1, M_2, M_3, comprising an act, are repeatedly elicited in a certain sequence through the activation of the appropriate sensory-motor coordination organizations (s–m) by effective sensory inflow (s_1, s_2, s_3). The same s–m coordination organizations may form a part of several act-assemblies.

While lesions of the motor cortex in man frequently result in paralyses, damage to the premotor cortex leads to disturbance in the sequential ordering of the components of acts. The main feature of the disturbance is that the successive movements do not form a smooth, unitary act, and tend to occur as isolated movements, with breaks and perseveration at the points of transition from one movement to the next. The disturbance is manifested most clearly as awkwardness of writing, difficulty in producing rhythms or tunes, and deficiency in terminating or controlling movements at the appropriate time. When the speech zone in the dominant hemisphere (Broca's area) is damaged, the patients show difficulty in pronouncing multisyllabic words, making errors of order and showing difficulty in transition from one sound (movement) to the next. In general, then, it is the disarrangement and lack of sequential integration of movements that characterizes patients with pre-motor lesions; this may be taken to reflect a disturbance of cortical act-assemblies. In contrast, cerebral deterioration of old age, as well as cellular degeneration of substantia nigra and globus pallidus seen in Parkinsonism, produce general slowing of the initiation and execution of acts rather than disarrangement and disintegration of movements (Hicks & Birren, 1970); this reflects disturbances of the more elementary processes involved in the production of individual movements.

Development of Act-Assemblies

How does an act-assembly become organized? It may be supposed that each sensory-motor coordination organization is connected, reciprocally, to certain neurons in the region of the brain where act-assemblies are formed. The neurons that happen to be repeatedly fired in a certain sequence (e.g., a certain sequence of arm or eye movements) become organized in an arrange-ment that corresponds to the movement sequence. As individual movements are repeatedly elicited in a certain sequence by appropriately ordered sensory inflow to particular sensory-motor organizations, the neurons corresponding to the sensory-motor organizations become organized for firing in the same sequential order. These sequentially ordered "act-assembly neurons" would now comprise a unified act-assembly, which, when activated, would produce the whole sequence of movements as a unitary act. The same act-assembly neurons may, of course, be parts of several different act-assemblies. Models of neuronal arrangements that could achieve such sequential ordering of the firing of act-assembly neurons have been proposed (e.g., Milner, 1961). However, a discussion of such mechanisms is beyond the scope of this work.

Note that no "reinforcement" or any type of sensory *outcome* is postu-lated for the organization of act-assemblies. It may be argued that even non-reinforcing sensory consequences of movements are not required for act shaping. It may be supposed that the central feedback connections of the motor system are such as to make the organization of act-assemblies possible without regard to the external consequences of the movements. The contribu-tion of the environmental stimulus input may reside only in the initial stimuli that elicit a certain sequence of movements and not in the sensory conse-quences of movement-produced stimuli. The integration of the movements in a sequence may thus occur through sheer practice or "exercise" of the sequence. The possibility that the motor system has the necessary central feedback loops to effect movement integration by sheer exercise has been suggested by K. U. Smith (1973) and Cohn, Jakniunas, and Taub (1972). However, at present there appear to be no clear ideas about the mechanisms that might make such loops important in the development of act-assemblies.

Some sequences of movements appear to become integrated with little or no practice, that is, without repeated sequential elicitation by particular stimulus configurations. This is particularly true of "circular reflexes," such as scratching, grasping, or babbling, in which a movement provides the stimulus for its own repetition. Rapid integration of movements into acts is also evident in the case of "chain reflexes," such as walking, micturition, copulation, or swallowing, in which each movement provides the stimulus for the following movement. The general point is that there may be marked differences in the ease with which acts involving certain movement sequences can be developed, and that these differences arise from the degree to which certain movement sequences either are integrated maturationally without any specific experience of sequential elicitation, or are preferentially elicited in a particular sequence owing to certain characteristics of the normal environment of the animal. Such differences in the readiness or "preparedness" (Seligman, 1970) for the development of certain types of acts are probably the basis of species differences in the typical forms of their consummatory, defensive, and exploratory (in general, "instinctive") actions. The particular acts that are shaped in a given situation depend on the species-typical movements elicited by the stimulus configurations of that situation. Prior exercise of individual movements of acts may, however, facilitate the emergence of what appear to be maturationally determined acts (Zelazo, Zelazo, & Kolb, 1972). The differences in the movements that comprise the "general activity" of particular species, and the related differences in the ease with which certain responses can be trained in those species (under a given set of experimental conditions), has been shown to be an important factor in determining the success or failure of training procedures (e.g., Bindra, 1961; Bolles, 1970; Breland & Breland, 1961; Hinde & Stevenson, 1970; Seligman, 1970).

MOVEMENT-CORRELATED INFORMATION: REAFFERENCE

A movement, even as it is being produced, has several consequences that may provide the brain with information about the progress and the environmental effects of the movement. Such movement-correlated feedback information has been called *reafference*, and is distinguished from *exafference*, or information that is unrelated to the animal's own movements, and is environmentally generated (Von Holst & Mittelstaedt, 1950).

Types of Reafference

There are two types of reafference, central or interneural, which is generated within the central nervous system, and peripheral or sensory, which requires receptors. Concepts such as "corollary discharge" (Held, 1961; Sperry, 1950), "efferenz-kopie" (Von Holst, 1954), and "sense of innervation" (Helmholtz, 1867), may be subsumed under the general label of central reafference.

When a motor command is activated, the efferent neural activity may activate collateral or other afferent fibers at various sites along the way, and this central reafference may provide information about the state of the motor outflow at certain points in time. When the efferent discharge activates muscle fibers, sensory reafference comes into play. Kinesthetic reafference may provide information about muscle contractions. The movement produced by muscle contractions in turn gives rise to proprioceptive, as well as vestibular and cutaneous, reafference, and this provides information about movement-correlated changes in the orientation and position of bodily parts. The movement may also be seen by the animal itself, and this visual reafference also provides information about the bodily motion and the changed relation of the body to environmental objects.

Taub, Bacon, and Berman (1965) have used the term *topographic* reafference to refer to reafference which corresponds to or depicts the spatial form of the movement from which it arises; typically, this would be central, proprioceptive, or visual. This may be distinguished from *nontopographic* reafference, which arises from consequences of the movement that bear no relation to its form (e.g., a click or a reward consequent upon a lever-press, clearer visual perception as one moves the head in the direction of a target).

Normally reafference is registered, that is, it provides an animal with utilizable information about certain consequences of its own movements. If a subject is blindfolded and one of his arms is lifted to a certain level and put in a certain position by the experimenter ("passive movement"), the subject knows the new location of the arm and hand without having to look at it; he can accurately point (by a finger of his other hand) to the new location of any part of the passively moved arm. Presumably proprioceptive (and perhaps, tactual) reafference from the shoulder and arm provides this information. Now, if the joint-capsule of an arm is anesthetized by procaine or a circulation-preventing cuff and then the limb is put in a new position by the experimenter, the subject is unable to tell accurately the new location of the moved limb. Thus, in the case of passive movement, peripheral reafference is required for telling limb position. However, if a subject with an anesthetized joint capsule is asked to raise his arm ("intentional movement") and, when it has reached a certain level, to stop, he has little difficulty in telling accurately the new location of the limb. Such observation (e.g., Gross, 1973; Paillard & Brouchon, 1968) point to the existence of some nonproprioceptive, centrally generated, reafferent information (or possibly kinesthetic information) in the case of intentional movements—information that is not generated in the case of passive movements. Since the activation of a sensory-motor coordination organization must be involved in intentional movement, but may not be in passive movement, it is probable that central reafference is generated by the efferent outflow from sensory-motor coordination organizations (Phillips, 1966).

Reafference and Behavior

What part does the movement-correlated reafferent information play in behavior? It is now known that normally reared adult animals can effectively perform well integrated responses in the absence of reafferent information about the responding limb from the somatosensory (proprioceptive, kinesthetic, cutaneous) and visual modalities (Gorska & Jankowska, 1961; Knapp, Taub, & Berman, 1958; Taub & Berman, 1963, 1968). For example, complete spinal deafferentation of limbs *and* blindfolding leave monkeys quite capable of walking, climbing, and performing fairly skillful instrumental responses (Cohn, Jakniunas, & Taub, 1972; Taub & Berman, 1968), though their level of spontaneous activity is much reduced. Clearly, peripheral reafferent information is not necessary in the adult for the accurate performance of acts. This could mean that, once an act has been integrated and practiced, the necessary motor outflow can be discharged in an organized way without the sensory feedback produced by the various individual movements as the act is being executed. It remains possible that central reafference produced by the efferent outflow of individual movements may be necessary for the performance of an act as a whole. There appears to be no readily available way of determining whether this is so.

The role of sensory reafferent information in the initial shaping of acts has also been studied. Taub, Ellman, and Berman (1966) have shown that spinal deafferentation performed on adult monkeys leaves them capable of *acquiring* a new instrumental act (e.g., grasping a cylinder to avoid an electric shock) in the absence of reafferent somatic or visual information from the responding limb. And recently, Taub, Perrella, and Barro (1973) have shown that spinal deafferentation at one day of age results in only minor retardation in the development of locomotory skills, even if the monkeys are reared without vision. These findings may, at first sight, suggest that peripheral reafference is not important even in the initial shaping of acts, but such a conclusion would be unwarranted. Take the experiment in which monkeys were spinally deafferented and then trained to perform an instrumental response (grasping a cylinder by flexion of the fingers) on the presentation of a signal (buzzer) in the absence of any visual information. During training, the performance of the act of grasping produced escape from or avoidance of an electric shock. In this case the termination or nonoccurrence of the shock would be movement-correlated consequence and would provide sensory reafferent information, and this must have played a part, if not in the shaping of the act, at least in providing the motivation for performing the response. Further, the response might well have been partly shaped in preliminary training before deafferentation.

What these deafferentation experiments may be taken to mean is that the intrinsic, topographic, sensory reafference (kinesthetic, proprioceptive, cutaneous, and visual) is not essential for the shaping of an act. This leaves open the possibility that some form of extrinsic, nontopographic sensory reafference may be essential for the shaping of acts. It may be that, as noted earlier, central, interneural reafference is sufficient for the shaping of an act, but that the extrinsic sensory reafference serves as a vehicle of motivational influences that determines the probability of occurrence of the act.

Whether sensory reafference turns out to be necessary for act shaping or not, the important role that sensory reafference, topographic or nontopographic, may normally play in the acquisition of acts is shown by several different kinds of findings. First, environmental stimuli that have been artificially correlated (nontopographic) with certain acts can be used to train highly refined responses. For example, by pairing the contraction of certain muscle fibers with a consistent "environmental feedback," such as the onset of a tone or a visual or auditory display of the electrical muscle potentials of the muscle activity, it is possible to train subjects to produce, on instruction, highly precise movements, including those involving the activation of a single motor neuron (Basmajian, 1963; Carlsöö & Edfeldt, 1963; Lloyd & Leibrecht, 1971). Further, in teaching deaf children to speak, extrinsic tactual or visual feedback produced by their random utterances may be used to facilitate the production of meaningful words (e.g., Kringlebotn, 1968). Similarly, the blind may be trained to identify distant objects by pairing their exploratory head movements with tactual input representing the features of environmental objects that are normally coded visually, such as shape, size, and distance (White, Saunders, Scadden, Bach-Y-Rita, & Collins, 1970).

Second, partial elimination of the normal topographic sensory reafference retards the acquisition of new responses. Thus prevention of the sight of one of its own arms during development makes a monkey less capable of performing visual-motor tasks, especially tasks involving the use of that arm (Held & Bauer, 1967). Conversely, by enhancing visual (topographic) reafference, the development of the ability to perform eye-hand coordination tasks can be reliably speeded in the human infant (White, Castle, & Held, 1964; White & Held, 1966).

Third, in the adult the acquisition and performance of highly refined responses may be disrupted in the absence of appropriate sensory reafference. For example, a normal rat can be readily trained to press a lever with a force between certain prescribed limits, say a force produced by a weight of between 10 and 15 gm on the lever. But desensitization of the responding limbs by injections of procaine disrupts the animal's performance (Notterman & Mintz, 1965). Further, performance on tasks that require time estimation is especially dependent on sensory reafference; enhancing sensory reafference by asking subjects to count aloud or to tap improves their estimates of time, while prohibiting the reafference-producing acts disrupts performance (see Schmidt, 1971).

Evidence pointing to the importance of central reafference comes from the finding that intentional movements contribute much more to shaping of acts than do passive movements. For example, passively produced movements are not as effective in the learning of "sensory-motor tasks" as are intentional movements. Held and Hein (1963) have shown that "yoked" cats, made to perform passively the same movements as the intentional movements of their paired "free" partners, benefit less from this training experience as judged by subsequent performance on new sensory-motor tasks. However, since passively produced movements probably generate neither central nor kinesthetic reafference, the relative importance of central and kinesthetic reafference in intentional movement remains to be elucidated.

A conclusion about the role of reafference in behavior that appears consistent with the available findings may be stated as follows: Sensory reafference plays an important part in the performance of integrated responses, but the sensory reafference need not be of the kind that is intrinsically or topographically related to the movements involved; any reafference consistently produced by the movements would improve performance. It is possible that central reafference is sufficient for the shaping of acts, but it is likely that topographic sensory reafference also contributes to act-shaping. Nontopographic, extrinsic reafference probably serves only as a motivational indicator and as such may determine the probability of occurrence of an act.

VOLITION: TRANSFER OF STIMULUS CONTROL

Hand-in-hand with the shaping of an act goes the development of volitional control of the act. For example, as an infant is developing the acts of reaching and grasping a feeding bottle, it also begins to perform the same act when it hears some characteristic sound (a conditioned stimulus) that normally precedes the visual presentation of the bottle. Thus, as it is being integrated, the act gradually appears to be internally controlled, occurring in the absence of the conditions that were initially necessary; it becomes voluntary.

Ideomotor Hypothesis

Most present-day discussions of voluntary action start from the ideomotor hypothesis of William James (1890). This hypothesis is that the idea or image of an act leads automatically to the efferent outflow that produces that act. A voluntary act is one that is preceded by the image of movements comprising that act; volition thus consists in activating images of movements. The image of a movement for James was the neural excitation of the sensory feedback (including proprioceptive and kinesthetic) normally generated by the internal and external consequences of that act; a particular arm movement is instigated by an image of what it felt like and looked like when that movement was made in the past. Thus, according to James, through learning, certain extraneous—conditioned—stimuli acquire the capability of activating the image (the central representation of the total feedback) of a movement. Then, if the activation of that image is the cause of the production of the movement, the movement may be said to be voluntary.

The process of acquiring voluntary movements proposed by James, and since elaborated by several authors (e.g., Greenwald, 1970; Kimble & Perlmuter, 1970; Konorski, 1967; Von Holst, 1954), is shown in Figure 4.3. In these accounts it has been customary to attribute the image of a movement mainly to the kinesthetic sensory feedback of the movement. Initially, a movement M is produced by the activation of a movement command m, by a stimulus configuration S, through innate neural paths P_1 and P_2. The sensory feedback S_K from the movement activates, through another innate path P_3, the image i_k of that movement—a kinesthetic image that has been developed on the basis of past experience. This kinesthetic image is capable of activating the central representation of the same movement through some innate mechanism involving a path P_4. Through repeated elicitation of the movement by the stimulus configuration S_1, a new learned path P_5 becomes capable of exciting the image, thereby activating the movement command m and producing the movement M. Produced through this new learned path P_5, the movement is voluntary. Other extraneous, initially ineffective (conditioned) stimuli, for example, S_2, also become capable of activating the image through learned paths, for example, P_6.

The main difficulty with the above view of the development of voluntary action is that it rests so heavily on sensory feedback and on the kinesthetic basis of the image that activates the movement command. It has been noted above that directed, instrumental, voluntary acts can be acquired in the total

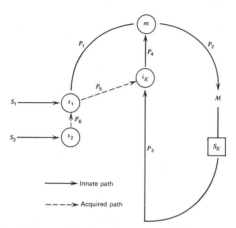

Figure 4.3. James' theory of voluntary movement. As a consequence of learning, a new path P_5, linked to an extraneous stimulus S_1, becomes capable of exciting the image i_K of a movement and thereby of producing the movement through a "voluntary channel". Note that path P_6 links a new, extraneous stimulus S_2 to the image i_K of the movement. [After James (1890) and Kimble and Perlmuter (1970).]

absence of the sensory reafference from the responding limb, that is, in the absence of any sensory basis for the image of the movement to be developed. Central, interneural reafference could, however, provide a basis for the development of an image of a movement. But then the basis of the image could hardly be kinesthesis (or any other sensory modality). And if the image is not kinesthetic (or based on some kind of topographic sensory feedback), it is hard to see in what sense the image could be regarded as an image of the *movement*. Further, if the image that activates a motor command includes nontopographic, arbitrary consequences of the movement (e.g., contact, food delivery), then the instigation of voluntary movement would result from a variety of neural influences and not only from the kinesthetic or any other topographic neural consequences of the movement. It seems reasonable to discard the idea that a voluntary movement is critically dependent on a specific image of that movement and to proceed on the broader assumption that a variety of neural influences combine to produce a movement. What remains tenable in James' theory of volition is the idea of the acquired role of extraneous (conditioned) stimuli in producing a major part of the neural influences that cause a movement. This idea of stimulus-control transfer appears to be sufficient as an explanation of the development of voluntary control.

Stimulus-Control Transfer

My view, then, is that the general idea of stimulus-control transfer provides a sufficient basis for explaining the development of voluntary acts. Because the particular stimulus configurations that acquire the capability of producing a given act depend on the individual experiences of animals, the relation between the act and the stimulus conditions under which it occurs cease to be species-specific and become highly variable and idiosyncratic. In the absence of knowledge of the effective conditioned stimuli, such acts appear to be voluntarily emitted operants rather than demonstrably elicited respondents (see Chapter 1). The process of the development of "voluntary control" is then essentially the process by which stimulus control of an act is transferred from the initial species-specific, unconditioned eliciting stimuli of movements to extraneous individual-specific, conditioned stimuli. The process underlying this learning will be discussed in later chapters. Here it is necessary only to consider some general ideas about such stimulus-control transfer.

The essential basis of stimulus-control transfer is that a new, conditioned stimulus configuration becomes capable of activating an act-assembly whose activation formerly required some other, species-specific, unconditioned stimulus configurations. In other words, the conditioned stimulus somehow becomes capable of generating a neural discharge that initially was generated by the unconditioned stimulus. The source of the conditioned excitatory discharge—the locus of learning—may be quite far removed from the act-assembly, but the consequence of conditioning is that an excitatory discharge sufficient to activate the act-assembly is somehow transmitted to the act-assembly.

In the adult animal the normal mode of the production of most acts is that of activation of act-assemblies by a variety of conditioned stimuli. Inasmuch as the stimulus control exercised by these stimuli is acquired through individual experience, the effectiveness of various stimuli depends on experiences that may vary greatly from one animal to another. Thus, when a number of adult animals of a species are presented with the same test stimuli, the acts they display (as a part of their "general activity") are likely to be quite variable from one animal to another. It is such observed idiosyncrasies of behavior that make adult behavior appear voluntary. In practice, then, the criterion of volition is this: How far is an observed action species-typical and therefore predictable on the basis of general knowledge about the species, and how far is it a characteristic of the individual as such and therefore unpredictable on the basis of general knowledge about the species? In the absence of knowledge about the causes of an individual's action, the more idiosyncratic and unpredictable an action—the more it sets an animal apart from other members of the species in similar circumstances—the more voluntary is that action judged to be. As Irwin (1942) has put it, voluntary behavior is "any behavior which exhibits a purpose ascribable to the behaving creature as an individual (1942, p. 132)." His main point is that the judgment that a certain action is voluntary or involuntary depends on the judge's knowledge and expectations about the typical behavior of the species and how far the action appears to be idiosyncratic rather than species-typical.

It follows that the more remote, unknown, or obscure the conditioned stimuli that acquire stimulus-control of an act through associative learning, the more unexpected the occurrence of that act would be to a casual observer, and the more likely he would be to ascribe to the animal voluntary control of that act. Conversely, the more an act remains under the control of the species-typical conditions of its occurrence, the less unexpected it would be to a casual observer, and the less likely he would be to ascribe voluntary control. This means that acts for which stimulus control cannot be readily transferred to conditioned stimuli would, in general, be regarded as involuntary. Thus we regard reflexes to be involuntary and mammals to be capable of greater voluntary control than other vertebrates. And species-typical consummatory actions, such as eating, drinking, copulation, are thought to be less voluntary than the more learnable and idiosyncratic instrumental actions that lead the animal to consummatory objects. When visceral reactions are produced by homeostatic autonomic reflexes or by species-typical environmental unconditioned stimuli, they are thought to be involuntary, but when they are produced as a consequence of individual training regimes, they are said to be voluntary (see Chapter 11). Actions performed upon instructions of a hypnotist may be considered voluntary by someone who regards hypnosis to be a phenomenon of social compliance and therefore the subject's actions to be unpredictable in detail, and as involuntary by someone who regards the subject to be under the hypnotist's control and therefore the subject's actions to be determined wholly by the hypnotist's will.

As will become evident in later chapters, my view is that the basis of a voluntary act lies not, as William James thought, in the conditioned excitation of the central representation of that *act*, but in the conditioned excitation of the central representation of the *stimulus configuration* that is effective in activating the act-assembly for that act.

CHAPTER 5

Knowledge of Stimuli

We would rarely mistake a pebble for a lost watch, a twig for a snake, or a stranger for a friend. We usually perceive objects correctly despite the stimulus features they may share with other objects. Since diverse environmental objects may activate some of the same feature detectors and thus produce similar sensory complexes, the distinctive knowledge that serves as the basis of correct identification must involve some additional processes that use the sensory information to generate knowledge of an object, as such. This chapter considers the processes involved in the generation of such "perceptual knowledge" of objects and other stimulus entities such as events, actions, and attributes.

To say that someone perceives a stimulus is to say that either the person has a conscious percept (awareness) of the stimulus, or that, under given conditions, the person can identify the stimulus as being this (e.g., belonging to class X) rather than not-this (e.g., not belonging to class X) or that the person can reliably point to or make some other discriminative response in relation to that stimulus. The discriminative, identifying response can occur only if the stimulus generates a distinctive neural pattern that is different from the neural patterns activated by other stimuli. I have coined the term *pexgo* to refer to such a presently excited, distinctive neural organization that underlies the identifying response made in relation to a stimulus entity, as well as the awareness (subjective experience described as percept or image) of that stimulus entity. The pexgo is a theoretical concept postulated to explain both the perceptual discrimination (identifying response) and the experienced awareness (percept). Pylyshyn (1973) has pointed out the confusion that arises when terms describing conscious entities, such as percept and image, are used both to describe the experience (conscious awareness) of stimuli and to designate theoretical, explanatory constructs. Though neologisms, like pexgo, are a burden in prose, it is really necessary here to invent a term that will clearly separate the explanatory construct from what is being explained.

WHAT IS PERCEPTION?

The idea that perception is not the same thing as sensation, that the percept or discriminative identification of an object can be meaningfully distinguished from the momentary sensory complex (of feature detectors) activated by that object, is both an old and well supported one. For one thing, percepts can apparently be experienced in the absence of appropriate sensory stimulation; the phenomena of eidetic images, hallucinations, and dreams as well as "phantom" experiences of amputated bodily limbs (Simmel, 1956a), suggest that percepts involve something more than the patterning of feature detectors activated by current stimulus inflow. Conversely, certain percepts may fail to be experienced even when the appropriate feature detectors have been activated; for example, the same speech sounds may be heard and identified as words when they form parts of a familiar language but not so heard or identified in unfamiliar sequences. For another, it seems that the same sensory input may produce markedly different percepts; a "reversible figure" may be seen now as a vase and now as two profiles (Rubin, 1921). In addition, the same percept may be produced by widely varying sensory information; the "constancy phenomena" illustrate this (Boring, 1946). Further, the elimination of certain sensory information may fail to disrupt the percept to which those features normally contribute; thus speech sounds that have been masked or replaced by a noise may be "perceptually restored," as judged by the identification of the complete phrase including the missing phonemes (Warren, 1970). Finally, percepts remain clear, stable, and unified in experience in spite of continual variations in sensory inflow caused by the unsteadiness of sense-organ mechanisms (Dodwell, 1971). Clearly, then, pexgo, the neural organization underlying perceptual experience and response, cannot be simply a primary sensory pattern but must involve something more.

Hypothesis of Sensory Organization

Early psychological theorists tended to work within the broad assumption that perception represents some kind of "organization" of the sensory elements (say, feature detectors) excited by the current sensory inflow. Associationists thought of this organization as resulting from associative activation of images and ideas of past sensory inputs (e.g., Titchener, 1918). Gestalt psychologists (e.g., Köhler, 1929; Köhler & Wallach, 1944) attributed perception to the organization of the cortical projection fields of sensory elements into certain sensory patterns by some (unspecified) direct-current dynamic field principles. A recent variation of the dynamic field view has been put forth by Pribram (1971). According to him perception represents sensory organization that may be described as interference patterns, like those produced in holographic photography, and these patterns are created by the ever slowing flow of impulses in the vastly arborizing axonal endings of neurons in the sensory cortex. Still another view is the "unit hypothesis," proposed by Barlow (1972) and questioned by M. J. Morgan (1975). According to this hypothesis, cells in the sensory system are hierarchically organized to such an extent that there actually exist single cells that are selectively responsive to very complicated environmental events, including objects, as such. The basic fallacy in all these views of sensory organization is the assumption that there is a place or places in the brain where pictorial or some form of life-like representations of stimuli are formed, whether by association, dynamic field principles, holographic interference patterns, or hierarchical arrangement of sensory neurons. The postulation of such life-like representations, rather than some form of abstract representations, requires the further postulation of an observing inner homunculus, and this offers no real solution to the problem but creates another one about the nature of the homunculus.

Another difficulty with the views that perception is essentially sensory organizations is that they do not take into account the involvement of motor processes in perceptual phenomena nor offer a plausible account of how perception is related to animal action. There is considerable evidence to show that the development of correct identification of objects is related to observational acts. When vision is restored in hitherto blind adults, they display observational acts in relation to objects before they begin to identify them visually (Von Senden, 1932, discussed by Hebb, 1949). Similarly, in learning to adapt to sensory rearrangement produced by wearing inverting lenses, the subject starts to make appropriate, directed movements before he reports seeing the world right-side up through the lenses (Kohler, 1951; Stratton, 1897; Taylor, 1962). The involvement of the motor processes in perception has been emphasized by many authors (E. J. Gibson, 1969; J. J. Gibson, 1966; Hebb, 1949; Sperry, 1952; Taylor, 1962), and this idea is clearly consistent with the biological consideration that perception unrelated to appropriate action would have no adaptive value. As Sperry put it, an animal perceives an object to the extent that it is ready to respond in relation to it. Considerations of this type have resulted in the formulation of views that attribute an important role to motor processes in the structuring of individual, distinctive perceptions (experienced percepts or identifying responses).

Hypothesis of Motor Organization

An outright motor view is presented in the "efference theory" of perception (Festinger, Ono, Burnham, & Bamber, 1967; Washburn, 1916). According to it, the basis of the percept and discriminative identification of a stimulus lies in the distinctiveness of the motor pattern generated by that stimulus. Sensory inflow partly determines the motor outflow pattern, but the critical correlate of perception is the motor outflow pattern, per se, however it gets determined. Note that the proposed critical correlate of perception is *not* the actual pattern of muscular activity or the sensory feedback from it, but the *central outflow* of a certain motor pattern. Festinger et al. (1967) have suggested, on the basis of incidental observations, that the following hypothetical experiment should work. If a patient who had recently suffered paralysis of his right arm were to be asked to close his eyes and raise his right arm, he would report an experience of the arm being lifted; on opening his eyes he would be surprised that the arm had not moved. If the same arm were to be moved passively without providing any proprioceptive or cutaneous cues, the patient would report no experience of arm motion. This suggests that the perception, arm-in-motion, is not dependent on sensory input arising from muscular activity, and implicates some central process, related to the efferent outflow normally required for producing the arm movement, as the basis of the perception.

Another type of evidence usually regarded as supporting the efference theory comes from experiments in which the subject is supplied with discordant sensory information. If a blindfolded man runs his fingers along the edge of a door, he can readily identify it as a straight (rather than a curved) edge. If allowed to see his fingers running along the edge, he still reports the edge as straight. But if he runs his fingers along the edge while looking through lenses that make the edge appear as curved, he reports the tactually felt edge to be curved (Gibson, 1933). This could mean that the reported experience of the edge—its identification as straight or curved—depends more on some central motor processes instigated by the visual information (edge curved) than on the concurrent tactual or reafferent sensory information (edge straight) accompanying the movement (Festinger et al., 1967). But the result could also be interpreted simply as the primacy of visual information over the tactual information under the conditions of the experiment (see Chapter 3).

Note that neither the above considerations nor the more recent experiments (e.g., Festinger & Easton, 1974) prove that the *efferent outflow* as such is the necessary basis of perception. What the evidence shows is that perception is not wholly dependent on the current sensory inflow, but may be closely tied to the motor outflow caused by the sensory information. If a distinctive pattern of motor outflow were the basis of each perception, disturbances of perception should result from damage to motor structures, but this does not appear to be the case. This difficulty may be avoided by suggesting that it is not efferent outflow but efferent "readiness" or "programming" that is the basis of perception (Festinger et al., 1967). But such a hypothesis would require specification of the meaning of efferent readiness and some indication as to how it differs from efferent outflow on the one hand and from sensory mechanisms on the other. Until this is done, efference theory remains at a standstill.

Hypothesis of Higher-Order Organization: Pexgo

If the basis of perception is neither purely sensory organizations nor purely efferent outflow patterns, what is it? The idea that still remains tenable is that proposed by Hebb (1949). In its general form, Hebb's idea is simply that motor processes play a part in the initial development of some higher-order neural organizations, called cell-assemblies; once developed, the activation of the different components of a cell-assembly in a certain sequence ("phase sequence") generates the appropriate perception. It is now possible to elaborate this general idea in several respects.

The first point to note is that it now appears reasonably certain that the neural substrate of perception lies outside the primary projection areas of the cortex, as shown in Figure 5.1. This is shown by the nature of the deficits produced by different sites of cortical damage (Teuber, 1960). For example, in man, circumscribed sensory deficits, such as visual-field deficits and scotomas, are associated with lesions in the primary visual projection of area 17 (Teuber, Battersby, & Bender, 1960). But perceptual deficits of identifying objects and patterns result from lesions of the secondary visual projections of areas 18 and 19. These clinical findings are supported by studies of sensory and perceptual deficits produced by experimental lesions in monkeys (Chow, 1952a, 1952b; Mishkin & Pribram, 1954; Weiskrantz, 1972). The fact that perceptual deficits can be relatively independent of sensory deficits suggests that perception involves some higher level neurons to which neurons of the primary sensory areas project. These higher-order neurons may be called "gnostic-neurons," following Konorski (1967). The fact that perception improves in the course of development—that pexgos of an object are generated more readily in mature and experienced individuals—indicates that gnostic-neurons become linked to form larger functional organizations. I shall call such a functional organization of gnostic-neurons a *gnostic-assembly*; with minor differences (to be noted later) the concept of gnostic-assembly is about the same as Hebb's (1949) concept of cell-assembly.

It may be assumed that a certain type of gnostic-neuron is activated by a particular combination of stimulus features through appropriate feature detectors, and that particular gnostic-neurons become linked to form gnostic-assemblies in the course of maturational growth. That certain stimulus feature combinations can be identified by the neonate is now well established. A human neonate reacts differently to visual stimuli of different colors and shapes (Bornstein, 1975; Kagan, 1971). Similarly, as shown in imprinting experiments, a newly hatched chick is more likely to fixate and follow certain moving or colorful stimuli than other visual stimuli (H. James, 1959; Kovach, 1971). What repeated experience with particular stimulus configurations does is to link the relevant gnostic-neurons together into gnostic-assemblies representing increasingly larger selections of sensory patterns representing stimulus configurations. Each member of a species may be assumed to be prepared with certain preexisting gnostic-neurons, representing phylogenetic selections of environmental stimulus features, and these gnostic-neurons will serve as a basis for the development of larger gnostic-assemblies representing the common combinations of stimulus features encountered by individual animals.

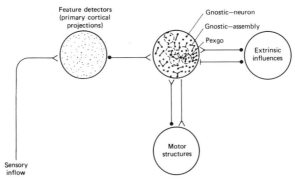

Figure 5.1. A schematic drawing of the hypothetical processes underlying perception. It is suggested that a pexgo is a pattern of neural firing produced when certain gnostic-neurons and gnostic-assemblies are activated by the momentary sensory inflow and various central influences.

As noted earlier (Chapter 2), the synaptic changes that constitute learning are a continuation of the changes at synaptic junctions that occur in the course of maturational growth. The assortments of gnostic-neurons that are activated by various recurring stimulus configurations of the environment will repeatedly be activated, and these neurons will develop more efficient synaptic connections with each other. Once such connections are developed, the neurons of a gnostic-assembly will tend to be activated as a unit, even if all the sensory elements initially required to activate the individual neurons are not present. This new functional unit is the gnostic-assembly. Through repeated experiences of particular combinations of stimulus features, individual gnostic-neurons are structured into larger gnostic-assemblies, which then serve as the elements from which pexgos of larger or more complex stimulus configurations (objects, events, etc.) may be quickly generated.

It is important to note that this view does *not* rest on the assumption that there develops a distinctive gnostic-assembly representing each stimulus entity or each potential perception. A gnostic-assembly is *not* the equivalent of the neural substrate of any one percept or identifying response; there is no such thing as a gnostic-assembly representing an apple or a triangle. If particular gnostic-assemblies represented particular stimulus configurations, there would have to be an infinitude of gnostic-assemblies to make possible the perception of each perceivable stimulus configuration; there would have to be a gnostic-assembly for a green, large, elongated, crinkly apple and one for a green, large, elongated, smooth apple, and so on. This is the fallacy of the "template matching" view of perception; it postulates a distinctive template for each identifiable stimulus configuration and then assumes that current sensory inflow activates one rather than another template on the basis of the degree of match between the feature detectors that comprise the template and the stimulus features represented in the current sensory inflow. The template matching idea belongs essentially to the sensory organization view of perception and suffers from all the shortcomings of that view (see above).

According to the hypothesis I am outlining here, a gnostic-assembly is not a substrate of any particular percept or identifying response, but is a higher-order functional element that, once developed, can represent certain combinations of features that occur together frequently, even when all the features are not present in the current sensory inflow. The distinctive basis of a perception is the pexgo, the neural organization consisting of gnostic-neurons and gnostic-assembly merely represents a certain combination of features that can be activated by a cue. A *cue* may be defined as any single feature or combination of features that can activate one or more gnostic-assemblies representing more stimulus features than those that comprise the cue. A pexgo is generated when certain cues, contained in the current sensory inflow, activate certain gnostic-assemblies. Thus, according to the present hypothesis, a pexgo is not a template or a previously formed neural entity to be activated by particular cues; each pexgo is a fresh construction whose characteristics depend on the particular assortment of gnostic-assemblies that are activated by the momentary sensory inflow and various central influences to be discussed later. A pexgo has no reality until it is actually generated; each pexgo is a new entity, not the replication of an existing standard or template.

ORGANIZATION OF GNOSTIC-ASSEMBLIES

How do gnostic-assemblies representing particular recurrent feature-combinations of an individual animal's environment come to be organized? Let us start with the assumption that the strengthening of synaptic connections between gnostic-neurons requires that they be activated simultaneously or in close temporal contiguity; the neurons that fire together develop stronger connections. Thus, in order for a gnostic-assembly to be organized to represent a certain combination of stimulus features that frequently occur together, it would be necessary that the various sensory patterns representing those stimulus features be activated closely in time, and this in turn would require that the stimulus features be *observed* closely in time. Gnostic-assemblies are organized on the basis of such contiguous observations, which involve some observational movements.

Role of Observational Movements

Though no sharp distinction can be drawn between observational movements and other types of movements, they may be roughly defined as those that displace sense organs in relation to the environment and thus direct them at certain parts of the environment. Eye and head movements of various types, ear-moving in certain rodents, sniffing, palpation and manipulation by fingers and hand are examples of observational movements. A good proportion of the waking hours of the early life of animals is spent observing the environment in this way. Further, it is known that different types of observational movements occur in the presence of different types of stimulus configurations. For example, human neonates show prolonged visual scanning along the horizontal axis when presented with a vertically split black-white field, but not when presented with a horizontally split black-white field. Similarly, the wandering gaze of a few-days-old infant is arrested by the vertex of a triangle and this may be followed by horizontal scans across the vertex (Bond, 1972; Salapatek & Kessen, 1966).

Not much seems to be known about the pattern of scanning of infants when they are presented with complex stimulus configurations. However, it is known that the course of visual scanning shown by a human adult when faced with large line drawings of faces depends on the configuration of the faces (Noton & Stark, 1971). Though reliable evidence is lacking, it would be reasonable to suppose that the nature of the observational movements involving the use of head, ears, hand, nose, etc., are also determined by the characteristics of stimulus configurations. It is conceivable, then, that observational movements may be involved in the linking together of certain parts of stimulus configurations by producing contiguous observation of those parts.

Some support for the idea that observational movements play an important part in the development of gnostic-assemblies comes from studies of the effects of damage to the neural structures involved in observational movements, such as the superior colliculus and the related motor nuclei of the midbrain. Such studies have shown (see Gordon, 1972) that collicular lesions impair the animal's ability to learn to discriminate between visual patterns when the identification of the patterns requires frequent changes of fixation point. However, lesions made after acquisition of such a task do not impair subsequent performance. This suggests that eye movements play a critical role in the organization of certain gnostic-assemblies, but once organized, the gnostic-assemblies may function relatively independently of eye movements. No assumption is made here that the pattern of observational movements involved in the organization of any given gnostic-assembly must be distinctive for each gnostic-assembly.

Further indirect evidence suggesting that observational movements may play a part in the development of gnostic-assemblies needed for normal perception comes from studies of subjects with sensory defects. For example, in haptic judgments of curvature, blind subjects tend to be more accurate than blindfolded normal subjects. Davidson (1972) has shown that blind subjects use a haptic "scanning" technique that is different from that used by normal subjects; normal subjects can be made to improve their judgments by requiring them to use the scanning technique characteristic of the blind. Similarly, the blind are known to make more effective use of auditory cues in avoiding obstacles than do blindfolded normal subjects, but normal subjects can also be trained to do so (Taylor, 1966).

There is also some clinical evidence that the pattern of eye movements of children with reading difficulties, as well as of certain neurological patients who have impaired visual perception (e.g., simultagnosia), is different from the normal eye-movement patterns (Yarbus, 1967). But whether these eye-movement differences are the causes or consequences of the perceptual impairment is not yet clear.

Now turn to the organization of gnostic-assemblies.

Structuring of Gnostic-Assemblies

What makes observational movements achieve a temporal linkage of the critical or distinctive features of a stimulus is that the movements are themselves elicited by particular features of the stimulus (as explained in Chapters 3 and 4). Observation of one stimulus feature may elicit a movement that leads to the observation of the next feature, which leads to another movement, and so on. Thus a certain sequence of movements will result in the observation of particular critical features of a stimulus in close temporal contiguity in a certain sequence, and this in turn will lead to the activation of particular gnostic-neurons in the same sequence. A new gnostic-assembly will thus get organized; the firing of individual neurons of the gnostic-assembly in certain sequences could now occur in the absence of the observational movements initially necessary for organizing the gnostic-assembly.

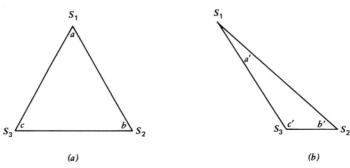

Figure 5.2.   Development of gnostic-assemblies representing parts of regular and irregular stimuli. (*a*) Equilateral triangle, (*b*) irregular triangle. Through repeated experience gnostic-assemblies representing various combinations of angles, *a–b–c, b'–c'–a'*, etc., are developed and they facilitate the generation of pexgos when appropriate sensory patterns are activated by the environmental stimulus.

Consider an example (see Figure 5.2). Let the three angles of a triangle be called, starting with a vertex and going clockwise, S_1, S_2, S_3. These three stimulus configurations give rise to corresponding sensory complexes, s_1, s_2, and s_3, each consisting of certain stimulus features (e.g., two lines of certain orientation, angle formed at the point of their junction). Suppose a human neonate happens to observe S_1 (that is, s_1 is potent enough to elicit a visual fixation). Now an eye-movement, M_1, may be elicited that consists of following the contour of the triangle from S_1 to S_2. This makes the infant look at S_2, and this in turn elicits the movement M_2 (S_2 to S_3), and so on. Looking at the triangle for a certain time, the infant may observe the three angles and the three lines of the triangle in succession, going sometimes in a clockwise and sometimes in an anticlockwise direction. Each critical feature of the triangle (e.g., the three angles) would activate particular types of gnostic-neurons, *a, b,* and *c,* in various orders. Through repeated activation in close temporal contiguity, these neurons would become organized in gnostic-assemblies; different gnostic-assemblies would develop for different orders: *a-b-c, a-c-b, b-c-a, b-a-c, c-a-b,* and *c-b-a.* Now, the firing of the first neuron of any of these assemblies might activate the whole sequence, and this, together with the representation of other stimulus features (e.g., the color, width, and length of lines forming the stimulus triangle), would comprise a pexgo of the triangle. For example, if the gnostic-neuron *a* is fired by the combination of feature detectors that make up S_1, then the whole of the gnostic-assemblies *a-b-c* or *a-c-b* may be activated. The exact pexgo generated would, of course, depend on the shape, size, etc., of the stimulus triangle, the the generation of the pexgo would be facilitated by the prior development of the gnostic-assemblies representing feature combinations that had frequently occurred together in the individual's life. In the case of an equilateral triangle (Figure 5.2a), since all the angles and lines are the same, the gnostic-neurons, a, b, c, would also be of the same type, and the six orders in which the three could be fired would be equivalent. In the case of an irregular triangle (Figure 5.2b) the gnostic-neurons fired would be of different types because of the differences in the angles, so that each of the six orders in which a', b', and c' are fired would be unique. Developing gnostic-assemblies that involve different types of gnostic-neurons may take longer than developing gnostic-assemblies with gnostic-neurons of only one type.

The above point suggests that it should be easier to generate a pexgo of a stimulus which has many redundant elements, and therefore involves the same type of gnostic-neurons, than for stimuli which have little or no redundancy. Thus, certain pexgos would be easier to generate than others; in general, stimuli such as circles, equilateral triangles, and squares should be easier to perceive than irregular forms such as complex arcs, obtuse-angle triangles, and miscellaneous quadrangles. These implications of the present hypothesis agree with the suggestion of Garner (1970) that what Gestalt psychologists called "good form" is a matter of low information content or redundancy.

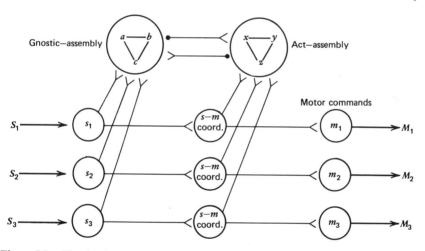

Figure 5.3. The development of gnostic-assemblies. The successive observational movements (M_1, M_2, M_3) elicited by particular stimulus features (S_1, S_2, S_3) have the effect of making the animal observe those stimulus features in close temporal contiguity; this results in the organization of gnostic-neurons into a gnostic-assembly.

On the assumption that gnostic-neurons of the same type are located closer to each other than gnostic-neurons of different types, and may be inherently connected to some extent, a neurophysiological basis may be found for the empirical laws of good form.

An implication of the above view that observational movements contribute to perception is that the development of act-assemblies and gnostic-assemblies goes hand-in-hand (see Figure 5.3). Just as certain movement sequences are repeatedly elicited and form unitary molar acts, so also individual gnostic-neurons are activated in certain sequences and develop into unitary, molar gnostic-assemblies. The elicitation of a certain movement sequence is dependent on certain stimulus features (Chapter 3), and the activation of certain gnostic-neurons in close temporal contiguity is also dependent on the same movement sequence. Thus, as an animal observes and acts in relation to a stimulus, it develops gnostic-assemblies and act-assemblies on the basis of a common set of elicited movements. It may be assumed that the gnostic-assemblies and act-assemblies that arise from a common set of movements become linked to each other through the selective strengthening of existing neural projections from gnostic-neurons to act-neurons. Thus a cue that activates a gnostic-assembly developed through certain movements would also be likely to activate an act-assembly consisting of the same movements. This linkage may be the basis of "ideomotor action"— the tendency to act in relation to a stimulus that is being perceived.

Intermodal Integration

An object such as a fruit, a predator, a nest, or an offspring can be the source of many diverse stimulus configurations. It can be looked at in the daylight or in the dark, from the front, from behind, from the sides, or from above, and these perspectives reveal different contours of shading, color, and texture; it can be touched and parts of it may be found to be rough, cold, or prickly; it can be smelled and tasted; it can be a source of different sounds; if lifted, it has a certain weight; and so on. Knowledge that animals acquire about the stable properties of a frequently encountered object is thus spread across sensory modalities. The general anatomical layout of the sensory systems indicates that the various stimulus features of a single object project to different parts of the brain, so that the sensory patterns arising from a given object may be widely dispersed. For example, the visual, tactual, and olfactory stimulus features of an apple would produce sensory patterns in the three anatomically distinct projection systems, and activate gnostic-neurons and gnostic-assemblies that are modality-specific. Unified knowledge about an object must thus emerge from some sort of integration of gnostic-assemblies across modalities.

Evidence of such integration of gnostic-assemblies of different modalities is provided by the phenomenon of cross-modality transfer. Human adults can readily tell whether an object they are observing, say, visually, is the same or not as the one they are exploring, say, haptically. This ability for making cross-modal judgments of object equivalence seems to be present in children about four years of age (A. D. Milner & Bryant, 1970). It has also been demonstrated in chimpanzees, orangutangs, and monkeys (e.g., Davenport & Rogers, 1970; Frampton, Milner, & Ettlinger, 1973). The suggestion that cross-modal transfer necessarily depends on the use of language, and arises from attaching the same name to different modality-specific percepts of an object, is made untenable by the demonstration of cross-modal transfer in nonhuman primates and preverbal human infants (Bryant, Jones, Claxton, & Perkins, 1972; Drewe, Ettlinger, Milner, & Passingham, 1970). Other findings show that differences in verbal ability make little difference in inter-modal transfer effects (Hermelin & O'Connor, 1964).

The idea that the development of cross-modal transfer of modality specific percepts results from making the same response to several different stimulus patterns, as well as its converse, that the differentiation of percepts results from learning to make different responses to similar stimulus patterns, is an old and popular one in psychology (e.g., James, 1890, p. 511; Gibson & Gibson, 1955; Dollard & Miller, 1950). Considerable experimental support has been adduced for this idea. Steady viewing of luminous figures in a dark room results in disruption of normal visual experience—the subject reports periodically that the figure or some part of it has disappeared (McKinney, 1963). This is the same type of effect as is obtained in retinal stabilization experiments (e.g., Pritchard, Heron, & Hebb, 1960). If two or more figures are presented in such a reduced stimulation experiment, the ones that are more similar in form to each other tend to disappear and reappear together (Donderi, 1966). Further, and this is the critical point, Donderi and Kane (1965) have shown that when a subject learns a common name for two elements of a three-element figure (e.g., three circles of different sizes or colors), the pair of common-name elements of the figure tend to disappear and remain visible together more frequently than any other pairs. It is also known that children who learn a common name for different geometrical figures tend to confuse these figures much more than children who learn different names for those figures (Katz, 1963). In general, the literature on "acquired distinctiveness of cues" (Lawrence, 1949, 1950; see also Sutherland & MacKintosh, 1971, Chap. 6), contains many observations showing that stimulus patterns can be made more or less equivalent by linking the same or different responses to them.

The basis of cross-modal transfer I want to propose is somewhat different from the above idea, though it also involves a response as the integrating agent. Imagine three different sets of gnostic-assemblies representing: A, smell of an apple; B, tactual smoothness of an apple; C, visual shape of an apple. If an animal eats an apple or has some other transaction with it as an object, all three types of gnostic-assemblies are likely to be activated simultaneously, through separate sensory systems. This will result in the strengthening of connections between the gnostic-assemblies, and this strengthening is likely to be bidirectional, that is, each stimulus configuration (A, B, C) would serve as a cue for the activation of all three types of gnostic-assemblies. After this inter-modal integration has occurred, the activation of any one set of gnostic-assemblies, say visual, would tend to activate or excite the gnostic-assemblies representing the critical olfactory and tactual features of the apple (see Figure 5.4). According to this interpretation, the importance of the response

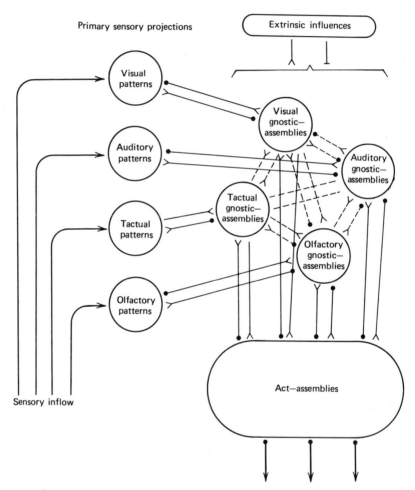

Figure 5.4. The relation of modality-specific sensory patterns and gnostic-assemblies to shared act-assemblies. Modality-specific gnostic-assemblies are separately connected to a common pool of act-assemblies. Modality-specific gnostic-assemblies also become linked to each other (broken lines) to form intermodal gnostic-assemblies representing objects as multimodal stimulus entities.

lies not in that it is in some sense "common" to the various modality-specific gnostic-assemblies, but in that the occurrence of the response makes inter-modal integration possible by activating the various modality-specific gnostic-assemblies in close temporal contiguity. *Any* response that leads to the contiguous activation of modality-specific gnostic-assemblies would suffice to produce intermodal integration.

The integration of gnostic-assemblies of different modalities with each other rests on the assumption that reciprocal synaptic connections exist among the various sites of modality-specific gnostic-assemblies, as shown in Figure 5.4. That such purely "perceptual" learning is possible is suggested by the demonstrations of sensory conditioning (e.g., Ellson, 1941; Jasper & Shagass, 1941; Thompson & Kramer, 1965). Since sensory projections of various modalities are likely to be distributed in varying degrees to any particular other sensory modality, it is to be expected that the ease of inter-modal integration of gnostic-assemblies would depend on the initial neural connectedness of the neurons forming the gnostic-assemblies. In other words, animals of a given species or strain may be more "prepared" to develop certain intermodal integrations, that is, to learn certain associations, than others.

Of course, normally several cues of different modalities are present simul-taneously, so that the inefficacy of certain sensory connections may make little difference in behavior. An apple may be identified and eaten on the basis of only its tactual cues, its visual cues, its olfactory cues, or any combination of these; and a passing train may be identified equally well on the basis of visual or auditory cues. Further, it is known that the simultaneous presence of cues of more than one modality facilitates identifying responses; for example, the detection of signals in a vigilance task is more efficient when both visual and auditory cues are provided than when cues of only one modality are provided (Brown & Hopkins, 1967). This substitutability and additivity of cues of different modalities in the production of an identifying response indicate that gnostic-assemblies of different modalities have separate access to the same act-producing structures, as shown in Figure 5.4.

The multiplicity of modality-specific pexgos that may underlie the percep-tion of a single object, and the separate connections by which the constituent gnostic-assemblies must reach various act-assemblies, indicates a considerable redundancy of routes by which environmental stimuli may be able to produce appropriate action. This is consistent with the findings that damage to indi-vidual sensory systems may often produce no clearly observable deficit in behavior. In the rat, for example, loss of *any* one or two sensory systems (e.g., vision and audition, vision and touch, touch and olfaction) does not necessarily lead to a decrement in the performance of a maze task learned before the sensory loss (DeFeudis, 1968; Honzik, 1936; Lashley & Ball, 1929).

The intactness of one or two of the sensory systems is, of course, necessary for the generation of some pexgos that could produce the (discriminative) response, but given this minimum the animal can perform normally in spite of major sensory damage.

PRODUCTION OF PERCEPTS

As noted earlier, a pexgo is not the same thing as a percept. A pexgo is only the first necessary step, not sufficient in itself, for producing particular percepts and identifying responses. My view is that a pexgo is generated by a combination of sensory and central influences, and the neural output of the pexgo then undergoes further neural interactions that form the basis of the reported percept and the overt identifying response. In trying to understand the relation between the pexgo—the distinctive presently excited gnostic organization—and the percept created by a certain stimulus, it may be instructive to examine what is known about the production of percepts.

Strength of Percept

Though the relation between perception and sensory events is not one-to-one, sensory projections are nevertheless normally the main basis of perception. In large measure, it is the relative potency (see Chap. 3) of various sensory representations of stimuli that determine the type and strength of the percept that will be produced.

Percept strength may reasonably be assumed to be reflected by the reported clarity of the conscious awareness of the stimulus, probability of correct detection (stimulus threshold measurement), or the speed of an arbitrary identifying response. The potency of the sensory representation is measured in terms of the magnitude of evoked potentials recorded from some part of the relevant sensory system or from the scalp of human subjects.

The change in electrical potentials evoked by a stimulus has several successive waves or components. The early components, say, those occurring within 70 msec of stimulus onset, comprise what may be called the sensory evoked potential (SEP), while the later components, say, those occurring from 120 to 400 msec after stimulus onset, are usually called the vertex evoked potentials (VEP) because typically they are recorded from the vertex of the scalp. Though the vertex potentials have been shown to be related to various attentional variables (see Sutton, 1969), they occur too late to contribute to the production of a percept; they are best regarded as reflecting the task significance or importance of the stimulus. Therefore, it is only the earlier (sensory evoked) potentials that we need to consider here.

Concerning the sensory evoked potentials recorded from the cortex, one important finding is that the magnitude of the potential is *inversely* related to the tonic level of arousal of the animal at the time of stimulus presentation (Thompson & Shaw, 1965). This inverse relation is seen clearly in the fact that the magnitude of sensory evoked potentials is greater during sleep and anesthesia than during the normal waking state, and greater during the normal waking state than during a state of excitement (Thompson & Shaw, 1965). However, for any given steady tonic level of arousal, the magnitude of the sensory evoked potentials tends to be directly proportional to the intensity of the stimulus. There have been only a few attempts to relate the magnitude of sensory evoked potentials directly to percept strength as measured by threshold of stimulus detection. In general, there does not appear to be a close relation between the probability of stimulus detection and the magnitude of cortical sensory evoked potentials so far as the initial or primary phase (about the first 30 msec) of the potential is concerned; even sub-threshold stimuli may evoke large primary sensory evoked potentials. There is thus no reason to believe that a primary sensory evoked potential of a certain amplitude is by itself sufficient for producing a percept.

The main positive finding about the events preceding the generation of a percept is that, on occasions when a stimulus *is* detected, there is a well-marked secondary phase (from 40 to 70 msec) of the sensory evoked potential (Libet, Alberts, Wright, & Feinstein, 1967). This secondary phase may represent a phasic excitation of the reticular activating system. If this is so, it may be supposed that the percept-producing capacity (or potency) of a sensory representation is indicated, not so much by the magnitude of the primary phase of its sensory evoked potential, as by the degree of the phasic increase in the activity of the reticular activating system, reflected in the secondary phase of the sensory evoked potential. This idea is supported by the finding that momentary electrical stimulation of the reticular activation system in an awake animal can improve performance in a tachistoscopic identification task (Fuster, 1958).

A tentative hypothesis about the process of perception may now be proposed. It may be supposed that any novel sensory representation, that is, a new test stimulus on a familiar stable background, leads to a phasic increase in activation level, and that this centrifugally induced phasic change in activation is projected back to the sensory systems generally. Such a phasic increase in activation enhances the strength of the sensory representation caused by the test stimulus and thus increases the probability of production of a certain pexgo of the test stimulus. Note that while a phasic increase in activation may influence the sensory cortex generally, it must have a more specific enhancing effect on the sensory representation of the novel, test stimulus, in order to make any relative difference. Note, too, that whether the test stimulus consists of the introduction of certain stimulus features or of their removal, the increase in activation takes place just the same (Weinberger & Lindsley, 1964). A possible neural mechanism for increasing the potency of a salient (intense or novel, or both) stimulus is shown in Figure 5.5.

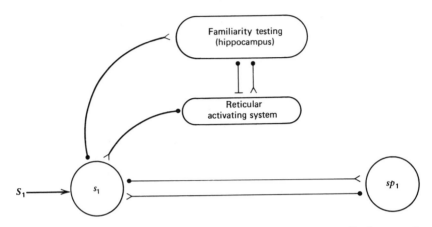

Figure 5.5. A hypothetical mechanism determining the potency or effectiveness of a stimulus configuration (S_1) and its corresponding sensory representation (s_1) in generating a sense-generated pexgo (sp_1). The potency is increased or decreased depending on the degree of habituation to (familiarity of) the stimulus. The hippocampus may be involved in the determination of the degree of familiarity and modulation of the reticular activating system.

According to this mechanism the sensory patterns are projected to the hippocampus from the sensory cortex. If the sensory input contains salient sensory features, the hippocampus sends impulses that raise the level of activation (or reduce the inhibition of activation); otherwise the hippocampus continues to send impulses that make no net effect on the activating system. This hypothesis rests on the findings that the hippocampus contains many neurons that respond to "sameness," or repetition of the same stimulus, and others that respond to "novelty," or a change in stimulation (Vinogradova, 1970), as well as on the suggestion that the hippocampus modulates the activity of the reticular activating system through fluctuations of an inhibitory discharge (Douglas, 1972). The essential idea here is that the stimulus as such, in the absence of central influences, is perceived only if it is sufficiently novel or intense, and can thereby increase the potency of its sensory representation through hippocampally induced increment in certain specific projections of the reticular activating system.

Time-Course of Percepts

If a subject is observing the location at which a stimulus will appear, and if the stimulus has moderate salience (sharp contours, distinctive sound frequencies, etc.), an exposure to the stimulus for only a few milliseconds may be sufficient to produce a percept. Identification of letters in a tachistoscopic display is possible with a flash exposure of even 1 msec, provided the flash is strong enough. Thus sufficient receptor information for the production of a percept can be provided by a very brief stimulus display. But the transduction, transmission, and transformation of the receptor information into a percept take considerably longer.

If, as suggested earlier, a percept depends on a centrifugally induced increase in activation level, as indicated by the secondary phase of the sensory evoked potential (from 40 to 80 msec), it may be guessed that it would take minimally 60 msec to perceive a stimulus after the appropriate receptor information has been provided. It is possible that the centrifugally induced increase in activation depends on the prior generation of a pexgo, so that it may take only 20–40 msec to generate a pexgo of a stimulus.

Once a percept has resulted from a momentary stimulus, how long does it persist? Estimates of percept persistence have been obtained by several methods. Using his method of partial report, Sperling (1960) found that a specified three-letter row of letters, which formed part of a letter square of nine letters, could be correctly reported if the row was specified up to one second after the offset of the stimulus display. By using flicker fusion as well as other methods, Haber and his coworkers (Haber, 1971) have estimated the duration of the percept to be well under 500 msec. By a method that required subjects to judge whether the offset of one stimulus and the onset of a succeeding stimulus were simultaneous or not, Efron (1970a; 1970b) found that the *minimum* duration of a percept following a momentary stimulus varies between 120 and 240 msec, depending on the modality (being shorter for audition than for vision) and on the subject. The higher estimate of Sperling may have been due to verbal rehearsal while the subject was waiting for the specification of the row to be recalled. Though more evidence is needed on this point, it may be tentatively concluded that a percept will persist for a period on the order of 200 msec, no matter how brief the stimulus which produces it.

Though a particular stimulus may not be consciously experienced as a percept, it may nevertheless generate a pexgo, as indicated by the occurrence of an appropriate identifying response. This is shown by an experiment by Fehrer and Raab (1962). In a reaction-time experiment they presented a masking stimulus following the reaction signal on certain trials. Under the conditions of their experiment the subject reported no percept of the signal stimulus on the trials with the masked stimulus. However, the speed of reactions to the masked signals was *not* lower than the speed of reactions to the unmasked signals. In interpreting these and other results, Fehrer and Biederman remark that a reaction can be ". . . initiated and determined by an event which is so successfully masked that it is often not detected by careful phenomenal observation" (Fehrer & Biederman, 1962, p. 130). This indicates that a pexgo can function effectively in producing an identifying (discriminative) response whether or not its excitation results in a conscious experience of the stimulus. Similar findings have been reported by Marcel (1974).

That a conscious percept need not be a condition of discriminative identification of a stimulus, and action in relation to it, is also shown by a case of visual field defect. Weiskrantz, Warrington, Sanders, and Marshall (1974) studied residual vision in a patient with right occipital lobe excision, which had produced a stable left hemianopia. When discriminanda were presented in this blind (so far as conscious awareness was concerned) field, the patient said he saw nothing at all. However, when forced to "guess" he could reliably discriminate the location, orientation, and shape of discriminanda so long as they were large and were presented for a certain duration. Acuity (minimal separation) in the "blind" part of the field was almost as good as in the intact field, but there was no conscious awareness of the discriminanda. Apparently, direct projections to secondary visual areas are sufficient for visual discriminations without awareness; however, primary visual areas somehow add conscious awareness of the discriminanda even if the acuity of discrimination is low.

IMAGES

We have seen above that a pexgo may be generated, as indicated by successful identification or some reliable influence on response, without any percept, as indicated by awareness of the stimulus. Now we consider cases in which a percept-like awareness is created in the absence of appropriate environmental stimulation. The reported experience of a stimulus that is not currently the source of an appropriate sensory input may be called an *image* of that stimulus. Note that the term "image" is used here to describe a reportable experience, an awareness like a percept, and not as a designation for an explanatory construct; pexgo is the explanatory construct.

Like percepts, images are produced by pexgos (they represent the excitation of an assortment of gnostic-assemblies) and, like percepts, images may be weak or strong, depending on the level of excitation of the pexgo that has been generated. The general idea that images are perceptions sans stimulus is old and has been reiterated by several writers (e.g., Hebb, 1968; James,

1890; Washburn, 1916). Since percepts proper are also only partly dependent on current sensory patterns, a sharp distinction between percepts and images is not possible. Several varieties of images may be recognized depending on the exact circumstances in which they are produced.

Varieties of Images

The type of image that is closest to a perception, and perhaps indistinguishable from it in experience, is the positive afterimage of a strong stimulus. Positive afterimages persist for about 250 msec after the termination of the stimulation and probably represent a brief continuation of sensory activity after stimulus termination. Negative afterimages are complementary to or opposite of the stimulus in certain respects (e.g., a red flag is seen as green in the negative afterimage), and persist for several seconds after stimulus termination. They appear to reflect some compensatory recuperative process that returns the stimulated sensory apparatus to the normal resting level after strong stimulation. Thus both positive and negative afterimages may be attributed to the persistence of initial or compensatory sensory processes that continue to occur for some time after stimulus termination. Afterimages move with the sense organs—they are projected wherever the eyes happen to be looking or the ears listening. This suggests that afterimages represent persistence of activity at fairly low levels of the sensory system, probably the sensory transduction apparatus. Consistent with this interpretation is the fact that an afterimage generated by the stimulation of one sense organ, say, an eye, shows no transfer to the other eye.

The images of missing limbs or the "phantom limb phenomena" are well documented. Typically, the subjects report an awareness of the missing limb, and sometimes pain or some form of discomfort is localized in the missing limb. Such experiences are reported by persons who have lost a limb through accident or amputation, but not by persons whose limbs have gradually absorbed, because of leprosy, lack of motor innervation, or some other chronic defect (Simmel, 1956a). There is little reason to doubt that the experience of phantom limb requires some adventitious activity in sensory nerves or nuclei that initially transmitted the somesthetic inflow from the missing limb or from intersensory interactions at higher sensory levels (Melzack & Schechter, 1965; Simmel, 1956b). However, several details of the phenomena of phantom limb require participation of higher levels of neural activity (Melzack & Bromage, 1973).

Eidetic images are clear and vivid images that may persist for a period of several seconds after the termination of a brief stimulus display. Unlike afterimages proper, eidetic images are not projected in the environment and do not move with the sense organs; they can be "read off" or "listened to" by appropriate eye and head movements. For example, after looking for 15 sec at a picture of a street scene a child may be able to spell, forward or backward, a long name on a sign post or to report accurately some other details of the scene. By adequate controls for memorizing and inference, it is possible to show that some children, but not adults, can generate stable images that are differentiated and vivid enough to allow them to read off the required detail (Haber & Haber, 1964; Leask, Haber, & Haber, 1969). Since eidetic images do not move with sense organs but can be inspected part-by-part, they seem to reflect persistence of activation of particular assortments of gnostic-assemblies comprising a pexgo, rather than of the sensory patterns as such. Why eidetic images should occur in only some children remains a mystery. Hypotheses of slight brain damage (Siipola & Hayden, 1965; Freides & Hayden, 1966) and of some kind of inhibitory defect (Hebb, 1968) have been suggested as possible bases of the persistence of neural activity.

Hallucinatory images share most of the characteristic clarity and vividness of eidetic images but are not a consequence of any specific stimulus input; the hallucinatory image may bear no resemblance to any recently encountered stimulus. Actually, hallucinatory images are likely to occur under conditions of perceptual isolation, monotony, loss of sleep, and weakness (Bexton, Heron, & Scott, 1954; Hartmann, 1967; Morris, Williams, & Lubin, 1960; Zubek, Aftanas, Kovach, Wilgosh, & Winocur, 1963). Since, like percepts and eidetic images, hallucinatory images do not move with sense organs but can be inspected, it is likely that hallucinatory images reflect activation of certain pexgos. Their activation is presumably a consequence of some sort of spontaneous central activity. The bizarreness of hallucinatory images indicates that the pexgos activated may not represent any specific stimulus object. Hebb (1968) has attributed hallucinatory images to a *"failure* of sensation": the absence of the modulating and organizing influence of sensory patterns presumably results in spontaneous, unorganized activation of gnostic-assemblies, leading to the generation of some pexgo that determines the characteristic of the hallucinatory images.

Dream images seem to differ from hallucinatory images only in that during sleep the dreamer does not distinguish between images and perceptions, and takes dream images as representing environmental stimulation. The exact content of hallucinatory and dream images may also be influenced by conditioned stimuli that have acquired the capability of centrally raising the level of excitation of particular gnostic-assemblies (see Chapters 7 and 8).

Memory images are images that are evoked centrally through association. For example, looking at some vegetation may lead an image of a field of grass, and this, through associatively related gnostic-assemblies (see Chapters 6 and 7) may lead to, successively, the images of a cow, a bottle of milk, a dairy, the workers at a dairy, and so on. Since there is no specific sensory basis for the production of the successive images, the images are likely to be more faint than vivid and are not likely to be projected into environment; they are experienced as being in the head.

Memory images and percepts may be regarded as reflecting the two extremes of a continuum of the strength of excitation of the pexgo. Memory images are generated mainly by central associative excitation of pexgos with a minimum of relevant sensory patterns, while percepts are generated mainly by the current inflow of sensory patterns with a minimum of associative excitation. There is perhaps no case of percept or image in which either the central or the sensory influence is wholly absent. There is thus no sharp distinction between the two; the differences between the different "types" of images lie essentially in relative proportions of the sensory and central influences and in the way in which these influences operate in any particular case. It is nonetheless useful to draw a distinction between *sense-generated pexgos* (sp) that underlie perceptions, and *centrally-generated pexgos* (cp) that underlie memory images (Hebb, 1968).

Functional Significance of Images

The test of the veridicality of a percept of a stimulus lies in the accuracy and reliability of the identifying response made in relation to the stimulus. It is the identifying response—whether the press of a key or a verbal response— that is publicly measurable in relation to other publicly observable events; we can find out that a person's color percepts are abnormal only by studying his color-identifying responses in relation to several colored stimuli presented under varying circumstances. The next question is whether the identifying response is in any way dependent on the percept, or, in other words, whether the conscious awareness of a stimulus contributes any specific influence (is causally related) to the production of an adaptive response in relation to that stimulus. This question is far from being resolved, but two points are worth considering here.

The first point to note is that a stimulus may not generate a specific, clear percept—an awareness or experiencing of it—and yet may influence behavior. As we go around performing various daily activities, such as driving to work, opening locks, and turning on a light switch, we do not perceive each stimulus (e.g., the road curb, the keyhole, the switch) on which our behavior can be shown to be dependent. If someone is whistling a tune near me, a few moments later I might whistle or hum the same tune without any awareness of having listened to the tune. Formal experiments have shown that the solution to a problem-solving task may be suggested by a hint of which the subject may remain unaware (Maier, 1931). It is possible that each stimulus in relation to which a subject acts is perceived or imaged at the time but that this fact is forgotten a few moments later when the subject is questioned. However, it is also possible, at least for responses that have become habitual, that the production of a response can be achieved without any percept or image of the stimulus in relation to which the response is made. This latter hypothesis is supported by the observations that clear percepts and images are generated usually when a response is interrupted or blocked or when no habitual response has yet developed (Sperry, 1952; Washburn, 1916). In the normal flow of well-practiced behavior, percepts and images of relevant stimuli are seldom formed.

The second point to note about the possible role of images in the production of adaptive responses is that the production of memory images need not contribute anything to the production of appropriate responses. On instruction a subject may experience an image of Michelangelo's statue, David, but may be unable to say whether David's head is turned to the right or left. As Hebb (1968) has pointed out, it is only upon closely questioning about particular details of an image that one can determine that a memory image may carry little or no utilizable information; a person who reports an image of a poem would most likely be unable to "read" the poem backwards from the image. In a study of recall of word groups, Baddeley and Warrington (1973) found that, while the recall was improved when word groups were formed on the basis of linguistic relations, grouping by composite visual images produced no advantage for recall even though images were reported. Conversely, absence of what might be considered appropriate images does not interfere with recall. Bugelski (1971) found that, in a paired-associate recall task, blind children could recall "visual words" (e.g., shadow, fog, blue) just as well as they could "auditory words" (e.g., music, whisper, echo) and "neutral words" (e.g., glove, key, sofa); the absence of visual images did not produce any selective deficit for recalling "visual words." Though such findings cannot be regarded as decisive, they are consistent with the tentative conclusion that memory images may contribute little or nothing to recall.

The above considerations indicate that the activation of a pexgo may be sufficient for producing appropriate behavior, whether or not the activation also produces a percept or an image. Conscious awareness of a real or imaged stimulus thus appears not to be an intrinsic or necessary part of the production of adaptive behavior.

STIMULUS ATTRIBUTES AND GENERALIZATION

While central representations of objects as unitary entities are being organized through the development of gnostic-assemblies and their intermodal integration, an apparently opposite development must also go on. This latter development has to do with the representation of "disembodied"stimulus dimensions, that is, of stimulus *features* as such, independent of the objects of which they are a part. The existence of such representations is indicated by the fact that we identify and recall without reference to particular objects, such (psychological) attributes as hue, brightness, pitch, form, sweetness, and roughness, whose values correspond to the values of certain (physical) dimensions of environmental stimuli. We are also able to imagine non-existent objects, such as a tiny pink elephant or a large purple unicorn, by combining particular attributes into new combinations. How is it possible to perceive an attribute that is independent of the object from which the attribute is derived?

Isolation of Stimulus Attributes

The problem of perceiving an attribute independent of any particular object is essentially that of isolating the representation of that attribute or stimulus feature from the representation of all the other attributes (stimulus features) of the object. The process by which an attribute may develop an isolated representation, that is, develop gnostic-assemblies representing that attribute as such, may be illustrated with reference to how the form (e.g., a triangle or letter) and orientation (i.e., degree of rotation about the origin of its horizontal and vertical axes) of a stimulus may be separated in perception.

Normal adults have no difficulty in identifying a form regardless of orientation in which the form is presented; perception is not orientation-specific, but is orientation-independent. It is known that children show an improvement with age (from about 2 to 14 years) in the ability to identify a form independently of orientation (Ghent & Bernstein, 1961). However, experiments with human infants show that even at six months of age they are quite capable of discriminating between different orientations of the same form, as well as of identifying different orientations of a form as the same form (McGurk, 1972). This suggests that the improvement in orientation-independent identification of form shown during childhood may have a different basis than the orientation-independent identification of which the infant is capable by six months of age. The former presumably represents the learning of verbally coded concepts of form and orientation, whereas the latter would seem to reflect the development of separate gnostic-assemblies representing the attributes of form and orientation. Here we are concerned with this latter development.

The development of separate form and orientation gnostic-assemblies seems to depend on the degree to which the two attributes vary with respect to each other in the stimulus configurations experienced by the infant. Suppose a triangle is repeatedly presented to an infant in four different orientations, with its vertex pointing north, south, east, or west. It will quickly be able to discriminate between the four orientations of the triangle but may not be able to discriminate between the triangle and, say, a square, even when they are presented in the same orientation. However, if the orientation were kept constant and the form varied (triangle, column, square, etc.), then the infant would be able to discriminate between forms but not between orientations. In other words, whatever attribute of the total stimulus configuration is varied will become discriminable—readily identifiable. Of course, both form and orientation are likely to vary independently of each other in the various stimulus configurations to which infants are normally exposed, so that both form and orientation would become independently discriminable. According to this account, the infant moves from a stage in which form and its orientation are treated as one (compound) stimulus, so that the identifications of form are orientation-specific and of orientation form-specific, to a stage at which form and orientation are treated as two separate stimulus features or attributes, so that the identifications of form are orientation-independent and of orientation form-independent.

The stimulus features or physical dimensions that are important in the differentiation of form and orientation are the spatial relations of the various form-determining contours of the stimulus and the "frame" in which the stimulus is presented. The frame may be one defined by the edges of the experimental visual field or one defined by the vertical and horizontal axes of the subject's head or eyes. Whatever the form, the physical dimensions relevant to orientation differentiation are the deviations from perfect alignment of the contours of the stimulus from those of the frame. If form is varied and orientation kept constant, the subject will learn to discriminate the attribute of form but not of orientation; the reverse will be the case when form is kept constant and orientation cues are varied. Essentially, then, any experimental stimulus may be regarded as a compound of several attributes (or features), and the subject learns to discriminate those attributes that are varied systematically with respect to the other attributes, which are either not varied at all or are varied randomly with respect to the critical attribute. If an experiment were arranged in which the critical stimulus attribute is form, random variations in orientation would have no effect on the identification of the form, and the identification of form would be orientation-independent. And if an experiment were arranged in which the critical stimulus attribute is orientation, random variations in form would have no effect on the identification of the orientation, and the identification of orientation would be form-independent.

The idea that spatial cues arising from the deviations in the alignment of a stimulus with a frame (or with some other stable aspect of a stimulus display) are important in the discrimination of orientation has been applied by

Bryant (1973) to an analysis of the frequently reported difficulty in the discrimination of a stimulus from its mirror image (Corballis & Beale, 1970). Working with children (about 4 to 7 years of age), Bryant showed that the successive discrimination of two oblique orientations of a line was no more difficult when the orientations were mirror-images of each other than when certain other (nonmirror-image) oblique orientations were presented. The critical factor seemed to be whether the oblique stimuli were aligned (parallel) in relation to each other or not. When no differential alignment cues were present, discriminations were difficult whether the orientations were mirror-image or not. Discrimination difficulty is not dependent on mirror-imageness as such, but on the extent to which differential spatial (alignment) cues are available. Thus the reported difficulty in the discrimination of mirror images may arise from the fact that the differential spatial cues are likely to be highly subtle when the form cues are exactly the same—as they must be in mirror-image discrimination tasks. Making use of the differential spatial cues requires aligning the stimuli with respect to each other or to a frame, and many subjects may not have learned the systematic use of alignment for producing differential spatial cues in the case of identical forms. Another reason for the difficulty of mirror-image discriminations may lie in the relative difficulty of remembering spatial cues in successive discrimination experiments. These considerations suggest that the discrimination of mirror images should be much easier when the discriminanda are presented simultaneously and the stimuli are presented in a frame in which they can be readily aligned to generate differential spatial cues.

Organization of Attribute Gnostic-Assemblies

Turn now to the question of the organization of gnostic-assemblies that would represent particular attributes of (compound) stimuli. As explained earlier, a gnostic-assembly does not represent an object as a whole, but only certain critical features that tend to occur together in the general experience of an animal with varieties of objects. The gnostic-assemblies activated, and the pexgo generated, and the resulting perception then, depend on the selection of gnostic-assemblies that are activated by the sensory inflow produced by a certain stimulus configuration. Applied to the central representation of attributes, this means that the critical stimulus features that define an attribute would become represented by specific gnostic-assemblies as an animal has repeated experience with different values of the physical dimensions that correspond to that attribute. It was noted in Chapter 2 that the more critical features in an environment tend to be those that change (assume different values) from time to time. Thus any physical dimension whose values have varied in the experience of an animal would lead to the organization of gnostic-assemblies representing different values of the dimension; such a set of gnostic-assemblies may be said to comprise a crude neural *attribute scale.*

How do value-differentiated gnostic-assemblies, comprising an attribute scale, become organized? A hypothetical answer to this question may be attempted as follows.

In the neonate, though there are no attribute scales, different values of particular stimulus dimensions are nevertheless differentially registered: observational reactions are undoubtedly different with different loudnesses, different degrees of circularity or angularity of forms, different hues, different degrees of tactual roughness, and so on. These initial differences in observational acts are, as noted earlier, dependent on the salience of the attribute values, as well as on the species-typical sensory-motor coordination organizations. These differential observational acts form the basis of the development of gnostic-assemblies representing particular values of a stimulus dimension. As an animal encounters different values of a certain stimulus dimension while other stimulus dimensions remain constant, the discriminative conditions necessary for the development of gnostic-assemblies representing particular values of the stimulus dimension are created (as explained above in connection with the orientation dimension). When a sufficient number of such gnostic-assemblies, each representing a particular range of a stimulus dimension, have been organized, a crude attribute scale may be said to have developed. Neurally, then, an attribute scale is a set of gnostic-assemblies ordered in terms of the value of the stimulus dimension they represent. The sensitivity of an attribute scale would of course depend on the number of different gnostic-assemblies that have been developed to represent a certain range of the stimulus dimensional values. Though several gnostic-assemblies representing a stimulus dimension are formed, it appears that the capability of identifying particular values in a successive discrimination task is quite limited (G. A. Miller, 1956); human subjects can barely cope with seven values of a dimension in such a task—a number that also describes the usual number of steps observed in a stimulus generalization gradient.

Stimulus Generalization

Different stimulus configurations activate different selections of sensory patterns and different assortments of gnostic-assemblies. Because potentially millions of different assortments of gnostic-assemblies may be activated by the ever-changing stimulus configurations of an animal's environment, there is in effect an infinitude of different pexgos—and perceptions—that can be generated. There is no reason to assume that a meaningful upper limit of possible percepts or discriminable entities is imposed by the number of sensory gnostic-neurons. However, because of the limitations of the motor system, the number and diversity of perceptions must far exceed the number and diversity of acts. Normally, several different stimuli may lead to the same response; this is the phenomenon of "stimulus equivalence." The fact that two stimuli are equivalent in that they evoke the same response does not, of course, mean that they necessarily activate the same gnostic-assemblies or generate identical pexgos. Common responses to different stimuli may be trained by making the stimuli equivalent in their functional use; thus J and j generate different percepts but usually evoke a common response, and the sight of an apple or of the letter sequence *a-p-p-l-e* may lead to the same verbal response. Stimulus equivalence as determined by common response may thus be attributable to similarity of function or meaning (see Chapter 8) of the stimuli. Here we are concerned with only those cases of stimulus equivalence in which the identity or similarity of response is dependent on the similarity of the stimulus configurations along a certain stimulus dimension; such cases are usually discussed under the rubric of "stimulus generalization."

The essential experimental paradigm for demonstrating stimulus generalization consists in showing that a response trained in relation to one stimulus, the training stimulus (say a triangle), is also elicitable at least to some degree, by some other stimulus, the test stimulus (say a smaller or a larger triangle), which differs from the training stimulus along a certain physical dimension (say, size). The response to the test stimulus is usually found to be crudely proportional to the similarity of the test stimulus to the training stimulus along the dimension on which the test stimulus is varied. There are two broad ways of accounting for the observed stimulus generalization. One is to assume that because the test and training stimuli are similar—share some sensory patterns—their gnostic-assemblies would also be quite similar, so that what is learned in relation to the training stimulus would also automatically be learned in relation to all the potential stimuli that share some gnostic-assemblies with the training stimulus. The degree of similarity of the response to the training and test stimuli would depend on the degree to which they activate common gnostic-assemblies. This "generalized-learning" view was essentially what was proposed by Pavlov (1927) and Hull (1943). The second way to account for stimulus generalization is to assume that, owing to the similarity of their sensory patterns, the animal confuses the test stimulus with the training stimulus; that is, not having learned to discriminate the dimension along which the training and test stimuli vary, the animal responds in the same way to the test stimulus as it does to the training stimulus. This "failure-of-discrimination" interpretation is what was proposed by Lashley and Wade (1946).

Though there has been much controversy between the proponents of these two views of stimulus generalization (see Prokasy & Hall, 1963), the two views can be readily integrated in terms of the proposed hypothesis about the organization of gnostic-assemblies. According to this, the degree of stimulus generalization observed depends on the extent to which the pexgos—i.e., the activated gnostic-neurons and gnostic-assemblies—generated by the training and test stimuli are similar, and this in turn depends on the extent to which the animal had previously developed separate gnostic-assemblies representing the different values of the dimensions along which the test stimuli are made different from the training stimulus. There is "generalized learning" because while training is given with the training stimulus, some of the gnostic-assemblies that are activated are those that will also be activated by the test stimulus. And there is "failure-of-discrimination" because the training and test stimuli, even though potentially discriminable, are not, at the time of test, represented by distinctive gnostic-assemblies; that is, the relevant attribute scale has not yet been developed. It follows that by giving discriminative training in relation to different values of the generalization dimension, stimulus generalization could be reduced to the threshold of discrimination; that is, the test stimulus could be made to look more and more like the training stimulus without eliciting the response trained to the training stimulus until the sensory patterns of the two stimuli are so alike as to be beyond the discrimination capability of the animal. There is considerable evidence to show that prior training to discriminate stimuli along the experimental stimulus dimension reduces stimulus generalization; for example, pigeons trained to discriminate between two wavelengths of light (say, 500 mμ positive and 600 mμ negative) give much sharper response gradient (show less stimulus generalization) than pigeons not given any special training (Guttman & Kalish, 1956; Tomie, Davitt, & Thomas, 1975). Conversely, lack of discriminative experience along a dimension makes the response gradients along that dimension quite flat (Jenkins & Harrison, 1962; Peterson, 1962).

CHAPTER 6

Knowledge of Spatial and Temporal Relations

The stimuli—objects, events, actions, etc.—that an animal encounters in its environment have a location in space as well as in time. It was noted in Chapter 2 that the spatial and temporal features of environmental stimuli are transmitted to the brain as a part of the sensory inflow. Here we examine the nature of the neural representation of the spatial and temporal location of stimuli; in other words, how are gnostic-assemblies representing the spatial and temporal features developed in the brain? The related question of the neural representation of the correlations between stimuli observed by an animal is also to be considered. I start with a brief account of what animals may know about the spatial and temporal aspects of their environments.

KNOWLEDGE ABOUT SPACE

Location in space cannot be defined absolutely, but only in relation to a reference point. In the study of behavior the reference point is usually the location of the head or eyes of the observer. In relation to the reference point the location of a specified object may be described in terms of the three spatial dimensions, lateral (left-right), sagittal (front-back), and vertical (up-down). The basic directional and distance information is contained in the current sensory inflow (see Chap. 2).

Knowledge that animals have about space can be determined by testing them on tasks requiring discrimination of particular spatial features. Though conceptually simple, such investigations have been difficult to conduct, and no coherent body of facts has yet emerged. A part of the difficulty undoubtedly lies in the ambiguity and vagueness of the terms used to describe discrimination tests. In the following account, my aim is to clarify the terminology and to indicate what appear to be the three main types of knowledge about space.

Types of Spatial Knowledge

The simplest type of knowledge about space is that of *spatial location* (in relation to the subject's body). Such knowledge may be demonstrated by a location-finding test. This test requires the subject to reach a certain object by going to a certain location from a given starting point in the absence of any current stimulus information from the object itself or from any distinctive cues along the path. For example, a hungry rat is put in a start box that opens into a round arena with several identical boxes arranged around its circumference. Food is hidden in a different goal box on each trial, but the goal box is always in the same position (say, at the 10 o'clock point on the circumference) in relation to the animal's starting point (which is also varied from trial to trial). When the gate of the start box is opened, the rat's task is to go to the goal box. If the rat can learn this task, that is, if it learns to go directly to the goal box regularly, and if it can be shown that the animal's response is not based on any current apparatus or extra-apparatus cues (e.g., sight or smell of food, or any distinctive cues correlated with the correct path), then the rat may be said to know the spatial location of the goal box. Since the correct response is not based on any current locational cues, the only basis for the animal to perform the task correctly is some central representation of a particular location with reference to its starting position. The usual delayed response test is an adaptation of the location-finding test for use with primates and other animals that are capable of one-trial observational learning.

The second type of spatial knowledge is that of *spatial relations*. A test of this would require the animal to differentiate between the spatial arrangements or relative positions of two (or more) objects in relation to each other, as they appear from the animal's position. For example, an animal may be required to show that it can differentiate AB from BA, that is, a stimulus A presented to the left (or above, or in front of) of stimulus B, and the same stimulus (A) presented to the right (or below, or in back of) of stimulus B. Since in such a test the possibility exists that the animal may respond correctly on the basis of location in relation to itself of only one of the stimuli (e.g., whether A is more or less to the left *of the animal*) rather than on the basis of the relative positions of the two stimuli, the location of the total stimulus array must be randomized with respect to the animal's position. Since the possibility also exists that during discrimination training the animal may learn simply to respond to the configuration (e.g., AB) that is followed by reward and ignore the other (incorrect) configuration altogether, it is desirable to arrange a successive discrimination task and require the animal to make two responses, both rewarded, one response (say, left turn) when one configuration is presented and the second (say, right turn) when the other is presented. Successful performance on such tests requires that the animal possess a central representation of the relative spatial locations of objects, with the animal's current position as the reference point. Appropriate tests have shown that birds and mammals can differentiate between different spatial configurations of the same stimuli (see Corballis & Beale, in press). In general, it has been found that discriminations involving configurations that juxtapose stimuli along the vertical (up-down) dimension (A/B vs. B/A) are more readily learned than those involving lateral (left-right: AB vs. BA) juxtapositions (L. J. Harris, 1972).

The third type of spatial knowledge is that of *spatial dimensions* as such. A test of this would require the animal to differentiate relative positions of two or more stimuli along a spatial dimension defined independently of the current position of the animal. In other words, successful performance on such a test would require knowledge of spatial dimensions with a moveable reference point—that is, without the use of the animal's own position as a reference point to define left-right, front-back, and up-down. For example, if two blocks, one red and one blue, are placed in front of a child, and he is asked whether the blue block would be on the right or left of the red block as observed from various assumed observation points, successful performance would indicate that the child has knowledge of the lateral dimension as such. Another method of demonstrating such knowledge is the three-object array method (Piaget, 1928). In this the subject is presented with three objects in the lateral plane, and he is asked to name the position (left or right) of the middle object in relation to each of the two side objects. Knowledge of spatial relations between stimuli that is independent of an animal's own current position may be said to be less "egocentric" or more perspectivist than the knowledge of spatial relations in reference to the observer's own body, and follows the acquisition of egocentric spatial knowledge (Laurendeau & Pinard, 1970; Piaget & Inhelder, 1956). Such abstract knowledge would seem to require a central representation of spatial dimensions from a variety of movable reference points. In this case too it has been shown that developing knowledge of the lateral dimension is more difficult than developing knowledge of the vertical dimension (L. J. Harris, 1972).

Representation of Spatial Knowledge

As noted in Chapter 2, sensory inflow contains not only information about the stimulus features of objects but also information about their spatial location. Just as gnostic-assemblies are organized that represent particular values of certain physical dimensions of the critical features of an object (color, shape, etc.), so, it may now be postulated, gnostic-assemblies are organized that represent particular values of spatial dimensions that define the location of the object in relation to the animal's current position.

If gnostic-assemblies representing particular locations-in-reference-to-the-observer are to be organized, the spatial information that is contained in specific receptor neurons (e.g., specific retinal points) must somehow be transformed into spatial information in reference to the animal's (head) position. Such transformations presumably take place as the receptor-topographic sensory activity of primary projection areas interacts with the secondary spatially coded projection areas, which receive inputs from the collicular structures. In primates, parts of the parietal cortex seem to be critically involved in the knowledge of spatial location (e.g., Critchley, 1953; Mendoza & Thomas, 1975). The neural mechanisms of such transformations are not known and are only beginning to be investigated (e.g., Milner, 1974).

It was noted in discussion of gnostic-assemblies representing an attribute scale that they are organized on the basis of discriminative experience with stimuli that lie at different values of a certain stimulus dimension. Similarly, it may be postulated that gnostic-assemblies representing different values of any spatial dimension are also organized on the basis of discriminative experience of particular stimulus locations varying along that spatial dimension. For example, if peanuts are presented to a monkey on a platform with each peanut placed at different left-to-right locations, the monkey will make different observational acts and will retrieve each peanut with a somewhat different retrieving action; a set of dimensional gnostic-assemblies representing the lateral dimension would thus get organized, as explained in Chapter 5. Gnostic-assemblies representing vertical and sagittal dimensions would be similarly organized on the basis of discriminative experience with locations varying in those dimensions. Since objects are always located in three-dimensional space, the dimensional gnostic-assemblies would be activated simultaneously, providing a unified representation in terms of spatial coordinates.

Further, just as gnostic-assemblies representing the stimulus features of objects are integrated intermodally, so the spatial gnostic-assemblies organized by the spatial information from the auditory, visual, and somatosensory modalities are also integrated intermodally. That the spatial information from different modalities is combined into an integrated representation of space is indicated by the accuracy of actions directed at a target location signaled now visually and now aurally, as well as by the ability to tell whether the locations of a visual and an auditory stimulus source are the same or different. The structural basis of a common response to different modality-specific spatial representations probably lies in the superior and inferior colliculi, which coordinate observational acts of eyes, ears, and head on the basis of directional information from visual, auditory, and somatosensory modalities. Some of this intermodal integration is clearly of maturational origin; eye movements aimed at the direction of a sound source can be observed in the human infant within minutes after delivery (Wertheimer, 1961). But whatever the basic mechanism of intermodal spatial integration, the integration of gnostic-assemblies of different modalities representing the same spatial location must continue throughout life, providing a basis for intermodal transfer of spatial information.

KNOWLEDGE ABOUT TIME

Like spatial location, location in time cannot be defined absolutely but only in relation to a reference event. Knowledge about the temporal aspects of environmental events may also be divided into three classes, each demonstrated by a different type of test.

Types of Temporal Knowledge

One type of knowledge about time is that of *temporal order*; did an event A occur before or after another event B? In order to demonstrate that a given animal is capable of temporal-order discrimination, it is necessary to train it to respond in a particular way to two stimuli presented in the order AB, and to respond in a different way when the same stimuli are presented in the order BA. However, such a training procedure leaves open the possibility that the animal may ignore one of the stimuli in a sequence-pair, for example, the animal may ignore the first stimulus and respond on the basis of the second (the last) stimulus of the pair (B or A) alone. This difficulty may be overcome by, for example, adopting a reproduction procedure which requires the animal to press keys that will reproduce the same order of stimuli (say, tones) which was presented a moment earlier. It has been found that cats and monkeys can learn temporal orders of tones, that such discriminations are more difficult to learn than are auditory intensity or frequency discriminations, and that localized ablations in the auditory cortex that leave the latter discriminations unaffected may greatly disrupt temporal-order discriminations (Cowey & Dewson, 1972).

The second type of knowledge about time is shown by the ability to discriminate *temporal duration*. It should be noted that the fact that the passage of time (i.e., time elapsed since a reference event) may influence behavior cannot be taken as proof that animals can discriminate particular temporal durations. Passage of time is a universal accompaniment of all biological (and other natural) processes, so that it is gratuitous to attribute any time-correlated change in a response to a discrimination based on knowledge of some temporal duration. For this reason a demonstration that variables, such as delay of reinforcement or the interval between the conditioned and unconditioned stimuli, can influence certain aspects of behavior, such as the rate of learning, speed of running, or rate of lever-pressing, cannot be considered as proof of temporal discrimination; what this proves is simply that certain processes in the animal change with the passage of time. The experiments that provide critical evidence of duration discrimination are those in which an animal is required to learn, for example, that a certain response would be rewarded only if the response occurs after the elapse of a specified duration, as is the case in the differential reinforcement of low rates (DRL) procedure. Successful performance of many animals in learning delayed or trace conditioned responses also indicates that they can discriminate particular durations of elapsed time. Another method is to train an animal to make one response (say, turning left in a T-maze) when it is exposed to one temporal duration (say, a forced waiting period of 4 sec) and another response (say, turning right in the T-maze) when it is exposed to another temporal duration (say, a forced waiting period of 30 sec). Such experiments (e.g., Anderson, 1932) show that with great difficulty rats can learn some crude discriminations of two temporal durations. The ability to discriminate temporal durations begins to appear in human children around the age of 5 years (Hermelin & O'Connor, 1971). A part of the difficulty of learning to discriminate between temporal durations may lie in the fact that the durations cannot be presented simultaneously, so that duration-discrimination tasks are necessarily successive discriminations tasks, which do not allow immediate comparison of stimuli.

The third type of knowledge about time is that of the *temporal dimension* as such, of time as a scale for quantifying durations. Knowledge of time as an abstract dimension can be demonstrated by showing that a subject can estimate different intervals of time. Thus, a subject may be asked to produce varied intervals (say, 10 or 20 sec) by pressing a key and keeping it pressed until he thinks the required interval has elapsed. Or he may be asked to reproduce a demonstrated interval, or to say how much time elapsed between two given events. Though these procedures yield somewhat different results (Bindra & Waksberg, 1956; Doob, 1971), they all demonstrate that at least adult human subjects have developed some kind of a temporal scale applicable to durations between events. As far as I know, no adequate test of the knowledge of time as a dimension has been devised for use with animals or children.

Representation of Temporal Knowledge

Any observed stimulus event may serve as the reference point for locating subsequent stimulus events in time. Thus if events *A*, *B*, *C*, and *D* occur at temporal separations shown in Figure 6.1, we may assume that *A* serves as a temporal reference point for *B*, *C*, and *D*, and that *B* serves as a temporal reference point for C and D, etc. As the memory of certain events fades, other more recent or more salient events become reference points for subsequent events. It was noted in Chapter 2 that certain "timing neurons" fire at fairly regular intervals. Suppose one such neuron fires every 2 sec. It would then fire twice between event A and event B, three times between A and C, seven times between A and D, once between B and C, five times between B and D, and four times between C and D. If a time frame—any discriminable time interval—is defined as 2 sec, then event A plus a tag of two time frames would coincide with time of occurrence of B, and event A plus a tag of three time frames, or event B plus a tag of one time frame, would coincide with the occurrence of event C, and so on. It seems reasonable to assume that the basic organization of temporal knowledge is in terms of temporal units made up of such event-plus-time-frame compounds.

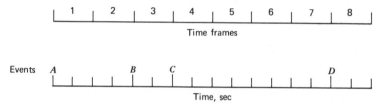

Figure 6.1. Representation of the location of events in time. If a time frame is defined as 2 sec, then the location of event B in time may be described as event A plus a tag of two time frames, location of C may be described as event A plus a tag of three time frames or event B plus a tag of one time frame, etc.

In the simplest case, discriminating temporal order, the discrimination would depend on whether there is a time frame separating the given events. If there is a temporal gap—an "empty" time frame—between two events, then they would be observed as successive, but it may still be difficult for the observer to differentiate their exact order, especially if the events are very brief. Differentiation of order may require a longer gap (about 20 msec for auditory stimuli) than that required for the identification of nonsimultaneity (about 2 msec for auditory stimuli). The exact values of these gaps varies with sense modality and various other experimental conditions (Hirsh, 1959; Rutschmann, 1966).

The discrimination of temporal durations would require some additive mechanism that counts the time frames separating the beginning and end of an interval. It may be assumed that, through experience with different durations marked by particular events, gnostic-assemblies are organized that represent particular temporal cues or durations of elapsed time since a particular marker or reference event. Such a temporal gnostic-assembly would be activated at a particular time after the occurrence of the reference event.

In the example shown in Figure 6.1, repeated exposure to the same sequence of events would result in the organization of gnostic-assemblies, $A + 2$ sec, $A + 3$ sec, $A + 7$ sec, etc., which would be excited, respectively, 2, 3, and 7 sec after A. Thus a rat that is rewarded for a left turn after a 4-sec delay following entry into a waiting chamber and is rewarded for a right turn after a 30-sec delay would form two gnostic-assemblies, $E + 4$ sec and $E + 30$ sec. Differential responding on the basis of temporal duration cues would thus become possible in much the same way as differential responding on the basis of other environmental cues.

Extensive experience with intervals of different durations would lead to the organization of a set of temporal gnostic-assemblies, each representing a particular duration and differentiated from each other in terms of the number of time frames each is removed from the reference event. Several such sets may be organized, each with a different time-frame base (e.g., 2 sec, 1 min, 1 hr). Such a collection of temporal gnostic-assemblies would amount to a rough interval scale of the time dimension, which would serve as the basis of performance in tasks requiring knowledge of time as an abstract dimension.

KNOWLEDGE ABOUT ENVIRONMENTAL CORRELATIONS

Animals continually encounter correlated events: The sunrise is correlated with increased brightness and warmth; onset of rain is correlated with wetness of ground and the wetness with slippery ground; eating the fruit of one plant is correlated with sweet taste, and of another with prickly thorns; pressing a lever is correlated with a clicking noise and the delivery of a food pellet. The basis of an observed correlation between two events may be either a natural law (e.g., the sun is correlated with warmth), or an experimental arrangement (e.g., a tone is correlated with food), or a chance coincidence (e.g., it happens to thunder when an animal rears or yawns). For the present purpose, such environmental correlations are best described as conditional relations or contingencies.

Contingencies, Predictive Value, and Imminence

A contingency between two events, E_1 and E_2, will be designated here as $E_1:E_2$; this reads, E_1, the first, independent, conditional, or predictor event signals a certain probability of occurrence of E_2, the second, dependent, signaled, predicted, or target event. The *conditional probability* is the probability that, given the occurrence of E_1, E_2 would occur within a certain specified interval of, say, 2 min; a conditional probability of .2 means that, in any 100 occurrences of E_1, E_2 would occur, within 2 min on 20 occasions.

A *base probability* of, say, .1 means that in any randomly selected 100 2-min intervals, E_1 or E_2 would occur on 10 occasions. The difference between the conditional and the base probability (.1 in this case) yields the *predictive value* of E_1 for predicting E_2 or the *dependency* of E_2 on E_1. If the difference, conditional probability minus base probability, is positive, that is, if E_1 predicts an increase in the probability of occurrence of E_2 above its base probability, then the predictive relation is said to be positive $(E_1:E_2+)$; if the difference is negative, that is, if E_1 predicts a decrease in the probability of occurrence of E_2 below its base probability, then the contingency is said to be negative $(E_1:E_2-)$; if the difference is zero, then there is no predictive relation between the two events $(E_1:E_20)$. The predictive value of E_1 for predicting E_2 is thus a measure of the dependence of the occurrence or nonoccurrence of E_2 on E_1. In terms of information theory, degree of dependence would correspond to the measure "information transmitted."

For the purpose of studying behavior it is not sufficient to note only the predictive value of E_1 for E_2, because predictive value indicates nothing about the temporal relation between the events, except in so far as any statement of conditional probability must assume a certain temporal limit within which E_2 must occur. For example, if in a delayed conditioning procedure a tone is sounded for 40 sec and food given at the end of it, and at no other time (base probability = zero), both the onset and termination of the tone would bear the same predictive relation to food delivery, but the tone termination would be temporally closer to food delivery than would tone onset. We may say in this case that the target event (food delivery) is more likely to occur at tone-onset-plus-40 sec than at tone onset. If we divide the 40-sec duration of the tone into 10 4-sec time frames, then we may say that the probability that food delivery would occur in any of the first nine time frames is zero, but the probability of occurrence of food delivery in the tenth time frame is 1.0. Essentially, then, we can divide the predictor event (E_1) into several discrete events in terms of time frames (E_{1a}, E_{1b}, E_{1c}, etc.) and ask, what is the probability of the occurrence of the target event E_2 in each of the defined time frames following the onset of the predictor event E_1. Or we can ask, in which time frame following the predictor event will the probability of occurrence of E_2 be maximum; the closer this time frame is to the onset of the E_1, the sooner, on the average, will the target event occur. The time frame in which E_2 is most likely to occur gives the most probable time of occurrence of E_2 in relation to E_1.

It may now be seen how a predictive value of E_1 for predicting E_2 together with the most probable time of occurrence of E_2 following E_1 can combine to yield the predicted *imminence* of E_2, given E_1. Suppose the predictive value of E_1 for E_2 is .5. This means that on the 50 per cent of occasions when

E_1 is followed by E_2 within a specified limit of, say, 3 min, the average time-elapse between E_1 and E_2 must be 3 min or less, say, 2 min; while on the 50 per cent of occasions when E_1 is not followed by E_2 within the time limit, the average time-elapse between E_1 and E_2 must be more than 3 min, say, 4 min. The average imminence of E_2, given E_1, would thus be roughly $[(50 \times 2) + (50 \times 4)]/100$, or 3 min. With the same predicted value of .5, the imminence of E_2 could vary within wide limits depending on the average interval between E_1 and E_2 and the time limit defining conditional probability. Conversely, with the same average interval between E_1 and E_2, imminence could vary within wide limits depending on the predictive value of E_1 for E_2. The imminence of occurrence of a traget event is the reciprocal of the average time between the onset of the predictor event and the time of occurrence of the target event. Predicted imminence, then, incorporates both the conditional and the temporal relations of two events within a single term; the same predicted imminence may be derived from many combinations of conditional and temporal variables.

The above analysis shows that there is no absolute difference between positive and negative contingencies. They both refer to predictive relations that vary along the common dimension of predicted imminence—they represent different "time windows" in which E_2 occurs following the occurrence of E_1. What is usually called a positive contingency has high predicted imminence—that is, the time window in which E_2 occurs is temporally rather close to E_1. What is usually called a negative contingency has low predicted imminence—that is, the time window in which E_2 occurs is temporally rather far removed from E_1. So far as the description of environmental correlations in physical terms is concerned, the point on the predicted imminence dimension at which positive contingencies become negative is strictly arbitrary. But, as we shall see below, different degrees of predicted imminence make a difference in the learning of predictive relations encountered in the environment.

Conditions of Contingency Learning

How does an objective predictive relation represented by a natural or arranged contingency between two events appear to an animal? What an animal *observes* is not a predictive relation as such, but only the individual instances of concomitant occurrences of certain events (E_1 with E_2) and individual instances of temporally separate occurrences of those events (E_1 alone and E_2 alone). Table 6.1 presents a hypothetical contingency table describing the relative frequency of observation of concomitant and temporally isolated occurrences of two events, E_1 and E_2, say, tone and food. Since a predictive relation is an average of the relative frequencies of such concomitant and isolated occurrences, it is only after an animal has observed a sufficient number of instances of the occurrences of the two events that it could possibly learn the true (i.e., the average) predictive relation between the two. Gradually, with repeated observations, the animal's experience of the relative frequencies will approximate the true contingency or predictive relation between the events. In general, the greater the relative frequency of isolated occurrences, the longer it will take to learn the predictive relation.

Table 6.1. Hypothetical Distributions of Relative Frequencies of Observations of Concomitance and Temporal Separation of Two Events, E_1 (Say, Tone) and E_2 (Say, Food). Each of the Four Large Squares Represents a Different Type of Causal Relation between E_1 and E_2

	E_2					E_2	
	Yes	No				Yes	No
Yes	$E_1:E_2$	$E_1:E_2$				$E_1:E_2$	$E_1:E_2$
	100	0		Yes		60	0
E_1	——	——		E_1		——	——
	$E_1:E_2$	$E_1:E_2$				$E_1:E_2$	$E_1:E_2$
No	0	0		No		40	0

[a] E_1 is a necessary and sufficient condition for the occurrence of E_2

[b] E_1 is not a necessary but is a sufficient condition for the occurrence of E_2

	E_2					E_2	
	Yes	No				Yes	No
	$E_1:E_2$	$E_1:E_2$				$E_1:E_2$	$E_1:E_2$
Yes	60	40		Yes		60	20
E_1	——	——		E_1		——	——
	$E_1:E_2$	$E_1:E_2$				$E_1:E_2$	$E_1:E_2$
No	0	0		No		20	0

[c] E_1 is a necessary but not a sufficient condition for the occurrence of E_2

[d] E_1 is neither a necessary nor a sufficient condition for the occurrence of E_2, but is a contributory condition

If the ratio $(E_1:E_2)/E_2$ is less than one, that is, if E_2 sometimes occurs in the absence of E_1, the rate of learning (but not necessarily the asymptote) would be less than the maximum; the rate would approach the maximum as the ratio approaches 1.0. This implication is supported by the finding that, in a classical conditioning experiment, the introduction of extra presentations of the unconditioned stimulus, temporally separated from the conditioned stimulus ("free-reinforcement" paradigm), produces less effective conditioning to the conditioned stimulus than when the unconditioned stimulus occurs only with the conditioned stimulus (Rescorla, 1968). Similarly, with extra occurrences of the conditioned stimulus (the "partial reinforcement" paradigm), that is, when the ratio $(E_1:E_2)/E_1$ is less than 1.0, the rate of learning (but not necessarily the asymptote) is lower than the rate when the ratio is 1.0 (e.g., Wagner, 1961).

The rate of contingency learning also depends on the amount of initial neural connectedness of the sensory modalities involved; the more extensive and direct the neural pathways that connect them, the higher the rate of learning. This assumption is supported by the finding that, in conditioning experiments, the rate of conditioning depends on the modalities of the conditioned and unconditioned stimuli. Thus Garcia, McGowan, Ervin, and Koelling (1968) have shown that the size of a food pellet (visual cues) can readily become a signal for an aversive electric shock but not so for aversive x-ray irradiation; conversely, the flavor of food (taste cues) can readily become a signal for x-ray irradiation, but not for electric shock. They suggest that such differences depend on the "central integration of the particular afferent channels through which the conditionally paired stimuli are presented" (Garcia et al., 1968, p. 795). Investigations are needed to confirm that the rate of learning predictive relations between stimuli of any two modalities parallel the central neuroanatomical arrangements of the modalities involved.

Concerning the learning of negative contingencies, it should be obvious that an animal can observe temporal separation only if it has some encounters with *both* the events E_1 and E_2, say, tone and food, in the same situation. A complete absence of food from the situation can provide the animal no basis for observing that food delivery is negatively related to the tone; temporal separation can be observed only if the animal has occasionally encountered food in the situation (base conditional probability of food), and now observes that the tone is accompanied by a decrease in the base probability of food. In other words, if the animal is to observe temporal separation and learn a negative contingency, the base probability of the target event must be substantially greater than zero, so as to allow a decrease in base probability to be noticeable. For this reason, the learning of a negative predictive relation would normally be a more difficult matter than the learning of a positive predictive relation, for the former requires the superimposition of negation (temporal separation) on an existing more general positive predictive relation (concomitance) between the situation as a whole and the test events.

The rate of learning of contingencies rests on the temporal separation between the observed events. Concomitance means that an event E_2 occurs within a certain time interval (1 sec, 15 sec, or 2 min) of the occurrence of event E_1, and temporal separation means that E_2 does not occur for a certain minimum time interval (1, 3, or 5 min) after the occurrence of E_1. The critical interval for the *observation* of concomitance or temporal separation ultimately depends on the period of time over which the animal integrates its observations. This presumably depends on the animal's integrational and memorial capabilities.

Nonetheless, other things being equal, contingencies between events closer to each other in time will be learned more readily than contingencies between events remote from each other in time. Further, it is possible that contingencies between remote stimuli are learned with the aid of contingencies between temporally closer stimuli. Thus, in a sequence $E_1-E_2-E_3-E_4$ the learning of the predictive relation between E_1 and E_4 may require the prior learning of the contingencies between adjacent stimuli. This means that contingencies between temporally remote events would be learned readily if the interval between them were bridged by certain consistently occurring events, and that the contingencies would be difficult to learn if the interval were filled with variable events. This implication is consistent with the fact that the learning of tasks involving long interevent delays, such as delayed conditioning, can be facilitated by starting with shorter intervals and gradually introducing the longer intervals (e.g., Pavlov, 1927). And, in general, learning takes longer when the learning situation contains events that are variable from trial to trial (I. MacKintosh, 1955).

The salience of stimulus events is a factor of primary importance in determining the rate of contingency learning. Salience is a joint function of stimulus intensity and novelty (see Chap. 2). It is well known that high-intensity stimulus events are more effective as conditioned stimuli than are less intense stimuli (Grice, 1968; Zielinsky, 1965). And a number of recent investigations have shown that familiarization with (or habituation to) certain stimulus events before they are used as conditioned stimuli renders them less effective as conditioned stimuli (Bateson, 1964; Lubow, 1973; Siegel, 1969). The intensity of unconditioned stimuli also bears a positive relation to the rate of conditioning (e.g., Kamin & Brimer, 1963), but this relation may depend on motivational differences rather than on the rate of contingency learning. It is possible that certain dramatic instances of one-trial aversive conditioning, some with long temporal separations of the stimulus events (see Garcia, Hankins, & Rusiniak, 1974), are explainable in terms of the salience (particularly the novelty) of conditioned stimuli and the strong motivational consequences of the unconditioned aversive stimuli (see Kalat, 1974; Krane & Wagner, 1975; Wydra, 1975).

Knowledge about "Causality"

All phenomena of nature have some causes, but causes are not observable. Causes are hypotheses, which may be correct or incorrect. What common sense takes to be "the cause" of an event is usually a hypothesis about the preceding or current conditions that best predict that event in a given situation. This use of the term "cause" has no reference to the mechanism underlying the predictive relation. What is usually accepted as a cause or explanation in science is the currently accepted hypothesis about some level of mechanism responsible for the predictive relation. Both common sense and scientific search for the cause of an event start with observational isolation of the "critical" condition required for the occurrence of the event to be explained. And the basis of observational isolation is contingency learning or the learning of predictive relations between particular events that occur in a situation. By observing a sufficient number of individual instances of concomitance and temporal separation of the target event, E_2, in relation to various other events that occur in the situation, we learn the correlation or predictive relation that best predicts E_2. Thus analysis or the isolation of critical variables that is the basis of science is ultimately an outcome of the learning of predictive relations encountered in one's natural or experimentally contrived environment.

We have already seen that the behavior of many species, such as the rat, is sensitive to variations in the degree of predictive relation between environmental events. The fact that an animal's behavior can be shown to change in a consistent way when the degree of predictive relation between certain events is varied, means that the correlative (predictive relations) has been isolated ("hypothesized") and is represented in the brain. Similarly, the fact that a human child may verbally describe a certain predictive relation as "E_1 is the cause of E_2" means that it has isolated (learned) a critical predictive relation; the use of the term "cause" in this context has no reference to underlying mechanism—the verbal label corresponds to the indicator response by which an animal indicates its sensitivity to changes in a predictive relation. Much of the work (for a review, see Larendau & Pinard, 1962) on the development of knowledge about "causality" also deals mainly with the ability to learn (isolate, "hypothesize") certain critical predictive relations and not with the understanding of or concern with the underlying mechanisms.

Predictive relations between two events may differ not only in respect to degree of correlation but also in respect to the type of predictive relation. For the simplest case of two events, different types of predictive relations may be described in terms of the relative frequencies of concomitant and temporally separated occurrences of the predictor and the predicted events, as shown in Table 6.1. Each of the four contingency squares describes a different type of predictive relation. Square A describes that E_1 is a necessary and a sufficient condition for the occurrence of E_2; Square B that E_1 is not a necessary, but is a sufficient condition for the occurrence of E_2; Square C that E_1 is a necessary but not a sufficient condition for the occurrence of E_2; and Square D that E_1 is neither a necessary nor a sufficient, but a contributory, condition for the occurrence of E_2. For an animal to discriminate between any of these types of predictive relations, it must integrate the total information in the four cells of the relevant contingency squares, rather than merely estimate the proportion of instances of concomitance of E_1 and E_2.

Proof that an animal is capable of discriminating between different types of predictive relations would rest in the demonstration that its behavior changes as the values in the cells of a contingency square are varied in a way that does not alter the degree of concomitance between the events. In the above table, for example, the $E_1:E_2$ degree of concomitance would be the same in Squares B, C, and D, but the types of predictive relations are quite different. It would be easy enough to show that animals can discriminate between the predictive relation described by Square A and that described by any of the other squares, but this discrimination would presumably be on the basis of the difference in degree of concomitance, not necessarily on the basis of the difference in the *type* of predictive relation. The critical test of knowledge of different types of predictive relation would lie in the animal's ability to discriminate between any two of the Squares B, C, and D. It is doubtful that even adult human beings normally acquire such knowledge in the absence of formal instruction (e.g., in logic) in discriminating between different types of predictive relations. We become familiar with many predictive relations, as seen by their influence on our behavior, but we seldom try to infer or abstract the differences between different types of learned predictive relations. Experiments on rule abstraction or conceptual learning (e.g., Bourne, 1966) indicate that even highly intelligent and educated adults tend not to draw inferences from predictive relations unless specifically instructed or prompted to do so. The development of the ability and habits of differentiating between different types of predictive relations would appear to be an important area of investigation. The interaction between "formal knowledge" acquired through verbal instruction and "concrete knowledge" acquired through adjusting to different types of predictive relations also appears to be a problem worthy of study.

NEURAL BASIS OF CONTINGENCY LEARNING

The central neural representation of a predictive relation as described by a contingency table (see Table 6.1) may be called a *contingency organization*. If a contingency organization is to represent a predictive relation between two events, it must somehow relate the pexgos of (gnostic-assembly complexes activated by) those events: p_1 representing the signal event, E_1, and p_2 or p_T representing the predicted target event, E_2 or E_T. The contingency organization representing the environmental correlation $E_1:E_2$ may thus be designated as $p_1:p_2$. How must such a contingency organization function so as to reflect the imminence of E_2 as it is predicted by E_1?

Excitatory and Inhibitory Processes

I start with the assumption (see Figure 6.2) that the statement "E_1 predicts a change in the imminence of E_2" is equivalent to the statement that E_1 activates p_1; a pexgo of E_1, and p_1, through the contingency organization $p_1:p_2$, developed in the course of contingency learning, alters the excitability level of p_2, a pexgo of E_2. If E_1 predicts an increase in the imminence of E_2, the excitability level of p_2 is increased, and if E_1 predicts a decrease in the imminence of E_2, the excitability of p_2 is decreased. Enhancement and diminution in the excitability level of p_2 may be effected by the modulation of either excitatory or inhibitory or both types of neural discharges from the contingency organization to p_2.

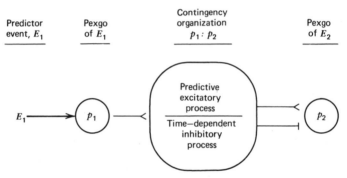

Figure 6.2. Functioning of a contingency organization. The organization activated by event E_1 and p_1 alters the excitation level of p_2, representing the predicted event E_2, by modulating excitatory or inhibitory outflow to p_2. When such a contingency organization has been developed, the excitation level of p_2 can be altered in the absence of E_2.

According to our earlier analysis of the factors that determine the imminence of a predicted event, there must be at least two separate sources of neural discharge from a contingency organization to p_2, one representing the predictive relation between the two events, E_1 and E_2 (and therefore between p_1 and p_2), and the other representing the temporal separation between E_1 and E_2. The former may be called the predictive discharge, because its magnitude depends on the predictive value of E_1 for predicting E_2, and the latter may be called a delay-related discharge, because its magnitude depends on the temporal separation between E_1 and E_2.

My second assumption is that predictive discharge from a contingency organization is excitatory (i.e., it enhances the excitability level of p_2), and the delay discharge is inhibitory (i.e., it diminishes the excitability level of p_2). A contingency organization must then consist of two separate sets of processes, one that represents the predictive value of E_1 for predicting E_2 and generates a corresponding magnitude of excitatory discharge, and one that is sensitive to elapsing time since the occurrence of E_1 and generates an inhibotory discharge that declines steadily from the time of occurrence of E_1 to the time of occurrence of E_2 (see Figure 6.3). Thus a contingency organization is so constructed that the activation of a signal pexgo p_1, representing E_1, leads immediately to an excitatory discharge to gnostic-assemblies comprising a pexgo of p_2, representing event E_2; at the same moment an inhibitory discharge is distributed to p_2, whose magnitude depends on the intervals separating E_1 and E_2, and which is dissipated at about the time of the normal occurrence of the predicted event E_2. The inhibitory delay-related discharge thus keeps the target gnostic-assemblies p_2 from getting activated too soon in relation to the time at which the predicted event normally occurs.

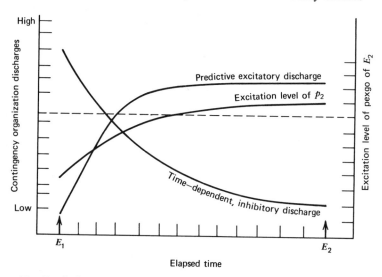

Figure 6.3. Predictive excitatory and inhibitory discharges (left ordinate) as a function of elapsed time since the occurrence of a signal event, E_1. The algebraic sum of the two determines the excitation level of the pexgo of E_2 (right ordinate), which is assumed to correspond to the imminence of E_2, as predicted by E_1.

Since one signal event, E_1, may have a predictive relation with several different events, E_2, E_3, E_4, etc., that occur at different times in a sequence (e.g., a tone may predict the onset of a light in 10 sec, a click in 20 sec, and food delivery in 30 sec), pexgos of the various predicted events, p_2, p_3, p_4, etc., may receive similar excitatory predictive discharges from the contingency organizations, $p_1:p_2$, $p_1:p_3$, $p_1:p_4$, etc., but may differ widely in the inhibitory delay-related discharges they receive from those organizations. In effect, then, the gnostic-assemblies comprising p_2, p_3, p_4, etc. would reach their maximum levels of excitation at different moments in time following E_1. Clearly, the proposed model of contingency organization allows for any one signal to predict simultaneously several different events at different points in time.

There are a couple of lines of evidence which suggest that the delay-related output of the contingency organization is inhibitory. One is that performance on tasks involving temporal discrimination is greatly affected by damage to frontal lobes, which are generally regarded as having an inhibitory influence on behavior. For example, damage to frontal lobes leads to hyperactivity, distractability, and emotional lability (Hebb & Penfield, 1940; Malmo, 1942; French & Harlow, 1955). More directly pertinent is the evidence that damage to the anterior frontal cortex, apart from producing deficits in coping with delayed-response tasks, disrupts performance on tasks requiring the animal to withhold a response or to execute a response at a slow rate, or to change from one response to another. These findings have been obtained from work with the dog (e.g., Lawicka, 1957), monkey (e.g., Pribram, 1958), and man (B. Milner, 1963; see P. M. Milner, 1970, Chap. 19). In general, they are consistent with the idea that frontal lobe damage makes animals respond inappropriately because their ability to impose temporal qualifications on the current test stimuli is impaired, and that an intrinsic aspect of this impairment is the inability to withhold or inhibit response tendencies produced by the test situation as a whole.

Another type of evidence for regarding the time-dependent output to be inhibitory is that young animals are frequently unable to learn tasks involving temporal discrimination. Correspondingly, it is known that inhibitory processes in the brain mature slowly and are not effectively in operation until fairly late in the maturational period (see Campbell, Lytle, & Fibiger, 1969; Mabry & Campbell, 1974). It seems reasonable then to proceed on the assumption that, where temporal variables are involved, contingency organizations generate a delay-related inhibitory output in addition to a predictive excitatory one.

Development of Contingency Organizations

It should be clear from the above discussion that the development of a contingency organization would require building neural representations of both predictive and temporal relations of particular events. Consider a concrete example. Imagine that in the classical Pavlovian conditioning situation, a hungry dog is given conditioning trials with a tone as the conditioned stimulus and food as the unconditioned stimulus. Say the tone sounds for 20 sec on each trial before a small piece of food is delivered. Conditioning is initially seen after 10 to 20 trials in the form of a conditioned salivary response that occurs within 2 or 3 sec of the onset of the tone—long before the food is to be delivered. This initial conditioning may be attributed to the development of the predictive structures involving a pexgo representing the tone (p_1) and a pexgo representing the food (p_2). If similar conditioning trials are continued, the dog's behavior changes. It now does not respond until about 7 sec have elapsed since the onset of the tone. This change from immediate responding during early training to delayed responding during later training would seem to represent the development of the time-sensitive inhibitory factor in relation to the contingency organization $p_1 : p_2$.

We have seen that the essential condition for the development of a predictive structure relating two events appears to be the observation of their concomitant and isolated occurrences. In general, the higher the probability that two pexgos p_1 and p_2, corresponding to two contiguous events E_1 and E_2, would be activated contiguously, the greater would be the excitation of p_2 by p_1 However, the degree of excitation of p_2 by p_1 also depends on the relative frequency of the isolated occurrences of E_1 and E_2, which reduce predicted imminence of E_2 by E_1, resulting in less excitation of p_2 than would otherwise be the case. Thus a neural structure must develop that reflects an average of the observed frequencies of the concomitant and separated occurrences of the two events, and that leads to the excitation of p_2 by p_1 only when p_1 has some predictive value. How such a predictive structure is put together neurally remains a matter for further speculation and investigation.

Concerning the development of delay-related inhibitory neural organizations, one line of speculation that appears worthwhile is as follows. Assume that any prolonged "empty" interval, containing only insignificant or nonsalient events (e.g., ones to which the animal has habituated), enhances the activity of some inhibitory mechanism. Other things constant, the longer the empty interval ("boredom") the greater the inhibition generated. Now, if the repeated occurrences of two salient events E_1 and E_2 are consistently separated by a certain interval of time but by no intervening salient events, the signal event E_1 may gradually acquire the capacity to excite a pexgo of the impending empty time interval even before the prolonged delay has actually occurred. Thus p_1 would not only excite p_2 but would also excite the gnostic-assemblies comprising a pexgo of the empty time, which in turn would enhance the inhibitory discharge to p_2. It may be assumed that this additional inhibitory discharge to p_2 would decline as time elapses until the excitatory discharge to p_2 is sufficient to bring p_2 to the critical level of excitation required for influencing behavior. The exact time at which this switch from the subthreshold excitation to suprathreshold excitation occurs is apparently somewhere between the times of occurrence of E_1 and E_2; early in learning, the switching point is closer to E_1, but gradually, presumably as the animal habituates more and the interval becomes increasingly "empty," it moves toward the end of the empty interval. However, unless highly specific temporal discrimination is taught, the animal responds well before the end of the empty interval; delay and trace conditioning are seldom perfect in regard to the required time of response.

The above rough speculations are offered merely to indicate that an account of contingency organizations in neural terms is not inconceivable. However, much detailed work at both behavioral and neurophysiological levels needs to be done for generating more clear hypotheses about the mechanisms underlying the representation of environmental correlations.

CHAPTER 7

Knowledge of Situations

If a banana is thrown among some monkeys, what a given monkey does depends on the location of the banana, on the area that is accessible to him for retrieving and eating unmolested, on who the other monkeys are and his status in relation to them, on the probability that more bananas will be thrown into the arena, and so on. In important respects the monkey's behavior is determined by the knowledge it has acquired about what happens, where, and when, in that kind of situation. Such knowledge about frequently-encountered situations goes beyond the information contained in the immediate stimulus input. Just as we can identify an object by only a few of its stimulus features, so too we can identify a situation as a dangerous situation, as a food situation, a copulation situation, etc., by observing briefly what has just happened, what is happening now, and extrapolating what is likely to happen next. Corresponding to neural pexgos representing objects, and neural contingency organizations representing predictive relations between events, there are thus neural schemas representing situations. This chapter is concerned with the development and neural organization of such situational schemas.

STRUCTURE OF SITUATIONS

A situation may be defined as any specified space that serves as the behavioral arena for a certain time period and all behaviorally significant events that happen in it during that period. Usually a situation consists of a large complex of fairly stable features, which serves as a static background for a smaller complex of changing features or events. Both the stable background and the passing events may be described in terms of the spatial and temporal structuring of stimulus features in the situational features.

Spatiotemporal Structure of a Situation

Spatially, a situation is a layout of various objects in a defined space; temporally, it is the succession of events that takes place in it over a defined time period. An event is any change (addition, subtraction, or rearrangement) in the stimulus features of the situation; it is described by specifying (a) the exact change in stimulus features of the situation that constitutes the event, (b) the spatial location of the event, and (c) the temporal location as well as the duration of the event.

Consider a concrete experimental situation. Say, we have a box, whose four wooden walls named, clockwise, A, B, C, and D, surround a space of 30 × 30 × 30 cm. The floor is made of wire grid and the roof has a one-way vision screen. Wall A has a continuously illuminated house light fixed to it. Wall B has a loudspeaker which can be used for sounding a tone. Wall C has a water-dispensing bottle. An experimenter has arranged a certain sequence of events to take place in this box during each session of 13.5 min. A session consists of 20 trials, each trial-cycle lasting 40 sec. Each trial-cycle begins with an empty pretrial or intertrial interval of 25 sec. At the end of 25 sec, a tone is sounded for 15 sec; the termination of the tone is accompanied by the delivery of one food pellet. Suppose the experimenter introduces a hungry rat into the above situation and starts a session. The events that occur in the situation are not only the stimulus events arranged by the experimenter but also the stimulus events arising from the animal's actions. The animal's nervous system thus receives continual sensory information about a variety of stimulus and response events.

Examine the important spatial and temporal aspects of the various events in relation to the target event of food delivery. The spatial aspect of this event is described by its location; food delivery always occurs in the receptacle attached to wall C. If the rat is facing wall D, the most direct way for it to reach the receptacle is by making a left (anticlockwise) turn, or a series of right turns, etc. All the walls, as well as other features of the box, bear a certain stable spatial relation to the food receptacle. The temporal relations of food delivery may be described in terms of the time intervals between food delivery and various other events in the situation; food delivery occurs 40 sec after the delivery of the food on the previous trial, about 40 sec after the rat has eaten the previous pellet, 15 sec after the onset of the tone, 10 sec after the tone has been on for 5 sec, and coincides with the termination of the tone. Thus, there are several overlapping time markers (tone onset, tone onset plus 5 sec, tone onset plus 10 sec, tone termination, etc.) which bear stable temporal relations to food delivery.

As an animal is repeatedly exposed to a situation like the above, it acquires knowledge of the situation as a whole. The stable, spatial aspects of the situation are typically learned first, during the early ("adaptation") sessions. The spatial aspect of the situation represents such relations as "the water bottle is on the right wall when the wall with the food tray is being faced" or "while wall A is being faced, the food tray is behind and the loudspeaker location is on the left," or "the lever is above the floor but is not as high as the house light," etc. The temporal aspect of the situational schema represents such relations as "food will be available from time to time in this situation," or "after a tone is sounded for 15 sec, a food pellet will be delivered," etc. When the main spatial and temporal relations that describe the behaviorally significant aspects of a situation have been learned by an animal, it may be said to know the situation well or to have a "cognitive map" (Tolman, 1948) of the situation.

The neural structures that become organized as representations of particular spatiotemporal aspects of situations are contingency organizations developed as representations of these aspects. The neural representation generated by any particular situation at a specific time may be called a *situational schema*. A situational schema is to contingency organizations what a pexgo is to object gnostic-assemblies. Even though an animal can receive stimulus information about only a small part of a situation at any one moment, an effective instantaneous representation of the whole situation may be gained through the generation of a situational schema by the activation of a complex of contingency organizations. The activation of a situational schema need not depend critically on any specific stimuli in the situation; any of a variety of stimuli, or their combinations, may activate it. Thus, once an animal has thoroughly explored a new experimental chamber, looking at any one corner or part of a wall, feeling the texture of any part of the floor, or smelling the chamber, may be sufficient to activate a schema. Note, again, a given situation does not have a permanent situational schema as its representation; a situation schema is generated when a certain group of contingency organizations are activated by some stimulus features of a situation. The same situation may generate somewhat different schemas on different occasions depending on the contingency organizations that get activated on each occasion; and different situations may activate several common contingency organizations.

Evidence for Situational Schemas

That behavior is, in fact, determined in important ways by the generation of some sort of situational schemas is indicated by evidence from several sources. This evidence shows, essentially, that several characteristics of behavior can be accounted for only by assuming that certain important spatial and temporal relations of recurring situations have become represented in the animal's brain.

Concerning the spatial aspect of schemas, one source of evidence is the experimental work on the effects of stimulus change or novelty on behavior. It is well known that unfamiliar situations and objects result in "novelty reactions," which range from complete arrest of behavior ("freezing") to locomotory exploration involving a variety of observational acts, such as sniffing, rearing, manipulating, scanning (see Welker, 1961), as well as a variety of autonomic changes sometimes collectively called "orientation reactions" (Sokolov, 1963). Such novelty reactions are produced when an unfamiliar object is placed at some location in a familiar situation (Bateson, 1973; Menzel, 1971; Sheldon, 1969). More important, novelty reactions also occur when an object is removed from a familiar situation or the location of a familiar object in a familiar situation is changed. For example, the rat shows investigatory responses when a familiar water tube is moved from one wall of a familiar cage to another wall, or is completely removed, and a chimpanzee shows surprised excitement when he sees a familiar laboratory attendant in clothes normally worn by another familiar attendant (Hebb, 1946). The fact that a change, not of objects but of their locations in a familiar situation, may produce novelty reactions clearly shows that the animal must be able to generate some kind of a schema or model in its brain that links each object with a certain location. A discrepancy between the spatial schema of the situation generated on the basis of past experience and the situation as it now appears is generally regarded as the basis of novelty reactions and investigative behavior (see Berlyne, 1960; Sokolov, 1963; Welker, 1961).

The existence of spatial schemas of wider areas has been demonstrated in field studies. In one such study, Menzel (1973) took young chimpanzees around a field to 18 different places where they observed food being hidden. They were then released and allowed to find the hidden foods. Their search patterns showed that they unerringly and directly approached the food sites and approximated an optimum routing, with little rechecking or duplication.

Temporal aspects of situational schemas are also demonstrable by the novelty reactions produced when the customary order of occurrence of a familiar stimulus is changed. If certain stimuli are usually presented in a certain sequence (e.g., 2, 4, 6, 8, 10, etc.), the presentation of a later or earlier stimulus at a given place in the sequence (e.g., presenting 8 instead of 6 in the third position) evokes orientation reactions (Unger, 1964). The existence of a temporal representation of specific intervals is shown by the results of certain reaction-time experiments. For example, reaction speed is higher for a series of trials in which each trial has a constant foreperiod (time interval between the ready signal and the presentation of the reaction signal) than for a series of trials in which each trial has a variable foreperiod (Klemmer, 1957). This could occur only if the subject were to build, during the early trials of a series, some representation of the intervals separating the ready signal and the reaction signal.

The phenomena of delayed and trace conditioning, as well as the pattern of responding seen in fixed-interval training procedures, also point to the existence of some sort of representation of the temporal aspects of the training situation. For example, if a thirsty rat is given water at the end of

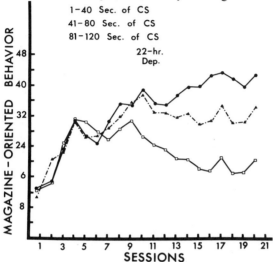

Figure 7.1.   Development of temporal discrimination. The unconditioned stimulus, water, was delivered at the end of 120 sec of the CS, a tone. The graph shows that temporal discrimination (decrease in response) starts to develop around the seventh training session, and that the rat learns the discrimination between the first 40-sec period of the tone and the later periods more readily than the discrimination between the two later periods. Squares: 1–40 sec of CS; triangles: 41–80 sec of CS; dots: 81–120 sec of CS. [Adapted from Baum & Bindra, 1968. Reprinted with permission of the Canadian Psychological Association.]

a 3-min period of the sounding of a tone (signal), within a few trials the animal becomes highly excited and approaches and sniffs the water magazine as soon as the tone is sounded. With continued training, the rat begins to show a delay in its excitement and water-oriented responses, corresponding to the interval between the tone-onset and water delivery. The results of one such experiment (Baum & Bindra, 1968) are shown in Figure 7.1. Note that the decline in water-oriented responses during the delay interval does not begin to appear until about the seventh session of training. Pavlov's (1927) conclusion that delayed conditioning involves learning to discriminate time intervals seems inescapable.

ACQUISITION OF SITUATIONAL KNOWLEDGE

The working assumption on which the following discussion rests is that the knowledge of a situation as a whole, its situational schema, is generated by the activation of several closely-integrated contingency organizations representing particular spatial and temporal relations of the situation. A spatial contingency is one that predicts a certain target location in relation to a reference location, and a temporal contingency is one that predicts a certain target time in relation to the time of a reference event. Thus the identification of a location L_1 may predict the existence of several other identifiable locations in that situation; for example, the presence of a light on the top of the right wall of a box may predict that the box has a water-delivery mechanism on the lower left wall. Similarly, an event E_1 at time T_1 may predict that the time of another event E_2 will be T_2; for example, the onset of a light may predict that food will be delivered 10 sec (or, say, two time frames) later. Consider now how repeated experience with particular spatial and temporal contingencies may lead to the integration of contingency organizations representing increasingly larger spatiotemporal segments of an animal's environment.

Spatial Integrations

How are spatial contingencies integrated into larger functional units, representing larger spatial segments of a situation? There are two types of integrations to be considered: intermodal integrations and integrations of discrete contingency organizations into coherent larger spatial organizations.

That the capacity to coordinate spatial knowledge of different modalities is acquired gradually in the course of maturation can be demonstrated easily. If a normal preschool child is blindfolded and is asked to point to a particular part of his body that has been identified by a light tap, the child is likely to make errors of pointing. These errors reflect a lack of integration of visual-visual spatial contingencies with visual-tactual spatial contingencies. Such cross-modal localization errors decrease progressively from the fourth to the eighth year of age, indicating increasing integration of spatial contingencies of different modalities. Similar experiments done on blind children show that their performance rests on proprioceptive-tactual integration rather than on proprioceptive-tactual-visual integration of spatial contingencies; this is suggested by McKinney's (1964) finding that, compared with the performance of normal children, that of blind children is more disrupted by the introduction of extraneous tactual and proprioceptive cues (e.g., holding or turning the hand just before the pointing test). These findings show that the intermodal integration of spatial information is produced on the basis of the spatial cues experienced in relation to each other during the developmental period. It seems reasonable to assume that the intermodal integration of spatial contingency organizations of different modalities is an outcome of the basic process of intermodal integration of gnostic-assemblies, as described in Chapter 5.

Turning to the development of coherent knowledge of larger spatial segments of the environment, we now consider the main question as to how individual spatial contingencies of various modalities are organized into larger functional units. The general answer would seem to be that the repeated observation of a location L_1 in close temporal contiguity with another location L_2 in a situation would lead to the development of a contingency organization linking the gnostic-assemblies (and hence pexgos) of the two, $pL_1:pL_2$. It is likely that in a situation containing L_1 and L_2 the animal would probably observe the two locations in both sequences, so that a contingency organization $pL_1:pL_2$, as well as $pL_2:pL_1$, would develop. The development of these contingency organizations means that pexgos of both the spatial locations could be excited by observing either one of the locations. In other words, the central representation of the two locations would be excited simultaneously as a consequence of the observation of only one of them; they would thus act as a unit, representing more than one location of the situation. With prolonged observational experience in the situation (e.g., sniffing, visually scanning and fixation, touching) each location, however identified, would, through certain actions, be observed contiguously with various other locations, and several interrelated clusters of spatial contingency organizations would develop, until each location of the situation would be related, however remotely, to every other location in the situation. Now, even a brief observation of any one location in the situation would excite the interrelated pexgos representing all varied locations of the situation. The simultaneous excitation of such interrelated contingency organizations that represent the spatial layout of the major identifiable location of a situation comprises a coherent spatial schema of that situation.

Temporal Integrations

It was explained in Chapter 6 that gnostic-assemblies representing particular order and durations of time in relation to particular reference events are developed as a consequence of discrimination learning. Accurate differentiation between temporal durations becomes possible only when gnostic-assemblies representing different values of the time dimension have developed. Children of about 5 years of age do not spontaneously differentiate between temporal durations but, when instructed, can learn to do so. The ability to make temporal judgments is acquired more readily when durations are presented as auditory stimuli than when they are presented as visual stimuli; nontemporal judgments show no such modality difference (Hermelin & O'Connor, 1971). Human adults are capable of highly refined temporal judgments; presumably they have developed the necessary gnostic-assemblies representing a fine scale of the time dimension through the same type of discrimination learning that leads to the development of scales of other physical dimensions (see Chap. 5).

How do individual temporal gnostic-assemblies become coordinated into a coherent temporal schema in which the order and duration of various events encountered by an animal are represented with a good deal of accuracy? The general answer again lies in the development of contingency organizations that represent the temporally contingent relations between events in the environment. The main point is that each event in a situation usually predicts not one but several subsequent events. This is because several overlapping or nested temporally contingent relations exist in a situation. Repeated encounters with the situation would result in the development of interrelated temporal organizations involving several common events as reference events. When this has happened, the occurrence of any event in the situation may excite pexgos of several contingently related events, so that an instantaneous representation of the events yet to occur is provided, their imminence being indicated by the degree of excitation of the pexgos. Such nested, interrelated contingency organizations that represent the temporal arrangement of the major events in a situation comprise a coherent temporal schema of that situation.

Schemas Involving Acts

It should be remembered that as an animal observes an act (its own or another animal's), gnostic-assemblies representing that act are developed. These act gnostic-assemblies represent the important stimulus features (visual, proprioceptive, cutaneous, etc.) of the act. A pexgo of an act functions in the same way as the pexgos of other events; that is, by occurring in predictive relations with other events, act pexgos too become parts of contingency organizations. This means that prior events bearing a predictive relation to an act form contingency organizations with both gnostic-assemblies (hence pexgos) of the stimulus configuration that normally evokes that act and the pexgo of the act itself.

Further, a pexgo of an act forms contingency organizations with pexgos of events that normally follow that act. This means that when an act occurs, its pexgo excites, through certain contingency organizations, pexgos of future events that have reliably followed the act (e.g., a click or food-delivery is a common consequence of lever-pressing). Thus pexgos of the consequences of an act are excited by an act serving as a conditioned (predictor) stimulus, and the level of excitation of the conditionally activated pexgos of subsequent events represents the imminence of their occurrence. The existence of such act-consequence contingency organizations is indicated by the surprise animals show when some usual consequence of an act fails to occur. Whereas William James invoked the conditioned excitation of an image of an act as the basis of the voluntary production of that act, the present suggestion is that a pexgo of an act is the basis only of the excitation of the *consequences* of that act, not of the production of the act itself.

In most cases the contiguous observation of two locations would require an intervening action, a right turn, eye-movements to the left, bending the neck back for looking up, etc. The gnostic-assemblies—as well as pexgos— representing such actions would thus also form a part of the contingency organizations. For example, looking at a stimulus, S_1, at location L_1, may give rise to a pexgo, pS_1L_1, which might excite a pexgo of an action, say a right turn, pA_r, and this might excite a pexgo of another stimulus, S_2, at location L_2, pS_2L_2. Repetition of this sequence would lead to the development of a contingency organization, $pS_1L_1:pA_R:pS_2L_2$; when this has happened, the observation of S_1 at L_1 would excite pexgos both of the action of turning right and of S_2 at L_2. Similarly, a certain event, E_1, occurring at time, T_1, may excite a contingency organization, $pE_1T_1:pA_x:pE_2T_2$, representing the environmental contingency that the occurrence of E_1 at T_1 is followed by action A_x, which is followed by the occurrence of E_2 at T_2.

SEQUENTIAL DEPENDENCIES AND CONTINGENCY CLUSTERS

The predictive relations that characterize a situation involve specific stimuli (objects, events, actions, etc.), specific locations, and specific times, and the corresponding contingency organizations link the gnostic-assemblies representing those stimuli, locations, and times. Thus, just as a situation is a collection of contingently related entities that form part of a defined spatio-temporal segment of the environment, so a situational schema may be thought of as a cluster of contingency organizations representing the variety of nested predictive relations that characterize the situation. Once such larger functional units or clusters of nested contingency organizations have become organized in an animal, the occurrence of each event in the situation would contribute to the prediction of the imminence of several subsequent events. The contribution that each event makes to the predicted imminence of particular subsequent events depends on the hierarchy of predictive relations that exists among those events.

Hierarchical Dependencies

Suppose a dog has repeatedly encountered and is now fully familiar with an experimental procedure consisting of the following events. Its cage door is opened (E_1), and the experimenter appears in front of the dog (E_2). The experimenter puts the dog on a leash (E_3) and walks it down a corridor (E_4) to an experimental room (E_5). The dog is then placed in an apparatus (E_6). A tone is sounded (E_7), it continues to sound (E_8) for some time, and then it terminates (E_9). The termination of the sound is accompanied by food delivery (E_{10}). There is then an intertrial interval of 2 min (E_{11}). Let us say that trial 2 is a negative contingency trial: Tone B (a CS$^-$) rather than tone A is presented as E_7, and it is not followed by food. Though there are many contingent relations in this situation, let us simplify the analysis by considering only the contingency between the target event of food delivery (E_{10}) and all the other events. The imminence of E_{10} predicted by each preceding event is shown in Table 7.1, with arbitrary values assigned to each degree of predicted imminence.

Table 7.1.   A Hypothetical Example of the Imminence of a Target Event (E_{10}) as Predicted by a Number of Sequentially Occurring Prior Signal Events

	Sequential Contingencies	Description of the Events	Approximate Time Interval between Signal Event and E_{10}	Cumulative Predicted Imminence of E_{01}
Pre-session	$E_1:E_{10}$	Opening the cage door	15 min	5
	$E_2:E_{10}$	Appearance of the experimenter	15 min	10
	$E_3:E_{10}$	Putting on the leash	14 min	15
	$E_4:E_{10}$	Walk down the corridor	12 min	20
	$E_5:E_{10}$	Experimental room	10 min	25
	$E_6:E_{10}$	Putting the dog in the apparatus	3 min	40
Trial 1	$E_{7A}:E_{10}$	Tone A onset (CS$^+$)	15 sec	70
	$E_{8A}:E_{10}$	Continued sounding of tone A	10 sec	80
	$E_{9A}:E_{10}$	Termination of tone A	1 sec	100
	E_{10}	Delivery of food	0 sec	100
Trial 2	$E_{11}:E_{10}$	Intertrial interval	2 min	50
	$E_{7B}:E_{10}$	Tone B onset (CS$^-$)	2 min 30 sec	45
	$E_{8B}:E_{10}$	Continued sounding of tone B	2 min 20 sec	45
	$E_{9B}:E_{10}$	Termination of tone B	2 min	50
Trial 3	$E_7 \ldots$			

The imminence of food delivery in the experimental chamber (E_{10}) predicted by the opening of the cage door (E_1) must be low. This is because the cage door is probably opened on occasions unrelated to the experimental procedure; the laboratory attendant and the veterinarian may open the door several times each day. Let us assign the arbitrary value of 1 to the imminence of E_{10} predicted by E_1. E_2, the appearance of the experimenter, may add only a small amount to the predicted imminence of E_{10}, because the same experimenter may occasionally handle the animal without taking it out of the cage. The (arbitrary) estimates of the cumulative predicted imminence following each event are shown in column 4 of the table.

A few points should be noted about the table. First, the signal events that occur later in the chain are closer to the target event and thus, in general, increase the predicted imminence, resulting in a progressive increase in predicted imminence from the beginning of an experimental session to the start of the trials. Then, in trial 1, with a positive CS (tone A), the predicted imminence is further increased, reaching the maximum (arbitrary) value of 100 at the moment of food delivery. After the animal has consumed the food, the predicted imminence is decreased, owing to the 2-min intertrial interval; the end of trial 1 signals a period of no food for 2 min, and this reduces the predicted imminence to a level similar to the one that prevails when the animal is first introduced into the experimental chamber (E_6) at the beginning of the session.

Second, when trial 2 is initiated, the negative CS (tone B) predicts a period of about 2 min and 30 sec until the next food delivery, so that the predicted imminence of food is reduced even below the level of the intertrial period (2 min). The main point to note is that the predicted imminence of the target event is changed (increased or decreased) by each signal event, and that the imminence predicted by any given signal event is determined by its average separation in time from the moment of food delivery. The positive and negative conditioned stimuli, as well as intertrial intervals, serve merely to modulate the predicted imminence of the target event above or below the average level of imminence predicted by the situation as a whole.

Third, in the above discussion we have been concerned only with the contingencies between the signal events and a specified target event. This was a matter of convenience only. Contingencies also exist between the signal events themselves, $E_1:E_2$, $E_1:E_3$, $E_1:E_4$, ... $E_2:E_3$, $E_3:E_4$, and so on. That contingency organizations representing all these contingent relations are developed is shown by the obvious surprise (novelty reactions) animals frequently show when any customary event in a sequence is omitted. The existence of these multiple overlapping contingencies means that, as a situation is enacted from the first signal event to the final target event, there is a progressive reduction in the number of different events that are predicted by each successive signal event. In the above example, E_1 (opening of the cage door) predicts a large number of different subsequent events, feeding, being taken for a walk, being cleaned, etc., E_6 (putting the animal in the apparatus) also predicts several subsequent events in that situation but fewer than the number predicted by E_1, and E_7 (sounding of tone A) predicts even fewer subsequent events. Thus each successive event in a situation channels the predictions to a progressively smaller number of subsequent events, and it is this channeling, combined with decreasing temporal remoteness of E_{10}, that forms the basis of the progressive increase in the predicted imminence of the specified target event. In other words, the earlier signal events predict the general characteristics of the situation, and the later signals predict more and more specific characteristics of the situation.

Fourth, the progressive increase in the predicted imminence of a target event in a situation rests on the existence of stable contingent relations between the various events that occur in the situation. The contribution that any specified signal event makes to the predicted imminence of a target event depends on the signal events that have preceded the specified event. Thus, in the above example, if the positive tone were sounded as soon as the dog was brought into the laboratory, before it had been placed in the experimental chamber, the contribution to the predicted imminence of food made by the tone may be expected to be much less than if the tone were presented in its regular place in the sequence. This means that the earlier events in a sequence comprise a "context" that determines what the contribution of a subsequent event to the prediction of the target event would be. The role of context in determining what a specified event would predict is clearly demonstrated by experiments in which the same signal event predicts different outcomes in different contexts. For example, in "switching experiments" (Asratyan, 1961) a dog may be trained to regard a tone as a signal for food in one experimental session (say, in the morning with experimenter A) and to regard the same tone as a signal for an electric shock in another experimental session (say, in the evening with experimenter B). In such experiments, it is apparent that the predictive significance of a given signal depends on the total sequence of events or context in which that signal occurs. The animal must learn the contingencies that context X plus signal event E_1 predicts target event T_1, while context Y plus signal event E_1 predicts target event T_2. For the present discussion, *context* may be regarded as any grouping of operative contingent relations (positive and negative) that determines the predictive significance of particular subsequent (signal) events.

It follows from the above discussion that each successive signal event adds to the context, and the new context then determines the predictive significance of the next signal event. Given a stable situation with the same recurring sequence of events, as each event occurs, the context—the grouping of operative contingent relations—becomes increasingly more constraining or limiting with respect to the events predicted. Each signal event further narrows—puts additional constraints on—an existing context. In this sense, increasing the predicted imminence of a target event means moving from a broad context to a progressively narrower context—one constrained by many contingent relations. For example, ask a subject to guess a target word (say, "psychology") as he is being sequentially shown the individual letters forming the word. When shown *P*, the subject's guess may be *pen, produce, psychology, psychiatry*, or numerous other words; when shown *PS*, the guesses may be *psalm, pseudo, psychology, or psychiatry*; when shown *PSY*, the guess may be *psyche, psychopath, psychology, psychiatry*; and so on. With each successive letter (signal event) there is progressive narrowing of context, with increasing probability that the target word would be correctly guessed or closely approximated. Presumably this is because there are contingent relations between individual letters and letter sequences, as well as between letter sequences and words. The word guessed on the presentation of each signal letter in the sequence depends on the context provided by the letters previously exposed. Another way of saying this is that the subject has learned certain sequential dependencies among letters, and the more these dependencies are brought into play by the signal letters, the easier becomes the prediction of the target word.

Neural Representation of Context

If an animal were exposed to a chain of events, a pexgo of the first event would activate various contingency organizations to which it bears predictive relations. The activation of the contingency organizations would result in excitatory or inhibitory discharges to gnostic-assemblies (i.e., potential pexgos) of the various predicted events. The occurrence of each successive predictive event would similarly excite or inhibit particular pexgos representing some of the subsequent situational events. To the extent that the earlier events may be contingently related to the same subsequent events (e.g., a target event), the excitatory and inhibitory influences produced by each sequentially activated contingency organization would tend to concentrate on certain potential pexgos. This means that repeated encounters with a stable situation would result in the excitation or inhibition of pexgos of certain subsequent (target) events by the earlier (signal) events in the situation. Thus the sequential dependencies between the signal and predicted events in a situation may be thought of as being represented in the brain as overlapping or nested clusters of contingency organizations, which, when activated, modulate the excitation level of potential pexgos of the predicted events. An activated cluster of contingency organizations may be called a *momentary determining set*, which determines what the predictive influence of the next event in the chain would be. A momentary determining set represents the momentary context of environmental events within which further predictive events occur. With succession of predictive events, as the environmental context becomes increasingly narrow or directed to specific target events, the momentary determining set also becomes narrow and directed to generating a particular target pexgo.

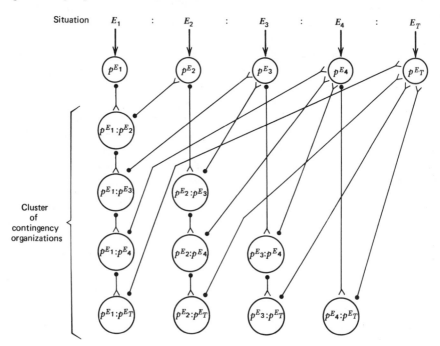

Figure 7.2. Neural representation of environmental context of sequential events. The occurrence of each event in the sequence activates a certain cluster of contingency organizations, comprising a momentary determining set, which determines what the influence of the next event in the sequence will be. Each successive event narrows the context and the momentary determining set. (For convenience, only excitatory connections of contingency organizations are shown.)

The process of modulation of the excitation level of a target pexgo by a sequence of prior signal events is depicted in Figure 7.2. This figure may be used to illustrate the process by which the context of a signal event influences the level of excitation of a target pexgo. For example, consider the event E_4 that immediately precedes the target event E_T. If E_4 were to occur without the prior occurrence of E_1, E_2, and E_3, it would increase the excitation level of a pexgo of the target event (p^{E_T}) to some extent, but the level of excitation achieved would be much lower than what would have been achieved if E_4 had occurred after the three events that normally precede it. Thus, though the contribution of E_4 to the excitation level of p^{E_T} may remain unchanged, the total level of excitation of pE_T achieved would be much lower than if E_4 had occurred at its normal place in the sequence.

The above analysis may be applied to context effects in the switching experiments of Asratyan. Let us say that the onset of a certain tone, E_4, signals an electric shock in one context (e.g., when preceded by E_{1A}, E_{2A}, and E_{3A}) but signals food in another context (e.g., when preceded by E_{1B}, E_{2B}, and E_{3B}). With such training, E_4 will excite the gnostic-assemblies of both shock (pE_{TX}) and food (pE_{TY}). However, the predictive significance of E_4, that is, the total level of excitation of pE_{TX} and pE_{TY} will be greater following E_{1B}, E_{2B}, and E_{3A}, and that of pE_{TY} will be greater following E_{1B}, E_{2B}, and E_{3B}.

Figure 7.2 also shows how, as the context narrows (the sequence of events gets closer to E_T), there would be increasing specification of the pexgo that would be maximally excited. It is apparent that E_1 leads to an increase in excitation level of four pexgos, E_2 influences only three, E_3 only two, and E_4 only one. Thus, as E_1 is followed by E_2, E_3, and E_4, more and more contingency organizations of a cluster are brought into play, so that the target pexgo of the cluster is excited to a greater and greater degree. As successive events of a recurring situation occur, the pattern of excitation of

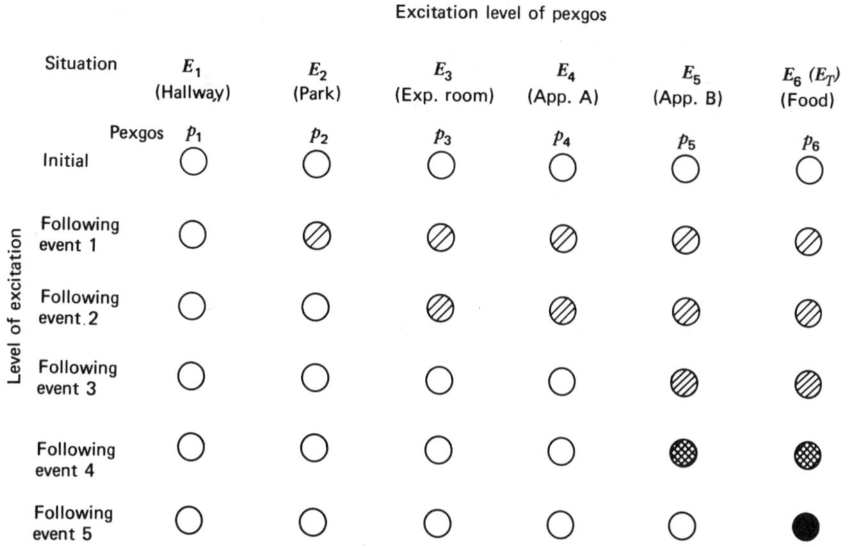

Figure 7.3. Progressive specification of a target pexgo. This example shows the progression from low-level excitation of pexgos of several events to a high-level excitation of pexgos of a smaller and smaller number of impending events as successive events bring more and more contingency organizations of a cluster into play (see text). The excitation level is indicated by the depth of shading.

pexgos moves from a low-level excitation of a large number of pexgos to increasingly higher levels of excitation of a progressively smaller number of pexgos—the momentary determining set narrows continually.

This process of the progressive reduction in the number of pexgos that reach a certain high level of excitation may be illustrated with reference to an example (see Figure 7.3). Take as the starting point the fact that a dog, healthy and awake, is sitting in its home cage. At this point, we may assume that a variety of potential pexgos representing certain stimuli frequently encountered by the dog (e.g., a hallway, a park, an experimental room, two apparatuses A and B, and food) are minimally excited; this is represented in the top row of Figure 7.3. Suppose an experimenter takes the dog out of its cage and makes it walk down the hallway (event 1). Now the pattern of excitation of various pexgos may change, with somewhat stronger excitation of the pexgos contingently related to the hallway. These may include the pexgos representing the objects in a certain experimental room and those representing a certain park where the experimenter sometimes takes the dog for a walk; this is represented in the second row of the figure. At a choice point in the hallway, the experimenter makes a left turn to the experimental room, rather than a right turn toward the park (event 2). The pattern of excitation of pexgos would now change radically, and those connected with the experimental room would become much more highly excited than the others; this is represented in the third row of the figure. The experimenter then puts the dog in an apparatus where food is usually given to the animal rather than in an apparatus where the dog is usually given electric shocks (event 3). Now the pattern of excitation of pexgos would be even more biased in that a pexgo representing food and food-related stimuli would become very highly excited and pexgos representing electric shock and related stimuli would decrease in excitability. Thus, an increase in the predicted imminence of food has come about through a process of continual and progressive excitation of more and more specific groups of pexgos. And this process of progressive specification would continue within the food apparatus in connection with particular food-related stimuli; for example, a food pexgo may be even more highly excited when the animal looks at the food bin rather than at some other part of the food apparatus.

Comparison with Other Models

The above account resembles various stochastic models of behavior in that there is an uncertainty about the outcome at each step where a prediction is made. The prediction depends on the sequence of events that has occurred and on the predictive relations (sequential dependencies) that the subject has previously learned. However, the present model differs from most earlier stochastic models (see Neimark & Estes, 1967; Restle, 1967; Vitz & Todd, 1969). In the earlier models each possible outcome remains rigidly tied to a certain combination or sequence of the predictive events; so that, for example, providing the letter N after B, L, and I may lead to the prediction of BLIND, but, if so, then it could not lead to the prediction of BLINKERS. We know that a subject on seeing *BLIN* may produce or predict BLIND when preoccupied by sensory handicaps, and the same subject may produce BLINKERS when preoccupied by traffic lights or head harnesses for horses. Such context effects cannot be interpreted in terms of linear models in which the predictive contribution of an event depends wholly on the chain of events preceding it.

A model presented by Norman and Rumelhart (1970) may appear to come closer to the present account of pexgo (or response) specification, but it too is fundamentally similar to the above models. According to it, the prediction, or the activation of a particular "memory attribute," depends on certain "contextual cues" to which it is linked. Each memory attribute has "attached to it information about the contexts in which it has occurred" (Norman & Rumelhart, 1970, p. 26). The recall of a memory (the prediction) consists of the activation of the required memory attributes by the given contextual cues. The main difficulty with this view is that it retains the idea that a specific contextual cue is linked to only a certain memory attribute, so that the activation of a memory is wholly dependent on the group of contextual cues provided for recall. In effect, then, a contextual cue remains rigidly linked to a certain memory; we might now say that $BLIN + X$ activates BLIND while $BLIN + Y$ activates BLINKERS, where X and Y are two different contextual cues. This scheme certainly makes for somewhat greater flexibility by attributing an important role to cues generated by the given context, but this only shifts the burden of explaining variable outcomes from specific recall cues to contextual cues. However, Norman and Rumelhart do not indicate how contextual cues are different from other recall cues, or how the two types of cues interact to activate a particular memory at a given time.

The general scheme I have proposed in the preceding pages is quite different in conception. First, it postulates multiple and overlapping linkages between particular pexgos and environmental cues; several different cues contribute to the excitation of the same pexgo, and a given cue may contribute to the excitation of several different pexgos. Second, the linkage between a pexgo and an environmental cue is not a simple association but involves a contingent relation, so that the exact influence a cue has on a certain pexgo depends on the properties of the contingency organization that links them. Third, the influence that a certain environmental cue has on the excitation levels of various pexgos depends on the momentary determining set—the cluster of contingency organizations excited by the prevailing situation or context. Fourth, the prevailing set continues to change, becoming increasingly narrow or directed, with each successive environmental cue; the set for any task is thus not a static entity but changes continually on the basis of interaction between the set of the moment before and the new environmental cue that has become effective at the given moment. These features of the present scheme overcome the major difficulties of other models and make the scheme capable of dealing with a variety of complex behavioral phenomena. The scheme will be further elaborated, and its applications explained, in later chapters.

CHAPTER 8

Meanings and Words

It is one thing to perceive something, quite another to comprehend its significance—to understand its meaning. There are neurological patients who may perceive a pen correctly, as judged, say, by the appropriateness of acts performed to pick it up from a table, but its significance may escape them, as judged by their inability to indicate the pen's components or function. Similarly, a patient may be able to copy a word or repeat a sentence but be unable to comprehend the word or the sentence. The significance or meaning that a stimulus (object, event, or word) has is thus something beyond its pexgo and separable from perception. There is reason to think that neural structures critically involved in generating the meanings of stimuli of a certain modality are different from the corresponding modality-specific perceptual structures. Studies of visual agnosias in monkeys and man implicate the inferotemporal cortex as the region of importance in generating the visual meaning of objects and situations (B. Milner, 1967; Weiskrantz, 1972). What is the nature of meaning, and in what sense does one comprehend or communicate the meaning of a given stimulus?

WHAT IS MEANING?

One main idea has repeatedly appeared in psychological discussions of meaning. This is the idea that the meaning of a stimulus consists of the domain of associations excited by that stimulus. This basic idea has been encapsulated in many definitions: Titchener (1918) said meaning is the associative context that accrues to a stimulus; Ogden and Richards (1923) suggested that meaning is a mediator or reference process in the head that mediates between the percepts and the referents (objects or events referred to); Bartlett (1932) thought of meaning as connectedness to something else; Osgood (1953) and Mowrer (1960a) call meaning an implicit, mediational response elicited by a stimulus; and Paivio (1971a) describes meaning in terms of overt

155

and covert reactions elicited by signs. The common features of these definitions are that they are applicable alike to verbal and nonverbal stimuli, and they regard the meaning of a stimulus as lying in the excitation of central processes that represent some other objects, events, actions, etc. Put another way, the meaning of a stimulus lies in the particular central representations or knowledge that it excites.

Meaning as Contingently Excited Pexgos

In terms of the present formulation, the above idea may be restated as follows: *Meaning of a stimulus (at any given moment) is the change in excitation level (excitatory or inhibitory) that the pexgo of that stimulus produces, through certain contingency organizations, in the gnostic-assemblies representing other objects, events, situations, words, etc.* This definition may be explicated in terms of the meaning of a specific stimulus, such as an apple, with the help of Figure 8.1. When a subject is shown an apple, a visual pexgo of that apple is generated in his visual perceptual system. This pexgo may associatively excite a number of other gnostic assemblies. Some of the associatively excited gnostic-assemblies may represent the tactual, gustatory, and olfactory features of apples. Others may represent somewhat remote entities, such as apple pie, apple tree, apple corner of a fruit store, a man drinking apple cider, and the like. Still other associatively excited gnostic-assemblies may represent written or spoken words and phrases, such as *apple orchard, Calvados, Adam and Eve, apple blossom,* etc. The degree to which the excitation level of various associated gnostic-assemblies is changed by a given stimulus depends on the contingency organizations that have been developed between the gnostic-assemblies representing the stimulus and gnostic-assemblies representing other stimuli. The principles governing the way in which contingency organizations determine the level of excitation of target gnostic-assemblies (see Chap. 7) apply here as well. The meaning of a stimulus is the excitation by its pexgo of certain other pexgos.

If, as shown in Figure 8.1, the meaning of a given test stimulus resides in the gnostic-assemblies it influences—the pexgos it generates—then the stimulus has not only one meaning but several different possible meanings. A pexgo of a test stimulus can potentially influence the excitation level of a wide range of gnostic-assemblies, and the assortment of potentially excitable pexgos may be said to comprise the "concept" of that stimulus. In the broadest sense, then, the concept of a stimulus is the entirety of its possible meanings. However, at any given time some of the pexgos would be excited much more than others, and it is the most highly influenced target pexgos that may be said to be the meaning of the test signal stimulus at that moment; the *momentary meaning* of a stimulus may thus vary from occasion to occasion.

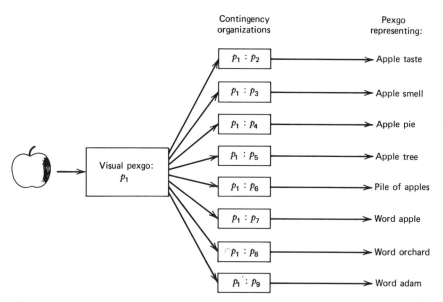

Figure 8.1. Meanings of Apple. Some hypothetical pexgos that might be excited (on the same or different occasions) by the visual pexgo of an apple.

As noted above, the visual pexgo of an apple as a test stimulus can influence the excitation level of many target pexgos—give rise to many meanings.

According to the ideas discussed in Chapter 7, the meaning of a test stimulus at any given moment would be determined not only by the contingency existing between the gnostic-assemblies representing features of that stimulus and the various target gnostic-assemblies but also by the sequential context in which the test stimulus is presented. Thus, during a discussion of cultivation and care of fruits, the visual pexgo of an apple may maximally excite target pexgos representing orchards, trees, or insecticides, but during a discussion of desserts, the visual pexgo of an apple may maximally excite target pexgos representing the aroma of a freshly baked apple pie, the sight of a sugar-glazed apple, or the name *apple strudel*. In the absence of any specific, explicitly contrived context, the momentary meaning of apple may be expected to vary greatly from time to time as well as from subject to subject. In general, the more narrowly specified the context, the more likely are the meanings of a stimulus to be the same for one subject at different times, as well as for different subjects on a given occasion.

Even within a given context the clarity of meaning may vary greatly. A test stimulus may result in the weak excitation of a large number of different types of pexgos or in relatively strong excitation of a limited class of pexgos; correspondingly the meaning would be less or more clear. Clarity of meaning may mean distinctiveness, invariance, stability, or vividness, or any combination of these. The *distinctiveness* of the meaning of a test stimulus depends on the distinctiveness of the target pexgos generated by the test stimulus; the greater the diversity of the pexgos generated at any moment, the more diffuse ("rich" or "connotative") the meaning, and the more limited the class of pexgos generated, the more sharp ("specific" or "denotative") the meaning. The *invariance* of meaning refers to the degree to which the pexgos generated by a test stimulus remain the same from occasion to occasion. If the pexgo of the odor of an apple excites a varying assortment of pexgos on different occasions, then the meaning of apple odor is more variable than if that odor were to excite the same set of pexgos on each occasion. The *stability* of meaning refers to the duration for which a particular meaning of a stimulus (i.e., the excitation of a particular pexgo) is maintained; if the target pexgos maximally excited do not keep changing in rapid succession, the meaning may be said to be relatively stable. The *vividness* of meaning refers to the degree of influence a signal pexgo has on the target-pexgo—the extent to which the excitation level is changed; if the visual pexgo of an apple increases the level of excitation of the pexgo representing an apple tree more than that of one representing apple pie, then the former meaning is more vivid than the latter.

The present proposal that the momentary meaning of a test stimulus is the collection of pexgos generated by that stimulus is consistent with, if not supported by, findings that perception of an object may be facilitated by the arousal of meaning that incorporates that object. For example, Potter (1975) asked subjects to identify a target picture from brief presentations (about 1/3 sec each) of a succession of pictures. She found that the target picture was identified almost as well when the subject had been told only its name (a boat, two men drinking beer, etc.) as when they had seen the picture itself in advance. Apparently, the meaning generated by the name led to the same facilitation of perceptual identification as did the prior perception of the picture itself. It is also known that, when it is not too complex, it is as easy to match a pattern and its verbal description as it is to match two patterns (Cohen, 1969a).

Acquiring Meaning-Word Contingencies

Words serve as signs for things, and things serve as signs for words; the word *apple* may generate as meaning the thing apple, and an apple may generate as meaning the word *apple*. How are such reversible sign-significate relations between particular words and meanings acquired?

The basic process of learning sign-significate relations is that of contingency learning, described in Chapters 6 and 7. If an infant, while observing an apple, hears the word *apple*, then an apple-thing:apple-word contingency

$(T:W)$ would develop, and if, while hearing the word *apple*, the infant observes an apple, a word:thing $(W:T)$ contingency would be developed. Since typically both types of sequences are likely to be repeated in the life of an infant, every infant would develop both the $T:W$ and $W:T$ contingency organizations. After such contingencies have been learned, the generation of a pexgo of the thing by a word would constitute the meaning of that word, and the generation of the pexgos of the word by the thing would be the basis of the production of the word—the name of that thing. Sometimes it is easier to generate a meaning from a given word than to produce the word from the given meaning, but sometimes it is easier to produce a word from a given meaning or referent than to produce a meaning from the given word. For example, the name of a man may readily evoke an image of him (or some other identifying response), while the name may be hard to evoke in the presence of the man; but equally likely a tree may fail to evoke its botanical name, while the botanical name may readily evoke an image of the tree. There is little doubt that normally a stimulus, word or nonword, can serve as both a sign and a significate; what is meaning at one moment can become a sign at the next, and vice-versa.

Consider some of the implications of this view for the learning of meanings and names. The first point to note is that learning the name of something requires considerable discriminative training, even when the name-word is used to refer to only one thing. Suppose a young child is trained to call his father *papa*. Though the training has involved a specific word-name for a specific referent, the child may well enunciate *papa* whenever any male figure enters the house, or when he sees anyone carrying a briefcase, etc. This "generalization" or failure of discrimination presumably rests on the commonality of certain features between the father and other figures. Only through discriminative training, which emphasizes the correctness of the word *papa* only for a certain specific figure, would the child learn to use the name correctly. In other cases, such generalization may not be inappropriate because the language community uses the word in a broader sense; the word *open*, first learned in relation to a particular door, may be generalized to all doors, to cupboards, drawers, and capped bottles. The breadth or narrowness of the range of referents for which a name is appropriate is learned by the child as it experiences particular instances of correct and incorrect uses of the word. It has been pointed out by Brown (1958) that the name by which an object is customarily called refers to those of its attributes that are important for its most frequent use. In terms of the present formulation, the learning of an appropriate name for a class of stimuli requires the development of contingency organizations which insure that the appropriate name-word pexgos would be excited only when the appropriate class of stimuli are present.

Further, it is rarely, if ever, that an object has only one name; a given apple is not only an *apple* but also a *fruit*, and it may be a *Mackintosh* or a *Russet*, and Mr. X is not only a man but also a *Homo sapiens*, a *Chinese*, an *accountant*, a *golfer*, a *husband*, etc. The name selected at a given moment to describe something obviously depends on what attributes of the object the speaker wants to draw attention to—what the speaker's intended specific referent is at the moment. The intended referent, of course, depends on what differentiation or comparison the speaker wants to specify or imply; to say that a man is an accountant is a way of emphasizing that he is not a doctor, lawyer, or engineer, or that he could serve as a consultant for calculating income tax, depending on the context of the speaker's utterance. Olson has summarized such observations by the statement that the name selected at any given time serves "to differentiate an intended referent from some perceived or inferred set of alternatives" (Olson, 1970, p. 257). The fact that the same word may be used without confusion in different contexts to refer to different things, or to different attributes of the same thing, shows the importance of the context in determining the momentary referent (object or attribute) of a word. Conversely, the selection of an appropriate word to describe an object or attribute at a given time reflects the differential excitation of the pexgos of that word by the contingency organizations that are activated by the contextual cues and the more specific test stimulus in the situation. The contingency organizations are developed through the observation of the contingent relations between words and the situational events in relation to which they are uttered in the linguistic community. Since the same name-meaning ($W:T$) and meaning-name ($T:W$) contingent relations are likely to be experienced by the members of a linguistic community, most children of the community learn the same names for particular attributes of things in particular contexts.

Another point to note is that when a child first hears something named, it may already know something about the referent. When a ball is called *ball*, the child is already familiar with many properties of the ball; ball, as seen or haptically perceived, has meanings before it has a name. In learning the name, the word *ball* acquires the meanings that the ball had for the child before learning the name. Thus, learning a name is not a process of "learning a meaning" of a word, but of attaching a word to some existing meanings. Macnamara (1972) has developed this point in connection with language acquisition. He has suggested that the adult speaker communicates his meaning to the child independently of language, and it is this meaning that the child then relates to the words heard. Indeed, both children and adults frequently use meaning to decipher what has been said; for example, in a noisy room it is only after hearing the word *dog* in the sentence "I have no desire to insult the vet for my dog today" that the listener may decide that the confusing word was *consult*, not *insult*.

PERCEPTION AND COMPREHENSION OF WORDS

Words are different from other environmental stimuli in that their meaning is arbitrary. While the meanings of most objects or events such as apples, stones, food, water, offspring arise from the experiences animals and man have with their intrinsic properties, the meanings of words depend, for the most part, not on their intrinsic stimulus properties but on the properties of entities to which they refer. Though both are acquired through individual experience, the meanings of objects and events tend to be universal, while those of words are culture-specific. Pavlov described words, and language generally, as the *second* signaling system. It would pay to give a closer examination to the problems of perception and comprehension of words as stimuli, and of the production of words as responses.

Words as Stimulus Configurations

The stimulus configuration of a word, as of all environmental objects and events, is a spatiotemporal array of certain stimulus features, which is represented in the brain as a sensory pattern—activation of certain feature detectors. When words are presented as speech, the modality of the sensory patterns is auditory; when words are presented in script, the sensory patterns are visual; when words are written on a part of the body without being seen (e.g., someone writes a word on your back), the sensory patterns are tactual; when a deaf child's hand is put against the throat of a speaker and he is made to "feel the words," the sensory pattern is haptic; and when a child's hand is moved by a teacher to form certain words, the sensory patterns representing the words may be proprioceptive. Just as an apple as an object may project sensory patterns in several modalities (e.g., visual, olfactory, tactual, gustatory), so *apple* as a word may also project sensory patterns in one or more of several modalities. The auditory modality is one that initially provides the sensory patterns of words, except in the congenitally deaf; the visual modality becomes more prominent as the child learns to read and write.

The sensory pattern of a word consists of many specific features, representing various details of the stimulus configuration. In the auditory modality, the stimulus configuration of a word consists of a temporal arrangement of a certain number of basic speech sounds or phonological features; in the visual modality, the stimulus configuration of a word may consist of a single ideographic character, as in hieroglyphics and the traditional Chinese and Japanese scripts, or of a spatial array of smaller units or letters, as in alphabetical scripts such as English. The stimulus features of a word, written as an ideograph, or alphabetically, are spatially arranged to form a unique configuration, but the spatial pattern is converted into a spatiotemporal arrangement when the words are read in a certain direction (e.g., left to right in English). The perception of words, whatever the stimulus modality in which they are presented, requires the integration of the various sensory features into unique pexgos.

Gnostic-Assemblies of Words

The integration of specific sensory features of a word into a unified auditory or visual pexgo requires the development of appropriate gnostic-assemblies in each modality. The process by which "word gnostic-assemblies" are developed is the same as described for "object gnostic-assemblies" described in Chapter 5. That word gnostic-assemblies are formed through experience is shown by the gradual improvement in word identification with increasing experience of the stimulus features of the words of a given language. This is evident in the increase in the speed of accurate identification as a child learns a language or as an adult learns a new language. More formally, it is known that training (hearing and speaking) certain speech sounds decreases their duration thresholds of identification (e.g., Postman & Rosenzweig, 1956). In conformity with this, identification thresholds are lower for words that have a greater frequency of occurrence in a language than for words that occur only rarely (Howes & Solomon, 1951; McGinnies, Comer, & Lacey, 1952). A more pertinent finding (Postman & Rosenzweig, 1956) is that visual identification thresholds (duration of tachistoscopic exposure) are no lower for three-letter English words (e.g., bun, pen) than they are for equally frequent three-letter syllables (e.g., sug; vit). This suggests that individuals develop gnostic-assemblies that represent the frequently occurring letter combinations in a language, whether or not those combinations have any meaning (Baron & Thurston, 1973). Thus, just as object gnostic-assemblies integrate the frequently recurring combination of object features an individual commonly encounters in its environment, so verbal gnostic-assemblies integrate the frequently recurring combinations of features the individual commonly encounters in spoken or written language.

Since gnostic-assemblies are modality-specific (see Chap. 5), the gnostic-assemblies that represent the important features of a word in different modalities must be separate. Evidence that this is so is provided by the clinical finding that an aphasic patient may be unable to identify a word presented aurally but may respond appropriately when the word is presented visually, and vice versa (Geschwind, 1965). It also appears that aural or visual training (hearing or reading) in the auditory identification of certain syllables does not greatly improve the identification of the same syllables presented in the other modality (Postman & Rosenzweig, 1956). Such transfer effects of training in one modality on identification in another that do occur are probably attributable to some intermodal transfer in the course of the experiment (see below). However, there can be little doubt that gnostic-assemblies representing the important features of a word in different modalities do not have a common locus.

How are verbal gnostic-assemblies developed? In other words, how are gnostic neurons of the auditory and visual systems organized into gnostic-assemblies representing modality specific combinations of stimulus patterns? One early idea (Liberman, Cooper, Shankweiler, & Studdert-Kennedy, 1967) was that an auditory word stimulus evokes certain specific articulatory movements in the listener (e.g., movements involved in pronouncing the same word), and that the proprioceptive feedback from these movements provides the basis for differential identification or percept of the word or word components. According to this "motor theory of speech perception" sensory or central feedback from articulatory movements (evoked automatically by a speech stimulus) would be essential for the development of verbal gnostic-assemblies. Apart from the general objections to the sensory feedback and the efferent outflow views of perception noted in Chapter 5, there are several other objections to the motor theory of speech perception. For one thing, neurological patients who suffer from "pure word deafness" (with normal performance on nonverbal tests) fail to identify spoken words though they can express themselves well in both speech and writing; conversely, there are cases of gross articulatory defect without loss of speech perception (Geschwind, 1965). For another, if articulatory mechanisms are required for speech perception, it is difficult to see how children without the ability to produce speech could learn to perceive speech, but they can (Fourcin, 1974; Lenneberg, 1962). Further, if articulatory movements required for speech perception are evoked by acoustic speech stimuli, it is difficult to see how deaf children could learn to make appropriate articulatory movements for producing speech, but they can. MacNeilage, Rootes, and Chase (1967) have described a case of a girl with severe speech-production deficit attributable to inability to control the spatiotemporal modulation of muscle contractions required for normal speech. This girl had normal speech perception even in characteristics that the motor theory would require to be aberrant. It therefore seems unlikely that speech perception requires reference to the mechanisms of speech production. The same conclusion is arrived at by Howes (1974) on the basis of an analysis of the distribution of word frequencies in spoken discourse.

According to the hypothesis about the development of gnostic-assemblies proposed in Chapter 5, the gnostic-neurons activated by particular components of a language become organized into assemblies of neurons that then tend to fire as a unit, in a certain sequence, even in the absence of some of the sensory inflow initially required for generating word pexgos. Verbal gnostic-assemblies are thus linkages of gnostic-neurons that are organized to fire in a sequence that represents the temporal arrangement in which the various stimulus components of a language appear commonly. In the case of a word presented as an acoustic stimulus, the sequence of word features are directly represented as the sequential firing of the particular gnostic-neurons representing those features; the sequential ordering is directly represented and leads directly to the sequential organization of the neurons. Thus gnostic-assemblies representing the more frequently occurring sequences in the language would get organized. And this would occur without the intervention of any observational or other acts to produce sequential and contiguous firing of the gnostic-neurons representing the phonological sequences.

Though spoken words are sequences of phonological features, these features are not normally encountered as isolated speech sounds. They typically occur in larger functional units, such as words and phrases. Gnostic-assemblies that are developed to represent certain speech-sound combinations, therefore, do not usually represent isolated phonological features, such as letters or bits of speech sounds, but the recurring *combinations* of features that make up the larger functional units. In general, then, it should be easier to identify words and phrases than to identify individual letters or fragmented speech sounds; this is usually the case (Savin & Bever, 1970; Warren, 1971). However, if specific discriminative training is given for the identification of certain smaller linguistic units as such, then gnostic-assemblies would develop for those particular smaller combinations, and their identification would become easier. Recall that the essential basis for the development of particular, refined gnostic-assemblies is discriminative experience (Chap. 5).

In the case of a word presented as a visual stimulus, either as a series of letters or as an ideograph, a sequential order of observation of the component graphemes would be imposed during reading. If the word is written as an ideograph, the order in which its components are scanned would provide the basis for the organization of the gnostic-neurons representing particular graphemic components into a unique order representing the ideograph, as explained in connection with the gnostic-assemblies of objects (Chap. 5). If the word is written as a sequence of letters, then in order to activate gnostic-neurons in a sequence corresponding to the sequence in which the letters form a word (say, left to right), it would be necessary that the letters be uniformly scanned in an invariant sequence. For example, gnostic-assemblies of written English words cannot develop until the reader has developed stable left-to-right reading habits; in contrast, the development of gnostic-assemblies of visually presented objects and pictures probably involves scanning patterns that vary greatly from one individual to another.

Experiments on the visual identification of English words show that it is the result of separate identifications of the sequences of features that make up different portions of the word, for example, the initial syllable, the end syllable, and the middle syllables (Nelson, Brooks, & Fosselman, 1972). Again, though letters are the units of the word as stimulus, people probably get more experience of reading words and phrases than of reading isolated letters. Identification of individual letters is made more difficult when they are embedded in letter sequences than when they are presented alone (Massaro, 1973); the reported facilitation of letter identification by word context seems to occur at the naming rather than the detection stage (Estes, 1975).

In summary, then, auditory and visual gnostic-assemblies representing common combinations of word features can develop without requiring articulation, and they can develop independently of each other. Therefore, no difficulty is presented by the facts that the dumb can learn to comprehend spoken words, the deaf can learn to speak them, and both can learn to read and write. Normally, however, the intactness of the auditory modality has an important role in both intermodal integration and speech production.

Intermodal Integration

The normal adult can readily tell whether the word presented to him in one modality, say, aurally, is the same as or different from the word presented to him in some other modality, say, visually, tactually, or proprioceptively. Such cross-modal transfer of perceptual information was attributed in Chapter 5 to intermodal integration of modality-specific gnostic-assemblies through their contiguous activation. Such contiguous activation may occur when, for example, a teacher shows a pupil the word *book* and at the same time speaks the same word, or a pupil is made to look at a word and to copy it while the teacher speaks the same word. Repeated experiences of this type would lead to the integration of the various modality-specific verbal gnostic-assemblies, so that a word presented in one modality would activate the gnostic-assemblies representing feature combinations of the same word in other modalities. As noted earlier, a common response (e.g., pronouncing or writing) is not required for such cross-modal transfer between different modalities, but a common response may facilitate intermodal integration by increasing the probability of contiguous occurrence of the different forms of the word stimulus.

In the course of normal development, the auditory gnostic-assemblies representing word features develop first, because words are heard before they are seen or felt. Auditory gnostic-assemblies may therefore play an especially important part in the development of cross-modal transfer. However, the development of auditory gnostic-assemblies is not necessary for cross-modal transfer; deaf children can learn to tell whether, say, a word presented visually is the same as a word presented tactually or proprioceptively, and persons who are both blind and deaf (e.g., Helen Keller) are probably capable of cross-modal transfer between the proprioceptive feedback arising from speaking a word and the tactual stimulation arising from haptically reading the same word in braille.

Comprehension of Words

Earlier in this chapter I suggested that the brain regions that determine the meanings of stimuli are probably different from the perceptual regions, and that the perceptual and meaning regions are modality-specific. If this is so, then there should be a number of modality-specific meaning regions. Damage to any one of these regions should produce a deficit in the comprehension of the meaning of stimuli of that modality only. Though pertinent information is not yet available, there is some indication that the modality-specific meaning regions lie in the parieto-temporal cortex. Lesions of particular parts of the parieto-temporal cortex produce deficits of comprehension that appear to be modality-specific.

When lesions of the parieto-temporal cortex are in the left hemisphere, there is a deficit of comprehending words. This has been most clearly demonstrated for lesions in Wernicke's area (see Figure 8.2), which is situated adjacent to the left Sylvian fissure. Damage to Wernicke's area results in a dramatic loss of ability to comprehend spoken or written words, without any impairment in the comprehension of the meanings of nonverbal stimuli. The significance of Wernicke's area in word comprehension may lie in that it serves as a specialized structure for determining the meaning of words ("secondary signals") as opposed to the meaning of objects and events. Further, since damage to Wernicke's area results in no deficit of fluency of speech and writing, it may be, as Howes (1967) has suggested, that Wernicke's area correlates the verbal system with the incoming sensory information on the basis of which words are selected. In other words, it may be the site of contingency organizations that link verbal and nonverbal stimuli to appropriate word pexgos. But if this is so, a "word" must be defined more broadly than an exclusively auditory or speech entity; it must include words presented in other modalities, including those presented (visually) in a sign language. It is now known that damage in or near Wernicke's area produces aphasic lack of comprehension of sign language in congenitally deaf signing adults (Douglass & Richardson, 1959; Sarno, Swisher, & Sarno, 1969). The major question that remains unanswered is this: What are the critical neural features that make a stimulus configuration (of any modality) into a "word" and thus involve the language structures of the left hemisphere?

PRODUCTION OF WORDS

In turning from the perception to the production of words, it may be helpful to start with outlining a tentative account of the neural substrate of word production.

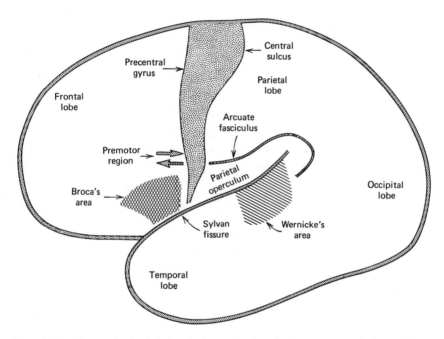

Figure 8.2. Human brain, left hemisphere, showing the four lobes and the pathways important in the comprehension and production of words. The parietal-temporal region appears to be important in comprehension. The precentral gyrus contains the classical motor cortex, whose lower end, near the Sylvian fissure, is the face area—the region controlling movements of the muscles of the face, jaw, tongue, palate, and vocal cords. (Reprinted by permission, *American Scientist*, journal of Sigma Xi, The Scientific Research Society of North America.)

Neural Substrate of Word Production

The act-assemblies for the production of words appear to lie in Broca's area, which is situated in the left frontal gyrus (see Figure 8.2). Thus Broca's area may not be so much a "speech" area as a "word articulation" area containing act-assemblies for the production of words involving different motor apparatuses. Damage to Broca's area produces no loss in the ability to perceive or comprehend words, or in the ability to select appropriate words, but produces marked articulation deficits; speech and writing become slow, labored, and "telegraphic." Since in such "expressive aphasias" both speech and writing are affected, it would appear that the efferent neurons of Broca's area project to parts of the parietal cortex that contain the sensory-motor coordination organizations for producing movements of jaw, tongue, palate, and larynx, as well as to parts which contain the sensory-motor coordination organizations for producing movements of arms, hands, and fingers. Whether there is, in fact, a differentiation within Broca's area between the speech and writing parts is not known, but the fact that the speech and writing deficits are not perfectly correlated would suggest that discrete, though anatomically overlapping, neuronal groups may exist in Broca's area.

While damage to Broca's area produces deficits of speech production, it does not produce any deficits of nonverbal movements involving the same muscular apparatus. For example, aphasics who are unable to speak fluently can nevertheless suck, chew, and swallow without difficulty, and deficits of writing do not seem to be accompanied by deficits of making nonverbal skilled movements (handling, picking, tapping) of hands and fingers. Broca's area thus seems to serve a higher-order, specifically word-production, function rather than being concerned with organizing movements of any particular muscular apparatus. Further, rather than producing paralysis or inability to produce components of words, patients with lesions of Broca's area have difficulty in producing words as units; each component seems to require separate effort. For example, in pronouncing a polysyllabic word, such as *modeling*, a patient may have difficulty in moving smoothly from *mo* to *del* to *ing* and may get stuck at the transition points, repeating a certain syllable as in stuttering. Such disjunctive and perseverative production of word components may also be seen in writing or drawing; every stroke seems to require a separate effort, and the patient's handwriting is greatly altered (Luria, 1973). Since patients remain capable of producing individual components of speech and writing, the disturbance is not one of producing components, but one of integrating them into larger units.

If the account of motor organization presented in Chapters 3 and 4 is correct in its general plan, then we should expect Broca's area, as a part of the premotor act-assembly region, to be the source of the sequentially organized neural discharges to the sensory-motor coordination organizations of the face and hand parts of the motor-sensory cortex. The sensory-motor coordination organizations would receive neural discharges not only from the act-assemblies for speaking and writing in Broca's area, but also from interneural and sensory circuits that provide information about the current state of the muscular apparatus. Further, the sensory-motor coordination organizations would continuously receive some part of the current sensory inflow from environmental bodily (somatosensory) stimuli. This scheme,

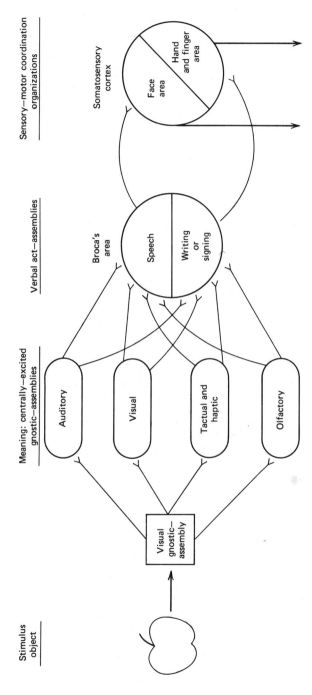

Figure 8.3. A hypothetical scheme describing how modality-specific word gnostic-assemblies can have independent influences on the production of speech and writing.

sketched in Figure 8.3, is broadly consistent with the account of speech production formulated by MacNeilage (1970) in his discussion of the problem of motor equivalence in speech production.

However, the critical question for the present purpose concerns not so much the projections from Broca's area that finally influence movement commands, but the projections *to* Broca's areas that determine what word act-assemblies will be activated there. Since words, whether spoken, written, or signed in a sign language, are normally produced to convey meanings of stimuli of various modalities, it must be assumed that neural discharges representing meanings of different modalities can reach verbal act-assemblies in Broca's area. In other words, the pexgos of various modalities that comprise the momentary meaning of a certain object, event, or word must be connected to Broca's area (as well as to the act-assemblies underlying various nonverbal acts). This arrangement is shown in Figure 8.3. Suppose a subject is shown an apple and is asked to describe it. The visual pexgo of the apple generated by the stimulus input from the apple itself will centrally excite, to varying degrees, various pexgos of visual and other modalities through the existing contingency organizations. This collection of centrally generated pexgos is the momentary meaning of the visually presented object, the apple. The neural output from these meaning pexgos (representing the taste, odor, texture, etc., of apples) will then reach Broca's area and selectively activate act-assemblies underlying the production of words.

Geschwind (1972) has suggested that the primary input to the word-production areas of the premotor region may be of auditory origin, at least in so far as spoken words are concerned, and that auditory perception is a requirement for appropriate speech production. Inputs from other modalities would then have to be translated into auditory pexgos before they could lead to production of appropriate words. This idea appears untenable. While it is true that most people first learn to speak on the basis of auditory input, it is also true that congenitally deaf persons can be trained to speak, read, and write correctly on the basis of visual or cutaneous guidance of word production. It is therefore likely that gnostic-assemblies of at least the visual and cutaneous sensory modalities also have independent connections to Broca's area. Without such connections it would be difficult to see how non-auditory pexgos could lead to an appropriate spoken or written response. With such connections it is easy to see why a patient may, for example, be unable to give an appropriate name when a test stimulus is presented visually but may be able to do so when the same stimulus is presented aurally or tactually.

Organization of Verbal Act-Assemblies

Turn next to the question of the development of act-assemblies that can produce words or word-components as integrated, unified wholes. How do they get organized in Broca's area? The general answer is the same as outlined in Chapter 4 in connection with the development of nonverbal act-assemblies. Essentially, the production of each word component requires that certain sensory-motor coordination organizations be activated, and initially this requires stimulation by particular types of stimulus configurations. When particular component-eliciting stimulus configurations occur in a certain sequence, words are formed. With repeated activation of the same sensory-motor coordination organizations in a certain sequence, superordinate act-assemblies would be organized, as explained in Chapter 4. Once organized, an act-assembly would be capable of generating sequentially organized discharges that would activate, in an appropriate sequence, particular sensory-motor coordinations, and hence produce a particular word. As noted before, an act-assembly, when triggered, can activate the whole sequence of sensory-motor coordination organizations without requiring all the eliciting stimuli initially needed to organize that act-assembly.

The essential condition for the development of verbal act-assemblies, then, is that the required eliciting stimulus configurations be provided in an appropriate sequence. Since normal infants spontaneously babble the elementary speech components or phonological elements required in the speech of all languages, but the speech of adults conforms to that of their linguistic community, it is to be expected that the words that a developing infant hears play an important part in determining the relative frequency of the various phonological elements it produces (see Lenneberg, 1967, Chap. 4). This suggests that the speech of the linguistic community provides the stimuli that are effective in eliciting certain speech sounds rather than others. There is considerable evidence from studies of human speech, as well as of bird songs, that individuals produce sound sequences that they have previously heard (Marler, 1970a, 1970b; Thorpe, 1961). The more frequently certain phonological sequences are used in the speech of a community, the more likely a child reared in that community would be to develop act-assemblies that integrate those sequences.

Important though auditory stimulation may be for the elicitation of speech sounds, it is not necessary either for the elicitation of speech sounds or for the development of verbal act-assemblies. The deaf do both. Apparently, the production of the normal range of speech sounds is not exclusively dependent on auditory stimulation. Infants of deaf parents start to babble in the same way as normal infants, though, understandably, differences in the patterns of sounds soon emerge (Lenneberg, Rebelsky, & Nichols, 1965). In general, speech movements are produced in the same spontaneous way as an infant produces other movements, and the specific eliciting stimulus configurations for different speech movements are not restricted to the auditory modality. Further, since the deaf can be taught to speak by substituting visual or tactual input in place of auditory stimulation, it is obvious that verbal act-assemblies can be organized through visual and tactual guidance of appropriate sound sequences. Auditory stimulation is normally important, but it is not indispensable for eliciting speech sounds and their sequences. The main route by which neural discharges from gnostic-assemblies of different modalities reach Broca's area appears to be the arcuate fasciculus (see Figure 8.2).

Since the same environmental speech sounds would normally form the basis of the development of both verbal gnostic-assemblies and verbal act-assemblies, there would be correspondence between the two types of assemblies. For example, persons reared in Chinese linguistic communities frequently fail to differentiate between *r* and *l* sounds in both perception and production of speech. In general, sound sequences we perceive best tend to be the ones that we produce best (Miller, Bruner, & Postman, 1954). However, this proposition should not be taken to mean that word perception is dependent upon word articulation, or vice versa. The relative separation of the functions of word perception and word production is clearly seen in neurological patients who can do one but not the other. For example, cases of alexia without agraphia have been reported (Geschwind, 1970), in which a patient is unable to read words but remains capable of copying the same words and of writing spontaneously. A case has also been reported (Geschwind, Quadfasel, & Segarra, 1968) of a woman who could not comprehend spoken words but could repeat them as well as complete common phrases and rhymes started by the examiner.

Verbal act-assemblies may be of varying size, representing combinations of different lengths. The more frequently certain speech-sound sequences occur in a language, the stronger will be the act-assemblies developed for producing those sequences. It should be noted that nominally the same sound may appear in different variations in different sequences; for example, the sound called *u* is pronounced differently in *put, but,* and *lute,* so that the *u* that forms a part of these different phonemic sequences is a different *u*. What is more important is that the same (nominal) sound may appear in different transitional variations in different sequences; for example, the sound *u* in *stu* (student) and in *stru* (strudel) are not quite the same, so that act-assemblies of *stu* and *stru* must have neural discharge to different combinations of sensory-motor coordinations resulting in the activation of different movement commands for the two variations of u, as explained in Chapter 3. It is clear that we must postulate that a great number of different act-assemblies, perhaps on the order of a million, capable of producing different combinations of frequently-occurring speech-sound sequences, short or long, get organized in the course of early development. Further, it is to be noted that certain general transformations of loudness, accent, nasality, rhythm, and so on, can be placed on speech; this implies that different calibration systems can be introduced into the movement-production process, as suggested in Chapter 3.

VERBAL COMMUNICATION

Words are arbitrary symbols used for communicating meaning. Minimally, verbal communication involves production of words that describe a certain meaning by an addressor and identification of those words and comprehension of their meaning by the addressee. The arbitrary or "symbolic" systems of communication that comprise human languages may involve hundreds of thousands of different words and many syntactical rules for combining the words. Such elaborate communication systems go far beyond emotional reactions and gestures as iconic signs representing situations. Symbolic communication could not have emerged without the evolutionary development of highly refined motor mechanisms for producing speech and highly refined perceptual mechanisms for perceiving and comprehending it. Speech multiplies the potential number of descriptions and makes the relation between the symbols and referents arbitrary rather than iconic.

Once a stable verbal communication system based on speech has developed within a group, speech may become an optional mode of communication. This is so because particular words, initially developed as unique speech-sound sequences, can now be represented by postural and manual signs or by written characters. Thus, dumb children can be taught to produce words ("talk") by sign language and by writing, and deaf children can be trained to identify spoken words by lip-reading and written words by reading characters. Within the limitation of their ability, some subhuman primates too can be taught to communicate symbolically by using a standard sign-language or some experimentally devised "language" in which words can be produced manually (Fouts, 1973; Gardner & Gardner, 1969; Premack, 1971). Clearly, given a language-community, neither the ability to produce speech nor the ability to perceive it is necessary for the acquisition of the capability of using the words of the language for symbolic communication. This is another way of saying that the communicative significance of words lies not in their own stimulus characteristics but in what they symbolize—their meaning.

Communication and Clarity of Meaning

The essential problem of communication resides in explaining how a certain meaning is transferred from the speaker to the listener (or from the writer to the reader). Verbal communication requires that the speaker utter words that capture the exact meaning of the referent he wants to communicate and that those words generate the same meaning in the listener. In terms of our analysis, this means that there must be a close correspondence between the pexgos (momentary meanings) that contribute to the production of a word by the speaker and the pexgos that are excited by that word in the listener. This correspondence can develop only through common experience, involving the organization of similar gnostic-assemblies and contingency organizations. The accuracy of communication thus is dependent on the degree of shared discriminative experience pertaining to the use of particular words.

Obviously, not all words are equally accurate for communication; some words (e.g., *piano, house, kangaroo, green*) may communicate the intended meaning quite precisely, while others (e.g., *justice, anxiety, bravery, amount*) may do so only roughly or not at all. The basis of such differences in communicative accuracy can be illustrated with reference to two words, *kangaroo* and *justice*. A child is likely to hear the word *kangaroo* as the name for an animal of a certain shape, size, posture, gait, etc., and learns (discriminatively) that the name is to be used only for an animal with these features. The discrimination learning is likely to be refined because, since the word refers to a concrete object that can be observed by the linguistic community, any errors of naming would be corrected quickly by adult members of the community. The meaning evoked by *kangaroo* would thus be clear (distinctive, invariant, etc.) and would be about the same for all normal members of the community in most contexts; it would be said to have a denotative meaning. In contrast, the word *justice* would be heard by a child in a variety of circumstances: when he passes a courthouse, or sees a judge giving a verdict, or is shown a policeman taking someone into custody, as well as parts of phrases, such as "liberty and justice." The meaning of the word would thus be highly variable from person to person and context to context. Even within a context (e.g., a courthouse), there would be no easy way of insuring that the child has learned to apply the word to attributes considered important by the community. The meaning of the word would thus lack clarity—it would be vague, variable, and unstable; it would be said to have a lot of connotations or to be rich in meaning. There would be little or no uniformity of evoked meaning for the members of the linguistic community even if the context were carefully controlled. Accurate communication may then be said to depend on the similarity between the "activated semantic fields" (Howes, 1974) in the speaker and the listener.

In general, words that signify concrete, pointable-at, palpable, or "objective" things, or refer to subjective entities (e.g., negative afterimage) describing events that occur in highly specified contexts (sequences, procedures, etc.), would make for accurate communication. Conversely, words that signify nonconcrete or amorphous entities, that are neither pointable-at nor palpable, nor defined in terms of highly specific contexts, would make for uncertain communication. The essential determinees of the uniformity of meaning between members of a linguistic community, and of clarity of meaning for an individual, are the details of discriminative training in the acquisition of the meanings of words and the similarity of contexts between the training and the test situations.

However, the difference in the uniformity of meaning between words describing concrete entities and those describing nonconcrete entities would in general hold for the members of a linguistic community. Thus certain words could be called "concrete words" and others "nonconcrete words" for a given community. The variable of specificity-abstractness of words per se should make no difference in the uniformity of meaning, except in so far as this variable may be related to the concrete-nonconcrete variable and thus to the type and extent of discriminative experience that defines a term for the members of a community. It may be, as Bugelski (1971) has suggested, that the words usually rated as abstract tend to be purely verbal substitutes for the words initially learned in relation to certain concrete referents, and may thus be far removed from discriminative experiences directly involving the referents. If *female person* is substituted for *girl*, *simian* for *monkey*, and *underprivileged* for *poor*, the substitutes would lack direct connection with the discriminative experience of the originals, would be called (relatively) abstract words, and would lack the uniformity of meaning of the original words. Concrete-nonconcrete and specific-abstract thus appear to be two separate but correlated variables.

Paivio (1968) has shown that concrete words, as compared to nonconcrete words (Paivio calls these "abstract" words) are more imageable; subjects can generate an image of a concrete word more quickly and the image is rated as more vivid. From the present viewpoint, concrete words are not more imageable as such, but the meaning they generate tends to be distinctive and stable, and uniform for different subjects. In contrast, the meaning generated by nonconcrete words is vague and fleeting, and lacks uniformity between subjects. Bugelski (1971) has given a similar interpretation of the apparent difference between the imageability of concrete and nonconcrete words. One implication of this interpretation is that, on average, the initial few word associations given to non-concrete words by members of a linguistic community would be much more diverse than those given to concrete words. Further, for a given individual, the initial word associations given to a nonconcrete word on different occasions would be more variable than those given to a concrete word. If this is so, then the diversity and variability of word associations may serve as an index of the richness (or vagueness) of the meaning of a word, while the constancy and speed of the initial associations may serve as an index of the clarity (and "imageability") of the meaning. These indices of the meaning of words are different from those arising from the idea that the "meaningfulness" of a word is given by the *number* of word associates elicited by the word (Noble, 1952).

Accuracy of Communication

The above discussion indicates that the accuracy of communication would be higher for words referring to stimuli that can be independently observed by others, so that a communal consensus of the meaning of the word can be arrived at by pointing to its referents. This means that words learned for describing the stimuli that are being directly observed are likely to be the most reliable. Such "public words" include those naming an object as a whole (apple, potato, tomato, etc.), describing its specific attributes of size, shape, color, weight, etc., and giving its spatial location; for example, "this potato is *on* the shelf but the other one is *in* the basket." Such words also include those that describe common actions, events, and comparisons, as well as their spatiotemporal properties; for example, "A *arrived before* B left," "the rat *lifted* its paw for a few seconds," or "the tone was *longer* in *duration* than the light." In general, then, nouns, adjectives, verbs—words describing objects, spatiotemporal relations, and results of comparisons—are likely to be more reliable means of communication.

In contrast, words learned for describing entities that cannot be independently observed by others would be less reliable for communication. Such "private words" describe internal states that are not directly observed by others, and thus cannot develop a communal consensus of precise meaning. Words such as anxiety, doubt, and joy, and words that describe meaning, as distinct from those that describe current stimuli, would fall in the category of private words. What little consensus is developed regarding the use of such words arises from the fact that the types of situations in which such states arise are known; for example, a mother who sees her child hesitate to go down the steps to a dark cellar may say "you are afraid," and the child may start using "afraid" to describe a certain kind of internal state that has probably also been experienced by others in a similar situation. This suggests that personal states and idiosyncratic meanings could some day be communicated reliably if the environmental conditions on which they depend become specified.

Science and Introspection

Science rests on reliable communication. Events are observed by investigators, the events are described in words, and these words are understood by other investigators as describing the observed events. This fundamental operation of science is the same in all disciplines, from physics to psychology. Perceived events, as described in public words or numerals, form the data of all science. A second common operation of science is inference; inferences are propositions, varying in speculativeness, about the causes that produce the observed data and their interrelations. The aim of science is to construct a picture of the reality underlying the apparent phenomena; reliable data and disciplined inference are its essentials.

The method of introspection employed systematically by a couple of generations of psychologists toward the end of the last century was a departure from the method of science, but not for the reasons usually given. What the method of introspection involved was (1) reporting the immediate experience—identifying the momentary perceptions, images, feelings—produced by the manipulation of environmental stimuli and other experimental conditions, and (2) inspecting the details of the immediate experience with the aim of finding, by direct inspection, the structure, nature, and mechanisms underlying the experience. It is this second aspect of the introspective method that made it different from the accepted method of science. For, essentially, the introspective method rested on the assumption that it is possible to replace inference (and consequent hypothesis testing) by direct inspection—that it is possible to find the reality (or laws of nature) underlying immediate experience by "looking inside" and describing what one "sees" there. This abandonment of the separation of data from inference, and the presumption that the causes of immediate experience are to be found by direct inspection rather than to be elucidated by careful testing of inferences by further data, are the primary shortcomings of the introspectionist method. The more recent attempts to replace inference by intuition (e.g., Chomsky, 1968) have the same defect of abandoning careful hypothesis testing for intuitions arising from the inspection of immediate experience of some observers.

Further, what the results of introspectionist studies showed was that the observers' descriptions of what their inspections revealed were frequently in disagreement. Apparently, the reason for the unreliability lies in the attempt to describe the meanings aroused by the stimuli in private words rather than to report the stimuli themselves in public words—as the physicist does. Since the meanings aroused by a stimulus are likely to be both idiosyncratic and changing from moment to moment, reliability of descriptions is hardly to be expected. However, stimuli themselves can be reported (identified) by public words and these reports may be expected to be reliable, within the limits of perceptual capabilities of man, physicist or psychologist. Indeed, when the introspectionist psychologists undertook psychophysical experiments, which require the subject to report stimuli in public words (e.g., *square, green, larger, the same, earlier, louder, less bright, seven point five*) of the type common to all science, their data and results were highly reliable. However, when the same psychologists inspected and described "the structure of an image," or the "elements of feeling," or "the transformation of sensations into a perception," their findings were understandably unreliable.

This unreliability led Watson (1913) to say that the introspective method should be discarded, and certainly the unreliability of the results was a sufficient reason for saying so. However, Watson based his attack on the point that introspection dealt with mental—private—events, and that the public psychological phenomena were those of behavior. This argument is not sound, for all scientific observations (reading a Geiger counter, recording the color of a chemical residue, drawing the shape of a paramecium seen under a microscope, etc.) involve immediate perceptual experience, which is private. The essential difference lies not in the private or public nature of *events*, but in the use of private or public vocabulary to describe them. If the vocabulary is public, well discriminated, and refined, the reports of events are likely to be reliable, regardless of whether the events are public (e.g., colors and meter readings) or private (e.g., images and feelings). Of course, the public vocabulary must be learned in relation to public events, but once the vocabulary has been well learned, it can be applied to the descriptions of other events, public or private. Watson was right in discarding the intro-spective method, but he was wrong in supposing that its fault lay in dealing with private events. The essential difference between the usual method of science and the introspective method is that the former constructs reality by inference and hypothesis testing while the latter hopes to find it ready-made simply by self-inspection.

CHAPTER 9

Motivation

For about 10 weeks in spring a dominant male sea lion makes its home in rugged rock, copulates incessantly with a harem of females, but hardly ever eats; for the rest of the year he roams the oceans, feeding and playing, with a pack of other males. In less dramatic forms, other animals too show that at particular times of day, or year, or life-cycle they are more likely to do certain things and less likely to do others. Whereas the variety of environmental demands might be expected to make the animal continually flit from one type of action to another, many animal actions show considerable persistence, some consistent aim, and a certain sense of completion. Such prolonged or repeated actions are typically performed in relation to particular classes of biologically or socially important stimuli. Examples include escaping from a predator and hiding, seeking food and eating, marking a territory and defending it, finding a sexual partner and copulating, protecting and nursing the offspring, and going to the post office and mailing a letter.

The phrase "motivational function" is a rough label for brain processes that are responsible for the maintenance of direction in behavior, frequently in spite of interruptions and hardship. This goal-directedness aspect of behavior points to the existence in the brain of certain relatively persisting central states or "affects" (see Tomkins, 1962), that motivate or bias the animal in favor of acting in relation to now one and now another class of objects. *A central motive state* may be defined as a set of neural processes that promote actions in relation to a particular class of environmental objects; it serves as a selective factor that enables the animal to overcome casual distractions and to persist in addressing its actions to particular environmental stimuli. This chapter is concerned with questions about (*a*) the nature of central motive states, (*b*) the manner in which central motive states influence behavior, and (*c*) the role of learning in relation to motivational states.

NATURE OF CENTRAL MOTIVE STATES

In order for a central motive state to bias behavior in an adaptively appropriate way, it is essential that the state be determined by both the current organismic condition (metabolic requirements) and incentive stimulation (the opportunities or dangers presented by biologically important environmental stimuli). I shall use the term *organismic condition* broadly to refer to such general variables as being awake or asleep, sick or well, excited or calm, as well as to the more specific physiological variations produced by water or food depletion, hormonal fluctuations, drug injections, fatigue, and so on. Particular organismic conditions are usually called "drives" (e.g., hunger, sex, or maternal drive). However, since the term drive is also used to refer to specific response tendencies (e.g., eating or copulation), ambiguity would be avoided by using the term organismic condition to refer to the metabolic-homeostatic changes (e.g., the physiological consequences of food deprivation or increase in estrogen level) without reference to animal actions, and by using specific terms (e.g., drinking, nursing, hoarding) to refer to action tendencies as such.

I shall use the term *incentive stimulus* as a rough label for such biologically important objects, events, and situations as foods, water, substances with odors and taste, sexual partners, nests, the calls of distressed offspring, crashing noises, predators, and injurious levels of heat or cold. Such stimuli are also called "affective," "hedonic," "emotional," "releasing," or "reinforcing" stimuli. They tend to be pleasing or discomforting; that is, generally they elicit appetitive or aversive reactions. They are contrasted with "neutral" stimuli, which are neither pleasant nor unpleasant, but hedonically neutral. Though there can be no sharp distinction between incentive and neutral stimuli, it is usual to assign the label incentive to those stimuli that, under certain specifiable organismic conditions, reliably elicit specific actions that are quite resistant to habituation decrement; in contrast, neutral stimuli do not reliably elicit specific actions, and whatever actions are elicited are quickly habituated by repetition of the stimulus (Glickman & Schiff, 1967; Hinde, 1970; Premack, 1959, 1969).

Generation of Central Motive States

Traditionally, the motivational influence on behavior was thought of either as provocation or elicitation of responses by attractive or repulsive aspects of various incentive stimuli (e.g., Spencer, 1872–73; Troland, 1932; Young, 1948), *or* as pushing or energizing of responses by various organismic conditions or "homeostatic or biological drives" (e.g., Woodworth, 1918;

Richter, 1927). Until recently those who stressed the situational incentive objects as the source of motivation had a rather minor impact on formal behavior theory. But now, owing mainly to the work on the role of sensory stimulation in the occurrence of foraging, defensive, aggressive, and sexual actions (e.g., Beach, 1942; Levison & Flynn, 1965; Hinde, 1970; McFarland, 1970; Tinbergen, 1951), the importance of incentive stimuli in motivational processes is being increasingly accepted. The view that has recently emerged (e.g., Bindra, 1968; R. W. Black, 1969; Flynn, 1967; Pfaff & Pfaffmann, 1969; Pfaffmann, 1969) is that the motivational processes are equivalent neither only to incentive provocation nor only to homeostatic energizing, but are generated jointly by these two sets of variables. The generation of a central motive state is thus regarded here as a joint function of the neural consequences of a particular kind of internal organismic condition and the neural consequences of a particular type of environmental incentive stimulus.

What requires emphasis, and distinguishes the new view from its ancestors (e.g., Morgan, 1943), is the stipulation that neither the appropriate organismic condition alone nor the appropriate incentive stimulation alone can generate a central motive state capable of promoting directed actions. For example, stomach emptiness and hypoglycemia are merely features of an organismic condition (food depletion or hunger) and as such should be incapable of producing food-directed behavior. A central motive state could be generated and food-directed behavior would ensue only if certain neural consequences of food depletion were to combine with certain features of appropriate incentive stimuli (such as the smell or sight of food or of some conditioned signals of food). Similarly, even a preferred (e.g., sweet) food would be incapable of generating an eating central motive state if the animal were hyperglycemic or uncomfortable from prior overeating. This means that of the many environmental objects potentially capable of generating a motivational state, only certain ones can be effective at a given time, and *which* ones are depends on the organismic conditions prevailing at the moment. In other words, no environmental incentive stimulus is capable of generating a central motive state under all circumstances; it becomes capable only under appropriate organismic conditions. And no organismic condition is capable of generating a central motive state under all circumstances; it becomes capable only when an appropriate incentive stimulus, unconditioned or conditioned, is present. The organismic condition may be said to serve as a "gate" that determines how effective a given incentive stimulation would be.

The above statements imply that there is always a minimum of incentive stimulation below which a given organismic condition cannot generate a relevant central motive state, and a minimum of a certain organismic variable below which a given incentive stimulation cannot generate the state. The exact way in which the two factors combine may be studied by asking two broad questions: (*a*) Given a certain incentive stimulation (e.g., a receptive sexual partner), what is the range of variation of an organismic variable (e.g., levels of gonadal hormones) within which a sexual central motive state could be generated (e.g., as indicated by copulation)? (*b*) Given a certain organismic condition (e.g., deficits of gonadal hormones), what is the range of incentive stimulation (e.g., a receptive sexual partner) that would generate a sexual central motive state? Thus, given a certain organismic condition, the readiness with which a certain incentive stimulus generates a central motive state and its attendant action (e.g., copulation) may be used as an indicator of the incentive value or motivation-generating capacity of that incentive stimulus. This means that in an animal with a certain degree of, say, food deprivation a sufficiently strong central motive state may be created for eating one food with certain stimulus features, but not for another food with other stimulus features. All objects, including neutral ones, have some minimal incentive value, especially when they are still novel and are able to create a central motive state that promotes exploration of the objects.

The organismic variables involved in the generation of any particular central motive state may be highly general, such as the metabolic rate or level of cerebral activation (sleep, wakefulness, excitement), or quite specific, such as changes in blood sugar level, cellular dehydration, hormonal changes associated with pregnancy, or hyperthyroidism. Similarly, the external stimuli involved in generating a particular central motive state may be of a highly nonspecific nature, such as the temperature, and sound and brightness levels that form background stimulation, or highly specific, such as particular objects of specific shapes, sizes, odors, and tastes. Correspondingly, a central motive state may be highly nonspecific, facilitating a great variety of non-specific actions, such as those involved in "general activity," or highly specific, facilitating only a particular set of actions, such as eating, attacking, or copulating.

Certain types of incentive stimulation are capable of creating a central motive state within a wide range of organismic conditions; this is particularly true of noxious stimuli and situations usually described as "emotional." For example, so long as the animal is awake and at a certain minimum activation level, an attacking predator will produce a central motive state ("defense"), as indicated by acts of withdrawal, crouching, etc. However, it is important to note that even such incentive stimuli do require a certain type of organismic condition (though not a highly specific one) for generating a central motive state. This is shown by such phenomena as premenstrual depression, androgen-induced aggression, and the reduction of fear responses by tran-quilizers; in all these cases changes in the organismic condition produce marked changes in the reactions to certain otherwise highly effective environmental stimuli. Thus there is no essential distinction between phenomena labeled "emotional" and "motivational" (Bindra, 1955, 1969; Gray, 1972). Though the external incentive stimulation is usually stressed in the descriptions of "emotional phenomena" (behaviors we call fear, anger, love, joy), and the internal organismic condition is stressed in discussions of "motivational phenomena" (eating, drinking, copulating, etc.), both certain types of organismic conditions and certain types of incentive stimulation are necessary in creating the appropriate central motive states for both classes of actions. The difference is one of degree and lies mainly in the greater specificity and cyclic nature of the organismic state in the case of the so-called "motivational phenomena."

Though an exact definition of a central motive state should include reference to the particular organismic variables and the incentive stimuli involved, for convenience central motive states may be classified in terms of the types of incentive stimuli involved or the types of transactional actions they promote. Central motive states common to mammals would include those of investigation, fear, irritation (anger), feeding, sex, nesting, and nursing. Those that involve attractive incentive stimuli may be grouped as appetitive states (e.g., investigatory, feeding, sexual, and maternal states), while those that involve repelling incentive stimuli may be grouped as aversive states (e.g., fear and irritation). Typically, adaptive actions involve two or more concurrent central motive states; for example, the "territorial defense" of a postparturient bitch may be the outcome of nursing, fear, and irritation motivational states, and "exploratory behavior" of a rat, say, in an open-field test, may involve investigatory and fear states (Glickman & Schiff, 1967; Montgomery, 1955).

Neural Substrate and Mechanisms

At which brain sites, and in what ways, are the various central motive states generated? Working within the broad assumption that the hypothalamic-limbic neural systems form the main loci of motivational processes, there are three specific questions that need to be answered: (a) What structures are the loci of the neural events representing various aspects of organismic state? (b) What structures are the loci of neural events representing various motivational features of incentive objects? (c) What are the manner and mechanisms of the interaction of the two sets of neural events? These questions may be discussed in relation to the working model shown in Figure 9.1.

According to this model, there exist at least three different types of structures in the hypothalamic-limbic system. First, there are structures whose neurons are sensitive to variations in the humoral aspects of organismic condition. When metabolic variation in a particular blood variable, such as the level of glucose, some hormone, or osmolarity, reaches a certain critical value, the neural activity in the relevant structure is changed; its altered neural output then usually results in certain regulatory viscerosomatic reactions. Such regulatory structures (e.g., the ventromedial and para-ventricular nuclei) lie mainly in the hypothalamus. Their destruction, or the interruption of their outflow, produces marked regulatory deficits (e.g., disorders of glucostatic, osmotic, liptostatic, and thermostatic controls) without permanently disrupting the mechanisms of directed actions such as the instrumental and consummatory acts of eating and drinking (see Hoebel, 1971; Epstein, 1971; Teitelbaum, Cheng, & Rozin, 1969). Thus, while their activity may influence behavior indirectly through regulatory changes in organismic condition, these regulatory structures are probably not themselves the loci of central motive states—the places of interaction of the neural representations of incentive and organismic variables.

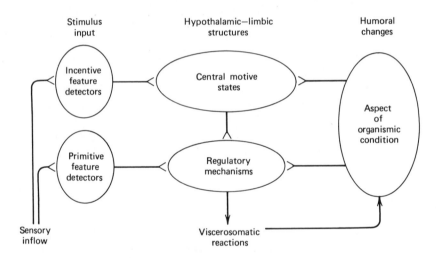

Figure 9.1.   A schematic plan of hypothalamic-limbic structures involved in the motivational function. It is suggested that while the hypothalamic structures serve mainly regulatory functions, the structures that are the main loci of central motive states are the forebrain limbic structures.

Structures of the hypothalamic-limbic system of the second type are "sensory regulatory," which receive neural impulses representing certain primitive aspects of environmental or internal stimulus changes. This sensory inflow is poorly differentiated (mainly gross quality and intensity) input from external and internal stimulus changes, such as those representing tastes, odors, light-intensity variations associated with the light-dark cycle, as well as various somesthetic stimuli representing states of gastric distension, muscle tonus, general malaise, etc. In recent years a substantial amount of evidence has accumulated showing the existence of paths of transmission to the hypothalamic-limbic system that are largely independent of the more highly differentiated "primary" pathways and thalamocortical projections (see Nauta & Haymaker, 1969). Olfacto-hypothalamic connections, retino-hypothalamic connections, gustatory-hypothalamic connections, and the connections between the central gray and the hypothalamus may be the transmission routes for such primitive motivational information. The structures that receive such information are presumably certain hypothalamic nuclei (Le Magnen, 1971; Snowden, 1970) that produce hormonal and other regulatory changes through the autonomic nervous system. Again, though the output of these structures may contribute to the generation of central motive states indirectly, it is unlikely that these structures themselves are the loci of central motive states.

The third type of hypothalamic-limbic structures are the ones containing the sites of various central motive states. According to the present view, neurons at these sites are specialized with respect to both their chemical properties and their sensory connections. This differentiation makes each site specially suited for combined representation of certain aspects of organismic variables and certain features of environmental objects. The features of objects represented in these structures are the incentive features—odors that please, tastes that displease, visual stimuli that are interesting, sounds that startle, etc. The pathways of hypothalamic-limbic representation of such incentive features of objects are probably different from the primary thalamo cortical projections that form the basis of finer discriminations of stimuli with respect to their location, quality, intensity, duration, and the like.

A line of experimental research suggested by this model would focus on elucidating the specific sites and mechanisms of neural interactions underlying various central motive states. The model requires that particular sites or neuronal groups in the hypothalamic-limbic system be differentiated in terms of their sensory connections and their chemical properties. Thus there are two experimental questions to ask: (a) Are the sensory consequences of incentive stimulation, in fact, represented in the hypothalamic-limbic structures—that is, does incentive stimulation reach the limbic system? (b) Are the neuronal groups at various limbic sites in fact distinguishable in terms of their chemical properties? These questions are being studied by several investigators and the general answer to them appears to be an affirmative one (e.g., Campbell, Bindra, Krebs, & Ferenchak, 1969; Krebs & Bindra, 1971; Krebs, Bindra, & Campbell, 1969; Norgren, 1970; Pfaff, 1968; Pfaff & Pfaffmann, 1969).

There is reason to believe that sites where central motive states are normally generated are more likely to be situated in the *forebrain* limbic structures, particularly the amygdaloid complex and the septal region, rather than in the hypothalamus. For one thing, circumsection of the hypothalamus does not permanently eradicate actions directed at particular classes of incentives, such as food (Ellison, 1968; Ellison, Sorenson, & Jacobs, 1970). For another, the "moods" that frequently persist following emotional or motivational arousal suggest that, once generated, a central motive state tends to persist for some time even after the generating conditions are no longer present. This implies that the relevant sites must lie in structures more susceptible than others to poststimulation reverberatory activity. And there is considerable evidence to show that, unlike the hypothalamus, the forebrain limbic structures are highly susceptible to poststimulation reverberatory activity (Racine, 1972; Walker & Udvarhelvi, 1965). Again, the species-typical actions produced by electrical stimulation of hypothalamic sites are highly "stimulation bound." For example, a satiated rat being stimulated in the lateral hypothalamus eats as long as the stimulation lasts, but, on its termination, immediately stops eating and displays no further interest in food until the stimulation is reapplied (N. E. Miller, 1957). Similarly, stimulation-induced copulation in the male rat is terminated as soon as the stimulation of the appropriate anterior hypothalamic site is stopped (e.g., Caggiula, 1970; Vaughan & Fisher, 1962). By contrast, the behavior produced by the electrical stimulation of the amygdaloid and septal sites, though quite variable, may be noted for several minutes after the cessation of stimulation. Psychiatric patients with electrode implantations in these forebrain limbic areas report the existence of a prolonged mood (usually unpleasant in the case of amygdaloid stimulation, and essentially pleasant in the case of septal stimulation) following the cessation of electrical self-stimulation (Heath, John, & Fontana, 1968; Stevens, Mark, Erwin, Pacheco, & Suematsu, 1969). Finally, conditioned stimuli paired with eating induced by hypothalamic stimulation do not become effective stimuli for producing eating, but conditioned stimuli paired with eating induced by hippocampal stimulation do become effective conditioned stimuli (Milgram, Grant, & Stockman, 1975). Thus it appears more likely that the forebrain limbic structures rather than the hypothalamus are the loci of sites of central motive states (Mogenson, 1974).

If the hypothalamus is not itself the locus of central motive states, what exactly is its contribution to motivational processes? Two fragments of an answer to this question are discernible in the current work. First, as noted above, the hypothalamus contains nuclei that are important in the regulation of organismic variables. Damage to these nuclei, or to their neural inputs or outputs, may be expected to disrupt normal motivational processes by producing abnormal organismic conditions (e.g., by increasing or decreasing the normal levels of insulin, glucose, gonadal hormones). Second, it has also been noted above that certain gross aspects of external and bodily stimuli may be projected to the hypothalamus. These exteroceptive and bodily sensory projections, apart from influencing regulatory functions, may also influence neural activity in the essential sites of central motive states. For example, sensory inflow arising from an empty stomach, taste of food, tumescent genital organs, or muscular tension may be transmitted through the hypothalamus to the forebrain limbic structures. The existence of several neurochemically distinguishable ascending pathways in the medial forebrain bundle (Ungerstedt, 1971) is consistent with the idea that the hypothalamus relays motivationally pertinent sensory inflow to the forebrain limbic structures, which contain the loci of central motive states. However, as I shall explain below, this idea should not be taken to mean that each neurochemically distinct pathway is exclusively tied to a particular motivational state, type of behavior, or function (e.g., reinforcement). The general working assumption that appears plausible is that the basis of the demonstrably important role of hypothalamus in the production of species-typical actions, as well as in intracranial self-stimulation, lies in the importance of the hypothalamus as the locus of motivationally pertinent ascending sensory inflow (Marshall & Teitelbaum, 1974). The traditional idea that the hypothalamus exerts its motivational influence primarily through descending neural discharge on specific motor structures (Glickman & Schiff, 1967) must now be considerably revised.

Note that while the present view postulates specific sites for each different class of central motive states, it recognizes that any given interactional variable may be represented at several sites and may contribute to the generation of different central motive states (see Figure 9.2). Thus, interactions between neural consequences of low blood-sugar level and of smell of food may take place at one site, while interactions between the neural consequences of low blood-sugar and an attack stimulus may take place at another site. The same organismic variable or incentive-stimulus features may enter into different interactions at different sites.

It should be noted also that typically two or more central motive states are active at the same time, and the behavioral outcome is influenced jointly by them. For example, in the course of moving around in its natural environment a squirrel may come across a piece of food. The squirrel may stop and sniff at the food and begin eating it. However, any unfamiliar passing sound or sight may make the animal stop eating, glance around, and quickly run up a tree, leaving the food behind. Eating in rodents is hardly ever an uninterrupted continuous affair. Apparently, in their natural environment, animals are alert to dangers at all times, and are capable of quickly switching, say, from eating to escaping, or eating to nesting, and vice versa. It must be

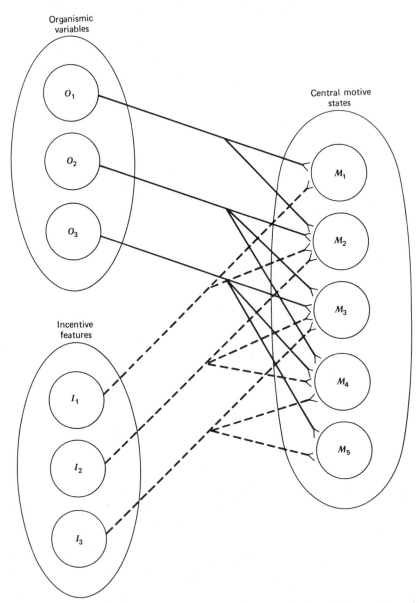

Figure 9.2. A schematic plan showing how the same organismic variables and incentive features may contribute to the generation of different central motive states, and how a certain response may be instigated by two or more different central motive states, acting alone or jointly.

assumed then that the array of various appetitive and aversive incentive stimuli may create several different central motive states of varying strengths, and that the observed action at any given moment is an outcome of the interaction of the separate influences of each central motive state on response producing mechanisms.

THE MODES OF MOTIVATIONAL INFLUENCE ON BEHAVIOR

The obvious next question concerns the processes by which a central motive state, once generated, promotes certain types of actions. There are two separate problems here: (1) the determination of the goal of the action—the object to which the behavior is addressed, and (2) the determination of the specific form of the instrumental, transactional, and regulatory outputs of the animal.

Determination of Goal Object

The essential question is this: How does it come about that, typically, an animal directs its actions in relation to an object that is appropriate to its current organismic condition? How does hunger make *food* the goal object, and thirst *water*, but not vice versa? This central question of motivation found no satisfactory answer in the traditional behavior theories, especially those that regarded homeostatic "drives"—organismic condition per se—as the main motivational factor (e.g., Hull, 1943; Mowrer, 1939; Spence, 1960). In general, the traditional theorists regarded motivational processes to be merely instigational, not directional in terms of what the animal would do; the directionality or response selection was attributed to the acquired stimulus-response organizations called "habits" (Hull, 1943) or means-end readinesses called "expectancies" (Tolman, 1932). They gave no systematic account of how response selection and motivation combine to make the animal act in relation to appropriate goal objects (for a fuller discussion of this point, see Bindra, 1969).

My view is that a goal-object is an (unconditioned or conditioned) incentive object. In other words, the object in relation to which the animal acts is the same incentive object some of whose stimulus features have contributed to the generation of the prevailing central motive state. For example, a food object provides the incentive stimuli required for generating an "eating" motive state (when the animal is food depleted), and also serves as the goal object to which an animal's approach and consummatory actions are addressed. Thus, in the present scheme there is no special problem of integrating the appropriate goal object with a given motivational state; normally, the goal itself is an object providing the incentive stimuli that, together with the organismic condition, create the central motive state that influences behavior in relation to those stimuli.

By what processes does a prevailing central motive state promote action in relation to the goal (incentive) stimuli that created the central motive state? Note that, in the absence of a particular central motive state (e.g., an eating state), the animal would not act in relation to a certain incentive object (e.g., food), but the animal would act in relation to the same object (approach it, sniff it, eat it, etc.) if that central motive state were generated. How does the central motive state enhance actions in relation to that object (e.g., food)? Does the motivational discharge (from a central motive state) act primarily on central motor processes or on central perceptual ones? Does the motivational discharge selectively raise the excitation level of certain motor commands, say, those of underlying transactional acts (e.g., the motor commands involved in biting, chewing, salivating, and swallowing in the case of an eating central motive state)? Or does the motivational discharge selectively raise the excitation level of certain gnostic-assemblies, say, those representing the important features of certain incentive objects? Or does motivational discharge influence both motor and perceptual processes?

It is unlikely that the motivational discharge directly excites motor commands. The actions performed in relation to an incentive object, such as food, may be highly variable. The exact course of instrumental acts may vary greatly depending on the location of the food in relation to the animal. Even consummatory acts may vary considerably depending on whether the food is in the form of hard pellets, a mash, or dissolved in a liquid. The actual acts that an animal may perform in relation to an incentive object may vary so greatly from occasion to occasion, or from one animal to another, that the motor-influence hypothesis would require one to postulate that every motivational influence has an excitatory influence on all motor commands. This may well be true, but it does not provide a basis for explaining the selective promotion by a motivational state of actions in relation to a particular class of incentive objects. Another argument against the motor influence hypothesis is that the creation of different motivational states in a given situation does not always produce different types of acts. For example, the patterns of general activity displayed by rats under motivational states of eating, drinking, and copulation do not differ from each other in a way that would suggest that different motor commands are being facilitated by each motivational state. The instrumental and consummatory acts shown when the animal is given access to an appetitive incentive object are of course quite different, but the anticipatory motivational excitement is characterized largely by the same types of acts in all cases. Thus, at least within the class of appetitive motivational states, the differential promotion of actions does not seem attributable to differential facilitation of specific motor commands.

It would appear then that the influence of motivational states is directed primarily at the central perceptual representation of the relevant goal (incentive) objects. It may be supposed that a central motive state, once generated by certain motivational properties of an object, excites the gnostic-assemblies representing the other important features of that object (see Figure 9.3). Thus, in the case of an eating central motive state (e), it may be supposed that the odor of food (f) may contribute to the generation of that state, and this means that the gnostic-assemblies representing the various important features of food (e.g., visual features) would become strongly excited, and thus the animal would act in relation to food rather than in relation to objects whose representations are less strongly excited.

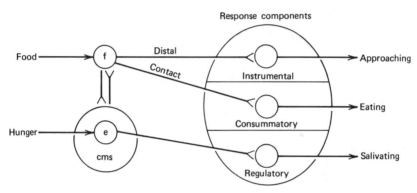

Figure 9.3. A schematic plan of the hypothetical process by which an unconditioned (incentive) stimulus produces particular viscerosomatic reactions and instrumental and transactional acts. The figure shows the consequences of the presentation of food when the organismic state is that of hunger. See text for further explanation. Copyright 1974 by the American Psychological Association. Reprinted by permission.

In effect, then, my hypothesis is that motivational processes influence behavior by modulating the degree of excitation of pexgos of (unconditioned or conditioned—see below) incentive stimuli. The potency of a pexgo in producing a response depends on its excitation level, and, as noted earlier, the excitation level is determined not only by stimulus intensity but also by the novelty (or familiarity) of the stimulus. Motivational processes may now be considered as another determinant of the level of excitation of gnostic-assemblies representing particular stimuli. The process by which a particular motivational state, say, eating, has a selective influence on the excitation level of a certain type of gnostic-assemblies (i.e., those representing food) is illustrated in Figure 9.3. Under the combined influence of hunger (food depletion) and incentive stimulation (say, smell of food), a strong eating central motive state is created and this selectively enhances the excitation level of the gnostic-assemblies of food odor. This activation of a strong pexgo of food odor is what makes food the goal object, that is, leads to action in relation to food. There may also be a general influence of the central motive state on a wide variety of sensory-motor coordinations usually involved in appetitive actions. However, the specific influences that lead to the occurrence of particular goal-directed acts arise from an enhancement of the perception of goal stimuli. In attributing the motivational influence on action to the generation of a strong pexgo of an incentive (or unconditioned) stimulus, the present approach resembles that of Asratyan (1974).

Processes Determining the Form of Action

Turn now to the motivational influence on response output: How does a central motive state influence the probability and promptness of the occurrence of particular aspects of actions in relation to the goal object of the moment? In broad terms, the answer I propose is that the exact way in which the motivational influence is exerted differs for the three major aspects of any animal action, viscerosomatic reactions, transactional acts, and instrumental acts. Consider these in turn.

Viscerosomatic Regulatory Reactions. There is considerable evidence to show that autonomic-somatic regulations linked to a central motive state may be dissociated from the particular instrumental and transactional acts promoted by that central motive state. For example, a conditioned stimulus that signals food typically leads to the onset of salivation *before* the animal makes any instrumental or consummatory responses. Further, in a fixed-ratio schedule of food reinforcement, the instrumental response may have to be repeated a number of times before food is delivered; in such cases salivation does not accompany each response but begins to occur toward the end of each fixed-ratio cycle (Ellison & Konorski, 1966). Similarly, in the case of learning to avoid an electric shock, the occurrence of each instrumental response may or may not be accompanied by autonomic-somatic changes (e.g., heart rate, breathing) that are produced by a conditioned signal for shock (e.g., A. H. Black, 1971; de Toledo & Black, 1966). These observations suggest that the neural pathways by which a central motive state produces internal autonomic-somatic reactions are probably different from those involved in transactional and instrumental acts in relation to environmental objects.

The simplest assumption to make in connection with viscerosomatic reactions is that each central motive state influences fairly directly certain autonomic mechanisms. The activation of each such mechanism would lead to a certain pattern of autonomic-somatic discharge, producing a variety of visceral reactions and tonic skeletal changes. There is probably a rough pattern of changes or "emotional expressions" corresponding to each major class of central motive state (Tomkins, 1962), but this is difficult to demonstrate because the same autonomic mechanisms are also influenced by the ongoing internal metabolic factors and by the metabolic consequences of the animal's ongoing muscular activity. Thus, a defensive central motive state may activate a certain specific pattern of autonomic discharge, but the observed reactions over time would also depend on the internal homeostatic mechanisms and on the consequences of fighting or other efforts of the animal. There are in fact marked individual differences in the intensity and the details of viscerosomatic changes accompanying central motive states (see Bindra, 1959, Chap. 8; Gellhorn & Loofbourrow, 1963). To the extent that viscerosomatic reactions are produced by a central motive state (i.e., by the interaction of incentive stimulation and the prevailing organismic state), they may be regarded as indices of emotional or motivational arousal. Though they are dependent on incentive stimulation, these motivationally produced reactions are not normally addressed or goal-directed in relation to any particular environmental object.

The mechanisms that produce the various patterns of autonomic-somatic changes presumably involve the nuclei of the midbrain reticular system. The descending input to these could come from the sites of central motive states through the periventricular zone of the hypothalamus, which appears to be involved in the homeostatic regulation of viscerosomatic regulations.

Transactional Acts. Though transactional acts appear to be as "automatic" as viscerosomatic reactions, the former are different in that they are addressed to specific (goal) objects in the environment. This means that transactional acts must be dependent, at least to some extent, on ongoing sensory information from the goal object, and any action must require moment-to-moment adjustments to the details of sensory input from the object. Acts of biting, chewing, and swallowing involved in eating food are guided by visual, cutaneous, and taste stimuli; consummatory and defensive acts involving two animals (e.g., copulation or fighting) require continual mutual adjustments of posture and action.

There is reason to believe that act-assemblies comprising most transactional acts may be located, for the most part, in the midbrain tegmental region. For one thing, electrical stimulation of certain sites in the tegmentum reliably produces fairly integrated components of various appetitive and aversive emotional expressions even in the absence of the relevant stimulus objects (Delgado, 1964); in contrast, stimulation of sites in the hypothalamic-limbic system seldom produces such components in the absence of appropriate stimulus objects (Flynn, 1967; Mendelson, 1972). For another, the type of contact stimuli that are frequently involved in the guidance of transactional acts are well represented in the tegmentum through afferents from the spino-thalamic tract (see Nauta & Haymaker, 1969).

If we assume, then, that most of the transactional act-assemblies are located in the midbrain tegmentum, it would seem reasonable to suggest that the motivational influence on these act-assemblies is transmitted through the descending components of the medial forebrain bundle and the dorsal longitudinal fasciculus. These descending components originate partly in the forebrain limbic structures and partly in the hypothalamus. An arrangement of this type would make the activation of any act-assembly dependent jointly on the nature of the prevailing central motive state and the discriminative properties of the contact (tactual, gustatory) stimuli arising from the goal objects. It would also make the occurrence of a transactional act independent of any specific instrumental acts, which typically involve distal stimuli and the refined discriminative apparatus of the cerebral cortex. This suggestion is supported by the fact that certain cortical lesions may make rats incapable of displaying instrumental acts in relation to food, without lowering their desire or ability to ingest food placed on the lips or tongue (Rice, 1971).

Thus, the pathways that carry neural influences from the sites of central motive states to the mesencephalic sites of viscerosomatic and transactional response components are very likely descending fibers from the forebrain limbic structure (Bergquist, 1970; Paxinos & Bindra, 1972; Routtenberg, 1971). In contrast, the act-assemblies involved in instrumental acts, involving the detailed discriminative aspects of stimuli, would appear to lie in the neocortex.

Instrumental Acts. While specific patterns of viscerosomatic reactions and transactional acts are, for the most part, closely linked to certain central motive states, instrumental actions do not bear such a close relation to particular motivational states. Thus, the same instrumental action (e.g., an approach or a lever-pressing response) may be used in relation to defensive, investigatory, feeding, sexual, or maternal motivational states. As well, the same motivational state may determine the occurrence of a variety of quite distinct instrumental actions. It is the processes and neural mechanisms underlying this flexible linkage of the various motivational states to a great variety of instrumental actions that are our primary concern.

The traditional views of instrumental behavior (e.g., Hull, 1943; Tolman, 1932) sought to explain flexible linkage of instrumental actions in terms of learned linkages of the response selection factor ("habit" or "expectancy"). However, since the early theorists made the response selection factor quite independent of the response instigational ("motivational") factor, they could not explain how a particular instrumental action gets linked to the appropriate motivational state in any given instance of behavior. Why does the feeding motivational state instigate an instrumental action that leads to food, and the sexual motivational state instigate an instrumental action that leads to a sexual partner? The problem is to explain flexible linkage as well as the appropriateness of the linkage for effective action on any given occasion.

According to the theoretical scheme proposed here, the forms of action— the activation of particular act-assemblies—is determined jointly by the current sensory input as it is modulated by the motivational influence of the prevailing central motive state or states. This means that the action performed is not first selected and then instigated by the motivational influence. Rather the selection of an action and its instigation go hand in hand; the motivational influence is an intrinsic part of the response selection processes.

While transactional acts are elicited by contact with primary incentive objects themselves, instrumental actions are directed toward stimuli that have become signals for the primary incentive objects. These signals or *conditioned incentive stimuli* serve as guides to the animal for the locations where, and times when, certain primary incentives are likely to be found. Distal stimuli (visual, auditory, olfactory) arising from an incentive object itself come to serve as conditioned or "secondary" incentive stimuli for all normal members of the species. Further, neutral stimuli (contact or distal), arising from nonincentive or neutral objects that happen to surround or be consistently related to the primary incentive objects, acquire conditioned incentive properties that vary from one member of the species to the next, according to individual experience.

The process by which initially neutral stimuli acquire incentive properties and acquire control over response output may be regarded as an extension of the motivational processes determining what the goal object would be. That is, a central motive state enhances the excitation level of pexgos of the same incentive stimuli that contributed to the generation of *that* central motive state. Consider a concrete example. A hungry rat is placed in a chamber to which it is well accustomed and in which it readily eats when food is delivered directly into its mouth. Now a light-panel is lighted for a few seconds before each delivery of food into the mouth. How does the light-panel acquire conditioned incentive properties and affect subsequent behavior of the rat?

After the conditioning has proceeded for some trials, the light-panel may not only excite its own pexgo but may also, through learned contingency organizations, excite pexgos representing gustatory incentive stimuli (in the absence of food in the mouth). This would result in the generation of a weak central motive state which in turn would enhance the pexgo of the light-panel as well as the pexgo of food (Figure 9.4). The enhancement of the light-panel pexgo would cause the animal to act in relation to the light-panel, and the general influence of the eating central motive state, including the enhanced excitation of the food pexgo, may cause the activation of some of the viscero-somatic and transactional components of eating (salivation, licking, biting). Thus the rat's behavior in relation to the light-panel is likely to be that of

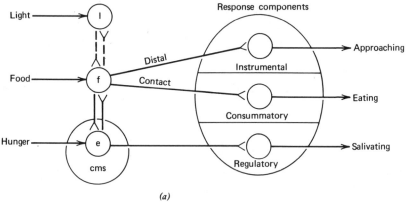

(a)

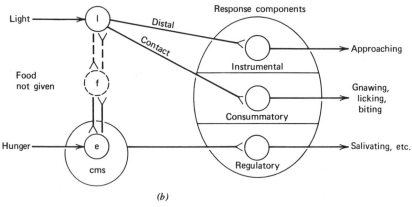

(b)

Figure 9.4. A schematic plan of the hypothetical process by which an initially neutral stimulus can become capable of producing a response. Section (*a*) shows what happens during the early stage of conditioning. The pairing of a light with food results in the learning of a CS:US contingency, which is shown as broken-line reciprocal connections between the central representations of light (*l*) and food (*f*). Section (*b*) shows what happens after conditioning has been successfully achieved. On a test trial, when the presentation of food is withheld, the central representation of light *l*, through its learned contingency with food, excites *f* and thereby creates the eating central motive state, which then enchances the excitation level of first *f* and then *l*. See text for further explanation. Copyright 1974 by the American Psychological Association. Reprinted by permission.

approach, investigation, licking, and biting. This would continue until the food is delivered in the mouth. As soon as the food is delivered, the degree of excitation of the food pexgo would become greater than that of the pexgo of light-panel. Hence the rat would now approach the food and start eating it, ignoring the light-panel.

THE PROBLEM OF ACQUIRED MOTIVATION

As explained above, stimuli that are initially motivationally neutral (non-incentive stimuli) may acquire motivational properties—capacity to generate central motive states—through individual experience of the animal. The next question is this: What changes in the animal are the basis of the motivation-generating capability by initially neutral, conditioned, stimuli?

There are three possibilities, and these may be discussed with reference to eating and food. The conditioned stimulus may acquire the property of producing either the neural consequences of the food depleted organismic condition (hunger), or of producing the neural consequences of incentive stimulation (food pexgo), or both. These three alternatives are shown in Figure 9.5. In the first alternative (*a*) the conditioned stimulus generates a food pexgo but does not produce hunger; according to this, the conditioned stimulus should be capable of creating the eating central motive state and food-oriented actions *in the absence of food*, so long as the animal is made hungry in the normal way. In the second alternative (*b*) the conditioned stimulus produces hunger, but does not generate a food pexgo; according to this, the conditioned stimulus should be capable of creating the eating central motive state and food-oriented actions *in a satiated animal*, so long as food itself is present. In the third alternative (*c*) the conditioned stimulus both generates a food pexgo and produces hunger; according to this the conditioned stimulus alone should be sufficient to create the eating central motive state and food-oriented behavior *in the absence of both hunger and food*. Now, the third possibility is clearly not correct. Conditioned stimuli do not generate motivational states and appropriate behavior in the absence of both hunger and food; for example, in Pavlovian experiments the metronome did not produce a conditioned salivation if the dog was neither hungry nor offered food. But the other two possibilities, *a* and *b*, are worth examining.

Acquired or Conditioned Incentives

Since the time of Wolfe's (1936) demonstration that monkeys would work for tokens that could be exchanged for a desired food, there has accumulated a great deal of evidence showing that initially neutral conditioned stimuli

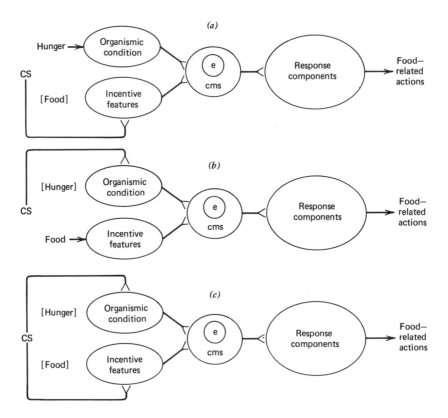

Figure 9.5. A schematic plan showing three possible mechanisms by which an initially neutral conditioned stimulus acquires motivational properties. It is suggested that the conditioned stimulus serves as a substitute for the incentive stimulus, as in (a), not for the organismic state, as in (b), or for both, as in (c).

that signal primary incentive objects soon acquire some of the motivational properties of the primary incentive object (for a review, see Wike, 1966). According to our earlier discussion, such conditioned incentive stimuli would be motivationally effective—would be capable of generating a central motive state—only under appropriate organismic conditions. A conditioned tone that has acquired food-incentive properties ceases to be effective in producing salivation or other food-related acts when the animal is not hungry, but becomes effective again as soon as the animal becomes hungry.

Note that the learning of the contingency between the conditioned stimulus (S_1) and a primary incentive stimulus (S_2) merely requires that the two occur contiguously and be observed to be concomitant (see Chapter 6), so that the pexgo of S_1 would be able to activate a pexgo of S_2. It is not necessary that S_2 be motivationally effective at the time of the contiguous occurrence of S_1 and S_2. For example, a tone (S_1) would become capable of activating a pexgo of food (S_2) even if the animal is not hungry at the time of the conditioning trials; later, when the animal is hungry, S_1 would be effective in generating the eating motivational state through its ability to activate the pexgo of food (S_2). That this is so is shown by certain types of latent learning experiments. If a rat, neither hungry nor thirsty, is exposed to food (not eaten) in one goal box of a Y-maze and to water (not drunk) in the other goal box, then on test trials when the rat is hungry or thirsty, it would go to the appropriate arm of the maze (Thistlethwaite, 1951). Apparently, when the animal is hungry, the sight of the food goal box but not of the water goal box creates the eating central motive state, and the animal then acts in relation to that box; the reverse happens when the animal is thirsty.

Experiments demonstrating sensory preconditioning (e.g., Brogden, 1947), also indicate that potentially motivating signal learning can occur in the absence of the generation of the central motive state that the signal would be able to generate after conditioning. For example, as a preconditioning stimulus, a tone (S_T) may be paired with a light (S_L) that signals an incentive stimulus (S^I) such as food or an electric shock. After this preconditioning training, the light may be paired with the incentive stimulus ($S_L:S^I$). In subsequent test trials with the tone, it is found that the tone has acquired motivational properties through its contingency with the light, even though the tone and light were never paired in the presence of the incentive stimulus.

The acquisition of incentive motivational properties by initially neutral conditioned stimuli does not mean that the acts performed in relation to the conditioned and primary incentive stimuli would be exactly the same. Only the instrumental acts are likely to be the same, because instrumental acts are performed in relation to distal incentive stimuli, and these acts would necessarily comprise general approach or withdrawal actions. Thus, a light-panel that signals food for a hungry animal, would make the animal move toward the light-panel, sniff the panel, manipulate it, etc., so long as the primary incentive, food, is *not* made available. These instrumental acts would be similar to the acts displayed in relation to food-at-a-distance. However, while on reaching and making contact with the food, the animal would begin to eat it, no similar consummatory acts would be shown in relation to the light-panel because it does not have the necessary stimulus features (odor, taste, etc.) of food. Thus, the animal's acts in relation to the conditioned stimuli would be restricted to whatever acts can be performed in relation to the light-panel; what the acquired incentive motivational properties of a conditioned stimulus do is simply make the animal act in relation to that stimulus rather than in relation to other stimuli in the situation, but the form of the acts remains dependent on the prevailing central motive state and sensory features of the conditioned stimulus, not on the features of the (absent) primary incentive object. However, if a conditioned incentive stimulus resembles the primary incentive object in some respects, the animal is likely to perform some components of consummatory acts in relation to the conditioned stimulus. For example, a hungry pigeon will peck at a round object resembling food more than at objects of other shapes (Blough, 1961; Breland & Breland, 1966); a hungry cow will lick the rope attached to the hopper of hay when the hopper is not yet open; and a monkey will chew and suck tokens that have been conditioned to food (in the absence of food itself). Viscerosomatic reactions, since they are the direct outcomes of the generation of a central motive state, would be the same when elicited by distal conditioned stimuli as when elicited by incentive stimuli. Thus changes in heart rate produced by the odor of a food would be similar to the change produced by a tone signal indicating food. However, when the animal makes contact with food, the additional taste and tactual factors would make the central motive state more intense, with a corresponding increase in the strength of viscerosomatic reactions.

Are Organismic Conditions Learnable?

If motivation can be learned in the sense that initially neutral stimuli may become conditioned incentive stimuli signaling primary incentives, can it also be learned in the sense that initially ineffective stimuli may become capable of producing specific organismic conditions? Can a conditioned stimulus become an effective stimulus for producing the organismic condition of, say, hunger, in the absence of the experimental manipulations (e.g., food deprivation) that normally produce that organismic condition? This question has traditionally been posed as: Are "drives" conditionable? Much confusion surrounds this question, some of which arises from the ambiguity of the term "drive."

The conditioning of a "drive," such as hunger, means essentially that a conditioned stimulus, such as a tone or a visual pattern, that is paired with the bodily condition produced by food deprivation, becomes capable of creating some of the neural consequences of that bodily condition even when the animal is not food deprived. The usual criterion of conditioned hunger is the promotion of eating by the conditioned stimulus when the animal is more or less satiated. A critical question is whether a conditioned increase in eating may be taken as a valid indicator of conditioned hunger. In order to use conditioned eating as an indicator of conditioned hunger, as opposed to conditioned incentive stimulation, it is necessary that the conditioned stimulus be paired with the bodily condition of food deprivation but *not* with food (or eating) in the conditioning situation. Experiments that have taken this precaution and have used appropriate control procedures have in general failed to show significant amounts of conditioned eating or conditioned drinking. At best the reported conditioned effects are brief and transitory, and completely negative results are frequently obtained. Conditioned increases in eating and drinking have been reported with the use of insulin or hypertonic saline as an unconditioned "stimulus." But these results appear to be outcomes of the distress-reducing effects of eating and drinking (avoidance learning) rather than of conditioned hunger or thirst as such (Mineka, Seligman, Hetrick, & Zuelzer, 1972; Siegel & Nettleton, 1970).

In general, those who have reviewed the literature on attempts to condition hunger or thirst have found no compelling evidence that such conditioning occurs at all or that it is an important aspect of the normal motivational processes (Cofer & Appley, 1964; Cravens & Renner, 1970; D'Amato, 1974). Put in the language of the traditional learning theory, the conclusion may be drawn that there is no such thing as conditioned or secondary hunger or thirst, but, as seen in the last section, there is such a thing as conditioned or secondary incentive stimulation (or reinforcement). The basis of conditioned central motive states of eating and drinking lies in conditioned incentive stimuli, not in conditioned "drives" or organismic conditions.

However, indirect evidence suggests that hunger or thirst might be conditionable. For example, if a conditioned stimulus regularly accompanies instrumental responses that lead to eating (produced by a central motive state generated by food-deprivation *and* food-incentive stimulation), the conditioned stimulus may continue to promote the instrumental responses even when the animal is satiated. By analogy to the persistence of instrumental responses in extinction, Morgan (1974) has called this phenomenon "resistance to satiation." It can be argued that such persistence or "functional autonomy" of instrumental behavior after satiation means that an appropriate central motive state is generated, and since the animal is satiated, the conditioned stimulus must have somehow created "hunger" in the (satiated) animal.

There are two points to note concerning an interpretation of resistance to satiation in terms of conditioned hunger. First, if a central motive state is created by a conditioned stimulus in the absence of food deprivation, the state is very weak and short-lived; for example, an animal, while satiated, may make some instrumental responses that lead to food, but it is not likely to eat the food when it reaches it, and even the instrumental responses are not likely to be repeated often. Since satiation is a matter of degree and the generation of a central motive state is a matter of interaction of the organismic condition with incentive stimulation, it is quite likely that a weak central motive state is generated on occasions even if the animal is relatively satiated. Second, it is possible to explain the persistence of instrumental responses in other terms, without invoking conditioned hunger. For example, it has been shown that animals develop preference for certain places that have become familiar or safe, or places where predictable or controllable events occur (Mitchell, Scott, & Williams, 1973; Wallace, Osborne, Norborg, & Fantino, 1973). An animal that has followed a certain consistent regime in a certain location may thus make instrumental responses to reach that location and perform instrumental responses that produce some predictable effects, without regard to food. This same interpretation may also apply to the phenomenon of "working" for food in the presence of free food (Wallace et al., 1973). While the phenomenon of resistance to satiation is an interesting one to unravel, and its parallels with resistance to extinction are intriguing, it cannot be regarded as providing decisive evidence for the conditionability of hunger (as an organismic condition).

In contrast to the lack of success in attempts to condition hunger and thirst, or the so-called "appetitive drives," it is often asserted that "aversive drives" can be readily conditioned. However, a closer examination shows some terminological confusion. What are called "aversive drives" are not produced by the normal metabolic processes such as those that produce the organismic conditions of hunger or thirst, but are produced by specific incentive stimuli that result in a distinctive sensory neural inflow to the central nervous system. Thus, when an animal is given an electric shock in contiguity with a tone as the conditioned stimulus, the tone acquires some of the (aversive) incentive properties of the shock through the contingency organization that links the pexgo of the tone to the pexgo of the discomfort produced by the shock. Clearly, this is not the conditioning of "drive" in the sense of an organismic condition, but the conditioning of an incentive-produced sensory input. Thus, the apparent difference in the conditionability of "appetitive drives" and "aversive drives" probably arises from a difference in the meaning of "drive" in the two cases; in the former case it means some organismic condition as such, while in the latter it means sensory input provided by an (aversive) incentive stimulus.

The interpretation of the conditioned effects of rewarding intracranial electrical stimulation parallels that of the conditioned effects of electric shock. The rewarding conditioned intracranial stimulation is incentive stimulation that produces a certain central appetitive motive state (when the animal is in a certain organismic condition). Whether the electrical stimulation produces some visceral reactions whose sensory feedback activates pleasurable effects, or whether the electrical stimulation directly activates the brain sites of the same visceral projections is not important from the present point of view. What is important is that the conditioned stimulus is consistently followed by the generation of a pleasurable effect, and it is this effect to which the pexgo of the conditioned stimulus becomes linked.

Thus, the conditioned stimulus should produce some of the same behavioral consequences (e.g., exploration) as are produced by the unconditioned electrical stimulation, and this does occur (e.g., Bindra & Campbell, 1967; Lenzer, 1972; Trowill, Panksepp, & Gandelman, 1969). Though the conditioning of rewarding intracranial stimulation is frequently classified as conditioning of "drive" as an organismic condition, the present analysis should make it clear that the basis of this conditioning is the contingency between the conditioned stimulus and the (electrical) incentive stimulation; no conditioning of drive in the sense of organismic conditions is involved.

In order to understand why organismic conditions such as hunger and thirst are not conditionable, it must be remembered (Chapter 6) that conditioning of an organismic condition can occur only if the neural representation of the conditioned stimulus (CS pexgo) is followed by the activation of the neural representation of the unconditioned stimulus (US pexgo) that would somehow produce the to-be-conditioned organismic condition. However, the bodily states of hunger and thirst are not normally produced by any particular (sensory) unconditioned stimulus, but by ongoing metabolic (rather than sensory) processes. Thus no neural basis exists for the conditioning of metabolically produced organismic conditions to a conditioned stimulus.

What can be conditioned are the changes in organismic conditions that are produced through sensory rather than metabolic influences on the autonomic nervous system. These organismic changes are viscerosomatic reactions, highly specific or quite general, produced by the activation of brain sites that control particular organismic factors such as perspiration, salivation, vasoconstriction, insulin release, epinephrine discharge, and changes in heart rate. These viscerosomatic reactions are conditionable only to the extent that their controlling brain (hypothalamic) sites are reached by the central representations (pexgos) of certain unconditioned stimuli. Many viscerosomatic reactions have been successfully conditioned to initially ineffective conditioned stimuli (see Bykov, 1957; Razran, 1961). The basis of the success of such conditioning can be elucidated by considering the Pavlovian conditioning of salivation to a conditioned stimulus, say a tone. The fact that after conditioning, the tone is effective in creating the eating motivational state, as shown by salivary secretion, does not mean that the tone creates the organismic condition of hunger, nor that it creates the neural consequences of food depletion. The instigation of salivation by the tone requires the *prior* existence of the organismic condition of hunger; the tone, which signals food, creates an eating central motive state only if the animal is already food deprived. The basis of the conditioning lies in the learning of a contingency between the conditioned stimulus and food or some other unconditioned stimulus (e.g., acid) that activates one of the autonomic regulating sites that produces salivation. The main point to note is that the conditioned visceral reaction that occurs depends on the linking of the central representation of the conditioned stimulus to central neural representations of the unconditioned stimulus, not on its linking to the neural control of that visceral reaction as such.

The above analysis helps to clarify some of the perplexities arising from the attempts to condition organismic factors by using drugs as the unconditioned agents. Consider studies designed to condition the organismic effects of insulin injections. The main immediate effect of an intraperitoneal insulin injection is hypoglycemia. Until a few years ago, many investigators believed that the hypoglycemic effects of insulin could be conditioned to initially ineffective conditioned stimuli; that a conditioned stimulus, paired with insulin injections leading to hypoglycemia, would also produce hypoglycemia—that is, a conditioned reaction that mimics the unconditioned hypoglycemic effect. However, from the present standpoint, since the circulating insulin produces hypoglycemia by direct action on bodily tissues (increasing their uptake of blood sugar), without requiring mediation through the central nervous system, there is no neural basis for the occurrence of a conditioned hypoglycemic effect, so long as the effect is produced metabolically (e.g., by insulin injection) and not through an unconditioned (environmental) stimulus. Though the evidence was unclear at first, it now seems established that the hypoglycemic effect produced by injecting insulin is not conditionable (Siegel, 1972, 1975). However, according to the above reasoning, a hypoglycemic effect should be conditionable when the conditioned stimulus is paired, not with an injection of insulin, but with some unconditioned stimulus that normally releases insulin through central neural mechanisms. Glucose and foods, given orally, are known to release insulin through a compensatory sugar-regulating mechanism, and thus they may be expected to serve as unconditioned stimuli for conditioning hypoglycemia. Several investigators have reported that such glucose-induced "compensatory" hypoglycemic effects can be reliably conditioned, and it has been shown that the effects are produced through a parasympathetic insulin-releasing mechanism (Deutsch, 1974; Woods, Alexander, & Porte, 1972; Woods & Porte, 1974).

Siegel (1972, 1975) has demonstrated in the rat that, after being paired with insulin injections, a conditioned stimulus produces *hyper*glycemia. The unconditioned stimulus for a hyperglycemic reaction may be provided by the malaise or visceral discomfort caused by insulin injections (Siegel & Nettleton, 1970). What the conditioned stimulus produces, then, is not the "mimicking" organismic change (hypoglycemia) that is directly produced by the peripheral action of insulin and may be intended by the experimenter to be the conditioned reaction, but the "compensatory" effect (hyperglycemia) that is mediated neurally through autonomic regulators that can be reached by environmental unconditioned stimuli.

The main point to note in the above analysis is that conditioned viscerosomatic reactions depend on the linking of the central neural representation of a conditioned stimulus with the central influence of an unconditioned stimulus that can produce autonomic discharges. The exact conditioned reaction that occurs as a consequence of a certain conditioning procedure depends on the nature and extent of the central unconditioned reactions produced. There is little point in arguing whether conditioned visceral reactions mimic unconditioned reactions or compensate for them. Conditioned reactions may be said to mimic the reactions produced by the central influence and to "compensate" for the reactions produced metabolically. Further, in many cases the terms mimicking and compensation may not apply; an insulin injection may lead to changes in vasoconstriction, heart rate, or muscular tremor, but it would be hard to classify these reactions as mimicking or compensatory in relation to the regulation of blood sugar level.

Several casual and experimental observations have shown that insulin release usually becomes conditioned to many environmental stimuli that normally precede food intake, for example, smell and taste of food, time of regular feeding, etc. (see Woods & Porte, 1974). It is possible that such a conditioned insulin-release reaction may generate a momentary tendency to eat even when the animal is relatively satiated (Reynier-Rebuffel, Louis-Sylvestre, & Le Magnen, 1974). According to the present analysis, this kind of conditioned phasic insulin release arises from the association between the conditioned stimuli and the unconditioned stimulus of food; the central reaction to food is insulin release. Such conditioning, therefore, does not contradict the earlier conclusion that organismic conditions produced by metabolic processes (e.g., the peripheral hyperglycemia produced by food) are not conditionable.

The view of the environmental control of drug-induced effects outlined above may prove useful in clarifying the results of experiments on the conditioning of the aversive, euphoric, and viscerosomatic consequences arising from the use of morphine and other opiates.

CHAPTER 10

Attention

As I sit at my desk and write, I am exposed to a barrage of enormously diverse stimulus input: the light in the room, the gurgle of the water flowing through the radiator, the noise of a passing aeroplane, the pressure and temperature gradients that surround my body, the feel of my joints and limbs, the emptiness of my stomach, the sight of the pencil-point on the paper, and so on. Of much of this background stimulation I am for the most part unaware. From time to time, for a moment or two, I may become aware of one of these background stimuli, and may perceive or remember that the light in the room is not strong enough, the radiator should be fixed, I have to make reservations for an aeroplane journey, my feet are too cold, my arthritis is beginning to hurt, I must get something to eat, this pencil needs sharpening, etc. But as I continue writing, the momentary intrusions again dissolve into unawareness. Such continual spontaneous shifts in momentary awareness are commonly described as attentional phenomena: a specific stimulus, memory, idea, etc., seems to get selected from a vast amorphous background of current stimulus input and previously acquired knowledge, is held in awareness as a clear figure for a moment or two, and is then replaced by something else.

This subjective phenomenon of "selective awareness" clearly parallels the behavioral observation that while a multiplicity of current stimuli and stored knowledge contribute to the organization of ongoing adaptive behavior, at any one moment an animal acts in relation to only one or a few of those stimuli, and its response is determined by only a few of the many associations that those stimuli may have with previously acquired knowledge. Such selection from impinging stimuli or "selective perception," as well as from existing knowledge or "selective recall," is essential for producing the specificity of action that is the basis of adaptive behavior. This chapter is concerned with understanding the processes underlying the selectivity in perception and recall.

SELECTIVE PERCEPTION

Without implying any fundamental distinction between the two, it is convenient to differentiate between two types of selective perception. One is selective perception of objects. Since different objects occupy spatially distinctive locations, their identification often involves orientations of the body and sense organs to produce greater stimulus input from certain locations than from others, for example, turning around and looking up to see a singing bird in a tree. The second is selective perception of attributes. Since stimulus attributes may have no spatially distinctive locus, their observation involves "tuning in" certain spatially undifferentiated aspects of a stimulus, for example, observing the color rather than the form of a pencil. Evidence for selective perception of objects is provided by observational acts, such as head turning, visual scanning, sniffing, licking, and manipulating, as they are displayed in exploration and discrimination experiments (Lovejoy, 1968; Mackintosh, 1965; Stollnitz, 1965). Evidence for the selective perception of attributes comes from experiments in which, for example, a subject, hearing several simultaneous conversations, is able to listen and comprehend anything said by a certain male voice, or anything dealing with a certain topic, etc., while ignoring the remaining equally audible conversations (Broadbent, 1958; Neisser, 1964). In selective perception of objects the observer makes certain objects or parts of a situation more effective through his observational acts, which overtly focus his sensory apparatus toward a certain source of stimulus input. In selective perception of attributes the observer utilizes certain aspects of the current sensory inflow more than other aspects through some totally central processes.

Development of Selective Perception

In trying to understand selective processes, it is best to begin by examining the development of the two types of selective perception. The general course of development appears to be one in which the relative control of selection is gradually shifted from the inherent properties of environmental stimuli ("involuntary" or imposed selection) to the slowly developing selective capacities of the observer ("voluntary" or self-controlled selection).

Development of Selective Perception of Objects. When the eyes of a few-days-old human infant are open, they move in conjugate, rhythmic saccades and receive stimulus input from various parts of the visual field (Trevarthen, 1974). If a stimulus of high salience, for example, one with sharp contours or one that is in motion, appears in the visual field, saccadic eye movements may stop and the eyes fixate or track the stimulus. Fixation time may be no more than a few seconds; the fixated stimulus is quickly "lost" by the infant (Kagan, 1971). Clearly whatever visual perception occurs at this stage is dependent on stimulus salience and consists in the elicitation of overt observational acts (eye movements) that are more flighty than stable. By the time the infant reaches the age of about four months, it begins to scan its visual field more systematically by joint head-and-eye saccades (Trevarthen, 1974) and fixates stimuli more effectively. The close relation between the location of visual fixation and location of the test object makes fixation time a good indicator of the duration of selective perception of objects in infants.

At the age of about 6 weeks, the infant begins to show habituation effects. If one of a pair of stimuli (e.g., a daffodil) is presented repeatedly over a few days and then the infant is tested with two stimuli (a daffodil, and, say, a tulip) presented simultaneously, the infant is likely to fixate the novel tulip for longer durations than the familiar daffodil. In one experiment, Weizmann, Cohen, and Pratt (1969, quoted by Kagan, 1971) found that 6-week-old infants looked longer at the familiar than at a novel stimulus, while 8-week-olds looked longer at the novel one, presumably owing to a higher rate of habituation in the older infants. Increasing stimulus complexity (e.g., length of contour) first increases and then decreases fixation time, and this too is a function of age (Karmel, 1969). The duration of observation is probably also determined by the incentive properties of the stimuli; other things constant, the observation of incentive stimuli should be less subject to habituation than is the observation of neutral stimuli. Also, owing to the approach tendencies they evoke, appetitive incentive stimuli (e.g., a smiling face or a milk bottle) may be observed more persistently than somewhat aversive incentive stimuli (e.g., a highly strange visage). These suppositions need to be investigated experimentally. At this point in development, then, selective visual perception would seem to depend not only on the distinctiveness of the test stimuli, but also on their relative familiarity or novelty (i.e., the degree of the infant's habituation to them) and on the degree and nature of their incentive properties.

Somewhat later in development, the persistence of visual observation of a test stimulus comes also to depend on stimulus discrepancy, that is, on change in the test stimulus. If an infant is exposed to a certain stimulus during several habituation trials and is then tested with the "same" stimulus but with some of its features changed, the infant's fixation time is likely to be considerably greater during the test than at the end of habituation. In a formal experiment, McCall and Kagan (1967) demonstrated that the duration of fixation on a multicomponent test object increased from test 1 to test 2 when, in the period between the two tests, the infant was repeatedly exposed to the test object with some of its components substituted or rearranged, or with some new components added. This experiment was done with infants who were about 4 months old. The fact that a change in a given test stimulus, regardless of the particular features rearranged, substituted, or added, can influence fixation time indicates that 4-month-old infants can react to a discrepancy between the test object as it is and as it is expected to be on the basis of the previous exposures to it. And this means that the infant must build an inner representation or model of the stimulus with which the new discrepant form of the stimulus is compared; fixation time is then determined by the results of the comparison on some same-different dimension (see Chapter 12). These models representing the expected form of a stimulus require contingency learning of the type discussed in Chapters 6 and 7. As the infant learns more and more of the contingent relations in a situation, fixation time will come to depend on more and more complex internalized models of the situation. Thus, when an infant has developed the spatial and temporal contingencies comprising a situational schema, any changes in the location or time of appearance of a certain test object may be expected to increase the duration for which that object or location is fixated. Discrepancies in spatial and temporal aspects of a test stimulus define the *unexpectedness* of the stimulus (Berlyne, 1960).

Further, since stimuli with incentive properties would, in general, elicit more observational reactions than would neutral stimuli, any neutral stimulus that bears a contingency with an incentive stimulus would come to elicit the same type of observational and instrumental acts as are elicited by the incentive stimulus (see Chapter 9). In the case of an appetitive incentive stimulus, for example, any initially neutral stimulus that becomes a conditioned signal for the incentive stimuli, would tend to be visually fixated and approached more than other neutral stimuli.

In general, then, the conditions that determine fixation time are primarily related to stimulus salience and incentive properties of stimuli in early infancy. As the infant becomes capable of long-term habituation, familiarity and novelty come also to determine fixation time. Then, as contingency learning proceeds, stimulus discrepancy, unexpectedness, and conditioned incentive properties also become important determinants of fixation time. As contingency learning becomes more and more complex, the fixation time is determined by more and more remote conditioned stimuli, so that, in the absence of highly salient, novel, or unexpected stimuli, it would be impossible to predict what the infant would fixate unless one knew the stimulus contingencies involved. A consequence of this development is that what is observed becomes proportionately more dependent on the internal processes (learned contingencies) of the observer and proportionately less dependent on the inherent salience and other properties of the stimuli; perception becomes more internally selective or voluntary and less externally imposed or involuntary. This development may be described as one giving conditioned observation-eliciting potency to neutral stimuli that otherwise would have lost their initial potency because of habituation. Voluntary selective perception is thus fundamentally a matter of acquiring conditioned incentive properties for initially neutral stimuli. Though the above account concerns visual perception, it is reasonable to suppose that the selective perception of stimuli of other modalities follows the same pattern of development.

Development of Selective Perception of Attributes. The term attribute is used here broadly to refer to aspects of a unitary stimulus (e.g., a pencil) as well as components of a compound stimulus (e.g., light plus tone). It is not easy to demonstrate that an observer while looking at a pencil is observing its color more closely than its length, or while haptically exploring an object is observing its roughness rather than its shape. Since there may be no overt observational acts that reliably reflect the selective observation of spatially undifferentiated attributes, careful experimental analysis is required to determine what specific attributes of a stimulus have been observed. The type of analysis required may be illustrated by an early experiment by Reynolds (1961). He trained pigeons to peck on keys consisting of a white triangle on a red background and used a key with a white circle on a green background as the negative stimulus. On later tests with the individual components of the discriminanda (white triangle only, red background only, white circle only, and green background only), he found that one pigeon treated the white triangle as the positive stimulus while another treated the red background as the positive stimulus. Though both these pigeons had been trained with white-triangle-on-red-background as the positive stimulus, presumably the white triangle was a more effective stimulus component or attribute for one bird and the red background for the other. Similar selective perception of attributes can also be shown in concept-identification and classification tasks. The essential feature of such demonstrations is that correct differential responses can be made on the basis of any one of two or more attributes, and tests are made to determine which of the "relevant" attributes (those that predict the outcomes) has in fact served as the basis of differential responding.

It has been found that, given the possibility of discrimination learning on the basis of two or more relevant attributes, animal and human subjects typically make use of only one attribute. Several factors determine which attribute gets selected as the basis of discrimination. Discriminability of the attributes is one factor (Archer, 1962; Imai & Garner, 1965; Trabasso, 1963). In general, an attribute that is usually highly discriminable (e.g., color or location) is more likely to be used as a discriminative cue than an attribute that is usually less discriminable (e.g., pitch or shape). Prior successful use of an attribute as a discriminative cue makes it more likely that the subject will use it preferentially in a new task; Lawrence (1949, 1950) called this phenomenon "learned distinctiveness of cues." Conversely, if an attribute has been an "irrelevant" attribute (i.e., does not predict outcomes) in prior experience, then the use of that attribute as a relevant attribute in a new task retards discrimination performance (Goodwin & Lawrence, 1955; Levine, 1962; Lovejoy, 1968; Mackintosh, 1964; Trabasso & Bower, 1968). Another factor that may be important in determining attribute selection is whether the attribute has previously been related to appetitive or aversive stimulation. Since an attribute associated with an aversive incentive will tend to be avoided, it might be less likely to be used as a discriminative cue in other discrimination tasks; systematic investigations of this point are needed. Individual difference in the preferential use of certain attributes may be assumed to be largely a consequence of differences in the details of prior experience with various attributes.

The question that is important here is that of the development of the capacity to observe particular attributes of a stimulus and to disregard others. No reliable information on this point appears to be available. It may be surmised that the young become capable of selective perception of attributes well after they are quite adept at selective perception of objects. Of course, they are probably quite capable of reacting differentially to particular values of attributes (e.g., to different shades of red) before they can selectively perceive those attributes. In the case of the human young, it is known that 3-year-old children can react to visual stimuli differentially on the basis of both color and form attributes, and that they show preferential use of the color attribute, while 6-year-old children utilize form more than color (Suchman & Trabasso, 1966). This reversal of "cue dominance" from age 3 to 6 is presumably dependent on the various experiential factors mentioned above. The developmental sequence in which various particular attributes begin to be utilized as discriminative cues has not been extensively studied.

Current Interpretations of Selective Perception

How is voluntary selective perception of objects and attributes to be explained? At any given moment, how does an observer act in relation to—select—one stimulus object or attribute rather than another? Before outlining my hypothesis, I believe it may be useful to examine some explanatory ideas that are now in circulation.

The concept that frequently appears in attempts to explain selective perception is that of selective sensory modulation. The relative intensity of certain components of sensory inflow, representing particular aspects of the total stimulus input, is thought to be modulated, attenuated or enhanced, by centrifugal influences arising from some higher, cognitive processes. According to this view, selection consists in making some sensory components relatively more effective than others in reaching the "perceptual stage," that is, generating a pexgo of a certain stimulus. Current ideas about the nature of the postulated selective sensory modulation have developed from Broadbent's (1958) "filter theory," which he proposed to account for the results of experiments on selective listening. Broadbent's early notion of sensory modulation was essentially one of exclusion of irrelevant sensory components by a central filter selectively "tuned" to allow the passage of only those sensory components (messages) that have been defined as relevant for a listener in terms of some specific attribute. The defining attribute of a message may be a sensory channel (e.g., one ear vs. the other), the location of the source of the message, voice quality, some aspect of the content of the message, etc.

The more recent versions of the filter model of attention (Broadbent, 1971; Treisman, 1964, 1969) suggest that the filter, rather than totally excluding, simply attenuates, the irrelevant messages (sensory components) at various stages of transmission from stimulus input to identification. This newer version also specifies the various types of factors (contextual relations, set, phonemic similarity, etc.) that determine the exact selective properties of the filter ("filter criteria") at each stage of attenuation (Treisman, 1969). This model has proved quite useful as a basis of experiments for isolating the contribution of particular variables in determining performance in certain attentional tasks. However, it remains a descriptive model, concerned more with the elucidation of filter properties than with the nature of the filter or the processes underlying filtering. The model does not provide an independent account either of the centrifugal cognitive influences that determine filter properties or of the tuning mechanisms of the filter.

The idea of selective sensory modulation may also be presented as one of sensory enhancement of the relevant message, after some preliminary ("preattentive") attenuational filtering has already taken place. The exact distribution of function between the filtering and the enhancement processes is left vague by Neisser (1967). His view seems to be that irrelevant messages can get rejected passively at several transmission stages on the basis of certain gross attributes, such as sensory modality and location, but that positive identification depends on the cognitive process of "analysis-by-synthesis," which is guided by whatever cues (from the relevant and the irrelevant messages) may remain available at the end of "preattentive processing." The evaluative comments made above on the filter theory apply as well to Neisser's view, for he too does not specify the basis of the centrifugal enhancement process in any independent terms.

The results of certain neurophysiological experiments have been taken by some as supporting the general sensory-modulation interpretation of selective perception. One set of frequently quoted experiments shows that evoked potentials produced by auditory clicks in the cochlear nucleus or nerve are markedly attenuated when the animal is distracted by interesting visual or olfactory stimuli (Hernández-Péon, Scheerer, & Jouvet, 1956; Horn, 1960). This finding has been interpreted by some as showing that the selective process ("attention") is a sensory gating (or filtering) process. But such a conclusion is unwarranted. What the experiments show is that distraction by ("attention to") a new, interesting stimulus of one modality may dampen certain other concurrent sensory inflow; the experiments tell us nothing about why the animal selectively perceives ("attends to") the distracting stimulus in the first place. It has been demonstrated that sensory transmission in one modality is inhibited by the presentation of a more interesting stimulus in the same or another modality, and this inhibition involves centrifugal neural influences on sensory inflow (Oatman, 1968). But this leaves unanswered the essential question of the basis of the distraction by the more interesting stimulus. What we need to know in order to explain selective perception are the neural events that *precede* the shift in perception to the distracting stimulus, not the neural consequences of the shift.

More recently two other views have been proposed, which are essentially different forms of the sensory modulation idea. Kahneman (1973) has suggested that the basis of selective perception lies in an increase in effort or arousal such that there is an increase in the number of sensory channels utilized by a certain stimulus input. According to him, a stimulus is attended to when some "spare" sensory channels are allocated to sensory input from that stimulus. Pribram and McGuinness (1975) have attributed selective perception to an increase in "competency" of sensory channels. By increased competency they seem to mean a reduction in clarity—they call it "equivocation" (noise and redundancy)—of the sensory inflow from a certain stimulus. Both of these views bring together several diverse behavioral and neurophysiological findings related to selectivity phenomena. But it remains to be seen whether these ways of restating the problem of selectivity will be helpful in formulating some explanatory hypotheses about how sensory modulation is made appropriately selective.

A New Hypothesis

The hypothesis I outline here does not make use of the idea of selective sensory modulation, but regards the voluntary selective perception of both objects and attributes as outcomes of *selective priming* of gnostic-assemblies. As we have seen (Chapter 5), the identification of any object or attribute rests on the generation of a pexgo, and a pexgo is generated when an assortment of gnostic-assemblies representing particular stimulus features-combinations is activated. Selective processes must then be processes that somehow enhance the relative probability of the activation of certain (target) classes of gnostic-assemblies. Recall also that a change in the probability of activation of a certain class of pexgo depends partly on the momentary sensory inflow and partly on the excitatory and inhibitory discharges its gnostic-assemblies receive from on-going central processes. And the amounts of excitatory and inhibitory discharges received depend on the contingent relations that exist between the target gnostic-assemblies, comprising the pexgo, and the other (nontarget) percept-assemblies activated in the given stimulus situation (Chapters 6, 7). The central point of the present hypothesis is that the selective activation of a pexgo of a target stimulus is a consequence of the priming of some of the pexgo's constituent gnostic-assemblies independently of and *prior* to the sensory inflow from that target stimulus (which is going to be selectively perceived). In other words, selective perception of a stimulus is determined, apart from the salience and habituation factors that determine imposed attention, by some advance excitatory discharges received by the target gnostic-assemblies from the activated pexgos of other stimuli that predict the target stimulus. Voluntary selective perception is thus seen here as dependent upon prior contingency learning, according to the principles outlined in Chapters 6 and 7.

Let us now examine how this general idea may apply to the selective perception of objects and attributes.

Selective Perception of Objects. Suppose a dog has been trained to salivate at the sound of a bell in a typical Pavlovian experiment (see Figure 10.1). It is known that during the intertrial interval the dog may look aimlessly around the experimental chamber and may, in passing, glance at the receptacle where the food is delivered, but at the onset of the bell the dog starts to look directly at the receptacle and keeps looking at it until the food is delivered (Zener, 1937). In explaining this selective perception of the food receptacle, it should be noted that the training procedure makes the experimental situation as a whole a signal for several more specific components of the situation, including the food receptacle; thus a pexgo of the food receptacle would be mildly excited as soon as the dog is placed in the situation. That same food-receptacle pexgo would be excited even more strongly when the bell is sounded. Further, since the food receptacle is associated with food, the excitation of the pexgo of the food receptacle will lead the dog to produce approach movements, including visually fixating the food receptacle and extending its neck toward the receptacle. With training, these movements will become organized into unitary acts in relation to the food receptacle, and would not require all the stimuli initially required for the production of each movement, as explained in Chapter 4. As soon as the dog is placed in the training harness, it would look at the various areas of positive incentive value, and, when the bell rings, the acts would become concentrated on the object of greatest motivational value at that time, namely, the food receptacle. The observational acts of looking and neck-extending, and perhaps licking the empty receptacle, are thus the outcome of the priming of the gnostic-assemblies representing that part of the situation by some other, prior, contingently related situational signals.

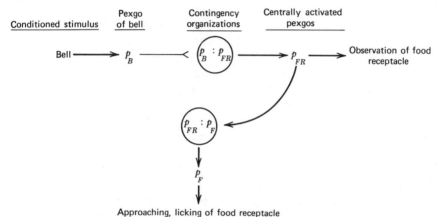

Figure 10.1.   The relation between priming of contingency organizations, centrally activated pexgos, and responses. They are related by virtue of their dependence on the generation of certain pexgos through contingency organizations that have been primed by a prior conditioned stimulus.

As noted earlier, the main characteristic of incentive stimuli is that animals are not as readily habituated to them as they are to neutral stimuli. Whatever reactions are elicited by an incentive stimulus (under appropriate organismic conditions), they continue to be elicited until there is a change in organismic state; and there is little or no accumulation of habituation in the case of incentive stimuli. Thus, with salience and familiarity equated, incentive stimuli would tend to elicit more observational acts than would neutral (non-incentive) stimuli. Further, since appetitive incentives elicit approach actions, while aversive incentives elicit defensive actions, it may be expected that the observational acts elicited by appetitive incentives would move from being distal (visual, olfactory, and auditory) acts to being contact (touch, tasting, manipulating, etc.) acts, while, in the case of aversive incentives, observational acts would be mainly acts elicited by distal aversive stimuli. Thus observational acts and selective perception would depend on the nature of the incentive stimuli predicted by the various situational conditioned stimuli.

Selective Perception of Attributes. Attribute selection may occur when the stimulus input cannot be manipulated by the animal's own observational acts, so that the selection is performed on the current sensory inflow rather than on the environmental stimuli themselves. The selection may be on the basis of a gross stimulus attribute; for example, stimulus input in one, say, the auditory modality, may be selected while that in another sense modality is ignored. Or the selection may be refined; for example, a subject may perceive only the stimulus input in one ear, or he may perceive the color but not the shape of an object. Since a subject can selectively perceive an arbitrarily defined target stimulus attribute from among several attributes of an object, it may be supposed that the selection is determined by central neural events beyond the sensory projection sites. Selective perception of attributes can be explained in terms of the priming of particular classes of gnostic-assemblies (see Chapter 5) by certain conditioned stimuli or contingently related aspects of the situation (including verbal signals).

How does an observer become capable of selectively perceiving one attribute of a display or object, that is, of increasing the probability of perceiving one attribute at the expense of the other attributes that occupy the same defined space and time, for example, identifying the form of the letter P rather than its color or size, or identifying the pitch of a tone rather than its loudness? According to the proposed hypothesis, there is no essential difference between the selective perception of objects and attributes; they both depend on the excitation of particular classes of gnostic-assemblies by specific prior, contingently related conditioned stimuli or cues. All that is required for developing the capability of selectively perceiving certain attributes is the establishment of certain contingent relations between certain prior cues and those attributes. The required discrimination is quite easy to arrange. For example, suppose we want an observer to perceive selectively the color of a target object on certain occasions and its shape on other occasions. The training would require that both color and form be varied; this would mean a minimum of four objects, say, a red ball, a green ball, a red cube, and a green cube. The training would also require two cues, say, a bell and a buzzer, each of which would be followed by the display of an appropriate object. If it is desired that color be identified when a bell has been sounded, and form when the buzzer has been sounded, then training contingencies might be arranged as follows:

Bell: red ball: Incentive
Bell: Red cube: Incentive
Bell: Green ball: No incentive
Bell: Green cube: No incentive
and

Buzzer: Red ball: Incentive
Buzzer: Red cube: No incentive
Buzzer: Green ball: Incentive
Buzzer: Green cube: No incentive

Such differential training would result in the observer treating color as the relevant attribute when the bell has been sounded, and form when the buzzer has been sounded. According to the present hypothesis, each differential cue would prime the gnostic-assemblies of a different attribute and thus would facilitate the perception of that attribute. The preparation or bias in favor of perceiving a certain attribute lies in the priming of a particular class of gnostic-assemblies by a certain cue.

There is little doubt that we learn many contingencies between particular cues and the relevance of certain attributes. As we approach any situation or task, we are prepared to perceive selectively certain attributes rather than others. For example, pigeons can be trained to discriminate between two tones ("attend to their differences") in the presence of a light of one color but to respond independently of their differences in the presence of a light of a different color (Heinemann, Chase, & Mandell, 1968). Similarly, we identify the size of stones when putting together a stone fence, and the color of stones when decorating a chimney; we identify body color when judging race, and body form when judging beauty; we judge similarities when instructed to abstract, and differences when instructed to differentiate. However, there has been little by way of systematic investigation of the development of such conditioned predispositions for selective perception of attributes, and the exact cues that normally prepare an observer for perceiving one rather than another attribute remain to be elucidated.

Some Implications

The hypothesis outlined above differs in two fundamental respects from any of the sensory modulation views of selective perception. First, the latter offer no causal hypothesis about selectivity, but merely state that certain unspecified attentional processes have a selective influence on sensory inflow—that "attention" is somehow "paid," "focused," or "allocated." The present hypothesis, on the other hand, suggests that the basis of selectivity lies in predictive processes arising from the contingency organizations developed as a consequence of experience with certain contingent relations in particular situations. Second, while the sensory modulation views regard the mechanism of selectivity to be sensory modulation, the present hypothesis regards the mechanism to be conditioned (anticipatory) priming of particular classes of gnostic-assemblies that lie beyond the sensory projections. The view of Kahneman (1973), as well as of Pribram and McGuinness (1975), attributes selectivity to enhancement in the discriminative *efficacy* of sensory *channels*, and not to alterations in the *content* of information being processed. On the contrary, the present hypothesis attributes (voluntary) selective perception to the prior predictive factors that prime particular gnostic-assemblies, making the activation of certain pexgos more likely, and not to alterations in the "discriminative efficacy" of the current sensory inflow. There is evidence to indicate that the manipulations, such as habituation repetition, that reduce the probability of perception do so without any attenuation of functional sensory intensity (Russo, Reiter, & Ison, 1975).

The conditioned priming hypothesis of selective perception is supported by studies of eye movements and fixations during the performance of perceptual tasks by human subjects. For example, in these studies it has been found that most of the visual fixations are centered on those stimulus features of a display that are contingently related to (that is, predict) the specified target stimuli (Mackworth & Morandi, 1967). Similarly, search time for target stimuli is reduced when the observer is given in peripheral vision certain subsidiary cues that signal (are contingently related to) the target (Williams, 1967). And Senders (1967) has shown that eye movements leading to a target are dependent on "other" aspects of the visual field that are correlated with the target. One implication of the present hypothesis is that the conditioned priming of any target pexgo would be at a peak value only for a certain time after the presentation of the stimulus to which it is contingently related. In general, the time of peak value would tend to coincide with the time at which the environmental stimulus represented by that pexgo usually appears—when the predicted imminence is at its highest (see Chapters 6 and 7); the level of priming of the pexgo should be less both before and after that particular point in time. This means that (selective) perception of a target stimulus would be most highly facilitated at the predicted time of its occurrence. This is consistent with the results of certain reaction-time experiments in which the foreperiod (the interval between the "ready" signal and the reaction stimulus) is systematically varied. These experiments show that the fastest reactions are obtained when the duration of the foreperiod equals the average duration of all the foreperiods used (e.g., Bevan, Hardesty, & Avant, 1965; Karlin, 1959; Klemmer, 1956, 1957). The learned temporal contingencies presumably lead to maximal priming at a particular moment that depends on the values and frequencies of the foreperiods experienced by the subject in that experimental situation.

The role of complex spatial and temporal contingencies—situational schemas—in selective priming is clearly seen in other reaction-time experiments. For example, in a discrete two-choice, reaction-time experiment a subject may be required to press one key, R_1, when he sees a stimulus in one location, say to the subject's left (S_L) and to press another key, R_2, when he

sees the same stimulus in another location, say to the subject's right (S_R).
Now, if instead of presenting the stimulus at the two locations (S_L and
S_R) with equal frequency, a series of trials is given in which the stimulus
occurs on the left more frequently (say 70 per cent of the trials) than on the
right, the reaction speed for S_L will become higher than that for S_R; and
the reverse would be true if the frequency of S_R would now be made relatively
greater than that of S_L (e.g., Geller, Whitman, & Farris, 1972). This means
that once the subject has had time to learn the probabilities of occurrence
of the stimulus in the two locations, his response to the stimulus on any given
trial is influenced by the spatial contingency organizations that represent the
relative probabilities of the occurrence of the stimulus in each location. The
effect of relative frequency is independent of the enhancing effect on reaction
speed of the subject's own correct prediction about where the *next* stimulus
would be presented; thus the relative frequency effect is the outcome of some
central facilitation—priming of a particular spatial pexgo on each trial—and
is not attributable to preparatory muscular readiness (Geller, Whitman,
Wrenn, & Shipley, 1971).

The influence of complex temporal schemas on selective priming is seen
in reaction-time experiments that study the effects of changes in the relative
frequency of occurrence of the two stimulus alternatives in a discrete two-
choice, reaction-time task. The reaction speed tends to be higher for the
relatively more frequently occurring stimulus alternative (e.g., Dillon, 1966;
Laming, 1969). Independent of relative frequency, sequential dependencies
can also affect reaction speed. Thus, if the alternative reaction stimuli occur
in a certain identifiable sequence, such as ABAB or AAABBABBABBAAA,
the average reaction speeds to A and B stimuli are likely to become quite
different as the subject becomes familiar with the rules (e.g., run lengths)
governing the stimulus sequence (Geller & Pitz, 1970). These results could
occur only if the subject were to build, quickly during the early trials of the
series, some schema of the sequential order of the components of the trial
series. Such a schema then influences reaction speed by selectively priming
the pexgo representing a particular stimulus alternative on each trial.

Note that the spatial and temporal features of a situation are not always
independent of each other; frequently they are correlated. For example, when
an animal looks at various stimuli at different locations in its visual field, the
layout of spatial locations looked at (A, B, C, D, etc.) corresponds to the
temporal sequence in which it looks at those stimuli. This redundancy of
spatial layout and temporal sequence is especially true when, as in reading
English and many other languages, the reader scans from left to right; here
the influence of spatial and temporal cues is completely confounded in the
sequence. However, in many other cases spatial-layout and temporal-
sequence cues can vary independently and have differential significance; for

example, one can easily learn that two different orders of durations of a tone sounded at the same location have different consequences.

In adult human subjects, a situational schema may be activated by the use of a word or phrase that describes or serves as a label for the situation. This is seen in experiments on "context effect" in the performance of various tasks. For example, telling subjects what the relative frequencies of reaction stimuli are in a choice reaction time experiment has the same enhancing effect on the reaction speed of the more frequent stimuli as does gaining familiarity with the relative frequencies through previous practice trials (Geller, et al., 1971). Similarly, the speed of identification of certain target stimuli in pictures is enhanced when subjects are presented words or sentences semantically related to the target stimuli (Cooper, 1974; Potter, 1975). A related finding is that a sentence, for example, "The baby vomited the milk," is comprehended (identified as meaningful or anomalous) more readily when the subject is first provided with the context, "A baby was given some milk before her nap" or "baby milk" than when no context is provided (Dooling, 1972). Presumably, the sentence or words activate a situational schema that primes the gnostic-assemblies related to the target stimuli whose perception or comprehension is under investigation.

Experimental instructions also serve as cues that may influence perception by priming. Consider an example. In visual search experiments (e.g., Moray, 1969; Neisser, 1967), a subject is instructed to say, for example, whether the letter P is present in a display of letters arranged in a succession of rows. The subject is quickly able to give the correct answer, for example, that the letter P appears in the tenth row, but he is not likely to be able to say what were the other letters in the display. This may be explained in the following way. The instructions, through the set they create, lead to the priming of the gnostic-assemblies of P, and, perhaps as well, an inhibition of the gnostic-assemblies of other letters. As the subject examines the display, the stimulus features of P represented in the sensory inflow would be more likely to be effective in activating a pexgo of P than would the letter features of any other letter, say, M, in the same sensory inflow be likely to activate a pexgo of M. Since identification of a stimulus depends on the activation of an appropriate pexgo, the letter P would be more likely to be identified than the other letters. To the extent that the letter features of, say, B and R, are similar to the letter features of P, the subject may falsely identify B or R as P, owing to the greater excitation (priming) of the gnostic-assemblies common to P, B and R (see Chapter 5). In general, the conditions that increase the speed of visual search are the conditions that favor the priming of gnostic-assemblies representing the distinctive features of the target stimulus—features that distinguish it from other stimuli in the display.

Selective Perception and Observational Acts

It is important to understand the exact relation between observational acts and selective perception and the implications of the relation. According to the conditioned priming hypothesis, voluntary selective perception of any target object or attribute would be possible only if the observer had previously learned that a certain cue bears a positive contingency to the target. Suppose that the cue is a bell and the target stimulus is a red ball that is displayed for a few seconds. After the contingency has been learned, a pexgo of the red ball will be primed when the bell is presented, that is, the observer will be more likely to perceive the red ball than other stimuli. Now, if the ball were to be displayed at a particular corner of the experimental chamber, say, the one on the observer's right, then the priming of a pexgo of the ball would also produce some observational acts (visually fixating, extending neck or hands, etc.) directed at the location where the ball is to appear. These anticipatory observational acts would be produced because, owing to that location's association with the ball, the location would also have acquired some incentive properties. But if the ball were to be displayed not at the same location each time but at varying locations within the chamber, the observational acts would also be directed at the varying locations where the ball had been displayed; the observer would then be said to be "searching." In either case the identification of the red ball would be facilitated by the selective priming of the relevant pexgo and the anticipatory observational acts. The point to note is that it is the bell as the cue that produces selective priming, and this priming underlies both the anticipatory observational acts and the facilitation of identification when the target is displayed. Priming is *not* a consequence either of observational acts or of the cues arising from the location observed; the location observed is determined by priming, not vice versa. Anticipatory observational acts are neither the cause of nor necessary for selective perception, but usually contribute to it when target stimuli occupy particular locations.

The above account of directed observational acts should be distinguished from Wyckoff's (1951, 1952) concept of "observing responses." There are two essential differences. First, Wyckoff defines an observing response as one that produces certain discriminative stimuli. For example, a hungry pigeon may be required to step on a pedal to produce, say, either a red key (S^D) or a green key (S^Δ); a response (e.g., pecking) in relation to one of the keys is then followed by food. In this case, the pedal-stepping response is called the observing response because it is instrumental in displaying the discriminanda. The concept of observational acts as used here does not refer to any specific act that *produces* certain particular discriminanda, but to acts involving movement of the sensory apparatus that may lead to the selective perception of one object rather than another; the observational act has no definitional reference to the production of any particular discriminanda. Second, Wyckoff's account of observing responses is not addressed to the problem of attention; he is not concerned with the acts of looking, listening, etc., that precede an instrumental response, but only with a prior instrumental response that provides the stimuli for further instrumental responding. Wyckoff's concept of observing responses has proved to be quite useful in the study of discrimination learning (e.g., see Dewson & Cowey, 1969; Stollnitz, 1965), but it has nothing to do with the problem of the nature of selective processes.

SELECTIVE RECALL

In discussions of selective perception we are interested in the conditions that enhance the probability of identifying a particular stimulus in a situation; the question we ask is: Why does the subject perceive this rather than something else? In discussions of selective recall, we are interested in the conditions that enhance the probability of remembering a particular past experience; the question we ask is: Why does the subject recall this rather than something else? Selective perception and selective recall go hand in hand and influence each other; noticing a book on one's desk may lead to the recall of the library from which it has been borrowed, and this may lead to the perception of a date on the desk calendar, and this to the recall of a birthday, and so on. This section explains that the basis of selective recall is the same as that of selective perception—conditioned priming of particular gnostic-assemblies that makes the generation of certain pexgos more likely.

Basis of Selective Recall

Any explanatory account of selective recall must deal with the fact that the same stimulus may lead to the recall of different items on different occasions. A tone may lead a dog to salivate (recall food) on one occasion and to freeze (recall of electric shock) on another. The word "pot" may lead to the recall of such items as kitchen and casserole on one occasion and to the recall of a fat person or marijuana on another. Because of multiple contingent relations among pexgos (of objects or words), it is necessary to explain why a pexgo of a particular class, and not any of the other possible ones, is associatively activated at a given time. How is the particular centrally activated pexgo—memory pexgo—that occurs at a given moment arrived at?

It is plausible to assume that the memory pexgo generated—the association produced—at any moment is a joint function of the prevailing determining set of the subject and the stimuli to which he is then exposed. When the prevailing set arises from an earlier conversation about cooking utensils, the new stimulus word "pot" may produce the association "roast," but when the prevailing set arises from an earlier conversation about obesity, then the same stimulus word produces the association "a fat person." As explained in Chapter 7, the determining set refers to a constellation of contingency organizations that have been excited or primed to varying degrees as a consequence of prior events up to a given moment. The presentation of a new stimulus at that moment then further leads to the excitation of some new contingency organizations, and the resultant momentary pattern of excitation leads to enhanced activation of some pexgo, which then determines the memory image and the associative response.

Usually, however, we are interested in recalling something specific rather than in seeing what association happens to come up next. The process that leads to the recall of a particular association is similar to that by which a player of the game "Twenty Questions" arrives at the name of an unknown object secretly specified by the opposing player. The guessing player asks the questions about the mystery object (Is it an animal? Is it in the western hemisphere? Is it an ornament currently used in personal adornment? And so on), and yes-or-no-answers to these questions enable the guesser to eliminate large subdomains of objects to which the mystery object does not belong. The progressive elimination of alternatives reduces the domain of objects to which the mystery object could belong, and players of this game get quite adept at naming the specified object well within twenty questions. The guessing player does not, of course, know what the eventual answer will be (there is no intention to reach any particular answer), yet he gradually gets increasingly closer to the correct answer; the answer is not pre-prepared, but is arrived at through progressive limitation of the possible alternatives, and the answer finally given is one that could not have been chosen with any certainty at the beginning. Correspondingly, the process of selective recall is usually one of progressive delimitation of the pexgos that continue to be primed more and more strongly under the given conditions until a certain pexgo—one meeting the specified characteristics—is activated. This implies a continual interaction between the varying excited contingency organizations that comprise the momentary determining set and those that are activated by new situational stimuli; the determining set moves progressively from being highly general to being increasingly more specific, as explained in Chapter 7. This interpretation will be applied to the analysis of various memory phenomena in Chapter 14.

Memory Pexgos and Observational Acts

The above analysis implies that the memory pexgo that is activated at a given time is the basis of both selective recall and selective identification. In other words, the memory pexgo activated at a given moment determines what the subject will selectively perceive at that moment. The associative activation of a pexgo thus determines both what the subject will recall and what the subject will perceive.

If memory pexgos are the same thing as perception pexgos, then there ought to be a relation between recall and observational acts, just as there is one between perception and observational acts. This prediction is supported by the results of experiments in which observational acts are recorded during the recall of items that had been presented in different locations. For example, Bryden (1961) found that in reporting a row of digits that had been presented tachistoscopically, subjects tended to fixate their eyes at the location where the digit being recalled had been placed. According to the present hypothesis, the correlation between the recall item and eye movements is a consequence of their dependence on the activation of a common pexgo. Since eye movements may also be determined by factors other than the priming of any specific pexgo, the correlation between eye movements and recall is not obligatory and need not be too close; recall does not depend on observational acts. Kahneman (1973) has reviewed several studies showing that reliable patterns of eye movements occur in a variety of thinking (i.e., directed recall) tasks, even though they cannot possibly facilitate performance. For example, if a subject is asked to recall names of automobiles, he may look steadily at the picture of *an* automobile even though this could not help him recall the names of other automobiles. Systematic eye movements also occur in auditory tasks requiring selective listening. Correlations have also been reported between dream images and eye movements (Jouvet, 1967). Congenitally blind subjects display haptic (observational) movements both during thinking and dreaming (Dement, 1965).

According to the present hypothesis, then, when observational acts occur in other than selective perception of spatially differentiated objects, they serve no useful function, but arise from the process of priming of pexgos that selective perception tasks share with various recall and thinking tasks. In other words, the occurrence of such observational acts in recall and thinking tasks is an "overflow" phenomenon, with no deeper significance. It corresponds to the phenomenon of implicit muscular contractions, say, in the right arm, when one is asked to think about lifting a weight with that arm (Jacobson, 1932). Observational acts could thus be considered as "ideomotor acts" instigated by pexgos when the parts of the motor system required for observational acts are not otherwise being used. At best, observational acts can *reflect* the locations (in relation to the observer) of the objects now being thought about; they cannot, of course, indicate anything about the content of the thoughts.

Limits of Selectivity

For how long does an entity remain in the focus of awareness before being replaced by something else? In other words, once a pexgo has been selectively activated, for how long does it "remain selected"? This broad question embodies several specific problems. Three of these are discussed here: (1) What are the factors that determine the rate of degradation of a sensory pexgo—one generated primarily through environmental stimulation—after the sensory inflow has ceased? This is the problem of so-called "short-term memory." (2) How many different memory pexgos can remain in active (relatively non-degraded) state at any one moment? This is the question of "holding capacity." (3) Under what conditions is it possible to do two or more discrete things concurrently? This is the problem of "divided attention" or "parallel processing."

Degradation of Pexgos

It is not easy to find out exactly how long after the termination of its relevant sensory input would a pexgo disappear—become too degraded to have any distinctive influence. The main difficulty lies in the fact that the behavioral determination of the duration of persistence of a pexgo involves recall tests at varying intervals after stimulus cessation. But performance in recall tests may be influenced by the conditioning of the pexgo to some situational or task cues, so that recall may result from pexgo *re*activation rather than from its persistence. The possibility of such associative conditioning may be minimized by using, as far as possible, discrete, unrelated stimuli, presenting each stimulus once briefly and including more stimuli than the subject can learn in one presentation. The paradigm that has these features is the "short-term memory experiment." In this paradigm, discrete stimulus items, such as unrelated digits or letters, are arranged in a list of, say, nine or ten items (more than the "span of immediate recall"), and the subject is required to repeat the items serially immediately after one presentation of the list.

However, even this type of experiment leaves the subject free to rehearse verbally the earlier items of the series so that recall may be improved by an indeterminate amount. Further, performance in the recall test is adversely affected by proactive and retroactive interference effects of both serial presentation and serial recall. The net effect of these various influences seems to be that, in a typical experiment, the subject shows better recall for the two or three initial items of the list ("primacy effect") as well as for the two or three items at the end of the list ("recency effect"). But, owing to the variety of factors that influence such performance, no unequivocal conclusions can be drawn about the spontaneous, or true, rate of degradation of the pexgo of each item. Improvements in the basic short-term memory experiment have been developed to minimize rehearsal by requiring the subject to perform a distracting task while being exposed to the list (Peterson & Peterson, 1959), and to minimize interference effects during recall by testing for the recall of only one probe item of a list (Waugh & Norman, 1965). While these improvements have proved useful for specification of the various conditions that influence the rate of degradation of a pexgo, they too have failed to produce any agreed account of the rate of "spontaneous" degradation of a pexgo, that is, degradation due to nonspecific factors. Estimates vary for particular conditions, ranging from about a few seconds to about a minute (Baddeley & Patterson, 1971).

Presumably, the rate of degradation of a pexgo depends on the initial strength (level of excitation) of the pexgo and the rate of its spontaneous decay, as well as on any interfering and reactivating influences. The initial strength of a pexgo may be expected to be a function of stimulus salience (see Chapter 2). Since stimulus intensity (relative to the background stimulation) is one determiner of salience, the persistence of a pexgo may be expected to be greater when the stimulus is more intense than when it is less so. And, in general, novel stimuli will produce greater pexgo strength than familiar ones; a novel stimulus presented in a list of familiar stimuli (e.g., a letter presented in a list of digits, or a digit written in a different ink) has a greater probability of recall than the familiar items.

The rate of spontaneous decay of a sensory pexgo would appear to depend on the efficiency of neural functioning. Any damage to or dysfunction of the structures that are the loci of gnostic-assemblies should alter the rate of decay, and thereby performance, in a short-term memory task. There is some evidence to support this. Warrington and Shallice (1969, 1972) have described a neurological patient, K. F., who could reliably repeat only one item of an aurally presented verbal list; though occasionally he managed to repeat correctly lists of two, three, or even four items, his performance remained considerably below normal. This impairment of immediate memory span or "repetition defect" was found not to be due either to any auditory dysfunction, because K. F could identify auditory stimuli well, or to any motor speech dysfunction, because he could repeat more items when the lists were visually presented. With auditory stimuli his performance remained poor when, instead of repeating the items, he was asked to match or recognize them. It is therefore reasonable to attribute K. F.'s impairment to rapid auditory pexgo degradation. The rapid degradation could have been due either to a high rate of spontaneous decay or to a loss of capacity to maintain (keep active) the items through rehearsal. Warrington and Shallice found that even with the presentation of a single item the forgetting was very rapid, which suggests that the primary deficit of K. F. was one of high rate of spontaneous decay of auditory pexgos. The damaged cortical area in this patient was identified as the left posterior parietal region, which is consistent with Geschwind's (1965) suggestion that this region is probably the critical site for perception of aurally presented words. A corresponding impairment of ability to read or interpret pictures, simultagnosia, has been reported by Kinsbourne and Warrington (1962, 1963) in a patient with a lesion of the left anterior occipital lobe, a region that might be considered as the locus of primarily visual pexgos.

The rate of spontaneous decay can perhaps also be influenced by certain stimulant and depressant drugs. For example, in normal human subjects, a mild dose of amphetamine (about 10 mg, or 1 mg/kg) reduces the duration of the inhibitory effect of masking stimulus on perception (Holland, 1963), and nitrous oxide has the reverse effect. It is also known that a stimulant drug like amphetamine can facilitate learning (see John, 1967; McGaugh & Petrinovitch, 1965), as well as performance in vigilance tasks (Mackworth, 1965). In general, it appears that performance in a task that requires the quick activation of a pexgo or its maintenance after the stimulus has ended may be improved by appropriate doses of central nervous system stimulant drugs, and adversely affected by depressant drugs.

Concerning interference effects on the degradation of a pexgo, it may be supposed that the activation of other, nontarget, pexgos would reduce the probability of activation of a target pexgo. Thus, in general, the greater the number of potent stimuli present concurrently or in close succession, the greater the interference effect and the lesser the probability of activation of a target pexgo. Note that the interference-induced increase in the rate of degradation is not attributed to any increase in the rate of spontaneous decay of the pexgo, but to a reduction in its level of excitation produced by a diminution of conditioned excitatory effects. The reduction in the probability of activation of a target pexgo would seem to be a function of three main factors: the number of other interfering pexgos activated, the times at which they are activated in relation to the time of activation of the target pexgo, and the relatedness of the interfering pexgos to the target pexgo, that is, the extent to which the activated gnostic-assemblies overlap. The influence of these variables on performance in memory tasks is well demonstrated. First, beyond the normal span of immediate recall of about six items, an increase in the number of items in the list leads to a reduction in the items correctly recalled. Second, by decreasing the interitem interval between the presentation of successive items, say, from 2 sec to 1/2 sec, the span of immediate recall can be considerably reduced (Warrington & Shallice, 1969). Third, by making the interfering stimuli more similar to the target stimulus along some relevant attributes (shape, color, sound-pattern, meaning, etc.), that is, by increasing the overlap among the activated gnostic-assemblies, it is possible to increase the number of confusions among items, thereby increasing the frequency of errors of recall (Baddeley, 1970; Conrad, 1964). Deutsch (1970) has shown that the recognition of a tone is impaired by presenting, during the interpolated interval, other tones but not by presenting digits.

The degradation of a pexgo may to some extent be counteracted by its reactivation. In the absence of the stimulus that generated the pexgo, it can be reactivated only if it continues to receive some fairly specific excitatory discharge. This could come from conditioned stimuli. In the case of human beings, since specific names are learned for particular objects, the name of an object would serve as a potent conditioned stimulus for activating a pexgo in the absence of the object itself. For example, if a subject is required to keep active the image of a book he has been shown, he can do so by pronouncing the word "book" repeatedly. Such verbal rehearsal appears possible only in human beings and provides them with the means of reactivating a pexgo from the word name of the corresponding object. Rehearsal facilitates recall, and the prevention of rehearsal produces rapid loss of the items (Brown, 1958). If opportunity to rehearse is provided by increasing the inter-item interval separating the items, recall is enhanced; the improvement is particularly evident in the recall of early parts of the list of items, which are usually rehearsed more often than the later items (Corballis, 1966). Rehearsal may consist in simply repeating each item discretely or in organizing the items into rhythmical or linguistic structures and then repeating those structures.

Holding Capacity

A related question concerns the number of different pexgos that can be concurrently maintained in a more or less distinctive state. Experiments on the span of immediate recall indicate that normally pexgos of about six discrete stimulus items can be held active enough for immediate recall; when the number of stimulus items is increased much beyond six, confusion results and the subject seems unable to hold even six. The term "holding capacity" is a rough label for the number of discrete pexgos that can, under given conditions, be maintained in a sufficiently distinctive state to be usable in the production of specific responses.

Perhaps the most important thing to note about holding capacity of a pexgo is that it is largely independent of the size or complexity of the stimulus it represents. Thus, a pexgo may vary from one representing a letter (e.g., *b*), or a three-letter word (e.g., *bad*), or a three-syllable word (e.g., *badminton*), and yet it would count as one item; so long as it is coherent and unitary, a pexgo functions as a single item in measures of holding capacity. Under one set of conditions Craik (1968) found that the holding capacity of his subjects remained at about three words while the number of syllables in the words varied from one to four. A unitary complex made up of smaller elements has been called a "chunk" (G. A. Miller, 1956), and holding capacity is said to be independent of the size of the chunks. Miller (1956) suggested that the holding capacity of adult human subjects is about seven, no matter what the size of the chunk or the nature (modality, attribute, etc.) of the items. In fact, holding capacity may vary considerably for different types of items (digits, syllables, colors, figures, etc.) and under different conditions (see Mandler, 1975; Simon, 1974). But the validity of Miller's general point that there is some fairly low limit on the number of different pexgos that a subject can hold active concurrently cannot be doubted.

There are two developmental questions here. First, how is the size of chunks enlarged through experience? This is essentially the problem of development of gnostic-assemblies, and has been considered before. The second question concerns the developmental changes in holding capacity. It seems well established that holding capacity, as measured by span of immediate recall, increases with age during childhood and declines in old age (Wimer & Wigdor, 1958; Woodworth & Schlosberg, 1955).

Dividing Attention

It is one thing to be able to hold a certain number of pexgos active at a given time, but quite another to think (have directed associations) about two or more things concurrently. The usual questions asked about the latter are: Can a subject do two things at the same time? Is parallel processing possible, or do mental activities have to be performed serially? Is attention unitary, or can it be divided?

On the face of it, there can be little doubt that human subjects can do two or more things concurrently. We can, for example, carry on a meaningful conversation while driving an automobile and eating peanuts. It is certainly true that several different movements can go on concurrently so long as they do not involve the same musculature; it is possible to talk while changing gears and even while chewing peanuts. There can also be little question that on occasions two mental activities can go on at the same time; we can formulate a reply concurrently with listening and comprehending, or do a crossword puzzle while listening to the radio. It is equally obvious that on other occasions two given mental activities cannot be carried on concurrently, or are carried on less efficiently than normally; it is impossible for most people to do mental arithmetic while listening to news on the radio, or to carry on a coherent conversation while eavesdropping on another. The question worth considering, then, is not whether it is possible to do two or more things at the same time but the conditions that facilitate or hinder doing more than one thing at a time.

Proficiency is perhaps the most important factor that makes it possible to perform two tasks concurrently. The more proficient a subject becomes at a task, the less is the performance of that task likely to interfere with his performance of another task. A practiced typist can follow a story or even carry on a conversation while transcribing, and an expert pianist can think up innovative variations while playing, but such feats are not possible while initially learning to typewrite or to play the piano. The more "automatic" or "thoughtless" a task becomes with practice, the more likely is the subject able to perform another task concurrently. Kahneman (1973) has suggested it is the momentary effort needed to perform a task that determines whether it will interfere with doing other things concurrently, and he relates momentary effort requirements to pressure resulting from time limits and related factors that make a task more difficult. Interest is another factor; if a subject is highly absorbed in a task, he is less likely to be able to do something else concurrently. It is customary to summarize such observations by saying that tasks that require a lot of "mental capacity" (or have a high "attentional requirement") because they are effortful or interesting do not leave sufficient mental capacity or "surplus attention" for doing anything else concurrently. However, this leaves unanswered the question of the conditions that determine the degree to which mental capacity is engaged in different tasks, and of the exact nature of the mental capacity that is engaged.

My view is that what requires the full mental capacity of a subject is the learning of a new relation between two or more events. While a relation is being learned, the subject can perform only the most automatic tasks (scratching, walking, etc.). The relation being learned may be between attributes of stimuli, their meaning, their names, etc. As we saw in Chapter 6, what is involved in learning the relation between two events is the development of a contingency organization that enables the first event to predict the spatial and temporal location of the second, the predicted, event. Thus when conditions exist that make it likely that a certain predictor event will be selectively perceived and be followed in time by the selective perception of a certain predicted event, the interval between those events will be the interval of maximum "attentional" or mental exercise. It is in this period of maximum preparation for selective perception of a predicted event that the subject would be less capable of selective perception of anything else or of performing any other than highly routinized actions. In other words, it is the period when the momentary determining set has become highly narrow, owing to a high level of selective priming of a small number of pexgos, that will be the period of maximum mental exercise or "attentional focus." The process underlying "mental effort" or "attentional focus" is thus one of progressive narrowing of determining set in the priming and activation of pexgos—the same process that is the basis of selective perception and recall.

As a relation between two events is experienced repeatedly, the period during which the determining set is narrow would become temporally differentiated. That is, the high level of selective priming of particular pexgos would occur for a shorter and shorter time as the temporal relation between the events becomes increasingly well learned. The subject would thus have more spare time in the situation, so that in the same time-span it would now become possible for him to observe and learn other relations concurrently. However, doing two things concurrently in this way does not mean they are being done simultaneously. What appear as two simultaneous operations ("parallel processing") may in fact be temporally separate operations ("serial processing") with rapid switching from one to the other. Though performed concurrently in the same overall time-span, the two operations may in fact be performed intermittently at temporally discrete points of a more refined time scale; things that look simultaneous in a scale of long time-frames may be found to be concurrent only when the time-frames for analysis are made shorter. While driving an automobile, we may stop talking, or even chewing peanuts, at the moment of shifting gears; shifting done, we may resume talking, and may utilize the pauses in talking for chewing. Like a computer serving many users concurrently, the function involved in learning new relations ("attentional capacity") may be said to be time-shared. As in the computer, time-sharing becomes possible because there is spare time between different operations.

The above time-sharing hypothesis of the ability to do two things concurrently is not meant to deny the possibility of simultaneous operation of certain functions or "parallel processing." Certainly the sensory inflow that results in sensory patterns representing particular environmental stimuli goes on simultaneously in different sensory modalities. Even in the case of more complex mental operations the possibility of simultaneous processing is a matter of degree; Kahneman (1973) has concluded that tasks and the circumstances determine how far parallel processing is possible and that performance is guided by a "flexible policy of attention allocation" (p. 177). What the present hypothesis says is simply that at moments when determining set required in a task becomes highly narrow or intense, the capacity for simultaneously performing other complex operations decreases, and that there is a level of task complexity beyond which the concurrent performance of more than one task would not be possible without spare time-frames. The chess master who can concurrently play against 20 opponents is able to do this because it has become possible for him to grasp, within a glance of 5 sec, the full layout of a chess game in progress and decide on the next move (De Groot, 1966). Shaffer (1973) has reported the case of a skilled typist who, while copying a visual text at a high speed, could concurrently perform another verbal task such as shadowing aurally presented prose or spelling dictated words. Apparently, in any time-span of a second or two, a skilled typist has sufficient spare time-frames to carry on another task. However, this seemed to be true only so long as the two tasks did not require the simultaneous (synchronous) use of the same mechanisms. When response units of the two tasks became similar, concurrent performance suffered; for example, the typist while typing IS HEREDITY and spelling OFFICE, typed OFF HEREDICY and spelled OFFICY. Performance also suffers when stimulus input for the two tasks becomes similar; for example, while reading aloud or reciting, the typist could more easily type from a visual text than from an aurally presented text. These observations suggest that concurrent performance of two tasks is not so much a matter of one of them becoming automatic, but of finely adjusted use of each time-frame for one task or the other, an adjustment that tends to break down when simultaneous use of a certain perceptual or response mechanism is required by both the tasks.

It may be supposed that as the infant develops and more and more of the normal adaptive activities are mastered and become temporally differentiated, the more adept it becomes at doing more than one thing concurrently. Further, for many types of recurrent situations the infant must also develop modes or strategies of time-sharing, so that several concurrent actions become possible. The exact course of this development would appear to be an important problem in the elucidation of the nature of intellectual abilities.

CHAPTER 11

Acquiring New Responses

Successful adaptation requires that the animal modify its behavior, as the circumstances of its existence change from time to time. Modifications of behavior that emerge as a consequence of an animal's encounters with particular types of situations are described as "learned modifications of behavior"; these are distinguished from behavioral modifications that arise from maturational growth or organismic variations. A learned behavioral modification may involve the acquisition of several new responses. In this chapter I give an account of how new responses are acquired in terms of the ideas outlined in previous chapters.

THE PROCESS OF ACQUIRING NEW RESPONSES

Acquiring a new "response" means changing an existing situation-response combination to a new one, that is an alteration of a functional relation between a specified set of stimulus conditions (S) and a certain response (R). The observed alteration that defines a response acquisition may involve an alteration from an existing stimulus-response relation, $S_1 \rightarrow R_1$, to a new relation with a different stimulus, $S_2 \rightarrow R_1$ (learning "stimulus control"), or an alteration from the existing relation, $S_1 \rightarrow R_1$, to a new relation with a different response, $S_1 \rightarrow R_2$ (learning new responses or "response shaping"). In nature, these two types of learning go hand in hand, but their study has until recently followed separate courses, and they have often been treated as fundamentally different forms of learning.

Pavlovian and Thorndikian Principles

Pavlov sought to study and isolate the process of stimulus control; this he did by making the occurrence of an incentive or "unconditioned stimulus" contingent on the occurrence of an arbitrarily selected, initially neutral, conditioned stimulus (CS:US). Thorndike sought to study and isolate the process of response shaping; he did this by making the occurrence of an incentive or "reinforcing," stimulus contingent on the occurrence of an arbitrarily selected instrumental response ($IR:S^{reinf.}$). Both the Pavlovian, or classical conditioning, and Thorndikian, or instrumental conditioning, procedures of training have been shown to be remarkably effective methods of obtaining behavior modifications. The classical procedure has been most successfully used in the training of autonomically controlled, "involuntary," viscerosomatic reactions that can be reliably elicited by known (unconditioned) stimuli, while the instrumental procedure has been most successfully used in the training of skeletal, "voluntary" responses, whose initial elicitors are largely unknown. In the former, the investigators have concentrated on understanding the stimulus control of a response; in the latter, on understanding the form of a response. Understandably, experimental work with the two procedures has led to two quite different views of learning.

The central difference between the two views lies in the characterization of the basis of the behavior modification produced by training (see Table 11.1). According to the main view derived from experiments with the classical-conditioning training procedure, what the animal learns is a stimulus-stimulus association between conditioned and unconditioned stimuli ($CS \rightarrow US$), and the basis of this association is the training contingency between these same stimuli ($CS:US$). According to the main view derived from experiments with the instrumental-conditioning training procedure, what the animal learns is a stimulus-response association between the stimulus situation and the instrumental response ($SS \rightarrow IR$), and the basis of this association is "response reinforcement", or the training contingency between the instrumental response and the reinforcing stimulus ($IR:S^{reinf.}$). The two views differ in regard to

Table 11.1. Difference Between the Classical and Instrumental Procedures and Principles[a]

Procedure	Arranged Contingency	Supposed Locus of Association	Supposed Principle of Learning
Classical (Pavlovian)	$[SS]CS:US$ or $[SS]S^N:S^I$	CS-US or S^N-S^I	Association between CS and US based on learning of the contingency $CS:US$ (or $S^N:S^I$) (signaling principle)
Instrumental (Thorndikian)	$[SS]IR:S^{reinf.}$ or $[SS]R:S^I$	SS-IR or SS-R	Association between SS and IR based on learning of the contingency $[SS]IR:S^{reinf.}$ (or $R:S^I$) (response-reinforcement principle)

[a] SS-stimulus situation or the background stimulation; CS or S^N: conditioned or neutral stimulus; US or $S^{reinf.}$ or S^I: unconditioned, reinforcing or incentive stimulus; IR or R: instrumental response.

both the locus of association and the training contingency that is critical in producing the association.

The principle of stimulus-stimulus (CS-US) association based on stimulus-stimulus (CS:US) contingency learning seems adequate to account for the acquisition of new stimulus control or signal learning (e.g., a bell becomes a signal for food); but, at first glance, this principle appears to be inadequate for dealing with the shaping of new forms of actions. How, for example, is maze learning or learning to press a lever for food to be explained merely in terms of the learning of CS:US contingencies? Conversely, the principle of stimulus-response (SS-IR) association based on response-reinforcement (IR:$S^{reinf.}$) contingency learning seems adequate to deal with response shaping, but it is not obvious how it could be used to deal with certain instances of acquiring stimulus control. How, for example, is the acquisition of stimulus control by a bell that is followed by food, regardless of the animal's response, to be explained in terms of IR:$S^{reinf.}$ (or response-reinforcement) contingencies?

The apparent inadequacy of either of the two views to provide a satisfactory account of both stimulus control learning and response shaping has led some to adopt the position that both stimulus-stimulus (CS:US), or signal-incentive (S^N:S^I), and instrumental response-reinforcement (IR:$S^{reinf.}$), or response-incentive (R:S^I), contingencies form the basis of observed learned modifications of behavior. This is the so-called "two-process theory" of learning. The commonest form of this view (e.g., Mowrer, 1947; Rescorla & Solomon, 1967; Solomon & Wynne, 1954) is that motivational or emotional arousal required for response production is achieved through CS:US (signal:incentive) contingencies, while instrumental response shaping is achieved through IR:$S^{reinf.}$ (response:incentive) contingencies. What this theory fails to explain is how the CS-induced motivational arousal and the reinforcement-induced response shaping are integrated to produce a response that is both motivationally and topographically appropriate. How, for example, does eating motivation link up with a response shaped for obtaining food, and sexual motivation with copulatory responses, and not vice versa? Without any specification about how the two processes are integrated, the two-process theory lacks the essentials of being an explanatory account of the acquisition of new responses.

Even if the above shortcoming were to be overcome, the two-process theory would be unacceptable because it incorporates the response-reinforcement principle, and the validity of this has been challenged on two important grounds. First, this principle requires that the acquisition of a new instrumental response should not be possible without the actual occurrence of that response; otherwise the necessary $IRS^{reinf.}$ contingency would be absent. But demonstrations of "response substitution" (e.g., Lashley & McCarthy,

1926; Macfarlane, 1930; quoted by Munn, 1950) and "learning without responding" (e.g., Dodwell & Bessant, 1960; Solomon & Turner, 1962) indicate clearly that a new stimulus-response relation may become functional without the occurrence of the response during training trials. Second, according to the response-reinforcement principle, it is necessary for the $IR:S^{reinf.}$ contingency to operate in order for a uniform and stable instrumental response to be shaped. However, the development of uniform and reliable instrumental responses in experiments on latent learning (see Kimble, 1961, Chap. 8) shows that new responses can be acquired without the reinforcement of those responses; this is also shown by the phenomena of "autoshaping" (Brown & Jenkins, 1968; Williams & Williams, 1969). Thus neither the occurrence of a response during training nor *its* reinforcement can be said to be necessary for the acquisition of that response.

A New Hypothesis

The central idea of the hypothesis elaborated below is that both forms of the acquisition of new responses—the acquisition of new stimulus control and the construction of new responses—are attributable exclusively to the learning of stimulus-stimulus contingencies, and that response-reinforcement contingencies as such do not contribute to learned behavior modifications. This hypothesis is different from the two-process theory (e.g., Mowrer, 1947; Rescorla & Solomon, 1967) in that the latter theory, while it considers stimulus-stimulus contingency learning to be important in motivational arousal, and hence in performance, it also regards response-reinforcement contingencies to be necessary for the construction of instrumental responses. The present hypothesis is also different from the views of Bolles (1972), Estes (1972), and Walker (1969) in that all of them, while emphasizing the role of stimulus-stimulus contingency learning, attribute some role also to response-reinforcement and other contingencies. The present hypothesis is closest in spirit to the "cognitive theory" of Tolman (1932) and the "emotion theory" of Mowrer (1960a, 1960b), in that they considered cognitions and emotions to be primarily a matter of stimulus-stimulus contingency learning. However, the theories of Tolman and Mowrer have remained quite vague, having failed to show in specific terms how cognitions or emotions may quickly produce instrumental responses of particular forms to suit the occasion. My task here is to try to show how the shaping of an appropriate response, as seen in the acquisition of new stimulus-response relations, may be explained in terms of the principles of (stimulus-stimulus) contingency learning, response production, and selective perception and recall presented in earlier chapters.

The present hypothesis may be outlined in terms of seven tentative assumptions or principles. These may be explained with reference to a concrete example. Consider how a hungry rat may acquire the response of leaving the start box of a runway, traversing the runway, and reaching food in the goal box at the other end.

(1) *Principle of Spontaneous Occurrence of Component Acts.* For the defined response to be completed, several acts, such as moving around, turning in the direction of the runway, approaching, stopping, etc., must be performed in a certain sequence. Apart from the acts that comprise the response and are therefore necessary, there are other "irrelevant" acts that the rat will probably perform from time to time (e.g., sniffing, grooming, rearing, biting a part of the runway, etc.). An act can occur only if a certain act-assembly is activated. As was explained in Chapter 4, an act-assembly may be activated either through the activation of neurons (gnostic-assemblies) that represent some inherently effective eliciting stimulus configurations or neurons that represent stimulus configurations that have acquired effectiveness through the process of stimulus-control transfer. Whatever the basis of the efficacy of the eliciting stimulus, inherent or acquired, no act can occur without an effective elicit- ing stimulus. In our example, then, the situation must contain the stimulus configurations capable of eliciting the required acts at appropriate places in the runway. Another way of saying this is that the "general" or "spontaneous" activity elicited in the training situation must contain the necessary acts if the desired response is to be constructed (Bindra, 1961).

In the case of an inexperienced rat, the "general activity matrix" displayed in a runway is likely to contain, apart from acts of "freezing," sniffing, orienting, grooming, etc., acts of approaching or withdrawing from particular areas of the runway that contain stimulus configurations of varying salience (intensity, novelty), which would initially have some incentive properties (motivational valence arising from novelty, etc.). As the animal becomes familiar with the situation, it will approach more and more novel aspects of the runway, that is, it will gradually move toward the as-yet-unfamiliar goal box. Let us say that there are four particular stimulus configurations, S_1, S_2, S_3, and S_4, that elicit approach acts, such that the rat ends up reaching the goal box (see Figure 11.1). Thus, even before the rat has discovered any food in the situation, it has completed the required response, though in a highly inefficient manner—with many irrelevant acts interspersed among the necessary ones. Whenever an animal of a given species is to be trained to a particular response, the trainer must arrange the physical features of the training situation in such a way that it contains all the stimulus configurations necessary for "spontaneously" eliciting all the required acts and as few as possible of the stimulus configurations that elicit irrelevant acts (Bindra, 1961; Breland & Breland, 1961).

(2) *Principle of Habituation of Spontaneous Activity.* With repeated exposure to the training situation, in the absence of any strongly rewarding or punishing incentive stimulation, there will be a gradual reduction in the efficacy of the various initially salient stimulus configurations, so that the acts elicited by them will decrease in frequency, resulting in a gradual decrease in the amount of general activity, as typically found in exploration experiments.

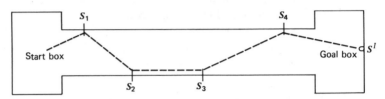

Figure 11.1.   Acquiring a runway response. The relative motivational valence of different stimulus configurations S_1, S_2, S_3, S_4, and S^I changes as a consequence of habituation and incentive stimulation in the course of training. See text for further explanation.

Such habituation is likely to lead first to a relatively greater decrease in irrelevant acts, but will gradually also spread to the relevant acts, those elicited by the salient stimuli specially arranged to facilitate the occurrence of the relevant acts. Thus, the speed of completing a defined response is first likely to increase, as irrelevant acts drop out, and later likely to decrease, as habituation extends to the relevant acts. In our example of the runway response, repeated trials of placing the rat in the start box, in the absence of any food in the goal box, should first lead to a gradual increase in the speed of completing the response and then to a decrease in both the speed and the likelihood of completing the response. After 15 or 20 trials the rat may simply sit in the start box, or in some other safe and comfortable corner of the runway, and may not complete the response at all. This decrease in exploratory activity may be taken to mean that the animal has developed a situational schema that represents spatial relations between the various important features of the situation. Any noticeable change in the physical characteristics or layout of the situation will result in a resumption of exploratory activity.

(3) *Principle of Motivational Arousal.* The essential requirement for training any response in a situation is, of course, that the animal keep producing the acts necessary for the construction of the response. Usually this means keeping active, but habituation results in decreased exploratory activity. However, the habituation decrement can be counteracted by introducing incentive stimuli into the situation in a way that would increase the probability of occurrence of the required acts. In general, the introduction of appetitive incentive stimuli results in a marked increase in general exploratory

activity, while the introduction of aversive incentive stimuli results in defensive acts of several varieties (e.g., freezing, hopping, squealing, spitting, biting, withdrawing). These effects of incentive stimulation occur whether or not the presentation of the incentive stimulation is made contingent on any response (Bindra & Palfai, 1967; Blanchard & Blanchard, 1969). In the present example of the hungry rat in a runway, the introduction of food in the goal box would result in an increase in exploratory activity after the rat has discovered the food in the goal box. Thus the decremental effects of habituation will be counteracted by motivational arousal generated by the food incentive in the current (hungry) organismic condition. If, as is usually the case, the food is introduced right at the beginning of training, then the observed exploratory activity will be a joint function of habituation decrement and motivational increment. If the food is not introduced until the rat has completely habituated to the situation, then it may take the rat several trials to discover the food, for it would have ceased to explore the whole situation on every trial.

(4) *Principle of Differential Motivational Valence.* The main thing required for the training of a specified response is that the particular stimulus configurations that elicit the necessary acts become more effective elicitors, while the stimulus configurations that elicit irrelevant acts become less effective. This differential in efficacy is produced by the learning of the contingent relations between the elicitors of necessary acts and some incentive stimulus, while the efficacy of irrelevant-act elicitors is being reduced through habituation. In the runway example, this means that the elicitors of necessary acts, S_1, S_2, S_3, and S_4 (Figure 11.1), must acquire additional motivational valence, that is, must become conditioned incentive stimuli, through the building of contingency organizations (as explained in Chapter 9) representing the contingent relations between these stimuli and the food incentive: $S_4:S^I$; $S_3:S^I$; $S_2:S^I$; and $S_1:S^I$. The learning of these specific contingencies (in addition to the general contingency between the situation as a whole or the background stimulation and food, $S_B:S^I$), would increase the efficacy of the eliciting stimuli, and the eliciting efficacy of each stimulus would be inversely proportional to its distance from the food. Now, when the rat is placed in the start box, S_1 would have greater appetitive motivational valence than the start box, and S_2 would have greater appetitive motivational valence than S_1, and so on; a rising gradient of appetitive motivational valence would exist between the start box and the goal box. Of course, the basis of the increased motivational valence of environmental stimuli lies not in the stimuli but in the animal's head—increased excitation of the pexgos of particular (conditioned) stimuli through the established contingency organizations (see Chapters 6 and 7).

(5) *Principle of Response Production.* The basic principle of response pro-

duction in a situation that is spatially differentiated with respect to motivational valence (eliciting efficacy) of its component stimulus configurations, is that the animal will move toward stimulus configurations of greater appetitive motivational valence or of lesser aversive motivational valence. In the present example, therefore, the rat would move from the start box to S_1, and from S_1 to S_2, and so on until it reaches the food, the area of greatest (appetitive) incentive value in the situation. If, on the other hand, the rat were given aversive stimulation in the start box, as in avoidance training, the rat would move in the direction of the goal box because it would represent the area of the least (aversive) incentive value ("the safest place") in the situation. In either event, the rat's behavior would first consist of several discrete acts, each moving the animal from one eliciting stimulus to another of greater appetitive motivational valence or lower aversive motivational valence. Note that the exact motivational valence of any particular stimulus may vary from moment to moment when temporal contingencies are involved. In the usual lever-pressing situation, for example, the motivational valence of the food receptacle may be expected to be greater *after* lever-pressing than before lever-pressing. In general, it may be said that a response (with a certain outcome) is produced when there exists a certain difference in the motivational valences of particular parts of the situation. In other words, the form of the response that emerges in a given training situation is determined by the spatiotemporal distribution of the various unconditioned and conditioned incentive stimuli in the situation.

(6) *Principle of Response Unification.* With increasing practice, a response tends to become increasingly more unified, or smooth and "ballistic." This is indicated by the fact that the response as a whole may then be triggered by the initial conditioned stimuli and may not require all the intermediate conditioned stimuli that initially guided particular act components of the response. Such response unification reflects the development of contingency organizations linking increasingly remote stimuli. In the runway example, with repeated training trials, the rat would learn not only the contingencies $S_1:S_2$, $S_2:S_3$, and $S_3:S_4$, but also $S_2:S_4$ and $S_1:S_4$. As these latter contingencies become strong, the percept of S_4 may be strongly excited by S_1, more strongly than the percept of S_2 or S_3, owing to the greater motivational valence of S_4. This means that on perceiving S_1 the rat may perceive S_4 and make an approach response directly to S_4; thus the wasteful acts of going to S_1, then S_2, etc., would be replaced by a more efficient sequence of acts that leads the rat directly to the goal box. The development of contingency organizations representing the more remote contingent relations ($S_2:S^I$; $S_1:S^I$, etc.), and the consequent progressively greater selective perception of the conditioned incentive stimuli closer to the food incentive, would

result in the progressive elimination of irrelevant acts, or progressive restriction of behavior to the acts necessary for completing the defined response. When this has happened, the response as a whole may be triggered by the initial conditioned stimuli (e.g., the start box), and all the intermediate conditioned stimuli would no longer be required for completing the response. With the repeated exercise of the $S_1:S^I$ contingency the motivational arousal produced by S_1 would also increase, so that the response will not only become more direct and unified, but will also be initiated earlier. Note that this account of response unification does not invoke an integration of discrete act-assemblies into larger and larger functional units; a unified response is not simply a speedier version of the initial sequence of acts, but is a new sequence of acts. Rather I attribute response unification to "short-circuiting" by the establishment of contingency organizations representing relations between remote stimuli, so that the animal's action (e.g., approach) is determined directly by more and more remote (i.e., closer to the food incentive) conditioned stimuli. The basis of this "short-circuiting" lies in selective perception—in the progressively greater priming of the pexgos of stimuli that lie further into the future than of those lying closer. This more efficient selective perception or anticipatory priming arises from the uniformity and stability of the situation, which make possible the learning of remote stimulus-stimulus contingencies. If the spatiotemporal distribution of unconditioned and conditioned incentives were to be changed (e.g., if food were given in the middle of the runway instead of in the goal box) the response form would also change, provided the selective perception habits of the animal did not prevent it from observing the changes.

(7) *Principle of Voluntary Action.* As a response is becoming unified, gnostic-assemblies representing various distinctive features of the response are also developing on the basis of the visual, tactual, proprioceptive, or other sensory consequences (feedback) of the occurrence of the components of the response. As noted in Chapter 5, through experience animals develop gnostic-assemblies of their own responses, which can then be activated to generate pexgos of the responses. A response pexgo, like other pexgos, becomes a part of the contingency organizations representing events that predict the response or are predicted by it. In a typical training situation, the main events that enter into contingency organizations are, say, the background situational complex (BS), the act-eliciting and later the response-triggering stimulus complex (ES), the occurrence of the trained response (TR), and the presentation of the incentive stimulation (S^I). The animal therefore not only learns the contingencies $BS:ES$, $BS:S^I$, and $ES:S^I$, which are the basis of priming the ES and S^I pexgos and thereby triggering the response, but also learns the contingencies $BS:TR$, $ES:TR$, and $TR:S^I$.

This means that BS would be capable of activating the pexgo of TR and TR would be capable of activating the pexgo of S^1. Thus, when a trained animal is placed in the situation, the pexgos ES, TR, and S^1 are activated. William James (1890) suggested that it is the conditioned excitation of the percept ("idea") of a *response* that is the basis of its production as a voluntary response ($BS:TR \rightarrow$ response production). But this is an incomplete account, for James failed to specify how the idea leads to the response. The present suggestion (see above) is that the basis of the production of a voluntary response lies in the conditioned excitation of the pexgos of the *stimulus configurations* that were initially capable of eliciting that response ($BS:ES \rightarrow$ response production) and that have been made salient through conditioned excitation of the gnostic-assemblies representing the eliciting stimulus (ES). The idea or percept (or pexgo) of a response is not the basis of its production.

What, then, is the role of the contingency organizations involving pexgos of the response? When a response is occurring, or when its pexgo has been contingently generated by the background stimulus complex, the pexgo of the response excites, through certain contingency organizations (e.g., $TR:S^1$), pexgos of future events that have reliably followed the response (e.g., a click or food-delivery as a consequence of lever-pressing). This means that pexgos of the consequences of a response are excited by a response serving as a conditioned (predictor) stimulus, and this is presumably the basis of the subjective experience of expectation that a certain response will produce particular consequences. Whereas William James invoked the conditioned excitation of the percept (idea) of a response as the basis of the voluntary action, the present suggestion is that the pexgo of a response, conditioned or unconditioned, is the basis of only the subjective experience of volition—expectation of certain consequences—but has nothing to do with the production of that response.

Though Tolman (1932) did not explain response production, he said that what animals learn are means-end cognition relations: Given this situation (BS), doing this (TR) would lead to that (S^1). The existence of such means-end cognitions, or response-consequence contingency organizations, is indicated by the surprise animals show when some usual consequences of a response fail to occur. If response-consequence contingencies are to be developed, animals should be able to discriminate between different responses of their own. This appears to be so. Beninger, Kendall, and Vanderwolf (1974) have shown that the rat is capable of responding differentially (on one of four levers) on the basis of what activity (sitting motionless, face-washing, walking, rearing) it happens to be engaged in at the moment of presentation of a discriminative signal for responding. They point out the similarity between such differential responses, based on knowledge of one's own action-in-progress, and self-report in man.

Since visceral reactions have no intrinsic sensory feedback, they would not be represented by any clear percepts that could become conditioned to situational stimuli or the consequences of the visceral reactions. According to the present view, then, the occurrence of conditioned visceral reactions would not be accompanied by an experience of volition, though it should be quite possible to produce particular visceral reactions by conditioned stimuli that predict the eliciting stimuli for those visceral reactions. In order to create an experience of voluntary control of visceral reactions, some extrinsic sensory feedback would have to be used or else the visceral reactions would have to be produced through postural and muscular adjustments.

The above seven principles comprise what may be called an incentive-motivational view of the acquisition of new responses. This view differs from other theoretical accounts of learned behavior modifications in important respects, and it may be useful to review briefly some of these differences.

SOME THEORETICAL ISSUES

I shall discuss five related issues here: (1) the issue of the critical contingencies in learning, (2) the issue of the essential difference between the classical and instrumental conditioning, (3) the issue of conditioning with compound stimuli, (4) the issue of the basis of serial ordering in response, and (5) the issue of the nature of response unification.

Critical Contingencies

According to the present formulation, the acquisition of a new response depends critically on the learning of the contingencies existing between *stimuli* in the training situation, that is, on the development of signal-incentive (stimulus-stimulus) contingency organizations. No role is attributed to any contingencies that might exist between situational stimuli and particular responses (stimulus-response contingencies) or between particular responses and incentive stimuli (response-incentive contingencies). Thus, the central idea of the Thorndikian or law-of-effect principle of learning—the learning of $S:R$ associations on the basis of response-reinforcement contingencies—is not included in the present formulation. In this respect, my account differs from several others (e.g., Bolles, 1972; Estes, 1969) that accept the idea that response-incentive contingencies may be sufficient for, or contribute to, the acquisition of new responses. Note too that the stimulus-stimulus contingencies considered critical in my formulation are not the contingencies between response-produced (or response feedback) stimuli and incentive stimuli, but the contingencies between response-eliciting stimuli and incentive stimuli.

The issue then is this: What are the precise roles of stimulus-incentive and response-incentive contingencies in the learning of new responses? Pavlovian experiments leave little doubt that a stimulus-incentive contingency can by itself be sufficient for the modification of viscerosomatic reactions. Further, the appearance of stable "instrumental" or operant components (e.g., head turning, neck stretching, and various superstitious and preparatory acts) in the course of classical conditioning indicate that the response-incentive contingencies may not be required for the learning of at least some operant responses. Finally, and more formally, recent analytic studies of the phenomenon of "auto-shaping" show that particular operant responses may be shaped and controlled by arranging response-independent, stimulus-incentive contingencies (Brown & Jenkins, 1968; Gamzu & Schwartz, 1973; Gamzu & Williams, 1973; Moore, 1973). What these observations mean is that stable operant responses can be acquired solely on the basis of stimulus-incentive contingencies existing between the response-eliciting stimuli and the incentive stimulation in a situation; a response-incentive contingency need not necessarily be required for the acquisition of new responses.

But even if not always required, might response-incentive contingencies be required in some cases of response acquisition? Without attributing at least a contributory role to response-incentive contingencies, how could one account for the various phenomena of instrumental learning (e.g., maze learning, lever-pressing for food, head-turning to look at something)? My general answer is this: The occurrence of any defined instrumental response (or some act component of it) at a given moment means that (the representation of) a certain stimulus configuration capable of eliciting that response has become highly potent through the operation of various contingency organizations and motivational mechanisms described earlier. The critical assumption here is that the response-eliciting stimulus complex is—must be—present in the training situation to begin with. Note that this assumption of the prior presence in the training situation of the response-eliciting stimulus complex is equally essential for the interpretation of instrumental learning in terms of the response-reinforcement view. This is so because in the Thorndikian instrumental training procedure the first reinforcement comes *after* the occurrence of the response to be reinforced, so that the first occurrence of the response must have some basis other than reinforcement. Though the first occurrence of the response-to-be-reinforced is usually attributed to "general activity" or "chance variation," it is evident that there must be some critical stimulus features that determine the first occurrence of a defined instrumental response or act (e.g., a lever-press, an approach-contact, grasping with the left hand), even as a part of general activity or chance variation. The fact that a trainer may spend considerable time in designing a training chamber in which the specified instrumental response is highly likely to occur "spontaneously" indicates that even in response-reinforcement procedures an implicit assumption is made that particular stimulus configurations of the situation determine the likelihood of occurrence of certain specified instrumental response components. The problem posed by the first occurrence of an instrumental act is usually ignored by response-reinforcement theorists, but it nevertheless remains a problem, and, within a deterministic framework, can be dealt with by making the assumption of act-eliciting stimulus configurations.

Once it is explicitly assumed that the production of any specific instrumental response or of some of its act components is linked to one or more particular eliciting stimulus configurations, then the way becomes clear for interpreting instrumental learning in terms of the learning of stimulus-stimulus contingencies alone. The problem of instrumental training then becomes one of making certain response-eliciting stimuli highly potent motivationally, and this can be done through stimulus-stimulus contingency learning between the response-eliciting stimulus and the incentive stimulus. This process was explained in Chapter 9.

Theoretically, then, it is possible that stimulus-incentive contingencies may be sufficient to explain the learning of instrumental responses. However the question remains whether response-incentive contingencies may, in themselves, also be sufficient for the acquisition of instrumental responses. An unequivocal answer to this question would require some way of isolating the effects of stimulus-incentive and response-incentive contingencies in the learning of a given instrumental response. Since the critical stimulus-incentive contingencies would involve the response-eliciting stimulus, which elicits the specified response before the first reinforcement, it seems impossible experimentally to separate the occurrence of the response from the perception of the eliciting stimulus, that is, to make the response-incentive contingency $(R:S^I)$ operate without simultaneously exercising the stimulus-incentive contingency $(ES:S^I)$; for example, an animal cannot learn to lever-press without perceiving the stimuli (e.g., the lever stimuli) that elicit that response. One way around this impasse is to try to add an explicit $R:S^I$ contingency to an existing $ES:S^I$ contingency and determine whether the addition of $R:S^I$ makes any difference in the form or frequency of the instrumental response.

Investigations that have examined this question show that the superimposition of a negative response-incentive contingency $(R:\overline{S^I})$ on a positive stimulus-incentive contingency $(ES:S^I)$ cannot fully counteract the effect of the latter contingency; however, the negative $R:\overline{S^I}$ contingency does reduce the frequency of occurrence of the instrumental response (Williams &

Williams, 1969). Further, the superimposition of a positive $R:S^I$ contingency on an $ES:S^I$ contingency results in a marked increase in the frequency of the instrumental response (Lajoie, 1975). The question raised by these findings is this: Is the change in instrumental responding produced by the addition of an $R:S^I$ contingency best interpreted as a consequence of the $R:S^I$ contingency per se, or of some change in the $ES:S^I$ contingency that accompanies the introduction of the former contingency?

My view is that the changes in instrumental responding are not attributable to the $R:S^I$ contingency, but arise from the requirement of greater stimulus discrimination imposed by the $R:S^I$ contingency procedure. What the addition of the $R:S^I$ contingency does is to restrict the range of stimuli perceived at the time of incentive stimulation. For example, in the case of the $ES:S^I$ contingency procedure, the incentive stimulation would occur not only when the animal is observing the response-eliciting stimulus, but also when it is observing other things (because the incentive stimulation is not dependent on the animal's behavior in any way); thus other stimuli (OS) would bear a contingent relation with incentive stimulation $(OS:S^I)$ in addition to the specific $ES:S^I$ that operates on the occasions when the animal is directly observing ES at the time of incentive stimulation. This means that a wide range of stimuli, including the response-eliciting stimulus, would serve to predict the incentive stimulation; ES would not be discriminated from OS. In the case of the response-reinforcement contingency, since the incentive stimulation occurs only when the animal has made the specified response—that is, when it has actually perceived the eliciting stimulus for that response—the contingency $ES:S^I$ will be learned more strongly than the contingency $OS:S^I$; ES would be discriminated from OS. Since response production is determined by the difference in the motivational valence of the various conditioned stimuli in the situation, the responding in the case of the response-incentive contingency procedure would be more concentrated on the specific ES (see Lajoie, 1975).

In view of the difficulties with the response-reinforcement view of instrumental learning, which were mentioned earlier in this chapter, it seems reasonable to adopt the working assumption that the critical contingencies underlying learned behavior modification are stimulus-incentive contingencies; response-incentive contingencies do not contribute to the learning or performance of instrumental responses.

Classical and Instrumental Procedures

The traditional view has been that the classical and instrumental training procedures produce different types of learned behavior modifications because the $CS:US$ contingency operates in the former and the $R:S^{reinf.}$ contingency operates in the latter. Actually it has long been recognized that both of the contingencies are usually present in each of the two procedures (Hebb, 1956; Konorski, 1948; Miller, 1951). However, according to the present formulation, the outcome differences arise wholly from the specific stimulus-stimulus contingencies that typically operate in the two procedures. In order to examine this issue it would be helpful to agree on a common terminology for the parallel contingencies of the two procedures. A simple scheme is presented in Table 11.2.

Table 11.2. Parallel Contingencies in the Classical and Instrumental Procedures

Contingency	Classical Procedure	Instrumental Procedure	Suggested Common Term
Between training stimulus and incentive stimulus	$CS:US$ (e.g., tone:food)	Miscellaneous chamber stimuli:$S^{reinf.}$ (ignored)	$TS:S^I$
Between training response and incentive stimulus	$CR:US$ Miscellaneous acts:US (ignored)	$IR:S^{reinf.}$ (e.g., lever-press:food)	$TR:S^I$
Between response-eliciting stimulus and incentive stimulus	$US:US$ (meaningless)	IR-eliciting stimulus:$S^{reinf.}$ (ignored)	$ES:S^I$
Discriminative training contingencies	CS or $CS^+:US$ no CS or $CS^-:US$	$S^D:IR:S^{reinf.}$ $S^\Delta:IR:S^{reinf.}$	$TS^+:S^I$ $TS^-:S^I$

In the typical classical conditioning experiment (say, Pavlov's salivation experiment) the experimenter's concern is with isolating and studying a change in stimulus control. He therefore arranges a contingency between a training stimulus (TS or CS, say, a tone) in relation to which the learned modification is to be measured and an incentive or unconditioned stimulus (S^I or US, say, food). The stimulus configuration (ES) that elicits the defined training response (e.g., salivation) is the unconditioned stimulus itself. Since ES is the same thing as US; the contingency $ES:S^I$ is meaningless and is ignored. Further, since the concern is with stimulus control, the contingency between the conditioned response (once it has begun to occur in response to CS) and US, as well as between miscellaneous other acts and US, is also ignored.

In the typical instrumental conditioning experiment (say, training a rat to press a lever to obtain food), the experimenter's concern is with changing response form. He therefore arranges to observe some change in behavior in an experimental chamber whose stimulus features are largely ignored so far as formal description is concerned. In fact, the experimenter does not know the precise stimulus configuration that would be effective in eliciting the defined instrumental response; he therefore waits until the animal happens to press the lever and then quickly presents the reinforcing or incentive stimulus (food). Clearly, the perception of the response-eliciting stimulus on the part of the animal must precede the occurrence of the first response and the reinforcing stimulation. This means that the so-called procedure of response-reinforcement contingency is in fact a procedure that results also in an unintended contingency between the response-eliciting *stimulus* and the reinforcing (incentive) stimulus ($ES:S^I$). In traditional accounts of learning, the $ES:S^I$ contingency was ignored: in descriptions of classical procedure, because $ES=US$, the contingency is meaningless; in descriptions of instrumental procedure, because there was little concern with how the first response happened to be performed, the first occurrence of the response was simply called "spontaneous occurrence."

According to the present view, the effective contingencies in both the procedures are stimulus-stimulus ($TS:S^I$ or $ES:S^I$) contingencies. In the classical procedure the experimenter knows the stimulus (CS) under whose control he wishes to bring a response, and also knows the stimulus (US) that will reliably produce that response. In the instrumental procedure he does not know the exact stimuli that would elicit the response he wishes to shape and therefore lets the "spontaneous" occurrence of the response provide the basis of perceiving the eliciting stimuli. The critical aspect of learning consists in the acquisition of incentive-motivational properties by CS or ES through their association with the incentive stimulation. If the experimenter knew and could manipulate the precise eliciting stimuli of an instrumental response, he would be able to train an instrumental response through the classical procedure. To some extent this is what happens in the auto-shaping procedure, in which TS is the same thing as ES, and its pairing with food results in approach responses in the absence of any response-incentive contingency.

These differences between the two procedures in the exact components of the critical stimulus-stimulus contingencies imply certain other characteristics usually identified with each procedure. First, it should be clear that the classical procedure can be best employed for the training of responses whose response-eliciting stimuli (i.e., unconditioned stimuli) are known *a priori*. This means, in effect, that viscerosomatic regulatory reactions and certain reflexive actions are the types of responses that could be readily trained (brought under new stimulus control) by the classical conditioning procedure.

Second, in the case of classical procedure, since the response-eliciting stimulus (US), as well as the training stimulus (TS or CS), is controlled by the experimenter, the occurrence of the response can be determined by the experimenter. In the instrumental procedure, since the experimenter does not know (as well) what the response-eliciting stimuli (ES) of the desired instrumental response are, and must withhold presenting S^I until the response-as-defined occurs "spontaneously," he cannot control the occurrence of the response. This means that any observed learned modification is readily attributable to distinctive and known stimuli in the case of classical conditioning, but this is not the case in instrumental training. Thus, the responses look like elicited respondents in the case of classical conditioning and emitted operants in the case of instrumental training. But in both cases the basic contingency learning is between two sets of stimulus events, TS and S^I in the case of classical conditioning, and ES and S^I in the case of instrumental training.

Third, an important difference between the two procedures lies in the fact that in classical conditioning the form of the conditioned response (e.g., salivation) is highly dependent on the nature of the incentive stimulus (S^I), and it occurs reliably only after the conditioned stimulus (CS or TS) has been paired with the incentive stimulus, whereas in instrumental training the response is specified by the experimenter and the incentive stimulus is not presented until the response as specified has already occurred because of certain unspecified eliciting stimuli. This means that the form of the *instrumental acts* (head turning, approaching, etc.) in classical conditioning may be quite variable, even though salivation occurs reliably, while in the case of instrumental training the desired response is specified in advance and the continuance of the experimental procedure is dependent on its occurrence in the form defined. Thus, in classical conditioning the experimenter can state what the conditioned incentive stimuli will be but cannot specify exactly what the animal will do (apart from the unconditioned response), while in instrumental training the experimenter can state what the animal will do but cannot specify exactly the effective conditioned incentive stimuli. It is understandable, then, why classical conditioning is said to lead to "stimulus control" learning and instrumental training is said to produce "response shaping."

The above interpretation of the apparent differences between classical conditioning and instrumental training paradigms implies that, by placing varying emphases on the specifications of the stimulus and response aspects of the experimental situation, it should be possible to obtain response shaping in classical conditioning experiments and stimulus control in instrumental training experiments. Indeed, the appearance of "instrumental components" (e.g., "superstitious" or "anticipatory" acts) in classical conditioning experiments (e.g., Skinner, 1948; Zener, 1937), and the appearance of "classical components" (e.g., conditioned anxiety) in instrumental training experiments (e.g., Miller, 1948; Mowrer, 1939) has been observed by many investigators. And several recent experimental demonstrations of "incidental" response shaping with the use of the "auto-shaping" procedure (Brown & Jenkins, 1968; Gamzu & Schwartz, 1973; Moore, 1971; Williams & Williams, 1969), and of "incidental" stimulus control with the use of the instrumental procedure (e.g., Kamin, Brimer, & Black, 1963), leave little doubt that the two procedures involve emphasis on different types of stimulus-stimulus contingencies rather than different fundamental learning processes.

It may be noted that, in terms of the proposed interpretation, no special significance need attach to the several recent demonstrations that autonomically controlled visceral reactions, such as tachycardia and vasodilation, can be trained by the instrumental procedure (see Miller, 1969). Whatever the eliciting stimuli that make a particular visceral reaction occur "spontaneously" for the first time in the instrumental training situation would become conditioned incentive stimuli when they are followed by some unconditioned incentive stimulus in the course of "instrumental training." And the process of learning from then on would be the same as in the case of skeletal responses, namely, a gradual increase in the conditioned incentive properties of whatever stimulus configurations are critical in the initial occurrence of the particular visceral reactions. As in all cases of instrumental training, the experimenter is ignorant of the exact response-eliciting stimuli, so that the occurrence of visceral reactions appears to be an operant rather than a respondent, "voluntary" rather than "involuntary." If the training of visceral reactions by the instrumental procedure is somewhat less reliable than the instrumental training of skeletal actions, it is because (1) there are stringent limits on the range of changes in visceral reactions that occur spontaneously in a recognizable form in a training situation, and (2) reflex regulatory mechanisms may mask the effects of conditioned visceral reactions. Thus, important though the recent demonstrations of modification of visceral reactions by instrumental procedure are from the viewpoint of traditional theoretical discussions, they are predictable from the ideas about the nature of learning proposed here. From the present viewpoint, the importance of the recent work, especially of the work of Miller and his collaborators (N. E. Miller, 1969), lies not so much in establishing that the instrumental procedure works for the modification of visceral reactions, but rather in the demonstration that autonomically controlled visceral reactions can be highly refined and differentiated—quite in contrast to the traditional accounts of the autonomic function as gross and diffuse.

Conditioning with Compound Stimuli

Consider the following experiment. A compound stimulus consisting of two components, say, a tone and a light, is paired in a classical conditioning procedure with a certain unconditioned stimulus, say, food or electric shock. After a reliable conditioned response has been established, test trials are given with each of the components, tone or light, alone. What would be the relative strength of the conditioned responses evoked by the two components individually? Pavlov (1927) observed that only one of the stimuli evoked a conditioned response; the other component remained ineffective, though, if used alone during conditioning, it too could be shown to be capable of evoking a strong conditioned response. The strength of conditioned responses evoked by a component of a compound conditioned stimulus thus depends on what other component is a part of the compound. In general, the relative strength of conditioned responses evoked by the components of a compound stimulus depends on the relative salience (intensity and novelty—see Chapter 4) of the two components (Kamin, 1969; Mackintosh, 1971); the relatively more salient component is said to "overshadow" the less salient component and thereby render it less effective as a conditioned stimulus.

Another factor that determines the relative efficacy of the components of a compound conditioned stimulus, as indicated by the strength of the conditioned response they evoke, is the relative priority of the two components in getting paired with the unconditioned or incentive stimulus. Of two components, A and B, if the component A alone is first paired with an incentive stimulus ($A:S^I$), and then the compound stimulus, AB, is paired with the same incentive stimulus ($AB:S^I$), subsequent tests with A alone and B alone would show that B evokes much weaker conditioned responses compared with A, and as compared with B in the absence of prior conditioning with A. In other words, with the same number of compound conditioning trials ($AB:S^I$) involving B, B would be a less potent conditioned stimulus if the compound conditioning trials had been preceded by a certain number of conditioning trials with A alone than if A had not had prior conditioning. The greater the prior conditioning with A alone, the less effective would be B in evoking the conditioned response (Kamin, 1969; Wagner, 1969). Since, after the conditioning of A alone, B *alone* remains conditionable to the same incentive stimulus, and the AB compound remains conditionable to other incentive stimuli, it seems reasonable to say that the prior conditioning with A "blocks" the subsequent conditioning of B in the AB compound (Kamin, 1969).

An explanation of the blocking phenomenon must indicate why the prior learning of a contingency $A:S^I$ reduces the conditionability of $B:S^I$ when A and B jointly make up the compound conditioned stimulus. One view is that the conditionability of B in the compound AB depends on the extent to which the previously conditioned component, A, predicts the occurrence of the incentive stimulus, S^I; if S^I is fully predicted by A when AB trials are introduced, no other contingency between that S^I and the other stimulus component (B) can be learned in the presence of A. This view was put forth by Kamin (1969), who suggested essentially that contingency learning takes place only while the unconditioned (incentive) stimulus is "surprising"—not predicted by the contingencies already learned. A more formal version of this view is that the potential conditioning capability of a given component is limited by the degree to which the incentive stimulus is already predicted by the total stimulus complex of the conditioning situation; the more an incentive stimulus is predicted by existing situational stimuli, the less effective any of its stimulus component would be as a conditioned stimulus (Rescorla & Wagner, 1972; Wagner & Rescorla, 1972). Essentially, then, this view attributes blocking to some kind of a "ceiling" of conditionability or contingency learning with a given incentive stimulus in a given situation. Another similar view is that stimuli compete with each other for association with a given incentive, and prior conditioning with A reduces the conditionability of B in the AB compound owing to "associative interference" from A (Revusky, 1971).

A somewhat different idea has been proposed by Wagner, Rudy, and Whitlow (1973). They suggest, essentially, that the reduction in the probability of learning the contingency $B:S^I$ arises from a decrease in the possibility of rehearsal that is normally required for the consolidation in memory of that contingency. The possibility of rehearsal in turn is linked to the surprisingness—unpredicted occurrence—of other episodes in the situation; a surprising episode commands greater rehearsal and therefore is more likely to be consolidated than a nonsurprising episode. In blocking experiments, the episode $AB:S^I$ is less surprising when the contingency $A:S^I$ has already been learned; hence the episode commands less rehearsal than it would without the prior learning of $A:S^I$, and this results in decreased consolidation (conditioning) of the $B:S^I$ contingency. A related formulation is that stimuli that predict new events command more "selective attention" than stimuli that predict events already predicted by other prior stimuli; thus the animal learns to "ignore" the stimuli that do not predict any change in the incentive stimulation in the given situation (Mackintosh, 1973; Mackintosh & Turner, 1971).

All the above views relate the blocking phenomenon to variations in some general hypothetical factors, such as ceiling of conditionability, competition for association, memory consolidation, and selective attention. However, none of them offer a plausible account of the processes underlying the factors, nor grounds for assuming why variations in the factors do or can lead to blocking. What is the justification for the assumption that there exists a conditionability ceiling, and even if such a ceiling exists why does it apply to the unconditioned (incentive) stimuli and not to conditioned stimuli? What exactly is competition for association, and why does associative interference block the conditioning of certain stimulus components and not of others? Is rehearsal the basis of memory consolidation, and, if it is, why do surprising events "command" rehearsal? What is the basis of selective attention and why does it favor salient and surprising stimuli? The proposed explanations of blocking need elaboration and specification. Further, more recent attempts to understand the phenomenon of blocking have produced a variety of new findings that are not neatly interpretable in terms of any of the above hypotheses (Mackintosh, 1974, 1975).

In terms of the ideas developed in this volume, the phenomena of compound conditioning, including blocking, are best seen as outcomes of the simultaneous operation of three processes: habituation, discrimination, and selective perception. The main point of my proposal is that the particular contingencies learned in a compound conditioning experiment depend on the strength of the pexgos of different potential conditioned stimuli generated during the conditioning trials. And the momentary strength of these pexgos is determined by the continual changes in the salience, discriminability, and stimulus selection that occur throughout the total procedure of an experiment. Consider a concrete example.

Suppose a rat is placed in a conditioning chamber and allowed, in two or three 30-min sessions, to become familiar with spatial layout and other features of the situation. Now we start presenting a brief compound stimulus periodically, say, on 10 occasions during each 30-min training session. The compound stimulus consists of a light (A) component and a tone (B) component. The first presentation of the compound stimulus in the by-now-familiar chamber would be very salient owing to its novelty, but its salience would decline with repetition as it becomes more familiar, even without any change in the intensity of the two components. Thus, in the absence of any other factor, the pexgo strength of the compound stimulus generated on its successive presentations would decline. As explained in Chapter 6, this habituation decrement in pexgo strength would make the compound stimulus progressively less conditionable to any incentive stimulus, such as an electric shock (S^I). The conditionability of each of the two components alone may also decline as a consequence of habituation to the compound, though not necessarily at the same rate for the two components. Note that these changes in conditionability would occur in the absence of any experience with an incentive stimulus, that is, in the absence of any formal conditioning procedure.

As the (unreinforced) presentations of the compound stimulus, AB, continue, gnostic-assemblies representing features of the light and tone would develop concurrently, resulting in a clearer identification (in relation to the background) of each of the two components. In other words, the two components, even though they are presented as parts of a compound, would gradually become more discriminable from each other and would become capable of serving as independent conditioned stimuli. The basis of the learning of such stimulus discrimination was explained in Chapter 5. Again, a noteworthy point is that the distinctiveness of a pexgo of a potential conditioned stimulus generated at any stage depends on the prior experience of the animal in the training situation, even when the experience does not involve exposure to any incentive stimulus.

Changes in selective perception of particular stimulus objects or stimulus attributes depend on the learning of contingencies that predict those stimuli and the incentive stimuli that are predicted by those stimuli. For example, the pexgo priming required for the selective perception of the compound AB would depend on the prior learning of the contingencies between other (background) situational events and AB ($S_B : AB$), as well as on the learning of contingencies between AB and the incentive stimuli it might predict ($AB : S^I$). According to the process of selective priming of pexgos explained in Chapter 10, conditioning trials, involving some incentive stimulation, would play an important (but not exclusive) part in the selective perception of the conditioned compound stimulus, AB. Further, conditioning with the individual components of the compound stimulus would influence the selective perception of the other component, as well as of other stimuli in the situation. For example, if component A is conditioned to shock ($A : S^I$), then the pexgo of A will come to be primed when the animal is placed in the experimental chamber, and selective perception of A will be facilitated. Now, if further conditioning trials are given with the compound AB ($AB : S^I$), the animal will selectively perceive A, so that the contingency $A : S^I$ will continue to be strengthened while the contingency $B : S^I$ may or may not be learned, depending on whether B is salient enough to overcome the priming advantage of the percept of A. Thus, *under certain circumstances*, the conditionability of B to the given incentive stimulus would be reduced, as found in the type of experiments on blocking described above.

However, this reduced conditionability of B may not apply to conditioning trials involving a new incentive stimulus (e.g., a stronger or a weaker shock), because the introduction of a strong novel stimulus, would mean a major change in the situation as previously experienced by the animal. Thus, conditioning trials with B and a new incentive stimulus would essentially mean a disruption of the context of the previously learned contingency ($A : S^I$). With the selective priming advantage of the pexgo of A gone, for even a few trials, there would be a strong possibility of learning the contingency between B

and the new incentive stimulus. The main point in which this interpretation differs from the ceiling-of-conditionability view is that conditionability is linked directly to the pexgo strength of the conditioned stimulus (compound or component), and not to any characteristic (limit of conditionabilit foy) the unconditioned incentive stimulus. Further, according to the present suggestion, changes in conditionability of the component of a compound stimulus may continue to occur, owing to the gradual development of distinctive gnostic-assemblies over many training trials of an experiment.

Thus, there are two clear implications of the present hypothesis. One is that variations in the conditionability of a component (A or B) of a compound stimulus (AB) may continue to occur much beyond the period over which training with the compound stimulus is usually given. The second is that some of the changes in conditionability would occur in the absence of any incentive stimulus, that is, as a consequence of repeated presentations of the compound stimulus without any unconditioned stimulus. Though detailed experimental tests of these implications remain to be made, I have come across one experiment that bears on the first of these implications. Gray and Lethbridge (in press) trained different groups of rats in conditioned suppression by pairing a compound conditioned stimulus (light-noise) with electric shock, and then compared the behavioral suppression-producing efficacy of the components across groups that had been given different numbers of conditioning trials (from 4 to 60). They found that, while after 8 or 12 conditioning trials each component was as effective (complete suppression) as the compound stimulus in producing suppression, the efficacy of both the components declined at an accelerating rate after 24, 40, and 60 conditioning trials with the compound stimulus; the compound stimulus, of course, continued to produce complete suppression. This finding may be interpreted as meaning that early in training the two components and the compound activate many common gnostic-assemblies, but later in training they are represented by more distinctive gnostic-assemblies, and that the development of more distinctive gnostic-assemblies proceeds in the absence of discriminative training—all conditioning trials were given with the compound stimulus and all trials were reinforced trials. This development of distinctive gnostic-assemblies could be due either to increasing differentiation of the component assemblies from the compound assemblies or to increasing integration of the component assemblies into common intermodal assemblies representing the compound stimulus (intermodal integration—see Chapter 5). The fact that the compound stimulus and the components show different eventual suppression-evoking properties suggests that both differentiation and integration are responsible for the increasing distinctiveness of the compound stimuli and component stimuli, as indicated by the differences in their suppression-producing efficacy. Whatever the basis of their differential efficacy, the main point for the present discussion is that progressive changes in the conditionability both of the components and of the compound stimulus are consistent with the present hypothesis, which proposes habituation (variations in salience), discrimination (development of distinctive gnostic-assemblies), and selective perception (conditioned priming of pexgos) as the critical determiners of the outcomes of compound conditioning experiments.

Serial Ordering in Response

A response is made up of many different acts that occur in a serial arrangement leading to a specific outcome. By what processes are the required acts produced in a sequential order that is appropriate for completing the response as a whole?

We have seen that serial ordering of acts in a response cannot be wholly accounted for in terms of either the order of presentation of the eliciting stimuli or the activation of particular associations between successive pairs of acts. Normally the production of successive acts in a response is too rapid and too flexible (X may be followed by Y on one occasion and by Z on another) to be accounted for in terms of particular act-eliciting stimuli or associations between particular acts. To explain the rapidity and flexibility of response structures, Lashley (1949) proposed that the neural arrangements (act-assemblies) representing the acts required in a response are first "primed" or "set" through associational and attentional processes, and then a "scanning" process imposes an activation-order on them, resulting in the flow of acts in the appropriate order. He thought of the scanning process, which imposes the order, as being independent of the act-assemblies and of the processes that prime them, so that the same acts could be scanned in different serial orders at different times. The difficulty with this view, as Bryden (1967) has pointed out, is that it begs the question. What, we may ask, is this scanning process? And how does it affect the order of production of certain acts when it is independent of those acts? Lashley (1949) posed the problem of serial ordering clearly enough but did not offer a satisfactory answer.

An alternative solution suggested by some (e.g., Bryden, 1967; Wickelgren, 1969) is that serial-ordering may be determined by particular associations whose activation is determined, not by a single prior act, but by the sequence of a number of prior acts. Such "context-sensitive coding" would make for some flexibility, because the same act, A, may activate any one of two or more (B or C or D, etc.) subsequent acts depending on the context in which A has occurred. But this flexibility is bought at the expense of greatly multiplying the number of distinctive context-sensitive associations that would have to be postulated to produce the innumerable different sequences in which any given act might occur. In effect, this proposal attempts to generate the diversity and appropriateness of observed sequences by multiplying the number of particular associations; it offers no new mechanisms that would guarantee genuine flexibility. This point has been elaborated by Halwes and Jenkins (1971) in connection with the serial-ordering of phonemes in the production of speech. Lashley postulated a nonassociative, truly flexible scanning process but failed to explain its workings.

According to the account of response production outlined earlier in this chapter, the basis of the occurrence of an act at a given moment lies in the activation of a pexgo representing the eliciting stimulus of that act. The occurrence of a succession of appropriate acts comprising a response would thus require the activation of each of the relevant pexgos at an appropriate moment in the sequence. As explained earlier (Chapters 6 and 7), the activation of a pexgo is determined, apart from the current sensory inflow, by the complex of contingency organizations that are active at the moment and comprise the momentary determining set. The mechanism of the production of an appropriate act at a given moment in a sequence of acts lies, then, in the pattern of contingency organizations that happen to be activated at that moment. This will be an ever changing pattern and would result in the priming or activation of a succession of pexgos corresponding to the succession of cues that were important in the initial stages of learning a response. According to the present formulation, then, serial ordering of acts in a response is the outcome of the repeated operation of the same processes (changing momentary determining set and changing cues) that generate individual acts. There is no serial ordering of acts apart from the mere occurrence of each act on the basis of the common process of act-production; no special process concerned only with imposing an order need be postulated.

Note that this view postulates no association between successive acts, taken singly or in groups. Nor does it claim that the activation of a particular pexgo leading to a certain act is determined associatively by a certain other pexgo. Rather it suggests that each of several contingency organizations, representing specific previously learned contingent relations, contributes to the priming or activation of the pexgos that produce particular acts. The occurrence of both correct and incorrect acts is to be accounted for in terms of the operating contingencies. The operating contingencies most important in determining a correct succession of acts are, of course, the temporal contingencies relating various situational events to each other in time. Lashley too thought the temporal features of stimuli to be important, but his account treated temporal features as static, associative elements rather than as dynamic features that created a continually changing, flexible determining set.

Consider how this set-cue interaction can lead to the typing of a word that appears in a visual display. Suppose the word is *look*. The typist reads the word, and the visual pexgo of the word primes several other pexgos through the contingency organizations of the word. Among the primed pexgos would be those representing the letters l, o, k. In the given typing situation, the set may lead to the activation of the pexgo of l that leads to the typing of l. The activation of this pexgo in the prevailing set would lead to a strong activation of a contingency organization of "double-letter" (repetition of a letter) as well as to the contingency organization $l:o$. As the pexgo o is activated, it, together with the activation of the double-letter $(X:X)$ contingency organization, would lead again to the activation of the pexgo of o—and so on until *look* has been typed. Now suppose that while the contingency organizations $o:o$ and $o:k$ are equally strong, and the contingency organization "double letter" is also activated by the word *look* or by the first o, then the typist is as likely to end up typing *lokk* as *look*. In order for the first o to be followed by the second o, and for the second o to be followed by k, the cues arising from the first o have to be distinguishable from the cues arising from the second o. But to the extent that a subject depends on proprioceptive cues (interneural or peripheral) for such differentiation, the typing of the same letter twice (pressing the same key with the same finger) would provide a very poor basis for distinguishing between the first and the second o. Thus the discrimination for producing the second o and k would have to be based on temporal order cues. Since temporal order cues are highly refined and easily missed, especially when one is trying to type fast, an inexpert typist may frequently make the error of typing *lokk* for *look*.

Three implications of this analysis should be noted. First, this kind of error is more likely to occur in typing than in cursive writing, because cues distinguishing the single from the double production of a letter are more likely to be readily discriminable in cursive writing. Second, this kind of error is less likely to occur when copy typing, which is visually guided, than when visual cues from the copy are lacking, as in dictation or composition. So far as I know, comparisons of errors of writing and typing, typing while composing, and typing while copying, have not been made. Third, errors of this type would be less likely to occur when the contingency which the letter that is repeated bears with the following letter is weak (e.g., $o:z$ in *ooze*) than when it is strong (e.g., $o:k$). With practice, the contingency organizations representing the common contingencies in a particular kind of material would be well learned, and an expert typist would make few errors in typing that kind of material. This same analysis would apply to most of what MacNeilage (1964) has called temporal errors of typing (e.g., reversal, omission, and anticipation errors), as well as to mistakes of order in speech, discussed by Lashley (1951).

Response Unification

In the early stages of training of a response, the necessary acts are mixed with several irrelevant acts, the acts occur individually in a haphazard and disjointed way, and the completion of the response becomes smooth and fast. This improvement in efficiency is reflected in the speeds of response initiation and response execution as well as in error reduction. The question at issue here is the basis of such response unification.

The traditional views of response unification (e.g., Bryan & Harter, 1897) have made use of the idea of integration of acts into larger units. It is suggested that, with practice, the successive acts in the sequence comprising a response form act-act linkages, so that one act leads directly to the next one without requiring the act-selection processes that are necessary in the early stages of learning. In this way acts are integrated into larger and larger sequences, which then serve as functional units such that the activation of the first act in the unit leads automatically to the execution of the whole sequence. The process of response unification is then one of developing larger and larger act-sequences that can operate as unitary wholes. In the case of learning Morse code, Bryan and Harter (1897) described the increasing integration as a progression from the letter-stage to the syllable stage, and from there to word and phrase stages. The central idea of this act-integration view is one of act-act linkages that come to operate largely independently of the sensory-perceptual processes necessary at the earlier stages of learning.

As we saw in Chapter 4, the idea of linkages between act-assemblies is not a plausible basis for interpreting response unification. Such linkages should make it difficult to obtain the type of flexible stimulus-response relations that characterize adaptive behavior. For example, if a strong integration of acts of typing *looking* exists, it is difficult to see how a typist would ever be able to stop at *look* or type *loot* or *lot*. Some sensory control of the determination of particular acts (letters in this case) must remain to produce the observed flexibility of act sequences.

Further, even a casual observation of a well-practiced response suggests that the processes that produce successive acts in the sequence comprising the response must overlap in time; processes that result in act *B* must get started considerably before act *A* has been executed. This is most clearly demonstrated in the analysis of tasks requiring a speedy succession of acts, such as typing or piano playing. Shaffer (1973) has reported the case of a typist who, under ideal conditions, could copy prose from a computer display at the rate of nine symbols per second (about 100 words per minute); that is, it took her about 110 msec to type one symbol. However, her reaction time for typing a single random symbol was about 500 msec. This means that the process resulting in the typing of a certain symbol in prose must start about

500 msec before that symbol is to be typed, but in this 500-msec period the typist would type at least four other symbols. Thus, the processes leading to the typing of five successive symbols may be "in the works" at any given moment. Actually, Shaffer's analysis shows that a typist's speed-per-symbol increases with pre-exposure of up to eight subsequent symbols in prose. Thus, the preparatory processes in the typing of a symbol (e.g., priming of relevant pexgos) may start almost 1 sec before that symbol is actively typed and during which time about seven other symbols are in various stages of production. Clearly, neural processes involved in the production of the serial components of a unified response overlap in time, and it may be supposed that the efficiency that comes with practice is attributable to some kind of improvement in the extent to which the neural processes underlying successive acts can be in operation concurrently.

On the basis of our earlier discussion, it may be assumed that the speed of motor output required for each act probably remains largely unaffected by practice. In the case of tasks, such as typing, that require movements of mainly hands and fingers, the interval between the activation of successive act-assemblies may be guessed to be of the order of 100 msec; the interval may be less in the case of, say, speech and more in the case of, say, boxing. Thus the bottleneck that determines the rate of act-production is the minimum interval required between the successive activation of two act-assemblies. The main improvement with practice would appear to lie in the processes that precede the activation of particular act-assemblies.

It seems reasonable to propose that a major part of the improvement in performance that has been described as response unification consists in increased speed of activation of pexgos on which the acts depend. As we saw in Chapter 5, with experience certain gnostic-assemblies become closely linked, so that pexgos of complex stimulus configurations can be quickly generated, as demonstrated by an improvement, with practice, in the speed of identifying individual faces, objects, drawings, etc. This means that the amount of input information per unit time of observation increases with practice. Related to the development of larger and larger gnostic-assemblies goes the learning of contingent relations between stimuli. The resulting contingency organizations make it possible to generate pexgos of familiar stimulus configurations, as well as situational schemas, with increasing speed. Further, the contingency organizations control selective perception (see Chapter 10) and this further improves the speed of effective information input—activation of appropriate pexgos. All this means that the speed of perceptual processes increases greatly with practice.

How is the gap between the increasing speed of perceptual processes and the constant speed of motor output from act-assemblies reconciled? In the case of typing, for example, a typist may read three words (15 to 20 symbols) in the 100 msec that it takes to type one symbol. And a typist may in fact read ahead, sometimes a whole line or two, beyond the letter that is being typed at the moment. This means that the words read must be held beyond the perceptual structures (to allow advance reading of the copy), and some process must feed letters one by one to the appropriate act-assemblies. The nature of this "buffer zone" where pexgos are translated into a sequence of letters and remain sequentially arranged for feeding into appropriate act-assemblies remains a mystery. It is likely that it is such buffer zones that make it possible for some typists to perform other tasks (e.g., carry on a conversation, shadow or monitor other perceptual material) while typing. This discrepancy between the slow speed of motor output and the high speed of perceptual input, must give the typist time periods of 100 to 200 msec during which other tasks can be concurrently performed without losing grasp on the speed and accuracy of typing.

While the exact processes cannot yet be specified, the above considerations indicate that response unification is primarily an outcome of increased speed of perceptual identification and some process that paces the translation of pexgos into the activation of individual acts. It is likely that practice results in an improvement in the pacing process as well.

CHAPTER 12

Routines: Their Acquisition, Control, and Extinction

Around midnight each night a farm rat follows a certain path to a particular storeroom, eats some grain or peanuts from a certain canister, and then spends a good deal of time transporting these materials to its hideout; we say that the rat has an instinct for hoarding food. A monkey occupies a shady perch every morning and then quietly moves away when, at sunny noon, a dominant monkey claims that place; we say that the monkeys have established a dominance-submission relation. A boy goes to the playground, runs, jumps, and practices on parallel bars; we say he is practicing athletic skills. A girl wakes up at six, studies until eight, and then bathes and takes the nine o'clock bus to school; we say this is her habit. A man is afraid of leaving his house and becomes panicky and paralyzed when forced to go out; we say he suffers from anxiety neurosis. All these things—instincts, patterns of interindividual relations, skills (athletic, social, or intellectual), habits, neuroses—are here subsumed under the rubric of "routines." A *routine* is a pattern of action developed in a recurring situation and performed, quite uniformly yet flexibly, whenever the same or similar situations are encountered. This chapter is concerned with illustrating how the principles of learned behavior modification discussed in the last chapter may be applied to acquisition, performance, and extinction of routines of various types.

DESCRIPTION OF TRAINING SITUATIONS

As explained in the last chapter, the response that emerges in any recurring (or training) situation is determined by the spatiotemporal distribution of the various situational stimuli that have acquired conditioned motivational properties. Let us start then by roughly classifying the main types of conditioned stimuli and the main forms of their spatiotemporal distribution.

Types of Conditioned Stimuli

A given conditioned stimulus can have four main types of contingent relations with a predicted or unconditioned stimulus, depending on whether the latter is a neutral stimulus or an incentive stimulus. Both CS and US may be incentive stimuli, $CS^I:US^I$; for example, the odor of food is followed by the taste of food. Both the stimuli may be neutral, $CS^N:US^N$; for example, a soft tone is followed by a dim light. The first stimulus may be an incentive stimulus and the second one not, $CS^I:US^N$; for example, the taste of food in the mouth is followed by a soft tone. And the first stimulus may be neutral and the second one may be an incentive stimulus, $CS^N:US^I$; for example, a soft tone is followed by food. The contingencies arranged in the usual laboratory studies belong mainly to the second, $CS^N:US^N$ (habituation paradigm), and the fourth, $CS^N:US^I$ (conditioning or training paradigm), types. The two other types of contingencies also exist, and are learned, but we shall ignore them in this discussion.

The contingency between CS^N and US^I may be positive, $CS:US^+$ (i.e., CS is followed by an increase in the probability of US during a certain time-span), or negative, $CS:US^-$ (i.e., CS is followed by a decrease in the probability of US during a certain time-span). In addition, the US may be an appetitive incentive stimulus ($US^{Iap.}$), an aversive incentive stimulus (US^{Iav}), or a neutral stimulus (US^N). For the present purpose, then, we may recognize six types of conditioned stimuli or motivational signals, and the corresponding six types of motivational influences (see Table 12.1).

First, a CS may be positively related to an appetitive incentive stimulus ($CS:US^{+Iap.}$); such a CS may be designated $CS^{+Iap.}$. A $CS^{+Iap.}$ would generate or enhance an appetitive central motive state, and this would promote some approach action in relation to the CS itself and other similar stimuli, so long as the $US^{Iap.}$ (the unconditioned appetitive incentive stimulus) is not present. Thus, a light that has been followed by an increase in the probability of presentation of food in a tray would generate an (appetitive) eating central motive state in a hungry animal, and this would promote approach acts (reaching, sniffing, touching, licking, pecking, etc.) toward the light and the empty food tray (e.g., Brown & Jenkins, 1968; Skinner, 1971; Zener, 1937). When the food is delivered, the same acts would be directed at the food, and the contact stimuli of food would then elicit the consummatory acts of eating.

Second, a CS may be positively related to an aversive incentive stimulus ($CS:US^{+Iav.}$); designate such a CS as $CS^{+Iav.}$. A $CS^{+Iav.}$ would generate or enhance an aversive central motive state, and this would promote some defensive action in relation to the CS itself and other similar stimuli, so long as the $US^{Iav.}$ (the unconditioned aversive incentive stimulus) is not present

Table 12.1.   Six Types of $CS\text{-}US$ Contingencies, the Corresponding Changes in Central Motive States Produced by CS (in the Absence of US), and Their Influence on Behavior

Type of Contingency	Designation of CS	Change in Central Motive State (cms)	Influence on Behavior
1. CS has a positive contingency with an appetitive incentive stimulus	$CS^{+Iap.}$	Generation or enhancement of an appetitive cms	Promoting approach action in relation to CS
2. CS has a positive contingency with an aversive incentive stimulus	$CS^{+Iav.}$	Generation or enhancement of an aversive cms	Promoting defensive action in relation to CS
3. CS has a negative contingency with an appetitive incentive stimulus	$CS^{-Iap.}$	Mitigation of an existing appetitive cms	Impeding approach action in relation to CS
4. CS has a negative contingency with an aversive incentive stimulus	$CS^{-Iav.}$	Mitigation of an existing aversive cms	Impeding defensive action in relation to CS
5. CS has a positive contingency with a neutral stimulus	CS^{+N}	Generation of a non-investigatory ("boredom") cms	Impeding exdolratory action in relation to CS
6. CS has a negative contingency with a neutral stimulus	CS^{-N}	Mitigation of an existing boredom cms	Promoting exploratory action in relation to CS

in the situation. Thus, a sound correlated with the presentation of an electric shock would generate an (aversive) fear central motive state in a rat, and this would promote defensive acts (freezing, crouching, escape attempts, etc.) in relation to the sound and other features of the situation (e.g., Bindra & Palfai, 1967; Blanchard & Blanchard, 1969; Ulm & Cicala, 1971). When the electric shock is delivered, the animal will direct vigorous defensive acts against the source of shock (e.g., biting the electric grid, squealing, jumping).

Third, a CS may be negatively related to an appetitive incentive stimulus ($CS\!:\!US^{-Iap.}$); such a CS may be designated $CS^{-Iap.}$. A $CS^{-Iap.}$ would generate some inhibitory process (see Chapter 7) that would attenuate the prevailing appetitive central motive state for a certain duration (what Mowrer has called "disappointment"), thereby impeding action normally performed in relation to the positive conditioned appetitive incentive stimuli in the situation. Thus, a stimulus correlated with the onset of a long period of absence of food, in a situation in which food is sometimes given, would attenuate the central motive state of eating and would impede approach acts in relation to the various conditioned incentive stimuli, such as the (empty) food tray, in the situation (e.g., Ferster, 1957).

Fourth, a CS may be negatively related to an aversive incentive stimulus $(CS:US^{-Iav.})$; such a CS may be designated $CS^{-Iav.}$. A $CS^{-Iav.}$ would generate some inhibitory process that would attenuate the prevailing aversive central motive state for a certain duration (what Mowrer has called "relief"), thereby impeding acts normally performed in relation to the positive conditioned aversive incentive stimuli in the situation. Thus, a stimulus correlated with the onset of a period of absence of electric shock ("safe period") would impede defensive actions normally shown in relation to various positively conditioned aversive incentive stimuli in the situation (e.g., Moscovitch & LoLordo, 1968).

Fifth, a CS may be positively related to a neutral stimulus, that is, a stimulus without marked or durable appetitive or aversive incentive properties $(CS:US^{+N})$; such a CS may be designated CS^{+N}. After a few presentations of CS and US^{N}, that is, after they cease to be novel in the situation, a CS^{+N} would generate a noninvestigatory central motive state (i.e., would produce "boredom" or lack of interest in the environment), thereby impeding exploratory acts in relation to the CS, and in relation to the US^{N} when it appears. Thus, a tone correlated with the onset of a weak light would not lead to any persistent specific acts beyond the few initial trials of the training session. The decline in response to the tone should parallel the decline in response to the repeated presentations of the weak light (US) itself. Studies of orientation reactions in habituation experiments on human subjects (e.g., J. A. Williams, 1963) suggest that the above prediction would be corroborated. A CS^{+N} may also attenuate some other central motive state prevailing at the moment, thus reducing the probability of action in relation to other conditioned stimuli—conditioned inhibition (Pavlov, 1927).

Sixth, a CS may be negatively related to a neutral stimulus $(CS:US^{-N})$; such a CS may be designated CS^{-N}. A CS^{-N} would mitigate the prevailing state of boredom (i.e., would revive interest in the environment) and would promote exploratory acts in relation to itself or other stimuli in the situation. Presumably a CS^{-N} would signal the end of a neutral US, that is, announce a novel stimulus that would occur at the termination of the time-span during which US^{N} is presented. Thus, a tone signaling the onset of a period of a novel stimulus would promote exploratory responses in relation to the CS^{-N}, as well as in relation to the novel stimulus when it occurs. Studies of orientation reactions in vigilance and disjunctive reaction time experiments (e.g., Blackman, 1966; Favreau, 1964), as well as in habituation experiments (e.g., Unger, 1964), suggest that this would be so. A CS^{-N} may enhance some other central motive state prevailing at the moment, thus increasing the probability of response in relation to certain other conditioned stimuli— "conditioned disinhibition."

To say that there are six types of conditioned stimuli is to simplify matters grossly. In fact, incentive stimuli are not only appetitive or aversive, but are appetitive or aversive in specific ways. Appetitive incentive stimuli include many foods with varied palatability values, as well as sexual stimuli, and a variety of olfactory and tactual stimuli. Similarly, aversive incentive stimuli not only include electric shock and predators, but also such things as visual cliff, and certain types of odors, sounds, and contrasts. Obviously the contingencies that determine habits may involve innumerable specific incentive stimuli, which may give rise to central motive states of varying degrees of specificity. Thus many subclasses of conditioned stimuli could be listed under each of the six categories of conditioned stimuli described in Table 12.1. However, the above account is sufficient for illustrating the role of conditioned stimuli in the acquisition of different types of routines.

Distribution of Conditioned Stimuli

Any training situation may be looked upon as consisting of a number of spatially distinct areas whose momentary motivational valence depends on the motivational properties of the various conditioned stimuli contained in them. As explained in Chapter 11, in general, the animal would approach areas of the training situation that at the moment are relatively more appetitive or less aversive than others. Thus, in a typical training situation, with only one clearly localized area of relatively high motivational valence, the animal would perform approach or withdrawal acts directly in relation to that area. But with a mixture of appetitive and aversive stimuli distributed over the whole situation (a circumstance common in nature), the form and direction of the animal's action could be predicted only with highly detailed and complex analyses. Experimental analysis of behavior in complex situations resembling the natural environment remain to be carried out. The considerations regarding the spatial and temporal distribution of unconditioned and conditioned incentive stimuli that must enter such analyses may be illustrated here.

The most important spatial relation is the one that exists between the locations of the CS and US. Since, as explained in Chapter 11, a conditioned stimulus may be either a training stimulus (TS), a response-eliciting stimulus (ES), or a discriminative stimulus (DS), several different types of CS-US spatial relations are possible. The simplest situation is one in which the only specific conditioned stimulus, presented on a familiar background stimulus complex (BS), is a training stimulus (TS), and in which the response to be trained (TR) does not require locomotion through space. This is the case in the Pavlovian simple conditioning experiment, where the eliciting stimulus (ES) for the training response is the US and there is no specific discriminative stimulus (DS). In such situations the training would, in general, be easier if TS and US appeared in fixed rather than variable locations and appeared in proximal rather than widely separated locations. If CS or US has no specific identifiable location outside the animal (e.g., if CS consists of intra-cranial stimulation of the visual cortex, or if food is placed directly in the mouth, or a loud aversive noise is aimed at the animal from all directions simultaneously), the TS-US spatial variable will obviously cease to be important.

There are situations (e.g., "auto-shaping") in which the same area of the training situation serves both as a TS (in relation to which the TR is measured) and ES (the stimulus that elicits the TR). In such cases the spatial relation between the location of TS-ES and the location of US can be important in two ways. If the specified TR requires doing something only at the TS-ES location but there is no particular US location (e.g., lever-pressing for intracranial or intravenous reward), then the important spatial relation is between the current location of the animal at the time of presentation or observation of TS-ES and the location of TS-ES. But if the specified TR requires doing something at both the TS-ES location and the US location (e.g., lever-pressing and then approaching the food receptacle and eating there), then the spatial relation between the TS-ES location and the US location also becomes important.

Situations in which the locations of TS and ES are separated (e.g., Pavlovian salivary conditioning, or lever-pressing for food measured in relation to a tone as the training stimulus) are discrimination situations with the TS as the positive discriminative stimulus (S^D or CS^+) and the situational background (BS) as the negative discriminative stimulus (S^Δ or CS^-). When two specific and explicit discriminative stimuli are used against a common background (e.g., Pavlovian differential conditioning, or lever-pressing that produces food when light A is on but not when light B is on), then the influence of the two discriminative stimuli may be measured in relation to baseline behavior seen when neither DS^+ nor DS^- is present. In all discrimination situations, the spatial relations between the starting location of the animal and the locations of the ES, the TS (DS^+ or DS^-, or both), and the US are important in determining the course of emergence of a stable routine. In general, the greater the spatial separation between these stimuli, the more difficult is the learning. For example, it takes a monkey longer to learn a discrimination task if the cues (training or discriminative stimuli), the manipulandum which releases the reward, and the reward appear in different locations than if they appear at the same location (e.g., Stollnitz, 1965; Cowey & Weiskrantz, 1968).

It is not only the spatial relations of the locations of different critical stimuli but also their temporal ordering that is important in determining the form of the response that emerges in a given situation. The temporal durations that separate TS (DS^+ or DS^-), ES, and US determine the moment-to-moment changes in the motivational value of the various stimuli, and this determines the order of what the animal does and hence the form of the trained response (TR) that will emerge. In a Pavlovian conditioned salivation experiment, for example, the food is presented after the onset of TS, and in lever-pressing experiments the food is presented after the lever stimulus complex has been effective in eliciting a lever-press. The routine response developed in these training situations would obviously be quite different if the order of these critical stimulus events were to be reversed or their time relation to each other altered (see Chapter 7). Temporal variables are not only important in determining the order and timing of acts, but also in that specific-temporal durations can serve as discriminative stimuli or cues that enter into contingencies learned by the animal (see Chapter 6).

ACQUISITION OF ROUTINES

We have seen that the form of response in a given training situation is determined by (1) the topographical arrangement of the various unconditioned stimuli and conditioned stimuli in the situation, (2) the learned temporal contingencies that determine the exact momentary motivational valence of each situational stimulus, and (3) the nature of the specific motivational properties (fear, irritability, desire for eating, sexual excitement, etc.) of the various stimuli in the situation. Now consider how these factors operate in the acquisition of certain commonly encountered forms of response routines.

Instinctive Actions

No sharp distinction can be drawn between instinctive actions and other forms of routines. They are all acquired through individual experience, as each animal, equipped with previously developed perceptual and action capabilities, repeatedly encounters a certain type of situation. Since all members of a species are likely to have developed similar perceptual and action capabilities at any given stage of development, and are likely to be exposed to similar organismic conditions and situations, most members of the species are likely to acquire similar routines. This is especially true in the case of routines acquired in connection with particular organismic states and particular incentive stimuli in the typical ("natural") environment of the species; it is these types of routines that are referred to as instinctive actions. In defining an instinctive action emphasis is placed on a certain organismic state (e.g., level of circulating estrogen) and the particular type of incentive object (e.g., sexual partner) in relation to which transactional acts (e.g., copulation) are performed; compared with other forms of routines, less emphasis is placed on the instrumental acts of approach or withdrawal in relation to the incentive object.

Three main features are usually considered as justifying a separate treatment of instinctive actions. (1) The general pattern of an instinctive action is species-typical; actions such as eating, copulating, and nursing the young tend to be performed in fairly uniform ways by most members of a species. (2) The whole action is displayed on the first (or an early) encounter with the appropriate situation (given a certain organismic state); the action appears to be "spontaneous," and there is little evidence of gradual acquisition of the routine as a consequence of repeated experiences with the situation. (3) The action tends to occur in a fairly fixed and stereotyped manner from one occasion to the next; instinctive actions appear to be much less flexible than other routines.

The general ideas about response construction outlined earlier can be directly applied to the interpretation of instinctive actions. The species-typical nature of instinctive actions may be linked to the common maturational and metabolic processes that generate the same organismic states in all members of a species at approximately the same age and at the same time in the diurnal and seasonal cycles, and to the species characteristics that make certain objects incentives for the species. Once an animal in a certain organismic state, comes in contact with an incentive object, the contact stimuli elicit specific types of viscerosomatic reactions and transactional acts (struggling, attacking, biting, licking, eating, copulating, etc.) that are common to the species by virtue of common brain properties.

The spontaneous—unrehearsed—occurrence of an effective pattern of action may be attributed to the existence of a highly appropriate spatio-temporal layout of the incentive (act-eliciting) stimuli in the situation. For example, in copulation, the male rat approaches, smells, and licks the genital area of an estrous female rat, and this stimulation then leads to the acts of mounting, biting the neck, and pelvic thrusting. If intromission is achieved, a few rapid thrusts may be elicited, which somehow result in dismounting, and the male rat then grooms its own genital area. The above sequence is then repeated until ejaculation occurs. If the critical stimuli are so distributed that the elicitation of each component act of the total action results in the animal receiving the stimuli that are appropriate for the next component, then the action would move to completion without any specific training. Of course, as the action is repeated, there will be considerable improvement in efficiency, but the whole action pattern may well be completed effectively, even if awkwardly, on the first occasion. The fixedness and stereotypy of instinctive actions may be attributed to the stability of the spatiotemporal relations of the critical stimuli in the situation. Like other actions, instinctive actions too may be readily disrupted by disarranging the appropriate spatiotemporal relations of the successive eliciting stimuli (e.g., by disrupting certain types of sensory input).

Consider how the above ideas apply to the instinctive action of "hoarding" as seen in some rodents. If a hungry rat in its home cage is placed at one end of a runway, with food pellets available in a bin at the other end, under certain known conditions, the rat is likely to bring back several pellets of food to its home cage within the first hour of exposure to that situation. With a 1-hr test session each day, while the rat is maintained on a food deprivation schedule, the pattern of transporting food pellets back to the home cage and piling them there improves in efficiency even though the daily accumulation of food is removed at the end of the session. In 4 or 5 days the rat may "hoard" as many as 200 pellets in one hour, spending only a fraction of the time in eating.

At one time this pattern of action was attributed to a "food-hoarding instinct" set into operation by a certain level of food deprivation (Morgan, Stellar, & Johnson, 1943). Such a view is untenable because rats will hoard more palatable or more visually attractive food even without any food deprivation (Bindra, 1948a; Licklider & Licklider, 1950). Since rats will also hoard water pellets when they are water deprived (an instinct to hoard water appears unlikely, for water is not normally found in a transportable form), nesting materials when they are cold, and neonatal pups when they are nursing their offspring, it is more reasonable to say that rats hoard whatever is valuable to them at the moment, that is, any object that by virtue of the current organismic state of the animal has strong appetitive incentive properties. Now, in order to explain the spontaneous emergence of the action sequence involved in "hoarding" (of any material), we should look at some of its component acts.

The first main component is leaving the cage to enter the runway. This may be attributed to the greater momentary motivational valence of some feature of the novel runway as compared to the main features of the familiar home cage. The novel features of the runway will elicit alternating approach and withdrawal acts, owing to the motivational gradients between the home cage and the various novel features. It may take the rat some time to emerge from the cage and to start exploring the runway; it will frequently run back to the home cage from various points in the runway, but will finally reach the end of the runway and discover the food. It may now pick up one pellet and start to eat it, but will soon run back to the home cage with the pellet still in its mouth. After eating a little of the pellet in the home cage, it may groom and explore a bit, and this may again lead it to the food bin. It will then bring back another pellet. The main point to note is that the hoarding situation is one with two attractive things, the home cage and the food bin, but the attractiveness of the food bin is marred by its unfamiliar location ("container neophobia"). The attractiveness of the home cage resides in the fact that it is a secure place with certain familiar odors and textures. The attractiveness of the food bin arises first from its novelty and then from the food pellets, but its location remains a much less secure place than the home cage. Thus the relative attractiveness of the home cage is greater when the rat is at the food bin, and the relative attractiveness of the food bin is greater when the rat is in the home cage—especially after it has eaten some of the food. The general principle that governs such novelty-related fluctuations in attractiveness has been formulated by Bateson (1973). His model shows how observed preference for an object is jointly determined by its familiarity and its novelty. Since there are no other locations of comparable attractiveness, the rat will continue running back and forth from the less secure to the more secure location. The essential point of this "security hypothesis" (Bindra, 1948b) of hoarding is that the action pattern that spontaneously emerges on the rat's first encounter with a situation is a direct outcome of the momentary relative motivational valences of the particular parts of the situation.

It follows from the above hypothesis that the emergence of the rat from the home cage may be delayed by making the runway very novel or unsafe (e.g., a wobbly plank separating the cage from the food bin), and it may be facilitated by making the runway more like the cage. It follows also that if the food bin area too is made very secure like the home cage, the rat may simply sit in the food bin and eat food there without hoarding any. It has been shown that "nonhoarders," rats which sit in the food bin and do not transport food to the home cage, can be made to hoard by shining a bright light on the food bin, that is, by making the food bin a less safe or attractive place and thus increasing the slope of the gradient of attractiveness between the food bin and the home cage (Bindra, 1948b). Since there are species and strain differences in "shyness" or timidity, a situation that is optimal for the emergence of hoarding behavior in one strain of rats may not be optimal for another. Thus a strain that is found to be "nonhoarder" in one testing situation may be shown to be "hoarder" in another. The differences in the speed with which hoarding behavior emerges are thus not attributable to strain differences in "strength of hoarding instinct" but to the particular situational arrangements that are optimal for creating the necessary attractiveness gradients in different strains (Bindra, 1948a). How instinctive hoarding is, or how "prepared" a species is for hoarding, depends both on the species' characteristics and the characteristics of the testing situation. This suggests that certain species (e.g., carnivores) that do not normally hoard materials could be made to do so by arranging appropriate situations and test materials.

As the hoarding action is repeated, it becomes more unified and stereotyped and progressively less dependent on the conditions that were critical in its initial emergence, including food deprivation. However, if food is removed from the food bin, or the animal is placed on an ad libitum eating schedule, hoarding gradually declines, showing a typical extinction curve. According to the principles of response unification discussed in the last chapter, the stability and uniformity of the hoarding action remains dependent on the stability and uniformity of the spatiotemporal features of the situation in which the action was developed. While several aspects of hoarding require more detailed study, the above general approach appears to be well suited to its analysis, as well as to the analysis of several other forms of instinctive actions that require commerce with specific environmental locations.

Maze Habits

A maze habit is the action of traversing the correct path to the goal (reward) box through a spatial arrangement of alleys, some of which are blind or incorrect. In the acquisition of the habit, the problem is essentially one of learning the contingencies between the stimulus features of the various alleys in the maze. After learning, at any choice point, looking into a correct alley (say, S_1) will activate the contingency $S_1:S^I$, while looking into a blind alley (say, S_2) will activate the contingency $S_2:\overline{S^I}$ (a delay or absence of reward). The exact stimulus complexes that serve as discriminative cues may differ depending on the nature of the maze. In a T-maze, for example, if there are clear extra-maze cues that can indicate the position of the goal box, the animal will probably follow these cues to the location of the box. If there are no extra-maze cues, the animal will learn the spatial relation between its initial position (start box) and the location at which the reward is given (right or left end box). If the goal box does not have a fixed position, then the animal will have to use the differential stimulus features of the two alleys (e.g., differences in their color or textures) as the basis for following the correct path.

In complex mazes with many blind alleys, the animal would have to use as discriminative cues, not only the intramaze stimulus features that differentiate correct and incorrect alleys, but also temporal cues of order that indicate, for example, that of the three alleys directed to the right, the first two are blind alleys but the third one is a part of the correct path. The difficulty of a maze thus may be increased by introducing incorrect alleys that can be differentiated from the correct path only on the basis of temporal-order cues. As errors (entries into incorrect alleys) are eliminated, the total response of running through the complex maze will be unified and the performance will become smooth and fast. The basis of this response unification lies in the shortcircuiting process described in Chapter 11.

The observed flexibility of maze habits is predictable from the above account of their acquisition. Since the response pattern developed is largely dependent upon the location of occurrence of particular incentive stimuli, any minor variation in the location of the critical conditioned stimuli would modify the response pattern; the exact response form of the habit would thus change from one occasion to the next, but the end result (e.g., reaching the goal box) would be achieved most efficiently. It should be noted that a given habit would remain flexible only in so far as the animal's behavior is guided by current stimuli. If large sections of the maze-traversed pattern become so unified that certain conditioned stimuli, initially required for the development of the pattern, now remain unobserved by the animal, then any variation in those stimuli may not produce any adjustments in the response pattern. For example, if after a rat has been well trained in a runway to obtain food at the goal box, some food is placed halfway down the runway on the floor at a location that is no longer looked at by the rat, then obviously the rat's response would not be modified until it happens, through some distraction, to discover the food at the new location. In other words, any given habit would remain flexible and efficient so long as the probability of the animal observing environmental changes (that call for adjustment) is not reduced.

However, the chief characteristic of habits is not that they are flexible but that their repeated occurrences appear to be uniform and automatic, or stereotyped. How is the stereotypy of habits to be explained? The source of stereotypy of a habit lies in the stability of the spatial arrangement of the incentive stimuli in the situation. The more the details of a situation are kept constant from occasion to occasion, the more stereotyped will a habit become. This follows from the proposed idea that the form of the habit pattern is determined by the relative location of incentive stimuli, so that the more stable the topographical and procedural features of the training are, the more stereotyped the habit will become. Conversely, the more variable the training situation is from occasion to occasion while a habit is being acquired (as may happen in the natural environment of the animal), the more flexible and stimulus-guided, rather than uniform and automatic, will the habit appear to be. It follows that the performance of a response would be disrupted more by a rearrangement of the critical stimuli in the situation than by damage to any particular muscular apparatus typically involved in the response. If the muscles commonly used in a component act (say, making a left turn) were paralyzed, the animal would continue acting in whatever way it could in relation to the critical conditioned incentive stimulus features of the choice point until some other movement (e.g., a right loop-turn) resulted in a left turn (Lashley & McCarthy, 1926).

The importance of the spatial relation of critical stimuli is shown by experiments in which the critical stimuli are rearranged after the response has been well practiced. Suppose a rat has learned a T-maze, with food as a reward, and now an extra supply of food is placed at the choice point. Since the strongest incentive stimulus (food) is now found before the goal box, the rat should be expected to stop at the choice point and eat the food without bothering to go to the goal box. But the rat may not do this immediately; it may take it several trials to switch to the new location of food. The main reason for this is not that the response is so well integrated that the rat can't stop, or that rats prefer to work for food (Stotz & Lott, 1964), but that, owing to shortcircuiting, the rat is no longer acting in relation to intermediate stimuli and it may take several trials for the rat to perceive clearly the food in the new location. Another reason is the incentive value of the habitual eating place, which is greater than the incentive value at other points in the runway; so that the rat might prefer to run a greater distance to eat in a habitual place than to eat in a nearer novel place—another instance of "container neophobia." Cohen-Salmon (1971) has shown that, if no food is given in the goal box but some food is placed in the middle of the runway, the rat will pick up a pellet of food, take it to the goal box, and eat it there. Preference for the habitual location of food has been demonstrated in other investigations (Mitchell, Scott, & Williams, 1973) and appears to be the most plausible explanation of the fact that sometimes an animal may spend greater effort to reach food than to eat more easily available food. Thus, though habits can be readily modified by altering the spatial arrangement of critical incentive stimuli, the specific changes are dependent on the incentive values of the stimuli at the time of the alteration.

Instrumental Skills (Finely Shaped Responses)

The present account of response production in terms of the spatiotemporal arrangement of incentive stimuli (conditioned and unconditioned) can readily account for instrumental locomotion (approach and withdrawal responses) in situations, such as mazes, where the incentive stimuli of varying values are distributed in a clear spatial layout. But how about responses that do not involve the locomotion of the animal-as-a-whole toward or away from particular incentive areas, but are apparently controlled from within the animal—responses such as turning head to the right, lever-pressing, chain-pulling, sitting motionless? The shaping of such responses—I shall call them instrumental skills—appears to involve "motor differentiation" rather than "stimulus differentiation" evident in the acquisition of approach and withdrawal. They seem to involve no obvious spatial areas of differential incentive values; the same training stimulus (e.g., a light onset) may be linked arbitrarily to a right head turn in one animal and to a left head turn in another. How may the shaping and performance of instrumental skills be explained in terms of conditioned incentive properties of environmental stimuli?

My view is that, contrary to appearances, skills are initially as much under the guidance of environmental incentive stimuli as are locomotory actions. The main difference between the two types of instrumental responses is that typically the components of a skilled response are small refined muscles, while instrumental locomotion involves displacement of the body as a whole and the large muscles of the body. A related difference is that the eliciting stimuli for the acts that comprise skills are highly detailed features of individual objects, while instrumental locomotion typically occurs in relation to easily recognizable and widely separated objects. For these two reasons the relation between environmental stimuli and the acts performed is more obscure in the case of instrumental skills. There is evidence that highly detailed features of a stimulus object can serve as differential eliciting stimuli. For example, Jenkins and Sainsbury (1969) have shown that pigeons will peck more at the quadrant of the pecking key that is correlated with the highest reward probability than at the other quadrants of the same key. Motor or response differentiation may thus be fundamentally stimulus differentiation.

Consider what appears to be a clear case of response differentiation. If a hungry rat in a lever box is rewarded with a pellet of food only when the lever is pressed with a certain force (to overcome a weight of about 20 gm), but lever-presses with a force higher (say, 30 gm) or lower (say, 10 gm) than the specified effective range are not rewarded, the rat will learn to press the lever within the required range of force (Notterman & Mintz, 1965; Trotter, 1956). The basis of this response differentiation lies, according to the present formulation, in the response eliciting stimuli (ES) for a lever-press of each force. The response-eliciting stimuli are partly the environmental eliciting stimuli for a lever-press and partly the proprioceptive stimuli representing the postural state of the limbs and body. It is the latter stimuli (they are not feedback stimuli but stimuli representing the static state of the musculature) that critically determine the exact form and force of the various acts involved in lever-pressing. It may be supposed that there are several different postural proprioceptive stimulus complexes (e.g., PS_1, PS_2, PS_3, etc.) that combine with the exteroceptive eliciting stimulus complex to produce a lever-press of a certain force. If all lever-presses were rewarded, then PS_1,

PS_2, and PS_3 would develop the same conditioned incentive properties, and their gnostic-assembly complexes would be equally likely to be activated by the background and the eliciting stimulus complexes. However, when only lever-presses with a certain force, say, that determined by PS_2, are rewarded, and lever-presses determined by PS_1 and PS_3 are not, then differential incentive values will be acquired by the various proprioceptive stimuli. This would mean that a pexgo of PS_2 would more likely be activated when the rat is placed in the situation, and together with the eliciting stimulus complex, it would make the lever-press of the specified force more likely to occur. According to this account, the acquisition of highly refined skills depends on conditioned activation of pexgos of proprioceptive stimuli by the situational background stimulus complex(S_B). It is the generation of the pexgos of highly specific postural or tonic muscular states at particular times that contributes to the production of response differentiations. The differentiatedness of the response depends on the differentiatedness of the momentary postural complex. In the training of fine skills, such as playing golf, juggling, and singing, the importance of "getting the right muscular feel" is commonly regarded as a prerequisite of accurate performance.

Note that the above account implies that, while the performance of a gross response such as a lever-press can be achieved by environmental eliciting stimuli, refined performance within specified limits of accuracy typically involves the proprioceptive sensory system. This implication is consistent with the fact that while deafferented monkeys can acquire gross instrumental responses (Taub & Berman, 1963), no claim seems to have been made that they are capable of acquiring finely differentiated acts, and it is likely that their manipulatory acts become crude, awkward, slow, and variable. However, it remains true that considerable response differentiation may be obtained on the basis of only exteroceptive eliciting stimuli.

The above interpretation also applies to the shaping of fine viscerosomatic reactions in relation to environmental stimuli ("instrumental conditioning of autonomic responses"). While several types of exteroceptive stimuli (e.g., "emotional" and pain stimuli) can induce specific viscerosomatic changes by generating particular central motive states (see Chapter 9), these reactions are also closely linked to particular postural and muscular states (Gellhorn, 1967; E. Jacobson, 1938; Obrist, Howard, Lawler, Galosy, Meyers, & Gaebelein, 1974; K. U. Smith, 1973). Thus it should be possible to produce certain types of specific alterations in viscerosomatic activity through changes in postural and muscular states. If, as shown above, certain specific postures and muscular states can be conditioned to certain situational stimuli, then it should be possible to obtain particular viscerosomatic changes by shaping the corresponding postural and muscular states. According to this view, the procedure used in "instrumental conditioning of autonomic reactions" is in fact one of rewarding those postural and muscular states that produce the autonomic reactions the experimenter has set out to "shape." What the conditioning procedure alters in these studies is not autonomic reactions directly but the postural and muscular states linked to those specific autonomic reactions. This view is consistent with the finding that it is difficult to shape finely differentiated autonomic reactions while the animal is under curare (N. E. Miller & Dworkin, 1974), as well as with the view that the reported instrumental shaping of viscerosomatic reactions is mediated through the central motor system involved in movement control (A. H.Black, 1974).

Two theoretical limits on the shaping of viscerosomatic reactions should be noted. First, there are several reflex mechanisms that normally keep particular viscerosomatic functions within a certain narrow range of activity; hyperactivity or hypoactivity beyond a certain level produce compensatory (homeostatic) adjustments. This means that the extent to which viscero-somatic reactions can be shaped in relation to environmental stimuli must always be limited by the levels of activity at which reflex mechanisms come into operation. Second, again because of compensatory mechanisms, it should not be possible to instrumentally condition an autonomic response consisting of several sequentially arranged individual viscerosomatic reactions. Conditioned production of viscerosomatic reactions is possible only with discrete individual reactions.

Routines under Reinforcement Schedules

The usual procedure of instrumental training (i.e., the reinforcement of each occurrence of a specified response) may be modified so that only certain occurrences of the specified response are reinforced (i.e., followed by the incentive stimulus). For example, in a lever-pressing situation only every fifth lever-press may be reinforced (a fixed-ratio schedule of five responses to one reinforcement), or only every response made after a defined interval of, say, 25 sec may be reinforced (a fixed-interval schedule of 25 sec). Such "schedules of reinforcement" may be complicated by using variable instead of fixed ratios or intervals, and by mixing them in various ways. Ferster and Skinner (1957) drew attention to the remarkable regularities of behavior that emerge under each schedule, and they considered the response routines produced by various schedules to be interpretable in terms of variations in the delay of response reinforcement, with the subsidiary principles of stimulus discrimination, secondary reinforcement, and response differentiation. An alternative interpretation outlined by Jenkins (1970) relies more heavily on variations in the temporal proximity of reinforced and nonreinforced responses to reinforcement but retains response-reinforcement as a central concept.

The approach suggested by the ideas proposed in this volume assumes that the response-reinforcement as such plays no part in producing the characteristic response routines observed under various schedules, but that the response patterns arise from the specific temporal contingencies that the animal learns under various schedules. The contingencies critical in producing schedule effects are those between the number of time frames elapsed since a reference event and the presentation of incentive stimulation. The basic assumption is that the actions of the animal during a cycle of any schedule depend on the momentary motivational valence of the various conditioned stimuli in the situation, and that their momentary motivational valence depends on the proportion of time frames that have elapsed since the reference event, which is usually the previous reinforcement. The relative motivational valence of the different situational stimuli during a given time frame determines the stimulus in relation to which the animal will act in that time frame. The essential feature of any reinforcement schedule is the time interval between successive reinforcements that comprise a cycle; the behavior in the cycle is determined by the temporal contingencies the animal has learned between the time frames of the cycle and the incentive stimulation that terminates the cycle. Since in the instrumental procedure the reinforcement (S^I) does not occur until the animal has made the specified response— that is, acted in relation to the response-eliciting stimulus (ES)—, the learning of temporal contingencies between time frames and S^I incorporates learning of the contingencies between time frames and ES. These temporal contingencies modulate the motivational valence of the response-eliciting stimulus (ES) in relation to which the specified response is to be made, as previously learned through $ES:S^I$ contingencies. In other words, the temporal contingencies modulate the relative strength of a pexgo of ES, and thereby determine the observed variations in response rate.

Consider what happens in a fixed-interval schedule. Suppose a hungry rat can obtain a pellet of food by the first response, say lever-pressing, after at least 30 sec have elapsed since the previous pellet was delivered. After some training on such a FI30-sec schedule, in a free operant situation, the characteristic "FI scallop" pattern of responding emerges: the rate of response is very low in the initial time frames of the 30-sec cycle, and then increases in a positively accelerated manner until the pellet is delivered. Assuming that each time frame is of 2-sec duration, we may expect each successive time frame to bear an increasingly stronger contingent relation with pellet-delivery; the predicted imminence of the reward will increase, in an accelerating manner, with each new time frame (see Chapter 6). Thus the observed FI scallop is a function of the increase in predicted imminence of incentive stimulation, hence of motivational arousal, during the various time frames of each cycle. Two other factors may also be expected to influence the pattern of responding. One is the postreinforcement pause (Staddon, 1974), the time of no responding (lever-pressing) following the consumption of the pellet delivered at the end of the previous cycle. The second is the level of ability of the animal to discriminate temporal intervals ("temporal sensitivity"); this will determine the slope of the scallop.

The above interpretation of the response pattern under a fixed-interval schedule makes no use of the idea of response-reinforcement. What the schedule determines is the progressive increase in the momentary motivational valence of the eliciting stimulus (some features of the lever complex), so that the animal allocates an increasing proportion of its time responding in relation to the lever; the increasing response rate is a reflection of the increasing time allocation. This interpretation is supported by the results of an experiment by M. J. Morgan (1970). He compared the pattern of lever-pressing obtained under a fixed-interval schedule with the pattern obtained under an equivalent time schedule in which a response made at any time *during* the interval was rewarded at the end of the interval (conjunctive schedule). By comparing the details of the delay of response reinforcement that actually prevailed in the two schedules, as well as the duration of post-reinforcement pauses in the two schedules, Morgan was able to argue that the pattern of responding in these schedules was influenced more by temporal than by response contingencies. Morgan's finding that the rate of lever-pressing in the fixed-interval schedule was higher than that in the conjunctive schedule may be attributed to the greater average motivational valence of the lever in the fixed-interval schedule. This greater motivational valence would arise from the shorter average delay between lever-press (observation of the eliciting stimulus complex) and food delivery in the fixed interval schedule than in the conjunctive schedule. This would be so because the final lever-press (the first after 30 sec have elapsed) leads immediately to food delivery in the case of the fixed-interval schedule, while a variety of stimuli intervene between the lever-press and food delivery in the case of the conjunctive schedule. The animal would thus allocate a greater proportion of its time to the lever in the case of the fixed-interval schedule.

Many different schedules of reinforcement have been contrived and studied. A detailed examination of the response patterns under the different schedules is outside the scope of this volume. The above account indicates roughly the approach implied by the ideas about learning and performance developed in the previous chapter. For a more formal and detailed account of behavior under schedules in terms of temporal variables the reader is referred to the work of Killeen (1975).

Learning by Observation of Models

The learning of a certain defined instrumental response by an animal may be facilitated if it observes another animal, usually a member of the same species, perform a similar response. Such learning by observing the performance of models has been experimentally demonstrated, not only in primates (e.g., Darby & Riopelle, 1959), but as well in the cat (e.g., John, Chesler, Bartlett, & Victor, 1968) and the rat (e.g., Church, 1957). Explanations of this phenomenon in terms of the traditional response-reinforcement principle (e.g., Miller & Dollard, 1941; Mowrer, 1950) have been shown to be quite inadequate (Bandura, 1962; Bandura & Walters, 1963; Estes, 1970). The main objection is that such an explanation is internally inconsistent, because while observational learning is learning without prior *occurrence* of the response-to-be-learned, the principle of response reinforcement requires that the response occur before—be instrumental in producing—the reinforcement. Further, the suggestion that observational learning may represent a "generalized response" to do what the model is doing merely begs the question; even if it is true that a generalized response is acquired through response reinforcement, it remains to be explained how such a generalized response facilitates the acquisition of a specific new instrumental response.

A different explanation of learning by observation of models is suggested by the present view that learned modifications of behavior rest on contingency learning and motivational arousal. Assume that the model is a strong conditioned appetitive incentive stimulus for the learner. For example, a rat pup learns the contingencies between the sight of its mother and the provision of safety, comfort, nourishment, warmth, and contact. This means that the rat pup would be attracted to the mother, and would tend to follow the mother, especially at times of danger, hunger, etc. The mother, in the course of its daily activities, itself explores and approaches various aspects of its surroundings. As it follows the mother, the pup would also approach the same locations and encounter the same objects; it would thus learn the contingencies between various environmental objects and the mother. Now, the mother, by performing certain actions in relation to some of the objects, would impart, so far as the pup is concerned, the same type of conditioned appetitive properties to those objects as those objects have for her; the more approach and contact transactions the mother has with an object, the greater would be the conditioned appetitive properties of that object for the pup. Thus the pup would also begin to act in relation to—approach or withdraw from—the same objects in relation to which the mother acts. This is one way in which the pup may be guided to discover the unconditioned incentive properties of various important objects in its surroundings. The particular actions performed by the rat pup would not always resemble those of the mother, but they would tend to resemble those of the mother if the pup's motivational state were the same as that of the mother at the time of observation, and if the pup were able to observe the specific stimulus features of the objects in relation to which the mother acts.

According to the present hypothesis, then, acquiring responses by observation of models involves three stages: (a) the learner learns the appetitive incentive properties of another animal, the model; (b) the learner learns (vicariously, by following the model) the incentive properties of various environmental stimuli by observing the model's transactions with those stimuli; and (c) the learner learns the unconditioned incentive properties of those stimuli by directly acting in relation to them. The particular actions performed by the learner depend, not on what the model did, but on the general principles determining the form of response, that is, on the spatio-temporal distribution of those and other (e.g., the model) stimuli in the learner's environment. Under certain conditions the learner's responses will be similar to those of the model and under other conditions not. Observational learning is not "response learning," nor is it learning to copy the actions of the model; rather, it is acquiring incentive value for various stimulus events vicariously through the observed transactions of an attractive (appetitive) model with those stimulus events. Once the learner has come in direct contact with the environmental stimuli, it may discover other properties—some unconditioned appetitive or aversive properties, such as sweet or foul odor—of the stimuli. Thus, the model may serve to draw the attention of the learner to certain unconditioned incentive stimuli by imparting some conditioned motivational properties to them.

Several recent experimental reports support the above hypothesis. Galef and Clark (1971) have shown that pups of wild rats will avoid a new diet that has been associated with poison for the adult rats of the colony, and that the adult rats influence the choice of food on which the pups first feed. In a supplementary experiment, Galef (1971) has shown that this adult influence arises from "a tendency on the part of the young to approach areas in which the adults are located and begin feeding there" (p. 358). Also Zentall and Levine (1972) have shown that the acquisition of a lever-press response by rats may be facilitated or retarded depending on whether they have observed models who acted in relation to the relevant stimuli (lever and reinforcement location) or have observed models who did not.

Evidence in support of the idea that the model's efficacy as a "demonstrator" depends on its appetitive incentive value for the learner comes from an early study by Bandura and Huston (1961); they found that nursery school children were more likely to be influenced by models with whom they had previously experienced nurturant interactions than by models with whom they had previously experienced nonnurturant interactions. A similar result has been obtained by Chesler (1969) in her study of the influence of observing the performance of an adult cat on the acquisition of a discriminative lever-pressing response by kittens. She found that kittens who observed the performance of their own mothers acquired the discriminative response sooner than kittens who observed the performance of strange female cats. The early dependence on, and attachment to, the mother would mean that the mother would have greater appetitive incentive value for the kittens than would the strange cats, and this would lead to closer observation of the mother as well as to greater imparted incentive value to the positive discriminative stimuli.

Further, in conformity with the present hypothesis, it has been shown that the benefit that the learner derives from observing the model is *not* dependent on observing the reinforcing (rewarding or punishing) consequences of the model's actions in relation to certain stimuli but merely on observing the model's contiguity with those stimuli (Groesbeck & Duerfeldt, 1971; Kohn & Dennis, 1972), that is, even when the learner does not get to observe the consequences of the model's actions. Those concerned with human social learning have developed several parallel theoretical ideas, such as the concepts of contiguous sensory stimulation, model characteristics, "channeling" of responses, and matching-to-sample (Bandura, 1962; Bandura & Walters, 1963; Gewirtz, 1971).

CONTROL OF ROUTINES

An animal may perform an avoidance or a food-getting response uniformly for several days and then, inexplicably, show a radical change in the level of performance on one day, only to return to its stable level on the following day. Spontaneous day-to-day exacerbation and amelioration of neurotic symptoms (e.g., anxiety, compulsive, or hysterical symptoms) is a similar phenomenon. In this section, I discuss some factors that control the readiness with which a response routine is likely to occur at a given time.

Effects of Extraneous Conditioned Stimuli on Routines

A rat has been trained to press a lever to obtain food. On a certain test day, under a particular set of conditions (hunger, palatability of the food delivered, force required to press the lever, etc.) the rat is observed to press the lever at a uniform rate of, say, 10 times per minute. Now, suppose an "extraneous" conditioned stimulus, say, a tone the animal has separately learned as a signal for something, is presented while the rat is pressing the lever. The extraneous conditioned stimulus is so called because it has not in any way been related to the initial training of the test response; it is a "response independent" conditioned stimulus. What effect will the extraneous conditioned stimulus, the tone, have on the previously stable rate of lever pressing? The obvious answer is that the effect will depend on *what* the extraneous conditioned stimulus signals; the effect may be expected to be different depending on whether the tone signals an electric shock, a food of higher palatability, a sexual partner, or an attackable object. This general prediction follows from the two-process learning theory, as developed by Mowrer (1947) and Solomon and Wynne (1954), which attributes variations in the strength of a response tendency to variations in emotional states generated by (classically) conditioned incentive-motivational stimuli.

Many experimental investigations of the effects of extraneous (response-independent) conditioned stimuli on previously acquired response routines have been inspired by the two-process theory (see Rescorla & Solomon, 1967; Trapold & Overmier, 1972). The working assumption for the experimental work has been that an extraneous positive conditioned aversive stimulus, $CS^{+Iav.}$ (e.g., a tone signaling an electric shock), should promote an aversive habit (e.g., an avoidance response) and impede an appetitive habit (e.g., a food-approach response). Conversely, an extraneous positive appetitive conditioned stimulus, $CS^{+Iap.}$ should impede an aversive habit and promote an appetitive one. The effect of conditioned extraneous negative conditioned stimuli, $CS^{-Iav.}$ or $CS^{-Iap.}$ would be expected to be the opposite of that produced by positive conditioned stimuli. Most studies support these predictions, but a substantial number do not; in general, the effects of extraneous conditioned appetitive stimuli appear not to be as uniform and clear-cut as those obtained with conditioned aversive stimuli.

As I have explained elsewhere (Bindra, 1974), the above working hypothesis needs to be amended in two ways. First, the effect on a response of an extraneous conditioned stimulus depends not only on whether that stimulus is appetitive or aversive, but also on the specific motivational state produced by it. It would make a difference whether a conditioned appetitive stimulus had been trained as a signal for a food of higher palatability, a food of lower palatability, a sexual partner, or access to an area where the animal's infant offspring are present. Similarly, it would make a difference whether a conditioned aversive stimulus had been trained as a signal for a predator, an aversive odor, or an electric shock.

Second, the effect on a response of an extraneous conditioned stimulus depends not only on the kind of response it is, but also on the exact spatial location and temporal frame in which the conditioned stimulus is introduced. Thus, in the case of an avoidance habit consisting of running from the start (shock) box to the goal (safe) box of a unidirectional alley, the effect of an extraneous conditioned aversive stimulus (e.g., a tone signaling a stronger electric shock) will depend on whether the tone is presented in the start box or in the goal box; in the former case the avoidance response should be promoted, and in the latter depressed. There is some evidence to support this type of prediction (Bolles & Grossen, 1970; Katzev, 1967). Similarly, the effect of the tone will also depend on the exact time at which it is presented; if it is presented in the start box before the onset of the avoidance response, it may be more likely to promote the response than if it is presented when the animal is in the middle of the runway.

The variability of the results of experiments with extraneous appetitive conditioned stimuli may be due to the fact that an appetitive conditioned stimulus will attract the animal to itself, and whether this promotes or impedes the test response will depend on the exact location and time of presentation of the conditioned stimulus (Rice, 1966). This factor is likely to be more important in the case of appetitive conditioned stimuli because, in typical experiments of this type, the extraneous conditioned stimulus is presented in a location (e.g., the start box) that is different from the location of the unconditioned incentive used in training an appetitive habit (e.g., goal box at the end of a runway). In the case of an aversive response, however, the location of the conditioned stimulus (e.g., the start box) is typically the same as the location of the unconditioned incentive stimulus (e.g., an electric shock) used in training the aversive response. Thus, in the former case the appetitive conditioned stimulus is likely to make the start box more attractive and thereby interfere with the response, while in the latter case the aversive conditioned stimulus is likely to make the start box more aversive and thereby promote the response.

It should be noted in passing that electric shock is employed as the aversive unconditioned stimulus in many investigations. Electric shock differs from most natural incentive stimuli in that it is not an object, such as food or a threatening enemy, but a disembodied stimulus, so that the animal has no way of acting in relation to electric shock as such, apart from acting in relation to the experimental location in which it is usually administered. Thus, in general, any increase in the strength of the central motive state produced by an extraneous aversive conditioned stimulus presented in the start box could do little else than facilitate withdrawal from the start box. If an aversive *object* were used as the unconditioned incentive stimulus, the possibility would exist for the animal to distinguish between the location of the unconditioned incentive object itself and the location of the conditioned stimulus (as is normally the case in studies with appetitive training). Under these conditions, the results of the studies with response-independent aversive conditioned stimuli may also be quite variable and parallel the results of the studies with response-independent appetitive conditioned stimuli.

Behavioral Contrast

Another possible source of fluctuations in the level of performance of a specified response may be illustrated with reference to the phenomenon of "behavioral contrast." The essential feature of the contrast experiment is that a change is made in the reinforcement density in one component (A) of a two-component (A-B) multiple schedule, and the effects of this change are studied on behavior in the other component (B). For example, a pigeon may be trained to peck key A when it is lighted on a reinforcement schedule of variable-interval 60 sec, and on key B when it is lighted on the same reinforcement schedule. The response rates in the two components A and B will reach a steady and equal level. Now, if the reinforcement schedule on key A is changed to variable-interval 120 sec (i.e., the average reinforcement density is halved), the pigeon's rate of pecking on key B, when that key is subsequently lighted, will be raised above its former steady level.

Such positive behavioral contrast effects may be explained as follows. A decrease in the density of reinforcement associated with key A results in a reduction in the motivational valence of that key. This means an increase in the *relative* motivational valence of key B; that is, there will be a steepening of the spatial gradient of motivational valence at the location of key B immediately after the component A has been in effect, as shown in Figure 12.1. Since time allocation is dependent on the steepness of the gradient (see Chapter 11), there will be an increase in the time allocation to key B, and hence an increase in the rate of responding to B. If only one response key is used (e.g., B. Schwartz, 1973), with the two components signaled by nonspatial cues (e.g., tones), the gradient of motivational valence will run between the key and the background (e.g., the wall on which the key is placed). And this gradient too will be steeper immediately after the reduced density of reinforcement associated with one of the discriminanda. However, this gradient will be less steep than that in the case of two response keys, and the contrast effects are likely to be less certain and less stable.

According to the present hypothesis the contrast effect should be largely independent of the responses actually emitted during the change in reinforcement density of component A. Bloomfield's (1969) review as well as the work of Halliday and Boakes (1972, 1974) and Keller (1974) shows that this is so. And, working with rats, Beninger and Kendall (1975) have shown that behavioral contrast can be demonstrated even when two topographically distinct responses (nose-key poking and lever-pressing) are required in different components of the multiple schedule. That the signal-incentive contingencies may be more important in producing contrast effects than response-incentive contingencies is beginning to be recognized (e.g., Rachlin, 1973). Further, according to the present hypothesis the contrast effect would occur with a purely classical conditioning procedure, in which no specific responses are trained and in which the contrast effect is measured in terms of relative preference for the signals or some autonomic correlate of motivational arousal.

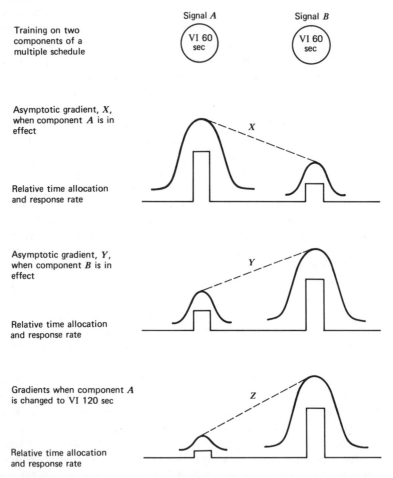

Figure 12.1. Explanation of contrast effect in terms of the slope of spatial gradient of motivational valence between the signals for the two components. Relative time allocation and response rates are a direct function of the relative motivational valence of the two signals.

Behavioral Conflict

Much of the early work on behavioral conflict placed a strong emphasis on the incompatibility of responses. Typically, a certain response (e.g., approach) was trained in a situation and then some stimulus that evoked an incompatible response (e.g., withdrawal) was introduced (e.g., N. E. Miller, 1944), or stimuli controlling two different responses (e.g., fighting and eating) were simultaneously presented to the animal (Tinbergen, 1951). The resulting behavior was compared with behavior in some comparable control situation, and any observed differences in the test response were attributed to the conflict between the two "response tendencies."

According to the present view, a conflict situation is one essentially like other behavioral situations in having a certain spatiotemporal distribution of incentive stimuli, but differs in that there are two or more incentive stimuli (unconditioned or conditioned) with a high motivational valence relative to other situational stimuli and roughly equal motivational valence relative to each other. In such a situation two or more strong central motivational states are aroused at the same time, or in quick succession, so that time allocation to various stimuli may occur in disjointed and interrupted ways, preventing the normal coherence and completion of actions. In the normal life of an animal, given a certain organismic state, several motivational states may be concurrently generated, as the animal is exposed now to one set of incentive stimuli and now to another. For example, a somewhat hungry bitch nursing its offspring in its "home area" may observe an intruding dog and also some food, so that irritability-defense and eating motivational states will be added to the prevailing nursing motivational state. Similarly, a male monkey having just finished fighting with another over the control of a piece of food or of a sitting perch, may come across a receptive female. And a human adolescent anxious about a job interview may find the interviewer to be an old family friend. Clearly, many different combinations of motivational states are possible, the particular combinations depending on the animal's current organismic state (hunger, hormonal level, pain, etc.) and on the various unconditioned and conditioned incentive stimuli in the situation. What are called the phenomena of behavioral conflict are characterized by lack of orderly succession of responses until a total action has been completed; they occur when different motivational states are aroused, prompting actions in relation to different stimuli concurrently. Motivational conflict, then, is a special case of motivational combinations that are a normal part of existence. This motivational view of behavioral conflict resembles the psychoanalytic view (Freud, 1920) in emphasizing the motivational origins of conflict, but differs from it in attributing the generation of motivational states to specific environmental incentive stimuli, which may be conditioned stimuli,—thus, in not regarding these states as wholly "intrapsychic" or "instinctive."

The behavioral effects of motivational combinations may be studied with an extension of the type of experimental method developed for the investigation of the effects of extraneous conditioned stimuli on trained responses. By manipulating relevant aspects of an animal's organismic state and the spatiotemporal distribution of unconditioned and conditioned incentive stimuli, it should be possible to produce different combinations of motivational states. The behavioral consequences of various motivational combinations could then be studied by comparing behavioral changes produced by certain combinations of motivational states with the changes produced by each of those motivational states alone. The exact form of the response produced at any given time would depend on the same principles of response production (see Chapter 11) that govern all response production: each successive response is determined by the specific momentary combinations of current motivational states, the situational contingencies that have been learned by the animal, and the spatiotemporal distribution of the incentive stimuli. There are no special principles governing "conflict behavior."

A phenomenon often discussed in relation to behavioral conflict is that of "collateral behavior." This refers to some fairly repetitive activities that are quite uniform for the members of a species, and occur spontaneously in conjunction with more formal instrumental actions but are not an intrinsic part of those actions. They include preening, grooming, pecking, grazing, "dancing," and the like. Since they are not part of any appropriate or expected response in the situation, they have been given various names, such as irrelevant behavior (e.g., Andrew, 1956), derived activities (Tinbergen, 1952), displacement phenomena (Bindra, 1959; N. E. Miller, 1948*b*), superstitious behavior (Skinner, 1948), adjunctive behavior (Falk, 1964, 1971), interim activities (Staddon & Simmelhag, 1971), and collateral behavior (Wilson & Keller, 1953). I use the last of these terms here because it has the least theoretical connotations.

There are two types of conditions under which collateral activities can be reliably obtained. First, if an animal is placed in a situation in which certain conditioned incentive stimuli generate or enhance a certain central motive state, but the particular stimulus in relation to which the defined, expected response is to be made (e.g., a lever if the response is lever-pressing, food if the response is eating, an adversary if the response is fighting) has been removed from, or has not yet been introduced into, the situation, then the animal is likely to display certain collateral activities. Second, if the contingency arranged by the experimenter has a temporal-delay feature, such as is characteristic of experiments involving differential reinforcement of slow rates (e.g., Kramer & Rilling, 1970; Pouthas & Cavé, 1972), fixed-interval reinforcement schedules (e.g., Staddon & Simmelhag, 1971), or negatively correlated reinforcement (Rashotte & Amsel, 1968), then the animal is likely to display collateral activities during the delay period. In both types of cases, the main feature of the situation is that while a central motive state has been aroused, the habitual response routine cannot occur because all the appropriate discriminative stimuli required for the response are not present at the moment, or some new, strong distracting stimuli are present. Under these conditions, according to the present view, the animal would act in relation to the various *other* (conditioned or unconditioned) stimuli that may momentarily have a relatively high motivational valence. The collateral responses usually made (e.g., grazing, preening) are those made in relation to stimuli that are almost always present in the situation (e.g., grass, one's own body). Collateral activities, then, are actions produced by the same principles of performance as govern any formally defined response, and they reflect the momentary motivational valences and distributions of incentive stimuli in the situation.

Effects of Drugs

Any observed effects of a drug on the performance of a response routine may arise from the influence that the drug has on any one or more of the processes involved in response production. The observed effects may arise from drug-induced changes in motor outflow, in motivational arousal, in contingency organizations, or in stimulus identification, or from any combination of these changes. Since a drug may influence neural activity in several different structures of the brain, it requires a good deal of experimental analysis to determine the exact basis of the behavioral effects of a drug. Though there is a great deal of reliable information on the influence of various drugs on different types of response routines (see Kumar, Stolerman, & Steinberg, 1970), little by way of reliable conclusions is available so far as the mechanisms underlying the behavioral effects are concerned. The phenomenon of state-dependent learning (see Chapters 2 and 14) is especially relevant to the search for the mechanisms of behavioral effects of drugs.

EXTINCTION

When an animal is reliably performing a certain response, the introduction of the extinction procedure—the withholding of the incentive stimulus on some or all of the trials—typically produces a marked decrement in responding as well as other changes in the response routine. Changes in behavior seen in the course of extinction seem to be best interpreted as reflecting alterations in the motivational valences of situational stimuli, which result from the modification of the contingent relations that were learned during the acquisition of the response routine. In essence, the extinction procedure creates conditions for the modification of existing contingency organizations into ones that better represent the new environmental contingencies; prior contingencies are not "unlearned" or "extinguished" in extinction but are modified by new additional experience.

Renewed Contingency Learning

Consider some possible contingency changes in the typical case of a rat's alley-running response acquired with food as the incentive stimulus. With the introduction of the extinction procedure, the most notable change in the experimental situation is the absence of food in the goal box. This would result in the gradual superimposition of the new contingencies—that alley stimuli are followed by no food $(S:\overline{S^I})$—on the previously existing positive contingencies $(S:S^I)$; the old positive contingencies would not be unlearned or obliterated, but they would be gradually modified by the accumulation of instances of disconcomitance between alley stimuli and food. This means that there would be a progressive decline in the conditioned motivational valences of the various situational stimuli, including the goal-box stimuli. The animal would thus be progressively less attracted to the goal box; response latencies and running times would increase.

Note that, while the contingencies between food and the various alley stimuli would be modified, the contingencies among the alley stimuli themselves would not be, for these stimuli would still hold the same location in relation to each other, appearing in the same order whenever the animal traverses the alley. It is only the motivational properties of the alley stimuli that would decline because those stimuli are no longer followed by food. Thus, during extinction, most of the previously learned contingencies that do not involve the incentive stimulus would remain intact, but the performance of the trained response would deteriorate owing to the weakening of the conditioned motivational properties of the alley and goal-box stimuli. The extinction procedure does not obliterate knowledge of the situation, but only modifies the part of knowledge that involves the incentive stimulus.

If the gradual decrement in the performance level of a response during extinction procedure is dependent on new learning that reduces the motivational valences of certain situational stimuli, then it should be possible to obtain a similar response decrement by any other procedure that would reduce motivational valences of the same stimuli. One procedure for achieving this is by reducing motivation by changing its organismic state (e.g., hunger) rather than by withholding the incentive (e.g., food). Thus, in the above example, if, instead of being deprived of food, the animal were satiated *before* the daily running trials to the goal box *with* food, the rat should show the same gradual decrement in performance level as is usually seen as a consequence of the extinction procedure. M. J. Morgan (1974) has shown that this is the case and has drawn attention to many parallels between the effects of extinction and satiation procedures on the pattern of response decrement.

As noted above, several contingencies inherent in the daily experimental routine may remain unaffected by the extinction procedure. The various regular events occurring for an hour or so before and after the training session proper are usually maintained during the extinction procedure. For example, it is customary to continue giving the animal its daily ration of food on a food stand soon after the training session, and this procedure is usually continued during extinction sessions. Thus, it is possible that the contingency between goal box and food-on-the-feeding-stand would continue to gain strength even during the course of extinction, and thus would enhance the conditioned motivational properties of the goal-box stimuli. If each rat is given an extinction session of 10 trials per day, then the food on the feeding stand (at the end of the session) may provide conditions for a fixed-ratio schedule of reinforcement, with one massive reinforcement per day—on the food stand—following 10 alley runs. It is also possible that during extinction the animal may gradually learn that the session is terminated quickly and food on the food stand is made available sooner following goal-box stimuli (i.e., when it runs down the alley) than following start-box stimuli (i.e., when it does not complete a run during the allotted time). These factors may operate to reinstate the prior speed of running after a certain number of extinction sessions; thus under certain conditions any substantial decrement in the performance level of the response may be difficult to obtain. What specific new contingencies are acquired during extinction would depend on the details of the total procedure. The main point here is simply that if new contingencies are acquired during extinction, and if some of these contingencies involve incentive stimuli, then the animal's behavior will be determined by the new spatiotemporal distribution of conditioned incentive stimuli. This interpretation of extinction as new contingency learning would predict that new patterns of response will emerge if extinction trials are continued over a prolonged period; indeed, some animals may resume performing the trained response at pre-extinction levels (e.g., Clark & Miller, 1966).

Though the present interpretation attributes extinction decrement to new learning, this is not the learning of a new competing *response* postulated in Guthrie's (1935) theory of extinction. Here the new learning refers to modification of the previously learned stimulus-stimulus contingencies on the basis of further experience in the situation; the previously acquired contingencies are not replaced or weakened but are built upon and elaborated. In other words, when a training procedure is changed to the extinction procedure, the animal "transfers" the previously acquired contingencies to the new task and continues learning. This transfer view is consistent with the "aftereffects hypothesis" of extinction proposed by Capaldi (1966) and his associates (Spivey, Hess, & Black, 1968). Since the concept of transfer emphasizes the modification or elaboration of existing contingencies rather than new learning from scratch, the proposed approach may also prove useful in the analysis of a variety of learning phenomena in which later learning of a specific task is facilitated by earlier experience—phenomena such as latent extinction, over-training reversal effect, learning sets, and behavioral contrast (see Dunham, 1968; Padilla, 1971; Sutherland & Mackintosh, 1971, Chap. 8). Finally, the idea of continuous elaboration of previously acquired contingencies provides a link with the transfer theory of the development of intellectual abilities in man (Ferguson, 1954).

Partial-Reinforcement and Extinction

Concerning the partial-reinforcement extinction effect (see G. A. Kimble, 1961, Chap. 10; Sutherland & Mackintosh, 1971, Chap. 10), the present interpretation would emphasize the fact that the contingencies learned in partial-reinforcement training are more numerous and complex than they are in the case of continuous reinforcement. For example, in the case of the alley-running situation described above, a rat being trained on a continuous reinforcement schedule would learn the contingencies between various alley stimuli (S_1, S_2, S_3, etc.), the sight of food, and the food itself, S^I. But a rat being trained on partial-reinforcement schedule would learn, in addition to the above contingencies, other contingencies in which the alley stimuli are not followed by the sight of food or food itself, but by the empty goal box, etc. Since the early parts of the chain are the same for both rats, their asymptotic response latencies and running times up to the goal box would be similar. However, owing to the lower correlation between goal-box stimuli and food in the case of the partial-reinforcement rat, it would take longer (more trials) to learn the (partial-reinforcement) contingencies between alley stimuli and food; the contingency would be learned faster by the continuous-reinforcement rat. With the introduction of an extinction procedure, the degree of correlation between alley-goal-box stimuli and food would decline to zero for both rats. However, more trials would be required to build up a sufficient number of instances of temporal separation between alley stimuli and food to modify the low-correlation partial-reinforcement contingencies. A rat in the partial-reinforcement condition would require at least as many trials to modify the existing low-correlation contingency as it took to learn that contingency initially. Thus, the resistance to extinction would be greater in the case of the partial-reinforcement condition.

The above interpretation superficially resembles the discrimination hypothesis of the partial-reinforcement extinction effect (e.g., Mowrer &

Jones, 1945; Gonzales & Bitterman, 1964). The discrimination hypothesis attributes the effect to greater difficulty of discrimination between the acquisition and extinction conditions in the case of partial-reinforcement acquisition than in the case of continuous-reinforcement acquisition. However, the present suggestion is that, because the acquisition conditions are more *variable* in the case of partial reinforcement, a more complex constellation of positive and negative contingencies is acquired, and this takes longer to develop and to modify than the contingencies learned in the case of continuous-reinforcement acquisition conditions. A corollary of the present hypothesis is that the greater the variation in training conditions, the greater would be the number and complexity of contingencies involving the incentive stimulus, the greater would be the number of trials required to modify the learned contingencies, hence the greater would be the resistance to extinction. There is some evidence to indicate that greater variability of stimulus conditions during acquisition leads to a greater resistance to extinction, even when no partial-reinforcement schedule is involved (I. Mackintosh, 1955). Since the present hypothesis regards extinction as involving further development of the prior contingencies of the stimuli concerned rather than a replacement of what has been learned before, it is consistent with the fact that the interpolation of some continuous-reinforcement trials after partial-reinforcement training does not abolish the partial-reinforcement extinction effect (e.g., Jenkins, 1962; Theios, 1962); this finding cannot be readily explained in terms of the discriminative hypothesis.

In short, the present view is that wherever partial-reinforcement training increases resistance to extinction, it does so because this procedure has resulted in the acquisition of more diverse and complex contingencies than is likely to be the case with the continuous reinforcement procedure. This hypothesis incorporates the idea that with partial-reinforcement training, the animal observes more cues than it does with continuous reinforcement training (e.g., McFarland, 1966; Sutherland & Holgate, 1966).

Extinction by Response Prevention ("Flooding")

If the basis of extinction is a learned modification of an existing stimulus-stimulus contingency, then it should be possible to produce extinction through exposure to the extinction contingency even if the animal is not allowed to make the trained response during exposure to the extinction contingency. Such "latent extinction," or extinction without responding, has been demonstrated often (see G. A. Kimble, 1961, Chap. 10). A special case of this is to be found in the recent attempts to develop new methods for producing desired behavioral modifications. Owing to the similarity of avoidance behavior as observed in animal experiments to phobias in human neurotics, the latent extinction method has attracted attention as a possible treatment for patients. Essentially, the method consists of exposure to the extinction contingency under conditions of response prevention so that the subject is forced to observe that the old contingency is no longer operative (Baum, 1970). Used clinically, the method is sometimes called "flooding" or "forced reality-testing."

Many animal experiments have shown that cessation of responding of a trained avoidance response (e.g., jumping from a dangerous to a safe chamber) is achieved much faster if the animal is prevented from making the avoidance response during some or all of the extinction trials than if it is allowed to make the response on all trials. Presumably, response prevention creates conditions under which the animal can observe and learn the new (extinction) contingency; if allowed to respond, the animal will observe the change only when, by fatigue, distraction, or reduced motivational arousal, it fails to respond. The observed faster extinction with response prevention is thus consistent with the stimulus-stimulus contingency view of acquisition and extinction of response routines. Another implication of this view is that by arranging an appetitive contingency, in addition to response prevention during extinction of an avoidance response, it should be possible to obtain even faster extinction of the avoidance response (e.g., the dangerous compartment would become a relatively pleasant place if the animal were given appetitive incentive stimulation there). The results of some experiments with appetitive and aversive intracranial stimulation during response prevention have been interpreted as being consistent with this implication (Baum, LeClerc, & St-Laurent, 1973; LeClerc, St-Laurent, & Baum, 1973).

CHAPTER 13

Choosing, Deciding, and Planning

The phrase "intelligent behavior" usually connotes thoughtful actions, those that rest on deliberation rather than on impulsiveness and are concerned with distant objectives rather than with immediate environmental demands. Such actions are commonly said to involve choosing, deciding, and planning. While it is useless to try to draw any sharp distinctions between them, it would be helpful to start with some rough definitions.

A "choice situation" may be described as one in which a subject selects one of two (or more) alternatives, and the selection of an alternative is quickly followed by a certain incentive outcome. *Choosing*, then, is making a selection between alternatives on the basis of their more or less immediate incentive outcomes. A "decision situation" may be described as one in which a subject makes some specified comparison and then selects one of two (or more) alternatives on the basis of the results of the comparison. *Deciding*, then, is making a selection between alternatives that rests on a comparison not directly involving the incentive outcomes of the alternatives. A "planning situation" may be described as one in which a subject makes several covert decisions related to a distant incentive outcome, but the action is delayed until most or all of the relevant decisions have been made. *Planning*, then, is making a prolonged succession of decisions prior to final action in relation to an incentive.

CHOICE SITUATIONS

Irwin (1971) has explained that choice implies that a subject has (1) an expectancy about the outcome of each choice alternative and (2) a preference for one of those outcomes. A choice situation, then, is one in which the subject's preference is examined in relation to two or more explicitly identified (unconditioned or conditioned) incentive-stimulus alternatives. By contrast, in the simple-responding or "non choice" situations, there is only one explicitly identified incentive stimulus and the subject's behavior is studied in relation to it alone. The meaningful measure for describing behavior in a choice situation is the relative preference for the various alternatives; in the non-choice situation the relevant measure is the degree of "strength" of responding in relation to the specified stimulus. It should be noted, as indeed it has been (Hull, 1943; Herrnstein, 1970), that even in a so-called nonchoice situation the strength of responding in relation to a specified stimulus is influenced by the strength of responding to all other behaviorally effective stimuli in the situation; when, for example, a hungry rat presses a lever, the rate of lever pressing is influenced by its exploratory and gnawing responses in relation to other situational stimuli. Thus, the behavior in a simple-responding situation may also be said to be determined by the preference for the specified stimulus relative to the preference for all the other stimuli. However, it is convenient to treat choice situations, with explicitly identified alternatives, separately.

The Matching Law

A method for studying the relative preference of alternatives that is being extensively used is that of "concurrent schedules of reinforcement." In a typical experiment, a hungry subject, say, a pigeon, is placed in a situation in which a different schedule of reinforcement is associated with each of two keys, the left key and the right key. Responses on the left key are reinforced, say, on a 2-min variable interval schedule (VI 2 min) and responses on the other (right) key are reinforced, say, on a 4-min variable interval schedule (VI 4 min). Each schedule is independent; that is, responses on one key have no influence on the schedule of the other key. In order to prevent the bird from being rewarded for switching from one key to the other, a changeover delay is introduced; this is the minimum interval during which reinforcement is not available on the key to which the bird has just switched. The measure of preference used is the relative frequency of responding on the two keys.

Herrnstein (1961) observed that under the above conditions the pigeon's responses on one of the two keys "match" the proportions of reinforcements obtained from pecking that key; the relative response rate equals the relative reinforcement rate. This so-called *matching law* is stated as follows:

$$\frac{R_L}{R_R} = \frac{S_L{}^{reinf.}}{S_R{}^{reinf.}}$$

where R_L equals overall response rate on the left key, R_R equals the overall response rate on the right key, $S_L{}^{reinf.}$ equals the rate of reinforcement on the left key, and $S_R{}^{reinf.}$ equals the rate of reinforcement on the right key.

Further analyses of responding in various types of concurrent schedules have shown that the matching law, stated in terms of response rate, holds true only under the specific conditions involving a concurrent variable-interval schedule and when responses during the changeover delay are included in the calculations. The matching law does not hold when certain fixed-interval concurrent schedules are used (e.g., Nevin, 1971), when certain chained schedules are used (Fantino & Duncan, 1972), or when responses during changeover delay are prevented by blackout of the experimental chamber (Silberberg & Fantino, 1970). A more fundamental difficulty with the matching law is the inadequacy of the ratio of response rates as a measure of preference, for this ratio is not invariant when absolute (baseline) response rates are changed by manipulations (e.g., alterations in the systems used for defining and counting responses) that should not affect preference (Lea & Morgan, 1972; Millenson & de Villiers, 1972). These types of considerations have led to the suggestion that the variable that may be meaningfully related to the relative reinforcement rate is the *relative time allocation* rather than the relative response rate (Baum & Rachlin, 1969; Premack, 1965; Rachlin, 1971). Thus, what started out to be a "law" matching relative response rate to relative reinforcement rate has been modified into a statement that replaces the relative response rate term by a relative time allocation term.

Another modification of the original matching law was required by the realization that it is not the mere rate of reinforcement associated with an alternative that determines preference, but the total "value" associated with the alternative (Baum & Rachlin, 1969). Thus, Rachlin (1971) suggested that the matching law should be restated as: $T_L/T_R = V_L/V_R$, where T_L and T_R are time allocations for the left and right keys, and V_L and V_R are the values associated with the two keys. But how does one estimate the total value of an alternative for a given subject? Presumably the value depends, apart from the quality and amount of the incentive stimulation that comprises a rein-forcement, on the rate and immediacy of its delivery, and on the effort required to produce the reinforcement. Further, the value of a given reinforce-ment for a certain animal depends upon the organismic state of the animal, as well as on miscellaneous other conditions prevailing at the time. This means that the total value of an alternative is a sum of several discrete quantities, each representing a certain point on a different "subjective scale" for different particular dimensions of the reinforcement (Killeen, 1972).

This idea of the value of an alternative resembles the concept of *utility* employed in "decision theory" (see Edwards, 1954) to refer to the algebraic sum of the desirable outcomes (benefit or positive value) and undesirable outcomes (cost or negative value) associated with an alternative. These con-siderations have led Killeen (1972) to suggest, essentially, that the older versions of the matching law be replaced by a statement that relative prefer-ence, as indicated by relative time allocation, T_L/T_R, is proportional to relative utility, U_L/U_R, as estimated from the appropriate subjective scales of value (benefits and costs). The exact relation between the ratios T_L/T_R and U_L/U_R may or may not be one of equality or "matching," but the equality relation appears to be a reasonable initial working assumption.

A third modification required in the current ideas about choice concerns the concept of "alternative." In the original response-ratio view of the matching law, the alternatives from which a choice is supposed to be made are different *responses*. The idea that the animal chooses between responses has persisted in the time-allocation view of the matching law; Rachlin (1971), for example, describes choice in terms of relative time allocation to the alternative *activities*. And the utility view of choice also considers utility to be an aspect of alternative responses. Against this prevailing view of choice alternatives as responses, my view is that choice alternatives are the unconditioned or conditioned incentive *stimuli* (the keys) in relation to which certain arbitrary indicator responses are defined and measured. As explained in Chapters 9 and 11, the basis of response production lies in the distribution of incentive stimuli in a situation; responses themselves are not pulled out of an existing storage but are constructed at the moment through the influence of incentive stimuli. In choosing, what a subject selects are stimuli, not responses.

The Process of Choice

Assume, then, that choice is a matter of preference between stimuli and that preference is a matter of relative utility of those stimuli. Now, if the relative preference for two alternative stimuli is determined by their relative utility, by what processes is the relative utility translated into relative preference? In other words, what is the basis of the relative time allocation to the stimuli in a choice situation?

The rough hypothesis I want to outline here is that the basis of relative utility lies in the relative motivational properties of the alternative (choice) stimuli. The choice stimuli are (unconditioned and conditioned) appetitive or aversive stimuli whose incentive properties attract or repel the animal to varying degrees. Since each stimulus may be a part of several contingencies that the animal has learned, it creates several specific changes in the motivational state of the animal. These changes fall into two main categories, motivation enhancing and motivation suppressing. The motivation enhancing effects of a stimulus depend on the nature and amount of the incentive stimulation it predicts, as well as on the delay of its occurrence (see Chapter 7). The motivation suppressing effects of the stimulus depend on the nature and degree of boredom (uneventful delay) and effort (fatigue) it predicts. The sum total of all these specific motivation enhancing and suppressing effects is the *net motivational valence* of that choice stimulus; this refers to the *type* (appetitive or aversive) and the *degree* (low or high) of the motivational arousal produced by a choice stimulus, and corresponds to its utility. Note that the net motivational valence will fluctuate continually, as the influences of various temporal contingencies come into play and then disappear; at any given time, a choice stimulus may be said to have a certain *momentary net motivational valence*. Remember too that the type and degree of motivational arousal produced by any given unconditioned or conditioned incentive stimulus is dependent on the prevailing organismic state of the animal (see Chapter 9). The concurrent presence of two or more such choice stimuli, each with its own temporal pattern of momentary net motivational valence, constitutes a choice situation.

Now consider an example. Suppose a hungry rat is placed in an experimental chamber fitted with two food receptacles, S_1 and S_2. Further, suppose that the animal is given a pellet of food at 60-sec intervals at each food receptacle, but the two deliveries occur at opposite phases of the 60-sec cycle, so that S_1 and S_2 deliveries are separated by 30 sec. Assume that the food pellets delivered in the two receptacles are identical, and that, under the given organismic conditions, each pellet has the same incentive (motivation arousing) value. Assume also that, on average, the effort required for going to each of the two food receptacles and eating a pellet of food is the same. The question we want to ask is this: after the animal has become thoroughly acquainted with the situation, what will be the pattern of its action in relation to the two receptacles, S_1 and S_2, and how would this pattern of action be arrived at? The simplest measure of action in relation to the two stimuli is the relative time spent in acting (e.g., sitting close to, sniffing, licking, gnawing, etc.) each of the receptacles. In general, the time allocated to the two goal stimuli, or conditioned-incentives, S_1 and S_2, would be proportional to their average motivational valence over an observation period; that is T^{S_1}/T^{S_2} would be proportional to M^{S_1}/M^{S_2}.

The details of pattern of time allocation or preference changes may be described with reference to Figure 13.1. The momentary net motivational valence of S_1 is the highest at the time T_0, when the food pellet is being delivered at that receptacle. As the food pellet is delivered, the stimulus with the highest motivational valence is the food pellet itself. After the food pellet has been consumed, say, at time T_5, the temporal relation between food consumption and a period (55 sec) of no food delivery will lead to a reduction in the motivational valence of S_1. Concurrently, the motivational valence of S_2 will gradually increase because of the temporal relation between the end of food consumption, T_5, and the delivery of another pellet 25 sec later, at T_{30}. At some time between T_5 and T_{30}, the animal will start acting in relation to S_2 (e.g., approaching, licking, etc.). The frequency and intensity of this behavior may increase until T_{30}, when food is delivered. The relative motivational valences of S_1 and S_2 would thus be in continuous flux, and the receptacle in relation to which the animal acts at any given moment would depend on their relative momentary net motivational valences.

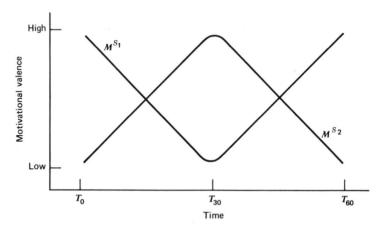

Figure 13.1. Hypothetical curves (with arbitrary units) of the variations in the motivational valences of two conditioned incentive-stimuli, M^{S_1} and M^{S_2}, which are related to food, presented at the opposite phases of a 60-sec cycle.

The exact time of changeover from S_1 to S_2, or vice versa, may be manipulated by varying the relative incentive value of food pellets (e.g., by making S_1 pellets larger or more palatable than S_2 pellets). The relative motivational valences may also be manipulated by varying the effort associated with reaching the two receptacles (e.g., one could be at the floor level and the other high on a wall). The time of changeover could also be manipulated by varying the interval between the two food deliveries, say by making S_1-S_2 interval 15 sec and S_2-S_1 interval 45 sec. It should be noted that the rat may, at times, act in relation to neither S_1 nor S_2 but to some other situational stimulus (e.g., a corner with a novel odor, or an accidental noise) whose net momentary motivational valence exceeds that of either of the specified choice stimuli at particular times during the cycle of situational events.

The above account of the type of processes that determine an animal's behavior in a choice situation is conceptually the same as the account of response production in a simple responding or nonchoice situation. In both cases the stimulus in relation to which the animal acts at a given moment is determined by the relative incentive properties of the spatiotemporal distribution of the various conditioned and unconditioned stimuli in the situation. The same fundamental choice process is involved in both. The main difference between the simple responding and choice situations is that in the former there is one dominant gradient of incentive value—the gradient between the specified test stimulus and the background stimulus complex of the situation, while in the latter there may be several important gradients of incentive value produced by the two or more choice stimuli on a common background. The outcomes of the interactions of the various gradients at any given moment are hard to predict in a choice situation, especially when choice is between stimuli with differential motivational properties (e.g., feeding, sexual, maternal, aggressive, exploratory, etc.). According to this proposal, then, the simple responding situation is essentially a simpler—much simpler—form of choice situation.

Transitivity in Choice

One implication of the above account of the process of choice is that the relative preference of a given set of stimulus alternatives in one situation may not be predictable from knowledge of the relative preference for the same stimuli in another situation. A female rat may prefer a saccharine solution to a saline solution normally, but may show a reversal in preference when pregnant; a male monkey may normally prefer a certain male companion to a certain female one, but may prefer the female when she is in estrus; and an adolescent boy may prefer a lemonade to whiskey in the presence of his father but whiskey to lemonade in the presence of his peers. This is so because the organismic-state variations as well as the contingency organizations activated by the same choice stimuli in different situations may produce different patterns of momentary net motivational valences. Clearly, according to this view, there is no such thing as an absolute level of motivational valence for any choice stimulus; the motivational valences of any two stimulus alternatives and hence their relative preference are always a function of the current organismic state and the spatiotemporal distribution of various incentive stimuli that make up the test situation.

A different view of choice assumes that there is something like an absolute valence of each choice alternative, and that relative preference of any two alternatives can be reliably predicted from knowledge of their absolute values or "strengths." This "constant ratio rule" has been used as the choice axiom by Luce and Suppes (1965) and Herrnstein (1970). It assumes that the relative preference of any two given alternatives is dependent only on their absolute or fixed values, and implies transitivity; if A is preferred to B and B to C, then A should be preferred to C. However, this is not always the case (Navarick & Fantino, 1972, 1974). As noted above, the momentary net motivational valence of any stimulus alternative is dependent on its spatiotemporal distribution in the situation, and fluctuates continually on the basis of temporal contingencies. Further, the subject's behavior in relation to an alternative depends on the momentary net motivational valence of other stimuli in the situation. According to the present view, then, transitivity of choice across alternative-combinations or across situations may or may not hold. Tversky's (1972) "elimination by aspects" model of choice is consistent with the process of choice being proposed here. According to his model the attributes (or contingencies) on the basis of which a choice is made shift with each new context or new combination of old choice alternatives.

DECISION TASKS

In a typical decision task, two or more given entities are first compared with respect to a certain specified quality (e.g., size, color, sameness, or meaning), the result of the comparison then determines the selective response, and the incentive outcomes depend on some arbitrary rule about the result of the comparison, as indicated by the selective response. For example, a child may be asked to compare two objects, A and B, with respect to weight, and then to press one key if A is heavier and another key if B is heavier; the incentive outcome may depend on the correctness of the judgment. The two objects are the comparison stimuli and the two keys are the choice alternatives; a response on one of the keys indicates the decision—the selection based on the comparison. In the choice situation the stimuli determining the selective response are themselves the choice alternatives, with defined incentive outcomes; in the decision situation the (comparison) stimuli determining the selective response are not themselves the choice alternatives, but they bear an arbitrary relation to the choice alternatives, and these in turn bear an arbitrary relation to incentive outcomes.

There are four main aspects or components of a decision. First, the subject must refrain from making the selective response until the required comparison has been made. He must withhold action until a decision has been reached. Second, the subject must obtain or recall and hold (see Chapter 10) the nformation necessary for making the required comparison. Third, a comparison must somehow be made and a result obtained, a decision reached. Fourth, the decision must be translated into a selective (indicator) response according to a certain specified transformational rule, such as "if the stimuli are the same, press the left key," or "if the noun is singular, put an s at the end of the verb." The following discussion is concerned with the type of processes in terms of which the above components of a decision may be understood.

Action-Control Processes

This name is given to processes that enable an animal to withhold action until the required comparison has been made and then quickly initiate the selective response. The existence of such processes is indicated by the various deficits of response withholding and response initiation. Deficits of response withholding are frequently observed following damage to frontal lobes, the hippocampus, and septal region. For example, exploratory activity and the performance of active avoidance responses are enhanced by dorsal frontal cortical lesions (e.g., Albert & Bignami, 1968; Butter, 1964), as well as by lesions of the dorsal hippocampus and of certain septal nuclei (Hamilton, Kelsey, & Grossman, 1970; Kimble, 1968; MacDougall, Van Hoesen, & Mitchell, 1969; Micco & Schwartz, 1971; Nadel, 1968). Similarly, perseverative tendencies and other deficits of withholding action in delayed-response tasks are a well-known consequence of damage to frontal lobes in primates (Butter, 1969; Goldman, Rosvold, Vest, & Galkin, 1971). Further, certain clinical syndromes, such as hyperactivity in children, are characterized by an inability to withhold responding—"to think before acting" (V. I. Douglas, 1972).

The contrary deficits of response initiation may also be observed following certain types of brain damage. For example, Vanderwolf (1963) has shown that medial thalamic lesions leave rats quite capable of making an active avoidance response, but the time taken by the animal to initiate the response is greatly increased. Similar increases in response latency, without impairment of response speed, have also been observed under the influence of tranquilizing drugs, such as chlorpromazine (Herr, Stewart, & Charest, 1961; Posluns, 1962). Clinical states of low arousal (e.g., catalepsy) and depression are also characterized by deficits of response initiation.

A reasonable working assumption is that these opposing deficits of response withholding and initiation are aspects of a single inhibitory action-control process (Bindra, 1968; R. J. Douglas, 1967, 1972; Gerbrandt, 1965; Kimble, 1968). Deficits of response withholding could represent a decrease in the output of an inhibition generating mechanism, and deficits of response initiation an increase in the output of the same inhibitory mechanism. The exact pathways and neural mechanisms of behavioral inhibition are not known, but increasingly it has begun to appear that inhibitory modulation of behavior arises fundamentally from interaction loops of the nigral, striatal, and dorsolateral frontal regions of the brain (Divac, 1972; Johnson & Rosvold, 1971; Johnson, Rosvold, & Mishkin, 1968; Ungerstedt, Butcher, Butcher, Andén, & Fuxe, 1969).

Normally, in the absence of lesions and other neural defects, the modulation of inhibitory control of action is highly selective and refined. For example, in a situation requiring a comparison of two stimuli, the subject's action is withheld until the needed information has been obtained and the comparison made; then the response is produced quickly. Even during the period of "action withholding" the subject may perform several observational and other acts; it is only the response indicating the decision that is withheld, and it is withheld in such a way that it can be quickly "released." This kind of selective and refined control would appear to be possible only through the learning of subtle contingencies of a decision task. The subject must learn that more decisions are correct if the response follows the required comparison than if the response is produced too quickly for an adequate comparison to have been made.

The degree to which a response is withheld in a decision task can of course be varied by manipulating experimental conditions. For example, if the subject is told that it is more important to be accurate than to be speedy (i.e., if the incentive value of "correct" verdict is raised and that of "fast" lowered by instructions), the response withholding will be markedly enhanced, so that response latency will be raised while errors are reduced. If speed is emphasized more than accuracy, response withholding will be markedly lowered, so that response latency will be lowered while errors are increased. The speed-accuracy trade-off for optimal performance will, of course, vary with the nature of the task requirements. Individuals differ greatly in the trade-off habits they bring to decision tasks, the two extreme types being the excessively action-inhibited, who delay and postpone action to avoid being wrong, and the excessively action-ready, who respond quickly but not too accurately. The maturational factors and early contingency learning that underlie such personality differences are worth investigating.

Preparatory Processes

Comparison processes may be studied by asking a subject to compare two entities (e.g., colors, objects, voices, words, values, or political philosophies) with respect to a certain attribute (e.g., hue of colors, weight of objects, sweetness of voices, abstractness of words, morality of values, or radicalism of political philosophies). The two comparison stimuli may be presented simultaneously or successively. The subject may be presented with only one stimulus at the time of comparison and asked to compare it with one he is to recall (are these raspberries more or less tasty than the ones you had last week?), or he may be asked to rate the presented stimulus on a seven-point scale (e.g., of tastiness) whose end points are identified. He may be asked to compare the stimuli with respect to an attribute that is unidimensional (e.g., hue) or with respect to an attribute that is multidimensional (e.g., volume, usefulness). The relevant attribute—along which the comparison is to be made—may be the only attribute with respect to which the comparison stimuli vary (e.g., hue), or there may also be variation with respect to one or more other attributes (e.g., size, shape). The subject may be told that he should be very accurate or told that the emphasis is on speed; that is, he may be encouraged (by instruction or reward contingencies) to adopt a stringent or a lax criterion, or confidence level, for the correctness of his judgments; and so on. There are many ways in which comparison tasks may differ from each other. The main measures of performance are response latency and errors.

What a subject says he does in making a comparison is this. He concentrates on the stimuli, as well as on the idea of comparing them with respect to the specified attribute at a certain level of accuracy. He lets a judgment emerge and then performs the response that corresponds to the judgment. What we are concerned with here is the nature of the preparatory processes by which the elements required for a comparison are isolated and held active for them to be compared. Perhaps the most fruitful way of exploring this question is to examine in detail what appears to be the simplest of comparisons, that is, the comparison involved in the decision whether two stimuli are the "same" or "different" with respect to a single, specified attribute.

Take the experiment by Bindra, Williams and Wise (1965) on same-different decisions. They presented two tones of equal intensity but different frequency; one was a 1.0-kHz tone (tone A) and the other a 1.6-kHz tone (tone B). Tone presentations were arranged in four pairs (AA, AB, BA, and BB), and, following each paired presentation, the subject was asked to indicate by pressing one of two keys whether the tones were the same (AA, BB) or different (AB, BA). On each trial, the tones were presented in succession, the first one for 4 sec, and the other one until the subject responded; the intertone interval was 1.0 sec. After some preliminary trials to acquaint them with the two tones and the required comparison, the subjects were given several trials under certain predetermined conditions. Mean response latencies and total errors were obtained separately for the same and different decisions under each condition. In general, the response latency was about 1 sec (measured from the time of onset of the second tone of the pair), and errors were few. The subjects were readily able to make the required comparison and to translate the resulting judgment quickly into the response of pressing the appropriate key.

Now, in order for a subject to be able to make a correct decision, he must hold the two tones in some sort of active, salient state that isolates them from other stimuli. This means that pexgos representing the two tones must be selectively activated. The pexgo of the first tone (A or B) would of course be highly activated during the 4 sec that it is being sounded, but, after the tone's termination, only a fading pexgo of the tone (decreasing excitation of the gnostic-assemblies representing the tone) would remain. The comparison, then, would be between the highly active pexgo of the second tone and the fading pexgo of the first tone. With simultaneous presentation of the comparison stimuli, of course, both the (sensory) pexgos would be simultaneously active at the time of comparison, and with a decision involving two recalled stimuli the comparison would be based on two (associatively) recalled pexgos. In general, the decisions would tend to be accurate and fast when they were based on sensory pexgos, and would tend to be inaccurate and slow when they were based on associative or otherwise degraded pexgos. Thus, in the above experiment, when the intertone interval was increased from 1.0 sec to 10.0 sec, the number of errors increased over threefold and the decision latency increased by about 25 msec. It may be expected that any condition that reduces the distinctiveness or strength of pexgos would impair performance.

The requirement to compare something with respect to a certain attribute may be assumed to lead to the excitation of pexgos representing various levels of that attribute. For example, the requirement to compare stimuli with respect to pitch or color would excite various pexgos representing different values of that attribute. These excited pexgos would form a scale, with the pexgos of different attribute-values serving as points of the scale as explained in Chapter 5). How refined or rough a scale would emerge depends on the discriminative experience of the subject with respect to that attribute, and on the requirements of the task. In the above experiment, where pitch is defined with reference to only two tones, the scale would be very limited in range and crude; but if one were to increase the number of tones from which the two comparison tones are selected for each trial, the scale activated would be much more extended or refined, or both. For several common attributes (e.g., size, color, weight, speed) adult human subjects appear to have well developed scales that they bring to various comparison and scaling tasks. Whatever the factors that determine the range and refinement of the attribute scale activated at a given time, the main point of the present hypothesis is that the central representation of the comparison attribute consists in the increased excitation of certain pexgos that represent different values of the attribute. The comparison attribute is centrally represented by the same sort of neural processes as are the comparison stimuli.

The Comparison Process

Turn now to the actual comparison. What exactly does a comparison mean neurally? A tentative hypothesis may be developed as follows. The outcome of a comparison is a neural discrepancy discharge representing a lack of commonality between the activated pexgos (sensory or associational) of the comparison stimuli. If the pexgos of the comparison stimuli involve largely common gnostic-assemblies—if they match—there is little discrepancy discharge, but, if they involve largely different gnostic-assemblies—if they mismatch—there is a great deal of discrepancy discharge. The discrepancy discharge may consist of the excitation of certain "novelty" or discrepancy neurons, which are excited by change or difference; these are presumably the same neurons that are activated when an animal comes across a novel stimulus or is exposed to a dishabituation or distracting stimulus. If the comparison stimuli are quite different, the rate of discrepancy discharge will be high; if the comparison stimuli are quite similar, the rate of discrepancy discharge will be low. These relations are shown in Figure 13.2.

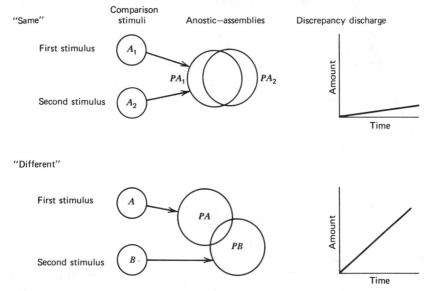

Figure 13.2. "Same" and "different" judgments rest on discrepancy discharge. The rate of discrepancy discharge depends on the extent to which the gnostic-assemblies excited by the two comparison stimuli are different.

When a subject is trained in preliminary or practice trials, in which he is told on each trial whether his decision is correct or incorrect, he learns the contingent relations between particular rates of discrepancy discharge and the verdicts ("correct" and "incorrect") of the experimenter. A high rate of discrepancy discharge would be positively correlated with the verdict "correct" on "different" trials, and a low rate of discrepancy discharge would be positively correlated with verdict "correct" on "same" trials. This means that, after some practice with a given set of comparison stimuli, a high rate of discrepancy discharge would lead to the judgment "different" and a low rate to the judgment "same." The rate of discrepancy discharge that serves as the end or the beginning point for a judgment is the criterion point for that judgment. The maximum rate of discrepancy discharge that results in mostly correct "same" judgments would become the end point for the judgment "same," and the minimum rate of discrepancy discharge that results in mostly correct "different" judgments would become the beginning point for the judgment "different." If the subject is required to give a decision on a long series of mixed (identical or dissimilar comparison stimuli) trials, then the two points are likely to represent an identical rate of discrepancy discharge, and this would be the common criterion point. The subject's judgments would, of course, be distributed around the criterion. Figure 13.3 shows the hypothetical relations between the rate of discrepancy discharge, the common criterion point, and the probability of "same" and "different" judgments. Since the criterion point is the point of maximum uncertainty, being equally related to the two judgments, the latency of decisions would be the highest for discrepancy rates around the criterion point.

If the criterion falls somewhere in the middle of the range of rates of discrepancy discharge produced by the identical and dissimilar pairs of stimuli, as shown in Figure 13.3a, the distribution of the same and different judgments around the common criterion point may be expected to be symmetrical. This would mean that the proportion of "same" and "different" judgments would be roughly equal and there would be no difference in the average latencies for "same" and "different" decisions. On the assumption of equal numbers of trials with the "same" and "different" pairs, the probabilities of erroneously calling an identical stimulus pair "different" (X-errors) or a dissimilar stimulus pair "same" (Y-errors) would also be roughly equal.

Now, suppose that the requirement for accuracy is relatively more stringent for "different" judgments than for "same" judgments—that is, the common criterion is set at a higher rate of discrepancy discharge, as shown in Figure 13.3b. There would now be proportionately fewer "different" judgments, the average latency of "different" decisions would be greater than the average latency of "same" decisions, and the probability of erroneously judging different stimuli as same (calling-"different"-"same" errors), or Y, errors would be greater than that of X-errors (calling-"same"-"different" errors). Conversely, suppose that the requirement for accuracy is more stringent for "same" judgments than for "different" judgments, that is, the common criterion is set at a lower rate of discrepancy discharge, as in Figure 13.3c. There would now be proportionately fewer "same" judgments, the average latency of "same" decisions would be greater than that of "different" decisions, and the probability of X-errors (calling-"same"-"different" errors) would be greater than that of Y-errors (calling-"different"-"same" errors). Thus the nature and speed of decision are related to the common criterion point, the value of discrepancy rate that separates the alternative judgments.

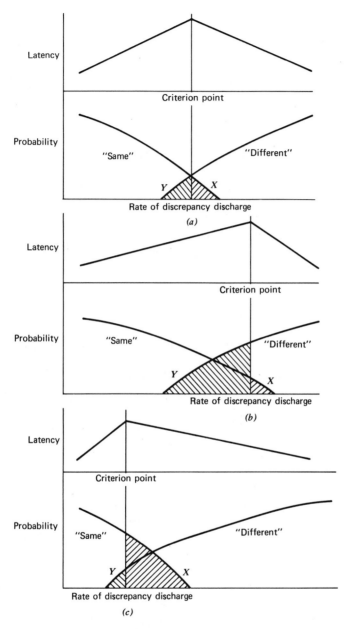

Figure 13.3. Probability and latency functions for "same" and "different" judgments, with judgments distributed around three different criterion points. (*a*) Medium criterion point, (*b*) high criterion point, (*c*) low criterion point. See text for further explanation.

If the experimenter makes the verdict "correct" more lax for "same" (i.e., more stringent for "different") judgments, the subject's criterion point will be raised; if the experimenter makes the verdict "correct" more stringent for "same" (i.e., more lax for "different") judgments, the subject's criterion point will be lowered. In other words, in a forced-choice two-alternative decision task, if the accuracy demands for one decision (e.g., "same") are made more stringent, the accuracy demands for the other decision (e.g., "different") automatically become more lax. It is thus *not* the criterion that determines the stringency or laxness of the accuracy standards adopted by the subject, but the accuracy standards operating in the subject (in consequence of his early experimental or pre-experimental experience), that determine what the criterion point will be. A criterion is simply a point on the discrepancy scale adopted as a point of reference by a subject under the requirements of a given decision task. The concept of criterion, as a critical determiner of the judgments made in a decision task, has been formally developed in signal-detection theory (Green & Swets, 1966; Swets, 1973; Swets, Tanner, & Birdsall, 1961).

In the experiment by Bindra, Williams, and Wise described above, it was found that the average latency of the "same" decisions was longer than that of "different" decisions, and the subjects made more errors of calling identical stimuli "different" than of calling dissimilar stimuli "same." In terms of the present formulation, these findings suggest that the subject operated on a higher standard of accuracy for "same" judgments than for "different" judgments; in other words, his criterion point was at a rather low level of discrepancy discharge, as seen in Figure 13.3c. There are many other studies of the "same"-"different" judgment in which the opposite results have been obtained (see Nickerson, 1972); in fact, longer latency for "different" decisions has been the commoner finding. In these latter studies, the subjects apparently operated on a higher standard of accuracy for "different" judgments than for "same" judgments, hence worked in relation to a criterion point that represented a relatively high level of discrepancy discharge.

What determines whether a subject will operate on a relatively higher standard of accuracy for the "same" judgment or for the "different" judgment? The commoner finding of higher accuracy standard for "different" has been obtained with stimuli that are complex patterns, such as alphanumeric characters (e.g., Nickerson, 1965; Posner & Mitchell, 1967; Sternberg, 1969) or words and objects (e.g., Fraisse, 1963; E. Smith, 1967; Tversky, 1969). The stimuli used in experiments in which the subjects operate on a higher accuracy standard for "same" have for the most part employed stimuli that vary along a single stimulus dimension whose different values are not independently identifiable, such as pitch of tones and length of lines (e.g., Bindra Donderi, & Nishisato, 1968; Bindra, Williams, & Wise, 1965). This suggests that it is the difference in the ease of discrimination between the comparison stimuli that underlies differences in the operative accuracy standard. Greater discrimination difficulty could mean that only a small discrepancy discharge is required for a correct "different" decision, so that the subject would have to consider as pertinent very small magnitudes of discrepancy discharge; this will happen if the experimenter gives a verdict of incorrect on many "same" judgments. In such a task, the criterion point that would emerge in preliminary trials would represent a rather low rate of discrepancy discharge (Figure 13.3c).

Discrimination difficulty could also be increased in other ways; for example, any degradation in the pexgo of the first comparison stimulus by the time the second stimulus is presented would increase discrimination difficulty and would lead the subject to a lower criterion point. In conformity with this implication, it may be expected that, as the interstimulus interval is increased, decision latency for the "same" judgment will increase relative to the decision latency for the "different" judgment; this appears to be the case (Entus & Bindra, 1970). The general point is that the criterion determining latencies and errors is a function of the standard of accuracy a subject adopts, and this depends on the difficulty of the comparison. The standards of accuracy the subject adopts may also be influenced by the penalties and rewards attached to correct and incorrect judgments—that is, by the "payoff matrix" (see Edwards, Lindman, & Phillips, 1965).

In the case of human subjects, one reason for the difference in discrimination difficulty of stimuli like objects, colors, and alphanumeric characters on the one hand, and of stimuli like tones and lines on the other, may be that the former are likely to have well-developed gnostic-assemblies possessing specific and rather unique features, so that they can be readily identified even in the absence of any reference stimulus. Individual pexgos of particular values of a single attribute, on the other hand, have no codable or distinctive meaning until they are compared with a reference stimulus or scale; they are thus more difficult to identify. "Codable" stimuli, then, would be more readily discriminable and yield shorter decision latencies, in general, and relatively shorter decision latencies for "same" judgments (Bindra, Donderi, & Nishisato, 1968; Cohen, 1969).

The above general account of decision-making may now be applied to situations in which the subject decides, not whether two stimuli are the same or different, but which one of any two specified entities is longer, shorter, more familiar, less meaningful, more aggressive, more entertaining, more consistent with an hypothesis, and so on. In all these cases, the essential comparison may be supposed to involve a discrepancy discharge arising from the juxtaposition of the pexgos of the two stimuli on a common attribute scale (e.g., one of length, familiarity, meaningfulness, relevance, etc.). The rate of discrepancy discharge is proportional to the difference between the two stimuli along the specified comparison attribute. For any given decision, particular rates of discrepancy discharge are associated with particular judgments, such as low, medium, and high, or points on a seven- or nine-category scale of the attribute. The main thing to note is that, regardless of what is being decided, the comparison is always between two pexgos.

Typically the pexgo of a stimulus is compared with an associatively generated pexgo of a certain comparison attribute. The particular comparison attribute and its different values are represented by certain pexgos, whose activation is determined by the important contingent relations specified by the decision task. Provided the subject has enough time to estimate the rate of discrepancy discharge, the rate is categorized on the basis of criterion points on the discrepancy-rate dimension. When a decision task involves three categories, two criterion points are required; for a scale of n categories, the number of criteria required is $n - 1$. The closer a certain rate of discrepancy discharge is to the mean rate for a certain category (or the midpoint between the criterion points defining a category), the faster the judgment will be made.

In decisions of everyday life, the comparison attribute, even though it may be given a single name, is likely to be a complex of several separate attributes. In deciding whether person A or B is more friendly, I may judge each on attributes of "good company," unselfishness, proneness to irritability, and expression of warmth. These initial judgments may then be combined to yield points on a global scale of friendliness. Suppose I decide that A is more friendly than B; and suppose I also decide that B is more friendly than C. Then, from the knowledge $A > B > C$, can it be concluded that, if I were asked to decide between A and C, I would find A more friendly than C? It is evident that one cannot make such a prediction with certainty; the presumed transitivity of the relation $A > B > C$ may not hold. For it may be that in deciding between B and C, my judgments of friendliness are based on only three of the above attributes (I disregard proneness to irritability), and in deciding between A and C my judgment may be based on a set that includes a new attribute, say, "arrogance." Apparently, I consider arrogance an important attribute when deciding between A and C, but not when deciding between A and B. It should be clear that because of shifting attributes on the basis of which we make everyday decisions, transitivity cannot be assumed. A formalization of this general approach to decisions about complex entities will be found in Tversky's (1972) model of decision making.

Response Selection

The response that defines a decision may be verbally saying "same" or "different," or pressing one of two keys, etc. The point is that reaching a judgment is followed by a separate step of translating the judgment into an appropriate indicator response. Different modes of indicator response may take different amounts of time (Seymour, 1969). For example, decisions requiring uttering the words "same" or "different" may take longer than decisions requiring pressing appropriately labeled keys; and pressing keys labeled "yes" (for "same") and "no" (for "different") may take less time than decisions requiring pressing keys labeled "no" for "same" and "yes" for "different" (Bindra, Williams, & Wise, 1965). These facts suggest that the decision response is not a simple continuation of the processes that result in judgment, but that some new process of translating the judgment into a motor pattern that indicates the judgment is involved in the making of the decision response. The translation process presumably rests on instructions and previous learning about the different stimuli in relation to which alternative decisions are to be indicated. Both the nature of the translation process and the particular movements (e.g., the particular fingers to be used for pressing a key) that make up the required response are important determinants of the total decision time.

One implication of the separation of the judgmental and response-selection processes in a decision task is that the making of judgments may be separated in time from response production. A person may decide that a motion picture X would be more enjoyable than Y long before he actually leaves for the appropriate motion-picture theater. The possibility of introducing a temporal gap between judgment and action brings us to the topic of planning.

PLANNED ACTIONS

The behavior of primates frequently consists of prolonged courses of action, continuous or interrupted, that appear to have been prepared in advance of their execution. It is as if the animal had decided on a final goal, prepared in its head an outline of the various steps required to achieve that goal, and then waited for an appropriate occasion for performing each step. A small monkey gradually inches his way close to an unfriendly, larger one who is eating some fruit; then, as soon as something distracts the larger monkey, the smaller one quickly grabs a piece of fruit and runs away. A chimpanzee goes to a water fountain and fills its mouth with water and sits nonchalantly near the entrance to his cage; when an attendant comes close, the chimpanzee spits the water at him and runs, amused, to the rear of the cage. A boy puts on his shoes, rides a bicycle to a store, buys some ice cream, rides back, and shares the ice cream with his sister.

Seen retrospectively, as a whole, the varied responses that make up each of the above instances of planned behavior are clearly related to a common, remote goal, and may be seen as involving a number of subgoals that are way stations for reaching the specified remote goal. Noting this hierarchical organization of the actions that make up any instance of planned behavior, Miller, Galanter, and Pribram (1960) defined the term *plan* as "any hierarchical process in the organism that can control the order in which a sequence of operations is to be performed," and conceived of this process as involving a flexible neural program. However, their account remained essentially retrospective and descriptive; they did not speculate about what the flexible neural programs might be, nor explain how a plan might be organized initially. Another problem with Miller, Galanter, and Pribram's concept of plan is that they use it to explain any prolonged course of action with a hierarchical organization, including instinctive actions, habits, and problem solving. Their concept of plan thus assumes the full burden of the explanation of all adaptive behavior, and ceases to have any special relevance to the distinctive feature of planning, namely, the temporal separation of decisions from action—the articulation of a plan now about something to be done in the future. In order to explain planned behavior we must have an account of how a plan is articulated, how it is executed.

The Articulation of a Plan

To articulate a plan is essentially to make a number of related decisions about alternatives likely to be encountered on the way to a goal or subgoal. Suppose I have just finished writing a letter and now want to mail it. The remote goal is putting the letter in a mail box. Several subgoals may be identified, such as getting up from my desk, preparing to go out, going to the post office, and putting the letter in a mail box. The articulation of a plan of mailing the letter means that, in advance of getting up from my desk, I make decisions about at least some of the alternatives I shall face on the way: whether to mail the letter now or later, if now, whether to walk to the post office or drive, etc. By thus deciding which of the alternatives I shall choose, I have prepared myself a rough "blueprint," indicating spatio-temporal arrangement of the important decisions and the particular alternative to be selected at each decision point. Now, if I can recall the decisions that comprise the plan at the appropriate place and time, I shall be able to execute the total action smoothly, without much overt trial and error or hesitation as I reach the actual, environmental choice points.

The articulation of a plan begins with the creation of a set dominated by the remote goal, that is, the activation of certain contingency organizations related to the goal. In the above example, seeing a completed letter might lead, through established or contingency organizations, to the idea of the letter being put in a mail box. Now the first decision issue arises: Should I mail the letter now or should I just finish the work I had sat down at my desk to do? This question would lead to a comparison of the two alternatives in terms of the expected utility (pleasure, satisfaction, etc.) I would receive from hearing my friend's reaction to my letter and from completing the work I have to do while I have some time to do it. Is my friend away on vacation? Has today's mail already been picked up? Would I have some time left for my work if I did go out to mail the letter now? How urgent is it that I finish the work? Questions like these would be important in reaching a judgment on the comparison of the utility of the two alternatives. Suppose I decide in favor of mailing the letter at once. I reach for stamps in the desk drawer and discover there are none left. So I would have to go to the post office to mail the letter.

Now I may go through the same comparison again with the alternatives of "going to the post office to mail the letter now" versus "working now and mailing the letter later." If I decide in favor of working now, the alternative of mailing the letter now would be abandoned, and the plan of mailing the letter would not be articulated any further—it would be aborted. If, on the other hand, I decide I shall go to the post office now, the plan would continue to be articulated. How should I get to the post office—by car or by walking? If I go by car, I would need a parking place but would not have to put on heavy outer garments, but if I walk I would not have to look for a parking place but will need to wear more clothes. At this point I might recall that my daughter is using the car, and realize that I must walk to the post office. What specific clothes should I wear? What is the weather like? It is raining. In that case perhaps I should wait until my daughter comes back—and perhaps she would go to the post office for me—and so on.

There is little reason to doubt that nonprimate mammals are capable of some planning. A dog, sitting in one room, may unexpectedly get up and walk down the hall to another room, look around the room for a certain shoe, and then take the shoe and offer it to its master as a plaything. It is hard to dismiss the interpretation that some event, perhaps the master's entry into the house, created the determining set of "playing" with the master, and that this goal, through learned contingencies, then produced a pexgo of the shoe, and this led to a pexgo of the usual location of the shoe (which room?), and so on. The remote goal of playing with the master may have instigated the planning that determined the subsequent course of action of the dog. This planning resembles human planning in that it is transitional (sitting in one room, the dog plans an action involving other rooms) and that its articulation is instigated by a remote goal. However, compared to man's, the dog's planning is obviously limited in the period of time spanned by the plan, that is, the number of steps or subgoals between the initial situation and the remote goal, as well as in the period of time that can separate the planning from the execution of the plan. In the above example, the dog's plan covers a period of only a minute or so, and there appears to be no marked temporal separation between the planning and the execution of the whole plan—there are no interruptions and resumptions of the type that characterize most human plans.

A chimpanzee is probably capable of planning that spans a longer period of time, as well as capable of separating the planning from the execution of the plan at least to some extent. The chimpanzee's "treacherous attack" (Hebb, 1946a) is a case in point: the chimpanzee acts friendly until the victim is in grasp and then attacks. Clearly, the type of rudimentary planning seen in the dog and the chimpanzee does not require language. But how far the human long-range planning and execution of actions intermittently over periods extending into days, months, and years is dependent on the use of language for coding the objects, events, and decisions involved in a plan is a question that requires study. It is likely that language is essential in planning over long periods of time as well as for planning that is highly detailed, requiring coding and recall of many decisions.

Planned action in the sense described above may also be called "intentional behavior," so long as it is understood that "intention" as an awareness is not being proposed as an explanatory process for dealing with planned actions. The word "intentional" is used here simply as a descriptive adjective to refer to courses of action related to a certain goal that can be demonstrated to have been planned in advance. The more detailed the planning, the more intentional the resulting behavior may be said to be; actions determined by vague plans are judged as less intentional than actions determined by detailed plans. Judgments of intentionality are retrospective judgments in terms of the detailedness of planning that preceded an action. In criminal courts the intentionality of a crime is judged on the basis of estimates of the degree of planning that must have been done in order for the crime to have been committed in exactly the way in which it was. Planned behavior and intentional behavior are thus synonymous terms from the present viewpoint. Irwin (1971) has described an intentional action as one that is chosen from a pair of alternative actions on the basis of the relative preference for the expected outcomes of the alternatives. Thus "choice" and "intentional behavior" would appear to be the same thing in his treatment. Irwin does not make a distinction between immediate choices and decisions about remote alternatives, a distinction that is critical in the concept of planning (or intentionality) as developed here.

The Process of Plan Articulation

The above descriptive account of what appears to be involved in the articulation of a plan indicates that the articulation starts with the remote goal. Having selected a remote goal, the subject then selects the subgoals that would lead to the remote goal. Articulation of a plan, then, is essentially the identifying of a "route" of subgoals that links the subject's present position with the remote goal. The end result of the deliberation of articulating a plan is a set of decisions about what to choose when; the considerations that led to each decision then become unimportant. Thus, the deliberation involved in the articulation of a plan is essentially the making of a number of decisions in the absence of any critical environmental comparison stimuli. The decisions will determine subsequent choices.

The question to be faced next concerns the process by which the remote goal and the present position jointly determine the identification of the subgoals. Only a few general points may be noted here. First, this process must be one that excites particular clusters of contingency organizations (see Chapter 7), which then serve as determining sets for the generation of particular pexgos representing the relevant comparison or choice stimuli. This determining set (e.g., sending a letter to a friend) must be maintained while a plan is being articulated. Second, the motivational arousal required for maintaining a certain set (e.g., for keeping occupied with the letter rather than with other things) is provided by the incentive value of the subgoals associated with the remote goal (e.g., influencing, amusing, hurting, etc., the person to whom the letter is addressed). Third, the time required for articulating a plan depends on how far certain decisions required for the plan have been made on previous occasions and no longer require fresh comparisons (e.g., decisions about the route to be followed to the post office, the most likely location for finding a parking place, etc.); the larger the components of the total plan for which decision outcomes are already well established, the smaller will be the number of new decisions required for articulating the plan—that is, the shorter the time required for planning. Fourth, the decisions made in articulating a plan concern the selection of stimuli in relation to which actions are to be performed at certain critical choice points; the exact responses will be selected during the actual execution of the plan. The articulation of a plan does not, therefore, preclude flexibility of responding when the successive choice situations are encountered. In general, considerable flexibility may be built into a plan by making partial decisions that can be made final when appropriate information becomes available (e.g., "If my daughter returns before it stops raining I'll ask her to go mail my letter; if it stops raining before she returns I'll go myself").

Through repeated encounters with the same types of situations, an individual may develop habitual plans for those situations. A habitual plan may consist of several alternative routinized ways or strategies for achieving particular subgoals (e.g., stealing a banana from another animal, reducing anxiety in a dentist's chair, winning friends, learning a list of nonsense syllables, playing chess). Such strategies may in turn consist of several alternative, routinized tactics (e.g., distracting the other animal, humming a soothing tune, ingratiation, repeating last syllables of a list first, castling the queen). A tactic may consist of many responses. The term "optimum strategy" is sometimes used to refer to a strategy that will lead to a goal or subgoal most efficiently (e.g., deliver a certain amount of food with a minimum effort or within minimum time, produce a certain profit with a minimum of capital yield recall of a list of names with a minimum of errors).

Execution of a Plan

Once a plan has been articulated, its execution may or may not be initiated immediately; even if initiated immediately, the execution of the total plan may require action over hours, days, or years. A long-term plan cannot be maintained in a state of activation until it has been executed or abandoned; from time to time it must be replaced by actions involved in other more pressing objectives. Thus, typically, a plan once articulated is "forgotten," and then portions of the plan (i.e., some of the decisions arrived at) are recalled periodically as opportunities for the execution of various steps of the plan arise. It is the possibility of repeated interruption and resumption of the execution of a plan that makes it possible to pursue a long-term goal without seriously jeopardizing all the other things that also have to be done in order to survive. Intermittent recall of a temporarily inactivated plan or subplan—its reentry from "inactive memory" to "active memory"—is clearly a prerequisite of planned behavior.

The basis of selective recall of a particular plan or subplan is the same as that of selective recall in general (see Chapter 10). Certain situations would contain stimuli that can activate the contingency organizations capable of exciting the pexgos related to a plan, and these in turn would lead to the recall of the decisions reached in connection with certain alternative stimuli. If some of the decision alternatives are present in the current situation, then an opportunity exists for execution of a part of the plan. In order to avoid missing an opportunity of executing a part of the plan, or undertaking some action in a wrong situation, it is essential that the decisions of a plan be "coded" appropriately for recall in situations relevant to the execution of that plan. For example, if I decide to go to one post office rather than another, the decision should be recalled—activated—when I reach the road-crossing at which the two routes separate.

The overt execution of a plan begins when stimulus alternatives about which decisions have been made during planning are actually encountered. In the example discussed above, the first stimulus alternatives are the "letter" (to be mailed) and "work papers" (to be studied). If the decision has been made to mail the letter now, then the letter may be said to be imbued with additional motivational valence, so that action will be performed in relation to the letter rather than the work papers; in other words, the letter will be chosen as the object of action. I will pick up the letter and place it on a table in the hall where I would pick it up on the way out. Now, I am faced with the choice of either putting on some heavy clothes for walking or driving to the post office dressed as I am. If the decision has been made to drive-as-I-am, then I will turn away from the clothes closet and start looking for the keys to the car; the decision to drive has increased the motivational valence of car keys over that of heavier clothes. And so on. The hypothesis is that (1) what a plan influences is the selection of the stimulus in relation to which action would occur, (2) the selection is influenced by an increase in the motivational valence of one of the stimulus alternatives relative to the others, and (3) the increase in relative motivational valence is produced by the recall of the prior decision pertaining to those stimuli. The ultimate source of the motivational valence that the decision distributes to choice stimuli lies in the degree of excitation of the pexgo of the goal (e.g., my friend chuckling on reading my letter and replying immediately).

Particular choices at choice points or strategies may deviate from the earlier decisions owing to conditions that were not anticipated. If I cannot find the car keys, I may now choose to walk, or to abandon temporarily the plan of mailing the letter. Sometimes a plan may be "tested" even before its execution has started. Testing a plan means going through the major decisions again with a somewhat different emphasis on the criteria for the decisions. For example, the above plan to mail a letter may be tested and possibly altered by considering the speed of mail transportation from the mail box to the destination (if the letter is mailed not today but tomorrow, will it make a difference in the time at which the letter reaches its destination?). In essence, testing a plan consists in making decisions about the same choice points (comparison stimuli) with somewhat different information, or criteria, or both. On the basis of such tests a plan may be abandoned or modified, or the ultimate goal may even be rejected as too costly to achieve.

CHAPTER 14

Remembering

If I were to ask you to name the object that was hanging on a certain wall of a certain room of a house that you had visited a day or two earlier, you might or might not be able to give the correct answer that I want. You might guess that the object was a "decorative piece." I might then ask, "What kind of a decorative piece? Was it an ornamental shield, a tapestry, or a painting?" Now you might reason, "Since I am interested in shields and tapestries, I certainly would have remembered seeing either of these, but since I don't remember seeing either, it must have been a painting." If I persist and ask, "What kind of painting, a water color or an oil?" you might confess ignorance, but assert, "All I remember is that it was a painting." "Was it a bright landscape or a blue still-life?" Prompted in this way, you might cheer up and say, "Yes, I have it now. It was a bright landscape by Van Gogh; it was hanging on a narrow wall under a light fixture; it showed a sunny harvesting scene near a canal with a bridge on it." I might then conclude that you do now remember what you saw on that wall, and tell you merely that you have added the canal and the bridge, which were not in *that* painting by Van Gogh. The processes underlying remembering of this type are the subject of this chapter.

ESSENTIALS OF EXPERIMENTS ON REMEMBERING

The above example illustrates three important features of memory tasks. First, successful performance in a test of remembering means producing a response that in some sense reflects knowledge of the test item. The test may require *recalling* the correct name or some other characteristic feature of the item, or *recognizing* the item from among a number of similar but incorrect items. The level of retention is assessed by determining how far the production of the response is determined by some specified prior experience (training) of the test item and how far by some extraneous factors that could also have produced the same response at that time.

Second, the above example shows that an appropriate (correct-as-defined) response may be produced by the subject on the basis of only general knowledge, in the absence of specific information about the test item; conversely, a subject may have a good deal of specific information about the item but not the particular detail the investigator has specified as the criterion of correctness. This means that the correctness of the subject's response is dependent on the stringency of the criterion of knowledge imposed by the investigator; the investigator may accept "a painting" as the correct answer, or he may want the subject to specify what kind of painting. The more stringent the criterion—the greater the amount of detailed information required of the subject—the poorer will be the measured performance.

Third, remembering is determined in important ways by the amount of information given to the subject at the time of the *test*. A subject might be unable to produce the correct response when asked, "What did you see on the wall?" but might recall successfully when asked, "Was the painting on the wall a landscape or a still-life?" When a large number of pertinent cues are provided at the time of the test, the subject may be able to produce the correct answer by guessing, even when there has been no retention of learning. The more numerous and pertinent the cues provided at the time of testing, the better will be the performance. Determining how much of a given level of performance reflects retention and how much, "guessing," requires experimental analysis.

The essential point is that remembering something means producing a response, and that the general principles of response production apply equally well to remembering. As in the case of other responses, the response in a recall or recognition test is determined as much by the conditions prevailing at the time of the test as by the relevant learning experience of the subject. In the study of remembering, the investigator's primary concern is with the relation of the response produced in the test to some specific prior training experience (the acquisition of the material to be retained). Therefore, it is the variables defining the training and the test procedures that are critical in the description of experiments on remembering.

The Critical Variables

Three main sets of variables define the similarities and differences of experimental paradigms used in the study of remembering. These are: acquisition or original-learning variables, retention-interval variables, and test-performance variables.

Original-learning variables determine how much of the test material (e.g., a list of digits, nonsense syllables, words, or phrases; face-name associations; a story; a poem) is acquired during the training phase of the experiment. The level of performance attained in one or more training trials depends, as noted in earlier chapters, on such factors as organismic conditions and motivational state of the subject, quantity and meaningfulness of the learning material, distinctiveness and salience of the discriminative cues, and rehearsal and organizational strategies used by the subject during the training period. Obviously, remembering at a later time would be critically dependent on the level of performance attained in training and the specific variables that contributed to that level of performance.

Retention-interval variables that influence performance in a later test of remembering include the duration of the interval, the nature and extent of new learning during the interval, and a variety of neurological factors. In general, test performance declines with increase in the elapsed interval between the end of training and the test, but the exact basis of the decline is not fully understood. Any new learning during the retention interval influences test performance, the exact effect depending on the relation of the new learning to the test material. If the new material learned is highly dissimilar or highly similar to the test material, the learning during the retention interval usually has little or no effect on performance; if the new material resembles the test material somewhat but is different from it (e.g., when the test material is a list of nonsense syllables and the new learning involves a different list of nonsense syllables), then the new learning usually results in a decrement in performance (Osgood, 1953).

Test-performance variables are as important in remembering as the above variables. It was noted in Chapter 11 that the producibility of learned response depends on the stability of the learning conditions. It follows that in remembering tasks the speed and accuracy with which a subject is able to produce some previously learned material would depend on the extent to which the conditions at the time of the test match those that prevailed during training. Changes in either the organismic or the situational factors would produce a decrement in performance.

The phenomenon of "drug dissociation" illustrates the importance for test performance of changes in the organismic state of the subject. If an animal is trained to make a certain response when it is under the influence of a certain drug (say, a barbiturate or alcohol) and is then tested for remembering when it is in the normal, no-drug, state (or is under the influence of a different drug), the animal's test performance will be less speedy and accurate than if it is tested under the influence of the drug used in training (Girden, 1942; Overton, 1964). Such performance decrement is not due to a drug-induced change in organismic state per se, but is due to the *change* in the organismic state of the animal. This is shown by the fact that the decrement occurs whether the training occurs in the normal or in the drug state, so long as the test is conducted in a state different from the one that prevailed during training; that is, transitions both from the no-drug to drug state and from the drug state to no-drug state produce a performance decrement. In human subjects, the amnesia that is sometimes observed in the normal state for events that had occurred during alcoholic intoxication, and vice versa, is probably a drug-dissociation phenomenon.

The situational factors can facilitate remembering to the extent that they are the same as those present during acquisition. The most important situational factors are discriminative cues—stimuli that differentially predict certain target events. It should be noted that the discriminative cues regarded by the investigator as the relevant ones are not necessarily the same as those on the basis of which the subject learned the test material. One subject, on being shown a number of paintings, may note their size, dominant color, composition, etc., but not notice the names of the painters, while another subject may not notice color or composition but note the names of the painters. Obviously, in a later test the cues that would aid (or hinder) the performance of the two subjects would be quite different; each subject's performance would depend on how far the test situation provided the discriminative cues that were used during acquisition. Further, the same individual discriminative cue when presented in different overall contexts may influence performance in different ways; for example, when the cue *Picasso* is presented as belonging to the class "abstract painters," it may hinder the production of the response *Goya*, but when *Picasso* is presented as belonging to the class "Spanish painters," it may make it easier to produce this response. Several formal experiments have demonstrated that recall is greatly influenced by the discriminative cues available or provided at the time of test and the context or "cognitive environment" in which the cue appears (Dolinsky, 1972; Runquist & Evans, 1972; Tulving & Thomson, 1971).

Long-Term and Short-Term Memory Experiments

Innumerable different classes of experiments may be designed by specifying different combinations of original-learning, retention-interval, and retention-test conditions. However, for the present purpose it is necessary only to consider two groups of experiments that have been important in theoretical discussions. The experiments in one group are labeled as *long-term memory experiments*, and in the other *short-term memory experiments*.

Ostensibly, the dichotomy of long-term and short-term memory experiments refers to the duration, long or short, of the retention interval used, whether the recall test is delayed or occurs immediately following the training trial or trials. In fact, however, there are several other differences between the experiments that are usually included in the two categories. In a typical long-term memory experiment, the subject is presented the test material repeatedly in several training trials until he reaches a certain fairly high criterion of acquisition. The material to be learned (e.g., nonsense syllables, words, a story, a path on a map, faces, etc.) is usually such as to be amenable to learning on the basis of a variety of discriminative cues representing shape, size, spatial location, temporal order, semantic association, rhyming or other phonological features, etc., of the test material, so that a great deal of organization of the material can take place during the acquisition phase of the experiment. Also, the material is usually presented in a way (slow speed of presentation, long intertrial intervals, etc.) that makes rehearsal possible in the course of learning. Further, frequently a somewhat stringent acquisition criterion is used, and training is continued until the criterion is met. All this means that in the long-term memory experiment the acquisition conditions are such as to promote a high level of original learning. As may be expected, then, the typical finding of such experiments is that remembering is accurate, "retention capacity" is large (i.e., the subject can learn and correctly remember a large amount of material), and forgetting is slow or nonexistent.

On the other hand, in a typical short-term memory experiment, the subject is presented with the test material only once or a few times, and no criterion of acquisition, stringent or lax, is specified. The material to be learned is usually a serial list of individual digits or letters, whose most distinctive feature is their temporal position in the series. We have already noted that acquisition is difficult and slow when temporal cues provide the main basis of learning. Further, the material is presented speedily (e.g., in a short-exposure visual or auditory display), so that rehearsal and organizational strategies in the course of the training trials, while not totally absent, are largely prevented by the interfering succession of items to be learned. For these reasons learning during training trial or trials is minimal. The typical finding of such experiments is, not unexpectedly, inaccurate remembering, small retention capacity, and fast forgetting. If the subject is unable to learn the material, his recall performance should be the same as his "immediate memory span," that is, whatever items in the early part of the list he has managed to rehearse or organize enough to learn, plus whatever items are still perceptually active; thus the subject is likely to produce some of the early items of the list ("primacy-effect") and the last two or three items of the list ("recency-effect").

It should be clear that what are called long-term memory experiments create conditions that promote the learning of the test material during the training trials, while the so-called short-term memory experiments create conditions that hinder acquisition, thereby limiting the subject's test performance to his immediate memory span. When conditions of a short-term memory experiment are changed to promote learning, for example, by increasing the number of training trials, encouraging the subject to employ rhymes, rhythms, and other grouping strategies, pacing the presentation of the material so as to make rehearsal possible, and so on, the performance of the subject begins to assume the characteristics of performance in a long-term memory experiment. For example, Hebb (1961) has shown that if a list of digits that, unknown to the subject, is repeated in a series of training-test trials, it is recalled with greater accuracy than other, nonrepeated lists in the series. Corballis (1966) has shown that providing opportunity for rehearsal improves test performance in a short-term memory task. And the influence on performance in short-term memory experiments of context at the time of test performance, known to be important in long-term memory experiments, has been demonstrated by Falkenberg (1972).

There is little doubt, then, that the typical short-term memory experiment lies at the low end of a continuum of the presence of conditions promoting acquisition during the training phase; this point has been made or implied by several investigators (e.g., Craik & Lockhart, 1972; Melton, 1963; Postman, 1964; Weiskrantz, 1970). Therefore, the distinction between long-term and short-term memory experiments is of no special significance so far as the understanding of the underlying processes is concerned. The question of the existence of two separate types of memory *processes*, a long-term memory process and a short-term memory process, is quite a different issue, though historically the latter distinction of processes developed as a way of explaining the difference in results obtained in the two types of experiments (Broadbent, 1958; Hebb, 1949). From the present viewpoint, what is called a short-term "memory" *process* is a special case of the perceptual-attentional processes discussed in Chapters 5 and 10 and the long-term "memory" *process* is a special case of the learning-extinction processes discussed in Chapters 11 and 12.

THE PROCESS OF REMEMBERING

Much of the recent analysis of remembering has been done within the broad information-processing model of human performance (see Norman, 1968, 1970; Tulving & Donaldson, 1972). The essential concepts of this model are memory trace, storage, retrieval, and coding. During training, a memory trace of test material is said to get stored, and during the recall test that memory trace is said to be retrieved. Accuracy and speed of test performance is determined by the "accessibility" of the trace, which is a function of the durability and strength of the trace as well as of the retrieval cues present at the time of the test; forgetting represents obliteration of the memory trace or inaccessibility to it (Shiffrin & Atkinson, 1969). Durability and strength of the trace may be enhanced by rehearsal and by coding (or recoding) the memory trace in terms of some organizational scheme. Further, some authors believe that there are two memory storage systems, "primary storage" and "secondary storage." Primary storage is able to preserve memory traces for only a brief period, lasting a few seconds (transient memory traces), whereas secondary storage contains memory traces that have become relatively durable through coding (lasting memory traces). The differences in the results of short-term and long-term remembering experiments are attributed to the differential involvement of the two storage systems. This has been a useful model for dealing with the phenomena of remembering within a common, coherent scheme, as well as for generating incisive experiments for isolating the variables that influence various aspects of recall and recognition.

The main shortcoming of the information model is that it fails to specify the exact meanings of its central concepts: What is a memory trace? In what sense is a memory trace storable, and what is a store? What is retrieved in retrieval, and how does retrieval function? What transformations does coding produce, and what determines how any given memory trace will be coded? It is not necessary to answer these questions if one's primary concern is with formulating descriptive principles of remembering. However, the above questions must be answered if the information model is to be developed into an explanatory scheme that tries to provide a theoretical basis for the descriptive principles.

The approach to the explanation of remembering I outline below does not employ concepts of storage or retrieval, although, of course, my account is much influenced by the experimental findings generated by the informational model. My aim is to show, in rough terms, how the processes of response production proposed in the earlier chapters may be used to derive the descriptive principles already discovered and to predict some new ones.

A New Account of Remembering

In a remembering experiment the subject is required to produce a response whose characteristics have been specified in advance by the experimenter— with or without the knowledge of the subject. What the experimenter specifies is the range or class of responses that would be regarded as correct, that is, acceptable as demonstrating retention (or "memory") of a certain prior learning experience. The form of the response that indicates correct remembering is not particular, for the test may require the subject to say something, write something, or to press a key to indicate recognition. Obviously, the subject does not reproduce or retrieve a response acquired during training, but produces a fresh response under the conditions of the prevailing test. The critical question then is: How does the subject manage to produce the correct response—one that reflects a certain degree of influence of the training experience—instead of producing any of the other responses that could be produced under the general test conditions? This question, as we saw in Chapters 7 and 11, is a general question that applies to the production of all responses. We start, then, with the assumption that the processes that govern the production of a response (correct or incorrect) in remembering need not be fundamentally different from the processes involved in response production generally.

For the subject's response to be correct, its production must be critically influenced by the central representation—the pexgo—of the item (object, event, word, etc.) being remembered. According to the formulation proposed in Chapter 7, the activation of a particular target pexgo is dependent on the net excitatory neural discharge received by the gnostic-assemblies that represent feature-combinations of the target item. The amount of net excitatory discharge received is determined by the excitation level of the sensory patterns linked to the target pexgo, as well as by the excitation levels of various contingently related pexgos that bear positive or negative contingencies with the target pexgo, and thus have an excitatory or inhibitory influence on it. Since in the typical experiment the current sensory inflow does not contain features that could directly activate the target pexgo, its excitation level is determined mainly by the neural discharges it receives from the activated contingency organizations. In other words, the cluster of contingency organizations activated at a given time, or the momentary determining set, largely determines the pexgo that would be maximally excited at a given moment. And, as we have seen (Chapters 7 and 10), the selective activation of a pexgo is a consequence of the progressive narrowing of the momentary determining set through continual interactions of the existing momentary determining sets and newly activated pexgos representing particular discriminative cues. Consider an example.

Suppose I, as an experimenter, bring you into a room in which you have previously performed some remembering tasks. You arrive in your usual midday organismic state and sit in the usual place, and the usual situational schema gets excited in the brain. I then say to you, "Today I would like to test your recall of one of the lists of names of living things that you have learned." This instruction would narrow your existing set by increasing the excitation of a certain differentiated cluster of contingency organizations representing "living things" (rather than cooking utensils, or articles used in sewing, or names of painters). Now I tell you, "Today we will concentrate on the lists of names describing animals in the sea." This more specific instruction, which provides the discriminative cue "sea animals," would serve further to narrow the set by increasing the excitation of a somewhat smaller cluster of contingency organizations representing "sea animals." Then I tell you, "The particular list I want you to recall now is the one you learned the day before yesterday." Assume that this instructional cue is sufficient for activating a pexgo representing some of the feature combinations of the particular list (e.g., that the list was about 10 items long, it was presented on a pink sheet of paper, items were typed vertically, the items were mainly large ocean animals, with a couple of dangerous ones). The activation of *The List* pexgo would then provide the discriminative cue that would narrow the set to a still smaller cluster of contingency organizations representing "Large Sea Animals."

Now, you as the subject, being familiar with the requirement that the names on the list have to be recalled in the proper order, ask yourself, "What was the *first name* on the list?" This cue, itself generated by the existing momentary determining set, may lead to the activation of the pexgo representing the top of the list, and this pexgo may activate an auditory pexgo of the word "Mammal." The cue "Mammal" then would further delimit the existing excited cluster by more strongly exciting a cluster representing "Large Sea Mammals." The cue "Mammal" would also lead you to ask, "What is a large sea mammal?" and this may quickly result in the activation of the pexgo of first the visual form of a whale and then of the name *Whale*, leading to an implicit verbal response "Whale." If the task instructions have stressed accuracy, a check or decision must now be made as to whether *Whale* was the first name on the list. This decision requires a comparison of the pexgo of the word Whale with whatever pexgo is generated as a consequence of the interaction of the pexgo of Whale with the pexgo of *The List*. The comparison may lead to a negative decision and also to the activation of a pexgo indicating that Whale occurred somewhere near the middle of the list.

This pexgo may suppress the excitation of Whale, before any overt response has been made, and activate a pexgo representing the fact that the first name on the list consisted of two words. Now you ask, "What is a large sea mammal with a two-word name?" This cue, with the cluster for large sea mammals already excited strongly, may quickly lead to the activation of a pexgo and implicit response "Sea Lion." Then you may decide whether *Sea Lion* was the first name on the list, and if no contradictory pexgo is strongly excited, you may decide affirmatively, and this would lead to the production of the overt response, "Sea Lion," in the specified form (saying, writing, etc.). Thus, the first name on the list is recalled.

Turn now to the recall of the second item on the list. Having produced the first name to your satisfaction (and, say, correctly), you may now ask, "What was the large sea animal after Sea Lion on that list?" This cue may activate the pexgo representing the early part of the list. This cue may then activate a pexgo representing the characteristic Dangerous. This cue would then result in the narrowing of the Large Sea Animal cluster to Dangerous, Large Sea Animal, and this may result in the activation of the pexgo of Shark. In trying to confirm Shark as the correct name for the second item on the list, you may come across no conflicting cue and thus make the overt response "Shark." This may in fact be incorrect because the correct name may have been that of another dangerous, large sea animal such as Barracuda, which could not be distinguished from Shark on the basis of the available discriminative cues. However, as you search for the third item on the list and discover it, say, *Tuna*, you may at once be reminded that the name before *Tuna* also had an open "a" at the end, and therefore the previous item might have been Barracuda rather than Shark. And so on. The cues that are effective in recall would, in general, be those in terms of which the material was learned during training.

The main point of the above analysis is to demonstrate that the production of responses in a memory task is the outcome of continual interactions between discriminative cues and the prevailing momentary determining set. The discriminative cues arise from instructions, from the task material itself, and from the subject's own activity or strategies. At each moment the new discriminative cues, working through their contingent relations, produce progressive narrowing of the prevailing set until a response is produced. When the task material has not been fully learned, the processes like the ones described above must occur in the course of the recall test. However, once the material has been learned verbatim, each item in the task material will act as a cue for the direct activation of the processes that lead to the second item. Thus, what in recall may appear to be a demonstration of rote learning, may in fact be the end result of complex processes that were essential in the early stages of learning.

Some Implications

The account of remembering outlined above differs in two important respects from the information-processing accounts. First, informational accounts make the assumption that a unique *trace*, representing an encoded or "pro-cessed" version of each *item*, is stored during the learning phase of an experiment. According to my account, learning an item means making a pexgo of that item a part of some new contingency organizations representing the particular situation and the contextual (e.g., interitem) relations. The combination of circumstances in which an item is presented may be said to comprise a unique "episode" (Tulving, 1972; Tulving & Thomson, 1973), but, if so, the episode does not, in my view, establish a unique trace. Rather, the representations of the contingent relations that describe the episode become a part of the existing contingency organizations representing the contingent relations of similar situations, similar contexts, similar items, etc. A pexgo of a learned item does not remain stored in the brain as a unique trace, but its contingent relations modify certain existing domains of knowledge or clusters of contingency organizations in particular ways, and thereby influence the subsequent activation of a pexgo of that item. By replacing the concept of the storage of a unique trace by that of modification of existing contingency organizations, my account implies no specific storage locus or unique engram for an item or episode. The perplexity about the locus of the engram raised by the work of Lashley (1949) and Chow (1967) therefore ceases to be a perplexity so far as remembering is concerned.

Second, because information-processing accounts look upon "memories" of learned items as the storage of unique traces, they are forced to show how a specific trace may be "retrieved" or reactivated in remembering. They suggest, in general, that "retrieval cues" present at the time of remembering provide "access" to what is stored, and reactivate the item. What retrieval cues would be effective in retrieval depend on what aspects of the item have been stored—on the coded trace. In my account, on the other hand, since there is no storage no retrieval is needed, and since there is no stored trace of the item to be retrieved, remembering does not involve access to or retrieval of the trace of the item. Remembering consists in the fresh production or construction of an item, not in the *re*activation of some permanent representation of the item as such, and what item is remembered—the response produced—is determined by the pexgo selectively activated at the time of remembering. The accuracy of remembering (resemblance of activated pexgo to the target pexgo) depends on how far the test-performance conditions (organismic state, situation, context, instructions, strategies, discriminative cues, etc.) can combine to recreate the conditions necessary for the activation of the contingency organizations that would lead to the activation of a pexgo falling within the acceptable range for correct recall or recognition. By replacing the concept of the retrieval of an item (or its pexgo) by that of production or construction of a pexgo, my account makes remembering a special case of the operation of the processes that determine selective activation of target pexgos (see Chapters 7 and 10).

The idea that the fundamental processes in remembering are the same processes as those involved in the selective activation of pexgos makes it possible to interpret performance in recall and recognition tests within a common framework. In the recall experiment the target pexgo is a pexgo of the item to be recalled, and this pexgo must be generated wholly associatively (centrally activated pexgo) through the contingency organizations activated by the performance-test conditions. In the recognition experiment, on the other hand, the pexgo of the item to be recognized is activated by the item itself, that is, through current sensory input (sensorily activated pexgo), and the subject's task is to generate another pexgo of some of the context (e.g., a word list of which the target item is a part) in which that item was learned. In recall, the subject is required to generate a pexgo of the target item from the context cues provided, while in recognition the subject is required to generate a pexgo of the context from the item cues provided. In general, then, recall should be more difficult than recognition because recall requires the generation of a more specific target pexgo. However, this is not necessarily the case. A recognition task may be made relatively more difficult by making the item cues less discriminable during learning—for example, by increasing the number, similarity, or speed of presentation of the items to be learned. Thus, while normally items that can be correctly recognized are not necessarily recallable, it should be possible to arrange experimental conditions that make correctly recallable words not recognizable. This has been demonstrated (Tulving & Thomson, 1973; Watkins & Tulving, 1975).

Another implication of the selective pexgo-generation view of remembering is that *any* established contingent relations of a pexgo of the target item are relevant to remembering, whether or not they were learned at the time of the "original learning" phase of an experiment. Thus, in a paired associate task, the word "Table" spoken at the time of a recall test may contribute to the recall of "Chair," even if in the original learning the paired-associate presented was "Bird"-"Chair." Several formal experiments have shown that prompting with extraneous (nonlist) words that are associatively related to a target word influences the recall of the latter (Bahrick, 1969; Bilodeau, 1967). Such influences of extraneous cues on remembering a specific learned material should also be demonstrable in recognition experiments, but I know of no specific experiments that bear on this point. It should be noted that the fact that extraneous cues at the time of test-performance influence that performance, may make it difficult to say how far a given level of performance is attributable to "retention," or the learning of some specific relation during original learning, and how far to "guessing," or the influence of extraneous cues unrelated to the original learning. Thus any conclusions about changes in retention from test-performance data must be drawn with great caution.

Impairment of Remembering

In a test of remembering, subjects frequently produce a wrong response, or take an unusually long time to produce the correct response, or altogether fail to produce a response within an experimentally specified interval. Such errors and increased response latencies may arise from several causes.

First, during training, the subject may not learn the contingencies that would be required for correct recall. Owing to distraction, or inadequate instruction, or insufficient exposure for learning a certain contingency, the subject may not observe the particular features of an item, or relations between items, that would be required for correct recall. Thus, subjects remember the exact wording of sentences better when they have learned the sentences under instructions to judge the grammatical features of the sentences than when they have learned the sentences under instructions emphasizing semantic analysis (Graesser & Mandler, 1975). It appears that normally (in the absence of any special biasing conditions) subjects favor the use of semantic cues, whether the material is acoustically or visually presented, and resort to the use of structural cues only when semantic cues are not available (Dolinsky, 1972).

Second, the subject may observe the appropriate contingent relations, but the effectiveness of these contingencies may be lost because of the "averaging" of the observed contingency with other contingencies involving the same items or discriminative cues. As noted in the discussion of extinction, the effect of each observed instance of concomitance or disconcomitance of events combines with the previously existing contingencies involving the same or similar events. Therefore, a new contingency involving a certain event must, as time passes, regress toward the mean of all the contingent relations of that event experienced until the time of recall; in other words, a contingency involving a certain event can remain distinctive only if experience with it is so extensive as to make all previous contingencies of the same event insignificant in comparison. Such a contingency-averaging process may be the basis of what is called "proactive interference"—the fact that some previously learned material may impair the learning and remembering of certain types of new material (Postman, 1971). It may also account for the "forgetting" of facts that are not consistent with one's well-developed hypotheses or biases. Of course, a previously learned contingency involving a certain event may also be obliterated by other contingencies involving that event experienced *subsequently*—during the retention interval. This corresponds to what is called "retroactive interference," the fact that the remembering of a certain previously learned material may be impaired by the subsequent learning of other material. Proactive and retroactive impairment of remembering have usually been attributed to "interference" during original learning or test performance (Underwood & Postman, 1960), but usually the basis of interference is not explained. The above interpretation provides an independent account of interference in terms of the development and modification of contingencies, and thus brings the explanation of proactive and retroactive interference within the general domain of processes involved in the learning and modification of contingency organizations.

Third, the subject may acquire the contingencies required for successful remembering and may, by rehearsal and organization, manage to prevent the obliteration of those contingencies, but his performance may still be impaired owing to conditions prevailing at the time of test. In general, any change in the conditions prevailing from the training to the recall situation would impair recall. The specific form of impairment (e.g., increased latency or errors) observed is probably related to the type of change in the conditions.

INTERPRETATION OF SOME PHENOMENA OF REMEMBERING

Consider now the application of the above view of remembering and its impairment to the interpretation of certain common phenomena.

Context Effects

Tulving and Thomson (1971) studied the recognition of certain test words as they altered cues at the time of test in different ways. They found that the recognition of a word (e.g., *water*) presented during training as a member of a pair (e.g., *whiskey-water*) is impaired when the other, the "context member" of the pair (i.e., *whiskey*), is removed or changed (e.g., ———-*water*, or *witness-water*). The impairment is greater when a weakly associated context word (e.g., *whiskey-water*) is replaced by a strongly associated context word (e.g., *lake-water*) than when the weakly associated context word is simply removed. This shows that, following constant training conditions, the recognition of previously seen items is influenced by the context cues present at the time of the test. Tulving and Thomson attribute the impairment to the change in context at the time of test.

According to the present explanatory scheme, the basis of such context effects lies in the change in discriminative cues, which results in the activation of contingencies leading to the excitation of a different group of pexgos than the pexgos excited by the cues present at the time of training. For example, pexgos that are likely to be strongly excited by the pair lake-water (e.g., canoe, ducks, trees) during the test are likely to be quite different from the pexgo of water as an ingredient of a drink excited by the pair *whiskey-water* during training. Therefore, the pexgo of water as an ingredient of a drink would not be available during the recognition test when the subject is presented with *lake-water*; *water* would thus be less likely to be recognized as an item seen before. According to this interpretation of the context effects, a change in context may result in no impairment of test performance if the changed test-material cues are so selected as to activate the same pexgos as were activated during training; for example, if in the above example *whiskey* were to be replaced by *rum* or *drink*, there might be no impairment in the recognition of *water*, and if a series of appropriate new cues is presented (e.g., *party*, *drink*) before the test pair *rum-water*, the recognition of *water* may be facilitated. Thus, the exact test responses (errors or correct responses) produced in remembering may be controlled by cues of known contingent relations presented at the appropriate moment during the test. Runquist and Evans (1972) have demonstrated both facilitation and impairment of recall by such manipulation of context cues.

A common parlor trick is to ask someone to tell you the pronunciation of P-O-K-E, S-T-R-O-K-E-, F-O-L-K, etc. Having thus established a "pronunciation context" with words ending with the sound *OKE*, you ask the person to say what the white of an egg is called. Typically, the answer given is "yolk," even though the subject could have given the correct answer if asked the test question without the previous context questions. Clearly, the recall of well learned material by a normally adequate test cue (the question) can be impaired by the set prevailing at the time of test. More formally, if the word *gold* is paired with *iron* in one list of paired associates, and with *bold* in another list, and the subject is later tested for recall of the paired associates of the first list within a "rhyming context" (created, say, by asking the subject to repeat pairs of words such as *key-tea*, *buy-lie*, *bell-sell*, etc.), then the subject may well respond to *gold* with the erroneous response *bold*, a word that belonged to a different list. Similarly, by testing the subject for the second list within a "metallurgical context," it may be shown that he is likely to respond to *gold* with *iron*—again erroneously. Such "intrusion errors" in recall may thus be interpreted as consequences of a context change from the training to the test conditions.

Prompting

It is common experience that difficulties in remembering may be overcome by prompting. A person who has been unable to produce the word *sharp* at an appropriate point in a list may produce it quickly if he hears the sound "SH" or is told that there is an R in the word, etc. The present interpretation of the efficacy of such prompting is as follows. Assuming that appropriate instructional and test-material cues are present, the inability to produce a certain word must mean the test conditions are insufficient to activate the appropriate pexgo (*sharp*), though presumably that pexgo is excited to some degree because it is a part of an appropriate determining set (e.g., "cutting things"). Now, giving the subject a prompt, *Sh* or *R*, means providing a part of the stimulus configuration that normally excites the pexgo of the word *sharp*. Though the part of the stimulus configuration provided in a prompt would not be sufficient normally to activate the appropriate pexgo, under the conditions of prior priming by the set and test-material cues, even a highly fragmentary prompt may prove effective. Thus, the efficacy of prompting comes as much from the current fragmentary stimulus input as from the priming of the appropriate pexgo by the set and cues prevailing at the time of test.

Weiskrantz and Warrington (1970) have shown that neurological patients with apparently total anterograde amnesia may demonstrate retention (learning) if they are trained and tested with the prompting method. This suggests that in such patients the appropriate pexgo cannot be activated on the basis of the instructional set and task cues, but may be activated by providing a fragment of the actual sensory pattern that comprises the sufficient sensory condition for the activation of that pexgo. The exact cause of the inability of these patients to utilize the instructions and cue information may vary greatly from patient to patient, but normally they all show marked learning deficits related to anterograde amnesia. Certain associative prompts may be just as effective as sensory prompts. Winocur and Weiskrantz (in press) made paired-associate items by combining words of similar meaning or sound (e.g., battle-soldier, tail-sail), and found that amnesic patients could learn a list of such items as well as control subjects. Apparently, by increasing the cues that can prime a target pexgo, considerable improvement in remembering can be achieved in patients who are totally amnesic under normal conditions.

Meaningfulness and Recall

Experiments with meaningful and nonmeaningful verbal material confirm everyday experience that the former is easier to remember than the latter; words are easier to remember than nonsense syllables, sentences than jumbled words, and a passage telling a story than a passage of disconnected sentences. The superior recall of meaningful verbal material is undoubtedly due to better learning during training. Why should meaningful material be more amenable to learning and recall?

As noted in Chapter 8, the meaningfulness of a word refers to the distinctiveness and reliability of pexgos it generates, and, in general, more meaningful words generate more distinctive and reliable pexgos than less meaningful ones. Because of this, the pexgos generated by more meaningful words are more likely to be characterized by more stable contingent relations with the pexgos of other parts of the test material than are the pexgos generated by less meaningful words; in other words, the more meaningful material is better organizable. Since the stability of contingent relations is essential for the development of contingency organizations during the learning phase, more meaningful material should be better learned. At the time of recall, the cues provided by the recall of any one item of the test material will tend to excite a highly specific group of pexgos in the case of more meaningful material, but will tend to excite a wide range of different and variable groups of pexgos in the case of less meaningful material. This means that in the case of more meaningful material, particular pexgos representing other items of the test material would be quickly activated. Thus recall would be more rapid and accurate in the case of more meaningful material.

It was noted in Chapter 7 that "concrete words" (i.e., words that name concrete objects, qualities or concepts) are, in general, more meaningful than "nonconcrete words" (i.e., words that name qualities or concepts not normally experienced concretely), in the sense that concrete words have clearer (distinctive, stable, invariable, and strong) meaning. According to the present analysis, then, task materials consisting largely of concrete words, should, in general, be more rememberable than task materials consisting largely of nonconcrete words. A number of investigations by Paivio and his coworkers have shown that this is so (Paivio, 1969, 1971a, 1971b). For example, they have found that "concrete sentences" (e.g., "The spirited leader slapped a mournful hostage.") are comprehended more quickly than are "nonconcrete sentences"—what they call "abstract sentences" (e.g., "The arbitrary regulation provoked a civil complaint."). They have also shown that, in a paired-associate memory task, lists containing concrete nouns and adjectives (e.g., blister, rusty) yield better recall performance than lists containing nonconcrete nouns and adjectives (e.g., explanation, basic). Further, working with connected discourses, Paivio's group has demonstrated that the content of "concrete passages" of prose is recalled better than the content of "nonconcrete passages." In the explanatory scheme proposed here, these findings may be interpreted in terms of the greater clarity of meaning of concrete words, that is, the strong and reliable associative excitation of particular pexgos by the pexgos of the cue word or words.

"Productive Recall"

So far we have considered mainly those memory tasks in which a fairly short, formal list consisting of a number of discrete items (digits, words, sentences, etc.) is used, and in which the subject is required to remember the list verbatim, and usually in a prescribed order. However, there are tasks in which the subject is exposed, usually only once, to a long, coherent passage (a story, an argument, a description of a scene, a joke, etc.) and is then asked to reproduce as much of it as he can. Such tasks resemble everyday demands of remembering and yield somewhat different results than the discrete-item tasks. The main finding with coherent passages is that the subject usually produces the main ideas and sense of the passage correctly, but frequently employs words and phrases that are quite different from those of the original passage. It appears that the subject grasps the gist or message of the passage and this is what he learns during exposure to the passage. Then, at the time of recall test, when the experimenter provides instructions and some cues (e.g., "Recall the story of the king and the clown"), the subject appears to remember only the gist of the passage and then proceeds to construct a coherent and comprehensible statement around it. Thus, with each recall test, given a few days apart, the gist remains constant but the words and phrases may vary greatly from occasion to occasion, but usually the statement assumes a stable form after several repetitions. Because of the obvious constructive or inventive nature of the performance in the early recall trials, the subject is said to show "productive recall" (Bartlett, 1932; Neisser, 1967), and this is usually distinguished from "rote recall" of discrete-item experiments. It is often suggested that productive recall involves "cognitive processes" while "rote recall" is simply a matter of retrieving items from memory storage.

From the present viewpoint, since all recall is considered to be productive, involving the production of appropriate responses at the time of the test, no special category of "productive recall" is needed. The apparent differences between the so-called productive and rote recalls may be attributed to differences in the conditions under which the two types of experiments are usually conducted. In the "productive recall" situation, verbatim reproduction is not emphasized, so that during training the subject typically does not even try to learn the exact phraseology, and in the recall test the experimenter typically adopts a lax criterion of recall. When the experimenter tells the subject to recall a certain material, say, a story, the instructions require or imply that a coherent, meaningful story has to be produced. The name of the story provides the initial cues for recall. These cues may be sufficient to activate pexgos representing the gist or point of the story, as well as pexgos representing some incidents in the story. As the subject begins to tell the story, he may realize that he is unable to recall certain parts that made the story meaningful. He may now begin to add new parts and eliminate others, so as to make his discourse into a meaningful story with the same gist or ending. The particular words and phrases that are produced are determined by the momentary requirements of producing sentences that would be comprehensible to the experimenter. The same story repeated to children or to a group of intimate friends would differ in its descriptive phraseology. The essential point, then, is that the requirement of telling the story about a recalled gist provides the main context for recall, and, within this context, the subject produces sentences on the basis of those intra-story cues that he used for the learning of contingencies among the events of the story.

In contrast, in "rote recall" situations the material is usually not immediately meaningful (e.g., multiplication tables), learning is extensive, and the recall criterion is stringent. In the early stages of what later appears to be rote recall, considerable inventiveness may be shown in developing mnemonic strategies (rhyming schemes, semantic associations, etc.), but after a great deal of practice, short-circuit association makes the recall appear to be thoughtless repetition. The same of course happens in cases of, say, an actor, who learns his lines so well as to be able to perform on the stage without much thought.

The above interpretation implies that, if the requirement for producing a coherent account of some incident is emphasized and if the subject is unable to recall some aspects of the incident on the basis of the available cues, he is likely to eliminate and add items that would make his discourse coherent. In other words, the tendency to distort is likely to be quite marked in those recall situations that emphasize coherence and listener interest more than accuracy. It is interesting to note that lack of information and the competition for telling "good stories" in a group are known to promote the creation and circulation of rumors (Allport & Postman, 1947). Clearly, productive recall as it occurs in everyday social situations is not merely an attempt to deny or mask memory gaps; it also involves instantaneous invention to suit the occasion. The basis of such imaginative creations lies in the same general principles of response production—interaction of momentary determining set and specific cues—that determine performance in other tasks. The distinguishing features of productive recall arise mainly from the greater variation and flexibility in task sets that are characteristic of recall situations with little instructional emphasis on accuracy.

Confabulation

The Wernicke-Korsakoff syndrome is a consequence of neurological deterioration usually, but not exclusively, associated with a prolonged history of alcoholism. The patient descends into general dementia and acute confusion, and displays a strange symptom, called confabulation. The patient is capable of talking fluently and is quite coherent in sentence structure, but his statements tend to be false, showing obvious factual inaccuracies and inconsistencies. The individual events described are those that have in fact been experienced by the patient, but the total account of a happening, the message, shows distortion of both sense and detail. Confabulation, thus, is absurd talk. This symptom gradually disappears when the patient, under care, comes out of the acute confusional state and settles into a chronic, deteriorated phase.

The verbal output of the patient is often so coherent and contains so many instantaneous inventions that the earlier investigators were inclined to attribute confabulation to deliberate fabrication in order to be sociable or to cover up memory gaps. However, more detailed observations indicate that the patient is unaware of the distortions as well as of the absurdity of some of his statements, so that confabulation is not fabrication. The patient at times may well falsify deliberately or try to cover up memory gaps, but these are distinguishable from the spontaneous, unintentional distortions of confabulation.

Careful work of Talland (1965) has demonstrated that the distortions that characterize confabulation are essentially a phenomenon of impaired recall; the patients also show marked retrograde and anterograde amnesia. Talland noted that the impaired recall reflects "inaccessibility of memories" rather than "their complete absence." He then suggested that the critical deficit of these patients lies in "sequential ordering of events" and "in the chronological placement of memories" (Talland, 1965, p. 280). This is consistent with the observation that they tend to misplace events in temporal as well as spatial context; the events recalled are accurate but they are referred to inappropriate contexts. According to Talland, the source of the impaired recall lies in the patients' inability to adopt different sets, to see the same information as a part of different patterns, to move from a "concrete attitude" to an "abstract attitude" (Goldstein, 1942).

According to the present formulation the impaired recall in confabulation is not so much a matter of inflexibility of set as of *inappropriateness* of set. The momentary determining set may be inappropriate either because of insufficient narrowing of the determining set to activate the exact target pexgos, or because of instability of set, that is, its not being maintained long enough for the recall to be successfully performed. In either case, the cause of the observed distorted recall is that an appropriate and sufficiently narrow determining set fails to be generated at the required time. For example, in a conversation about World War II, the set created may be one of "a war," so that the patient may carry on a conversation indiscriminately referring to events from several different wars. The vagueness and the general "all-over" quality of confabulatory conversation would be expected from the hypothesis of inadequate narrowing of the determining set. Further, inaccuracies of detail and inconsistencies *within* the description of an incident would also be expected to occur as a consequence of the lack of an adequately narrow set for each of the various details of the incident. From the present viewpoint, then, impaired recall that is seen as confabulation occurs when appropriate and adequately narrow sets that are needed at each point in a conversation fail to be created; the broad determining set leads to intrusion errors from similar but irrelevant events, and these errors give the recall its characteristic confabulatory character. Warrington and Weiskrantz's (1970, 1971) interpretation of amnesia syndromes in terms of "failure of internal inhibition" appears to be consistent with this idea.

What prevents the determining set from becoming sufficiently narrow to produce correct recall? Since the generation of an appropriate and sufficiently narrow set depends on the interaction of a prevailing momentary determining set with particular discriminative cues, the lack of generation of appropriate sets at different points in a conversation could result either from an inappropriate and fixed initial set or from inadequate utilization of the normal conversational cues, or from both these factors. The cause seems to lie largely in inadequate utilization of normal spatial and temporal discriminative cues that arise as a conversation is being carried on. These patients also show marked spatial and temporal transpositions in other aspects of behavior (e.g., in recall or word lists); thus it is likely that they have a deficit of spatiotemporal discrimination. As we have seen (Chapters 6 and 7), discrimination along the spatial and temporal dimensions plays an important role in the production of refined differentiated response, so that the impaired recall in confabulation may well arise from a basic deficit of spatiotemporal discrimination. In a conversation the patient may comprehend the verbal cues referring to things or events but may be unable to comprehend the significance of spatiotemporal words such as *on, below, after, before, when, if,* etc.

CHAPTER 15

Problem-Solving

The supreme mark of the flexibility and innovativeness of adaptive behavior is seen in the ability to cope with new problems. A new problem is one which cannot be dealt with, at least not obviously, by the direct application of any previously developed routines; it requires a new solution, though some elements of the required solution may be already familiar. We continually face new problems: "perceptual problems" of identifying new things, or recognizing old things in strange contexts, and doing this under unfamiliar pressures of time and incentive; "abstractional problems" of extracting the attributes or rules by which a collection of things (stones, dresses, animal species, etc.) is or may be classified; and "extrapolational problems" of explicating or extending the relation between certain givens. Most problem-solving tasks are, of course, mixed, requiring all the above types of problem-solving. Completing a crossword puzzle, showing that $(a + b)^2 = a^2 + b^2 + 2ab$, obtaining a certain effect on a canvas by mixing colors, working out an analogy, formulating a principle that handles certain data, etc., all have perceptual, abstractional, and extrapolational elements. The adjectives "perceptual," "abstractional," and "extrapolational" are used here as convenient rubrics for tasks of different types, involving more or less of each type of problem-element. In this chapter, I start with a general account of what is involved in problem-solving, and then discuss a few examples of the above categories of problems.

THE PROCESS OF SOLVING PROBLEMS

Problem-solving begins with the subject's—problem solver's—confrontation with a problem and ends with either failure or the development of a successful or correct solution. Repeated experience with problem-solving tasks of a similar type usually enables the subject to complete the task successfully with progressively greater speed and efficiency, until a stable procedure for dealing with that particular type of task develops. Then the task no longer remains a problem-solving task. Instead of requiring the development of a new solution, the task now requires only the application of a previously mastered procedure; an innovation becomes a routine. The crux of explaining problem-solving obviously lies in the processes leading to the initial emergence of a solution, rather than in those involved in the application of a previously perfected procedure.

Both the self-analyses by certain exemplary problem solvers (e.g., Poincaré, 1930) and laboratory studies (e.g., Maier, 1930, 1931) indicate that there are two main steps in problem solving. When a subject is given a problem-solving task, he must first formulate the problem in a form in which he will work on it; this requires translating the task, as presented, into more familiar terms that define the approach by which the gap between the givens and the solution might be closed. The second step is that of generating specific solutions and testing them one by one until a correct solution is demonstrated or failure is evident.

Formulation of the Problem

Suppose a dog that habitually obtains food by following a certain path is one day prevented by a wood fence from reaching the location of the food. As the dog reaches the fence, it sees that the fence stands between it (the dog) and the food. Now, if the dog attempts to climb over the fence, or go under it, or bite and shake it, it may be surmised that the dog sees the problem as one of overcoming an obstruction. The investigator may see the same problem as a "detour problem" because he hopes that the dog will reach the food by walking along the fence until it reaches an end and then going around the fence, and thereby discover a new solution—a successful path to the food. With some difficulty, dogs can discover the detour solution (C. L. Morgan, 1903).

There are two essential elements of the problem formulation phase in the above example. First, the dog sees or expects the food to be at a certain location, which is now behind the fence, and the observation of food in that situation leads to the idea of the objective—the dog being on the food-side of the fence; the objective describes the general form of the required solution. Second, the observation of certain new situational features (e.g., the fence) leads to the priming of certain clusters of contingency organizations, comprising a momentary determining set (see Chapter 7). The set may consist predominantly of contingency organizations developed in relation to obstruction situations, avoidance situations, or other detour situations that the animal has previously experienced. The process of the formulation of a problem is fundamentally one of the activation of a set; whether the problem is seen as one of obstruction, avoidance, or detour depends on the primed contingency organizations that comprise the momentary set, and this depends on the complex of interrelated contingent relations that the animal has previously encountered in similar situations.

The formulation of a workable problem from a given task thus rests on two things. First a pexgo of the objective—the general form of the solution—has to be activated, and, second, this pexgo must interact with the representation of the somewhat discrepant or unexpected situation as it actually exists at the moment. This interaction generates a certain initial set, which represents the formulation ("obstruction," "avoidance," "detour," etc.) on the basis of which the animal will try to find a solution to the problem. The initial momentary determining set may be considered as the basis of what Newell and Simon (1971) have called the "problem space," or the way a particular subject defines a given problem-solving task. The set defines the domain within which the animal will try to generate particular solutions. How useful a particular set is for successfully completing a given task depends on how far the set contains the contingency organizations required for producing a correct solution.

To illustrate with another example, suppose a child is asked, "Someone gave me five dollars and then two more dollars, how many dollars in all did he give me?" In order to find the correct solution, a pexgo of the objective must first be activated. This pexgo would represent a number of dollars (unknown) that is greater than either of the numbers mentioned in the question. The activated pexgo, together with certain cues contained in the instructions—the fact that the question mentions "two *more* dollars," as well as "how many dollars *in all*"—would generate an "addition set" involving contingency organizations developed in relation to summing tasks. If the instructions had been, "Someone gave me five dollars every time I met him and I met him two *times*, how many dollars in all did he give me?" then the initial set would have consisted of contingency organizations developed in multiplication tasks.

Whatever the initial set may be, it forms the basis of the child's search for the particular required answer to the question. In the case of addition, the emergence of the correct solution depends on the prior generation of an "addition set" by the instructional cues and the interaction of this set with the specific cues, the numbers (five and two) provided in the instructions. This interaction may quickly lead to the answer "seven." If the instructional cues erroneously lead to the generation of a "multiplication set" or a "subtraction set," the child will fail to come up with the correct answer except by accident or by an error of calculation. The more clearly a subject isolates the critical elements of the task as indicated in instructions, that is, the more pertinent the initial set, the greater the probability of success.

Perspicacity in isolating pertinent information is a part of "sagacity," which was thought by William James (1890) to be the basis of successful problem-solving.

Search for a Solution

The search for a correct solution involves the generation of a solution and the testing of that solution; an alternating sequence of the operations of generating and testing solutions continues until a correct solution is discovered or the problem abandoned. The solutions that are generated, as well as their testing, are limited by the nature of the initial set ("problem space"). In the example of the detour problem, if an "obstruction set" is activated (instead of a "detour set"), then solutions that would emerge are likely to be those of climbing over the fence, squeezing under the fence, pushing apart the planks of the fence, biting and pulling the fence, etc. As it emerges, each solution may be tested by the dog and given up when it proves unsuccessful. If an "avoidance set" is created, the dog may abandon the problem altogether. The importance of the initial set in determining the direction of search for a solution was recognized by the earliest of experimental investigators (Duncker, 1945; Luchins, 1942; Maier, 1930, 1931; Wertheimer, 1945), but no explicit hypotheses have been proposed concerning the processes underlying the generation of particular solutions.

A hypothesis suggested by the theoretical ideas outlined in this volume is that the generation of any particular solution is a consequence of progressive narrowing of the determining set by the continual interactions of the momentary determining set with "data cues" provided by various features of the task. A solution is the activation of the pexgos of certain cues by a momentary determining set; this renders the cues so salient that the probability of the subject's acting in relation to those cues is increased. Thus certain data cues become "solution cues"—in relation to which the subject acts. In the detour problem, for example, given an initial "obstruction set," when the dog observes some small openings at the bottom edge of the fence, these data cues would delimit the initial set by increased excitation of the contingency organizations related to holes or narrow passages; this would amount to a further—more specific—definition of the problem as one of "obstruction-to-be-overcome-by-squeezing-through-at-the-bottom." The new, delimited set may then be sufficient to make the openings at the bottom of the fence so salient as to produce some action in relation to them. When this fails, the dog may notice the open top of the fence, or some openings between the planks of the fence, etc., and these data cues will result in different delimitations of the initial "obstruction set" and correspondingly different actions.

Each solution is the result of an interaction of an ongoing determining set, consisting of certain excited contingency organizations, and the contingency organizations that are freshly excited by certain data cues that have just been observed or whose representations have just been activated associatively. What is called the generation of a solution is the progressive delimitation of an initial set by interaction with data cues to a sufficient degree to lead to action in relation to certain environmental cues. No internal agent or homuncular problem-solver that generates solutions needs to be assumed. What the information-processing theorists (e.g., Broadbent, 1971; Miller, Galanter, & Pribram, 1960; Neisser, 1967; Newell & Simon, 1971) call a "rule" is the existing initial set, and what they call an operator is a newly observed data cue. They seem to assume an internal agent that "uses" rule-operator interactions to generate a solution; they characterize the process of problem-solving but do not give an explanatory hypothesis. My hypothesis is that solutions are the outcomes of continual interactions between a progressively narrowing determining set and newly observed data cues, as previously discussed in Chapters 7, 10, 11, and 14.

The testing of a solution is a direct result of the generation of a solution specific enough to lead to action in relation to particular solution cues. If the action leads to success (for example, if the dog is able to reach the food by squeezing through the fence), a solution to the problem will have been demonstrated. If the action does not lead to success, then a new problem set will be activated as the dog observes some other data cues, and the process of the generation of a solution will be resumed. Essentially, then, the testing of a solution is determining whether a particular action made in relation to certain solution cues is successful or not. This determination may be made overtly, or, typically in human subjects, covertly by judgmental decisions about the chances of success.

If the above task for the dog is arranged in such a way that it can be solved only by a detour, then all the solutions generated by the "obstruction set" will end in failure, and the dog, frustrated and fatigued, may abandon the problem for a while. As the "obstruction set" begins to disintegrate, some other "initial set" may take form, for example, a set that promotes exploring the topography of the area. This new "investigatory set" may be activated by such specific cues as the pattern and odor of the wood planks that make up the fence, which the dog happens to observe as the obstruction set is dissolved. The investigatory set interacting with the various specific fence cues may lead the dog to the end of the fence, from where it may get an uninterrupted view of the food; it may then approach the food directly and promptly. A new, or "creative" solution to the problem would have emerged. But the dog is likely to require considerable practice at the same task before the rather general investigatory set would be replaced by a more specific "detour set." When the observation of the fence begins to activate a detour set promptly, together with the corresponding detour behavior, the dog would have learned to deal with the problem by the detour solution; its behavior would no longer be called problem-solving behavior but a routine or habit. If now the dog is given another task that can also be solved by a detour solution, it is likely that the detour set will be generated much sooner than would have been the case without the prior learning of the detour solution. When the animal employs the detour solution in dealing with a new problem (that is, shows transfer), its detour actions might be called a strategy. What are called strategies in problem-solving tasks are solutions that have been developed in previous problem situations and are now quickly reinstated in a new, similar task.

To turn to the addition problem discussed earlier, if the child fails to come up with the correct answer owing to an inappropriate (e.g., a multiplication) set, then further instructions may be required to shift to an "addition set." The activation of the appropriate set depends critically on the learned contingent relations between the instructional cues provided in the task and some of the contingency organizations that comprise an "addition set." If the child is unable to comprehend the instructional cues, or has not yet developed specific contingent relations between those types of cues and an "addition set," then a correct solution will not be consistently produced. The errors that a problem-solver makes do not represent random "trial-and-error," but reflect the inappropriate momentary set or data cues.

Any conditions that prevent the activation of an appropriate set would hinder the generation of a correct solution (Scheerer, 1963). If a particular set has been created in a subject by prior experience with certain problem-solving tasks, then that set may be maintained for a new problem even though it is now inappropriate. What is called "rigidity" or "mechanization" in problem-solving (Luchins, 1942) is frequently a consequence of lack of flexibility in shifting from determining sets that, though appropriate for prior tasks, are not appropriate for a new one. The lack of flexibility may arise from lack of comprehension of instructional cues or from habits of selective perception that prevent the observation of new data cues, or from a combination of these factors. Rigidity in this sense will make for efficient problem-solving so long as the particular problems do not require different initial sets or data cues, but would hinder the generation of correct solutions to problems that required different initial sets or data cues.

SOME EXAMPLES OF PROBLEM-SOLVING

Now we may examine how the proposed ideas may apply to certain kinds of problem-solving tasks. Consider one example from the area of perception, one from the area of rule learning, and one from the studies of multiple-step problem-solving tasks.

Perceptual Search

Suppose a subject is given a sheet with 100 letters printed on it, arranged in a table consisting of 20 rows of six letters each, and is told that the letter C appears once in the table and his task is to identify the location of that letter as quickly as possible, starting when a "go" signal is sounded. Basically, this is a variation of the same-different comparison task discussed in Chapter 13. On receiving the instructions, the subject is likely to formulate this visual search problem as one of reading each letter until he reaches the target letter C, and then pressing a key that identifies the letter's location. This formulation of the problem would generate a "reading set" involving the excitation of contingency organizations that determine the direction of reading (say, left to right and down the rows), as well as a set involving a pexgo of the letter C. When the "go" signal is sounded, the subject starts reading each letter until he reaches the letter C and then presses the key corresponding to its location, say, the row number. If the letter C is distributed at random among the other letters, the subject may complete the task (find the location of the letter) at the average rate of covering each row in about 4 seconds. His speed of performance is known to depend on several factors, such as the number of different nontarget letters that are included in the table, the exact forms of the nontarget letters in terms of their resemblance to C (e.g., whether the irrelevant letters are mostly like A and N, or like G and O), the uniformity and clarity with which the letter is printed, and so on. Under any given combination of conditions, the subject improves quickly with practice trials, each involving a different random display of the target (C) and non-target letters. His final average speed may reach about 1/2 sec per row (Neisser, 1964; Rabbitt, 1964).

The improvement that the subject shows may be accounted for in terms of learning new contingent relations peculiar to the task material. For example, if the nontarget letters were mainly angular, then the judgment whether each letter read is a C or not-C could be made on the basis of the roundness of the character, so that the judgments could be made without actually reading each letter. If the nontarget letters were also rounded in appearance (e.g., G, O), then the judgment could be made on the basis of the shape of the opening of C and roundedness could be ignored. In either case, as the subject isolated the features that distinguish the target letter from the nontarget letters, he would be able to scan each row, or part of a row, for the distinctive feature, and the average speed would improve. Thus, as the subject learned new contingencies relating specific features to the pexgos of the target and nontarget letters, his performance would continue to improve. It might take over 100 trials to reach an asymptotic speed.

Note that the observed improvement in the speed of perceptual identification is limited by the initial determining set that has been generated on the basis of the task instructions. Suppose the experimenter now changes the rules without revising his instructions to the subject. Instead of distributing C randomly through the letter-table display, he now restricts its location to the first three columns of the table. As the subject now practices under the new conditions, he will gradually learn the contingency that the letter C will appear only in the initial three places of any row, not at the end of the rows. This would result in the selective observation (see Chapter 10) of the initial part of each row, and may end with vertical scanning of the first three columns, yielding great advantage in speed. Thus the subject would have solved the new problem by learning a new tactic of vertical scanning as a part of the general strategy of scanning the table quickly. An analysis of eye-movement during scanning over the practice trials may confirm the change in tactic from horizontal to vertical scanning.

Now let us apply this general contingency-learning interpretation to a point of dispute about visual search for multiple targets—identifying the location of any one of two or more particular letters, say, C, M, P, or Z. Under this condition, Neisser, Novick, and Lazar (1963) found that there was no increase in search time as the number of target letters increased; whether the subject was required to identify one particular letter or eight particular letters made no difference in his search speed. Rabbitt (1964), however, found that search time increased as the number of target letters was increased. According to the present analysis such a discrepancy in results should be interpretable in terms of the particular contingencies that the subjects were likely to learn in the two experiments. In both experiments, the subjects presumably generated pexgos of all the target letters and scanned the display systematically. But the detailed requirements of the two tasks were different. In Neisser's experiment, the display was a continuous string of letters arranged in tightly packed rows, and the subject's task was merely to identify the row in which any one of the target letters appeared. Under these conditions, the subject could continue scanning until he came across a target letter; he could maintain one problem-set until the trial was completed. Assuming that the pexgos of all the target letters are maintained in an activated state during the brief trial period, it should make little difference (after sufficient practice) how many different letters are being searched.

In Rabbitt's experiment, on the other hand, the display was a card with nine well spaced letters, and the subject's task was to sort the cards into two categories, those containing any one of the target letters and those not containing any. Under these conditions the subject had to decide and make a differential response for each card of the pack (trial), and then resume the search. There were thus repeated changes required from a "search set" to the set required for deciding in which category to put a given card. If we assume that it would take a subject longer to regenerate pexgos of four or eight target letters before each trial (for each new card) than to regenerate pexgos of one or two target letters, then it is readily seen that the search time would be greater as the number of relevant letters is increased. However, with continued practice with the same target letters, the simultaneous generation of several pexgos should become easier, and the difference between the search speeds for small versus large numbers of target letters should decline and eventually disappear. This apparently is the case (P. M. A. Rabbitt, personal communication).

The general point is that the exact basis of performance in a perceptual problem can be only partially understood in terms of strategies and tactics that the subject may be presumed to bring to the task; fuller understanding comes from a consideration of the tactics that develop in the course of practice on the basis of the precise contingencies operating in the task. It is the development of the contingency organizations representing the intra-task contingent relations that is responsible for the considerable improvement that continues to occur for a long time during continued practice on a new task or some variation of an old task.

Abstraction Tasks

There are tasks in which the subject is required to identify the basis on which a given stimulus population (objects, events, ideas, etc.) has been partitioned or classified. At the simplest, a stimulus population may be partitioned into two classes; for example, automobiles may be partitioned into those with four doors and those with not-four doors, or toys into green ones and not-green ones. The basis of partition involves, minimally, an attribute or dimension along which the given stimulus population can be differentiated (e.g., four-doorness or greenness), as well as a rule that relates the relevant attributes to the two classes (e.g., if an automobile has four doors it belongs to class X, otherwise to class not-X, or Y). Thus any partitioning of stimulus items into two categories must specify certain "relevant" attribute or attributes (other attributes, such as the size, horsepower, or name of automobiles, are "irrelevant" attributes) as well as one or more rules (e.g., if an automobile is green, or if it is not-green and has three doors, it belongs to class X) that describe how the attributes are to be used for partitioning (see Bourne, 1966, 1970).

In such abstractional tasks, the subject may be given a rule by instructions or example and then asked to discover the relevant attributes as he observes positive (e.g., four-door automobiles) and negative (e.g., not-four-door automobiles) instances of a predetermined class-concept; this kind of task may be described as an *attribute extraction task*. Alternatively, the subject may be told the relevant attributes and then asked to discover the rule as he observes positive and negative instances of the class-concept (e.g., four-door automobiles belong to class X, all others to class not-X); this kind of task may be described as a *rule extraction task*. The so-called concept attainment tasks may involve either or both of attribute extraction and rule extraction.

Abstractional tasks are essentially discrimination tasks with the difference that (*a*) the relevant stimuli (discriminanda) may be mixed with certain irrelevant stimuli, (*b*) the sample stimuli are not fixed but vary from trial to trial, and (*c*) the rules of partition tend to be more complex. The essential thing the subject "learns" in discrimination tasks and "extracts" in the abstraction tasks is the predictive relation between certain signals (stimulus patterns or dimensions) and certain target events; identification or classification response based on the predictive relation is then shown to be correct or incorrect.

The idea that abstraction tasks are essentially complex discrimination tasks is supported by some findings of Carter and Eckerman (1975). They trained pigeons in a matching-to-sample task. On each trial a sample stimulus and two comparison stimuli were presented, and the bird was required to choose (i.e., peck at) the comparison stimulus that was identical to the sample stimulus. In one task both sample and comparison stimuli were colors of different hues, in another task they were lines of different orientations. Performance of birds on this similarity-matching (or similarity-discrimination) task was compared to their performance in a "symbolic-matching" (or rule-extraction) task. In the latter task, colors were used as sample stimuli, and vertical or horizontal lines were used as comparison stimuli; for example, with a sample of color *A* pecking at the vertical line was rewarded, with a sample of color *B* pecking at the horizontal line was rewarded. In other words, in this task the birds had to learn or extract the rule governing the delivery of the reward. The pigeons were able to learn this. What Carter and Eckerman were able to demonstrate by comparing the rate of learning in the two types of tasks was that symbolic matching (rule extraction) is not necessarily more difficult than similarity matching (similarity discrimination). The basis of the observed differences in the rate of learning of the two tasks lies in differences in the inherent discriminability of stimulus dimensions used as samples and comparison stimuli; the level of task difficulty is independent of the similarity between the sample and comparison stimuli—the variable that distinguishes the two tasks. This suggests that both similarity matching and symbolic matching involve the same process of learning predictive "if . . . then . . ." relations; that is, performance in both discrimination and rule-extraction tasks rests on the principles of contingency learning that were discussed in Chapters 6 and 7.

Thus, what is called "stimulus discrimination" in discrimination learning literature is fundamentally the same thing as attribute extraction in concept-formation literature; and what is called "conditional discrimination" (Nissen, 1951) in discrimination learning literature is the same thing as rule extraction in concept-formation literature. In the simplest discrimination task there is only one stimulus attribute that varies, it predicts the target event (i.e., there are no irrelevant attributes), and the rule is the simplest affirmative rule (if A, then B). As irrelevant dimensions are added to diriminanda (or examples) and the rules become more complex (overlappings positive and negative contingent relations), a discrimination task becomes more like an abstractional task. Stimulus discrimination or attribute extraction means learning to differentiate between discriminanda or instances; conditional discrimination or rule extraction means learning to differentiate between contingent relations or rules (see discussion of causality in Chapter 6).

Next, consider some aspects of a typical human rule-learning task with reference to one of Bourne's (1970) experiments. In this experiment Bourne examined the relative difficulty of learning four primary bidimensional rules, conjunction, disjunction, conditionality, and biconditionality, when the two attributes that defined a class-concept were given to the subjects in preliminary instructions. A description of these four rules in relation to the simple affirmative rule is presented in Table 15.1.

Bourne used four groups of subjects, one for each of the four rules. Each subject was given a series of nine problems based on the same rule. Though the concept involved only two attributes, the population of geometrical designs from which examples were drawn varied on four dimensions: color (red, green, and blue), form (square, triangle, hexagon), number (one, two, and three), and size (large, medium, small). The two attributes that were to serve as relevant attributes for a given problem were told to the subject, and his task was to learn the rule that would allow an errorless partition of the stimuli into two classes. On the presentation of each pattern (positive or negative instance) the subject made a "class response" by pressing one of two keys, and was immediately informed whether his response was correct. The sequence of trials continued with the presentation of other instances until the subject responded correctly on 16 consecutive trials. Bourne found that the average number of trials required for rule learning was the lowest in the conjunction group, and this was followed by the disjunction, conditional, and biconditional groups, respectively ($Cj < Dj < Cd < Bd$); the number of trials required declined sharply in the later problems of a series and all subjects performed errorlessly after six problems on the same rule. Thus, there were clear initial differences in the difficulty of learning the four rules, but these differences disappeared with practice, indicating marked interproblem transfer effects.

Table 15.1. Conceptual Rules Describing Binary Partitions of a Stimulus Population[a]

	Primary Rule	
Name	Symbolic description[b]	Verbal Description
Affirmative	R	All red patterns are examples of the concept
Conjunctive	R ∩ S	All patterns which are red and square are examples
Inclusive disjunctive	R ∪ S	All patterns which are red or square or both are examples
Conditional	R → S [R̄ ∪ S]	If a pattern is red then it must be square to be an example
Biconditional	R ↔ S [(R ∩ S) ∪ (R̄ ∩ S̄)]	Red patterns are examples if and only if they are square

[a] From L. E. Bourne, Jr., Knowing and using concepts, *Psychological Review*, 1970, **77**, 546–556. Copyright 1970 by the American Psychological Association. Reprinted by permission.

[b] R and S stand for red and square (relevant) attributes, respectively.

Bourne notes that the obtained order of relative difficulty ($Cj < Dj < Cd < Bd$) cannot be explained in terms of hypotheses that ascribe such differences to possible differences in the proportion of positive instances in the stimulus population used in a problem, or the "natural primitiveness" of certain rules (e.g., conjunction). Recognizing that conjunctive arrangements are more familiar to adult subjects, Bourne suggests that the observed differences in the difficulty of learning different rules could be interpreted in terms of the degree of departure from the conjunctive rule required by each of the other three rules. This general idea can be elaborated further in terms of the idea of contingency learning discussed in Chapter 7.

If we call the first relevant attribute R (redness) and the second relevant attribute S (squareness), then the attribute combinations that would be correct for the four rules would be as shown in Table 15.2. In order for a subject to show that he has mastered the required rule, he must discriminate errorlessly between the positive and negative instances. This means that he must learn the contingency between the attribute combinations and the verdict ("correct" or "incorrect"). Table 15.2 shows that in the case of the conjunctive rule, the subject could perform errorlessly by learning only that the RS combination is positive and all other combinations are negative (R̄S̄+; R̄S̄−), without learning specifically what the "other" combinations (RS, R̄S, R̄S̄) are. Similarly, in the case of the disjunctive rule, the subject could perform errorlessly by learning only that the R̄S̄ combination is negative and all other combinations (R̄S, R̄S̄, RS) are positive. The disjunctive rule should take somewhat longer to learn because it involves negative contingencies, which can be learned only after some background positive contingencies have been learned (see Chapter 6). Nevertheless, both these rules would be considerably easier to learn than the conditional and biconditional rules, each of which requires the learning of certain complex contingencies.

Table 15.2. Correct Attribute Combinations for the Four Bidimensional Rules[a]

Rule	Combinations for Positive Instances	Combinations for Negative Instances
Conjunctive	RS	R̄S or RS̄ or R̄S̄
Inclusive disjunctive	R̄S or RS̄ or RS	R̄S̄
Conditional	RS or R̄S or R̄S̄	RS̄
Biconditional	RS or R̄S̄	R̄S or RS̄

[a]R means stimulus pattern is red, R̄ that it is not red, S means stimulus pattern is square, S̄ that it is not square.

The conditional rule requires either the learning of one negative combination, RS̄, or the learning of the three positive combinations, RS, R̄S, and R̄S̄. Even if the subject learns the one negative combination, the rule will be more difficult to learn than the disjunctive rule, for in the latter case both elements of the negative combination (R̄ and S̄) are negatively related to the criterion instances, while in the conditional case one element (S̄) is negatively related and the other (R) is positively related. The biconditional rule is still more difficult, for it requires the learning of at least two contingencies regardless of whether the subject learns the positive or the negative combinations. The biconditional rule would also require more trials to learn than the conditional rule because the former involves the learning of two contradictory contingencies—both RS and R̄S̄ are positive combinations. Thus the order of difficulty of learning the four rules predicted by the contingency-learning hypothesis is the same as that found by Bourne in his experiment.

Another factor that would determine the difficulty of learning a rule is the suitability of the strategy used to approach the problem, which in turn depends on the initial set generated by the instructions and the problem cues operating in the early trials. Since positive contingencies are primary in the sense that they must be learned before any negative contingencies involving the same stimuli can be learned, it is reasonable to expect that the subjects in abstractional tasks would observe the concomitance (conjunction) of the test attributes before they would observe the separation (disjunction) of the attributes. Thus, in general, subjects would tend to adopt a conjunctive strategy (or hypothesis) first. This priority of the conjunctive strategy must, to varying degrees, interfere with the emergence of disjunctive and conditional solutions.

The initial set may, of course, be varied with special experimental manipulations. For example, if a subject is given conjunctive-rule problems before being switched to a conditional-rule problem, the problem set likely to be generated would be one of finding the positive combinations and treating all "other" combinations as negative; however, the reverse may be the case if the subject is given several disjunctive-rule problems before the conditional-rule problem. The exact factors that determine the initial strategy in approaching a concept-learning task require further study.

This analysis suggests that there can be several levels of "knowing" a rule. In the above example, a subject could solve conjunctive-rule problems errorlessly by specifically learning only the positive combination and treating all the negative combinations as the same. Clearly, another subject who not only learns this but also learns the specific contingencies of *each* of the negative combinations may be thought of as knowing the meaning of conjunction better than the first subject. Thus, errorless performance according to a rule indicates correct application of the rule but does not prove comprehension of the rule as might be indicated by, say, verbal or mathematical formulation of the rule as described in Table 15.1. It is likely that many reported examples of rule learning in monkeys and children reflect rule abstraction only in the sense of correct rule application but not in the sense of rule formulation in a formal language; the latter formal or "abstract knowledge" may depend on language and specific training in logical relations. Even adult human subjects frequently fail to formulate the simple conjunctive and disjunctive rules although they perform errorlessly.

Multiple-Step Problems

So far I have discussed behavior in simple problem-solving situations where a single solution is required. However, in most problem-solving tasks, especially those that confront human adults, the problem consists of several subproblems, so that a solution to each of the subproblems has to be found, and then the various solutions have to be put together into a total-problem solution. In such multiple-step problems or "thinking" tasks (e.g., playing chess, solving cryptarithmetic problems, discovering proofs in logic), each step involves the formulation of the subproblem and search for a solution to it. But in addition to these processes, they also depend heavily on "memory"—the capability of remembering which subproblems have been worked on and what subsolutions arrived at.

An idea that is important in dealing with multistep problems is that of *progress* toward the total solution. As a solution emerges for a subproblem, the problem-solver arrives at a new "knowledge-state" (Simon & Newell, 1971), which serves as a node or decision point for choosing the next step. This choice is determined by a decision based on some judgment about the relative usefulness of various possible alternatives—how much closer would a particular step bring the problem-solver to the total solution, or by how much would the discrepancy between the desired solution and the present knowledge state be reduced by a particular step. The next step may be to start working on a new subproblem (generating a new problem set) or to try out a new operator (act in relation to some new data cues) on a current subproblem. The general strategy of deciding what to do next—what the next subproblem is or how it should be attacked—has been called "means-ends analysis," and this is an important concept in theoretical accounts of human problem-solving (e.g., Duncker, 1945; Newell & Simon, 1971).

It should be clear that each judgment about the relative usefulness of the various alternative steps would require selective recall of what progress has already been made on the different subproblems, and what types of "next steps" have already been tried and found to be more or less useful. The ability to "hold" the various components (subproblems, subsolutions, data cues, etc.) and other attentional (or "short-term memory") processes would also be important in determining the efficiency of solving a multistep problem. Of course, selective holding and remembering are also important in simple problem-solving tasks, but the "memory load" is a more critical factor in multiple-step problem-solving. Note that selective processes have two separate roles to play in problem-solving. First, the contingency organizations that comprise an activated problem set represent prior experience, and hence involve selective recall. Second, decisions about the appropriate next step, as well as the recall and collation of the solutions already arrived at, require continual selective holding by rehearsal or other means. The "memory load" of a problem-solving task may be reduced by increasing the number of overt steps required to arrive at the total solution (Greeno & Simon, 1974).

It is doubtful that most multiple-step problem tasks could be solved without the use of language. Language provides labels for environmental cues that make it easy to link data cues to a variety of contingency organizations representing past experience, as well as labels that can quickly activate particular problem sets. Further, language cues can be a great help in the coding and recall of various aspects of a task in the course of problem-solving.

With practice at a particular type of multiple-step problem task, a subject would learn the most effective way of solving that kind of problem. In other words, he would develop a plan indicating the decisions to be made at each node; such a plan would consist of subplans or strategies dealing with particular subproblems or groups of subproblems.

Consider an example. Suppose a subject is asked to solve the problem $637 \times 9 = ?$ "mentally." The multiplication sign would create a "multiplication-problem set," involving the activation of some multiplication sets. The subject's first step might be to decide which procedure of multiplication to use: to round off the numbers, multiply, and then make appropriate additions and subtractions, or to multiply "long-hand." Estimating the relative difficulty of the two procedures with the given numbers, he may decide to use the "long-hand" procedure. A more specific "multiplication long-hand problem set" would now develop, and looking at the numbers, the subject might go through the following sequence: "nine times seven is . . . sixty-three, put down three and carry six; nine times three is . . . twenty-seven, and I was carrying . . . six, so that makes thirty-three; the new three goes next to the other three, and I carry three; nine times six is . . . fifty-four, and I was carrying . . . three, so that makes fifty-seven, which goes in front of the two threes, making five-seven-three-three; so the answer is 5733." Clearly, there are several steps, and at each step the subproblem is one of arriving at a one-digit number as a result of multiplication and adding whatever was being carried; further, as each subproblem is being worked on, the earlier subsolutions (digits arrived at) are recalled at appropriate times, as required for the momentary operations. The general account of problem-solving outlined earlier in this chapter—that at each step a subsolution emerges as a consequence of an interaction between the continually changing momentary determining set and the momentary data cues—applies to the above example.

The rapid emergence of the subsolution at each step, of course, depends on prior mastery of multiplication and addition operations as well as of the rules of sequential progression from one step to the next. If the subject has not mastered these, for example, if the subject does not know multiplication tables and has to multiply by adding, then the memory load would be high and the subject might be unable to find the solution to the above problem "mentally." The greater the rapidity with which the successive operations are performed, and the fewer the discrete steps, the less the memory load of a task would be. Rehearsal, organization, and other methods of improving recall (see Chapters 11 and 14), as well as keeping a written record, may be used to cope with the memory requirements of a multiple-step task. As in the case of other types of perceptual and abstractional problem-solving, the efficiency of multiple-step problems or "thinking" depends on practice; Bartlett (1958) called thinking a "high-level skill" dependent on "well informed practice" (p. 11).

A detailed analysis of complex multiple-step problems, such as those in games (e.g., Duncker, 1945), logical exercises (e.g., Newell & Simon, 1971), and science (e.g., Bartlett, 1958) falls outside the scope of this work. The main point made here is simply that the elementary steps in all forms of problem-solving, including "creative problem-solving," involve the iterative operation of the same fundamental process of interaction of narrowing momentary determining sets with a succession of data cues.

CHAPTER 16

Summary and Conclusion

Philosophers of the seventeenth and eighteenth centuries gave sanction to the notion that man's actions are attributable to three sets of mental processes: cognitive, affective, and conative. Cognitive processes produce knowledge of the world, affective processes generate emotions or motivation, and conative processes control the initiation and execution of actions. Influences that subsequently shaped ideas about the nature of knowledge, motivation, and action came from several disciplines, including philosophy, physics, biology, neurophysiology, neurology, psychology, ethology, psychiatry, and, lately, linguistics. Understandably, this diversity of influences led to a multiplicity of descriptive and explanatory concepts, whose use remained largely restricted to separate, and often isolated, domains of study. The commonality of problems and the similarity of concepts have remained somewhat obscured by the differences of terminology, method, and rhetoric that developed in each discipline.

In this volume my aim has been to pose the main questions that must be dealt with in any complete theory of adaptive behavior, and, by trying to answer them, to indicate the general outline of a theoretical scheme that might guide the formulation of detailed and unified explanatory accounts of behavior in diverse contexts. I have tried to characterize the processes underlying knowledge, motivation, and action, and to show how they might combine to produce goal-directed, foresightful, and intentional actions in animals and man. In this final chapter I want to summarize the main points of my theoretical scheme and to indicate some of its implications for certain recurrent issues.

THE THEORETICAL SCHEME

The theoretical scheme may be summarized by reiterating a few points in terms of which it differs from certain other historical and current theoretical approaches to explaining intelligent behavior.

358

Knowledge

Perception, learning (or memory), and meaning are the main historical concepts that have been used in describing what someone knows about the environment. All these aspects of knowledge may be supposed to be generated by activation in the head of certain knowledge or "gnostic" structures. Broad agreement may be also assumed on some points concerning the postulated gnostic structures. First, whether we call these structures "mental," "behavioral," "cognitive," or "informational," ultimately gnostic structures must be regarded as *neural*. Second, gnostic structures *develop* during the life of the individual animal from simpler and less efficient structures to complex and more efficient structures; this development parallels the observed improvement in perceptual-cognitive capabilities during infancy and childhood. Third, the development of gnostic structures involves the *organization* of certain kinds of elements into structures of greater complexity, which come to serve as higher-level functional units; the same elements may enter into the organization of different gnostic structures.

Within this area of common understanding, several different views of the neural, developmental, and organizational aspects of gnostic structures may be and have been held. I have suggested that the basic functional unit of the immediate or perceptual knowledge of the environment is the "pexgo." I have coined this term to differentiate the critical functional unit (pexgo) from both correct stimulus identification or perceptual response and experienced stimulus percept or perceptual awareness. The pexgo in my account is a purely theoretical concept, and is clearly distinguished from the phenomena of identifying response, percept generation, and imagery, which it is designed to explain. What I propose is that the generation of a pexgo is a necessary condition for both correct identification and awareness of a given stimulus, but that perceptual response and perceptual awareness, as well as imagery, require particular additional processes.

A *pexgo* is defined as a presently generated neural entity that represents sufficient characteristics (shape, size, roughness, pitch, taste, spatial location, etc.) of a stimulus for it to be identified as distinct from certain other stimuli. The same stimulus may generate different pexgos on different occasions. An apple may generate a visual "apple pexgo" on one occasion and a tactual or olfactory one on another occasion. Further, several different apple pexgos of a single modality may be generated on different occasions. The generation of a pexgo involves a fresh neural construction, not the activation of a pre-existing neural entity.

A pexgo is not a *sensory* pattern, as the "perceptron" and "template-matching" models of stimulus identification might regard it. Nor is a pexgo a *motor* pattern, as the "efference theories" might suggest; the close relation between perception and action can be explained in another way. A pexgo is generated in the secondary projection areas of the brain as a consequence of certain interactions involving sensory patterns and information about the position of sense organs as well as of other parts of the body. A pexgo thereby represents a stimulus-in-space, not in terms of the points on the receptor surface stimulated, but in a spatially differentiated manner that depicts the spatial position of the stimulus in relation to the animal. Thus two identical but separate stimuli can simultaneously generate separate pexgos without confusion.

The neural organizations whose activation generates a pexgo are called "gnostic-assemblies"; they are organizations of gnostic neurons of the secondary, modality-specific projection areas. Each *gnostic-assembly* is an integrated group of gnostic-neurons, which have become integrated by species-typical maturation and individually-specific experience. Thus like Hebb's cell-assembly, my concept of gnostic-assembly refers to a higher-level functional unit that is developed by an integration of varied assortments of neural elements (gnostic-neurons); these represent stimulus-feature *combinations* that are characteristic of the objects that an animal frequently encounters in its environment. The generation of a pexgo of any given stimulus (e.g., an apple) would typically involve several gnostic assemblies, activated by the summation of neural influences produced directly by the current sensory inflow and neural influences produced indirectly by miscellaneous prevailing central factors. The particular complex of gnostic-assemblies activated would vary from occasion to occasion, depending on the current sensory inflow and central factors. Thus, each time a pexgo of a stimulus is generated it may involve a different assortment of gnostic-assemblies.

It is important to note that I have *not* proposed that there is a particular gnostic-assembly (or a single gnostic neuron) corresponding to each distinguishable object or that the activation of a given gnostic-assembly must generate a pexgo representing a particular object. In my view the gnostic-assembly represents feature combinations or dimensions, not objects as such; in this respect my view differs from the early cell-assembly model and the new "single-unit hypothesis" of perception, which assume a one-to-one correspondence between a neural structure and an environmental object. The view proposed here is that no object *has* a unique or permanent pexgo, whose activation results in its perception. A pexgo of an object is a fresh and different construction on each occasion, its exact neural structure depending on what particular stimulus features are presented and what specific assortment of gnostic-assemblies are activated by the sensory patterns of those stimulus features, as well as by various central influences. The idea that there exists a unique and rather permanent neural representation of environmental stimuli has been a source of much confusion in attempts to understand the basis of perceptual knowledge. The alternative idea offered here, that the representation—a pexgo—has no existence until it is generated briefly by a unique confluence of sensory and central neural discharges, appears to overcome the traditional difficulties.

I have followed Hebb in proposing that larger neural functional units—gnostic-assemblies—develop as a consequence of the contiguous activation of their constituent gnostic-neurons and smaller gnostic-assemblies. I have further suggested that observational acts (e.g., eye movements or haptic exploratory movements) play an essential part in this development, not because motor elements "mediate" the integrated activation of certain gnostic-assemblies, but because they bring the activation of the gnostic-neurons representing different features of a stimulus into closer temporal contiguity. Observational acts are thus necessary for the initial integration of certain gnostic-assemblies, but once organized, the sequence can be activated as a whole by an appropriate sensory pattern without requiring any motor mediation. Some correspondence between perception and observational acts remains, even when the former is no longer dependent on the latter, because some of the stimulus features that are represented in gnostic-assemblies are also the ones that evoke the observational acts.

Finally, it should be noted that by suggesting that pexgo generation is only the first necessary, but not sufficient, step in producing the phenomena of stimulus identification and conscious awareness (percepts and images), I have tried, as many others have done before, to dispel the notion that some miniaturized lifelike representation, rather than an abstract translation, is generated in the brain. The former notion, common to the mentalistic, Gestalt, and holographic accounts of perception is untenable because it assumes an unexplained inner "perceiver." This notion is also a source of many pseudoproblems, from Kepler's paradox (why do we see rightside up when the image on the retina is upside down?) to the currently voiced "overlap problem" (how do we succeed in identifying stimuli that are partially hidden?). The notion of lifelike representation must be discarded in favor of the idea that stimuli are represented in abstract codes and that the phenomena of perception rest not on an inner perceiver, but on the successive neural transformations of the sensory inflow produced by a stimulus. Both aspects of perception, conscious percept and identifying response, are end products; pexgo generation is only an initial step in the determination of perception and action, and even pexgo generation depends on important on-going central influences other than those produced by any current stimulus input.

In explaining the learning of the correlations that exist between particular environmental events—what goes with what—I have suggested a further organization of pexgos (i.e., of gnostic-assemblies) that typically represent certain correlated events. Pexgos of correlated events $(E_1:E_2)$ become organized, through observation of their concomitant and disconcomitant occurrences, into higher-level gnostic structures, called *contingency organizations*. A contingency organization represents a certain predictive relation between two events, such that a pexgo p_1 generated by E_1, the predictive event, leads to changes in the excitation level of a pexgo p_2 of E_2, the predicted event. I have proposed a mechanism by which changes in the imminence of occurrence of the predicted event (E_2) are reflected as changes in the level of excitation of p_2. The activation of a contingency organization is regarded as the basis of the subjective experience of an "idea" of a relation between two events, as well as the basis of anticipatory action directed at the predicted event, before its actual occurrence.

The spatial and temporal relations between the early or signal events and the later or target events in a stably recurring situation come to be represented in the brain as overlapping or nested clusters of contingency organizations; they are called *situational schemas* (or "cognitive maps"). An activated cluster of contingency organizations is called a *momentary determining set*, and this concept is used to explain the fact that it is the context or situation in which an event occurs that determines the exact predictive significance of that event. Thus, the predictive influence of any given event is not fixed, but depends on the momentary determining set at the time of its occurrence. When a certain specific target event (e.g., food delivery) is part of a situation, the occurrence of each of the earlier signal events (in that context) results in a progressive increase in the level of excitation of a pexgo of the target event, corresponding to its predicted imminence. The basis of this progressive increase in the excitation level of a pexgo of the target event lies in the progressive narrowing of the momentary determining set through continual interactions between the determining set of a moment ago and the new environmental signal events that become effective at each moment. This formulation, with its emphasis on multiple, nested contingency organizations, is able to handle complex context effects on behavior, which cannot be plausibly interpreted in terms of linear models in which the predictive contribution of each event depends wholly on the chain of specific events preceding it.

I have used the above scheme to deal with the general problem of selectivity in behavior. For example, in a discussion of meaning, I have suggested that the basis of meaning of a given stimulus (object, event, action, or word) lies in the excitation of certain pexgos of *other* stimuli through the various contingency organizations activated by the given stimulus. Since a stimulus (e.g., an apple or the word *apple*) can generate many different pexgos, and since any pexgo may be a part of several contingency-organizations, each object can generate several different meanings. The momentary meaning generated or "selected" at a certain time depends on the context and the other general factors determining the contingency organizations that will be activated and the pexgos that will be generated. How clear the momentary meaning of a stimulus is depends on the specificity or narrowness of the range of pexgos generated at a particular moment. I have used the same fundamental concept—progressive narrowing of a momentary determining set through continual interactions with new stimulus events (cues or data)— to explain selectivity in perception (selective perception or "attention") and in remembering (selective recall).

Motivation

The term motivation serves as a rough label for the relatively persisting states that make an animal initiate and maintain actions leading to particular outcomes or goals. The older philosophical view was that motivational states are generated by environmental incentive objects—those that give pleasure or pain. Then, around the beginning of the present century, owing perhaps to the popularity of mechanical drive systems, the physiologists and psychologists came to attribute motivational changes to alterations in internal organismic conditions or "biological drives" (e.g., hunger, thirst, hormonal fluctuations). The latter view remained dominant until about the 1940s, when the importance of environmental incentive stimuli (variously called "affective," "emotional," "reinforcing," or "releasing" stimuli) began to be re-emphasized in the writings of ethologists and psychologists. Now it has become widely accepted that motivational states are jointly determined by the prevailing internal organismic conditions *and* the environmental stimulation from different classes of incentive objects. This is the broad assumption within which I have formulated certain hypotheses about the basis of the motivational control of behavior.

The main concept I have used is *central motive state*. A particular central motive state (e.g., one promoting eating, copulation, attack, or avoidance) is generated by the joint influence of certain specific organismic-state factors (e.g., hypoglycemia, hormonal levels, sickness) and certain specific types of incentive stimulation (odor of food, sight of a sexual object, noise made by an intruder). The neural consequences of organismic-state fluctuations and the neural consequences of incentive stimulation presumably reach the same neural structures and interact there to produce a persisting change in neural activity. Unlike certain cybernetic theories that attribute motivational fluctuations to feedback from the consequences of responses made in relation to incentive objects, my formulation attributes motivational fluctuations to direct influence of changes in environmental incentive stimulation on neural activity at particular sites in the brain.

Concerning the mechanism of motivational influence on behavior, I have proposed that a central motive state promotes action in relation to a certain class of incentive objects by increasing the excitation of pexgos of those objects, thereby rendering them more salient and potent response elicitors. The basis of this selective pexgo excitation lies in the fact that the objects whose pexgos are excited are the same ones that have played a part in the generation of the central motive state; for example, certain stimulation from food (e.g., its odor) generates the central motive state of eating (under certain organismic conditions), and this central motive state in turn excites a pexgo of food, so that food becomes more salient relative to other stimuli in the situation. This mechanism makes it possible to explain why an eating central motive state leads to actions in relation to food and a copulation central motive state leads to action in relation to a sexual object, but not vice versa. The correspondence between motivation and action has not been satisfactorily explained by earlier theories of motivation.

The particular form of the action (e.g., approach, withdrawal) produced under given organismic conditions is determined by the nature (e.g., appetitive or aversive) of the incentive objects present in the situation. While viscerosomatic reactions and transactional (consummatory or rejectional) acts tend to be fairly uniform for a given central motivational state, the instrumental responses tend to vary considerably. The latter are determined by the spatiotemporal arrangement of the relevant incentive stimuli in the situation. The specific instrumental response produced in a given situation is a fresh construction, each time it occurs, created by the momentary motivational states and the spatiotemporal distribution of various (unconditioned and conditioned) incentive stimuli in the situation. In the normal life of an animal two or more motivational states are likely to be concurrently active, so that the response constructed at a given moment may depend on the situational arrangement of different types of incentive objects. For example, a hungry she-wolf's response may be determined at a given moment by its offspring in the nest, food nearby, and a predator or intruder not too far away.

The term "learned motivation" is used to describe the generation of a central motive state associatively by a certain stimulus that was initially neutral motivationally. The critical question about learned motivation is this: When a motivationally neutral or conditioned stimulus becomes capable of contributing to the generation of a central motive state through its association with that state, what new capability does the conditioned stimulus acquire? Does the conditioned stimulus become capable of producing the organismic conditions required for the given central motive state? Does the conditioned stimulus become capable of representing the unconditioned, incentive stimulation required for generating that central motive state? Or do both these things happen?

I have argued that the conditioned stimulus substitutes for incentive stimulation, *not* for organismic conditions. For example, in conditioning the central motive state of eating, the conditioned stimulus substitutes for (i.e., generates a pexgo of) food, but the animal must be actually food-deprived if the conditioned stimulus is to become an effective motivator; neural consequences of food deprivation cannot be produced by conditioned stimuli. While phasic viscerosomatic reactions (e.g., salivation, hypoglycemia) can be readily conditioned, a careful analysis of recent attempts to condition "drives" shows that the behavioral changes taken as evidence of drive conditioning are probably consequences of other, adventitious factors. It appears, then, that incentive stimuli are conditionable, but the organismic factors that are relevant to the generation of motivational states are not; there is such a thing as a secondary or conditioned incentive (or reinforcing) stimulus, but no such thing as a secondary or conditioned organismic factor or biological drive. These ideas provide a basis for resolving certain controversies about the conditionability of hunger, thirst, and drug states.

When the pexgo of a certain target (e.g., incentive) stimulus is excited through conditioning, the excitation occurs in advance of the actual occurrence of that stimulus; the basis of learned motivation, then, is anticipatory excitation or priming of the pexgo of a target stimulus by some other, conditioned stimulus. Since the excitation of a pexgo of a stimulus contributes to the readiness with which that stimulus is perceived (identified or experienced), conditioned priming of a pexgo may also be the mechanism of selective perception. Thus, I have proposed that the type of increased readiness for perceiving certain stimuli that has traditionally been described as "selective attention" arises from conditioned priming of pexgos. The phenomena of selective attention and learned motivation are therefore both regarded here as the outcomes of the process of selective priming of particular pexgos by conditioned stimuli. Which pexgo will be primed at any given moment depends on the same principles of contingency organization and determining set that determine selectivity generally. This view makes it unnecessary to attribute attentional phenomena to filtering or enhancement of current sensory inflow, and it makes any particular observational acts a consequence rather than a cause of the selective activation of a certain pexgo. This formulation can plausibly deal with most known phenomena of "selective attention."

Production of Action

Traditionally, there has been little interest in the problem of how actions appropriate for the prevailing states of knowledge and motivation are produced. Cartesian dualism had ascribed initiation of human actions to the soul, which was the pontif that willed certain actions to be performed. The important thing was for the pontif to gain knowledge about the environment and about the bodily perturbations related to passions, and to arrive at a decision about what to do. Once the decision had been made and a certain action willed, the execution of the action through nerves and muscles was thought to be automatic. This general attitude was what the early psychologists inherited. They too regarded the motor apparatus as the slave of a higher "self" or executive. Understandably, then, the (sensory) input to the executive and the nature of thinking and feeling remained the main problems of interest; the functioning of the motor apparatus was regarded as a secondary matter and largely ignored. Interest in detailed studies of the motor apparatus and the production of action grew largely from physiological studies of the motor system, neurological examinations of disorders of voluntary action, and more recently from neurophysiological analyses of the mechanisms controlling the motor outflow from the brain. The basic question about the production of actions may be posed as follows: How are neural events organized to yield the spatiotemporal ordering of acts that make up the adaptive actions of animals.

An *act*, such as lever pressing or speaking a short word, consists of several movements produced in a certain spatiotemporal arrangement. Initially an act occurs as a series of disjointed, slow, individually-elicited movements, but with practice it begins to appear as unified, efficient, and voluntary; a series of "respondents" are integrated into an "operant." There are several reasons for discarding the older views that the integration of movements into an act reflects the formation of neural links between successive movement commands, or between the sensory feedback of a previous movement and the movement command of the following movement. Proprioceptive feedback from limbs is not necessary for the development of normal locomotory acts. The acquisition of somewhat more skilled acts seems to require some sensory feedback, though not necessarily proprioceptive. Once a certain act has been developed, sensory feedback is not necessary for its performance, except in the case of responses requiring highly refined movements. In general, there is now little doubt that once appropriate neural structures have been formed, long sequences of acts can be performed normally without the necessity of any sensory feedback.

A workable hypothesis seems to be that the shaping of an act reflects the development of a new, higher-level organization which I have called the *act-assembly*. Such an organization would make it possible for the specific movements to be substituted even while the act, as defined by its outcome, remains the same. Another reason for postulating act-assemblies is that disorders of act production—failure of the proper sequential patterning of the movements that make up an act—may occur independently of any deficits in the production of individual movements. While some primitive act-assemblies (e.g., those involved in locomotion, micturition, and certain aspects of copulation) are presumably maturationally organized and are located in subcortical structures, other act-assemblies are certainly dependent on individually specific experience and are probably located in the premotor areas of the cortex.

I have proposed that the development of act-assemblies closely parallels the development of gnostic-assemblies. The particular sequences of stimulus configurations that result in the activation of a certain sequence of movement commands form the basis of the development of both certain gnostic-assemblies (representing the important features of those stimulus configurations) and certain act-assemblies (representing the movement sequence that makes up an act). This common basis of perceptual-motor development insures that aspects of the environment that we learn to perceive well are the same aspects in relation to which we learn to perform acts. Though gnostic-assemblies are separate from act-assemblies, some "ideomotor" tendencies presumably persist as a consequence of their common heritage.

If a situation remains stable, and the conditions are so arranged that the same sequence of movements is repeatedly elicited (as in a typical learning experiment), smaller act-assemblies coalesce into larger ones, and the sequences of movements that could be produced as a unit become longer and longer. In this way a whole response, as defined for the experiment (e.g., reaching the end of a runway, opening a lock, reciting a poem), may occur as a serially-ordered, unified, and ballistic output. However, such serially-ordered responses are maintained only so long as the contingent relations that make up the situational schema remain unaltered; otherwise they are readily disrupted. For example, any change in the arrangement of the parts of the runway disrupts the running response, and a delay in the auditory feedback of one's speech disrupts speech. Thus some flexibility in serial-ordering remains even after act-assemblies seem to have coalesced into larger units; serial ordering is not simply a matter of integration of act-assemblies. The stereotypy of the serial-ordering in responses seen in most skills and habits arises from the stability of the situational cues and their contingent relations. The more typical response production in the normal life of an animal involves a flexible and changing serial-ordering of acts (as in exploratory behavior or communicative speech), which depends on continually changing patterns of activation of contingency organizations by stimuli of varying significance for the animal, which produce continual changes in momentary determining sets.

The development of volition—the emergence of acts that appear "voluntary"—may be explained by considering that the occurrence of any act would also result in the generation of a pexgo of that act. As an act-assembly is being formed and the act is repeated often, gnostic-assemblies representing that act are also developed; these gnostic-assemblies represent the important stimulus features (visual, proprioceptive, cutaneous, etc.) of the act. A pexgo of an animal's own act functions in the same way as the pexgos of objects and other events; for example, by occurring in predictive relations with other, prior events, act pexgos too become parts of contingency organizations. This means that prior events (i.e., conditioned stimuli) become linked both to the pexgo of the stimulus configuration necessary to activate the act-assembly for that act and to the pexgo of the act itself. In this way it becomes possible for an act to be produced by conditioned stimuli that precede, by a considerable time, the stimulus configuration that was initially the sole activator of the act-assembly. When an act is thus produced by remote, idiosyncratic conditioned stimuli, in the absence of any known, universal eliciting stimuli, the act appears to be "voluntary" or an emitted "operant," rather than "involuntary" or an elicited "respondent." William James suggested that it is the conditioned excitation of the central representation ("idea") of the *act* that is the basis of a voluntary act. The present suggestion is that the basis of a voluntary act lies in the conditioned excitation, *not* of the representation (pexgo) of that act, but of the pexgo of that *stimulus configuration* effective in activating the act-assembly for that act. When an act is occurring, *its* pexgo excites, through certain contingency organizations, pexgos of future events that have reliably followed the act (e.g., a click or food-delivery is a common consequence of lever-pressing). This means that pexgos of the consequences of an act are excited by an act serving as a conditioned (predictor) stimulus, and this may be the basis of the subjective experience of expectation that a certain act will produce particular consequences. The basis of voluntary action and expectancy may thus be quite different.

Choice implies a preference for an alternative on the basis of its expected utility (benefits minus costs) relative to the expected utility of the other alternatives. A choice may be roughly differentiated from a decision in that a choice is a selection between alternatives that have fairly immediate and certain utility outcomes, while a decision is a selection between alternatives with remote and uncertain utility outcomes. The alternatives from which the selection is made are usually thought to be response alternatives and are talked about as *doing* this rather than that, but I have proposed that the selection is not between responses as such but between stimulus alternatives that predict different utility outcomes (though response effort may enter as a factor in determining the predicted utility of each stimulus alternative). A convenient measure of choice—relative preference—is the relative time allocated to transactions with the various stimulus alternatives. I have tried to show how relative time allocation may be determined by the momentary net motivational valences (representing utility) of the alternatives. The momentary net motivational valence of a stimulus alternative in turn depends on the contingency organizations it activates at that time in that situation. This account of the choice process implies lack of transitivity of preference relations; that is, the relative preference of two stimulus alternatives may change in different contexts and in different combinations of other alternatives. This fact has been an embarrassment to the usual reinforcement views of choice.

The important feature of a decision is that it involves a *comparison* of stimuli with respect to some specified dimension or dimensions, and the choice is then determined by the outcome of the comparison; a decision based on the comparison of certain stimuli determines what relative preference will be shown to some subsequent choice stimuli. Minimally, a comparison requires the activation of the pexgos of the stimuli to be compared and the generation of a neural discrepancy discharge proportional to their dissimilarity. The judgment arising from a comparison depends on the differentness (or rate of discrepancy discharge) of the stimuli on some specified dimension and the criterion values of rate of discrepancy discharge that that define each judgment category. The criterion values may be affected by the pay-off matrix—the utility (incentive) consequences of each alternative—and this is the way in which expected utility can influence a judgment. Most decisions of everyday life involve complex comparison attributes, each of which may involve several separate judgments on different subattributes. It may thus be possible to interpret complex decision making in terms of the general principles of knowledge and motivation proposed earlier.

My account of planning is linked to that of decision making. Planning is the preparation of a course of action leading to a certain goal. The subject, animal or man, prepares in its head an outline of the various steps required to achieve a goal, and then performs those steps when appropriate occasions arise. The preparation or plan is made up of a number of subgoals that are way stations for reaching the specified remote goal. The articulation of a plan requires that a general determining set involving pexgos of the goal or a subgoal be created and maintained. The motivational arousal required for maintaining a certain set is generated through the incentive (unconditioned or conditioned) of the goal stimuli. The decisions made in articulating a plan determine the relative preference to be shown at particular choice points. The relative preference is determined by modulation of the motivational valence of the choice alternatives through the recall of the relevant decision. In this way a plan provides for the execution of an appropriate course of action by influencing, at appropriate choice points, the relative preference for choice stimuli. Planned action is intentional action. To show that someone is capable of intentionality is to show that the creature is able to make decisions about future choices in advance of encountering the actual choice stimuli, and is able to recall and follow those decisions during the execution of the planned action.

This, then, is the rough scheme about how the processes underlying knowledge, motivation, and action combine to produce intelligent behavior. Three chapters of this volume are devoted to an application of the scheme to the understanding of certain commonly studied behavioral phenomena. One of these chapters deals with routine actions (instincts, habits, etc.) developed in relation to recurring situations. A second deals with the phenomena of memory, and the third with certain instances of problem-solving.

SOME GENERAL IMPLICATIONS

Finally, consider briefly some implications of the above scheme for four recurring issues in the study of behavior. These concern the concept of association, the problem of the executive, the investigation of brain function, and the enigma of consciousness.

Association

Association means joining. The doctrine of associationism, which flourished from the seventeenth to the nineteenth centuries, held that knowledge consists of ideas, and that simple or elementary ideas may, through experience, be joined together into larger ideas. A larger idea may involve the simultaneous association of two or more elementary ideas (e.g., the idea of furniture is a collection of ideas of chair, table, bed, etc.), or a larger idea may involve the successive association of ideas (e.g., the idea of cloud leads to the idea of rain, and the idea of rain to the idea of umbrella, etc.). In either event, the association (joining or linking) of ideas results in larger functional units, making mental operations more efficient with experience. Behaviorism replaced "ideas" by "responses" as the associative elements and suggested that adaptive capabilities improve as individuals develop larger sensory-motor functional units or habits.

There can be no issue about the use of the term association, in its common-sense meaning, to describe entities that usually or frequently occur together. The issues that have arisen concern mainly two questions, not wholly unrelated. First, what is the basis of the observed associations between entities, be they ideas, responses, objects, events, or any other types of elements? Second, what is the role of experience in the development of the larger functional units or organizations that make mental functioning or adaptive processes more efficient?

Concerning the basis of association, connectionism has been commonly invoked since the beginning of this century. The connectionistic view is that the neural representations of certain behavioral elements are either inherently linked together or become linked together through contiguous experience of those events. The degree of association between any two behavioral or experiential elements depends on the strength of some fairly direct and specific neural connections between the representations of those elements. It was pointed out in Chapter 2 that the connectionistic explanation of observed associations, whether the elements are regarded as stimuli, or responses, or both, is inadequate to deal with the flexibility observed in behavior. What, then, is the basis of association?

The answer I have proposed is essentially this: What we ordinarily call an association may reflect either a combination relation or a predictive relation. When B is said to be associated with A, it may mean that A produces the neural combination ab, or it may mean that A produces the neural events that predict B ($a:b$). Connectionism is quite adequate for explaining combinational associations, that is, for explaining the existence and development of gnostic-assemblies, intermodal gnostic-assemblies, and act-assemblies. However, connectionism is inadequate for explaining the development of contingency organizations underlying predictive associations. I do not deny that the acquisition of any new, long-lasting association requires the strengthening of some neural connections. What I emphasize is that the type of neural organizations that develop to represent predictive associations are complex interactional organizations involving much more than the transmission of impulses along fairly specific neurons from the neural representation of one event to the neural representation of another. The basis of combinational associations lies in relatively direct linkages between representations of the associated events, whereas the basis of predictive associations lies largely in linkages that produce complex interactions between neural structures other than those that directly represent the (predictively) associated events. The improvements with experience that occur in perception (identification of objects and events) and in the integration of unified acts (skilled directed action) largely reflect predictive associations produced by the strengthening of diverse connections underlying the development of contingency organizations.

Concerning the origin of the neural organizations required for proficient mental functioning or adaptiveness, it is obvious that individual experience plays a necessary part in their development. It is also obvious that neural substrates underlying such neural organizations are already rich in connections formed through species-typical maturation. What individual experience does is to *strengthen* selectively particular neural connections, thereby converting a pluripotent, diffusely connected neural substrate into specific functional organizations with particularized functions. It was explained in Chapter 2 that species-typical maturation and individual experience (or learning) are both parts of the same continuous process of neuronal growth and branching that are the basis of the development of all functional neural connections. Development is not an alternative to learning, as some present-day "cognitivists" appear to believe, but includes both maturation and learning. All this means that the suggestion that the development of new neural organizations is wholly or largely a matter of learning is as absurd as the suggestion that it is wholly or largely a matter of maturation. Since both are always implicated, it is equally absurd to ask whether any given behavioral capability is innate ("wired-in") *or* learned.

What can be a subject for meaningful discussion and investigation is the question of the range of variation in a given behavioral characteristic that may be produced by manipulating individual experience at a certain stage of maturation, or conversely, that may be produced by manipulating maturation at a certain stage without altering subsequent individual (learning) experience. Any behavioral characteristic that can be made to assume a wide range of arbitrary forms through differential learning experiences may then be said to be a more learnable characteristic than one that remains relatively fixed in spite of differential learning experiences given at the same stage of maturation. Note that the universality of any behavioral characteristic is no indication of the degree of its learnability, for the types of environmental encounters that result in development of a certain type of behavioral characteristic may be universally experienced. For example, objects of certain sizes, shapes, and colors, their spatial relations (up-down, right-left), and their predictive relations with other objects and events are a part of everyone's experience. Discussions in earlier chapters (mainly Chapters 5, 6, and 7) leave little doubt that the neural organizations underlying the perception of objects, the generation of meaning, and the operation of predictive rules remain highly modifiable throughout life, while the neural organizations involved in the generation of sensory patterns and the production of certain specific movements and primitive acts become relatively fixed early in life.

The Executive

Descartes regarded the soul as an executive that collates information, makes decisions, and wills action. This idea that there exists an inner, "real" self which somehow makes use of and controls the knowledge, motivation, and action possibilities represented in the brain, at once raises the problem of explaining the workings of such an inner homuncular executive—a brain within the brain—and leads to an explanatory infinite regress. Physiologists and neurologists around the turn of this century tried to get around this diffi-culty by suggesting that the "higher brain centers" are capable of achieving the type of neural integration required for intelligent actions. But by what processes do the higher centers achieve the higher levels of integration? The hierarchical model of brain function (see Chapter 2) provided no plausible answer to this, and the higher centers came to be treated essentially as a hierarchy of executives. This thinking is represented in the information-processing accounts of behavior, in which sensory input is said to be analyzed, coded, filtered, stored, retrieved, etc., by some "mini-executives" at different stages of neural processing. The same thinking is represented in neuro-behavioral accounts in which certain brain sites are identified as eating, copulation, aggression, or planning loci or centers. If soul, as an explanatory concept, was an embarrassment to the nineteenth century thinkers, so are the executive, mini-executives, and brain centers becoming an embarrassment today.

It is customary to think about an executive, locus, or center as an operator that performs certain operations on its input (or information), and thereby transforms (analyzes, codes, groups, etc.) the input in some way; this trans-formed information is then fed into another operator to undergo further transformation, and so on, until a response is produced. In neural terms, this means that an operator is something that acts on new information—neural input generated by environmental cues—and transforms it in some way; in other words the influence of a cue on behavior is determined by what the prevailing operator is and what kind of transformation it produces. I have suggested, essentially, that the prevailing operator at any moment is the momentary determining set, and it determines how the incoming information will be transformed. To call an operator a momentary determining set in itself is no different from calling it an executive. What makes the concept of momentary determining set more interesting is that, within the present frame-work, a plausible account may be given of how the momentary determining set is itself determined. The suggestion is that the momentary determining set is a collection of activated contingency organizations representing the critical predictive relations in the situation at that moment. The operator or the executive thus need not remain a magic black box, but the basis of its operations may now be studied. A way is thus provided to continue the search for causal processes beyond the executives of the day. The executive is not the final cause—it need not be the end of the explanatory line. It is important to keep on moving, trying to undo each executive as it seems to be getting reified.

Brain Function

By emphasizing integrative *centers* at various levels, the earlier connection-istic model of brain function (see Chapter 2) steered the study of brain func-tion mainly to the examination of the effects of lesions and stimulation of particular structures on specified types of behavior. Though important and necessary, this approach is clearly not sufficient for discovering how the brain produces adaptive actions. We need also to know what all the other structures not manipulated experimentally contribute to the specified behavior, and how the manipulated structures influence other types or aspects of behavior not under scrutiny in a given study.

The emergence of the interactional model of brain function, which attributes adaptive behavior to concurrent activity in several different reciprocally connected structures of the brain, and emphasizes multiple interactions between them, suggests a somewhat different approach for elucidating how the brain produces behavior. An implication of the interactional model is that there is no single site, center, or locus that is the basis of only one type of *behavior* (eating, copulating, choosing, planning, etc.). Nor do the functions of any particular part of the brain correspond to any exclusive category of mental or behavioral function (e.g., attention, motivation, perception, etc.). Different forms of adaptive behavior are produced by a common set of brain processes, and each of these processes is the outcome of neural interactions among several parts of the brain. There is no one center or pontifical point that itself produces any particular behavioral process, let alone any particular type of behavior. The problem of explaining any given type of behavior thus requires, *not* identifying particular controlling centers, but giving a plausible account of what concurrent sequences of neural interactions and transformations lead to its production. A potentially fruitful approach to the study of brain function would therefore seem to lie in the simultaneous examination of neural activity in neuronal groups in diverse parts of the brain while an awake animal is performing particular adaptive responses under controlled conditions. Though technically difficult, this approach is potentially capable of yielding a spatiotemporally differentiated picture of neural events in relation to the performance of different types of adaptive responses.

Consciousness

In phylogenesis, the capacity for intelligent actions and the capacity for conscious awareness appear to have shown parallel courses. Noting this, post-Darwinian thinkers postulated "consciousness" as a special biological function concerned with producing intelligent behavior, and sought to determine the stage in phylogenesis where the consciousness function might have emerged. Because conscious awareness in other animals (including other human beings) cannot be directly observed, the capacity of associative learning was assumed to be the criterion of the existence of consciousness. This assumption served as a useful rationale for comparing the learning ability of species. But since there was no independent proof of the validity of this assumption, nor any unambiguous methods of differentiating levels of the capacity for associative learning, there was no sound basis for deciding where in phylogenesis consciousness emerged or for saying what consciousness is.

It is important to distinguish between the fact of conscious awareness (or subjective experience) and the postulate of consciousness as a special, higher-level function. Though the two propositions are separate and must be examined independently, it is undeniable that in everyday observation conscious awareness (a perception, emotion, choice, intention, etc.) seems to accompany our more intelligent actions. It is probable that this common observation formed the basis of the postulate that consciousness is a special function, with the implication that conscious awareness plays a causal role in the production of intelligent actions.

There is little to support this hypothesis. First, important aspects of behavior may be determined by certain stimuli, without any awareness of them. For example, correct identifying responses may be made without any awareness (reported experience) of the stimuli being identified (see Chapter 5). Second, what may be regarded as a relevant conscious awareness may occur without influencing response. For example, memory images that are experienced and reported may have no influence on recall performance. Third, fairly complex actions become "automatic," so that a subject can perform them while thinking about (having conscious awareness of) something else (see Chapter 10). Fourth, the emergence of solutions in problem-solving indicates that it is the end products of thinking that appear in conscious awareness; the thinking processes themselves, which might be presumed to require the consciousness function, are for the most part carried on unconsciously. This is also true in those reaction-time and word-association experiments that require particular thinking operations to be performed before responding. Fifth, a distinct emotional experience can be shown to emerge considerably after some adjustive responses and (unconscious) intellectual assessment of the situation have already taken place. Clearly, a distinctive conscious awareness of some particular entity cannot be said to be a necessary condition for the occurrence of a given type of intelligent action. It appears more likely that distinctive awareness (perceptions, images, emotions, etc.) are an optional accompaniment of the processes that produce adaptive responses rather than an essential causal link in the chain of those processes.

Concerning the basis of conscious awareness or subjective experience, the main thing to note is that awareness is always of something, an object, action, or internal visceral state. In other words, an awareness is either a percept, however vague or specific, involving current sensory inflow, or an image generated in the absence of appropriate sensory inflow. Thus, in the present scheme, an awareness must involve the excitation of certain gnostic-assemblies.

This minimal condition is clearly not sufficient, for awareness may be absent even when the excitation of gnostic-assemblies has contributed to an appropriate identifying response. One suggestion is that awareness of something is determined by a "selective input" to an action system that involves that entity. If this were true, a subject should always be aware of the stimulus in relation to which he is acting at the moment, and be unaware of stimuli in relation to which he is not acting. But this is not the case, for a proficient performer can and usually does act in relation to certain stimuli while thinking about other things. Another possibility is that awareness is generated when several interrelated gnostic-assemblies are concurrently activated, either through intermodal connections or through contingency organizations. Elucidation of the basis of conscious awareness would require much more detailed studies of the relation between moment-to-moment changes in awareness and the course of simultaneous neural and behavioral events. Such studies of awareness in situations in which states of consciousness can be manipulated (e.g., hypnosis, split-brain patients) may prove to be enlightening.

Conscious experience remains an enigma, as do many aspects of intelligent behavior. To explain them in a coherent and satisfactory scheme that makes sense both behaviorally and neurally is an enduring challenge. It will probably continue to engage the best efforts of generations of scientists.

References

Albert, M., & Bignami, G. Effects of frontal, median cortical and caudate lesions on two-way avoidance learning by rats. *Physiology and Behavior*, 1968, **3**, 141–147.

Allport, G. W., & Postman, L. *The psychology of rumour*. New York: Henry Holt, 1947.

Anderson, A. C. Time discrimination in the white rat. *Journal of Comparative Psychology*, 1932, **13**, 27–55.

Andrew, R. J. Normal and irrelevant toilet behaviour in Emberize spp. *British Journal of Animal Behaviour*, 1956, **4**, 85–91.

Archer, E. J. Concept identification as a function of obviousness of relevant and irrelevant information. *Journal of Experimental Psychology*, 1962, **63**, 616–620.

Asanuma, H., & Rosen, I. Functional role of afferent inputs in the monkey motor cortex. *Brain Research*, 1972, **40**, 3–5.

Asanuma, H., Stoney, S. D., Jr., & Abzug, C. Relationship between afferent input and motor outflow in cat motor-sensory cortex. *Journal of Neurophysiology*, 1968, **31**, 670–681.

Asratyan, E. A. The initiation and localization of cortical inhibition in the conditioned reflex arc. *Annals of the New York Academy of Sciences*, 1961, **92** (art. 3), 1141–1159.

Asratyan, E. A. Conditional reflex theory and motivational behavior. *Acta Neurobiologia Experimentalis*, 1974, **34**, 15–31.

Baddeley, A. D. Effects of acoustic and semantic similarity on short-term paired-associate learning. *British Journal of Psychology*, 1970, **61**, 335–343.

Baddeley, A. D., & Patterson, K. The relation between long-term and short-term memory. *British Medical Bulletin*, 1971, **27**, 237–242.

Baddeley, A. D., & Warrington, E. K. Memory coding and amnesia. *Neuropsychologia*, 1973, **11**, 159–165.

Bahrick, H. P. Measurement of memory by prompted recall. *Journal of Experimental Psychology*, 1969, **79**, 213–219.

Bandura, A. Social learning through imitation. In M. R. Jones (Ed.), *Nebraska symposium on motivation*. Lincoln, Nebr.: University of Nebraska Press, 1962. Pp. 211–269.

Bandura, A., & Huston, A. C. Identification as a process of incidental learning. *Journal of Abnormal and Social Psychology*, 1961, **63**, 311–318.

Bandura, A., & Walters, R. H. *Social learning and personality development*. New York: Holt, Rinehart, & Winston, 1963.

Barlow, H. B. Single units and sensation: A neuron doctrine for perceptual psychology. *Perception*, 1972, **1**, 371–394.

Barlow, H. B., Blakemore, C., & Pettigrew, J. D. The neural mechanism of binocular depth discrimination. *Journal of Physiology*, 1967, **193**, 327–342.

Baron, J., & Thurston, I. An analysis of the word-superiority effect. *Cognitive Psychology*, 1973, **4**, 207–288.

Bartlett, F. C. *Remembering: A study in experimental and social psychology*. Cambridge: Cambridge University Press, 1932.

Bartlett, F. C. *Thinking: An experimental and social study*. New York: Basic Books, 1958.

Basmajian, J. V. Control and training of individual motor units. *Science*, 1963, **141**, 440–441.

Bateson, P. P. G. Relation between conspicuousness of stimuli and their effectiveness in the imprinting situation. *Journal of Comparative and Physiological Psychology*, 1964, **58**, 407–411.

Bateson, P. P. G. Preferences for familiarity and novelty: A model for the simultaneous development of both. *Journal of Theoretical Biology*, 1973, **41**, 249–259.

Baum, M. Extinction of avoidance through response prevention (flooding). *Psychological Bulletin*, 1970, **74**, 276–284.

Baum, M., & Bindra, D. Conditioned incentive motivation, spontaneous behaviour, and inhibition of delay. *Canadian Journal of Psychology*, 1968, **22**, 323–335.

Baum, M., Leclerc, R., & St-Laurent, J. Rewarding vs. aversive intracranial stimulation administered during flooding (response prevention) in rats. *Psychological Reports*, 1973, **32**, 551–558.

Baum, W. M., & Rachlin, H. C. Choice as time allocation. *Journal of the Experimental Analysis of Behavior*, 1969, **12**, 861–874.

Beach, F. A. Analysis of the stimuli adequate to elicit mating behavior in the sexually inexperienced male rat. *Journal of Comparative Psychology*, 1942, **33**, 163–207.

Beninger, R. J., & Kendall, S. B. Behavioral contrasts in rats with different reinforcers and different response tendencies. *Journal of the Experimental Analysis of Behavior*, 1975, **24**, 267–280.

Beninger, R. J., Kendall, S. B., & Vanderwolf, C. H. The ability of rats to discriminate their own behaviours. *Canadian Journal of Psychology*, 1974, **28**, 79–91.

Bergquist, E. H. Output pathways of hypothalamic mechanisms for sexual, aggressive, and other motivated behaviors in opossum. *Journal of Comparative and Physiological Psychology*, 1970, **70**, 389–398.

Berlyne, D. E. *Conflict, arousal, and curiosity*. New York: McGraw-Hill, 1960.

Berlyne, D. E., McDonnell, P., Nicki, R. M., & Parham, L. C. C. Effects of auditory pitch and complexity on EEG desynchronization and on verbally expressed judgments. *Canadian Journal of Psychology*, 1967, **21**, 346–367.

Bevan, W., Hardesty, D. L., & Avant, L. L. Response latency with constant and variable interval schedules. *Perceptual and Motor Skills*, 1965, **20**, 969–972.

Bexton, W. H., Heron, W., & Scott, T. H. Effects of decreased variation in the sensory environment. *Canadian Journal of Psychology*, 1954, **8**, 70–76.

Bilodeau, E. A. Experimental interference with primary associates and their subsequent recovery with rest. *Journal of Experimental Psychology*, 1967, **73**, 328–332.

Bindra, D. The nature of motivation for hoarding food. *Journal of Comparative and Physiological Psychology*, 1948, **41**, 211–218. (*a*)

Bindra, D. What makes rats hoard? *Journal of Comparative and Physiological Psychology*, 1948, **41**, 397–402. (*b*)

Bindra, D. Organization in emotional and motivated behaviour. *Canadian Journal of Psychology*, 1955, **9**, 161–167.

Bindra, D. *Motivation, a systematic reinterpretation*. New York: Ronald, 1959.

Bindra, D. Components of general activity and the analysis of behavior. *Psychological Review*, 1961, **68**, 205–215.

Bindra, D. Neuropsychological interpretation of the effects of drive and incentive-motivation on general activity and instrumental behavior. *Psychological Review*, 1968, **75**, 1–22. (*a*)

Bindra, D. Drive, incentive-motivation and reinforcement. *Neurosciences Research Program Bulletin*, 1968, **6**, 67–72. (*b*)

Bindra, D. The interrelated mechanisms of reinforcement and motivation, and the nature of their influence on response. In W. J. Arnold & D. Levine (Eds.), *Nebraska symposium on motivation*. Lincoln, Nebr.: University of Nebraska Press, 1969. (*a*) Pp. 1–33.

Bindra, D. A unified interpretation of emotion and motivation. *Annals of the New York Academy of Sciences*, 1969, **159**, 1071–1083. (*b*)

Bindra, D. The problem of subjective experience: Puzzlement on reading R. W. Sperry's "A modified concept of consciousness." *Psychological Review*, 1970, **77**, 581–584.

Bindra, D. A motivational view of learning, performance, and behavior modification. *Psychological Review*, 1974, **81**, 199–213.

Bindra, D., & Campbell, J. F. Motivational effects of rewarding intracranial stimulation. *Nature*, 1967, **215**, 375–376.

Bindra, D., Donderi, D. C., & Nishisato, S. Decision latencies of "same" and "different" judgments. *Perception & Psychophysics*, 1968, **3**, 121–130.

Bindra, D., & Palfai, T. Nature of positive and negative incentive-motivational effects on general activity. *Journal of Comparative and Physiological Psychology,* 1967, **63**, 288–297.

Bindra, D., & Spinner, N. Response to different degrees of novelty: The incidence of various activities. *Journal of the Experimental Analysis of Behavior,* 1958, **1**, 341–350.

Bindra, D., & Waksberg, H. Methods and terminology in studies of time estimation. *Psychological Bulletin,* 1956, **53**, 155–159.

Bindra, D., Williams, J. A., & Wise, J. S. Judgments of sameness and difference: Experiments on decision time. *Science,* 1965, **150**, 1625–1627.

Bishop, P. O. Beginning of form vision and binocular depth discrimination in cortex. In F. O. Schmitt (Ed.), *The neurosciences.* Second Study Program. New York: Rockefeller University Press, 1970. Pp. 471–485.

Black, A. H. Autonomic aversive conditioning in infrahuman subjects. In F. R. Brush (Ed.), *Aversive conditioning and learning.* New York: Academic Press, 1971. Pp. 3–104.

Black, A. H. Operant autonomic conditioning: The analysis of response mechanisms. In P. A. Obrist, A. H. Black, J. Brener, & L. V. DiCara (Eds.), *Cardiovascular psychophysiology: Current issues in response mechanisms, biofeedback and methodology.* Chicago: Aldine, 1974. Pp. 229–250.

Black, A. H., & De Toledo, L. The relationship among classically conditioned responses: Heart rate and skeletal behavior. In A. H. Black and W. F. Prokasy (Eds.), *Classical conditioning II: Current theory and research.* New York: Appleton-Century-Crofts, 1972. Pp. 290–311.

Black, R. W. Incentive motivation and the parameters of reward in instrumental conditioning. In W. J. Arnold and D. Levine (Eds.), *Nebraska symposium on motivation: 1969.* Lincoln Nebr.: University of Nebraska Press, 1969. Pp. 85–141.

Blackman, R. The effect of the orienting reaction on disjunctive reaction time. *Psychonomic Science,* 1966, **4**, 411–412.

Blakemore, C. The representation of three-dimensional visual space in the cat's striate cortex. *Journal of Physiology* (London), 1970, **209**, 155–178.

Blakemore, C., & Cooper, G. F. Development of the brain depends on the visual environment. *Nature,* 1970, **228**, 477–478.

Blanchard, R. J., & Blanchard, D. C. Crouching as an index of fear. *Journal of Comparative and Physiological Psychology,* 1969, **67**, 370–375.

Bloomfield, T. M. Behavioural contrast and the peak shift. In R. M. Gilbert and N. S. Sutherland (Eds.), *Animal discrimination learning.* London: Academic Press, 1969. Pp. 215–241.

Blough, D. S. Experiments in animal psychophysics. *Scientific American,* 1961, **205**, 113–122.

Bolles, R. C. Species-specific defense reactions and avoidance learning. *Psychological Review,* 1970, **77**, 32–48.

Bolles, R. C. Reinforcement, expectancy, and learning. *Psychological Review*, 1972, **79**, 394–409.

Bolles, R. C., & Grossen, N. E. Function of the CS in shuttle-box avoidance learning by rats. *Journal of Comparative and Physiological Psychology*, 1970, **70**, 165–169.

Bolles, R. C., & Woods, P. J. The ontogeny of behaviour in the albino rat. *Animal Behaviour*, 1964, **12**, 427–441.

Bond, E. K. Perception of form by the human infant. *Psychological Bulletin*, 1972, **77**, 225–245.

Bonin, G. von. The frontal lobe of primates: Cytoarchitectural studies. *Proceedings of the Association for Research in Nervous and Mental Disease*, 1948, **27**, 67–83.

Boring, E. G. The perception of objects. *American Journal of Physics*, 1946, **14**, 99–107.

Bornstein, M. H. Qualities of color vision in infancy. *Journal of Experimental Child Psychology*, 1975, in press.

Bourne, L. E., Jr. *Human conceptual behavior*. Boston: Allyn & Bacon, 1966.

Bourne, L. E., Jr. Knowing and using concepts. *Psychological Review*, 1970, **77**, 546–556.

Breland, K., & Breland, M. The misbehavior of organisms. *American Psychologist*, 1961, **16**, 681–684.

Breland, K., & Breland, M. *Animal behavior*. New York: Macmillan, 1966.

Bridgeman, B. Visual receptive fields sensitive to absolute and relative motion during tracking. *Science*, 1972, **178**, 1106–1108.

Bridges, K. M. B. Emotional development in early infancy. *Child Development*, 1932, **3**, 324–341.

Brinkman, J., & Kuypers, H. G. J. M. Splitbrain monkeys: Cerebral control of ipsilateral and contralateral arm, hand, and finger movements. *Science*, 1972, **176**, 536–539.

Broadbent, D. E. *Perception and communication*. London: Pergamon, 1958.

Broadbent, D. E. *Decisions and stress*. London: Academic Press, 1971.

Broadbent, D. E., & Gregory, M. Donder's B- and C-reactions and S-R compatibility. *Journal of Experimental Psychology*, 1962, **63**, 575–578.

Broadbent, D. E. *In defence of empirical psychology*. London: Methuen & Co. Ltd., 1973.

Brodmann, K. *Vergleichende Lokalisationslehre der Grosshirnrinde in ihren Prinzipien dargestellt auf Grund des Zellenbaues*. Leipzig: Barth, 1909.

Brogden, W. J. Sensory pre-conditioning of human subjects. *Journal of Experimental Psychology*, 1947, **37**, 527–539.

Brown, A. E., & Hopkins, H. K. Interaction of the auditory and visual sensory modalities. *Journal of the Acoustical Society of America*, 1967, **41**, 1–6.

Brown, P. L., & Jenkins, H. M. Auto-shaping of the pigeon's key-peck. *Journal of the Experimental Analysis of Behavior*, 1968, **11**, 1–8.

Brown, R. *Words and things.* New York: Free Press, 1958.

Bruner, J. On perceptual readiness. *Psychological Review*, 1957, **64**, 123–152.

Bruner, J., & Kehoe, J. Long-term decrements in the efficacy of synaptic transmission in molluscs and crustaceans. In G. Horn & R. A. Hinde (Eds.), *Short-term changes in neural activity and behaviour.* Cambridge: Cambridge University Press, 1970. Pp. 323–359.

Bryan, W. L., & Harter, N. Studies in the physiology and psychology of the telegraphic language. *Psychological Review*, 1897, **4**, 27–53.

Bryant, P. E. Discrimination of mirror images by young children. *Journal of Comparative and Physiological Psychology*, 1973, **82**, 415–425.

Bryant, P. E., Jones, P., Claxton, V., & Perkins, G. M. Recognition of shapes across modalities by infants. *Nature*, 1972, **240**, 303–304.

Bryden, M. P. The role of post-exposural eye movements in tachistoscopic perception. *Canadian Journal of Psychology*, 1961, **15**, 220–225.

Bryden, M. P. A model for the sequential organization of behaviour. *Canadian Journal of Psychology*, 1967, **21**, 37–56.

Bugelski, B. R. The definition of the image. In S. J. Segal (Ed.), *Imagery: Current cognitive approaches.* New York: Academic Press, 1971. Pp. 49–68.

Burke, R. E. Control systems operating on spinal reflex mechanisms. *Neurosciences Research Program Bulletin*, 1971, **9**, 60–85.

Burnham, W. H. Retroactive amnesia: Illustrative cases and tentative explanation. *American Journal of Psychology*, 1903, **14**, 118–132.

Burns, B. D. *The uncertain nervous system.* London: Edward Arnold, 1968.

Butter, C. M. Habituation of responses to novel stimuli in monkeys with selective frontal lesions. *Science*, 1964, **144**, 313–315.

Butter, C. M. Perseveration in extinction and in discrimination reversal tasks following selective frontal ablations in Macaca mulatta. *Physiology and Behavior*, 1969, **4**, 163–171.

Bykov, K. M. *The cerebral cortex and the internal organs.* Translated by W. H. Gantt. New York: Chemical Publishing Company, 1957.

Caggiula, A. R. Analysis of the copulation-reward properties of posterior hypothalamic stimulation in male rats. *Journal of Comparative and Physiological Psychology*, 1970, **70**, 399–412.

Campbell, B. A., Lytle, L. D., & Fibiger, H. C. Ontogeny of adrenergic arousal and cholinergic inhibitory mechanisms in the rat. *Science*, 1969, **166**, 635–637.

Campbell, B. A., Misanin, J. R., White, B. C., & Lytle, L. D. Species differences in ontogeny of memory: Indirect support for neural maturation as a determinant of forgetting. *Journal of Comparative and Physiological Psychology*, 1974, **87**, 193–202.

Campbell, B. A., & Spear, N. E. Ontogeny of memory. *Psychological Review*, 1972, **79**, 215–236.

Campbell, J. F., Bindra, D., Krebs, H., & Ferenchak, R. P. Responses of single units of the hypothalamic ventromedial nucleus to environmental stimuli. *Physiology and Behavior*, 1969, **4**, 183–187.

Capaldi, E. J. Partial reinforcement: A hypothesis of sequential effects. *Psychological Review*, 1966, **73**, 459–477.

Carlsöö, S., & Edfeldt, A. W. Attempts at muscle control with visual and auditory impulses as auxiliary stimuli. *Scandinavian Journal of Psychology*, 1963, **4**, 231–235.

Carter, D. E., & Eckerman, D. A. Symbolic matching by pigeons: Rate of learning complex discriminations predicted from simple discriminations. *Science*, 1975, **187**, 662–664.

Castellucci, V., Pinsker, H., Kupfermann, I., & Kandel, E. R. Neuronal mechanisms of habituation and dishabituation of the gill-withdrawal reflex in aplysia. Science, 1970, **167**, 1745–1748.

Chesler, P. Maternal influence in learning by observation in kittens. *Science*, 1969, **166**, 901–903.

Chomsky, N. *Language and mind*. New York: Harcourt, Brace & World, 1968.

Chorover, S. L., & Schiller, P. H. Reexamination of prolonged retrograde amnesia in one-trial learning. *Journal of Comparative and Physiological Psychology*, 1966, **61**, 34–41.

Chow, K. L. Further studies on selective ablation of associative cortex in relation to visually mediated behavior. *Journal of Comparative and Physiological Psychology*, 1952, **45**, 109–118. (*a*)

Chow, K. L. Conditions influencing the recovery of visual discriminative habits in monkeys following temporal neocortical ablations. *Journal of Comparative and Physiological Psychology*, 1952, **45**, 430–437. (*b*)

Chow, K. L. Effects of ablations. In G. C. Quarton, T. Melnechuk, & F. O. Schmitt (Eds.), *The neurosciences*. New York: Rockefeller University Press, 1967. Pp. 705–713.

Chow, K. L., & Leiman, A. L. The structural and functional organization of the neocortex. *Neurosciences Research Program Bulletin*, 1970, **8**, 153–220.

Church, R. M. Transmission of learned behavior between rats. *Journal of Abnormal and Social Psychology*, 1957, **54**, 163–165.

Chute, D. L., & Wright, D. C. Retrograde state dependent learning. *Science*, 1973, **180**, 878–880.

Clark, J. W., & Miller, S. B. The development of rapid running in T-mazes in the absence of obvious rewards. *Psychonomic Science*, 1966, **4**, 127–128.

Cofer, C. N., & Appley, H. M. *Motivation: Theory and research*. New York: Wiley. 1964.

Cohen, G. Pattern recognition: Differences between matching patterns to patterns and matching descriptions to patterns. *Journal of Experimental Psychology*, 1969, **82**, 427–434. (*a*)

Cohen, G. The effect of codability of the stimulus on recognition reaction times. *British Journal of Psychology*, 1969, **60**, 25–29. (*b*)

Cohen-Salmon, C. Influence d'une discrimination de parcours sur le transport de la nourriture chez le rat. *L'Année Psychologique*, 1971, **71**, 381–391.

Cohn, R., Jakniunas, A., & Taub, E. Summated cortical evoked response testing in the deafferented primate. *Science*, 1972, **178**, 1113–1115.

Colonnier, M. L. The structural design of the neocortex. In J. C. Eccles (Ed.), *Brain and conscious experience*. New York: Springer-Verlag, 1966. Pp. 1–23.

Condon, W. S., & Sander, L. W. Neonate movement is synchronized with adult speech: Interactional participation and language acquisition. *Science*, 1974, **183**, 99–101.

Conrad, R. Acoustic confusions in immediate memory. *British Journal of Psychology*, 1964, **55**, 75–84.

Cooper, R. M. The control of eye fixation by the meaning of spoken language: A new methodology for the real-time investigation of speech perception, memory, and language processing. *Cognitive Psychology*, 1974, **6**, 84–107.

Corballis, M. C. Rehearsal and decay in immediate recall of visually and aurally presented items. *Canadian Journal of Psychology*, 1966, **20**, 43–51.

Corballis, M. C., & Beale, I. L. Monocular discrimination of mirror-image obliques by pigeons: Evidence for lateralized stimulus control. *Animal Behaviour*, 1970, **18**, 563–566.

Corballis, M. C., & Beale, I. L. *The psychology of left and right*. New York: Lawrence Erlbaum & Associates, 1976, in press.

Cowan, W. M. Axodendritic synapses in the hippocampus. In M. V. Edds, Jr., D. S. Barkley, and D. M. Fambrough (Eds.), Genesis of neuronal patterns. *Neurosciences Research Program Bulletin*, 1972, **10**, 268–271.

Cowey, A., & Dewson, J. H. Effects of unilateral ablation of superior temporal cortex on auditory sequence discrimination in macaca mulatta. *Neuropsychologia*, 1972, **10**, 279–289.

Cowey, A., & Weiskrantz, L. Varying spatial separation of cues, response, and reward in visual discrimination learning in monkeys. *Journal of Comparative and Physiological Psychology*, 1968, **66**, 220–224.

Craik, F. I. M. Two components in free recall. *Journal of Verbal Learning and Verbal Behavior*, 1968, **7**, 996–1004.

Craik, F. I. M., & Lockhart, R. S. Levels of processing: A framework for memory research. *Journal of Verbal Learning and Verbal Behavior*, 1972, **11**, 671–684.

Cravens, R. W., & Renner, K. E. Conditioned appetitive drive states: Empirical evidence and theoretical status. *Psychological Bulletin*, 1970, **73**, 212–220.

Critchley, M. *The parietal lobes*. Baltimore: Williams & Wilkins, 1953.

D'Amato, M. R. Derived motives. *Annual Review of Psychology*, 1974, **25**, 83–106.

Darby, C. L., & Riopelle, A. J. Observational learning in the Rhesus monkey. *Journal of Comparative and Physiological Psychology*, 1959, **52**, 94–98.

Darwin, C. *On the origin of species.* London: Murray, 1859.

Davenport, R. K., & Rogers, C. M. Intermodal equivalence of stimuli in apes. *Science,* 1970, **168,** 279–280.

Davidson, P. W. Haptic judgments of curvature by blind and sighted humans. *Journal of Experimental Psychology,* 1972, **93,** 43–55.

DeFeudis, P. A. The role of sensory factors in the organization of instrumental response. Unpublished master's thesis, McGill University, 1968.

De Groot, A. D. Perception and memory versus thought: Some old ideas and recent findings. In B. Kleinmuntz (Ed.), *Problem solving: Research, methods, and theory.* New York: Wiley, 1966.

Delgado, J. M. R. Free behavior and brain stimulation. *International Review of Neurobiology,* 1964, **6,** 349–449.

Delgado, J. M. R. Sequential behavior induced repeatedly by stimulation of the red nucleus in free monkeys. *Science,* 1965, **148,** 1361–1363.

Dement, W. C. An essay on dreams: The role of physiology in understanding their nature. In F. Barron, W. C. Dement, W. Edwards, H. Lindman, L. D. Phillips, J. Olds, & M. Olds (Eds.), *New directions in psychology II.* New York: Holt, Rinehart and Winston, Inc., 1965. Pp. 135–211.

Denney, D., & Adorjani, C. Orientation specificity of visual cortical neurons after head tilt. *Experimental Brain Research,* 1972, **14,** 312–317.

Deutsch, D. Tones and numbers: Specificity of interference in immediate memory. *Science,* 1970, **168,** 1604–1605.

Deutsch, J. A. *The structural basis of behavior.* Chicago: University of Chicago Press, 1960.

Deutsch, R. Conditioned hypoglycemia: A mechanism for saccharin-induced sensitivity to insulin in the rat. *Journal of Comparative and Physiological Psychology,* 1974, **86,** 350–358.

Dewson, J. H., III, & Cowey, A. Discrimination of auditory sequences by monkeys. *Nature,* 1969, **222,** 695–697.

Diamond, I. T., & Hall, W. C. Evolution of neocortex. *Science,* 1969, **164,** 251–262.

Dillon, P. J. Stimulus versus response decisions as determinants of the relative frequency effect in disjunctive reaction-time performance. *Journal of Experimental Psychology,* 1966, **71,** 321–330.

Divac, I. Neostriatum and functions of prefrontal cortex. *Acta Neurobiologia Experimentalis,* 1972, **32,** 461–477.

Dobzhansky, T. G. *Mankind evolving.* New Haven, Conn.: Yale University Press, 1962.

Dodwell, P. C. On perceptual clarity. *Psychological Review,* 1971, **78,** 275–289.

Dodwell, P. C., & Bessant, D. E. Learning without swimming in a water maze. *Journal of Comparative and Physiological Psychology,* 1960, **53,** 422–425.

Dolinsky, R. Clustering and free recall with alternative organizational cues. *Journal of Experimental Psychology,* 1972, **95,** 159–163.

Dollard, J., & Miller, N. E. *Personality and psychotherapy*. New York: McGraw-Hill, 1950.

Donderi, D. C. Visual disappearances caused by form similarity. *Science*, 1966, **152**, 99–100.

Donderi, D. C., & Kane, E. Perceptual learning produced by common responses to different stimuli. *Canadian Journal of Psychology*, 1965, **19**, 15–30.

Doob, L. W. *Patterning of time*. New Haven, Conn.: Yale University Press, 1971.

Dooling, D. J. Some context effects in the speeded comprehension of sentences. *Journal of Experimental Psychology*, 1972, **93**, 56–62.

Doty, R. W., & Boxma, J. F. An electromyographic analysis of reflex deglutition. *Journal of Neurophysiology*, 1956, **19**, 44–60.

Douglas, R. J. The hippocampus and behavior. *Psychological Bulletin*, 1967, **67**, 416–442.

Douglas, R. J. Pavlovian conditioning and the brain. In R. A. Boakes and M. S. Halliday (Eds.), *Inhibition and learning*. New York: Academic Press, 1972. Pp. 529–553.

Douglas, V. I, Stop, look and listen: The problem of sustained attention and impulse control in hyperactive and normal children. *Canadian Journal of Behavioural Science*, 1972, **4**, 259–282.

Douglass, E., & Richardson, J. C. Aphasia in a congenital deaf-mute. *Brain*, 1959, **82**, 68–80.

Drewe, E. A., Ettlinger, G., Milner, A. D., & Passingham, R. E. A comparative review of the results of neuropsychological research on man and monkey. *Cortex*, 1970, **6**, 129–163.

Duncker, K. On problem-solving. *Psychological Monographs*, 1945, **58** (5, Whole No. 270).

Dunham, P. J. Contrasted conditions of reinforcement: A selective critique. *Psychological Bulletin*, 1968, **69**, 295–315.

Edds, M. V., Jr., Barkley, D. S., & Fambrough, D. M. Genesis of neuronal patterns. *Neurosciences Research Program Bulletin*, 1972, **10**, 254–367.

Edwards, W. The theory of decision making. *Psychological Bulletin*, 1954, **51**, 380–417.

Edwards, W., Lindman, H., & Phillips, L. D. Emerging technologies for making decisions. In F. Barron, W. C. Dement, W. Edwards, H. Lindman, L. D. Philipps, J. Olds, & M. Olds (Eds.), *New directions in psychology II*. New York: Holt, Rinehart, & Winston, 1965. Pp. 259–325.

Efron, R. The minimum duration of perception. *Neuropsychologia*, 1970, **8**, 57–63. (*a*)

Efron, R. The relationship between the duration of a stimulus and the duration of perception. *Neuropsychologia*, 1970, **8**, 37–55. (*b*)

Efstathiou, A., Bauer, J., Greene, M., & Held, R. Altered reaching following adaptation to optical displacement of the hand. *Journal of Experimental Psychology*, 1967, **73**, 113–120.

Ellison, G. D. Appetitive behavior in rats after circumsection of the hypothalamus. *Physiology and Behavior*, 1968, **3**, 221–226.

Ellison, G. D., & Konorski, J. Salivation and instrumental responding to an instrumental CS pretrained using the classical conditioning paradigm. *Acta Biologiae Experimentalis*, 1966, **26**, 159–165.

Ellison, G. D., Sorenson, C. A., & Jacobs, B. L. Two feeding syndromes following surgical isolation of the hypothalamus in rats. *Journal of Comparative and Physiological Psychology*, 1970, **70**, 173–188.

Ellson, D. G. Hallucinations produced by sensory conditioning. *Journal of Experimental Psychology*, **1941**, **28**, 1–20.

Entus, A., & Bindra, D. Common features of the "repetition" and "same-different" effects in reaction time experiments. *Perception and Psychophysics*, 1970, **7**, 143–148.

Epstein, A. N. The lateral hypothalamic syndrome: Its implications for the physiological psychology of hunger and thirst. In E. Stellar and J. M. Sprague (Eds.), *Progress in Physiological psychology*. New York: Academic Press, 1971. Pp. 263–317.

Estes, W. K. Reinforcement in human learning. In J. Tapp (Ed.), *Reinforcement and behavior*. New York: Academic Press, 1969. Pp. 63–94.

Estes, W. K. *Learning theory and mental development*. New York: Academic Press, 1970.

Estes, W. K. Reinforcement in human behavior. *American Scientist*, 1972, **60**, 723–729.

Estes, W. K. The locus of inferential and perceptual processes in letter identification. *Journal of Experimental Psychology: General*, 1975, **1**, 122–145.

Evarts, E. D. Feedback and corollary discharge: A merging of concepts. *Neurosciences Research Program Bulletin*, 1971, **9**, 86–112.

Falk, J. L. Studies on schedule-induced polydipsia. In M. J. Wayner (Ed.), *Thirst: Proceedings of the First international symposium on thirst in the regulation of body water*. New York: Pergamon, 1964. Pp. 95–116.

Falk, J. L. The nature and determinants of adjunctive behavior. *Physiology and Behavior*, 1971, **6**, 577–588.

Falkenberg, P. R. Recall improves in short-term memory the more recall context resembles learning context. *Journal of Experimental Psychology*, 1972, **95**, 39–47.

Fantino, E., & Duncan B. Some effects of interreinforcement time upon choice. *Journal of the Experimental Analysis of Behavior*, 1972, **17**, 3–14.

Fantz, R. L. Pattern vision in newborn infants. *Science*, 1963, **140**, 296–297.

Favreau, O. Proactive decremental effects on response speed in a continuous DRT task. *Psychonomic Science*, 1964, **1**, 319–320.

Fehrer, E., & Biederman, I. A comparison of reaction time and verbal report in the detection of masked stimuli. *Journal of Experimental Psychology*, 1962, **64**, 126–130.

Fehrer, E., & Raab, D. Reaction time to stimuli masked by metacontrast. *Journal of Experimental Psychology*, 1962, **63**, 143–147.

Feigley, D. A., Parsons, P. J., Hamilton, L. W., & Spear, N. E. Development of habituation to novel environments in the rat. *Journal of Comparative and Physiological Psychology*, 1972, **79**, 443–452.

Ferguson, G. On learning and human ability. *Canadian Journal of Psychology*, 1954, **8**, 95–112.

Ferster, C. B. Withdrawal of positive reinforcement as punishment. *Science*, 1957, **126**, 509.

Ferster, C. B., & Skinner, B. F. *Schedules of reinforcement*. New York: Appleton-Century-Crofts, 1957.

Festinger, L., & Easton, A. M. Inferences about the efferent system based on a perceptual illusion produced by eye movements. *Psychological Review*, 1974, **81**, 44–58.

Festinger, L. Ono, H., Burnham, C. A., & Bamber, D. Efference and the conscious experience of perception. *Journal of Experimental Psychology Monograph*, 1967, **74** (4, Whole No. 637). Pp. 1–36.

Flynn, J. P. The neural basis of aggresions in cats. In D. C. Glass (Ed.), *Neurophysiology and emotion*. New York: Rockefeller University Press, 1967. Pp. 40–60.

Fourcin, A. J. Language development in the absence of expressive speech. In E. H. Lenneberg and E. Lenneberg (Eds.), *Foundations of language development: A multidisciplinary approach*. New York: Unipub, 1974.

Fouts, R. S. Acquisition and testing of gestural signs in four young chimpanzees. *Science*, 1973, **180**, 978–980.

Fraisse, P. *The psychology of time*. New York: Harper & Row, 1963.

Frampton, G. G., Milner, A. D., & Ettlinger, G. Cross-modal transfer between vision and touch of go, no-go discrimination learning in the monkey. *Neuropsychologia*, 1973, **11**, 231–233.

Freeman, R. D., & Thibos, L. N. Electrophysiological evidence that abnormal early visual experience can modify the human brain. *Science*, 1973, **180**, 876–878.

Freides, D., & Hayden, S. P. Monocular testing: A methodological note on eidetic imagery. *Perceptual and Motor Skills*, 1966, **23**, 88.

French, G. M., & Harlow, H. F. Locomotor reaction decrement in normal and brain-damaged rhesus monkeys. *Journal of Comparative and Physiological Psychology*, 1955, **48**, 496–501.

Freud, S. *A general introduction to psychoanalysis*. Translated by J. Rivière. New York: Boni and Liveright, 1920.

Frigyesi, T. L., & Machek, J. Basal ganglia diencephalon synaptic relations in the cat. II. Intracellular recordings from dorsal thalamic neurons during low frequency stimulation of the caudato-thalamic projection systems and the nigro-thalamic pathway. *Brain Research*, 1971, **27**, 59–78.

Fuster, J. M. Effects of stimulation of the brain stem on tachistoscopic perception. *Science*, 1958, **127**, 150.

Gaito, J. *DNA complex and adaptive behavior*. Englewood Cliffs, N. J.: Prentice-Hall, 1971.

Galef, B. G., Jr. Social effects in the weaning of domestic rat pups. *Journal of Comparative and Physiological Psychology*, 1971, **75**, 358–362.

Galef, B. G., Jr., & Clark, M. M. Social factors in the poison avoidance and feeding behavior of wild and domesticated rat pups. *Journal of Comparative and Physiological Psychology*, 1971, **75**, 341–357.

Gamzu, E., & Schwartz, B. The maintenance of key pecking by stimulus-contingent and response-independent food presentation. *Journal of the Experimental Analysis of Behavior*, 1973, **19**, 65–72.

Gamzu, E., & Williams, D. R. Associative factors underlying the pigeon's key pecking in autoshaping procedures. *Journal of the Experimental Analysis of Behavior*, 1973, **19**, 225–232.

Garcia, J., Hankins, W. G., & Rusiniak, K. W. Behavioral regulation of the milieu interne in man and rat. *Science*, 1974, **185**, 824–831.

Garcia, J., McGowan, B. K., Ervin, F. R., & Koelling, R. A. Cues: Their relative effectiveness as a function of the reinforcer. *Science*, 1968, **160**, 794–795.

Gardner, R. A., & Gardner, B. T. Teaching sign language to a chimpanzee. *Science*, 1969, **165**, 664–672.

Garner, W. R. Good patterns have few alternatives. *American Scientist*, 1970, **58**, 34–42.

Gaze, R. M. *The formation of nerve connections*. New York: Academic Press, 1970.

Geller, E. S., & Pitz, G. F. Effects of prediction, probability, and run length on choice reaction speed. *Journal of Experimental Psychology*, 1970, **84**, 361–367.

Geller, E. S., Whitman, C. P., & Farris, J. C. Probability discrimination indicated by stimulus predictions and reaction speed: Effects of S-R compatibility. *Journal of Experimental Psychology*, 1972, **93**, 404–409.

Geller, E. S., Whitman, C. P., Wrenn, R. F., & Shipley, W. G. Expectancy and discrete reaction time in a probability reversal design. *Journal of Experimental Psychology*, 1971, **90**, 113–119.

Gellhorn, E. *Principles of autonomic-somatic integrations*. Minneapolis: University of Minnesota Press, 1967.

Gellhorn, E., & Loofbourrow, G. H. *Emotions and emotional disorders: A neuro-physiological study*. New York: Harper & Row, 1963.

Gerbrandt, L. K. Neural systems of response release and control. *Psychological Bulletin*, 1965, **64**, 113–123.

Geschwind, N. Disconnexion syndromes in animals and man. Part I. *Brain*, 1965, **88**, 237–294.

Geschwind, N. Disconnexion syndromes in animals and man. Part II. *Brain*, 1965, **88**, 585–644.

Geschwind, N. The organization of language and the brain. *Science*, 1970, **170**, 940–944.

Geschwind, N. Some differences between human and other primate brains. In L. E. Jarrard (Ed.), *Cognitive processes of nonhuman primates*. New York: Academic Press, 1971. Pp. 149–154.

Geschwind, N. Language and the brain. *Scientific American*, 1972, **226**, 76–83.

Geschwind, N. The apraxias: Neural mechanisms of disorders of learned movement. *American Scientist*, 1975, **63**, 188–195.

Geschwind, N., & Levitsky, W. Human brain: Left-right asymmetries in temporal speech region. *Science*, 1968, **161**, 186–187.

Geschwind, N., Quadfasel, F. A., & Segarra, J. M. Isolation of the speech area. *Neuropsychologia*, 1968, **6**, 327–340.

Ghent, L., & Bernstein, L. Influence of the orientation of geometric forms on their recognition by children. *Perceptual and Motor Skills*, 1961, **12**, 95–101.

Gibson, E. J. *Principles of perceptual learning and development*. New York: Appleton-Century-Crofts, 1969.

Gibson, J. J. Adaptation, after-effect and contrast in the perception of curved lines. *Journal of Experimental Psychology*, 1933, **16**, 1–31.

Gibson, J. J. *The senses considered as perceptual systems*. Boston: Houghton-Mifflin, 1966.

Gibson, J. J., & Gibson, E. J. What is learned in perceptual learning? A reply to Professor Postman. *Psychological Review*, 1955, **62**, 447–450.

Girden, E. The dissociation of pupillary conditioned reflexes under erythroidine and curare. *Journal of Experimental Psychology*, 1942, **31**, 322–332.

Glickman, S. E. Perseverative neural processes and consolidation of the memory trace. *Psychological Bulletin*, 1961, **58**, 218–233.

Glickman, S. E., & Schiff, B. B. A biological theory of reinforcement. *Psychological Review*, 1967, **74**, 81–109.

Globus, A., Rosenzweig, M. R., Bennett, E. L., & Diamond, M. C. Effects of differential experience on dendritic spine counts in rat cerebral cortex. *Journal of Comparative and Physiological Psychology*, 1973, **82**, 175–181.

Goldman, P. S., Rosvold, H. E., Vest, B., & Galkin, T. W. Analysis of the delayed-alternation deficit produced by dorsolateral prefrontal lesions in the rhesus monkey. *Journal of Comparative and Physiological Psychology*, 1971, **77**, 212–220.

Goldstein, K. Die Lokalisation in der Grosshirnrinde. In A. Bethe et al. (Eds.), *Handbuch der normalen und pathologischen Physiologie. Vol. 10.* Berlin: Springer, 1927. Pp. 600–842.

Goldstein, K. *Aftereffects of brain injuries in war*. New York: Grune & Stratton, 1942.

Gonzalez, R. C., & Bitterman, M. E. Resistance to extinction in the rat as a function of percentage and distribution of reinforcement. *Journal of Comparative and Physiological Psychology*, 1964, **58**, 258–263.

Goodwin, G. M., McCloskey, D. I., & Matthews, P. B. C. The persistence of appreciable kinesthesia after paralysing joint afferents but preserving muscle afferents. *Brain Research*, 1972, **37**, 326–329. (*a*)

Goodwin, G. M., McCloskey, D. I., & Matthews, P. B. Proprioceptive illusions induced by muscle vibration: Contribution by muscle spindles to perception? *Science*, 1972, **175**, 1382–1384. (*b*).

Goodwin, W. R., & Lawrence, D. H. The disfunctional independence of two discrimination habits associated with a constant stimulus situation. *Journal of Comparative and Physiological Psychology*, 1955, **48**, 437–443.

Gordon, B. The superior colliculus of the brain. *Scientific American*, 1972, **227**, 72–82.

Gorska, T., & Jankowska, E. The effect of deafferentiation on instrumental (type II) conditioned reflexes in dogs. *Acta Biologiae Experimentalis*, 1961, **21**, 219–234.

Graesser, A. II, & Mandler, G. Recognition memory for the meaning and surface structure of sentences. *Journal of Experimental Psychology: Human Learning and Memory*, 1975, **104**, 238–248.

Gray, J. A. The mind-brain identity theory as a scientific hypothesis. *Philosophical Quarterly*, 1971, **21**, 247–254. (*a*)

Gray, J. A. Medial septal lesions, hippocampal theta rhythm and the control of vibrissal movement in the freely moving rat. *Electroencephalography and Clinical Neurophysiology*, 1971, **30**, 189–197. (*b*)

Gray, J. A. The structure of the emotions and the limbic system. In Ciba Foundation symposium 8, *Physiology, emotion, and psychosomatic illness*. Amsterdam: Asp. (Elsvier Excerpta Medica), 1972. Pp. 87–129.

Gray, T., & Lethbridge, D. A. Configural conditioning in the CER: Loss of element strength after repeated reinforced compound CS trials. In press.

Green, D. M., & Swets, J. A. *Signal detection theory and psychophysics*. New York: Wiley, 1966.

Greeno, J. G., & Simon, H. A. Processes for sequence production. *Psychological Review*, 1974, **81**, 187–198.

Greenwald, A. G. Sensory feedback mechanisms in performance control: With special reference to the ideo-motor mechanism. *Psychological Review*, 1970, **77**, 73–99.

Grice, G. R. Stimulus intensity and response evocation. *Psychological Review*, 1968, **75**, 359–373.

Groesbeck, R. W., & Duerfeldt, P. H. Some relevant variables in observational learning of the rat. *Psychonomic Science*, 1971, **22**, 41–43.

Gross, Y. Central and peripheral determinants of localization of body parts. Unpublished doctoral dissertation, McGill University, 1973.

Groves, P. M., & Thompson, R. F. Habituation: A dual-process theory. *Pscho-logical Review*, 1970, **77**, 419–450.

Guthrie, E. R. *The psychology of learning*. New York: Harper & Row, 1935.

Guttman, N., & Kalish, H. I. Discriminability and stimulus generalization. *Journal of Experimental Psychology*, 1956, **51**, 79–88.

Haber, R. N. Where are the visions in visual perception? In *Imagery: current cognitive approaches*. New York: Academic Press, 1971. Chap. 3.

Haber, R. N., & Haber, R. B. Eidetic imagery: I. Frequency. *Perceptual and Motor Skills*, 1964, **19**, 131–138.

Halliday, M. S., & Boakes, R. A. Discrimination involving response-independent reinforcement: Implications for behavioral contrast. In R. A. Boakes and M. S. Halliday (Eds.), *Inhibition and learning*. New York: Academic Press, 1972. Pp. 73–97.

Halliday, M. S., & Boakes, R. A. Behavioral contrast without response-rate reduction. *Journal of the Experimental Analysis of Behavior*, 1974, **22**, 453–462.

Halwes, T., & Jenkins, J. J. Problem of serial order in behavior is not resolved by context-sensitive associative memory models. *Psychological Review*, 1971, **78**, 122–129.

Hamilton, L. W., Kelsey, J. E., & Grossman, S. P. Variations in behavioral inhi-bition following different septal lesions in rats. *Journal of Comparative and Physiological Psychology*, 1970, **70**, 79–86.

Hardt, M. E., Held, R., & Steinbach, M. J. Adaptation to displaced vision: A change in the central control of sensorimotor coordination. *Journal of Experi-mental Psychology*, 1971, **89**, 229–239.

Harlow, H. F. Learning set and error factor theory. In S. Koch (Ed.), *Psychology: A study of a science. Vol. 2*. New York: McGraw-Hill, 1959. Pp. 492–537.

Harper, L. V. Role of contact and sound in eliciting filial responses and develop-ment of social attachments in domestic guinea pigs. *Journal of Comparative and Physiological Psychology*, 1970, **73**, 427–435.

Harris, C. S. Perceptual adaptation to inverted, reversed, and displaced vision. *Psychological Review*, 1965, **72**, 419–444.

Harris, L. J. Discrimination of left and right, and the development of the logic of relations. *Merrill-Palmer Quarterly of Behavior and Development*, 1972, **18**, 307–320.

Hartmann, E. *The biology of dreaming*. Springfield, Ill. Charles C. Thomas, 1967.

Head, H. *Studies in neurology*. London: Oxford University Press, 1920. Vol. 2.

Heath, R. G., John, S. B., & Fontana, C. J. The pleasure response: Studies by stereotaxic technics in patients. In Kline & Laska (Eds.), *Computers and electronic devices in psychiatry*. New York: Grune & Stratton, 1968.

Hebb, D. O. Behavioral differences between male and female chimpanzees. *Bulletin of the Canadian Psychological Association*, 1946, **6**, 56–58. (*a*)

Hebb, D. O. On the nature of fear. *Psychological Review*, 1946, **53**, 259–276. (*b*)

Hebb, D. O. *Organization of behavior*. New York: Wiley, 1949.

Hebb, D. O. The distinction between "classical" and "instrumental." *Canadian Journal of Psychology*, 1956, **10**, 165–166.

Hebb, D. O. Distinctive features of learning in the higher animal. In J. F. Delafresnaye (Ed.), *Brain mechanisms and learning*. A symposium. Oxford: Blackwell, 1961, Pp. 37–51.

Hebb, D. O. Concerning imagery. *Psychological Review*, 1968, **75**, 466–477.

Hebb, D. O. What psychology is about. *American Psychologist*, 1974, **29**, 71–79.

Hebb, D. O., & Penfield, W. Human behavior after extensive bilateral removal from the frontal lobes. *Archives of Neurology and Psychiatry*, 1940, **44**, 421–438.

Heinemann, E. G., Chase, S., & Mandell, C. Discriminative control of "attention." *Science*, 1968, **160**, 553–554.

Held, R. Sensory deprivation: Facts in search of a theory. Exposure-history as a factor in maintaining stability of perception and coordination. *Journal of Nervous and Mental Disease*, 1961, **132**, 26–32.

Held, R., & Bauer, J. A., Jr. Visually guided reaching in infant monkeys after restricted rearing. *Science*, 1967, **155**, 718–720.

Held, R., & Hein, A. Movement-produced stimulation in the development of visually guided behavior. *Journal of Comparative and Physiological Psychology*, 1963, **56**, 872–876

Helmholtz, H. L. F., von *Handbuch der physiologischen Optik*. Vol. 3. Leipsig: Leopold Voss, 1867.

Hermelin, B., & O'Connor, N. Cross-modal transfer in normal, subnormal and autistic children. *Neuropsychologia*, 1964, **2**, 229–235.

Hermelin, B. M., & O'Connor, N. Children's judgements of duration. *British Journal of Psychology*, 1971, **62**, 13–20. (*a*)

Hermelin, B., & O'Connor, N. Spatial coding in normal, autistic and blind children. *Perceptual and Motor Skills*, 1971, **33**, 127–132. (*b*)

Hernández-Péon, R., Scherrer, R., & Jouvet, M. Modification of electric activity in cochlear nucleus during "attention" in unanesthetized cats. *Science*, 1956, **123**, 331–332.

Herr, F., Stewart, J., & Charest, M-P. Tranquilizers and antidepressants: A pharmacological comparison. *Archives internationales de pharmacodynamie et de thérapie*, 1961, **134**, 328–342.

Herrnstein, R. J. Relative and absolute strength of response as a function of frequency of reinforcement. *Journal of the Experimental Analysis of Behavior*, 1961, **4**, 267–272.

Herrnstein, R. J. On the law of effect. *Journal of the Experimental Analysis of Behavior*, 1970, **13**, 243–266.

Herrnstein, R. J., & Boring, E. G. *A source book in the history of psychology.* Cambridge, Mass.: Harvard University Press, 1965.

Hicks, L. H., & Birren, J. E. Aging, brain damage, and psychomotor slowing. *Psychological Bulletin*, 1970, **74**, 337–396.

Hinde, R. A. Behavioural habituation. In G. Horn & R. A. Hinde (Eds.), *Short-term changes in neural activity and behaviour.* Cambridge, Mass.: Cambridge University Press, 1970. Pp. 3–40.

Hinde, R. A., & Stevenson, J. G. Goals and response control. In L. R. Aronson, et al. (Eds.), *Development and evolution of Behavior.* San Francisco: Freeman, 1970. Pp. 216–237.

Hine, B., & Paolino, R. M. Retrograde amnesia: Production of skeletal but not cardiac response gradient by electroconvulsive shock. *Science*, 1970, **169**, 1224–1226.

Hirsh, I. J. Auditory perception of temporal order. *Journal of the Acoustical Society of America*, 1959, **31**, 759–767.

Hirsch, H. V. B., & Spinelli, D. N. Visual experience modifies distribution of horizontally and vertically oriented receptive fields in cats. *Science*, 1970, **168**, 869–871.

Hodos, W. Evolutionary interpretation of neural and behavioral studies of living vertebrates. In F. O. Schmitt (Ed.), *The neurosciences: Second program.* New York: Rockefeller University Press, 1970. Pp. 26–39.

Hodos, W., & Campbell, C. B. G. Scala Naturae: Why there is no theory in comparative psychology. *Psychological Review*, 1969, **76**, 337–350.

Hoebel, B. G. Feeding: Neural control of intake. *Annual Review of Physiology*, 1971, **33**, 533–568.

Holst, E., von. Relations between the central nervous system and the peripheral organs. *British Journal of Animal Behaviour*, 1954, **2**, 89–94.

Holst, E., von, & Mittelstaedt, H. Das reafferenzprinzip (Wechselwirkungen zwischen Zentralnervensystem und Peripherie). *Die Naturwissenschaften*, 1950, **37**, 464–476.

Honzik, C. H. The sensory basis of maze learning in rats. *Comparative Psychology Monographs*, 1936, **13**, (Whole No. 64). P. 113.

Horn, G. Electrical activity of the cerebral cortex of unanesthetized cats during attentive behaviour. *Brain*, 1960, **83**, 57–76.

Horn, G., & Hill, R. M. Modifications of receptive fields of cells in the visual cortex occurring spontaneously and associated with bodily tilt. *Nature*, 1969, **221**, 186–188.

Horn, G., Rose, S. P. R., & Bateson, P. P. G. Experience and plasticity in the central nervous system. *Science*, 1973, **181**, 506–514.

Horridge, G. A. *Interneurons. Their origin, action, specificity, growth, and plasticity.* San Francisco: Freeman, 1968.

Howes, D. Hypotheses concerning the functions of the language mechanisms. In *Research in verbal behavior and some neurophysiological implications.* New York: Academic Press, 1967.

Howes, D. H. The link between speech production and speech perception. In H. R. Moskowitz et al. (Eds.), *Sensation and measurement.* Dordrecht, Holland: D. Reidel Publishing Co., 1974.

Howes, D. H., & Solomon, R. L. Visual duration threshold as a function of word-probability. *Journal of Experimental Psychology,* 1951, **41**, 401–410.

Hubel, D. H., & Wiesel, T. N. Binocular interaction in striate cortex of kittens reared with artificial squint. *Journal of Neurophysiology,* 1965, **28**, 1041–1059.

Hubel, D. H., & Wiesel, T. N. Receptive fields and functional architecture of monkey striate cortex. *Journal of Physiology* (London), 1968, **195**, 215–243.

Hull, C. L. *Principles of behavior.* New York: Appleton-Century-Crofts, 1943.

Hunter, W. S. The sensory control of the maze habit in the white rat. *The Pedagogical Seminary and Journal of Genetic Psychology,* 1929, **36**, 505–537.

Imai, S., & Garner, W. R. Discriminability and preference for attributes in free and constrained classification. *Journal of Experimental Psychology,* 1965, **69**, 596–608.

Irwin, F. W. The concept of volition in experimental psychology. In F. P. Clark & M. C. Nahm (Eds.), *Philosophical essays in honor of Edgar Arthur Singer, Jr.* Philadelphia: University of Pennsylvania Press, 1942. Pp. 115–137.

Irwin, F. W. *Intentional behavior and motivation: A cognitive theory.* Philadelphia, Pennsylvania: Lippincott, 1971.

Jacobson, E. The electrophysiology of mental activities. *American Journal of Psychology,* 1932, **44**, 677–694.

Jacobson, E. *Progressive relaxation.* 2nd ed. Chicago: University of Chicago Press, 1938.

Jacobson, M. Development of specific neuronal connections. *Science,* 1969, **163**, 543–547.

Jackson, J. H. Remarks on evolution and dissolution of the nervous system (1887). In J. Taylor (Ed.), *John Hughlings Jackson: Selected writings.* Vol. 2. London: Hodder & Stoughton, 1932.

James, H. Flicker: An unconditioned stimulus for imprinting. *Canadian Journal of Psychology,* 1959, **13**, 59–67.

James, W. *The principles of psychology.* Vol. 2. New York: Holt, 1890.

Jasper, H. H. Recent advances in our understanding of ascending activities in the reticular system. In H. H. Jasper (Ed.), *Reticular formation of the brain.* Boston: Little, Brown, 1958.

Jasper, H., & Shagass, G. Conditioning the occipital alpha rhythm in man. *Journal of Experimental Psychology.* 1941, **28**, 373–388.

Jenkins, H. M. Resistance to extinction when partial reinforcement is followed by regular reinforcement. *Journal of Experimental Psychology*, 1962, **64**, 441–450.

Jenkins, H. M. Sequential organization in schedules of reinforcement. In W. N. Schoenfeld (Ed.), *Theory of reinforcement schedules*. New York: Appleton-Century-Crofts, 1970. Pp. 63–109.

Jenkins, H. M., & Harrison, R. H. Generalization gradients of inhibition following auditory discrimination learning. *Journal of the Experimental Analysis of Behavior*, 1962, **5**, 435–441.

Jenkins, H. M., & Sainsbury, R. S. The development of stimulus control through differential reinforcement. In N. J. Mackintosh & W. K. Honig (Eds.), *Fundamental issues in associative learning*. Halifax: Dalhousie University Press, 1969. Pp. 123–161.

Jerison, H. J. Brain evolution and dinosaur brains. *American Nature*, 1969, **103**, 575–588.

Jerison, H. J. *Evolution of the brain and intelligence*. New York: Academic Press, 1973.

John, E. R. *Mechanisms of memory*. New York: Academic Press, 1967.

John, E. R. Switchboard versus statistical theories of learning and memory. *Science*, 1972, **177**, 850–864.

John, E. R., Chesler, P., Bartlett, F., & Victor, I. Observation learning in cats. *Science*, 1968, **159**, 1489–1491·

Johnson, T. N., & Rosvold, H. E. Topographic projections on the globus pallidus and the substantia nigra of selectively placed lesions in the precommissural caudate nucleus and putamen in the monkey. *Experimental Neurology*, 1971, **33**, 584–596.

Johnson, T. N., Rosvold, H. E., & Mishkin, M. Projections from behaviorally defined sectors of the prefrontal cortex to the basal ganglia, septum, and diencephalon of the monkey. *Experimental Neurology*, 1968, **21**, 20–34.

Jones, E. G., & Powell, T. P. S. The ipsilateral cortical connexions of the somatic sensory areas in the cat. *Brain Research*, 1968, **9**, 71–94.

Jouvet, M. Mechanisms of the states of sleep: A neuropharmacological approach. In S. S. Kety, E. V. Evarts, & H. L. Williams (Eds.), *Sleep and altered states of consciousness*. Baltimore: Williams & Wilkins, 1967.

Julesz, B. Binocular depth perception without familiarity cues. *Science*, 1964, **145**, 356–362.

Kagan, J. *Change and continuity in infancy*. New York: Wiley, 1971.

Kagan, J., Henker, B. A., Hen-Tov, A., Levine, J., & Lewis, M. Infants' differential reactions to familiar and distorted faces. *Child Development*, 1966, **37**, 519–532.

Kahneman, D. *Attention and effort*. Englewood Cliffs, N. J.: Prentice-Hall, 1973.

Kalat, J. W. Taste salience depends on novelty, not concentration, in taste-aversion learning in the rat. *Journal of Comparative and Physiological Psychology*, 1974, **86**, 47–50.

Kamin, L. J. Predictability, surprise, attention, and conditioning. In R. Church, & B. Campbell (Eds.), *Punishment and aversive behavior*. New York: Appleton-Century-Crofts, 1969.

Kamin, L. J., & Brimer, C. J. The effects of intensity of conditioned and unconditioned stimuli on a conditioned emotional response. *Canadian Journal of Psychology*, 1963, **17**, 194–200.

Kamin, L. J., Brimer, C. J., & Black, A. H. Conditioned suppression as a monitor of fear of the CS in the course of avoidance training. *Journal of Comparative and Pyhsiological Psychology*, 1963, **56**, 497–501.

Kandel, E. R., & Tauc, L. Mechanism of heterosynaptic facilitation in the giant cell of the abdominal ganglion of *Aplysia depilans*. *Journal of Physiology* (London), 1965, **181**, 28–47.

Karlin, L. Reaction time as a function of foreperiod duration and variability. *Journal of Experimental Psychology*, 1959, **58**, 185–191.

Karmel, B. Z. Complexity, amounts of contour, and visually dependent behavior in hooded rats, domestic chicks, and human infants. *Journal of Comparative and Physiological Psychology*, 1969, **69**, 649–657.

Katz, P. Effects of labels on children's perception and discrimination learning. *Journal of Experimental Psychology*, 1963, **66**, 423–428.

Ka⁺zev, R. Extinguishing avoidance responses as a function of delayed warning signal termination. *Journal of Experimental Psychology*, 1967, **75**, 339–344.

Keller, K. The role of elicited responding in behavioral contrast. *Journal of the Experimental Analysis of Behavior*, 1974, **21**, 249–257.

Kennedy, D. Input and output connections of single arthropod neurons. In F. D. Carlson (Ed.), *Physiological and biochemical aspects of nervous integration*. Englewood Cliffs, N. J.: Prentice-Hall, 1968. Pp. 285–306.

Killackey, H., & Ebner, F. Convergent projection of three separate thalamic nuclei on to a single cortical area. *Science*, 1973, **179**, 283–285.

Killeen, P. The matching law. *Journal of the Experimental Analysis of Behavior*, 1972, **17**, 489–495.

Killeen, P. On the temporal control of behavior. *Psychological Review*, 1975, **82**, 89–115.

Kimble, D. P. Hippocampus and internal inhibition. *Psychological Bulletin*, 1968, **70**, 285–295.

Kimble, G. A. *Hilgard and Marquis' conditioning and learning*. (2nd ed.), New York: Appleton-Century-Crofts, 1961.

Kimble, G. A., & Perlmuter, L. C. The problem of volition. *Psychological Review*, 1970, **77**, 361–384.

Kimmel, H. D. Instrumental conditioning of autonomically mediated behavior. *Psychological Bulletin*, 1967, **67**, 337–345.

Kinsbourne, M., & Warrington. E. K. A disorder of simultaneous form perception. *Brain*, 1962, **85**, 461–486.

Kinsbourne, M., & Warrington, E. K. A study of visual perseveration. *Journal of Neurology, Neurosurgery, and Psychiatry*, 1963, **26**, 468–475.

Klemmer, E. T. Time uncertainty in simple reaction time. *Journal of Experimental Psychology*, 1956, **51**, 179–184.

Klemmer, E. T. Simple reaction time as a function of time uncertainty. *Journal of Experimental Psychology*, 1957, **54**, 195–200.

Knapp, H. D., Taub, E., & Berman, A. J. Effect of deafferentation on a conditioned avoidance response. *Science*, 1958, **128**, 842–843.

Kohler, I. *Über Aufbau und Wandlungen der Wahrnehmungswelt*. Vienna: R. M. Rohrer, 1951.

Köhler, W. *Gestalt psychology*. New York: Liveright, 1929.

Köhler, W., & Wallach, H. Figural after-effects: An investigation of visual processes. *Proceedings of the American Philosophical Society*, 1944, **88**, 269–357.

Kohn, B., & Dennis, M. Observation and discrimination learning in the rat: Specific and nonspecific effects. *Journal of Comparative and Physiological Psychology*, 1972, **78**, 292–296.

Komisaruk, B. R. Synchrony between limbic system theta activity and rhythmical behavior in rats. *Journal of Comparative and Physiological Psychology*, 1970, **70**, 482–492.

Konorski, J. *Conditioned reflexes and neuron organization*. Cambridge: Cambridge University Press, 1948.

Konorski, J. *Integrative activity of the brain*. Chicago: University of Chicago Press, 1967.

Koppenaal, R. J., Jogoda, E., & Cruce, J. A. J. Recovery from ECS produced amnesia following a reminder. *Psychonomic Science*, 1967, **9**, 293–294.

Kovach, J. K. Effectiveness of different colors in the elicitation and development of approach behavior in chicks. *Behaviour*, 1971, **38**, 154–168.

Kramer, T. J., & Rilling, M. Differential reinforcement of low rates: A selective critique. *Psychological Bulletin*, 1970, **74**, 225–254.

Krane, R. V., & Wagner, A. R. Taste aversion learning with a delayed shock US: Implications for the "generality of the laws of learning." *Journal of Comparative and Physiological Psychology*, 1975, **88**, 882–889.

Krebs, H., & Bindra, D. Noradrenaline and "chemical coding" of hypothalamic neurones. *Nature New Biology*, 1971, **229**, 178–180.

Krebs, H., Bindra, D., & Campbell, J. F. Effects of amphetamine on neuronal activity in the hypothalamus. *Physiology and Behavior*, 1969, **4**, 685–691.

Kringlebotn, M. Experiments with some visual and vibrotactile aids for the deaf. *American Annals of the Deaf*, 1968, **113**, 311–317.

Külpe, O. *Outlines of psychology*. Translated from the German (1893) by E. B. Titchener. London: Swan Sonnenschein & Co., 1901.

Kumar, R., Stolerman, I. P., & Steinberg, H. Psychopharmacology. *Annual Review of Psychology*, 1970, **21**, 595–628.

Lajoie, J. Roles of stimulus-incentive and response-incentive contingencies in the learning of an approach response. Ph.D. thesis, McGill University, 1975.

Laming, D. R. J. Subjective probability in choice-reaction experiments. *Journal of Mathematical Psychology*, 1969, **6**, 81–120.

Lashley, K. S. Studies of cerebral function in learning. V. The retention of motor habits after destruction of the so-called motor areas in primates. *Archives of Neurology and Psychiatry*, 1924, **12**, 249–276.

Lashley, K. S. The mechanism of vision: IV. The cerebral areas necessary for pattern vision in the rat. *Journal of Comparative Neurology*, 1931, **53**, 419–478.

Lashley, K. S. Persistent problems in the evolution of mind. *Quarterly Review of Biology*, 1949, **24**, 28–42.

Lashley, K. S. The problem of serial order in behavior. In L. A. Jeffress (Ed.), *Cerebral mechanisms in behavior*. New York: Wiley, 1951. Pp. 112–136.

Lashley, K. S., & Ball, J. Spinal conduction and kinesthetic sensitivity in the maze habit. *Journal of Comparative Psychology*, 1929, **9**, 71–105.

Lashley, K. S., & McCarthy, D. A. The survival of the maze habit after cerebellar injuries. *Journal of Comparative Psychology*, 1926, **6**, 423–433.

Lashley, K. S., & Wade, M. The Pavlovian theory of generalization. *Psychological Review*, 1946, **53**, 72–87·

Laurendeau, M., & Pinard, A. *Causal thinking in the child*. New York: International Universities Press, 1962.

Laurendeau, M., & Pinard, A. *The development of the concept of space in the child*. New York: International Universities Press, 1970.

Lawicka, W. The effect of prefrontal lobectomy on the vocal conditioned reflexes in dogs. *Acta Biologiae Experimentalis*, 1957, **17**, 317–325.

Lawrence, D. H. Acquired distinctiveness of cues: I. Transfer between discriminations on the basis of familiarity with the stimulus. *Journal of Experimental Psychology*, 1949, **39**, 770–784.

Lawrence, D. H. Acquired distinctiveness of cues: II. Selective association in a constant stimulus situation. *Journal of Experimental Psychology*, 1950, **40**, 175–188.

Lea, S. E. G., & Morgan, M. J. The measurement of rate-dependent changes in responding. In R. M. Gilbert and J. R. Millenson (Eds.), *Reinforcement: Behavioral analyses*. New York: Academic Press, 1972. Pp. 129–145.

Leask, J., Haber, R. N., & Haber, R. B. Eidetic imagery in children: II. Longitudinal and experimental results. *Psychonomic Monograph Supplements*, 1969, **3**, (3, Whole No. 35). Pp. 28–45.

Leclerc, R., St-Laurent, J., & Baum, M. Effects of rewarding aversive, and neutral intracranial stimulation administered during flooding (response prevention) in rats. *Physiological Psychology*, 1973, **1**, 24–28.

Le Magnen, J. Advances in studies on the physiological control and regulation of food intake. In E. Stellar & J. M. Sprague (Eds.), *Progress in physiological psychology.* New York: Academic Press, 1971. Pp. 203–261.

Lenneberg, E. H. Understanding language without ability to speak: A case report. *Journal of Abnormal and Social Psychology,* 1962, **65,** 419–425.

Lenneberg, E. H. *Biological foundations of language.* New York: Wiley, 1967.

Lenneberg, E. H., Rebelsky, F. G., & Nichols, I. A. The vocalization of infants born to deaf and to hearing parents. (Vita Humana) *Human Development,* 1965, **8,** 23–37.

Lenzer, I. I. Differences between behavior reinforced by electrical stimulation of the brain and conventionally reinforced behavior: An associative analysis. *Psychological Bulletin,* 1972, **78,** 103–118.

Levine, M. Cue neutralization: The effects of random reinforcements upon discrimination learning. *Journal of Experimental Psychology,* 1962, **63,** 438–443.

Levison, P. K., & Flynn, J. P. The objects attacked by cats during stimulation of the hypothalamus. *Animal Behaviour,* 1965, **13,** 217–220.

Lewis, D. J. Sources of experimental amnesia. *Psychological Review,* 1969, **76,** 461–742.

Lewis, D. J., & Maher, B. A. Neural consolidation and electroconvulsive shock. *Psychological Review,* 1965, **72,** 225–239.

Lewis, D. J., Miller, R. R., & Misanin, J. R. Control of retrograde amnesia. *Journal of Comparative and Physiological Psychology,* 1968, **66,** 48–52.

Liberman, A. M., Cooper, F. S., Shankweiler, D. P., & Studdert-Kennedy, M. Perception of the speech code. *Psychological Review,* 1967, **74,** 431–461.

Libet, B., Alberts, W. W., Wright, E. W., Jr., & Feinstein, B. Responses of human somatosensory cortex to stimuli below threshold for conscious sensation. *Science,* 1967, **158,** 1597–1600.

Licklider, L. C., & Licklider, J. C. R. Observations on the hoarding behavior of rats. *Journal of Comparative and Physiological Psychology,* 1950, **43,** 129–134.

Lloyd, A. J., & Leibrecht, B. C. Conditioning of a single motor unit. *Journal of Experimental Psychology,* 1971, **88,** 391–395.

Logan, F. A. Decision making by rats: Uncertain outcome choices. *Journal of Comparative and Physiological Psychology,* 1965, **59,** 246–251.

Lorenz, K. The comparative method in studying innate behavior patterns. In *Symposia of the Society for Experimental Biology.* Vol. 4. Cambridge: Cambridge University Press, 1950.

Lorenz, K. *On aggression.* Translated by M. K. Wilson. New York: Harcourt, Brace & World, 1966.

Lovejoy, A. O. *The great chain of being.* Cambridge, Mass.: Harvard University Press, 1936.

Lovejoy, E. *Attention in discrimination learning.* San Francisco: Holden-Day, 1968.

Lubow, R. E. Latent inhibition. *Psychological Bulletin,* 1973, **79,** 398–407.

Luce, R. D., & Suppes, P. Preference, utility, and subjective probability. (1959). In R. D. Luce, R. R. Bush, & E. Galanter (Eds.), *Handbook of mathematical psychology*, Vol. 3. New York: Wiley, 1965. Pp. 249–252.

Luchins, A. S. Mechanization in problem solving—the effect of Einstellung. *Psychological Monographs*, 1942, **54** (Whole No. 248). Pp. 95.

Luria, A. R. *Higher cortical functions in man.* Translated by B. Haigh. New York: Basic Books, 1966.

Luria, A. R. *The working brain: An introduction to neuropsychology.* Translated by B. Haigh. London: Penguin Books, 1973.

Mabry, P. D., & Campbell, B. A. Ontogeny of serotonergic inhibition of behavioral arousal in the rat. *Journal of Comparative and Physiological Psychology*, 1974, **86**, 193–201.

MacCorquodale, K., & Meehl, P. E. Preliminary suggestions as to a formalization of expectancy theory. *Psychological Review*, 1953, **60**, 55–63.

MacDougall, J. M., Van Hoesen, G. W., & Mitchell, J. C. Anatomical organization of septal projections in maintenance of DRL behavior in rats. *Journal of Comparative and Physiological Psychology*, 1969, **68**, 568–575.

Macfarlane, D. A. The role of kinesthesis in maze learning. *University of California Publications in Psychology*, 1930, **4**, 277–305.

Mackintosh, I. The resistance to extinction of responses acquired under irregular conditions of learning. *Journal of Comparative and Physiological Psychology*, 1955, **48**, 363–370.

Mackintosh, N. J. Overtraining and transfer within and between dimensions in the rat. *Quarterly Journal of Experimental Psychology*, 1964, **16**, 250–256.

Mackintosh, N. J. Selective attention in animal discrimination learning. *Psychological Bulletin*, 1965, **64**, 124–150.

Mackintosh, N. J. Analysis of overshadowing and blocking. *Quarterly Journal of Experimental Psychology*, 1971, **23**, 118–125.

Mackintosh, N. J. Stimulus detection: Learning to ignore stimuli that predict no change in reinforcement. In R. A. Hinde & J. Stevenson-Hinde (Eds.), *Constraints on learning.* London: Academic Press, 1973. Pp. 75–96.

Mackintosh, N. J. *The psychology of animal learning.* New York: Academic Press, 1974.

Mackintosh, N. J. A theory of attention: Variations on the associability of stimuli with reinforcement. *Psychological Review*, 1975, **82**, 276–298.

Mackintosh, N. J., & Turner, C. Blocking as a function of novelty of CS and predictability of UCS. *Quarterly Journal of Experimental Psychology*, 1971, **23**, 359–366.

Mackworth, J. F. The effect of amphetamine on the detectability of signals in a vigilance task. *Canadian Journal of Psychology*, 1965, **19**, 104–110.

Mackworth, N. H., & Morandi, A. J. The gaze selects informative details within pictures. *Perception and Psychophysics*, 1967, **2**, 547–552.

Macnamara, J. Cognitive basis of language learning in infants. *Psychological Review*, 1972, **79**, 1–13.

MacNeilage, P. F. Typing errors as clues to serial ordering mechanisms in language behavior. *Language and Speech*, 1964, **7**, 155–159.

MacNeilage, P. F. Motor control of serial ordering of speech. *Psychological Review*, 1970, **77**, 182–196.

MacNeilage, P. F., Rootes, T. P., & Chase, R. A. Speech production and perception in a patient with severe impairment of somesthetic perception and motor control. *Journal of Speech and Hearing Research*, 1967, **10**, 449–467.

Maier, N. R. F. Reasoning in humans. I. On direction. *Journal of Comparative Psychology*, 1930, **10**, 115–143.

Maier, N. R. F. Reasoning in humans. II. The solution of a problem and its appearance in consciousness. *Journal of Comparative Psychology*, 1931, **12**, 181–194.

Malmo, R. B. Interference factors in delayed response in monkeys after removal of frontal lobes. *Journal of Neurophysiology*, 1942, **5**, 295–308.

Mandler, G. Memory storage and retrieval: Some limits on the reach of attention and consciousness. In P. M. A. Rabbit and S. Dornic (Eds.), *Attention and performance V*. London: Academic Press Inc. (London) Ltd., 1975. Pp. 499–516.

Marcel, A. Perception with and without awareness. Paper presented to the Experimental Psychology Society, Stirling, England, July, 1974.

Marler, P. A comparative approach to vocal learning: Song development in white-crowned sparrows. *Journal of Comparative and Physiological Psychology Monographs*, 1970, **71**, (Whole No. 2, Part 2). (*a*)

Marler, P. Birdsong and speech development: Could there be parallels? *American Scientist*, 1970, **58**, 669–673. (*b*)

Marsden, C. D., Merton, P. A., & Morton, H. B. Servo action and stretch reflex in human muscle and its apparent dependence on peripheral sensation. *Journal of Physiology* (London), 1971, **216**, 21P–22P.

Marsden, C. D., Merton, P. A., & Morton, H. B. Changes in loop gain with force in the human muscle servo. *Journal of Physiology* (London), 1972, **222**, 32P–34P.

Marshall, J. F., & Teitelbaum, P. Further analysis of sensory inattention following lateral hypothalamic damage in rats. *Journal of Comparative and Physiological Psychology*, 1974, **86**, 375–395.

Massaro, D. W. Perception of letters, words, and nonwords. *Journal of Experimental Psychology*, 1973, **100**, 349–353.

Masserman, J. H. *Behavior and neurosis*. Chicago: Chicago University Press, 1943.

Masterton, B., & Skeen, L. C. Origins of anthropoid intelligence: Prefrontal system and delayed alternation in hedgehog, tree shrew, and bush baby. *Journal of Comparative and Physiological Psychology*, 1972, **81**, 423–433.

Masterton, R. B., & Berkley, M. A. Brain function: Changing ideas on the role of sensory, motor, and association cortex in behavior. *Annual Review of Psychology*, 1974, **25**, 277–312.

McCall, R. B., & Kagan, J. Attention in the infant: Effects of complexity, contour, perimeter, and familiarity. *Child Development*, 1967, **38**, 939–952.

McFarland, D. J. The role of attention in the disinhibition of displacement activities. *Quarterly Journal of Experimental Psychology*, 1966, **18**, 19–30.

McFarland, D. J. Recent developments in the study of feeding and drinking in animals. *Journal of Psychosomatic Research*, 1970, **14**, 229–237.

McFarland, D. J. *Feedback mechanisms in behavior.* London: Academic Press, 1971.

McGaugh, J. L. Time-dependent processes in memory storage. *Science*, 1966, **153**, 1351–1358.

McGaugh, J. L., & Petrinovitch, L. Effects of drugs on learning and memory. *International Review of Neurobiology*, 1965, **8**, 139–196.

McGinnies, E., Comer, P. B., & Lacey, O. L. Visual-recognition thresholds as a function of word length and word frequency. *Journal of Experimental Psychology*, 1952, **44**, 65–69.

McGurk, H. Infant discrimination of orientation. *Journal of Experimental Child Psychology*, 1972, **14**, 151–164.

McKenzie, B. E., & Day, R. H. Object distance as a determinant of visual fixation in early infancy. *Science*, 1972, **178**, 1108–1110.

McKinney, J. P. Disappearance of luminous designs. *Science*, 1963, **140**, 403–404.

McKinney, J. P. Hand schema in children. *Psychonomic Science*, 1964, **1**, 99–100.

Melton, A. W. Implications of short-term memory for a general theory of memory. *Journal of Verbal Learning and Verbal Behavior*, 1963, **2**, 1–21.

Melzack, R., & Bromage, P. R. Experimental phantom limbs. *Experimental Neurology*, 1973, **39**, 261–269.

Melzack, R., & Schechter, B. Itch and vibration. *Science*, 1965, **147**, 1047–1048.

Mendelson, J. Ecological modulation of brain stimulation effects. *International Journal of Psychobiology*, 1972, **2**, 285–304.

Mendoza, J. E., & Adams, H. E. Does electroconvulsive shock produce retrograde amnesia? *Physiology and Behavior*, 1969, **4**, 307–309.

Mendoza, J. E., & Thomas, R. J., Jr. Effects of posterior parietal and frontal neocortical lesions in the squirrel monkey. *Journal of Comparative and Physiological Psychology*, 1975, **89**, 170–182.

Menzel, E. W., Jr. Group behavior in young chimpanzees: Responsiveness to cumulative novel changes in a large outdoor enclosure. *Journal of Comparative and Physiological Psychology*, 1971, **74**, 46–51.

Merton, P. A. Human position sense and sense of effort. Society of Experimental Biology Symposia 18, *Homeostasis and feedback mechanisms.* Cambridge: Cambridge University Press, 1964. Pp. 387–400.

Micco, D. J., & Schwartz, M. Effects of hippocampal lesions upon the development of Pavlovian internal inhibition in rats. *Journal of Comparative and Physiological Psychology*, 1971, **76**, 371–377.

Milgram, N. W., Grant, D. P., & Stockman, S. M. Situational control over electrically induced ingestive behavior: A comparison of hippocampal and hypothalamic feeding. *Physiological Psychology*, 1975, **3**, 337–339.

Millenson, J. R., & de Villiers, P. A. Motivational properties of conditioned anxiety. In R. M. Gilbert & J. R. Millenson (Eds.), *Reinforcement: Behavioral analyses*. New York: Academic Press, 1972. Pp. 97–128.

Miller, G. A. The magical number seven, plus or minus two: Some limits on our capacity for processing information. *Psychological Review*, 1956, **63**, 81–97.

Miller, G. A., Bruner, J. S., & Postman, L. Familiarity of letter sequences and tachistoscopic identification. *Journal of General Psychology*, 1954, **50**, 129–139.

Miller, G. A., Galanter, E., & Pribram, K. H. *Plans and the structure of behavior*. New York: Holt, Rinehart & Winston, 1960.

Miller, N. E. Experimental studies of conflict. In J. McV. Hunt (Ed.), *Personality and the behavior disorders*. Vol. 1. New York: Ronald, 1944. Pp. 431–465.

Miller, N. E. Studies of fear as an acquirable drive: I. Fear as motivation and fear-reduction as reinforcement in the learning of new responses. *Journal of Experimental Psychology*, 1948, **38**, 89–101. (*a*)

Miller, N. E. Theory and experiment relating psychoanalytic displacement to stimulus-response generalization. *Journal of Abnormal and Social Psychology*, 1948, **43**, 155–178. (*b*)

Miller, N. E. Learnable drives and rewards. In S. S. Stevens (Ed.), *Handbook of experimental psychology*. New York: Wiley, 1951.

Miller, N. E. Experiments on motivation. Studies combining psychological, physiological, and pharmacological techniques, *Science*, 1957, **126**, 1271–1278.

Miller, N. E. Learning of visceral and glandular responses. *Science*, 1969, **163**, 434–445.

Miller, N. E., & Dollard, J. *Social learning and imitation*. New Haven, Conn.: Yale University Press, 1941. Chap. 2.

Miller, N. E., & Dworkin, B. R. Visceral learning: Recent difficulties with curarized rats and significant problems for human research. In P. A. Obrist, A. H. Black, J. Brener, & L. V. DiCara (Eds.), *Cardiovascular psychophysiology: Current issues in response mechanisms, biofeedback and methodology*. Chicago: Aldine, 1974. Pp. 312–331.

Miller, R. R., Misanin, J. R., & Lewis, D. J. Amnesia as a function of events during the learning-ECS interval. *Journal of Comparative and Physiological Psychology*, 1969, **67**, 145–148.

Milner, A. D., & Bryant, P. E. Cross-modal matching by young children (1968). *Journal of Comparative and Physiological Psychology*, 1970, **71**, 453–458.

Milner, B. Effects of different brain lesions on card sorting. *Archives of Neurology*, 1963, **9**, 90–100.

Milner, B. Brain mechanisms suggested by studies of temporal lobe. In C. H. Millikan, F. Darley (Eds.), *Brain mechanisms underlying speech and language*. New York: Grune & Stratton, 1967. Pp. 122–145.

Milner, P. M. The cell-assembly: Mark II. *Psychological Review*, 1957, **64**, 242–252.

Milner, P. M. Learning in neural systems. In M. C. Yovitz & S. Cameron (Eds.), *Self-governing systems*. New York: Pergamon, 1960. Pp. 190–202.

Milner, P. M. A neural mechanism for the immediate recall of sequences. *Kybernetik*, 1961, **1**, 76–81.

Milner, P. M. *Physiological psychology*. New York: Holt, Rinehart & Winston, 1970.

Milner, P. M. A model for visual shape recognition. *Psychological Review*, 1974, **81**, 521–535.

Mineka, S., Seligman, M. E. P., Hetrick, M., & Zuelzer, K. Poisoning and conditioned drinking. *Journal of Comparative and Physiological Psychology*, 1972, **79**, 377–384.

Misanin, J. R., Miller, R. R., & Lewis, D. J. Retrograde amnesia produced by electroconvulsive shock after reactivation of a consolidated memory trace. *Science*, 1968, **160**, 554–555.

Mishkin, M., & Pribram, K. H. Visual discrimination performance following partial ablations of the temporal lobe: I. Ventral vs. lateral. *Journal of Comparative and Physiological Psychology*, 1954, **47**, 14–20.

Mitchell, D., Scott, D. W., & Williams, K. D. Container neophobia and the rat's preference for earned food. *Behavioral Biology*, 1973, **9**, 613–624.

Mogenson, G. J. Changing views of the role of the hypothalamus in the control of ingestive behaviors. In K. Lederis and K. E. Cooper (Eds.), *Proceedings of the International Symposium on Recent Studies of Hypothalamic function, Calgary, 1973*. Basel, Switzerland: S. Karger, 1974. Pp. 268–293.

Montgomery, K. C. The relation between fear induced by novel stimulation and exploratory drive. *Journal of Comparative and Physiological Psychology*, 1955, **48**, 254–260.

Moore, B. R. On directed respondents. Unpublished doctoral dissertation, Stanford University, 1971.

Moore, B. R. The role of directed Pavlovian reactions in simple instrumental learning in the pigeon. In R. A. Hinde & J. Stevenson-Hinde (Eds.), *Constraints on Learning*. London: Academic Press, 1973. Pp. 159–188.

Moray, N. *Attention: Selective processes in vision and hearing*. London: Hutchinson Educational, 1969.

Morgan, C. L. *Introduction to comparative psychology*. (2nd ed.) London: Scott, 1903.

Morgan, C. T. *Physiological psychology*, New York: McGraw-Hill, 1943.

Morgan, C. T., Stellar, E., & Johnson, O. Food deprivation and hoarding in rats. *Journal of Comparative and Physiological Psychology*, 1943, **35**, 275–295.

Morgan, M. J. Fixed interval schedules and delay of reinforcement. *Quarterly Journal of Experimental Psychology*, 1970, **22**, 663–673.

Morgan, M. J. Resistance to satiation. *Animal Behaviour*, 1974, **22**, 449–466.

Morgan, M. J. Single units and the identity hypothesis. Unpublished mimeo, 1975.

Morris, G. O., Williams, H. L., & Lubin, A. Misperception and disorientation during sleep deprivation. *AMA Archives of General Psychiatry*, 1960, **2**, 247–254.

Moscovitch, A., & LoLordo, V. M. Role of safety in the Pavlovian backward fear conditioning procedure. *Journal of Comparative and Physiological Psychology*, 1968, **66**, 673–678.

Mountcastle, V. B. Some functional properties of the somatic afferent system. In W. A. Rosenblith (Ed.), *Sensory communication*. Cambridge, Mass.: Massachusetts Institute of Technology, 1961. Pp. 403–436.

Mowrer, O. H. A stimulus-response analysis of anxiety and its role as a reinforcing agent. *Psychological Review*, 1939, **46**, 553–565.

Mowrer, O. H. Preparatory set (expectancy)—some methods of measurement. *Psychological Monographs*, 1940, **52** (2, Whole No. 233). Pp. 1–43.

Mowrer, O. H. On the dual nature of learning—a re-interpretation of "conditioning" and "problem-solving." *Harvard Educational Review*, 1947, **17**, 102–148.

Mowrer, O. H. *Learning theory and personality dynamics*. New York: Ronald, 1950.

Mowrer, O. H. *Learning theory and the symbolic processes*. New York: Wiley, 1960 (*a*).

Mowrer, O. H. *Learning theory and behavior*. New York: Wiley, 1960 (*b*).

Mowrer, O. H., & Jones, H. Habit strength as a function of the pattern of reinforcement. *Journal of Experimental Psychology*, 1945, **35**, 293–311.

Muir, D. W., & Mitchell, D. E. Visual resolution and experience: Acuity deficits in cats following early selective visual deprivation. *Science*, 1973, **180**, 420–422.

Munn, N. L. *Handbook of psychological research on the rat*. Boston: Houghton Mifflin 1950.

Muram, D., & Carmon, A. Behavioral properties of somatosensory-motor interhemispheric transfer. *Journal of Experimental Psychology*, 1972, **94**, 225–230.

Nadel, L. Dorsal and ventral hippocampal lesions and behavior. *Physiology and Behavior*, 1968, **3**, 891–900.

Nauta, W. J. H., & Haymaker, W. Hypothalamic nuclei and fiber connections. In W. Haymaker, E. Anderson, & W. J. H. Nauta (Eds.), *The hypothalamus*. Springfield, Ill.: Thomas, 1969. Pp. 136–209.

Navarick, D. J., & Fantino, E. Transitivity as a property of choice. *Journal of the Experimental Analysis of Behavior*, 1972, **18**, 389–401.

Navarick, D. J., & Fantino, E. Stochastic transitivity and unidimensional behavior theories. *Psychological Review*, 1974, **81**, 426–441.

Neimark, E. D., & Estes, W. K. (Eds.). *Stimulus sampling theory*. San Francisco: Holden-Day, 1967.

Neisser, U. Visual search. *Scientific American*, 1964, **210**, 94–102.

Neisser, U. *Cognitive psychology*. New York: Appleton-Century-Crofts, 1967.

Neisser, U., Novick, R., & Lazar, R. Searching for ten targets simultaneously. *Perceptual and Motor Skills*, 1963, **17**, 955–961.

Nelson, D. L., Brooks, D. H., & Fosselman, J. R. Words as sets of features: Processing phonological cues. *Journal of Experimental Psychology*, 1972, **92**, 305–312.

Nevin, J. A. Rates and patterns of responding with concurrent fixed-interval and variable interval reinforcement. *Journal of the Experimental Analysis of Behavior*, 1971, **16**, 241–247.

Newell, A. You can't play 20 questions with nature and win: Projective comments on the papers of this symposium. In W. G. Chase (Ed.), *Visual information processing*. New York: Academic Press, 1973.

Newell, A., & Simon, H. A. *Human problem solving*. Englewood Cliffs, N. J.: Prentice-Hall, 1971.

Nickerson, R. S. Response times for "same"-"different" judgments. *Perceptual and Motor Skills*, 1965, **20**, 15–18.

Nickerson, R. S. Binary-classification reaction time: A review of some studies of human information-processing capabilities. *Psychonomic Monograph Supplements*, 1972, **4** (Whole No. 65), 275–318.

Nissen, H. W. Analysis of a complex conditional reaction in chimpanzee. *Journal of Comparative and Physiological Psychology*, 1951, **44**, 9–16.

Noble, C. E. An analysis of meaning. *Psychological Review*, 1952, **59**, 421–430.

Norgren, R. Gustatory responses in the hypothalamus. *Brain Research*, 1970, **21**, 63–77.

Norman, D. A. Toward a theory of memory and attention. *Psychological Review*, 1968, **75**, 522–536

Norman, D. A. (Ed.). *Models of human memory*. New York: Academic Press, 1970.

Norman, D. A., & Rumelhart, D. E. A system for perception and memory. In D. A. Norman (Ed.), *Models of human memory*. New York: Academic Press, 1970. Pp. 19–64.

Noton, D., & Stark, L. Scanpaths in eye movements during pattern perception· *Science*, 1971, **171**, 308–311.

Notterman, J. M., & Mintz, D. E. *Dynamics of response*. New York: Wiley, 1965.

Oatman, L. C. The effect of attention on auditory evoked potentials in unanesthetized cats. *Dissertation Abstracts*, 1968, **29**, 2223–B

Obrist, P. A., Howard, J. L., Lawler, J. E., Galosy, R. A., Meyers, K. A., & Gaebelein, C. J. The cardiac-somatic interaction. In P. A. Obrist, A. H. Black, J. Brener, & L. V. DiCara (Eds.), *Cardiovascular psychophysiology: Current issues in response mechanisms, biofeedback and methodology.* Chicago: Aldine, 1974. Pp. 136–162.

Ogden, C. K., & Richards, I. A. *The meaning of meaning.* New York: Harcourt Brace, 1923.

Olson, D. R. Language and thought: Aspects of a cognitive theory of semantics. *Psychological Review*, 1970, **77**, 257–273.

Osgood, C. E. *Method and theory in experimental psychology.* New York: Oxford University Press, 1953.

Overton, D. A. State-dependent or "dissociated" learning produced with pentobarbital. *Journal of Comparative and Physiological Psychology*, 1964, **57**, 3–12.

Padilla, A. M. Analysis of incentive and behavioral contrast in the rat. *Journal of Comparative and Physiological Psychology*, 1971, **75**, 464–470.

Paillard, J., & Brouchon, M. Active and passive movements in the calibration of position sense. In S. J. Freedman (Ed.), *The neuropsychology of spatially oriented behavior.* Homewood, Ill.: Dorsey Press, 1968. Pp. 37–55.

Paivio, A. A factor-analytic study of word attributes and verbal learning. *Journal of Verbal Learning and Verbal Behavior*, 1968, **7**, 41–49.

Paivio, A. Mental imagery in associative learning and memory. *Psychological Review*, 1969, **76**, 241–263.

Paivio, A. *Imagery and verbal processes.* New York: Holt, Rinehart, & Winston, 1971 (*a*).

Paivio, A. Imagery and language. In S. J. Segal (Ed.), *Imagery: Current cognitive approaches.* New York: Academic Press, 1971. Pp. 7–32(*b*).

Parker, C. E. Behavioral diversity in ten species of nonhuman primates. *Journal of Comparative and Physiological Psychology*, 1974, **87**, 930–937.

Parsons, P. J., Fagan, T., & Spear, N. E. Short-term retention of habituation in the rat: A developmental study from infancy to old age. *Journal of Comparative and Physiological Psychology*, 1973, **84**, 545–553.

Passingham, R. E. Anatomical differences between the neocortex of man and other primates. *Brain, Behavior and Evolution*, 1973, **7**, 337–359.

Pavlov, I. P. *Conditioned reflexes.* Translated by G. V. Anrep. London: Oxford University Press, 1927.

Paxinos, G., & Bindra, D. Hypothalamic knife cuts: Effects on eating, drinking, irritability, aggression, and copulation in the male rat. *Journal of Comparative and Physiological Psychology*, 1972, **79**, 219–229.

Penfield, W., & Rasmussen, T. *The cerebral cortex of man.* New York: Macmillan, 1950.

Peterson, L. R., & Peterson, M. J. Short-term retention of individual verbal items. *Journal of Experimental Psychology*, 1959, **58**, 193–198.

Peterson, N. Effect of monochromatic rearing on the control of responding by wave-length. *Science*, 1962, **136**, 774–775.

Pfaff, D. W. Autoradiographic localization of radioactivity in rat brain after injection of tritiated sex hormones. *Science*, 1968, **161**, 1355–1356.

Pfaff, D., & Pfaffmann, C. Behavioral and electrophysiological responses of male rats to female rat urine odors. In C. Pfaffmann (Ed.), *Olfaction and taste III. Proceedings of the third International Symposium.* New York: Rockefeller University Press, 1969, Pp. 258–267.

Pfaffmann, C. (Ed.). *Olfaction and taste III. Proceedings of the third International Symposium.* New York: Rockefeller University Press, 1969.

Phillips, C. G. Changing concepts of the precentral motor area. In J. C. Eccles (Ed.), *Brain and conscious experience.* New York: Springer-Verlag, 1966. Pp. 389–421.

Piaget, J. *Judgment and reasoning in the child.* Translated by M. Warden. London: Routledge & Kegan Paul, 1928.

Piaget, J. *The psychology of intelligence.* Translated by M. Piercy, & D. E. Berlyne. London: Routledge & Kegan Paul, 1947.

Piaget, J. *The origin of intelligence in children.* Translated by M. Cook. New York: International Universities Press, 1952.

Piaget, J., & Inhelder, B. Translated by F. J. Langdon & J. L. Lunzer. *The child's conception of space.* London: Routledge & Kegan Paul, 1956.

Pinneo. L. R. Electrical control of behaviour by programmed stimulation of the brain. *Nature*, 1966, **211**, 705–708.

Pohl, W. Dissociation of spatial discrimination deficits following frontal and parietal lesions in monkeys. *Journal of Comparative and Physiological Psychology*, 1973, **82**, 227–239.

Poincaré, H. *Science et méthode.* Paris: Flammarion, 1930.

Pomeranz, B., & Chung, S. H. Dendritic-tree anatomy codes form-vision physiology in tadpole retina. *Science*, 1970, **170**, 983–984.

Porter, R. Functions of the mammalian cerebral cortex in movement. *Progress in Neurobiology*, 1973, **1**, 1–51.

Posluns, D. An analysis of chlorpromazine-induced suppression of the avoidance response. *Psychopharmacologia*, 1962, **3**, 361–373.

Posner, M. I. & Mitchell, R. F. Chronometric analysis of classification. *Psychological Review*, 1967, **74**, 392–409.

Postman, L. Short-term memory and incidental learning. In A. W. Melton (Ed.), *Categories of human learning.* New York: Academic Press, 1964. Pp. 145–201.

Postman, L. Organization and interference. *Psychological Review*, 1971, **78**, 290–302.

Postman, L., & Rosenzweig, M. R. Practice and transfer in the visual and auditory recognition of verbal stimuli. *American Journal of Psychology*, 1956, **69**, 209–226.

Potter, M. C. Meaning in visual search. *Science*, 1975, **187**, 965–966.

Pouthas, V., & Cavé, C. Evolution de deux conduites collatérales au cours d'un conditionnement au temps chez le rat. *L'année psychologique*, 1972, **1**, 17–24.

Powers, W. T. *Behavior: The control of perception*. Chicago, Ill.: Aldine, 1973.

Premack, D. Toward empirical behavior laws. I. Positive reinforcement. *Psychological Review*, 1959, **66**, 219–233.

Premack, D. Reinforcement theory. In D. Levine (Ed.), *Nebraska symposium on motivation: 1965*. Lincoln, Nebr.: University of Nebraska Press, 1965. Pp. 123–180.

Premack, D. Catching up with common sense or two sides of a generalization: Reinforcement and punishment. Paper read at a Conference on The Nature of Reinforcement, University of Pittsburgh, June, 1969.

Premack, D. Language in chimpanzee? *Science*, 1971, **172**, 808–822.

Pribram, K. H. Neocortical function in behavior. In H. F. Harlow & C. N. Woolsey (Eds.), *Biological and biochemical bases of behavior*. Madison: University of Wisconsin Press, 1958. Pp. 151–172.

Pribram, K. H. *Languages of the brain*. Englewood Cliffs, N. J.: Prentice-Hall, Inc., 1971.

Pribram, K. H., & McGuinness, D. Arousal, activation, and effort in the control of attention. *Psychological Review*, 1975, **82**, 116–149.

Pritchard, R. M., Heron, W., & Hebb, D. O. Visual perception approached by the method of stabilized images. *Canadian Journal of Psychology*, 1960, **14**, 67–77.

Prokasy, W. F., & Hall, J. F. Primary stimulus generalization. *Psychological Review*, 1963, **70**, 310–322.

Purpura, D. P. Dendritic spine "dysgenesis" and mental retardation. *Science*, 1974, **186**, 1126–1128.

Purpura, D. P., Frigyesi, T. L., McMurtry, J. G., & Scarff, T. Synaptic mechanisms in thalamic regulation of cerebello-cortical projection activity. In D. P. Purpura & M. D. Yahr (Eds.), *The thalamus*. New York: Columbia University Press, 1966. Pp. 153–170.

Pylyshyn, Z. W. What the mind's eye tells the mind's brain: A critique of mental imagery. *Psychological Bulletin*, 1973, **80**, 1–24.

Quartermain, D., Paolino, R. M., & Miller, N. E. A brief temporal gradient of retrograde amnesia independent of situational change. *Science*, 1965, **149**, 1116–1118.

Rabbitt, P. M. A. Ignoring irrelevant information. *British Journal of Psychology*, 1964, **55**, 403–414.

Rabbitt, P. M. A. Learning to ignore irrelevant information. *American Journal of Psychology*, 1967, **80**, 1–13.

Rachlin, H. Contrast and matching. *Psychological Review*, 1973, **80**, 217–234.

Rachlin, H. On the tautology of the matching law. *Journal of the Experimental Analysis of Behavior*, 1971, **15**, 249–251.

Racine, R. J. Modification of seizure activity by electrical stimulation. I. After-discharge threshold. *Electroencephalography and Clinical Neurophysiology,* 1972, **32,** 269–279. (*a*)

Racine, R. J. Modification of seizure activity by electrical stimulation. II. Motor seizure. *Electroencephalography and Clinical Neurophysiology,* 1972, **32,** 281–294. (*b*)

Rashotte, M. E., & Amsel, A. Transfer of slow-response rituals to extinction of a continuously rewarded response. *Journal of Comparative and Physiological Psychology,* 1968, **66,** 432–443.

Razran, G. The observable unconscious and the inferable conscious in current Soviet psychophysiology: Interoceptive conditioning, semantic conditioning, and the orienting reflex. *Psychological Review,* 1961, **68,** 81–147.

Rescorla, R. A. Probability of shock in the presence and absence of CS in fear conditioning. *Journal of Comparative and Physiological Psychology,* 1968, **66,** 1–5.

Rescorla, R. A., & Solomon, R. L. Two-process learning theory: Relationships between Pavlovian conditioning and instrumental learning. *Psychological Review,* 1967, **74,** 151–182.

Rescorla, R. A., & Wagner, A. R. A theory of Pavlovian conditioning: Variation in the effectiveness of reinforcement and nonreinforcement. In A. H. Black & W. F. Prokasy (Eds.), *Classical conditioning II: Current research and theory.* New York: Appleton-Century-Crofts, 1972.

Restle, F. Grammatical analysis of the prediction of binary events. *Journal of Verbal Learning and Verbal Behavior,* 1967, **6,** 17–25.

Revusky, S. H. The role of interference in association over a delay. In W. Honig & H. James (Eds.), *Animal memory.* New York: Academic Press, 1971.

Reynier-Rebuffel, A.-M., Louis-Sylvestre, J., & Le Magnen, J. Conditioned insulin release: Effect on food intake. In *XXVI International Congress of Physiological Sciences, Jerusalem Satellite Symposia,* October 1974.

Reynolds, G. S. Attention in the pigeon. *Journal of the Experimental Analysis of Behavior,* 1961, **4,** 203–208.

Rice, R. W. Incentive motivation and approach-avoidance tendencies. Unpublished Master's thesis, McGill University, 1966.

Rice, R. W. Effects of cortical lesions on eating produced by hypothalamic stimulation. Unpublished doctoral dissertation, McGill University, 1971.

Richter, C. P. Animal behavior and internal drives. *Quarterly Review of Biology,* 1927, **2,** 307–343.

Rock, I., & Harris, C. S. Vision and touch. *Scientific American,* 1967, **216,** 96–104.

Romanes, G. J. *Animal intelligence.* New York: D. Appleton, 1883.

Rosenzweig, M. R., Bennett, E. L., & Diamond, M. C. Chemical and anatomical plasticity of brain: Replications and extensions, 1970. In J. Gaito (Ed.),

Macromolecules and behavior. (2nd ed.), New York: Appleton-Century-Crofts, 1972. Pp. 205–277.

Routtenberg, A. Forebrain pathways of reward in Rattus Norvegicus. *Journal of Comparative and Physiological Psychology,* 1971, **75,** 269–276.

Rubin, E. *Visuell wahrgenommene Figuren: Studien in psychologischer Analyse.* Teil I. Berlin: Gyldendalske Boghandel, 1921.

Runquist, W. N., & Evans, A. Stimulus recognition and associative coding. *Journal of Experimental Psychology,* 1972, **95,** 242–244.

Russo, J. M., Reiter, L. A., & Ison, J. R. Repetitive exposure does not attenuate the sensory impact of the habituated stimulus. *Journal of Comparative and Physiological Psychology,* 1975, **88,** 665–669.

Rutschmann, R. Perception of temporal order and relative visual latency. *Science,* 1966, **152,** 1099–1101.

Salapatek, P., & Kessen, W. Visual scanning of triangles by the human newborn. *Journal of Experimental Child Psychology,* 1966, **3,** 155–167.

Sarno, J. E., Swisher, L. P., & Sarno, M. T. Aphasia in a congenitally deaf man. *Cortex,* 1969, **5,** 398–414.

Savin, H. B., & Bever, T. G. The nonperceptual reality of the phoneme. *Journal of Verbal Learning and Verbal Behavior,* 1970, **9,** 295–302.

Sasaki, R., Matsuna, Y., & Mizuno, N. Distribution of cerebellar-induced responses in cerebral cortex. *Experimental Neurology,* 1973, **36,** 342–354.

Scheerer, M. Problem-solving. *Scientific American,* 1963, **208,** 118–128.

Schmidt, R. A. Proprioception and the timing of motor responses. *Psychological Bulletin,* 1971, **76,** 383–393.

Schneider, G. E. Two visual systems. *Science,* 1969, **163,** 895–902.

Schneirla, T. C. An evolutionary and developmental theory of biphasic processes underlying approach and withdrawal. In M. R. Jones (Ed.), *Nebraska symposium on motivation: 1959.* Lincoln, Nebr.: University of Nebraska Press, 1959. Pp. 1–42.

Schneirla, T. C. Aspects of stimulation and organization in approach/withdrawal processes underlying vertebrate behavioral development. In D. S. Lehrman, R. A. Hinde, & E. Shaw (Eds.), *Advances in the study of behavior,* Vol. I. New York: Academic Press, 1965. Pp. 1–74.

Schuell, H., Jenkins, J. J., & Jimenéz-Pabón, E. *Aphasia in adults: Diagnosis, prognosis, and treatment.* New York: Hoeber, 1964.

Schwartz, B. Maintenance of key pecking by response-independent food presentation: The role of the modality of the signal for food. *Journal of the Experimental Analysis of Behavior,* 1973, **20,** 17–22.

Sechenov, I. M. *Reflexes of the brain.* Cambridge, Mass.: Massachusetts Institute of Technology Press, 1965. First published 1886.

Seligman, M. E. P. On the generality of the laws of learning. *Psychological Review,* 1970, **77,** 406–418.

Semmes, J., Weinstein, S., Ghent, L., & Teuber, H-L. Correlates of impaired orientation in personal and extra-personal space. *Brain*, 1963, **86**, 747–772.

Senders, J. W. On the distribution of attention in a dynamic environment. *Acta Psychologica* (Amsterdam), 1967, **27**, 349–354.

Seymour, P. H. K. Matching latencies for word-shape pairs. *Quarterly Journal of Experimental Psychology*, 1969, **21**, 312–321.

Shaffer, L. H. Multiple attention in continuous verbal tasks. Paper presented at the Stockholm Conference on Attention and Performance, July, 1973.

Shallice, T. Dual functions of consciousness. *Psychological Review*, 1972, **79**, 383–393.

Sharpless, S. K. Reorganization of function in the nervous system—use and disuse. *Annual Review of Physiology*, 1964, **26**, 357–388.

Sheldon, A. B. Preference for familiar vs. novel stimuli as a function of the familiarity of the environment. *Journal of Comparative and Physiological Psychology*, 1969, **67**, 516–521.

Sherrington, C. S. *The integrative action of the nervous system*. New Haven, Conn.: Yale University Press, 1961. First published 1906.

Shiffrin, R. M., & Atkinson, R. C. Storage and retrieval processes in long-term memory. *Psychological Review*, 1969, **76**, 179–193.

Siegel, S. Effect of CS habituation on eyelid conditioning. *Journal of Comparative and Physiological Psychology*, 1969, **68**, 245–248.

Siegel, S. Conditioning of insulin-induced glycemia. *Journal of Comparative and Physiological Psychology*, 1972, **78**, 233–241.

Siegel, S. Conditioning insulin effects. *Journal of Comparative and Physiological Psychology*, 1975, **89**, 189–199.

Siegel, S., & Nettleton, N. Conditioning of insulin-induced hyperphagia. *Journal of Comparative and Physiological Psychology*, 1970, **72**, 390–393.

Siipola, E. M., & Hayden, S. D. Exploring eidetic imagery among the retarded. *Perceptual and Motor Skills*, 1965, **21**, 275–286.

Silberberg, A., & Fantino, E. Choice, rate of reinforcement, and the changeover delay. *Journal of the Experimental Analysis of Behavior*, 1970, **13**, 187–197.

Simmel, M. L. Phantoms in patients with leprosy and in elderly digital amputees. *The American Journal of Psychology*, 1956, **69**, 529–545. (*a*)

Simmel, M. L. On phantom limbs. *A.M.A. Archives of Neurology and Psychiatry*, 1956, **75**, 637–647. (*b*)

Simon, H. A. How big is a chunk? *Science*, 1974, **183**, 482–488.

Simon, H. A., & Newell, A. Human problem solving: The state of the theory in 1970. *American Psychologist*, 1971, **26**, 145–159.

Simon, J. R., Hinrichs, J. V., & Craft, J. L. Auditory S-R compatibility: Reaction time as a function of ear-hand correspondence and ear-response-location correspondence. *Journal of Experimental Psychology*, 1970, **86**, 97–102.

Simpson, G. G. *The meaning of evolution.* (rev. ed.), New Haven, Conn.: Yale University Press, 1967.

Simpson, G. G. *Principles of animal taxonomy.* New York: Columbia University Press, 1961.

Skavenski, A. A. Inflow as a source of extraretinal eye position information. *Vision Research,* 1972, **12,** 221–229.

Skinner, B. F. *The behavior of organisms: An experimental analysis.* New York: Appleton-Century-Crofts, 1938.

Skinner, B. F. "Superstition" in the pigeon. *Journal of Experimental Psychology,* 1948, **38,** 168–172.

Skinner, B. F. *Science and human behavior.* New York: Macmillan, 1953.

Skinner, B. F. Behaviorism at fifty. *Science,* 1963, **140,** 951–958.

Skinner, B. F. Autoshaping. *Science,* 1971, **173,** 752.

Smith, E. E. Effects of familiarity on stimulus recognition and categorization. *Journal of Experimental Psychology,* 1967, **74,** 324–332.

Smith, K. *Behavior and conscious experience: A conceptual analysis.* Athens, Ohio: Ohio University Press, 1969.

Smith, K. U. Physiological and sensory feedback of the motor system: Neural-metabolic integration for energy regulation in behavior. In J. D. Maser (Ed.), *Efferent organization and the integration of behavior.* New York: Academic Press, 1973. Pp. 19–66.

Snowden, C. T. Gastrointestinal sensory and motor control of food intake. *Journal of Comparative and Physiological Psychology,* 1970, **71,** 68–76.

Sokolov, E. N. *Perception and the conditioned reflex.* Translated by S. W. Waydenfeld. New York: Pergamon, 1963.

Sokolov, E. N. *Neuronal mechanisms of the orienting reflex.* Moscow: Proceedings of the 18th International Psychology Congress, Symposium 5, 1966. P. 3.

Solomon, R. L., & Turner, L. H. Discriminative classical conditioning in dogs paralyzed by curare can later control discriminative avoidance responses in the normal state. *Psychological Review,* 1962, **69,** 202–219.

Solomon, R. L., & Wynne, L. C. Traumatic avoidance learning: The principles of anxiety conservation and partial irreversibility. *Psychological Review,* 1954, **61,** 353–385.

Sommerhoff, G. *Analytical biology.* London: Oxford University Press, 1950.

Spence, K. W. *Behavior theory and learning.* Selected Papers. Englewood Cliffs, N.J.: Prentice-Hall, 1960.

Spencer, H. *The principles of psychology.* Vols. 1 & 2. New York: Appleton, 1872–1873.

Sperling, G. The information available in brief visual presentations. *Psychological Monographs,* 1960, **74,** (11, Whole No. 498).

Sperry, R. W. Neural basis of the spontaneous optokinetic response produced by visual neural inversion. *Journal of Comparative and Physiological Psychology*, 1950, **43**, 482–489.

Sperry, R. W. Neurology and the mind-brain problem. *American Scientist*, 1952, **40**, 291–312.

Sperry, R. W. A modified concept of consciousness. *Psychological Review*, 1969, **76**, 532–536.

Spivey, J. E., Hess, D. T., & Black, D. Response decrement as a function of extinction or shift in reinforcement schedule. *Psychonomic Science*, 1968, **13**, 143–144.

Staddon, J. E. R. Temporal control, attention, and memory. *Psychological Review*, 1974, **81**, 375–391.

Staddon, J. E. R., & Simmelhag, V. L. The "superstition" experiment: A re-examination of its implications for the principles of adaptive behavior. *Psychological Review*, 1971, **78**, 3–43.

Stanley, W. C., Barret, J. E., & Bacon, W. E. Conditioning and extinction of avoidance and escape behavior in neonatal dogs. *Journal of Comparative and Physiological Psychology*, 1974, **87**, 163–172.

Stephan, H., & Andy, O. J. Quantitative comparative neuroanatomy of primates: An attempt at phylogenetic interpretation. In J. M. Petras & C. R. Noback (Eds.), Comparative and evolutionary aspects of the vertebrate central nervous system. *Annals of the New York Academy of Sciences*, 1969, **167**, 370–387.

Sternberg, S. The discovery of processing stages: Extensions of Donders' method. In W. G. Koster (Ed.), *Attention and performance. II.* Amsterdam: North Holland, 1969. Pp. 276–315.

Stevens, J. R., Mark, V. H., Erwin, F., Pacheco, P., & Suematsu, K. Deep temporal stimulation in man. *Archives of Neurology*, 1969, **21**, 157–169.

Stollnitz, F. Spatial variables, observing responses, and discrimination learning sets. *Psychological Review*, 1965, **72**, 247–261.

Stolz, S. B., & Lott, D. F. Establishment in rats of a persistent response producing a net loss of reinforcement. *Journal of Comparative and Physiological Psychology*, 1964, **57**, 147–149.

Stratton, G. M. Vision without inversion of the retinal image. *Psychological Review*, 1897, **4**, 341–360.

Stumpf, C. Drug action on the electrical activity of the hippocampus. *International Review of Neurobiology*, 1965, **8**, 77–138.

Suchman, R. G., & Trabasso, T. Color and form preference in young children. *Journal of Experimental Child Psychology*, 1966, **3**, 177–187. (a)

Suchman, R. G., & Trabasso, T. Stimulus preference and cue function in young children's concept attainment. *Journal of Experimental Child Psychology*, 1966, **3**, 188–198. (b)

Sullivan, A. M., & Skanes, G. R. Differential transfer of training in bright and dull subjects of the same mental age. *British Journal of Educational Psychology*, 1971, **41**, 287–293.

Sutherland, N. S., & Holgate, V. Two-cue discrimination learning in rats. *Journal of Comparative and Physiological Psychology*, 1966, **61**, 198–207.

Sutherland, N. S., & Mackintosh, N. J. *Mechanisms of animal discrimination learning.* New York: Academic Press, 1971.

Sutton, S. The specification of psychological variables in an average evoked potential experiment. In E. Donching, & D. B. Lindsley, (Eds.), *Average evoked potentials. Methods, results, and evaluation.* NASA SP-191. Washington, D.C.: U.S. Government Printing Office, 1969. Pp. 237–297.

Swets, J. A. The relative operating characteristic in psychology. *Science*, 1973, **182**, 990–1000.

Swets, J. A., Tanner, W. P., Jr., & Birdsall, T. G. Decision processes in perception. *Psychological Review*, 1961, **68**, 301–340.

Talland, G. A. *Deranged memory: A psychonomic study of the amnesic syndrome.* New York: Academic Press, 1965.

Taub, E. Prism compensation as a learning phenomenon: A phylogenetic perspective. In S. J. Freedman (Ed.), *The neuropsychology of spatially oriented behavior.* Homewood, Ill.: Dorsey Press, 1968. Pp. 77–106.

Taub, E., Bacon, R. C., & Berman, A. J. Acquisition of a trace-conditioned avoidance response after deafferentation of the responding limb. *Journal of Comparative and Physiological Psychology*, 1965, **59**, 275–279.

Taub, E., & Berman, A. J. Avoidance conditioning in the absence of relevant proprioceptive and exteroceptive feedback. *Journal of Comparative and Physiological Psychology*, 1963, **56**, 1012–1016.

Taub, E., & Berman, A. J. Movement and learning in the absence of sensory feedback. In S. J. Freedman (Ed.), *The neuropsychology of spatially oriented behavior.* Homewood, Ill.: Dorsey Press, 1968. Pp. 173–192.

Taub, E., Ellman, S. J., & Berman, A. J. Deafferentation in monkeys: Effect on conditioned grasp response. *Science*, 1966, **151**, 593–594.

Taub, W., Perrella, P., & Barro, G. Behavioral development after forelimb deafferentation on day of birth in monkeys with and without blinding. *Science*, 1973, **181**, 959–960.

Taylor, I. K. What words are stuttered? *Psychological Bulletin*, 1966, **65**, 233–242.

Taylor, J. G. *The behavioral basis of perception.* New Haven, Conn.: Yale University Press, 1962.

Teitelbaum, P., Cheng, M-F., & Rozin, P. Stages of recovery and development of lateral hypothalamic control of food and water intake. *Annals of the New York Academy of Sciences*, 1969, **157**, 849–860.

Teuber, H. L. Perception. In J. Field, H. W. Magoun, & V. E. Hall (Eds.), *Handbook of physiology: Neurophysiology.* Vol. 3. Washington, D.C.: American Physiological Society, 1960. Pp. 1595–1668.

Teuber, H.L., Battersby, W. S., & Bender, M. B. *Visual field defects after penetrating missile wounds of the brain.* Cambridge, Mass.: Harvard University Press, 1960.

Theios, J. The partial reinforcement effect sustained through blocks of continuous reinforcement. *Journal of Experimental Psychology*, 1962, **64**, 1–6.

Thistlethwaite, D. A critical review of latent learning and related experiments. *Psychological Bulletin*, 1951, **48**, 97–129.

Thompson, C. I., & Grossman, L. B. Loss and recovery of long-term memories after ECS in rats: Evidence for state-dependent recall. *Journal of Comparative and Physiological Psychology*, 1972, **78**, 248–254.

Thompson, R. F., Johnson, R. H., & Hoopes, J. J. Organization of auditory, somatic, sensory, and visual projection to association fields of cerebral cortex in the cat. *Journal of Neurophysiology*, 1963, **26**, 343–364.

Thompson, R. F., & Kramer, R. F. Role of association cortex in sensory precon-ditioning. *Journal of Comparative and Physiological Psychology*, 1965, **60**, 186–191.

Thompson, R. F., Mayers, K. S., Robertson, R. T., & Patterson, C. J. Number coding in association cortex of the cat. *Science*, 1970, **168**, 271–273.

Thompson, R. F., & Shaw, J. A. Behavioral correlates of evoked activity recorded from association areas of the cerebral cortex. *Journal of Comparative and Physiological Psychology*, 1965, **60**, 329–339.

Thompson, R. F., & Spencer, W. A. Habituation: A model phenomenon for the study of neuronal substrates of behavior. *Psychological Review*, 1966, **73**, 16–43.

Thompson, W. D., Stoney, S. D., Jr., & Asanuma, H. Characteristics of projections from primary sensory cortex to motorsensory cortex in cats. *Brain Research*, 1970, **22**, 15–27.

Thorpe, W. H. *Bird song*. Cambridge: Cambridge University Press, 1961.

Tinbergen, N. *The study of instinct*. Oxford: Clarendon Press, 1951.

Tinbergen, N. Derived activities; their causation, biological significance, origin, and emancipation during evolution. *Quarterly Review of Biology*, 1952, **27**, 1–32.

Titchener, E. B. *A beginner's psychology*. New York: Macmillan, 1918.

Toledo, L. de, & Black, A. H. Heart rate: Changes during conditioned suppression in rats. *Science*, 1966, **152**, 1404–1406.

Tolman, E. C. *Purposive behavior in animals and men*. New York: Century, 1932.

Tolman, E. C. Cognitive maps in rats and men. *Psychological Review*, 1948, **55**, 189–208.

Tomie, A., Davitt, G. A., & Thomas, D. R. Effects of stimulus similarity in dis-crimination training upon wavelength generalization in pigeons. *Journal of Comparative and Physiological Psychology*, 1975, **88**, 945–954.

Tomkins, S. S. *Affect, imagery, consciousness*. Vol. 1. *The positive affects*. New York: Springer, 1962.

Towe, A. L. Motor cortex and the pyramidal system. In J. D. Maser (Ed.), *Efferent organization and the integration of behavior.* New York: Academic Press, 1973. Pp. 67–97.

Trabasso, T. R. Stimulus emphasis and all-or-none learning in concept identification. *Journal of Experimental Psychology,* 1963, **65,** 398–406.

Trabasso, T. R., & Bower, G. H. *Attention in learning: Theory and research.* New York: Wiley, 1968.

Trapold, M. A., & Overmier, J. B. The second learning process in instrumental learning. In A. H. Black & W. F. Prokasy (Eds.), *Classical conditioning II: Current research and theory.* New York: Appleton-Century-Crofts, 1972. Pp. 427–452.

Treisman, A. M. Verbal cues, language, and meaning in selective attention. *The American Journal of Psychology,* 1964, **77,** 206–219.

Treisman, A. M. Strategies and models of selective attention. *Psychological Review,* 1969, **76,** 282–299.

Trevarthen, C. L'action dans l'espace et la perception de l'espace. *Mécanismes cérébraux de base.* Discussion du rapport de J. Paillard. In *De l'espace corporel a l'espace écologique.* Symposium de l'Association de psychologie scientifique de langue française, Bruxelles, 1972. Vendôme, France: Presses Universitaires de France, 1974. Pp. 65–80.

Troland, L. T. *The principles of psychophysiology.* Vol. 3. New York: D. Van Nostrand, 1932. Chapter 23.

Trotter, J. R. The physical properties of bar-pressing behaviour and the problem of reactive inhibition. *Quarterly Journal of Experimental Psychology,* 1956, **8,** 97–106.

Trowill, J. A., Panksepp, J., & Gandelman, R. An incentive model of rewarding brain stimulation. *Psychological Review,* 1969, **76,** 264–281.

Tulving. E. Episodic and semantic memory. In E. Tulving & W. Donaldson (Eds.), *Organization of memory.* New York: Academic Press, 1972. Pp. 381–403.

Tulving, E., & Donaldson, W. (Eds.). *Organization of memory.* New York: Academic Press, 1972.

Tulving, E., & Thomson, D. M. Retrieval processes in recognition memory: Effects of associative context. *Journal of Experimental Psychology,* 1971, **87,** 116–124.

Tulving, E., & Thomson, D. M. Encoding specificity and retrieval processes in episodic memory. *Psychological Review,* 1973, **80,** 352–373.

Tversky, A. Elimination by aspects: A theory of choice. *Psychological Review,* 1972, **79,** 281–299.

Tversky, B. Pictorial and verbal encoding in a short-term memory task. *Perception & Psychophysics,* 1969, **6,** 225–233.

Ulm, R. R., & Cicala, G. A. Reliable immobility and activity enhancement are produced by a fear CS. *Psychonomic Science,* 1971, **24,** 143–144.

Underwood, B. J., & Postman, L. Extraexperimental sources of interference in forgetting. *Psychological Review,* 1960, **67,** 73–95.

Ungar, G. Biological assays for the molecular coding of acquired information. In J. Gaito (Ed.), *Macromolecules and behavior*. (2nd ed.) New York: Appleton-Century-Crofts, 1972. Pp. 83–98.

Unger, S. M. Habituation of the vasoconstrictive orienting reaction. *Journal of Experimental Psychology*, 1964, **67**, 11–18.

Ungerstedt, U. Stereotaxic mapping of the monoamine pathways in the rat brain. *Acta Physiologica Scandinavica*, 1971, Supp. **367**, 1–48.

Ungerstedt, U., Butcher, L. L., Butcher, S. G., Anden, N-E., & Fuxe, K. Direct chemical stimulation of dopaminergic mechanisms in the neostriatum of the rat. *Brain Research*, 1969, **14**, 461–471.

Uttal, W. R. *The psychobiology of sensory coding*. New York: Harper & Row, 1973.

Valverde, F. Apical dendritic spines of the visual cortex and light deprivation of the mouse. *Experimental Brain Research*, 1971, **3**, 337–352.

Van der Loos, H., & Woolsey, T. A. Somatosensory cortex: Structural alterations following early injury to sense organs. *Science*, 1973, **179**, 395–398.

Vanderwolf, C. H. The effect of medial thalamic lesions on previously established fear-motivated behaviour. *Canadian Journal of Psychology*, 1963, **17**, 183–187.

Vaughan, E., & Fisher, A. E. Male sexual behavior induced by intracranial electrical stimulation. *Science*, 1962, **137**, 758–760.

Vinogradova, O. S. Registration of information and the limbic system. In G. Horn & R. A. Hinde (Eds.), *Short-term changes in neural activity and behaviour*. Cambridge: Cambridge University Press, 1970. Pp. 95–140.

Vitz, P. C., & Todd, T. C. A coded element model of the perceptual processing of sequential stimuli. *Psychological Review*, 1969, **76**, 433–449.

Volkmar, F. R., & Greenough, W. T. Rearing complexity affects branching of dendrites in the visual cortex of the rat. *Science*, 1972, **176**, 1445–1447.

Wagner, A. R. Effects of amount and percentage of reinforcement and number of acquisition trials on conditioning and extinction. *Journal of Experimental Psychology*, 1961, **62**, 234–242.

Wagner, A. R. Stimulus validity and stimulus selection in associative learning. In N. J. Mackintosh and W. K. Honig (Eds.), *Fundamental issues in associative learning*. Halifax, N. S.: Dalhousie University Press, 1969. Pp. 90–122.

Wagner, A. R., & Rescorla, R. A. Inhibition in Pavlovian conditioning: Application of a theory. In A. H. Black & W. F. Prokasy (Eds.), *Classical conditioning II: Current research and theory*. New York: Appleton-Century-Crofts, 1972.

Wagner, A. R., Rudy, J. W., & Whitlow, J. W. Rehearsal in animal conditioning. *Journal of Experimental Psychology*, 1973, **97**, 407–426.

Walker, A. E., & Udvarhelyi, G. B. The generalization of a seizure. *Journal of Nervous and Mental Disease*, 1965, **140**, 252–271.

Walker, E. L. Reinforcement—"the one ring." In J. T. Tapp (Ed.), *Reinforcement and behavior*. New York: Academic Press, 1969. Pp. 47–62.

Wallace, R. F., Osborne, S., Norborg, J., & Fantino, E. Stimulus change contemporaneous with food presentation maintains responding in the presence of free food. *Science*, 1973, **182**, 1038–1039.

Wallace, R. J. S-R compatibility and the idea of a response code. *Journal of Experimental Psychology*, 1971, **88**, 354–360.

Wallace, R. J. Spatial S-R compatibility effects involving kinesthetic cues. *Journal of Experimental Psychology*, 1972, **93**, 163–168.

Warren, J. M. Primate learning in comparative perspective. In A. M. Schrier, H. F. Harlow, & F. Stollnitz (Eds.), *Behavior of nonhuman primates: Modern research trends*. New York: Academic Press, 1965. Pp. 249–281.

Warren, R. M. Perceptual restoration of missing speech sounds. *Science*, 1970, **167**, 392–393.

Warren, R. M. Identification times for phonemic components of graded complexity and for spelling of speech. *Perception and Psychophysics*, 1971, **9**, 345–349.

Warrington, E. K., & Shallice, T. The selective impairment of auditory verbal short-term memory. *Brain*, 1969, **92**, 885–896.

Warrington, E. K., & Shallice, T. Neuropsychological evidence of visual storage in short-term memory tasks. *Quarterly Journal of Experimental Psychology*, 1972, **24**, 30–40.

Warrington, E. K., & Weiskrantz, L. Amnesic syndrome: Consolidation or retrieval? *Nature*, 1970, **228**, 628–630.

Warrington, E. K., & Weiskrantz, L. Organizational aspects of memory in amnesic patients. *Neuropsychologia*, 1971, **9**, 67–73.

Washburn, M. F. *Movement and mental imagery*. New York: Houghton Mifflin, 1916.

Watkins, M. J., & Tulving, E. Episodic memory: When recognition fails. *Journal of Experimental Psychology: General*, 1975, **104**, 5–36.

Watson, J. B. Psychology as the behaviorist views it. *Psychological Review*, 1913, **20**, 158–177.

Watson, J. B. *Psychology from the standpoint of a behaviorist*. (3rd ed.) Philadelphia: Lippincott, 1929.

Waugh, N. C., & Norman, D. A. Primary memory. *Psychological Review*, 1965, **72**, 89–104.

Weinberger, N. M., & Lindsley, D. B. Behavioral and electroencephalographic arousal to contrasting novel stimulation. *Science*, 1964, **144**, 1355–1357.

Weiskrantz, L. Experimental studies of amnesia. In C. N. M. Whitty & O. L. Langwill (Eds.), *Amnesia*. London: Butterworth, 1966. Pp. 1–35.

Weiskrantz, L. A long-term view of short-term memory in psychology. In G. Horn & R. A. Hinde (Eds.), *Short-term changes in neural activity and behaviour*. Cambridge: Cambridge University Press, 1970. Pp. 63–74.

Weiskrantz, L. Behavioural analysis of the monkey's visual nervous system. *Proceedings of the Royal Society* (London), 1972, **182**, 427–455.

Weiskrantz, L., & Warrington, E. K. A study of forgetting in amnesic patients. *Neuropsychologia*, 1970, **8**, 281–288.

Weiskrantz, L., Warrington, E. K., Sanders, M. D., & Marshall, J. Visual capacity in the hemianopic field following a restricted occipital ablation. *Brain*, 1974, **97**, 709–728.

Weizmann, F., Cohen, L. B., & Pratt, R. J. Novelty, familiarity, and the development of infant attention. Unpublished manuscript, 1969.

Welker, W. I. An analysis of exploratory and play behavior in animals. In D. W. Fiske & S. R. Maddi (Eds.), *Functions of varied experience*. Homewood, Ill.: Dorsey Press, 1961. Pp. 175–226.

Wertheimer, M. *Productive thinking*. New York: Harper, 1945.

Wertheimer, M. Psychomotor coordination of auditory and visual space at birth. *Science*, 1961, **134**, 1692.

White, B., Castle, P., & Held, R. Observations on the development of visually directed reaching. *Child Development*, 1964, **35**, 349–364.

White, B. L., & Held, R. Plasticity of sensorimotor development. In J. F. Rosenblith & W. Allinsmith (Eds.), *The causes of behavior: Readings in child development and educational psychology*. (2nd ed.) Boston: Allyn & Bacon, 1966. Pp. 60–70.

White, B. L. *Human infants. Experience and psychological development*. Englewood Cliffs, N. J.: Prentice-Hall, 1971.

White, B. W., Saunders, F. A., Scadden, L., Bach-Y-Rita, P., & Collins, C. C. Seeing with the skin. *Perception and Psychophysics*, 1970, **7**, 23–27.

Wickelgren, W. A. Context-sensitive coding, associative memory, and serial order in (speech) behavior. *Psychological Review*, 1969, **76**, 1–15.

Wiesel, T. N., & Hubel, D. H. Effects of visual deprivation on morphology and physiology of cells in the cat's lateral geniculate body. *Journal of Neurophysiology*, 1963, **26**, 978–993.

Wiesel, T. N., & Hubel, D. H. Comparison of the effects of unilateral and bilateral eye closure on cortical unit responses in kittens. *Journal of Neurophysiology*, 1965, **28**, 1029–1040.

Wike, E. L. *Secondary reinforcement: Selected experiments*. New York: Harper & Row, 1966.

Williams, D. I. The overtraining reversal effect in the pigeon. *Psychonomic Science*, 1967, **7**, 261–262.

Williams, D. R., & Williams, H. Auto-maintenance in the pigeon: Sustained pecking despite contingent non-reinforcement. *Journal of the Experimental Analysis of Behavior*, 1969, **12**, 511–520.

Williams, J. A. Novelty, GSR, and stimulus generalization. *Canadian Journal of Psychology*, 1963, **17**, 52–61.

Wilson, M. P., & Keller, F. S. On the selective reinforcement of spaced responding. *Journal of Comparative and Physiological Psychology*, 1953, **46**, 190–193.

Wimer, R. E., & Wigdor, B. T. Age differences in retention of learning. *Journal of Gerontology*, 1958, **13**, 291–295.

Winocur, G., & Weiskrantz, L. An investigation of paired-associate learning in amnesic patients. *Neuropsychologia*, 1976, **14**, 97–110.

Wolfe, J. B. Effectiveness of token rewards for chimpanzees. *Comparative Psychology Monographs*, 1936, **12** (5, Whole No. 60). Pp. 1–72.

Woods, S. C., Alexander, K. R., & Porte, D., Jr. Conditioned insulin secretion and hypoglycemia following repeated injections of tolbutamide in rats. *Endocrinology*, 1972, **90**, 227–231.

Woods, S. C., & Porte, D., Jr. Neural control of the endocrine pancreas. *Physiological Reviews*, 1974, **54**, 596–619.

Woodworth, R. S. *Dynamic psychology*. New York: Columbia University Press, 1918.

Woodworth, R. S., & Schlosberg, H. *Experimental psychology*. (rev. ed.). New York: Henry Holt and Co., 1955.

Woody, C. D. Aspects of the electrophysiology of cortical processes related to the development and performance of learned motor responses. *The Physiologist*, 1974, **17**, 49–69.

Woody, C. D., & Engel, J., Jr. Changes in unit activity and thresholds to electrical microstimulation at coronal-pericruciate cortex of cat with classical conditioning of different facial movements. *Journal of Neurophysiology*, 1972, **35**, 230–241.

Woolsey, T. A., & Van der Loos, H. The structural organization of layer IV in the somatosensory region (SI) of mouse cerebral cortex. The description of a cortical field composed of discrete cytoarchitectonic units. *Brain Research*, 1970, **17**, 205–242.

Wyckoff, L. B., Jr. The role of observing responses in discrimination learning: Part II. Unpublished Ph.D. thesis, Indiana University, 1951.

Wyckoff, L. B., Jr. The role of observing responses in discrimination learning. Part I. *Psychological Review*, 1952, **59**, 431–442.

Wydra, A. Conditioned aversion to visual cues. M.A. thesis. McGill University, 1975.

Yarbus, A. L. *Eye movements and vision*. Translated by B. Haigh. New York: Plenum Press, 1967.

Yerkes, R. M. Animal psychology and the criteria of the psychic. *Journal of Philosophy, Psychology, and Scientific Methods*, 1905, **2**, 141–149.

Young, P. T. Appetite, palatability and feeding habit: A critical review. *Psychological Bulletin*, 1948, **45**, 289–320.

Zelazo, P. R., Zelazo, N. A., & Kolb, S. "Walking" in the newborn. *Science*, 1972, **176**, 314–315.

Zener, K. The significance of behavior accompanying conditioned salivary secretion for theories of the conditioned response. *American Journal of Psychology*, 1937, **50**, 384–403.

Zentall, T. R., & Levine, J. M. Observational learning and social facilitation in the rat. *Science*, 1972, **178**, 1220–1221.

Zieliński, K. The direction of change versus the absolute level of noise intensity as a cue in the CER situation. *Acta Biologiae Experimentalis*, 1965, **25**, 337–357.

Zubek, J. P., Aftanas, M., Kovach, K., Wilgosh, L., & Winocur, G. Effect of severe immobilization of the body on intellectual and perceptual processes. *Canadian Journal of Psychology*, 1963, **17**, 118–133.

Zucker, E., & Welker, W. I. Coding of somatic sensory input by vibrissae neurons in the rat's trigeminal ganglion. *Brain Research*, 1969, **12**, 138–156.

Zucker, I., & Bindra, D. Peripheral sensory loss and exploratory behaviour. *Canadian Journal of Psychology*, 1961, **15**, 237–243.

Author Index

Subject Index